RUNNING
LINUX

RUNNING
LINUX

Third Edition

MATT WELSH, MATTHIAS KALLE DALHEIMER,
AND LAR KAUFMAN

O'REILLY®

Beijing · Cambridge · Farnham · Köln · Paris · Sebastopol · Taipei · Tokyo

Running Linux, Third Edition

by Matt Welsh, Matthias Kalle Dalheimer, and Lar Kaufman

Published by O'Reilly & Associates, Inc., 101 Morris Street, Sebastopol, CA 95472.

Editor: Andy Oram

Production Editor: Jeffrey Liggett

Printing History:

May 1995:	First Edition.
November 1995:	Minor corrections.
August 1996:	Second Edition.
August 1999:	Third Edition.

ISBN: 1-56592-469-X

[M]

[5/00]

TABLE OF CONTENTS

PREFACE

This is a book about Linux, a free implementation of Unix for Intel 386 (or higher), Alpha, SPARC, PowerPC, Motorola 680x0 (m68k), and other personal computer and server architectures. In this book, we want to show how you can completely change the way you work with computers by exploring the world of a powerful and free operating system—one that goes against the grain of the traditional PC world. Setting up and running a Linux system can be challenging, rewarding, and a lot of fun; we think that Linux brings a great deal of excitement back into computing. We invite you to dive in, enjoy yourself, and be the first on your block to know what it means to tweak your dot clocks and *rdev* your kernel image.

We aim this book at readers who are inquisitive and creative enough to delve full-tilt into the world of Linux. Linux represents something of a rebellion against commercial operating systems, and many of its users are the kind of people who like living on the edge of the latest technological trends. Sure, the casual reader can set up and run a Linux system (or hundreds of them!) without much trouble, but the purpose of this book is to dig deeper into the system and bring you completely into the Linux mentality. Rather than gloss over the messier details, we explain the concepts by which the system actually works, so that you can troubleshoot problems on your own. By sharing the accumulated expertise of several Linux experts, we hope to give you enough confidence so that one day you can call yourself a true Linux Guru.

This is the third edition of *Running Linux*. In this edition, we have completely updated the installation, configuration, and tutorial information to be up-to-date with the latest Linux software distributions (including Red Hat, SuSE, and Debian) and many application packages. The core of the book, however, has not changed much. This was intentional: in the first two editions we made a great effort to make the book as robust as possible, even though Linux itself is under constant development. This philosophy worked remarkably well and has been preserved in this new, updated edition. We think this book will be of use to you for a long time to come.

This book concentrates on the version of Linux for the Intel x86 family of processors (the 386/486, Pentium, Pentium Pro, and Pentium II/III chips). We have also included appendices detailing the installation and basic configuration procedures for several other architectures, including Alpha, SPARC, m68k, and PowerPC ports of Linux. However, apart from the basic installation procedures, the rest of this book, which focuses on using the system, applies to any port of Linux.

Kalle Dalheimer has joined Matt Welsh and Lar Kaufman as co-authors for this third edition. Kalle has been active in the Linux community for some time and was instrumental in the development of KDE (a popular desktop environment for Linux). Kalle has authored most of the new material in this edition, and his particular expertise has brought a fresh perspective to the technical aspects of this book.

In the preface to the first edition, we said that "Linux has the potential to completely change the face of the PC operating system world." Looking back, we think it's obvious that this has already happened. Linux has erupted into the computing mainstream with an amazing force: it has been covered by every major media channel, has helped usher in the so-called "Open Source Revolution," and is widely claimed as the most viable competitor to Microsoft's dominance in the operating systems market. Today, most estimates place the number of Linux users worldwide at over 10 million. Linux has matured to the point where many people don't need to know much about their systems: they can simply install the software and use it. So, perhaps you will find much of the detailed advice in this volume superfluous; at the very least, retain it for historical evidence.

In writing this book, we wanted to make Linux a real choice for the many personal computer users who find themselves trapped within the limitations of commercial operating systems. Because of the cooperative nature of the system, certain aspects of Linux can be confusing or apparently ad hoc. In this book, we've attempted to condense as much wisdom as possible based on correspondence with thousands of users worldwide (and far too much time playing with our own Linux systems). Linux really can change the way you think about computing—this book will show you how.

The world of Linux has changed a lot between the previous edition of *Running Linux* and this one. But most of these changes have been in its image rather than its substance: Forbes magazine and the Economist are excited about the growth of Linux, major computer companies like IBM, Hewlett Packard, Oracle, and Compaq are supporting Linux in various ways, and the "open source" model (originally known as free software) that Linux exemplifies is all over the news.

Linux itself has improved along the way, and the programs you run on Linux have matured impressively. Linux can now be used for massive, mission-critical servers with multiple processors, clusters, and RAID disk arrays. Since this is a getting-started book, we don't talk about those things. Rather, we concentrate on the more introductory aspects of the system, but we do cover several server-related topics (specifically, setting up Samba and web servers).

A major new development covered in this third edition is KDE. KDE (and GNOME, a similar project) has brought a new, modern look-and-feel to the Linux desktop, making the system poised to conquer the personal productivity computing market once and for all.

In addition to new sections on KDE and Samba, this edition offers introductions to PPP and to building Java™ programs on Linux. Of course, all the other information has been completely updated as well.

Why People Like Linux

Why on earth would you want to run Linux? Good question. What you have now works, doesn't it? Windows 98 is a good operating system, but it has a lot of limitations. Being tailored for low-end home users, Windows doesn't deliver the performance or flexibility that many people expect out of a PC operating system. Here are a few reasons why people are switching to Linux:

It's free.

That is, Linux is a freely redistributable clone of the Unix operating system (OS). You can get Linux free from someone who has it, from the World Wide Web, or you can buy it at a reasonable price on CD-ROM from a vendor who has packaged it (probably with added value), possibly with support services.

It's popular.

It runs on inexpensive Pentium Pro, Pentium II, AMD, and Cyrix chips, and even older 386/486 machines. Linux also runs on personal PCS based on the Intel Pentium architecture, higher-end workstations based on the SPARC or Alpha architecture, PowerPCs, and 68k-based Macs. Linux supports a broad range of video cards, sound cards, CD-ROM and disk drives, printers, scanners, and other devices.

Linux has an enormous user community presence on the World Wide Web, with many web sites devoted to providing information and discussion about the system. A growing number of commercial software vendors are developing applications for Linux, including Corel WordPerfect, the StarOffice suite from Star Division, and a number of database products from big names such as Oracle, Informix, and IBM.

It's powerful.

You will be pleased to see how fast the system runs, even with many processes running and with multiple windows open. Linux makes excellent use of the hardware. Many commercial operating systems (including Windows 98) make little use of the advanced multitasking capabilities of the Pentium processor. Linux is native to this architecture and uses them all. A Linux machine with a reasonably fast processor and a sufficient amount of RAM can perform as well, or better, than Unix workstations costing $10,000 or more.

It is of good quality, and runs high-quality software applications.

Linux is being developed publicly with hundreds of programmers and users refining it, but with the individual vision and focus of its originator, Linus Torvalds. It incorporates the work of universities, companies, and individuals in the form of highly developed compilers, editors, utilities, and scripts that have been developed over the last quarter century. Unlike other new operating systems, Linux already has an enormous base of applications freely available for your use—from major scientific applications, to multimedia tools, to games.

It has full Unix features.

Linux is a true multiuser, multitasking operating system that supports multiple processors on some systems. It uses the X Window System graphical user interface (GUI) and offers several different integrated desktop environments, including KDE and GNOME. Full networking support (TCP/IP, SLIP, PPP, and UUCP, among others) is available.

It's highly compatible with Windows 95/98, Windows NT, and MS-DOS.

You can install Linux along with other disk partitions that contain Windows 98 or other operating systems. Linux can directly access files on Windows systems from the floppy or hard drive. Developers are working on emulators for both Windows 98 and MS-DOS, so that eventually you can run commercial applications built for Windows under Linux. Linux does not run under Windows; it is completely independent of it, but features have been added to allow the separate systems to work together.

It is small.

The basic OS will run on 8 MB of system memory, including a GUI and window manager. A good basic system will fit in 10 to 20 MB of disk storage. (If this seems like a lot of disk space, it's because Linux provides a lot of utilities.) Linux has even been tuned to run on low-memory embedded systems (such as those used in network routers or robots), and in hand-held Personal Digital Assistants such as the PalmPilot!

It is big.

Some of the larger distributions fill more than 1 GB of uncompressed disk storage in binary files alone. (Full source code is freely available for Linux and is included in many CD-ROM distributions of the software.) The number of powerful utilities and applications ported to Linux grows constantly. You could probably fill several gigabytes of hard disk with them, even without loading up on graphics and audio files. Linux has even been used to build some of the largest supercomputers in the world by networking together dozens of PCs, each running Linux, and using them as one large computer.

Most Linux users can run a complete system in 300 MB or so of disk space. This includes all the basics, as well as nice extras such as the X Window System GUI, text-processing tools, and development utilities such as compilers and libraries. But if you're a real power user, much more is available.

It's supported.

The biggest line of support is the many web sites devoted to Linux (along with thousands of newsgroup participants), but you can also contract for support from an independent company or buy a supported version of Linux from one of its distributors.

It's well-documented.

There is this book (an excellent start!), which is also available in French, German, Japanese, and Chinese. The Linux development community established the Linux Documentation Project (LDP) early on, which maintains a large amount of online documentation about the system. The many books, FAQ lists, and "how-to" documents from the LDP can guide you through almost any task that needs to be done under Linux. Once you get over a few installation humps, Linux is more or less like any other Unix system, so the many general books about Unix use and administration will give you all the help you need. Finally, there is the popular press, which has written hundreds of books on Linux—both introductory and advanced—which have been translated into most major languages around the world.

Organization of This Book

Each chapter of this book contains a big chunk of information. It takes you into a world of material that could easily take up several books. But we move quickly through the topics you need to know.

Chapter 1, *Introduction to Linux*, tries to draw together many different threads. It explains why Linux came to be and what makes it different from other versions of Unix as well as other operating systems for personal computers.

Chapter 2, *Preparing to Install Linux*, describes preliminary tasks that you may have to do before installation, such as partitioning your disk (in case you want to run another operating system as well as Linux).

Chapter 3, *Installation and Initial Configuration*, is a comprehensive tutorial on installing and configuring Linux on your system.

Chapter 4, *Basic Unix Commands and Concepts*, offers a system administrator's introduction to Unix, for people who need one. It is intended to give you enough tools to perform the basic tasks you'll need to do throughout the book. Basic commands are covered, along with some tips for administrators and some concepts you should know.

Chapter 5, *Essential System Management*; Chapter 6, *Managing Filesystems, Swap, and Devices*; Chapter 7, *Upgrading Software and the Kernel*; and Chapter 8, *Other Administrative Tasks*, cover system administration and maintenance. These are perhaps the most important and useful chapters of the book; they cover user account management, backups, software upgrading, building a new kernel, and more.

Chapter 9, *Editors, Text Tools, Graphics, and Printing*, introduces you to the most popular and commonly used text tools and editors on Linux—*vi* and Emacs—and shows you how to print a document and how to use various graphics programs.

Chapter 10, *Installing the X Window System*, shows you how to install and configure the X Window System, a powerful GUI for Linux and Unix systems. We show you how to overcome problems you might encounter when your distribution installs the software and how to configure it for the best performance on your video hardware.

Chapter 11, *Customizing Your X Environment*, shows you how to set up your own visual environment under the X Window System, covering a wide range of the powerful customizations the system makes available, the KDE desktop, and a few useful programs that run under X.

Chapter 12, *Windows Compatibility and Samba*, presents various tools for interfacing with DOS and Windows systems, particularly the Samba server that integrates Linux with other users running PCs.

Chapter 13, *Programming Languages*, and Chapter 14, *Tools for Programmers*, are for programmers. Compilers, interpreters, debuggers, and many other tools for programming under Linux are presented.

Chapter 15, *TCP/IP and PPP*, tells you how to set up your all-important connection to the outside world. It shows you how to configure your system so it can work on a local area network or communicate with an Internet service provider using PPP.

Chapter 16, *The World Wide Web and Electronic Mail*, goes beyond basic network configuration and shows you how to configure electronic mail, set up the Elm and Netscape mail readers, and even run your own World Wide Web server.

Appendix A, *Sources of Linux Information*, tells you about other useful documentation for Linux and other sources of help.

Appendix B, *The GNOME Project*, contains information on the GNOME project.

Appendix C, *Installing Linux on Digital/ Compaq Alpha Systems*, shows you how to install Linux on the first non-Intel system that supported it, the 64-bit Digital Alpha machine.

Appendix D, *LinuxPPC: Installing Linux on PowerPC Computers*, shows how to install Linux on the popular PowerPC platform.

Appendix E, *Installing Linux/m68k on Motorola 68000-Series Systems*, shows how to install Linux on systems using the Motorola 680x0 (m68k) processor, like the Amiga, Atari, and some Apple Macintosh models.

Appendix F, *Installing Linux on Sun SPARC Systems*, shows how to install Linux on powerful Sun SPARC systems.

Appendix G, *LILO Boot Options*, lists LILO boot options.

Appendix H, *Zmodem File Transfer*, describes tools for telecommunication using a modem.

The Bibliography lists a number of books, HOWTOs, and Internet RFCs of interest to Linux users and administrators.

Conventions Used in This Book

The following is a list of the typographical conventions used in this book:

Bold
: is used for machine names, hostnames, usernames, and IDs.

Italic
: is used for file and directory names, program and command names, command-line options, email addresses and pathnames, site names, and new terms.

`Constant Width`
: is used in examples to show the contents of files or the output from commands, to indicate environment variables and keywords that appear in code, and for Emacs commands.

`Constant Italic`
: is used to indicate variable options, keywords, or text that the user is to replace with an actual value.

`Constant Bold`
: is used in examples to show commands or other text that should be typed literally by the user.

 The bomb icon in the left margin is for Caution: you can make a mistake here that disables or damages your system or is hard to recover from.

[0]Biblio
Chapter 0
manpage(1)

The book icon indicates a reference to another part of this book or to another source of information. The citation string (or strings) underneath the book may be a number and key for a book, HOWTO article, or RFC listed in the Bibliography; a pointer to another chapter or appendix in this book; or a referral to a particular program's manual page.

How to Contact Us

We have tested and verified the information in this book to the best of our ability, but you may find that features have changed (or even that we have made mistakes!). Please let us know about any errors you find, as well as your suggestions for future editions, by writing to:

O'Reilly & Associates, Inc.
101 Morris Street
Sebastopol, CA 95472
1-800-998-9938 (in the U.S. or Canada)
1-707-829-0515 (international or local)
1-707-829-0104 (FAX)

You can send us messages electronically. To be put on the mailing list or request a catalog, send email to:

info@oreilly.com

To ask technical questions or comment on the book, send email to:

bookquestions@oreilly.com

We have a web site for the book, where we'll list examples, errata, and any plans for future editions. You can access this page at:

http://www.oreilly.com/catalog/runux3/

For more information about this book and others, see the O'Reilly web site:

http://www.oreilly.com

Acknowledgments

This book is the result of many people's efforts, and as expected, it would be impossible to list them all here. First of all, we would like to thank Andy Oram, who did an excellent job of editing, writing, and whip-cracking to get this book into shape. Apart from being the overall editor, Andy contributed the Unix tutorial chapter as well as material for the X and Perl sections. It was Andy who approached us about writing for O'Reilly in the first place, and he has demonstrated the patience of a saint when waiting for our updates to trickle in.

Those of you who are already familiar with Linux may notice that some portions of this book, such as the introductory and installation chapters, have been released as part of *Linux Installation and Getting Started*, a free book available via the Internet. O'Reilly allowed us to release those portions (originally written for this book) to the I&GS, so they could benefit the Internet-based Linux community and we would get feedback and corrections from its readership. Thanks to everyone who contributed edits to those sections.

We would also like to thank the following people for their work on the Linux operating system—without all of them, there wouldn't be anything to write a book about: Linus Torvalds, Richard Stallman, Donald Becker, Alan Cox, Remy Card, Eric Raymond, Ted T'so, H.J. Lu, Miguel de Icaza, Ross Biro, Drew Eckhardt, Ed Carp, Eric Youngdale, Fred van Kempen, Steven Tweedie, Patrick Volkerding, Dirk Hohndel, Matthias Ettrichand, and all of the other hackers, from the kernel grunts to the lowly docos, too numerous to mention here.

Special thanks to the following people for their contributions to the Linux Documentation Project, technical review of this book, or general friendliness and support: Phil Hughes, Melinda McBride, Bill Hahn, Dan Irving, Michael Johnston, Joel Goldberger, Michael K. Johnson, Adam Richter, Roman Yanovsky, Jon Magid, Erik Troan, Lars Wirzenius, Olaf Kirch, Greg Hankins, Alan Sondheim, Jon David, Anna Clark, Adam Goodman, Lee Gomes, Rob Walker, Rob Malda, Jeff Bates, and Volker Lendecke. We are grateful to Shawn Wallace and Umberto Crenca for the gorgeous shot in Chapter 9 of The Gimp in use.

For the third edition, we thank Phil Hughes, Robert J. Chassell, Tony Cappellini, Craig Small, Nat Makarevitch, Chris Davis, Chuck Toporek, Frederic HongFeng, and David Pranata for wide-ranging comments and corrections. Particularly impressive were the efforts put in by an entire team of Debian developers and users, organized for us by Ossama Othman and Julian T. J. Midgley. Julian set up a CVS repository for comments and the book was examined collectively by him, Chris Lawrence, Robert J. Chassell, Kirk Hilliard, and Stephen Zander.

As you can see from a glance at the first pages of the appendices, we had a lot of contributions from porters and developers to document Linux support and installation on non-Intel systems. Barrett G. Lyon and Richard Payne (Alpha), Jason Haas (LinuxPPC), Chris Lawrence (Linux/m68k), and David S. Miller (SPARC) all gave up a lot of their personal time to create the appendices. Kostas Gewrgiou, Jambi Ganbar, Sanjeev Gupta, Roman Hodek, Geert Uytterhoeven, Jes Sorensen, Hubert Figuiere, and Christopher F. Miller reviewed the appendices for various systems and offered corrections.

If you have questions, comments, or corrections for this book, please feel free to get in touch with the authors. Matt Welsh can be reached on the Internet at *mdw@cs.berkeley.edu*. Lar Kaufman can be reached at *lark@conserve.org*. Kalle Dalheimer can be reached at *kalle@dalheimer.de*.

CHAPTER ONE

INTRODUCTION
TO LINUX

This is a book about Linux, a free Unix clone for personal computer systems that supports full multitasking, the X Window System, TCP/IP networking, and much more. Hang tight and read on: in the pages that follow, we describe the system in meticulous detail.

Linux has generated more excitement in the computer field than any other development of the past several years. Its surprisingly fast spread and the loyalty it inspires recall the excitement of do-it-yourself computing that used to characterize earlier advances in computer technology. Ironically, it succeeds by rejuvenating one of the oldest operating systems still in widespread use, Unix. Linux is both a new technology and an old one.

In narrow technical terms, Linux is just the operating system kernel, offering the basic services of process scheduling, virtual memory, file management, and device I/O. In other words, Linux itself is the lowest-level part of the operating system.

However, most people use the term "Linux" to refer to the complete system—the kernel along with the many applications that it runs: a complete development and work environment including compilers, editors, graphical interfaces, text processors, games, and more.

This book will be your guide to Linux's shifting and many-faceted world. Linux has developed into an operating system for businesses, education, and personal productivity, and this book will help you get the most out of it.

Linux can turn any personal computer into a workstation. It will give you the full power of Unix at your fingertips. Businesses are installing Linux on entire networks of machines, using the operating system to manage financial and hospital records, distributed-user computing environments, telecommunications, and more. Universities worldwide are using Linux for teaching courses on operating-systems programming and design. And, of course, computing enthusiasts everywhere are using Linux at home, for programming, document production, and all-around hacking.

Apart from workstation and personal use (many people find it convenient to run Linux on their laptop computers), Linux is also being used to drive big servers. Increasingly, people are discovering that Linux is powerful, stable, and flexible enough to run the largest disk arrays and multiprocessor systems—with applications ranging from World Wide Web servers to corporate databases. Scientists are wiring together arrays of Linux machines into enormous "clusters" to solve the most computationally intensive problems in physics and engineering. With the latest release of the Samba software suite, Linux can even act as a Windows file and print server—with better performance than Windows NT!

What makes Linux so different is that it's a *free* implementation of Unix. It was and still is developed by a group of volunteers, primarily on the Internet, who exchange code, report bugs, and fix problems in an open environment. Anyone is welcome to join in the Linux development effort: all it takes is interest in hacking a free Unix clone and some kind of programming know-how. This book is your tour guide.

In this book, we assume you're comfortable with a personal computer (running any operating system, such as Windows 95, or some other version of Unix). We also assume that you're willing to do some experimentation to get everything working correctly—after all, this is half of the fun of getting into Linux. Linux has evolved into a system that is amazingly easy to install and configure, but because it is so powerful, some details are more complex than you'll find in the Windows world. With this book as your guide, we hope you'll find that setting up and running your own Linux system is quite easy and a great deal of fun.

About This Book

This book is an overview and entry-level guide to the Linux system. We attempt to present enough general and interesting information on a number of topics to satisfy Unix novices and wizards alike. This book should provide sufficient material for almost anyone to install and use Linux and get the most out of it. Instead of covering many of the volatile technical details—those things that tend to change with rapid development—we give you enough background to find out more on your own.

This book is geared for those people who really want to exploit the power that Linux provides. Rather than gloss over all of the tricky details, we give you enough background to truly understand how the various parts of the system work, so you can customize, configure, and troubleshoot the system on your own.

Linux is not difficult to install and use. However, as with any implementation of Unix, there is often some black magic involved to get everything working correctly. We hope this book will get you on the Linux tour bus and show you how cool this operating system can be.

In this book, we cover the following topics:

- What is Linux? The design and philosophy of this unique operating system, and what it can do for you.

- All the details needed to run Linux, including suggestions on what kind of hardware configuration is recommended for a complete system.

- How to obtain and install Linux. We cover the Red Hat, SuSE, and Debian distributions in more detail than others, but the background here should be adequate to cover any release of the system.

- For new users, an introduction to the Unix system, including an overview of the most important commands and concepts.

- The care and feeding of the Linux system, including system administration and maintenance, upgrading the system, and how to fix things when they don't work.

- Getting the most out of your Linux system, with "power tools" such as TEX, Emacs, KDE, and more.

- The Linux programming environment. The tools of the trade for programming and developing software on the Linux system. We introduce compilation and debugging of C and C++ programs, Java, Perl, shell scripts, and Tcl/Tk.

- Using Linux for telecommunications and networking, including the basics of TCP/IP configuration, PPP for Internet connectivity over a modem, ISDN configuration, email, news, and Web access—we even show how to configure your Linux system as a web server.

There are a million things we'd love to show you how to do with Linux. Unfortunately, in order to cover them all, this book would be the size of the unabridged *Oxford English Dictionary* and would be impossible for anyone (let alone the poor authors) to maintain. Instead we've tried to include the most salient and interesting aspects of the system and show you how to find out more.

Chapter 4
Chapter 5

While much of the discussion in this book is not overly technical, it helps to have previous experience with another Unix system. For those who don't have Unix experience, we have included a short tutorial in Chapter 4, *Basic Unix Commands and Concepts*, for new users. Chapter 5, *Essential System Management*, is a complete chapter on systems administration, that should help even seasoned Unix users run a Linux system.

Appendix A

If you are new to Unix, you'll want to pick up a more complete guide to Unix basics. We don't dwell for long on the fundamentals, instead preferring to skip to the fun parts of the system. At any rate, while this book should be enough to get you running, more information on using Unix and its many tools will be essential for most readers. See Appendix A, *Sources of Linux Information*, for a list of sources of information.

A Brief History of Linux

Unix is one of the most popular operating systems worldwide because of its large support base and distribution. It was originally developed as a multitasking system for minicomputers and mainframes in the mid-1970s. It has since grown to become one of the most widely used operating systems anywhere, despite its sometimes confusing interface and lack of central standardization.

The real reason for Unix's popularity? Many hackers feel that Unix is the Right Thing—the One True Operating System. Hence, the development of Linux by an expanding group of Unix hackers who want to get their hands dirty with their own system.

Versions of Unix exist for many systems, ranging from personal computers to supercomputers such as the Cray Y-MP. Most versions of Unix for personal computers are quite expensive and cumbersome. At the time of this writing, a one-machine version of AT&T's System V for the 386 runs at about $US1500.

Linux is a freely distributable version of Unix, originally developed by Linus Torvalds, who began work on Linux in 1991 as a student at the University of Helsinki in Finland. Linus now works for Transmeta Corporation, a start-up in Santa Clara, California, and continues to maintain the Linux *kernel*, that is, the lowest-level core component of the operating system.

Linus released the initial version of Linux for free on the Internet, inadvertently spawning one of the largest software-development phenomena of all time. Today, Linux is authored and maintained by a group of several thousand (if not more) developers loosely collaborating across the Internet. Companies have sprung up to provide Linux support, to package it into easy-to-install distributions, and to sell workstations pre-installed with the Linux software. In March 1999, the first Linux World Expo trade show was held in San Jose, California, with reportedly well over 12,000 people in attendance. Most estimates place the number of Linux users worldwide somewhere around the 10 million mark (and we expect this number will look small by the time you read this).

Inspired by Andrew Tanenbaum's Minix operating system (another free Unix for PCs—albeit a very simple one), Linux began as a class project in which Linus wanted to build a simple Unix system that could run on a 386-based PC. The first discussions about Linux were on the Usenet newsgroup *comp.os.minix*. These discussions were concerned mostly with the development of a small, academic Unix system for Minix users who wanted more.

The very early development of Linux dealt mostly with the task-switching features of the 80386 protected-mode interface, all written in assembly code. Linus writes:

> After that it was plain sailing: hairy coding still, but I had some devices, and debugging was easier. I started using C at this stage, and it certainly speeds up development. This is also when I start to get serious about my megalomaniac ideas to make "a better Minix than Minix." I was hoping I'd be able to recompile *gcc* under Linux some day ...

> Two months for basic setup, but then only slightly longer until I had a disk driver (seriously buggy, but it happened to work on my machine) and a small filesystem. That was about when I made 0.01 available [around late August of 1991]: it wasn't pretty, it had no floppy driver, and it couldn't do much anything. I don't think anybody ever compiled that version. But by then I was hooked, and didn't want to stop until I could chuck out Minix.

No announcement was ever made for Linux Version 0.01. The 0.01 sources weren't even executable: they contained only the bare rudiments of the kernel source and assumed that you had access to a Minix machine to compile and play with them.

On October 5, 1991, Linus announced the first "official" version of Linux, version 0.02. At this point, Linus was able to run *bash* (the GNU Bourne Again Shell) and *gcc* (the GNU C compiler), but not much else was working. Again, this was intended as a hacker's system. The primary focus was kernel development; none of the issues of user support, documentation, distribution, and so on had even been addressed. Today, the situation is quite different—the real excitement in the Linux world deals with graphical user environments, easy-to-install distribution packages, and high-level applications such as graphics utilities and productivity suites.

Linus wrote in *comp.os.minix*:

> Do you pine for the nice days of Minix-1.1, when men were men and wrote their own device drivers? Are you without a nice project and just dying to cut your teeth on an OS you can try to modify for your needs? Are you finding it frustrating when everything works on Minix? No more all-nighters to get a nifty program working? Then this post might be just for you.

> As I mentioned a month ago, I'm working on a free version of a Minix-lookalike for AT-386 computers. It has finally reached the stage where it's even usable (though may not be depending on what you want), and I am willing to put out the sources for wider distribution. It's just version 0.02 ... but I've successfully run *bash*, *gcc*, GNU *make*, GNU *sed*, *compress*, etc. under it.

After Version 0.03, Linus bumped the version number up to 0.10, as more people started to work on the system. After several further revisions, Linus increased the version number to 0.95, to reflect his expectation that the system was ready for an "official" release very soon. (Generally, software is not assigned the version number 1.0 until it's theoretically complete or bug-free.) This was in March 1992. Almost a year and a half later, in late December 1993, the Linux kernel was still at Version 0.99.pl14—asymptotically approaching 1.0. Version 1.0 appeared in March 1994. As of the time of this writing (March 1999), the current kernel version is 2.2.6, while the 2.3 kernel versions are being concurrently developed. (We'll explain the Linux versioning conventions in detail later.)

Chapter 13

Linux could not have come into being without the GNU tools created by the Free Software Foundation. Their *gcc* compiler, which we'll discuss in Chapter 13, *Programming Languages*, gave life to Linus Torvalds's code. GNU tools have been intertwined with the development of Linux from the beginning. Because of the critical contributions of these tools, the Free Software Foundation even requests that distributions of Linux with accompanying utilities be called GNU/Linux.

Berkeley Unix (BSD) has also played an important role in Linux—not so much in its creation, but in providing the tools that make it popular. Most of the utilities that come with Linux distributions are ported from BSD. Networking daemons and utilities are particularly important. The kernel networking code for Linux was developed from the ground up (two or three times, in fact), but the daemons and utilities are vintage BSD.

Today, Linux is a complete Unix clone, capable of running the X Window System, TCP/IP, Emacs, Web, mail and news software, you name it. Almost all major free software packages have been ported to Linux, and commercial software is becoming available. In fact, many developers start by writing applications for Linux, and port them to other Unix systems later. More hardware is supported than in original versions of the kernel. Many people have executed benchmarks on Linux systems and found them to be faster than workstations from Sun Microsystems and Compaq, and Linux performs better than or as well as Windows 98 and Windows NT on a wide range of benchmarks. Who would have ever guessed that this "little" Unix clone would have grown up to take on the entire world of personal and server computing?

Who's Using Linux?

Application developers, system administrators, network providers, kernel hackers, multimedia authors: these are a few of the categories of people who find that Linux has a particular charm.

Unix programmers are increasingly using Linux because of its cost—they can pick up a complete programming environment for a few dollars and run it on cheap PC hardware—and because Linux offers a great basis for portable programs. It's a modern operating system that is POSIX-compliant and looks a lot like System V, so code that works on Linux should work on other contemporary systems. Linux on a modest PC runs faster than many Unix workstations.

Networking is one of Linux's strengths. It has been adopted with gusto by people who run community networks like Free-Nets or who want to connect nonprofit organizations or loose communities of users through UUCP. Linux makes a good hub for such networks. Since Linux also supports Network File System (NFS) and Network Information Service (NIS), you can easily merge a personal computer into a corporate or academic network with other Unix machines. It's easy to share files, support remote logins, and run applications on other systems. Linux also supports the Samba software suite, which allows a Linux machine to act as a Windows file and print server—many people are discovering that the combination of Linux and Samba for this purpose is faster (and cheaper) than running Windows NT.

Kernel hackers were the first to come to Linux—in fact, the ones who helped Linus Torvalds create Linux—and are still a formidable community. If you want to try tuning buffer sizes and the number of table entries to make your applications run a little faster, Linux is one of your best choices. You'll get a lot of sympathy on the Net when things go wrong, too.

Finally, Linux is becoming an exciting forum for multimedia. This is because it's compatible with an enormous variety of hardware, including the majority of modern sound and video cards. Several programming environments, including the MESA 3D toolkit (a free OpenGL implementation), have been ported to Linux. The GIMP (a free Adobe Photoshop work-alike) was originally developed under Linux, and is becoming the graphics manipulation and design tool of choice for many artists. For example, during the production of the movie "Titanic," Linux machines (with Alpha processors) were used to render some of the trick effects.

Linux has also had some real-world applications. Linux systems have traveled the high seas of the North Pacific, managing telecommunications and data analysis for an oceanographic research vessel. Linux systems are being used at research stations in Antarctica. On a more basic level, several hospitals are using Linux to maintain patient records. One of the reviewers of this book uses Linux in the U.S. Marine Corps. Linux is proving to be as reliable and useful as other implementations of Unix.

So Linux is spreading out in many directions. Even naive end users can enjoy it if they get the support universities and corporations typically provide their computer users. Configuration and maintenance require some dedication. But Linux proves to be cost-effective, powerful, and empowering for people who like having that extra control over their environments.

System Features

Linux supports most of the features found in other implementations of Unix, plus quite a few not found elsewhere. This section is a nickel tour of the Linux kernel features.

A Note on Linux Version Numbers

One potentially confusing aspect of Linux for newcomers is the way in which different pieces of software are assigned a version number. When you first approach Linux, chances are you'll be looking at a CD-ROM distribution, such as "Red Hat Version 5.2" or "SuSE Linux Version 6.0." It's important to understand that these version numbers only relate to the particular distribution (which is a prepackaged version of Linux along with tons of free application packages, usually sold on CD-ROM). Therefore, the version number assigned by Red Hat, SuSE, or Debian might not have anything to do with the individual version numbers of the software in that distribution. Don't be fooled—just because one distribution company uses a higher version number than another doesn't mean that the software is any more up-to-date.

The Linux kernel, as well as each application, component, library, or software package in a Linux distribution, generally has its *own* version number. For example, you might be using *gcc* Version 2.7.2.3, as well as the XFree86 graphical user interface Version 3.3.1. As you can guess, the higher the version number, the newer the software is. By installing a distribution (such as Red Hat and SuSE), all of this is simplified for you since the latest versions of each package are usually included in the distribution.

The Linux kernel has a peculiar version numbering scheme that you should be familiar with. As mentioned before, the kernel is the core operating system itself, responsible for managing all of the hardware resources in your machine—such as disks, network interfaces, memory, and so on. Unlike Windows systems, the Linux kernel doesn't include any application-level libraries or graphical user interfaces. In some sense, as a user you will never interact with the kernel directly, but rather through interfaces such as the shell or the GUI (more on this later).

However, many people still consider the Linux kernel version to be the version of the "entire system," which is somewhat misleading. Someone might say, "I'm running kernel Version 2.3.32," but this doesn't mean much if everything else on the system is years out of date.

The Linux kernel versioning system works as follows. At any given time, there are *two* "latest" versions of the kernel out there (meaning available for download from the Internet)—the "stable" and "development" releases. The stable release is meant for most Linux users who aren't interested in hacking on bleeding-edge experimental features, but who need a stable, working system that isn't changing underneath them from day to day. The development release, on the other hand, changes very rapidly as new features are added and tested by developers across the Internet. Changes to the stable release consist mostly of bug fixes and security patches, while changes to the development release can be anything from major new kernel subsystems to minor tweaks in a device driver for added performance. The Linux developers don't guarantee that the development kernel version will work for everyone, but they do maintain the stable version with the intention of making it run well everywhere.

The stable kernel release has an even minor version number (such as 2.2), while the development release has an odd minor version number (such as 2.3). Note that the current development kernel always has a minor version number exactly one greater than the current stable kernel. So, when the current stable kernel is 2.4, the current development kernel will be 2.5. (Unless, of course, Linus decides to rename Version 2.4 to 3.0—in which case the development version will be 3.1, naturally).

Each of these kernel versions has a third "patch level" version number associated with it, such as 2.2.19 or 2.3.85. The patch level specifies the particular revision of that kernel version, with higher numbers specifying newer revisions. As of the time of this writing in July 1999, the latest stable kernel is 2.2.10 and the latest development kernel is 2.3.11.

A Bag of Features

Linux is a complete multitasking, multiuser operating system (just like all other versions of Unix). This means that many users can be logged into the same machine at once, running multiple programs simultaneously. Linux also supports multiprocessor systems (such as dual-Pentium motherboards), with support for up to 16 processors in a system, which is great for high-performance servers and scientific applications.

The Linux system is mostly compatible with a number of Unix standards (inasmuch as Unix has standards) on the source level, including IEEE POSIX.1, System V, and BSD features. Linux was developed with source portability in mind: therefore, you will probably find features in the Linux system that are shared across multiple Unix implementations. A great deal of free Unix software available on the Internet and elsewhere compiles on Linux out of the box.

If you have some Unix background, you may be interested in some other specific internal features of Linux, including POSIX job control (used by shells such as the C shell, *csh*, and *bash*), pseudoterminals (*pty* devices), and support for national or customized keyboards using dynamically loadable keyboard drivers. Linux also supports *virtual consoles*, which allow you to switch between multiple login sessions from the system console in text mode. Users of the *screen* program will find the Linux virtual console implementation familiar.

Linux can quite happily co-exist on a system that has other operating systems installed, such as Windows 95/98, Windows NT, OS/2, or other versions of Unix. The Linux boot loader (LILO) allows you to select which operating system to start at boot time, and Linux is compatible with other boot loaders as well (such as the one found in Windows NT).

Linux can run on a wide range of CPU architectures, including the Intel x86 (386, 486, Pentium, Pentium Pro, II, and III), SPARC, Alpha, PowerPC, MIPS, and m68k. Ports to various other architectures are underway, and it is expected that Linux will run just fine on Intel's next-generation "Merced" processors. There has even been work to port Linux to embedded processors, such as the one found in the 3Com PalmPilot personal digital assistant.

Chapter 3
Chapter 5

Linux supports various filesystem types for storing data. Some filesystems, such as the Second Extended (*ext2fs*) filesystem, have been developed specifically for Linux. Other filesystem types, such as the Minix-1 and Xenix filesystems, are also supported. The MS-DOS filesystem has been implemented as well, allowing you to access Windows and DOS on hard drive or floppy directly. Support is included for OS/2, Apple, Amiga, and Windows NT filesystems as well. The ISO 9660 CD-ROM filesystem type, which reads all standard formats of CD-ROMs, is also supported. We'll talk more about filesystems in Chapter 3, *Installation and Initial Configuration*, and Chapter 5.

Chapter 15

Networking support is one of the greatest strengths of Linux, both in terms of functionality and performance. Linux provides a complete implementation of TCP/IP networking. This includes device drivers for many popular Ethernet cards, PPP and SLIP (allowing you to access a TCP/IP network via a serial connection), Parallel Line Internet Protocol (PLIP), and the NFS Network File System. The complete range of TCP/IP clients and services is supported, such as FTP, Telnet, NNTP, and Simple Mail Transfer Protocol (SMTP). The Linux kernel includes complete network firewall support, allowing you to configure any Linux machine as a firewall (which screens network packets, preventing unauthorized access to an intranet, for example). It is widely held that networking performance under Linux is superior to other operating systems. We'll talk more about networking in Chapter 15, *TCP/IP and PPP*.

Kernel

The *kernel* is the guts of the operating system itself; it's the code that controls the interface between user programs and hardware devices, the scheduling of processes to achieve multitasking, and many other aspects of the system. The kernel is not a separate process running on the system. Instead, you can think of the kernel as a set of routines, constantly in memory, that every process has access to. Kernel routines can be called in a number of ways. One direct method to utilize the kernel is for a process to execute a system call, which is a function that causes the kernel to execute some code on behalf of the process. For example, the *read* system call will read data from a file descriptor. To the programmer, this looks like another C function, but in actuality the code for *read* is contained within the kernel.

Kernel code is also executed in other situations. For example, when a hardware device issues an interrupt, the interrupt handler is found within the kernel. When a process takes an action that requires it to wait for results, the kernel steps in and puts the process to sleep, scheduling another process in its place. Similarly, the kernel switches control between processes rapidly, using the clock interrupt (and other means) to trigger a switch from one process to another. This is basically how multitasking is accomplished.

The Linux kernel is known as a *monolithic* kernel, in that all device drivers are part of the kernel proper. Some operating systems employ a *microkernel* architecture whereby device drivers and other components (such as filesystems and memory management code) are *not* part of the kernel—rather, they are treated similarly to regular user applications. There are advantages and disadvantages to both designs: the monolithic architecture is more common among Unix implementations and is the design employed by classic kernel designs, such as System V and BSD. Linux does support loadable device drivers (which can be loaded and unloaded from memory through user commands); this is the subject of the section "Loadable Device Drivers" in Chapter 7, *Upgrading Software and the Kernel.*

Chapter 7

The kernel is able to emulate FPU instructions itself on many architectures, so that systems without a math coprocessor can run programs that require floating-point math instructions.

The Linux kernel on Intel platforms is developed to use the special protected-mode features of the Intel 80x86 processors (starting with the 80386). In particular, Linux makes use of the protected-mode descriptor-based memory management paradigm and many of the other advanced features of these processors. Anyone familiar with 80386 protected-mode programming knows that this chip was designed for a multitasking system such as Unix (it was actually inspired by Multics). Linux exploits this functionality.

The Linux kernel supports demand-paged loaded executables. That is, only those segments of a program that are actually used are read into memory from disk. Also, if multiple instances of a program are running at once, only one copy of the program code will be in memory.

In order to increase the amount of available memory, Linux also implements disk paging: that is, a certain amount of *swap space** can be allocated on disk. When the system requires more physical memory, it will swap out inactive pages to disk, thus allowing you to run larger applications and support more users at once. However, swap is no substitute for physical RAM; it's much slower due to the time required to access the disk.

---

* Technically speaking, swap space is inappropriately named: entire processes are not swapped, but rather individual pages of memory are paged out. Of course, in many cases, entire processes will be swapped out, but this is not necessarily always the case.

The kernel also implements a unified memory pool for user programs and disk cache. In this way, all free memory is used for caching, and the cache is reduced when the processor is running large programs.

Executables use dynamically linked shared libraries, meaning that executables share common library code in a single library file found on disk, not unlike the SunOS shared library mechanism. This allows executable files to occupy much less space on disk, especially those files that use many library functions. This also means that a single copy of the library code is held in memory at one time, thus reducing overall memory usage. There are also statically linked libraries for those who wish to maintain "complete" executables without the need for shared libraries to be in place. Because Linux shared libraries are dynamically linked at runtime, programmers can replace modules of the libraries with their own routines.

Chapter 14

To facilitate debugging, the Linux kernel does core dumps for post-mortem analysis. Using a core dump and an executable linked with debugging support, you can determine what caused a program to crash. We'll talk about this in the section "Examining a Core File" in Chapter 14, *Tools for Programmers*.

Software Features

In this section, we'll introduce you to many of the software applications available for Linux and talk about a number of common computing tasks. After all, the most important part of the system is the wide range of software available for it. What's even more impressive on Linux is that most of this software is freely distributable.

Basic Commands and Utilities

Chapter 4

Virtually every utility you would expect to find on standard implementations of Unix has been ported to Linux. This includes basic commands such as *ls*, *awk*, *tr*, *sed*, *bc*, *more*, and so on. There are Linux ports of many popular software packages including Perl, Python, the Java Development Kit, and more. You name it— Linux has it. Therefore, you can expect your familiar working environment on other Unix systems to be duplicated on Linux. All of the standard commands and utilities are there. (Novice Unix users should see Chapter 4 for an introduction to these basic Unix commands.)

Many text editors are available, including *vi* (as well as "modern" versions, such as *vim*), *ex*, *pico*, and *jove*, as well as GNU Emacs and variants, such as XEmacs (which incorporates extensions for use under the X Window System) and *joe*. Whatever text editor you're accustomed to using has more than likely been ported to Linux.

The choice of a text editor is an interesting one. Many Unix users still use "simple" editors such as *vi* (in fact, the authors wrote this book using *vi* and Emacs under Linux). However, *vi* has many limitations due to its age, and more modern (and complex) editors, such as Emacs, are gaining popularity. Emacs supports a complete LISP-based macro language and interpreter, a powerful command syntax, and other fun-filled extensions. Emacs macro packages exist to allow you to read electronic mail and news, edit the contents of directories, and even engage in an artificially intelligent psychotherapy session (indispensable for stressed-out Linux hackers). In Chapter 9, *Editors, Text Tools, Graphics, and Printing*, we include a complete *vi* tutorial and describe Emacs in detail.

Chapter 9

One interesting note is that most of the basic Linux utilities are GNU software. These GNU utilities support advanced features not found in the standard versions from BSD or AT&T. For example, GNU's version of the *vi* editor, *elvis*, includes a structured macro language, which differs from the original AT&T version. However, the GNU utilities strive to remain compatible with their BSD and System V counterparts. Many people consider the GNU versions of these programs superior to the originals. An example of this are the GNU *gzip* and *bzip2* file-compression utilities, which compress data much more efficiently than the original Unix *compress* utility.

The most important utility to many users is the *shell*. The shell is a program that reads and executes commands from the user. In addition, many shells provide features such as *job control* (allowing the user to manage several running processes at once—not as Orwellian as it sounds), input and output redirection, and a command language for writing *shell scripts*. A shell script is a file containing a program in the shell command language, analogous to a "batch file" under MS-DOS.

There are many types of shells available for Linux. The most important difference between shells is the command language. For example, the C shell (*csh*) uses a command language somewhat like the C programming language. The classic Bourne shell uses a different command language. One's choice of a shell is often based on the command language it provides. The shell that you use defines, to some extent, your working environment under Linux.

No matter what Unix shell you're accustomed to, some version of it has probably been ported to Linux. The most popular shell is the GNU Bourne Again Shell (*bash*), a Bourne shell variant. *bash* includes many advanced features, such as job control, command history, command and filename completion, an Emacs-like (or optionally, a *vi*-like) interface for editing the command line, and powerful extensions to the standard Bourne shell language. Another popular shell is *tcsh*, a version of the C shell with advanced functionality similar to that found in *bash*. Other shells include the Korn shell (*ksh*), BSD's *ash*, *zsh*, a small Bourne-like shell, and *rc*, the Plan 9 shell.

What's so important about these basic utilities? Linux gives you the unique opportunity to tailor a custom system to your needs. For example, if you're the only person who uses your system, and you prefer to use the *vi* editor and the *bash* shell exclusively, there's no reason to install other editors or shells. The "do it yourself" attitude is prevalent among Linux hackers and users.

Text Processing and Word Processing

Almost every computer user has a need for some kind of document preparation system. (How many computer enthusiasts do you know who still use pen and paper? Not many, we'll wager.) In the PC world, *word processing* is the norm: it involves editing and manipulating text (often in a "What-You-See-Is-What-You-Get" [WYSIWYG] environment) and producing printed copies of the text, complete with figures, tables, and other garnishes.

In the Unix world, *text processing* is much more common, which is quite different from the classical concept of word processing. With a text-processing system, the author enters text using a "typesetting language" that describes how the text should be formatted. Instead of entering the text within a special word processing environment, the author may modify the source with any text editor, such as *vi* or Emacs. Once the source text (in the typesetting language) is complete, the user formats the text with a separate program, which converts the source to a format suitable for printing. This is somewhat analogous to programming in a language such as C, and "compiling" the document into a printable form.

There are many text-processing systems available for Linux. One is *groff*, the GNU version of the classic *troff* text formatter originally developed by Bell Labs and still used on many Unix systems worldwide. Another modern text-processing system is TEX, developed by Donald Knuth of computer science fame. Dialects of TEX, such as LATEX, are also available.

Text processors such as TEX and *groff* differ mostly in the syntax of their formatting languages. The choice of one formatting system over another is also based upon what utilities are available to satisfy your needs, as well as personal taste.

For example, some people consider the *groff* formatting language to be a bit obscure, so they use TEX, which is more readable by humans. However, *groff* is capable of producing plain ASCII output, viewable on a terminal, while TEX is intended primarily for output to a printing device. Still, various programs exist to produce plain ASCII from TEX-formatted documents or to convert TEX to *groff*, for example.

Another text-processing system is Texinfo, an extension to TEX used for software documentation by the Free Software Foundation. Texinfo is capable of producing a printed document, or an online-browsable hypertext "Info" document from a single source file. Info files are the main format of documentation used by GNU software, such as Emacs.

Text processors are used widely in the computing community for producing papers, theses, magazine articles, and books. (In fact, this book was originally written in the LATEX format, filtered into a home-grown SGML system, and printed from *groff*.) The ability to process the source language as a plain-text file opens the door to many extensions to the text processor itself. Because source documents are not stored in an obscure format, readable only by a particular word processor, programmers are able to write parsers and translators for the formatting language, thus extending the system.

What does such a formatting language look like? In general, the formatting language source consists mostly of the text itself, along with "control codes" to produce a particular effect, such as changing fonts, setting margins, creating lists, and so on.

The most famous text formatting language is HTML, which now has a younger cousin in XML; HTML is descended from the SGML in which this book is maintained. The particular tags used in this book (like <PARA> and <TITLE>) come from Docbook, a kind of industry-standard set of tags for marking up technical documentation, which is used in official Linux documentation (to be discussed later in this chapter). Here is a typical section beginning in Docbook:

```
<sect2><title>Basic Commands and Utilities</title>

<para>

Virtually every utility you would expect to find on standard
implementations of Unix has been ported to Linux. This
includes basic commands such as <command>ls</command>,
<command>awk</command>, <command>tr</command>,
<command>sed</command>, <command>bc</command>,
<command>more</command>, and so on.  There are Linux ports
of many popular software packages including Perl, Python,
the Java Development Kit, and more. You name it—Linux has
it.  Therefore, you can expect your familiar working
environment on other Unix systems to be duplicated on
Linux. All of the standard commands and utilities are
there.
(Novice Unix users should see
<xref linkend="X-100-3-chap-basic"> for an introduction to
these basic Unix commands.)

</para>
```

At first glance, the typesetting language may appear to be obscure, but it's actually quite easy to learn. Using a text-processing system enforces typographical standards when writing. For example, all enumerated lists within a document will look the same, unless the author modifies the definition of the enumerated list "environment."

The primary goal of typesetting languages is to allow the author to concentrate on writing the actual text, instead of worrying about typesetting conventions. When the example just shown is printed, the commands in <command> tags will be printed using whatever font, color, or other convention the publisher has chosen, and a command index can easily be generated too. Furthermore, the correct chapter number and title are plugged in where the strange-looking <xref&> tag was written, so they are correct even if the authors reorder the chapters after writing the paragraph.

While there are WYSIWYG editors for HTML (and even a few for SGML) getting used to entering tags by hand, like those in the previous example, actually takes only a little practice. Tools can then generate output in a standard format like PostScript or PDF and display it on the author's screen or send it to a printer. Text-processing systems illustrated in Chapter 9 include LaTeX, its close cousin Texinfo, and *troff*.

WYSIWYG word processors are attractive for many reasons; they provide a powerful, and sometimes complex, visual interface for editing the document. However, this interface is inherently limited to those aspects of text layout that are accessible to the user. For example, many word processors provide a special "format language" for producing complicated expressions such as mathematical formulae. This format language is identical to text processing, albeit on a much smaller scale.

The subtle benefit of text processing is that the system allows you to specify exactly what you mean. Also, text processing systems allow you to edit the source text with any text editor, and the source is easily converted to other formats. The tradeoff for this flexibility and power is the lack of a WYSIWYG interface.

Many users of word processors are used to seeing the formatted text as they edit it. On the other hand, when writing with a text processor, one generally doesn't worry about how the text will appear once it's formatted. The writer learns to expect how the text should look from the formatting commands used in the source.

There are programs that allow you to view the formatted document on a graphics display before printing. One example is the *xdvi* program, which displays a "device independent" file generated by the TeX system under the X Window System. Other software applications, such as *xfig*, provide a WYSIWYG graphics interface for drawing figures and diagrams, which are subsequently converted to the text-processing language for inclusion in your document.

There are many other text-processing utilities available. The powerful METAFONT system, used to design fonts for TeX, is included with the Linux port of TeX. Other programs include *ispell*, an interactive spell checker; *makeindex*, an index generator for LaTeX documents; and many *groff* and TeX-based macro packages for formatting various types of documents and mathematical texts. Conversion programs are available to translate between TeX or *groff* source and many other formats.

Chapter 9

In Chapter 9, we discuss LaTeX, *groff*, and other text-formatting tools in detail.

Commercial Applications

Commercial software vendors are becoming increasingly interested in making their products available for Linux. These products include office productivity suites, word processors, network administration utilities, and large-scale database engines. In the first two editions of this book, we couldn't say much about commercial application availability, but this is rapidly changing—so much so that by the time you read this, we believe that a host of other commercial application packages will have been ported to Linux.

Star Division (*http://www.stardivision.com*) has released the Star Office v5.0 office productivity suite for Linux (also available for Windows 98, Windows NT, and other Unix systems). This suite is more or less a clone of Microsoft Office, including a word processor, spreadsheet, HTML editor, presentation manager, and other tools. It is capable of reading file formats from a wide range of similar applications (including Microsoft Office) and is available for free download for non-commercial use.

Corel has ported WordPerfect 8 for Linux, which includes a word processor, spreadsheet, presentation software, personal information manager, and other applications. It is free for personal use. A single-user license for non-personal use is $US49.95 if bought from a retailer or $US69.95 if bought directly from Corel.

Companies such as Oracle, IBM, Informix, Sybase, and Interbase have released (or have announced plans to release) commercial database engines that have been ported to Linux. IBM has released a beta Linux version of its DB2 database server, available for free download from IBM's website (*http://www.ibm.com*). This beta release does not support clustering or several of the higher-end features found in other versions of DB2, but it does exploit multiprocessors. IBM has also announced that it will provide a Linux version of the popular AFS network filesystem.

Caldera has released NetWare for Linux 1.0, allowing Linux servers to host NetWare file, print, and directory services, and share data with Novell NetWare-based servers. It's compatible with NetWare 4.10b and NetWare clients for Windows 3.1/95/98, DOS, Linux, Macintosh, and UnixWare.

Programming Languages and Utilities

Linux provides a complete Unix programming environment, including all of the standard libraries, programming tools, compilers, and debuggers that you would expect to find on other Unix systems. Within the Unix software development world, applications and systems programming is usually done in C or C++. The standard C and C++ compiler for Linux is GNU's *gcc*, which is an advanced, modern compiler supporting many options. It's also capable of compiling C++ (including AT&T 3.0 features) as well as Objective-C, another object-oriented dialect of C.

Java, a relative newcomer on the programming-language scene, is fully supported under Linux. Sun's Java Development Kit Version 1.2 (also known as "Java 2") has been ported to Linux and is fully functional. Java is an object-oriented programming language and runtime environment that supports a diverse range of applications like web page applets, Internet-based distributed systems, database connectivity, and more. Programs written for Java can be run on any system (regardless of CPU architecture or operating system) that supports the Java Virtual Machine. There has been a great deal of excitement in the marketplace over the possibilities presented by Java.

Besides C, C++, and Java, many other compiled and interpreted programming languages have been ported to Linux, such as Smalltalk, FORTRAN, Pascal, LISP, Scheme, and Ada. In addition, various assemblers for writing machine code are available, as are Unix-hacking favorites such as Perl (the script language to end all script languages), Tcl/Tk (a shell-like command-processing system that includes support for developing simple X Window System applications), and Python (the first scripting language to be designed as object-oriented from the ground up).

The advanced *gdb* debugger has been ported, which allows you to step through a program to find bugs or examine the cause for a crash using a core dump. *gprof,* a profiling utility, will give you performance statistics for your program, letting you know where your program is spending most of its time. The Emacs text editor provides an interactive editing and compilation environment for various programming languages. Other tools that have been ported to Linux include GNU *make* and *imake,* used to manage compilation of large applications, and RCS, a system for source locking and revision control.

Linux is ideal for developing Unix applications. It provides a modern programming environment with all of the bells and whistles. Professional Unix programmers and system administrators can use Linux to develop software at home and then transfer the software to Unix systems at work. This not only can save a great deal of time and money, but also lets you work in the comfort of your own home.* Computer science students can use Linux to learn Unix programming and to explore other aspects of the system, such as kernel architecture.

With Linux, not only do you have access to the complete set of libraries and programming utilities, but you also have the complete kernel and library source code at your fingertips.

Chapter 13
Chapter 14

Chapters 13 and 14 are devoted to the programming languages and tools available for Linux.

---

* The authors use their Linux systems to develop and test X applications at home, which can then be directly compiled on workstations elsewhere.

The X Window System

The X Window System is the standard graphics interface for Unix machines. It's a powerful environment supporting many applications. Using X, the user can have multiple terminal windows on the screen at once, each window containing a different login session. A pointing device, such as a mouse, is generally used with the X interface.

One of the real strengths of the X Window System is that its "look and feel" is greatly customizable. It's possible to emulate the Windows 95/98, Macintosh, and NeXTStep environments under X, as well as to create totally novel desktop configurations (many Linux users prefer to make up their own).

Many X-specific applications have been written, such as games, graphics utilities, programming and documentation tools, and so on. With Linux and X, your system is a bona fide workstation. Coupled with TCP/IP networking, you can even display X applications running on other machines on your Linux screen, as is possible with other systems running X.

The X Window System, originally developed at MIT, is freely distributable. However, many commercial vendors have distributed proprietary enhancements to the original X software. The version of X available for Linux is known as XFree86, a port of X11R6 made freely distributable for PC-based Unix systems, such as Linux. XFree86 supports a wide range of video hardware, including VGA, Super VGA, and a number of accelerated video adaptors. XFree86 is a complete distribution of the X software, containing the X server itself, many applications and utilities, programming libraries, and documentation.

Standard X applications include *xterm* (a terminal emulator used for most text-based applications within an X window), *xdm* (the X Session Manager, which handles logins), *xclock* (a simple clock display), *xman* (an X-based manual page reader), and more. The many X applications available for Linux are too numerous to mention here, but the base XFree86 distribution includes the "standard" applications found in the original MIT release. Many others are available separately, and theoretically any application written for X should compile cleanly under Linux.

The look and feel of the X interface is controlled to a large extent by the *window manager*. This friendly program is in charge of the placement of windows, the user interface for resizing, iconifying, and moving windows, the appearance of window frames, and so on. The standard XFree86 distribution includes *twm*, the classic MIT window manager, although more advanced window managers, such as the Open Look Virtual Window Manager (*olvwm*), are available as well. One window manager that is popular among Linux users is *fvwm2*. This is a small window manager, requiring less than half of the memory used by *twm*. It provides a 3D appearance for windows, as well as a virtual desktop; if the user moves the mouse to the edge of the screen, the entire desktop is shifted as if the display were much larger than it actually is. *fvwm2* is greatly customizable and allows all functions to be accessed from the keyboard as well as from the mouse. Many Linux distributions use *fvwm2* as the standard window manager.

The XFree86 distribution contains programming libraries and includes files for those wily programmers who wish to develop X applications. Various widget sets, such as Athena, Open Look, and Xaw3D, are supported. All of the standard fonts, bitmaps, manual pages, and documentation are included. PEX (a programming interface for 3D graphics) is also supported, as is Mesa, a free implementation of the OpenGL 3D graphics primitives.

Chapter 10
Chapter 11

In Chapter 10, *Installing the X Window System* and Chapter 11, *Customizing Your X Environment*, we'll discuss how to install and use the X Window System on your Linux machine.

KDE and GNOME

KDE and GNOME are two new and noteworthy projects generating a lot of excitement in the Linux world. Both systems intend to produce a complete integrated graphical desktop environment, running on top of the X Window System. By building up a powerful suite of development tools, libraries, and applications that are integrated into the desktop environment, KDE and GNOME aim to usher in the next era of Linux desktop computing. Both systems provide a rich GUI, window manager, utilities, and applications that rival or exceed the features of systems such as the Windows 98 desktop.

With KDE and GNOME, even casual users and beginners will feel right at home with Linux. Most distributions automatically configure one of these desktop environments during installation, making it unnecessary to ever touch the text-only console interface.

While both KDE and GNOME aim to make the Unix environment more user-friendly, they have different emphases. KDE's main goals are ease-of-use, stability, and user-interface compatibility with other computing environments (such as Windows 95). GNOME, on the other hand, aims more at good looks and maximum configurability.

Networking

Linux boasts one of the most powerful and robust networking systems in the world—so much so that more and more people are finding that Linux makes an excellent choice as a network server. Linux supports the two primary networking protocols for Unix systems: TCP/IP and UUCP. TCP/IP (Transmission Control Protocol/Internet Protocol, for acronym aficionados) is the set of networking paradigms that allows systems all over the world to communicate on a single network known as the Internet. With Linux, TCP/IP, and a connection to the network, you can communicate with users and machines across the Internet via the Web, electronic mail, Usenet news, file transfers with FTP, and more.

Most TCP/IP networks use Ethernet as the physical network transport. Linux supports many popular Ethernet cards and interfaces for personal computers and laptops. Linux also supports Fast Ethernet, Gigabit Ethernet, ATM, ISDN, wireless LAN adapters, Token Ring, packet radio, and a number of high-performance network interfaces.

However, because not everyone has an Ethernet drop at home, Linux also supports PPP and SLIP, allowing you to connect to the Internet via modem. In order for you to use PPP or SLIP, your ISP will have to provide you with an account on their dial-in server, Many businesses and universities provide dial-in PPP or SLIP access. In fact, if your Linux system has an Ethernet connection as well as a modem, you can configure it as a PPP/SLIP server for other hosts.

Linux supports a wide range of web browsers (including Netscape Navigator, the free Mozilla spin-off, and the text-based Lynx browser). With a web browser and a Linux machine connected to the Internet, you can engage in Web surfing, email, chat, news, and many other web-based services.

Chapter 16

Linux also hosts a range of web servers (including the popular and free Apache web server). In fact, it's estimated that Apache running on Linux systems drives more web sites than any other platform in the world. Apache is easy to set up and use; we'll show you how in Chapter 16, *The World Wide Web and Electronic Mail.*

Samba is a package that allows Linux machines to act as a Windows file and print server. NFS allows your system to share files seamlessly with other machines on the network. With NFS, remote files look to you as if they were located on your own system's drives. File Transfer Protocol (FTP) allows you to transfer files to and from other machines on the network.

A full range of mail and news readers are available for Linux, such as Elm, Pine, *rn, nn,* and *tin.* Whatever your preference, you can configure your Linux system to send and receive electronic mail and news from all over the world.

Other networking features include NNTP-based electronic news systems such as C News and INN; the *sendmail, exim* and *smail* mail transfer agents; *telnet, rlogin, ssh,* and *rsh,* which allow you to log in and execute commands on other machines on the network; and *finger,* which allows you to get information on other Internet users. There are tons of TCP/IP-based applications and protocols out there.

If you have experience with TCP/IP applications on other Unix systems, Linux will be familiar to you. The system provides a standard socket programming interface, so virtually any program that uses TCP/IP can be ported to Linux. The Linux X server also supports TCP/IP, allowing you to display applications running on other systems on your Linux display. Administration of Linux networking will be familiar to those coming from other Unix systems, as the configuration and monitoring tools are similar to their BSD counterparts.

Chapter 15

In Chapter 15, we'll discuss the configuration and setup of TCP/IP, including PPP, for Linux. We'll also discuss configuration of web browsers, web servers, and mail software.

UUCP (Unix to Unix Copy) is an older mechanism used to transfer files. UUCP machines are connected to each other over phone lines via modem, but UUCP is able to transport over a TCP/IP network as well. If you do not have access to a TCP/IP network or a PPP server, you can configure your system to send and receive files and electronic mail using UUCP.

Telecommunications and BBS Software

Telecommunications software under Linux is very similar to that found under Windows or other operating systems. Anyone who has used a telecommunications package will find the Linux equivalent familiar. If you have a modem, you will be able to communicate with other machines using one of the telecommunications packages available for Linux. Many people use telecommunications software to access bulletin board systems (BBSes), as well as commercial online services. Other people use their modems to connect to a Unix system at work or school. You can even use your modem and Linux system to send and receive facsimiles.

Appendix H

One of the most popular communications packages for Linux is Seyon, an X application providing a customizable, ergonomic interface, with built-in support for various file-transfer protocols such as Kermit, Zmodem, and so on. Other telecommunications programs include C-Kermit, *pcomm*, and *minicom*. These are similar to communications programs found on other operating systems and are quite easy to use. Zmodem for Linux is described in Appendix H, *Zmodem File Transfer*.

If you do not have access to a PPP server (see the previous section), you can use *term* to multiplex your serial line. *term* allows you to open multiple login sessions over the modem connection to a remote machine. *term* also allows you to redirect X client connections to your local X server through the serial line, enabling you to display remote X applications on your Linux system. Another software package, KA9Q, implements a similar SLIP-like interface.

If you do not have access to a TCP/IP network or UUCP feed, Linux allows you to communicate with a number of BBS networks, such as Fidonet, with which you can exchange electronic news and mail via the phone line.

Interfacing with Windows and MS-DOS

Various utilities exist to interface with the world of Windows 95, Windows 98, and MS-DOS. The most well-known application is a project known as Wine—a Microsoft Windows emulator for the X Window System under Linux. The intent of this project, which is still under development, is to allow Microsoft Windows applications to run directly under Linux. This is similar to the proprietary WABI

Windows emulator from Sun Microsystems. Wine is in a process of continual development, and now runs a wide variety of Windows software, including many desktop applications and several games. See *http://www.winehq.com* for details of the project's progress.

Linux provides a seamless interface for transferring files between Linux and Windows systems. You can mount a Windows partition or floppy under Linux, and directly access Windows files as you would any others. In addition, there is the *mtools* package that allows direct access to MS-DOS–formatted floppies, as well as *htools*, which does the same for Macintosh floppy disks.

Another application is the Linux MS-DOS Emulator, which allows you to run many MS-DOS applications directly from Linux. Although Linux and MS-DOS are completely different operating systems, the x86 protected-mode environment allows certain tasks to behave as if they were running in 8086-emulation mode, as MS-DOS applications do.

The MS-DOS emulator is still under development, yet many popular applications run under it. Understandably, however, MS-DOS applications that use bizarre or esoteric features of the system may never be supported, because it's only an emulator. For example, you wouldn't expect to be able to run any programs that use x86 protected-mode features, such as Microsoft Windows (in 386-enhanced mode, that is).

Applications that run successfully under the Linux MS-DOS Emulator include 4DOS (a command interpreter), Foxpro 2.0, Harvard Graphics, MathCad, Turbo Assembler, Turbo C/C++, Turbo Pascal, Microsoft Windows 3.0 (in *real* mode), and WordPerfect 5.1. Standard MS-DOS commands and utilities, such as *PKZIP*, work with the emulator as well.

The MS-DOS Emulator is meant mostly as an ad hoc solution for those people who need MS-DOS only for a few applications, but use Linux for everything else. It's not meant to be a complete implementation of MS-DOS. Of course, if the Emulator doesn't satisfy your needs, you can always run MS-DOS as well as Linux on the same system (but not at the same time). Using the LILO boot loader, you can specify which operating system to start at boot time. Linux can coexist with other operating systems, such as OS/2, as well.

Chapter 12

We'll show you how to use the MS-DOS emulator in the section "DOS Emulators: Dosemu and xdos" in Chapter 12, *Windows Compatibility and Samba*, along with other ways to interface Linux with Windows.

Other Applications

A host of miscellaneous applications are available for Linux, as one would expect from such a hodgepodge operating system. Linux's primary focus is currently for personal Unix computing, but this is rapidly changing. Business and scientific software is expanding, and commercial software vendors are beginning to contribute to the growing pool of applications.

Scientific computing applications include FELT (a finite element analysis tool), *gnuplot* (a plotting and data analysis application), Octave (a symbolic mathematics package, similar to MATLAB), *xspread* (a spreadsheet calculator), *xfractint* (an X-based port of the popular Fractint fractal generator), *xlispstat* (a statistics package), and more. Other applications include Spice (a circuit design and analysis tool) and Khoros (an image/digital signal processing and visualization system).

Of course, there are many more such applications that have been, and can be, ported to run on Linux. Whatever your field, porting Unix-based applications to Linux should be straightforward. Linux provides a complete Unix programming interface, sufficient to serve as the base for any scientific application.

As with any operating system, Linux has its share of games. These include classic text-based dungeon games such as Nethack and Moria; MUDs (multiuser dungeons, which allow many users to interact in a text-based adventure) such as DikuMUD and TinyMUD; and a slew of X games, such as *xtetris*, *netrek*, and *Xboard* (the X11 front-end to *gnuchess*). There has been increasing commercial interest in graphics-intensive games under Linux, and iD Software has produced Linux versions of Quake, Quake II, Quake III, and Doom. A number of other PC game vendors are providing Linux versions as well, and many of them admit to developing their software almost entirely under Linux!

For audiophiles, Linux has support for various sound cards and related software, such as CDplayer (a program that can control a CD-ROM drive as a conventional CD player, surprisingly enough), MIDI sequencers and editors (allowing you to compose music for playback through a synthesizer or other MIDI-controlled instrument), and sound editors for digitized sounds.

Can't find the application you're looking for? Freshmeat, found on the Web at *http://www.freshmeat.net*, is a popular directory of free software, nearly all of which runs under Linux. While this directory is far from complete, it contains a great deal of software. Take a look at it just to see the enormous amount of code that has been developed for Linux.

If you absolutely can't find what you need, you can always attempt to port the application from another platform to Linux. Or, if all else fails, you can write the application yourself. That's the spirit of Free Software—if you want something to be done right, do it yourself!

About Linux's Copyright

Linux is covered by what is known as the GNU *General Public License*, or *GPL*. The GPL, which is sometimes referred to as a "copyleft" license, was developed for the GNU project by the Free Software Foundation. It makes a number of provisions for the distribution and modification of "free software." "Free," in this sense, refers to freedom, not just cost. The GPL has always been subject to misinterpretation, and we hope that this summary will help you to understand the extent and goals of the GPL and its effect on Linux. A complete copy of the GPL is available at *http://www.gnu.org/copyleft/gpl.html.*

Originally, Linus Torvalds released Linux under a license more restrictive than the GPL, which allowed the software to be freely distributed and modified, but prevented any money changing hands for its distribution and use. The GPL allows people to sell and make profit from free software, but doesn't allow them to restrict the right for others to distribute the software in any way.

First, we should explain that "free software" covered by the GPL is *not* in the public domain. Public domain software is software that is not copyrighted and is literally owned by the public. Software covered by the GPL, on the other hand, is copyrighted to the author or authors. This means that the software is protected by standard international copyright laws and that the author of the software is legally defined. Just because the software may be freely distributed doesn't mean it is in the public domain.

GPL-licensed software is also not "shareware." Generally, "shareware" software is owned and copyrighted by the author, but the author requires users to send in money for its use after distribution. On the other hand, software covered by the GPL may be distributed and used free of charge.

The GPL also allows people to take and modify free software, and distribute their own versions of the software. However, any derived works from GPL software must also be covered by the GPL. In other words, a company could not take Linux, modify it, and sell it under a restrictive license. If any software is derived from Linux, that software must be covered by the GPL as well.

People and organizations can distribute GPL software for a fee and can even make a profit from its sale and distribution. However, in selling GPL software, the distributor can't take those rights away from the purchaser; that is, if you purchase GPL software from some source, you may distribute the software for free or sell it yourself as well.

This might sound like a contradiction at first. Why sell software for profit when the GPL allows anyone to obtain it for free? When a company bundles a large amount of free software on a CD-ROM and distributes it, they need to charge for the overhead of producing and distributing the CD-ROM, and they may even decide to make profit from the sale of the software. This is allowed by the GPL.

Organizations that sell free software must follow certain restrictions set forth in the GPL. First, they can't restrict the rights of users who purchase the software. This means that if you buy a CD-ROM of GPL software, you can copy and distribute that CD-ROM free of charge, or you can resell it yourself. Second, distributors must make it obvious to users that the software is indeed covered by the GPL. Third, distributors must provide, free of charge, the complete source code for the software being distributed, or they must point their customers on demand to where the software can be downloaded. This will allow anyone who purchases GPL software to make modifications of that software.

Allowing a company to distribute and sell free software is a very good thing. Not everyone has access to the Internet to download software, such as Linux, for free. The GPL allows companies to sell and distribute software to those people who do not have free (cost-wise) access to the software. For example, many organizations sell Linux on floppy, tape, or CD-ROM via mail order, and make profit from these sales. The developers of Linux may never see any of this profit; that is the understanding that is reached between the developer and the distributor when software is licensed by the GPL. In other words, Linus knew that companies may wish to sell Linux and that he may not see a penny of the profits from those sales.

In the free software world, the important issue is not money. The goal of free software is always to develop and distribute fantastic software and to allow anyone to obtain and use it. In the next section, we'll discuss how this applies to the development of Linux.

Open Source and the Philosophy of Linux

When new users encounter Linux, they often have a few misconceptions and false expectations of the system. Linux is a unique operating system, and it's important to understand its philosophy and design in order to use it effectively. At the center of the Linux philosophy is a concept that we now call Open Source Software.

Open Source is a term that applies to software for which the source code—the inner workings of the program—is freely available for anyone to download, modify, and redistribute. Software covered under the GNU GPL, described in the previous section, fits into the category of Open Source. Not surprisingly, though, so does a lot of other software that uses copyright licenses similar, but not identical, to the GPL. For example, software that can be freely modified but that does not have the same strict requirements for redistribution as the GPL is also considered Open Source.

The so-called "Open Source development model" is a phenomenon that started with the Free Software Foundation and which was popularized with Linux. It's a totally different way of producing software that opens up every aspect of development, debugging, testing, and study to anyone with enough interest in doing so. Rather than relying upon a single corporation to develop and maintain a piece of software, Open Source allows the code to evolve, openly, in a community of developers and users who are motivated by desire to *create good software*, rather than simply make a profit.

O'Reilly & Associates, Inc., has published a book, *Open Sources*, which serves as a good introduction to the Open Source development model. It's a collection of essays about the Open Source process by leading developers (including Linus Torvalds and Richard Stallman) and was edited by Chris DiBona, Sam Ockman, and Mark Stone.

Open Source has received a lot of media attention, and some are calling the phenomenon the "next wave" in software development, which will sweep the old way of doing things under the carpet. It still remains to be seen whether that will happen, but there have been some encouraging events that make this outcome seem not so unlikely. For example, Netscape Corporation has released the code for their web browser as an Open Source project called Mozilla, and companies such as Sun Microsystems, IBM, and Apple have announced plans to release certain products as Open Source in the hopes that they will flourish in a community-driven software development effort.

Open Source has received a lot of media attention, and Linux is at the center at all of it. In order to understand where the Linux development mentality is coming from, however, it might make sense to take a look at how commercial Unix systems have traditionally been built.

In commercial Unix development houses, the entire system is developed with a rigorous policy of quality assurance, source and revision control systems, documentation, and bug reporting and resolution. Developers are not allowed to add features or to change key sections of code on a whim: they must validate the change as a response to a bug report and consequently "check in" all changes to the source control system, so that the changes can be backed out if necessary. Each developer is assigned one or more parts of the system code, and only that developer may alter those sections of the code while it is "checked out."

Internally, the quality assurance department runs rigorous test suites (so-called "regression tests") on each new pass of the operating system and reports any bugs. It's the responsibility of the developers to fix these bugs as reported. A complicated system of statistical analysis is employed to ensure that a certain percentage of bugs are fixed before the next release, and that the operating system as a whole passes certain release criteria.

In all, the process used by commercial Unix developers to maintain and support their code is very complicated, and quite reasonably so. The company must have quantitative proof that the next revision of the operating system is ready to be shipped—hence the gathering and analyzing of statistics about the operating system's performance. It's a big job to develop a commercial Unix system, often large enough to employ hundreds (if not thousands) of programmers, testers, documenters, and administrative personnel. Of course, no two commercial Unix vendors are alike, but you get the general picture.

With Linux, you can throw out the entire concept of organized development, source control systems, structured bug reporting, or statistical analysis. Linux is, and more than likely always will be, a hacker's operating system.*

Linux is primarily developed as a group effort by volunteers on the Internet from all over the world. There is no single organization responsible for developing the system. For the most part, the Linux community communicates via various mailing lists and web sites. A number of conventions have sprung up around the development effort: for example, programmmers wanting to have their code included in the "official" kernel should mail it to Linus Torvalds. He will test the code and include it in the kernel (as long as it doesn't break things or go against the overall design of the system, he will more than likely include it).

The system itself is designed with a very open-ended, feature-rich approach. While recently the number of new features and critical changes to the system has diminished, the general rule is that a new version of the kernel will be released about every few weeks (sometimes even more frequently than this). Of course, this is a very rough figure; it depends on several factors, including the number of bugs to be fixed, the amount of feedback from users testing prerelease versions of the code, and the amount of sleep that Linus has had that week.

Suffice it to say that not every single bug has been fixed and not every problem ironed out between releases. As long as the system appears to be free of critical or oft-manifesting bugs, it's considered "stable" and new revisions are released. The thrust behind Linux development is not an effort to release perfect, bug-free code; it's to develop a free implementation of Unix. Linux is for the developers, more than anyone else.

Appendix A

Anyone who has a new feature or software application to add to the system generally makes it available in an "alpha" stage—that is, a stage for testing by those brave users who want to bash out problems with the initial code. Because the Linux community is largely based on the Internet, alpha software is usually uploaded to one or more of the various Linux web sites (see Appendix A), and a message is posted to one of the Linux mailing lists about how to get and test the code. Users who download and test alpha software can then mail results, bug fixes, or questions to the author.

After the initial problems in the alpha code have been fixed, the code enters a "beta" stage, in which it's usually considered stable but not complete (that is, it works, but not all of the features may be present). Otherwise, it may go directly to a "final" stage in which the software is considered complete and usable. For kernel

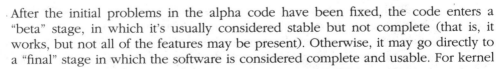

---

* What we mean by "hacker" is a feverishly dedicated programmer—a person who enjoys exploiting computers and generally doing interesting things with them. This is in contrast to the common connotation of "hacker" as a computer wrongdoer or an outlaw.

code, once it's complete, the developer may ask Linus to include it in the standard kernel, or as an optional add-on feature to the kernel.

Keep in mind these are only conventions—not rules. Some people feel so confident with their software that they don't need to release an alpha or test version. It's always up to the developer to make these decisions.

What happened to regression testing and the rigorous quality process? It's been replaced by the modality of "release early and release often." The users are the best testers, because they try out the software in a variety of environments and a host of demanding real-life applications that can't be easily duplicated by any software Quality Assurance group. One of the best features of this development and release model is that bugs (and security flaws) are often found, reported, and fixed within *hours*—not days or weeks.

You might be amazed that such a nonstructured system of volunteers programming and debugging a complete Unix system could get anything done at all. As it turns out, it's one of the most efficient and motivated development efforts ever employed. The entire Linux kernel was written *from scratch*, without employing any code from proprietary sources. A great deal of work was put forth by volunteers to port all the free software under the sun to the Linux system. Libraries were written and ported, filesystems developed, and hardware drivers written for many popular devices.

The Linux software is generally released as a *distribution*, which is a set of prepackaged software making up an entire system. It would be quite difficult for most users to build a complete system from the ground up, starting with the kernel, then adding utilities, and installing all necessary software by hand. Instead, there are a number of software distributions including everything you need to install and run a complete system. Again, there is no standard distribution; there are many, each with their own advantages and disadvantages. In this book, we describe how to install the Red Hat, SuSE, and Debian distributions, but this book can help you with any distribution you choose.

Despite the completeness of the Linux software, you still need a bit of Unix knowhow to install and run a complete system. No distribution of Linux is completely bug-free, so you may be required to fix small problems by hand after installation.

Hints for Unix Novices

Installing and using your own Linux system doesn't require a great deal of background in Unix. In fact, many Unix novices successfully install Linux on their systems. This is a worthwhile learning experience, but keep in mind that it can be very frustrating to some. If you're lucky, you will be able to install and start using your Linux system without any Unix background. However, once you are ready to delve into the more complex tasks of running Linux—installing new software, recompiling the kernel, and so forth—having background knowledge in Unix is going to be a necessity. (Note, however, that many distributions of Linux are as easy to install and configure as Windows 98 and certainly easier than Windows NT.)

Chapter 4
Chapter 5

Fortunately, by running your own Linux system, you will be able to learn the essentials of Unix necessary to perform these tasks. This book contains a good deal of information to help you get started. Chapter 4 is a tutorial covering Unix basics, and Chapter 5 contains information on Linux system administration. You may wish to read these chapters before you attempt to install Linux at all; the information contained therein will prove to be invaluable should you run into problems.

Nobody can expect to go from being a Unix novice to a Unix system administrator overnight. No implementation of Unix is expected to run trouble and maintenance free. You must be aptly prepared for the journey that lies ahead. Otherwise, if you're new to Unix, you may become overly frustrated with the system.

Hints for Unix Gurus

Even those people with years of Unix programming and system-administration experience may need assistance before they are able to pick up and install Linux. There are still aspects of the system Unix wizards need to be familiar with before diving in. For one thing, Linux is not a commercial Unix system. It doesn't attempt to uphold the same standards as other Unix systems you may have come across, but in some sense, Linux is *redefining* the Unix world, by giving all other systems a run for their money. To be more specific, while stability is an important factor in the development of Linux, it's not the *only* factor.

More important, perhaps, is functionality. In many cases, new code will make it into the standard kernel even though it's still buggy and not functionally complete. The assumption is that it's more important to release code that users can test and use than delay a release until it's "complete." Nearly all Open Source software projects have an alpha release before they are completely tested. In this way, the Open Source community at large has a chance to work with the code, test it, and develop it further, while those who find the alpha code "good enough" for their needs can use it. Commercial Unix vendors rarely, if ever, release software in this manner.

If you have been a Unix system administrator for more than a decade, and have used every commercial Unix system under the sun (no pun intended), Linux may take some getting used to. The system is very modern and dynamic, with a new kernel release approximately every few months and new utilities constantly being released. One day your system may be completely up to date with the current trend, and the next day the same system is considered to be in the Stone Age.

With all of this dynamic activity, how can you expect to keep up with the ever-changing Linux world? For the most part, it's best to upgrade incrementally; that is, upgrade only those parts of the system that *need* upgrading, and then only when you think an upgrade is necessary. For example, if you never use Emacs, there is little reason to continuously install every new release of Emacs on your system. Furthermore, even if you are an avid Emacs user, there is usually no reason to upgrade it unless you find that some feature is missing that is in the next release. There is little or no reason to always be on top of the newest version of software.

We hope that Linux meets or exceeds your expectations of a home-brew Unix system. At the very core of Linux is the spirit of free software, of constant development, and of growth. The Linux community favors expansion over stability, and that is a difficult concept to swallow for many people, especially those steeped in the world of commercial Unix. You can't expect Linux to be perfect—nothing ever is in the free software world (or any other world, for that matter). However, we believe that Linux really is as complete and useful as any other implementation of Unix.

Differences Between Linux and Other Operating Systems

It's important to understand the differences between Linux and other operating systems, such as Windows 95/98, Windows NT, OS/2, and other implementations of Unix for the personal computer. First of all, it should be made clear that Linux will coexist happily with other operating systems on the same machine: that is, you can run Windows NT and OS/2 along with Linux on the same system without problems. There are even ways to interact between the various operating systems, as you'll see.

Why Use Linux?

Why use Linux instead of a commercial operating system? We could give you a thousand reasons. One of the most important, however, is that Linux is an excellent choice for personal Unix computing. If you're a Unix software developer, why use Windows at home? Linux will allow you to develop and test Unix software on your PC, including database and X applications. If you're a student, chances are that your university computing system runs Unix. With Linux, you can run your own Unix system and tailor it to your own needs. Installing and running Linux is also an excellent way to learn Unix if you don't have access to other Unix machines.

But let's not lose perspective. Linux isn't just for personal Unix users. It's robust and complete enough to handle large tasks, as well as distributed computing needs. Many businesses are moving to Linux in lieu of other Unix-based workstation environments. Linux has an excellent price-performance ratio, is one of the most stable and powerful operating systems available, and because of its Open Source nature, is completely customizable for your needs. Universities are finding Linux to be perfect for teaching courses in operating systems design. Larger commercial software vendors are starting to realize the opportunities a free operating system can provide.

Linux Versus Windows 95 and 98

It's not uncommon to run both Linux and Windows 95/98 on the same system. Many Linux users rely on Windows for applications such as word processing and productivity tools. While Linux provides its own analogs for these applications (for example, TEX), and commercial software support for Linux is increasing, there are various reasons why a particular user would want to run Windows as well as Linux. If your entire dissertation is written using Microsoft Word, you may not be able to easily convert it to TEX or some other format (although the Star Office suite for Linux can probably do the trick). There are many commercial applications for Windows that aren't available for Linux, and there's no reason why you can't use both.

As you might know, Windows 95 and 98 do not fully utilize the functionality of the x86 processor. On the other hand, Linux runs completely in the processor's protected mode and exploits all of the features of the machine, including multiple processors.

We could debate the pros and cons of Windows and Linux for pages on end. However, suffice it to say that Linux and Windows are completely different entities. Windows is inexpensive (compared to other commercial operating systems) and has a strong foothold in the PC computing world. No other operating system for the PC has reached the level of popularity of Windows, largely because the cost of these other operating systems is unapproachable for most personal computer users. Very few PC users can imagine spending a thousand dollars or more on the operating system alone. Linux, however, is free, and you finally have the chance to decide.

We will allow you to make your own judgments of Linux and Windows based on your expectations and needs. Linux is not for everybody. But if you have always wanted to run a complete Unix system at home, without the high cost of other Unix implementations for the PC, Linux may be what you're looking for.

There are tools available to allow you to interact between Linux and Windows. For example, it's easy to access Windows files from Linux. Development is proceeding on the Wine Windows emulator, which allows you to run many popular applications.

Linux Versus Windows NT

A number of other advanced operating systems are on the rise in the PC world. Specifically, Microsoft's Windows NT is becoming very popular for server computing.

Windows NT, like Linux, is a full multitasking operating system, supporting multiprocessor machines, several CPU architectures, virtual memory, networking, security, and so on. However, the real difference between Linux and Windows NT is that Linux is a version of Unix and hence benefits from the contributions of the Unix community at large.

There are many implementations of Unix from many vendors. There is a large push in the Unix community for standardization in the form of open systems, but no single corporation controls this design. Hence, any vendor (or, as it turns out, any hacker) may implement these standards in an implementation of Unix.

Windows NT, on the other hand, is a proprietary system. The interface and design are controlled by a single corporation, Microsoft, and only that corporation may implement the design. (Don't expect to see a free version of Windows NT anytime in the near future.) In one sense, this kind of organization is beneficial: it sets a strict standard for the programming and user interface unlike that found even in the open systems community. NT is NT wherever you go.

It seems likely that in the coming years, Linux and Windows NT will be battling it out for their share of the server computing market. Windows NT has behind it the full force of the Microsoft marketing machine, while Linux has a community of thousands of developers helping to advance the system through the Open Source model. So far, benchmarks of Linux versus Windows NT have demonstrated that each system has its strengths and weaknesses; however, Linux wins hands-down in a number of areas, most notably networking performance. Linux is also much smaller than Windows NT, has a much better price-performance ratio, and is generally seen as more stable. (While Windows NT is known to crash quite often, Linux machines run continuously for months.) It might seem amazing that "little" Linux gives Microsoft serious competition, but it's not surprising when you realize how effective the Open Source development process really is.

Other Implementations of Unix

There are several other implementations of Unix for the personal computer. The Intel x86 architecture lends itself to the Unix design, and a number of vendors have taken advantage of this, including Sun (with Solaris x86), SCO, and BSDI.

In terms of features, other implementations of Unix for the PC are quite similar to Linux. You will see that almost all commercial versions of Unix support roughly the same software, programming environment, and networking features. However, there are some major differences between Linux and commercial versions of Unix. This stems primarily from Linux's roots as a "personal" Unix system, rather than one that runs only on large servers (although Linux is perfectly at home in either environment).

First of all, Linux supports a much wider range of hardware than other Unix implementations, simply because there is more demand under Linux to support every crazy brand of sound, graphics, network, and SCSI board. Plus, under the Open Source model, anyone with enough time and interest to write a driver for a particular board is able to do so. We'll cover the hardware requirements for Linux in the next section.

The most important factor to consider for many users is price. The Linux software is free if you have access to the Internet (or another computer network) and can download it. If you do not have access to such a network, you may need to purchase it via mail order on CD-ROM, and such packages often include bundled documentation and support. Of course, you may copy Linux from a friend who may already have the software or share the cost of purchasing it with someone else. If you are planning to install Linux on a large number of machines, you need only purchase a single copy of the software; Linux is not distributed with a "single machine" license.

The value of commercial Unix implementations should not be demeaned: along with the price of the software itself, you usually pay for documentation, support, and assurance of quality. These are important factors for large institutions, but personal computer users may not require these benefits. A number of companies, including Red Hat and LinuxCare, are now providing commercial Linux support. Caldera, another Linux distributor, offers 24x7 support. In any case, many businesses and universities are finding that running Linux in a lab of inexpensive personal computers is preferable to running a commercial version of Unix in a lab of workstations. Linux can provide the functionality of a workstation on PC hardware at a fraction of the cost.

There are other free or inexpensive implementations of Unix for the x86. One of the most well known is FreeBSD, an implementation and port of BSD Unix for the 386. FreeBSD is comparable to Linux in many ways, but deciding which one is "better" depends on your own needs and expectations. The only strong distinction we can make is that Linux is developed openly (where any volunteer can aid in the development process), while FreeBSD is developed within a closed team of programmers who maintain the system. Because of this, serious philosophical and design differences exist between the two projects. The goals of the two projects are entirely different: the goal of Linux is to develop a complete Unix system from scratch (and have a lot of fun in the process), and the goal of FreeBSD is in part to modify the existing BSD code for use on the x86.

NetBSD is another port of the BSD NET/2 distribution to a number of machines, including the x86. NetBSD has a slightly more open development structure and is comparable to FreeBSD in many respects. OpenBSD is still another version of BSD.

Another project of note is the HURD, an effort by the Free Software Foundation to develop and distribute a free version of Unix for many platforms. Contact the Free Software Foundation for more information about this project. At the time of this writing, HURD is still in early stages of development and interest in it has been mostly superseded by Linux.

Other inexpensive versions of Unix exist as well, such as Minix (an academic but useful Unix clone upon which the early development of Linux was based). Some of these implementations are of mostly academic interest, while others are full-fledged systems for real productivity. But many personal Unix users are moving to Linux.

Hardware Requirements

Now, you must be convinced of how wonderful Linux is and of all the great things that it can do for you. However, before you rush out and install the software, you need to be aware of its hardware requirements and limitations.

Keep in mind that Linux was developed by its users. This means, for the most part, that the hardware supported by Linux is that which users and developers actually have access to. As it turns out, most of the popular hardware and peripherals for 80x86 systems are supported (in fact, Linux probably supports more hardware than any commercial implementation of Unix). However, some of the more obscure and esoteric devices, as well as those with proprietary drivers for which the manufacturers do not easily make the specifications available, aren't supported yet. As time goes on, a wider range of hardware will be supported, so if your favorite devices aren't listed here, chances are that support for them is forthcoming.

Another drawback for hardware support under Linux is that many companies have decided to keep the hardware interface proprietary. The upshot of this is that volunteer Linux developers simply can't write drivers for those devices (if they could, those drivers would be owned by the company that owned the interface, which would violate the GPL). The companies that maintain proprietary interfaces write their own drivers for operating systems, such as Microsoft Windows; the end user (that's you) never needs to know about the interface. Unfortunately, this does not allow Linux developers to write drivers for those devices.

Little can be done about the situation. In some cases, programmers have attempted to write hackish drivers based on assumptions about the interface. In other cases, developers work with the company in question and attempt to obtain information about the device interface, with varying degrees of success.

Linux includes a number of laptop-specific features, such as PCMCIA (or "PC Card") support and APM. The PCMCIA Tools package for Linux includes drivers for many PCMCIA devices, including modems, Ethernet cards, and SCSI adaptors; the PCMCIA HOWTO is the document that you need to get started.

APM allows the kernel to keep track of the laptop's battery power and perform certain actions (such as an automated shutdown) when power is low; it also allows the CPU to go into "low power" mode when not in use. This is easy to configure as a kernel option. Various tools interact with APM, such as *apm* (which displays information on battery status) and *apmd* (which logs battery status and can be used to trigger power events). These should be included with most Linux distributions.

[68] Hardware HOWTO

In the following sections, we'll attempt to summarize the hardware requirements for Linux. The Linux Hardware HOWTO (see the section "Sources of Linux Information" later in this chapter for an explanation of HOWTOs) contains a more complete listing of hardware supported by Linux.

Chapter 2

NOTE   A good deal of hardware support for Linux is currently in the development stage. Some distributions may or may not support these experimental features. This section primarily lists hardware that has been supported for some time and is known to be stable. When in doubt, consult the documentation for the distribution of Linux you are using (see the section "Distributions of Linux" in Chapter 2, *Preparing to Install Linux*) for more information on Linux distributions).

Another caveat to watch out for: occasionally hardware suppliers will substitute the latest version of a system component (such as a network board) regardless of what you originally ordered. When in doubt, be sure to check the particular hardware that you have.

Motherboard and CPU Requirements

Linux currently supports systems with an Intel 80386, 80486, Pentium, Pentium Pro, Pentium II, and Pentium III CPU. This includes all variations on this CPU type, such as the 386SX, 486SX, 486DX, and 486DX2. Non-Intel "clones," such as AMD and Cyrix processors, work with Linux as well.

Linux has been ported to a number of non-Intel architectures. These include the Alpha AXP, MIPS, PowerPC, SPARC, and Motorola 68K. At the time of this writing, some of these ports are more mature than others. Red Hat ships both SPARC and

Appendix E

Alpha versions of its distribution in addition to the Intel x86 versions, as does Debian. SuSE has an Alpha version at well, and Debian even provides a Motorola 68K distribution. (See Appendix E, *Installing Linux/m68k on Motorola 68000-Series Systems.*) In this book, we concentrate on the version of Linux for Intel x86 systems. Apart from hardware requirements and basic installation you should find that the majority of this book is just as relevant to ports of Linux to other architectures.

If you have an older 80386 or 80486SX, you may also wish to use a math coprocessor, although one isn't required (the Linux kernel can do FPU emulation if you do not have a math coprocessor). All standard FPU couplings are supported, such as IIT, Cyrix FasMath, and Intel coprocessors.

The system motherboard must use ISA, EISA, PCI, or MicroChannel (MCA) bus architecture. These terms define how the system interfaces with peripherals and other components on the main bus.

Systems that use a local bus architecture (for faster video and disk access) are supported as well. It's suggested that you have a standard local bus architecture, such as the VESA Local Bus (VLB).

Memory Requirements

Linux requires very little memory to run compared to other advanced operating systems. You should have at the very least 8 MB of RAM; however, it's strongly suggested that you have at least 16 MB. The more memory you have, the faster the system will run.

Linux can support the full 32-bit address range of the 80x86; in other words, it will utilize all of your RAM automatically. Amounts of RAM greater than 64 MB need a boot-time parameter.

Linux will run happily with only 8 MB of RAM, including all of the bells and whistles such as the X Window System, Emacs, and so on. However, having more memory is almost as important as having a faster processor. Sixteen megabytes is just enough for personal use; 32 MB or more may be needed if you are expecting a heavy user load on the system. Linux systems can, of course support systems with very large amounts of memory—including 1 GB or more.

Chapter 2

Most Linux users allocate a portion of their hard drive as swap space, which is used as virtual RAM. Even if you have a great deal of physical RAM in your machine, you may wish to use swap space. While swap space is no replacement for actual physical RAM, it allows your system to run larger applications by swapping out inactive portions of code to disk. The amount of swap space you should allocate depends on several factors; we'll come back to this question in the section "Linux Partition Requirements" in Chapter 2.

Hard Drive Controller Requirements

You do not need a hard drive to run Linux, in fact; you can run a minimal system completely from floppy! However, using Linux with a hard disk is the standard way of doing things. Linux should support all MFM, RLL, and IDE controllers. Most, but not all, ESDI controllers are supported—only those which do ST506 hardware emulation.

The general rule for non-SCSI hard drive and floppy controllers is that if you can access the drive from Windows or another operating system, you should be able to access it from Linux.

Linux also supports a number of popular SCSI drive controllers, although support for SCSI is more limited because of the wide range of controller interface standards. Supported SCSI controllers include the Adaptec AHA2940, AHA3940 AHA1542B, AHA1542C, AHA1742A (BIOS Version 1.34), AHA1522, AHA1740 (SCSI-2 controller, BIOS Version 1.34 in Enhanced mode); Future Domain 1680, TMC-850, TMC-950; Seagate ST-02; UltraStor SCSI; and Western Digital WD7000FASST. Clones that are based on these cards should work as well. This list is just a sampling; the number of supported SCSI drives is too great to enumerate here.

Hard Drive Space Requirements

Of course, to install Linux, you'll need to have some free space on your hard drive. Linux will support multiple hard drives in the same machine; you can allocate space for Linux across multiple drives if necessary.

The amount of hard drive space you will require depends greatly on your needs and the amount of software you're installing. Linux is relatively small as Unix implementations go; you could run a complete system in 10 to 20 MB of space on your drive. However, if you want to have room for expansion, and for larger packages, such as the X Window System, you need more space. If you plan to allow multiple users to use the machine, you need to allocate storage for their files.

Chapter 6

In addition, you'll more than likely want to allocate swap space on your hard drive to be used as virtual RAM. We will discuss the details of installing and using swap space in the section "Managing Swap Space" in Chapter 6, *Managing Filesystems, Swap, and Devices*.

Each distribution of Linux comes with some literature that should help you to gauge the precise amount of storage required depending on the amount of software you plan to install. You can run a minimal system with less than 20 MB; a complete system with all of the bells and whistles in 300 MB or less; and a very large system with room for many users and space for future expansion in 1 GB. Again, these figures are meant only as a ballpark approximation; you must look at your own needs and goals in order to determine your specific storage requirements.

Monitor and Video Adapter Requirements

Linux supports all standard Hercules, CGA, EGA, VGA, IBM monochrome, and Super VGA video cards and monitors for the default text-based interface. In general, if the video card and monitor coupling works under another operating system such as Windows, it should work fine with Linux. Original IBM CGA cards suffer from "snow" under Linux, which is unpleasant. (If you have one of these cards, you might want to donate it to a museum anyway.)

Chapter 10

Graphical environments, such as the X Window System, have video hardware requirements of their own. Instead of listing these requirements here, we relegate the discussion to the section "Hardware Requirements" in Chapter 10. In short, to run the X Window System on your Linux machine, you need one of the video cards listed in that section. The good news is that nearly all graphics boards (including high-end ones) are supported.

Miscellaneous Hardware

The previous sections described the hardware required to run a Linux system. However, most users have a number of "optional" devices such as tape and CD-ROM storage, sound boards, and so on, and are interested in whether or not this hardware is supported by Linux. Read on.

Mice and other pointing devices

For the most part, you will be using a mouse only under a graphical environment, such as the X Window System. However, several Linux applications not associated with a graphics environment also use a mouse.

Linux supports all standard serial mice, including Logitech, MM series, Mouseman, Microsoft (two-button), and Mouse Systems (three-button). Linux also supports Microsoft, Logitech, and ATIXL busmice. The PS/2 mouse interface is supported as well.

All other pointing devices, such as trackballs, which emulate the mice just listed, should work as well.

CD-ROM and DVD-ROM storage

Most CD-ROM drives sold today use the near-universal IDE/ATAPI CD-ROM standard, which is fully supported under Linux. Many CD-ROM drives use the SCSI interface instead, and as long as you have a SCSI adaptor supported by Linux, your CD-ROM drive should work.

Linux supports the standard ISO-9660 filesystem for CD-ROMs, including the Microsoft filename extensions.

In addition to the CD-ROM drives, Linux supports a number of CD-R and CD-RW drives that you can use to make your own CD-ROMs.

Various DVD-ROM drives are supported in Linux kernel version 2.2; however, filesystems allowing direct access to the DVD contents are not yet included. By the time you read this, we expect them to be fully supported.

Tape drives and removable storage

There are several types of tape drives available on the market. Many use the SCSI interface, all of which should be supported by Linux. QIC-02 and so-called "floppy tape" devices (which hang off of the floppy controller) are well-supported, as are various kinds of removable storage media, such as DAT, and the Iomega ZIP drive.

Printers

Linux supports the complete range of parallel printers. If you are able to access your printer via the parallel port from Windows or another operating system, you should be able to access it from Linux as well. The Linux printing software consists of the Unix standard *lp* and *lpr* software. This software also allows you to print remotely via the network, if you have one available.

Modems

As with printer support, Linux supports the full range of serial modems, both internal and external. If your modem is accessible from another operating system on the same machine, it is likely that you can access it from Linux with no difficulty. However, Linux does not support so-called "Winmodems," a kludge where the operating system has to take over many of the modem's tasks. In addition, some internal PCI modems are not supported.

Ethernet, Fast Ethernet, and Gigabit Ethernet Cards

Linux supports nearly every Ethernet and Fast Ethernet card available for the PC platform, and those that are not supported are more than likely being worked on as this is being written. Linux kernel Version 2.2 includes drivers for a number of high-performance network interfaces as well, including the Packet Engines G-NIC, Alteon AceNIC, and 3Com 3C985 PCI Gigabit Ethernet adaptors. A number of token ring and ATM interface cards are supported, as are various System Area Networks, such as Myricom's Myrinet.

Sources of Linux Information

As you have probably guessed, there are many sources of information about Linux available apart from this book.

Online Documents

If you have access to the Internet, you can get many Linux documents via web and anonymous FTP sites all over the world. If you do not have direct Internet access, these documents may still be available to you; many Linux distributions on CD-ROM contain all the documents mentioned here and are often available off the retail shelf. Also, they are distributed on many other networks, such as Fidonet and CompuServe.

Appendix A

There are a great number of web and FTP archive sites that carry Linux software and related documents. Appendix A contains a listing of some of the Linux documents available via the Internet.

Examples of available online documents are the Linux FAQ, a collection of frequently asked questions about Linux; the Linux HOWTO documents, each describing a specific aspect of the system—including the Installation HOWTO, the Printing HOWTO, and the Ethernet HOWTO; and the Linux META-FAQ, a list of other sources of Linux information on the Internet.

Most of these documents are also posted regularly to one or more Linux-related Usenet newsgroups; see the section "Usenet Newsgroups" later in this chapter.

The Linux Documentation home page is available to web users at *http://www.linuxdoc.org*. This page contains many HOWTOs and other documents, as well as pointers to other sites of interest to Linux users, including the Linux Documentation Project manuals (see the following section).

Books and Other Published Works

The bibliography at the end of this book points you to a wealth of sources that will help you use your system. There are a number of published works specifically about Linux. Most noteworthy are the books from the Linux Documentation Project (LDP), a project carried out over the Internet to write and distribute a bona fide set of "manuals" for Linux. These manuals are analogs to the documentation sets available with commercial versions of Unix: they cover everything from installing Linux to using and running the system, programming, networking, kernel development, and more.

Bibliography

The Linux Documentation Project manuals are available via the Web, as well as via mail order from several sources. The Bibliography lists the manuals that are available and covers the means of obtaining them in detail. O'Reilly & Associates has published the *Linux Network Administrator's Guide* from the LDP.

Aside from the growing number of Linux books, there are a large number of books about Unix in general that are certainly applicable to Linux—as far as using and programming the system is concerned, Linux doesn't differ greatly from other implementations of Unix in most respects. In fact, this book is meant to be complemented by the large library of Unix books currently available; here, we present the most important Linux-specific details and hope you will look to other sources for more in-depth information.

Armed with a number of good books about using Unix, as well as the book you hold in your hands, you should be able to tackle just about anything. The Bibliography includes a list of highly recommended Unix books, for Unix newcomers and wizards alike.

There are at least two monthly magazines about Linux: *Linux Journal* and *Linux Magazine*. These are an excellent way to keep in touch with the many goings-on in the Linux community.

Usenet Newsgroups

Usenet is a worldwide electronic news and discussion forum with a heavy contingent of so-called "newsgroups"—discussion areas devoted to a particular topic. Much of the development of Linux has been done over the waves of the Internet and Usenet, and not surprisingly, there are a number of Usenet newsgroups available for discussions about Linux.

There are far too many newsgroups devoted to Linux to list here. The ones dealing directly with Linux are under the *comp.os.linux.advocacy* hierarchy, but you'll probably find others on related topis like *comp.windows.x*.

Internet Mailing Lists

If you have access to Internet electronic mail, you can participate in a number of mailing lists even if you do not have Usenet access. If you are not directly on the Internet, you can join one of these mailing lists as long as you are able to exchange electronic mail with the Internet. (For example, UUCP, Fidonet, CompuServe, and other networks all have access to Internet mail.)

Getting Help

You will undoubtedly require some degree of assistance during your adventures in the Linux world. Even the most wizardly of Unix wizards is occasionally stumped by some quirk or feature of Linux, and it's important to know how and where to find help when you need it.

The primary means of getting help in the Linux world are Internet mailing lists and Usenet newsgroups. If you don't have online access to these sources, you might be able to find comparable Linux discussion forums on other online services, such as on local BBSes, CompuServe, and so on.

A number of businesses provide commercial support for Linux. A "subscription fee" allows you to call consultants for help with your Linux problems. Several vendors provide commercial support. However, if you have access to Usenet and Internet mail, you may find the free support found there just as useful.

Keeping the following suggestions in mind should improve your experiences with Linux and guarantee you more success in finding help to your problems:

Consult all available documentation first.

Appendix A

The first thing to do when encountering a problem is consult the various sources of information listed in the previous section and Appendix A. These documents were laboriously written for people like you—people who need help with the Linux system. Even books written for Unix in general are applicable to Linux, and you should take advantage of them. Impossible as it might seem, more than likely you will find the answer to your problems somewhere in this documentation.

If you have access to the Web, Usenet news, or any of the Linux-related mailing lists, be sure to actually read the information there before posting for help with your problem. Many times, solutions to common problems are not easy to find in documentation and are instead well-covered in the newsgroups and mailing lists devoted to Linux. If you only post to these groups, and don't actually read them, you are asking for trouble.

If you can't find what you're looking for, web search engines, and the DejaNews (*http://www.dejanews.com*) Usenet archive site are great places to start.

Learn to appreciate self-maintenance.

In most cases, it's preferable to do as much independent research and investigation into the problem as possible before seeking outside help. Remember that Linux is about hacking and fixing problems yourself. It's not a commercial operating system, nor does it try to look like one. Hacking won't kill you. In fact, it will teach you a great deal about the system to investigate and solve problems yourself—maybe even enough to one day call yourself a Linux guru. Learn to appreciate the value of hacking the system and fixing problems yourself. You can't expect to run a complete, home-brew Linux system without some degree of handiwork.

Remain calm.

It's vital to refrain from getting frustrated with the system. Nothing is earned by taking an axe—or worse, a powerful electromagnet—to your Linux system in a fit of anger. The authors have found that a large punching bag or similar inanimate object is a wonderful way to relieve the occasional stress attack. As Linux matures and distributions become more reliable, we hope that this problem will go away. However, even commercial Unix implementations can be tricky at times. When all else fails, sit back, take a few deep breaths, and go after the problem again when you feel relaxed. Your mind will be clearer, and your system will thank you.

Refrain from posting spuriously.

Many people make the mistake of posting or mailing messages pleading for help prematurely. When encountering a problem, do not—we repeat, do *not*—rush immediately to your nearest terminal and post a message to one of the Linux Usenet newsgroups. Often, you will catch your own mistake five minutes later and find yourself in the curious situation of defending your own sanity in a public forum. Before posting anything to any of the Linux mailing lists or newsgroups, first attempt to resolve the problem yourself and be absolutely certain what the problem is. Does your system not respond when you turn it on? Perhaps the machine is unplugged.

If you do post for help, make it worthwhile.

If all else fails, you may wish to post a message for help in any of the number of electronic forums dedicated to Linux, such as Usenet newsgroups and mailing lists. When posting, remember that the people reading your post are not there to help you. The network is not your personal consulting service. Therefore, it's important to remain as polite, terse, and informative as possible.

How can one accomplish this? First, you should include as much (relevant) information about your system and your problem as possible. Posting the simple request "I can't seem to get email to work" will probably get you nowhere unless you include information on your system, what software you are using, what you have attempted to do so far, and what the results were. When including technical information, it's usually a good idea to include general information on the version(s) of your software (Linux kernel version, for example), as well as a brief summary of your hardware configuration. However, don't overdo it—including information on the brand and type of monitor that you have is probably irrelevant if you're trying to configure networking software.

Second, remember that you need to make some attempt—however feeble—at solving your problem before you go to the Net. If you have never attempted to set up electronic mail, for instance, and first decide to ask folks on the Net how to go about doing it, you are making a big mistake. There are a number of documents available (see the previous section "Sources of Linux Information") on how to get started with many common tasks under Linux. The idea is to get as far along as possible on your own and *then* ask for help if and when you get stuck.

Also remember that the people reading your message, however helpful, may occasionally get frustrated by seeing the same problem over and over again. Be sure to actually read the Linux HOWTOs, FAQs, newsgroups, and mailing lists before posting your problems. Many times, the solution to your problem has been discussed repeatedly, and all that's required to find it is to browse the current messages.

Third, when posting to electronic newsgroups and mailing lists, try to be as polite as possible. It's much more effective and worthwhile to be polite, direct, and informative—more people will be willing to help you if you master a humble tone. To be sure, the flame war is an art form across many forms of electronic communication, but don't allow that to preoccupy your and other people's time. The network is an excellent way to get help with your Linux problems—but it's important to know how to use the network *effectively*.

## CHAPTER TWO

PREPARING TO INSTALL LINUX

This chapter represents your first step in installing Linux. We'll describe how to obtain the Linux software, in the form of one of the various prepackaged distributions, and how to prepare your system. We'll include ways to partition disks so that Linux can coexist with Windows, OS/2, or another operating system.

As we have mentioned, there is no single "official" distribution of the Linux software; there are, in fact, many distributions, each of which serves a particular purpose and set of goals. These distributions are available via anonymous FTP from the Internet, on BBS systems worldwide, and via mail on floppy, tape, and CD-ROM.

Distributions of Linux

Because Linux is free software, no single organization or entity is responsible for releasing and distributing the software. Therefore, anyone is free to put together and distribute the Linux software, as long as the restrictions in the GPL are observed. The upshot of this is that there are many distributions of Linux, available via anonymous FTP or mail order.

You are now faced with the task of deciding on a particular distribution of Linux that suits your needs. Not all distributions are alike. Many of them come with just about all of the software you'd need to run a complete system—and then some. Other Linux distributions are "small" distributions intended for users without copious amounts of disk space. Many distributions contain only the core Linux

Chapter 5

software, and you are expected to install larger software packages, such as the X Window System, yourself. (In Chapter 5, *Essential System Management*, we'll show you how.)

The Linux Distribution HOWTO contains a list of Linux distributions available via the Internet as well as mail order.

How can you decide among all of these distributions? If you have access to Usenet news, or another computer conferencing system, you might want to ask there for personal opinions from people who have installed Linux. Even better, if you know someone who has installed Linux, ask them for help and advice. In actuality, most of the popular Linux distributions contain roughly the same set of software, so the distribution you select is more or less arbitrary.

Getting Linux via Mail Order or Other Hard Media

If you don't have Internet or BBS access, you can get many Linux distributions via mail order on floppy, tape, or CD-ROM. Many distributors accept credit cards as well as international orders, so no matter where you live, you should be able to obtain Linux in this way.

Linux is free software, but distributors are allowed by the GPL to charge a fee for it. Therefore, ordering Linux via mail order might cost you between US $5 and US $150, depending on the distribution. However, if you know people who have already purchased or downloaded a release of Linux, you are free to borrow or copy their software for your own use. Linux distributors are not allowed to restrict the license or redistribution of the software in any way. If you are thinking about installing an entire lab of machines with Linux, for example, you need to purchase only a single copy of one of the distributions, which can be used to install all of the machines. There is one exception to this rule, though: in order to add value to their distribution, some vendors include commercial packages that you might not be allowed to install on several machines. If this is the cas, it should be explicitly stated on the package.

Many Linux user groups offer their own distributions; see if there's a user group near you. For special platforms like Alpha, a user group may be an excellent place to get Linux.

Getting Linux from the Internet

If you have access to the Internet, the easiest way to obtain Linux is via anonymous FTP.* One major FTP site is *ftp://metalab.unc.edu*, and the various Linux distributions can be found there in the directory */pub/Linux/distributions*.

---

* If you do not have direct Internet access, you can obtain Linux via the FTPMAIL service, provided that you have the ability to exchange email with the Internet.

Many distributions are released via anonymous FTP as a set of disk images. That is, the distribution consists of a set of files, and each file contains the binary image of a floppy. In order to copy the contents of the image file onto the floppy, you can use the *RAWRITE.EXE* program under MS-DOS. This program copies, block-for-block, the contents of a file to a floppy, without regard for disk format. *RAWRITE.EXE* is available on the various Linux FTP sites, including *ftp://meta-lab.unc.edu* in the directory */pub/Linux/system/Install/rawwrite*.

Be forewarned that this is a labor-intensive way of installing Linux: the distribution can easily come to more than 50 floppies.

Therefore, in many cases, you simply download the set of floppy images, and use *RAWRITE.EXE* with each image in turn to create a set of floppies. You boot from the so-called "boot floppy," and you're ready to roll. The software is usually installed directly from the floppies, although some distributions allow you to install from an MS-DOS partition on your hard drive. Some distributions allow you to install over a TCP/IP network. The documentation for each distribution should describe these installation methods if they are available.

Other Linux distributions are installed from a set of MS-DOS formatted floppies. For example, the Slackware distribution of Linux requires *RAWRITE.EXE* only for the boot and root floppies. The rest of the floppies are copied to MS-DOS format-ted floppies using the MS-DOS COPY command. The system installs the software directly from the MS-DOS floppies. This saves you the trouble of having to use *RAWRITE.EXE* for many image files, although it requires you to have access to an MS-DOS system to create the floppies.

If you have access to a Unix workstation with a floppy drive, you can also use the *dd* command to copy the file image directly to the floppy. A command such as `dd of=/dev/rfd0 if=foo bs=18k` will "raw write" the contents of the file *foo* to the floppy device on a Sun workstation. Consult your local Unix gurus for more information on your system's floppy devices and the use of *dd*.

Each distribution of Linux available via anonymous FTP should include a *README* file describing how to download and prepare the floppies for installation. Be sure to read all available documentation for the release you are using.

When downloading the Linux software, be sure to use binary mode for all file transfers (with most FTP clients, the command *binary* enables this mode).

Getting Linux from Other Online Sources

If you have access to a BBS system, there may be a means to download the Linux software from this source. Not all Linux distributions are available from these com-puter networks, however; many, especially the various CD-ROM distributions, are available only via mail order.

Preparing to Install Linux

After you have obtained a distribution of Linux, you're ready to prepare your system for installation. This takes a certain degree of planning, especially if you're already running other operating systems. In the following sections, we'll describe how to plan for the Linux installation.

Installation Overview

While each release of Linux is different, in general the method used to install the software is as follows:

1. *Repartition your hard drive(s).* If you have other operating systems already installed, you will need to repartition the drives in order to allocate space for Linux. This is discussed in the section "Repartitioning Your Drives" later in this chapter. In some distributions, this step is integrated into the installation procedure. Check the documentation of your distribution to see whether this is the case. Still, it won't hurt you to follow the steps given here and repartition your hard drive in advance.

2. *Boot the Linux installation media.* Each distribution of Linux has some kind of installation media—usually a "boot floppy"—or a bootable CD-ROM that is used to install the software. Booting this media will either present you with some kind of installation program, which will step you through the Linux installation, or allow you to install the software by hand.

Chapter 3

3. *Create Linux partitions.* After repartitioning to allocate space for Linux, you create Linux partitions on that empty space. This is accomplished with the Linux *fdisk* program, covered in the section "Creating Linux Partitions" in Chapter 3, *Installation and Initial Configuration* or some other distribution-specific program like the *Disk Druid* that comes with Red Hat Linux.

4. *Create filesystems and swap space.* At this point, you will create one or more filesystems, used to store files, on the newly created partitions. In addition, if you plan to use swap space, you will create the swap space on one of your Linux partitions. This is covered in the sections "Creating Swap Space" and "Creating the Filesystems," both in Chapter 3.

5. *Install the software on the new filesystems.* Finally, you will install the Linux software on your newly created filesystems. After this, if all goes well, it's smooth sailing. This is covered in the section "Installing the Software" in Chapter 3. Later, in the section "Running Into Trouble," also in Chapter 3, we describe what to do if anything goes wrong.

People who want to switch back and forth between different operating systems sometimes wonder which to install first: Linux or the other system? We can testify that some people have had trouble installing Windows 95 after Linux. Windows 95 tends to wipe out existing boot information when it's installed, so you're safer installing it first and then installing Linux afterward using the information in this chapter.

We don't know whether Windows 98 will demonstrate the same cavalier behavior as Windows 95. Windows NT seems to be more tolerant of existing boot information.

Many distributions of Linux provide an installation program, that will step you through the installation process and automate one or more of the previous steps for you. Keep in mind throughout this chapter and the next that any number of the previous steps may be automated for you, depending on the distribution.

Important hint: While preparing to install Linux, the best advice we can give is to take notes during the entire procedure. Write down everything you do, everything you type, and everything you see that might be out of the ordinary. The idea here is simple: if (or when!) you run into trouble, you want to be able to retrace your steps and find out what went wrong. Installing Linux isn't difficult, but there are many details to remember. You want to have a record of all these details so that you can experiment with other methods if something goes wrong. Also, keeping a notebook of your Linux installation experience is useful when you want to ask other people for help, for example, when posting a message to one of the Linux-related Usenet groups. Your notebook is also something you'll want to show to your grandchildren someday.*

Repartitioning Concepts

In general, hard drives are divided into *partitions*, where one or more partitions are devoted to an operating system. For example, on one hard drive, you may have several separate partitions—one devoted to, say, Windows, another to OS/2, and another two to Linux.

If you already have other software installed on your system, you may need to resize those partitions in order to free up space for Linux. You will then create one or more Linux partitions on the resulting free space for storing the Linux software and swap space. We call this process *repartitioning*.

Many MS-DOS systems utilize a single partition inhabiting the entire drive. To MS-DOS, this partition is known as C:. If you have more than one partition, MS-DOS names them D:, E:, and so on. In a way, each partition acts like a separate hard drive.

On the first sector of the disk is a *master boot record* along with a *partition table*. The boot record (as the name implies) is used to boot the system. The partition table contains information about the locations and sizes of your partitions.

---

* Matt shamefully admits that he kept a notebook of all of his tribulations with Linux for the first few months of working with the system. It is now gathering dust on his bookshelf.

There are three kinds of partitions: *primary*, *extended*, and *logical*. Of these, primary partitions are used most often. However, because of a limit on the size of the partition table, you can only have four primary partitions on any given drive. This is due to the poor design of MS-DOS; even other operating systems of the same era do not have such limits.

The way around this four-partition limit is to use an extended partition. An extended partition doesn't hold any data by itself; instead, it acts as a "container" for logical partitions. Therefore, you could create one extended partition, covering the entire drive, and within it create many logical partitions. However, you may have only one extended partition per drive.

Linux Partition Requirements

Chapter 3

Before we explain how to repartition your drives, you need an idea of how much space you will be allocating for Linux. We will be discussing how to create these partitions later, in the section "Creating Linux Partitions" in Chapter 3.

On Unix systems, files are stored on a *filesystem*, which is essentially a section of the hard drive (or other medium, such as CD-ROM or floppy) formatted to hold files. Each filesystem is associated with a specific part of the directory tree; for example, on many systems, there is a filesystem for all the files in the directory */usr*, another for */tmp*, and so on. The *root filesystem* is the primary filesystem, which corresponds to the topmost directory, /.

Under Linux, each filesystem lives on a separate partition on the hard drive. For instance, if you have a filesystem for / and another for */usr*, you will need two partitions to hold the two filesystems.

Before you install Linux, you will need to prepare filesystems for storing the Linux software. You must have at least one filesystem (the root filesystem), and therefore one partition, allocated to Linux. Many Linux users opt to store all their files on the root filesystem, which, in most cases, is easier to manage than several filesystems and partitions.

Chapter 6

However, you may create multiple filesystems for Linux if you wish—for example, you may want to use separate filesystems for */usr* and */home*. Those readers with Unix system administration experience will know how to use multiple filesystems creatively. In the section "Creating Filesystems" in Chapter 6, *Managing Filesystems, Swap, and Devices*, we discuss the use of multiple partitions and filesystems.

Why use more than one filesystem? The most commonly stated reason is safety; if, for some reason, one of your filesystems is damaged, the others will (usually) be unharmed. On the other hand, if you store all your files on the root filesystem, and for some reason the filesystem is damaged, you may lose all your files in one fell swoop. This is, however, rather uncommon; if you back up the system regularly, you should be quite safe.*

On the other hand, using several filesystems has the advantage that you can easily upgrade your system without endangering your own precious data. You might have a partition for the users' home directories, and when upgrading the system, you leave this partition alone, wipe out the others, and reinstall Linux from scratch. Of course, nowadays distributions all have quite elaborate update procedures, but from time to time, you might want a "fresh start."

Another reason to use multiple filesystems is to divvy up storage among multiple hard drives. If you have, say, 100 MB free on one hard drive, and 2 GB free on another, you might want to create a 100-MB root filesystem on the first drive and a 2-GB */usr* filesystem on the other. Currently it is not possible for a single filesystem to span multiple drives; if your free hard drive storage is fragmented between drives, you need to use multiple filesystems to use all the storage.

In summary, Linux requires at least one partition, for the root filesystem. If you wish to create multiple filesystems, you need a separate partition for each additional filesystem. Some distributions of Linux automatically create partitions and filesystems for you, so you may not need to worry about these issues at all.

Another issue to consider when planning your partitions is swap space. You have two options. The first is to use a *swap file* that exists on one of your Linux filesystems. You will create the swap file for use as virtual RAM after you install the software. The second option is to create a *swap partition*, an individual partition to be used only as swap space. Most people use a swap partition instead of a swap file.

A single swap file or partition may be up to 128 MB (more with the latest kernels).† If you wish to use more than 128 MB of swap (hardly ever necessary), you can create multiple swap partitions or files—up to 16 in all. For example, if you need 256 MB of swap, you can create two 128-MB swap partitions.

Chapter 3
Chapter 6

Setting up a swap partition is covered in the section "Creating Swap Space" in Chapter 3, and setting up a swap file in the section "Managing Swap Space" in Chapter 6.

Therefore, in general, you will create at least two partitions for Linux: one for use as the root filesystem, and the other for use as swap space. There are, of course, many variations on partitioning, but this is the minimal setup. You are not required to use swap space with Linux, but if you have less than 32 MB of physical RAM, it is strongly suggested that you do.

Of course, you need to know how much *space* these partitions will require. The size of your Linux filesystems (containing the software itself) depends greatly on

---

* Matt uses a single 200-MB filesystem for all his Linux files and hasn't had any problems (so far).

† This value applies to machines with Intel processors. On other architectures like the Alpha, it can be higher.

how much software you're installing and what distribution of Linux you are using. Hopefully, the documentation that came with your distribution will give you an approximation of the space requirements. A small Linux system can use 40 MB or less; a larger system anywhere from 100 to 300 MB, or more. Keep in mind that in addition to the space required by the software itself, you need to allocate extra space for user directories, room for future expansion, and so forth.

If you use several partitions, you can use a rather small partition for the root directory. 32 MB should suffice—use at least 30-50 MB more if you keep */var* on the same partition, as most people do. On the other hand, you will probably want to have a largish */usr* partition.

The size of your swap partition (should you elect to use one) depends on how much virtual RAM you require. A rule of thumb is to use a swap partition that is twice the space of your physical RAM; for example, if you have 4 MB of physical RAM, an 8-MB swap partition should suffice. Of course, this is mere speculation; the actual amount of swap space you require depends on the software you will be running. If you have a great deal of physical RAM (say, 64 MB or more), you may not wish to use swap space at all.

 Because of BIOS limitations, it is usually not possible to boot from partitions using cylinders numbered over 1023. Therefore, when setting aside space for Linux, keep in mind you may not want to use a partition in the over-1023 cylinder range for your Linux root filesystem. Linux can still *use* partitions with cylinders numbered over 1023, but you may not be able to *boot* Linux from such a partition. This advice may seem premature, but it is important to know when planning your drive layout, and today, many people have large disks with more than 1023 cylinders.

If you absolutely must use a partition with cylinders numbered over 1023 for your Linux root filesystem, you can always boot Linux from floppy. This is not so bad, actually; it takes only a few seconds longer to boot than from the hard drive. At any rate, it's always an option.

Repartitioning Your Drives

In this section, we'll describe how to resize your current partitions (if any) to make space for Linux. If you are installing Linux on a "clean" hard drive, skip this section and proceed to Chapter 3.

The usual way to resize an existing partition is to delete it (thus destroying all data on that partition) and recreate it. Before repartitioning your drives, *back up your system*. After resizing the partitions, you can reinstall your original software from the backup. However, there are several programs available for MS-DOS that resize partitions nondestructively. One of these is known as FIPS and can be found on many Linux FTP sites.

Also, keep in mind that because you'll be shrinking your original partitions, you may not have space to reinstall everything. In this case, you need to delete enough unwanted software to allow the rest to fit on the smaller partitions.

The program used to repartition is known as *fdisk*. Each operating system has its own analogue of this program; for example, under MS-DOS, it is invoked with the FDISK command. You should consult your documentation for whatever operating systems you are currently running for information on repartitioning. Here, we'll discuss how to resize partitions for MS-DOS using *fdisk*, but this information should be easily extrapolated to other operating systems.

The *fdisk* program (on any operating system) is responsible for reading the partition table on a given drive and manipulating it to add or delete partitions. However, some versions of *fdisk* do more than this, such as adding information to the beginning of a new partition to make it usable by a certain operating system. For this reason, you should usually only create partitions for an operating system with the version of *fdisk* that comes with it. You can't create MS-DOS partitions with Linux *fdisk*; partitions created in this way can't be used correctly by MS-DOS (actually, if you really know what you are doing, you might be lucky in creating MS-DOS partitions from Linux, but we would not advise doing so). Similarly, MS-DOS *fdisk* may not be able to recognize Linux partitions. As long as you have a version of *fdisk* for each operating system you use, you should be fine. (Note that not all systems name this program *fdisk*; some refer to it as a "disk manager" or "volume manager.")

Later, in the section "Creating Linux Partitions" in Chapter 3, we describe how to create new Linux partitions, but for now we are concerned with resizing your current ones.

Chapter 3

Please consult the documentation for your current operating systems before repartitioning your drive. This section is meant to be a general overview of the process; there are many subtleties we do not cover here. You can lose all the software on your system if you do not repartition the drive correctly.

Let's say that you have a single hard drive on your system, currently devoted entirely to MS-DOS. Hence, your drive consists of a single MS-DOS partition, commonly known as `C:`. Because this repartitioning method will destroy the data on that partition, you need to create a bootable MS-DOS "system disk," which contains everything necessary to run FDISK and restore the software from backup after the repartitioning is complete.

In many cases, you can use the MS-DOS installation disks for this purpose. However, if you need to create your own system disk, format a floppy with the command:

```
FORMAT /s A:
```

Copy onto this floppy all necessary MS-DOS utilities (usually most of the software in the directory *DOS* on your drive), as well as the programs *FORMAT.COM* and *FDISK.EXE*. You should now be able to boot this floppy and run the command:

```
FDISK C:
```

to start up FDISK.

Use of FDISK should be self-explanatory, but consult the MS-DOS documentation for details. When you start FDISK, use the menu option to display the partition table, and write down the information displayed there. It is important to keep a record of your original setup in case you want to back out of the Linux installation.

To delete an existing partition, choose the FDISK menu option "`Delete an MS-DOS Partition or Logical DOS Drive`." Specify the type of partition you wish to delete (primary, extended, or logical) and the number of the partition. Verify all of the warnings. Poof!

To create a new (smaller) partition for MS-DOS, choose the FDISK option "`Create an MS-DOS Partition or Logical DOS Drive`." Specify the type of partition (primary, extended, or logical) and the size of the partition to create (specified in megabytes). FDISK should create the partition, and you're ready to roll.

After you're done using FDISK, exit the program and reformat any new partitions. For example, if you resized the first DOS partition on your drive (`C:`), you should run the command:

```
FORMAT /s C:
```

You may now reinstall your original software from backup.

CHAPTER THREE

INSTALLATION AND INITIAL CONFIGURATION

Appendix A

A t this point, you should have your Linux distribution and have disk space set aside for Linux. In this chapter, we present a general overview of the installation process. Each distribution has its own installation instructions, but armed with the concepts presented here, you should be able to feel your way through any installation. Appendix A, *Sources of Linux Information*, lists sources of information for installation instructions and other help, if you're at a total loss.

Different Linux distributions store files in different locations, which can make it hard to describe how to administer Linux. For instance, the same files may be found on Red Hat, SuSE, and Debian systems, but they may be under the */etc* directory on one system and the */sbin* directory under another. Gradually, the vendors are standardizing the set of locations listed in a document called the Filesystem Hierarchy Standard, but in this book we'll just try to deal with lagging discrepancies by listing the locations of the most important files in the version of each major distribution that we checked.

Installing the Linux Software

After resizing your existing partitions to make space for Linux, you are ready to install the software. Here is a brief overview of the procedure:

1. Boot the Linux installation media.

2. Run *fdisk* under Linux to create Linux partitions.

3. Run *mke2fs* and *mkswap* to create Linux filesystems and swap space.

4. Install the Linux software and configure it.

5. Finally, either install the LILO boot loader on your hard drive, or create a boot floppy in order to boot your new Linux system.

As we have said, one (or more) of these steps may be automated for you by the installation procedure, depending on the distribution of Linux you are using. Please consult your distribution's documentation for specific instructions.

Booting Linux

The first step is to boot the Linux installation media. In most cases, this is either a boot floppy, which contains a small Linux system or a bootable CD-ROM. Upon booting the floppy or the CD-ROM, you are presented with an installation menu of some kind that leads you through the steps of installing the software. On other distributions, you are presented with a login prompt when booting this floppy. Here, you usually log in as **root** or **install** to begin the installation process.

The documentation that comes with your particular distribution will explain what is necessary to boot Linux from the installation media.

Most distributions of Linux use a boot floppy that allows you to enter hardware parameters at a boot prompt to force hardware detection of various devices. For example, if your SCSI controller is not detected when booting the floppy, you will need to reboot and specify the hardware parameters (such as I/O address and IRQ) at the boot prompt. Likewise, IBM PS/1, ThinkPad, and ValuePoint machines do not store drive geometry in the CMOS, so you must specify it at boot time.

The boot prompt is often displayed automatically when booting the boot floppy or CD-ROM. This is the case for the Red Hat distribution. With distributions that do not show the prompt by default, you need to hold down the Shift or Control key or press the Scroll Lock key while booting the floppy or CD-ROM if you want to enter something at the boot prompt. If successful, you should see the prompt:

```
boot:
```

and possibly other messages. What you are seeing here is a boot prompt presented by LILO (the LInux LOader), a program used to boot the Linux operating system and specify hardware-detection parameters at boot time. After you have installed Linux, you may wish to install LILO on your hard drive, which allows you to select between Linux and other operating systems (such as MS-DOS) when the system is booted.

At this point you have several options. You can press the Enter key to simply boot Linux from the floppy with no special parameters. (You should try this first, and if installation seems to go well, you're all set.) Or, just wait until the installation proceeds, today's distributions set a timeout for the boot prompt, and when you do not enter anything for some time, they just continue booting. Otherwise, you may have to specify hardware-detection parameters at this boot prompt, to force the system to properly identify the hardware installed in your system.

If you don't want to try any hardware-detection parameters now, just press Enter at the boot prompt. Watch the messages as the system boots. If you have an SCSI controller, for example, you should see a listing of the SCSI hosts detected. If you see the message:

```
SCSI: 0 hosts
```

then your SCSI controller was not detected, and you will have to use the hardware detection procedure we'll describe in a moment.

Most new distributions often follow a different path of choosing hardware. They come with a minimal kernel on the boot disk and then load so-called *kernel modules* from either a second floppy disk or a CD-ROM. In this case, you will probably be dropped into some menu where you can select additional modules to be probed. Even specifying modules is largely automated: you just ask the installation program to probe for SCSI adapters and see whether yours is found. The same goes for Ethernet cards and other devices that are needed for the installation process. Devices that are not needed during the installation, such as sound boards, are unlikely to be detected at this point of the installation. You will probably be given the option to configure them later.

If the automated hardware detection procedures do not work for you (which normally is the case only if you have very old, very new or very unusual hardware), you will have to help Linux a bit by forcing hardware detection.

To force hardware detection, you must enter the appropriate parameters at the boot prompt, using the following syntax:

```
linux parameters
```

There are many such parameters, some of which are listed below. We don't expect you to understand what all of these parameters mean or are used for; rather, you should be able to determine which of these hardware options corresponds to your own system. For example, if you have an AHA152x-based SCSI controller, and you know that under MS-DOS you must configure the board for a particular I/O address and IRQ, you can use the corresponding option (`aha152x=`) here. In fact, many of these boot options are simply unnecessary for initial installation. We are presenting a more comprehensive list here, in one place, as you may find them useful later on.

One other piece of advice: write down and remember the boot options you use to get your system running. After you have installed Linux, you'll need to use the same boot options in order for your hardware to be properly detected each time you boot. If you install the LILO loader on your hard drive, you can configure it to automatically use a certain set of boot options so you won't have to type them each time.

no387
> Disables the 80387 math coprocessor; circumvents some buggy coprocessors when used in protected mode.

`no-hlt`

> Disables use of the HLT instruction; used to place the CPU into a low-power state when the system is idle. Some early 486DX-100 chips have a problem using this instruction.

`root=device`

> Specifies the device to use as the root filesystem when booting the system. For initial installation this should not be used; after installaton of the system you can use this to override the default location of your Linux root filesystem.

`ro` Mounts the root filesystem in a read-only state; used for system maintenance.

`lock`

> Saves the boot parameters for the future so that you do not have to enter them each time you are booting the system.

`rw` Mounts the root filesystem in a read-write state; used for system maintenance.

`debug`

> Forces the kernel to print verbose debugging messages to the console as the system runs.

`ramdisk=kilobytes`

> Tells the system to reserve the given number of kilobytes for a ramdisk. This is often used by installation boot floppies that load an entire filesystem image into memory. You don't want to use this option for initial installation, but if you want to experiment with ramdisks at a later date, this is the option to use.

`mem=size`

> The system BIOS in most PCs only reports up to 64 MB of installed RAM; Linux uses this information to determine the amount of installed memory. If you have more than 64 MB and use an older kernel, you may need to use this parameter to allow the rest of system memory to be used. The size parameter can be a number with `k` or `M` appended; for example, `mem=96M` would specify a system with 96 MB of RAM installed. Note that if you tell the system it has more memory than is actually installed, Bad Things will eventually happen.

`hd=cylinders,heads,sectors`

> Specifies the hard drive geometry for IDE and standard ST-506 drives (not SCSI drives). Required for systems such as the IBM PS/1, ValuePoint, and ThinkPad. For example, if your drive has 683 cylinders, 16 heads, and 32 sectors per track, use:

```
ramdisk hd=683,16,32
```

> This option can also be used as `hda=`, `hdb=`, `hdc=`, or `hdd=` to specify the geometry for a particular IDE drive. Note that use of the `hd=` option may be necessary if you are using a large IDE drive (over 1024 cylinders). If Linux has problems recognizing the geometry of your drive (you'll know when you try to partition the disk for Linux), try using this option.

`max_scsi_luns=`*num*

If *num* is 1, the system won't probe for SCSI devices that have a Logical Unit Number (LUN) other than zero. This parameter is required for some poorly designed SCSI devices that lock up when probed at non-zero LUNs. Note that this does not have anything to do with the SCSI device ID; LUNs allow the addressing of multiple logical units or subdevices within a single SCSI device, such as a disk drive.

`aha152x=`*iobase,irq,scsi-id,reconnect,parity*

Specifies parameters for Adaptec AHA151x, AHA152x, AIC6260, AIC6230, and SB16-SCSI interfaces. *iobase* must be specified in hexadecimal, as in `0x340`. All arguments except *iobase* are optional.

`aha1542=`*iobase*

Specifies the I/O base, in hex, for Adaptec AHA154x SCSI interfaces.

`aic7xxx=`*extended,no-reset*

Specifies parameters for Adaptec AHA274x, AHA284x, and AIC7xxx SCSI interfaces. A non-zero value for *extended* indicates that extended translation for large disks is enabled. If *no-reset* is non-zero, the driver will not reset the SCSI bus when configuring the adapter at boot time.

`buslogic=`*iobase*

Specifies the I/O base, in hex, for Buslogic SCSI interfaces.

`tmc8xx=`*mem-base,irq*

Specifies the base of the memory-mapped I/O region (in hex) and IRQ for Future Domain TMC-8xx and TMC-950 SCSI interfaces.

`pas16=`*iobase,irq*

Specifies the I/O base (in hex) and IRQ for Pro Audio Spectrum SCSI interfaces.

`st0x=`*mem-base,irq*

Specifies the base of the memory-mapped I/O region (in hex) and IRQ for Seagate ST-0x SCSI interfaces.

`t128=`*mem-base,irq*

Specifies the base of the memory-mapped I/O region (in hex) and IRQ for Trantor T128 SCSI interfaces.

`aztcd=`*iobase*

Specifies the I/O base (in hex) for Aztech CD-ROM interfaces.

`cdu31a=`*iobase,irq,pas*

Specifies the I/O base (in hex) and IRQ for CDU-31A and CDU-33A Sony CD-ROM interfaces. These options are used on some Pro Audio Spectrum sound cards, as well as boards from Sony. The *irq* and *pas* parameters are optional.

If *irq* is 0, interrupts are not supported (as is the case with some boards). The only valid value for the *pas* option is PAS, indicating that a Pro Audio Spectrum card is being used.

soncd535=*iobase,irq*
> Specifies the I/O base (in hex) and IRQ (optional) for Sony CDU-535 interfaces.

gscd=*iobase*
> Specifies I/O base (in hex) for GoldStar CD-ROM interfaces.

mcd=*iobase,irq*
> Specifies the I/O base (in hex) and IRQ (optional) for Mitsumi standard CD-ROM interfaces.

optcd=*iobase*
> Specifies the I/O base (in hex) for Optics Storage Interface CD-ROM interfaces.

cm206=*iobase,irq*
> Specifies the I/O base (in hex) and IRQ for Philips CM206 CD-ROM interfaces.

sjcd=*iobase,irq,dma*
> Specifies the I/O base (in hex), IRQ, and DMA channel for Sanyo CD-ROM interfaces. The *irq* and *dma* parameters are optional.

sbpcd=*iobase,type*
> Specifies the I/O base in hex for SoundBlaster Pro and compatible CD-ROM interfaces. The *type* parameter must be SoundBlaster, LaserMate, or SPEA, based on what type of board you have. Note that this option specifies parameters *only* for the CD-ROM interface, not for the sound hardware on the board.

ether=*irq,iobase,parameters...*
> Specifies the IRQ and I/O base for Ethernet cards. If you are having problems detecting your Ethernet card and wish to use it for installation (e.g., via FTP or NFS), check out the Linux Ethernet HOWTO that describes the various boot options for Ethernet cards in much detail. There are too many to detail here.

floppy=thinkpad
> Tells the floppy driver that you have a ThinkPad; necessary for floppy access on ThinkPad systems.

floppy=0,thinkpad
> Tells the floppy driver that you do not have a ThinkPad, in case it's confused.

bmouse=*irq*
> Specifies IRQ for busmouse* interface.

---

* A busmouse is a mouse attached to the system bus, instead of a serial port or a PS/2-style mouse port.

`msmouse=`*`irq`*
   Specifies IRQ for Microsoft busmouse interface.

Quite a few other options are available; the previous options should be those that are generally necessary for normal use of your system. (For example, we have left out the many parameters available for sound card drivers; we urge you to read the appropriate HOWTO documents if you have a life-threatening situation involving use of your sound card.)

For each of these, you must enter *linux* followed by the parameters you wish to use.

[69] SCSI
HOWTO
[71] CD-ROM
HOWTO

If you have questions about these boot-time options, read the Linux Bootprompt HOWTO, Linux SCSI HOWTO, and Linux CD-ROM HOWTO. These three documents should be available on any Linux FTP site (as well as most Linux CD-ROMs) and describe the LILO boot arguments in more detail.

Drives and Partitions Under Linux

Many distributions require you to create Linux partitions by hand using the *fdisk* program. Others may automatically create partitions for you. Either way, you should know the following information about Linux partitions and device names. (This information applies only to Intel and Alpha systems; other systems like PowerPC, SPARC, and m68k do not have logical and extended partitions.)

Drives and partitions under Linux are given different names from their counterparts under other operating systems. Under MS-DOS, floppy drives are referred to as A: and B:, while hard drive partitions are named C:, D:, and so on. Under Linux, the naming convention is quite different.

Device drivers, found in the directory */dev*, are used to communicate with devices on your system (such as hard drives, mice, and so on). For example, if you have a mouse on your system, you might access it through the driver */dev/mouse*. Floppy drives, hard drives, and individual partitions are all given individual device drivers of their own. Don't worry about the device-driver interface for now; it is important only to understand how the various devices are named in order to use them. The section "Device Files" in Chapter 6, *Managing Filesystems, Swap, and Devices*, talks more about devices.

Chapter 6

Table 3-1 lists the names of these various device drivers where multiple names can be created with increasing numbers (0, 1, etc.). One or two are shown in the table as examples.

Table 3-1: Linux Partition Names

Device	Name
First floppy (A:)	*/dev/fd0*
Second floppy (B:)	*/dev/fd1*
First hard drive (entire drive)	*/dev/hda*
First hard drive, primary partition 1	*/dev/hda1*
First hard drive, primary partition 2	*/dev/hda2*
First hard drive, primary partition 3	*/dev/hda3*
First hard drive, primary partition 4	*/dev/hda4*
First hard drive, logical partition 1	*/dev/hda5*
First hard drive, logical partition 2	*/dev/hda6*
⋮	
Second hard drive (entire drive)	*/dev/hdb*
Second hard drive, primary partition 1	*/dev/hdb1*
⋮	
First SCSI hard drive (entire drive)	*/dev/sda*
First SCSI hard drive, primary partition 1	*/dev/sda1*
⋮	
Second SCSI hard drive (entire drive)	*/dev/sdb*
Second SCSI hard drive, primary partition 1	*/dev/sdb1*
⋮	
First SCSI CD-ROM drive	*/dev/scd0*
Second SCSI CD-ROM drive	*/dev/scd1*
⋮	
First generic SCSI device (like scanners, CDR writers, etc.). Note that newer systems use numbers instead of letters (i.e., */dev/sg0* instead of */dev/sga*).	*/dev/sga*
Second generic SCSI device	*/dev/sgb*
⋮	

A few notes about this table: */dev/fd0* corresponds to the first floppy drive (A: under MS-DOS), and */dev/fd1* corresponds to the second floppy (B:).

Also, SCSI hard drives are named differently from other drives. IDE, MFM, and RLL drives are accessed through the devices */dev/hda*, */dev/hdb*, and so on. The individual partitions on the drive */dev/hda* are */dev/hda1*, */dev/hda2*, and so on. However, SCSI drives are named */dev/sda*, */dev/sdb*, and so on, with partition names such as */dev/sda1* and */dev/sda2*.

Most systems, of course, do not have four primary partitions. But the names */dev/hda1* through */dev/hda4* are still reserved for these partitions; they cannot be used to name logical partitions.

Here's an example. Let's say you have a single IDE hard drive, with three primary partitions. The first two are set aside for MS-DOS, and the third is an extended partition that contains two logical partitions, both for use by Linux. The devices referring to these partitions would be:

Device	Name
First MS-DOS partition (C:)	*/dev/hda1*
Second MS-DOS partition (D:)	*/dev/hda2*
Extended partition	*/dev/hda3*
First Linux logical partition	*/dev/hda5*
Second Linux logical partition	*/dev/hda6*

Note that */dev/hda4* is skipped; it corresponds to the fourth primary partition, which we don't have in this example. Logical partitions are named consecutively starting with */dev/hda5*.

Creating Linux Partitions

Now you are ready to create Linux partitions with the *fdisk* command. In general, you need to create at least one partition for the Linux software itself and another partition for swap space.

Here we are describing the basic text-mode usage of *fdisk* which should be available with all distributions. Many distributions nowadays provide a more user-friendly interface to *fdisk*. While those are usually not as flexible as plain *fdisk*, they can help you make the right choices more easily. Whatever tool you use, this section is helpful for understanding the underlying concepts. The tools all do more or less the same things in the end; some simply have more sugar-coating than others. You can also make use of the information presented here for fixing or checking something that you suspect didn't go right with the graphical tool.

After booting the installation media, run *fdisk* by typing:

```
fdisk drive
```

where *drive* is the Linux device name of the drive to which you plan to add partitions (see Table 3-1). For instance, if you want to run *fdisk* on the first SCSI disk in your system, use the command:

```
# fdisk /dev/sda
```

/dev/hda (the first IDE drive) is the default if you don't specify one.

If you are creating Linux partitions on more than one drive, run *fdisk* once for each drive:

```
# fdisk /dev/hda
```

```
Command (m for help):
```

Here *fdisk* is waiting for a command; you can type m to get a list of options:

```
Command (m for help): m
Command action
   a   toggle a bootable flag
   d   delete a partition
   l   list known partition types
   m   print this menu
   n   add a new partition
   p   print the partition table
   q   quit without saving changes
   t   change a partition's system id
   u   change display/entry units
   v   verify the partition table
   w   write table to disk and exit
   x   extra functionality (experts only)

Command (m for help):
```

The n command is used to create a new partition. Most other options you won't need to worry about. To quit *fdisk* without saving any changes, use the q command. To quit *fdisk* and write the changes to the partition table to disk, use the w command. This is worth repeating: So long as you quit with q without writing, you can mess around as much as you want with *fdisk* without risking harm to your data. Only when you type w, you can cause potential disaster to your data if you do something wrong.

The first thing you should do is display your current partition table and write the information down for later reference. Use the p command to see the information. It is a good idea to copy the information to your notebook after each change you have made to the partition table. If, for some reason, your partition table is damaged, you will not access any data on your hard disk any longer, even though the data itself is still there. But by using your notes, you might be able to restore the partition table and get your data back in many cases by running *fdisk* again and deleting and recreating the partitions with the parameters you previously wrote down. Don't forget to save the restored partition table when you are done.

Here is an example of a printed partition table:

```
Command (m for help): p

Disk /dev/hda: 16 heads, 38 sectors, 683 cylinders
Units = cylinders of 608 * 512 bytes
   Device Boot  Begin    Start      End  Blocks   Id  System
/dev/hda1    *       1        1      203   61693    6  DOS 16-bit >=32M

Command (m for help):
```

In this example, we have a single MS-DOS partition on */dev/hda1*, which is 61693 blocks (about 60 MB).* This partition starts at cylinder number 1 and ends on cylinder 203. We have a total of 683 cylinders in this disk; so there are 480 cylinders left to create Linux partitions on.

To create a new partition, use the n command. In this example, we'll create two primary partitions (*/dev/hda2* and */dev/hda3*) for Linux:

```
Command (m for help): n
Command action
   e   extended
   p   primary partition (1-4)
   p
```

Here, *fdisk* is asking which type of the partition to create: extended or primary. In our example, we're creating only primary partitions, so we choose p:

```
Partition number (1-4):
```

fdisk will then ask for the number of the partition to create; since partition 1 is already used, our first Linux partition will be number 2:

```
Partition number (1-4): 2
First cylinder (204-683):
```

Now, we enter the starting cylinder number of the partition. Since cylinders 204 through 683 are unused, we'll use the first available one (numbered 204). There's no reason to leave empty space between partitions:

```
First cylinder (204-683): 204
Last cylinder or +size or +sizeM or +sizeK (204-683):
```

fdisk is asking for the size of the partition we want to create. We can either specify an ending cylinder number, or a size in bytes, kilobytes, or megabytes. Since we want our partition to be 80 MB in size, we specify +80M. When specifying a partition size in this way, *fdisk* will round the actual partition size to the nearest number of cylinders:

---

* A block, under Linux, is 1024 bytes.

```
Last cylinder or +size or +sizeM or +sizeK (204-683): +80M
```

```
Warning: Linux cannot currently use 33090 sectors of this partition
```

If you see a warning message such as this, it can be ignored. *fdisk* prints the warning because it's an older program and dates back before the time that Linux partitions were allowed to be larger than 64 MB.

Now we're ready to create our second Linux partition. For sake of demonstration, we'll create it with a size of 10 MB:

```
Command (m for help): n
Command action
   e   extended
   p   primary partition (1-4)
p
Partition number (1-4): 3
First cylinder (474-683): 474
Last cylinder or +size or +sizeM or +sizeK (474-683): +10M
```

At last, we'll display the partition table. Again, write down all of this information—especially the block sizes of your new partitions. You'll need to know the sizes of the partitions when creating filesystems. Also, verify that none of your partitions overlap:

```
Command (m for help): p

Disk /dev/hda: 16 heads, 38 sectors, 683 cylinders
Units = cylinders of 608 * 512 bytes
   Device Boot   Begin    Start    End   Blocks   Id   System
/dev/hda1    *       1        1    203    61693    6   DOS 16-bit >=32M
/dev/hda2          204      204    473    82080   83   Linux native
/dev/hda3          474      474    507    10336   83   Linux native
```

As you can see, */dev/hda2* is now a partition of size 82080 blocks (which corresponds to about 80 MB), and */dev/hda3* is 10336 blocks (about 10 MB).

Note that most distributions require you to use the t command in *fdisk* to change the type of the swap partition to "Linux swap," which is numbered 82. You can use the L command to print a list of known partition type codes, and then use the t command to set the type of the swap partition to that which corresponds to "Linux swap."

This way the installation software will be able to automatically find your swap partitions based on type. If the installation software doesn't seem to recognize your swap partition, you might want to rerun *fdisk* and use the t command on the partition in question.

In the previous example, the remaining cylinders on the disk (numbered 508 to 683) are unused. You may wish to leave unused space on the disk, in case you wish to create additional partitions later.

Finally, we use the w command to write the changes to disk and exit *fdisk*:

```
Command (m for help): w
#
```

Keep in mind that none of the changes you make while running *fdisk* take effect until you give the w command, so you can toy with different configurations and save them when you're done. Also, if you want to quit *fdisk* at any time without saving the changes, use the q command. Remember that you shouldn't modify partitions for operating systems other than Linux with the Linux *fdisk* program.

You may not be able to boot Linux from a partition using cylinders numbered over 1023. Therefore, you should try to create your Linux root partition within the sub-1024 cylinder range which is almost always possible (e.g., by creating a small root partition in the sub-1024 cylinder range). If for some reason, you cannot or do not want to do this, you can simply boot Linux from floppy.

Some Linux distributions require you to reboot the system after running *fdisk* to allow the changes to the partition table to take effect before installing the software. Newer versions of *fdisk* automatically update the partition information in the kernel, so rebooting isn't necessary. To be on the safe side, after running *fdisk* you should reboot the installation media before proceeding.

Creating Swap Space

Chapter 6

If you are planning to use a swap partition for virtual RAM, you're ready to prepare it.* In the section "Managing Swap Space" in Chapter 6, we discuss the preparation of a swap file, in case you don't want to use an individual partition.

Many distributions require you to create and activate swap space before installing the software. If you have a small amount of physical RAM, the installation procedure may not be successful unless you have some amount of swap space enabled.

The command used to prepare a swap partition is *mkswap*, and it takes the following form:

```
mkswap -c partition size
```

where `partition` is the name of the swap partition, and `size` is the size of the partition in blocks.† For example, if your swap partition is */dev/hda3* and is 10336 blocks in size, use the command:

```
# mkswap -c /dev/hda3 10336
```

The *-c* option tells *mkswap* to check for bad blocks on the partition when creating the swap space. Bad blocks are spots on the magnetic media that do not hold the

---

* Again, some distributions of Linux prepare the swap space for you automatically, or via an installation menu option.

† This is the size as reported by *fdisk*, using the p menu option. Again, a block under Linux is 1024 bytes.

data correctly. This occurs only rarely with today's hard disks, but if it does, and you do not know about it, it can cause you endless trouble. Always use the *-c* option to have *mkswap* check for bad blocks. It will exclude these from being used automatically.

If you are using multiple swap partitions, you need to execute the appropriate *mkswap* command for each partition.

After formatting the swap space, you need to enable it for use by the system. Usually, the system automatically enables swap space at boot time. However, because you have not yet installed the Linux software, you need to enable it by hand.

The command to enable swap space is *swapon*, and it takes the following form:

```
swapon partition
```

After the *mkswap* command shown, we use the following command to enable the swap space on */dev/hda3*:

```
# swapon /dev/hda3
```

Creating the Filesystems

Chapter 2

Before you can use your Linux partitions to store files, you must create filesystems on them. Creating a filesystem is analogous to formatting a partition under MS-DOS or other operating systems. We discussed filesystems briefly in the section "Linux Partition Requirements" in Chapter 2, *Preparing to Install Linux*.

There are several types of filesystems available for Linux. Each filesystem type has its own format and set of characteristics (such as filename length, maximum file size, and so on). Linux also supports several "third-party" filesystem types, such as the MS-DOS filesystem.

Chapter 6

The most commonly used filesystem type is the *Second Extended Filesystem*, or *ext2fs*. The *ext2fs* is one of the most efficient and flexible filesystems; it allows filenames of up to 256 characters and filesystem sizes of up to 4 terabytes. In the section "Filesystem Types" in Chapter 6, we discuss the various filesystem types available for Linux. Initially, however, we suggest you use the *ext2fs* filesystem.

To create an *ext2fs* filesystem, use the command:

```
mke2fs -c partition size
```

where `partition` is the name of the partition, and `size` is the size of the partition in blocks. For example, to create an 82080-block filesystem on */dev/hda2*, use the command:

```
# mke2fs -c /dev/hda2 82080
```

If you're using multiple filesystems for Linux, you need to use the appropriate *mke2fs* command for each filesystem.

If you have encountered any problems at this point, see the section "Running Into Trouble" later in this chapter.

Installing the Software

Finally, you are ready to install the software on your system. Every distribution has a different mechanism for doing this. Many distributions have a self-contained program that steps you through the installation. On other distributions, you have to *mount* your filesystems in a certain subdirectory (such as */mnt*) and copy the software to them by hand. On CD-ROM distributions, you may be given the option to install a portion of the software on your hard drive and leave most of the software on the CD-ROM. This is often called a "live filesystem." Such a live filesystem is convenient for trying out Linux before you make a commitment to install everything on your disk.

Some distributions offer several different ways to install the software. For example, you may be able to install the software directly from an MS-DOS partition on your hard drive instead of from floppies. Or you may be able to install over a TCP/IP network via FTP or NFS. See your distribution's documentation for details.

For example, the Slackware distribution requires you to do the following:

1. Create partitions with *fdisk*.

2. Optionally create swap space with *mkswap* and *swapon* (if you have 16 MB or less of RAM).

3. Run the *setup* program to install the software. *setup* leads you through a self-explanatory menu system.

The exact method used to install the Linux software differs greatly with each distribution.

You might be overwhelmed by the choice of software to install. Modern Linux distributions can easily contain a thousand or more packages spread over several CD-ROMs. There are basically three methods for selecting the software package:

Selection by task
> This is the easiest means of selection for beginners. You don't have to think about whether you need a certain package, you just pick whether your Linux computer should act as a workstation, a development machine, or a network router, and the installation program will pick the appropriate packages for you. In all cases, you can then either refine the selection by hand or come back to the installation program later.

Selection of individual packages by series
> With this selection mechanism, all the packages are grouped into series like "Networking," "Development," or "Graphics." You can go through all the series and pick the individual packages there. This requires more decisions

than if you select it by task, because you still have to decide whether you need it or not, but you can skip an entire series when you are sure that you are not interested in the functions it offers.

Selection of individual packages sorted alphabetically
This method is useful only when you already know which packages you want to install; otherwise you won't see the forest for the trees.

Chosing one selection method does not exclude the use of the others. Most distributions offer two or more of the aforementioned selection mechanisms.

It might still be difficult to decide which package to pick. Good distributions show a short description of each package on screen to make it easier for you to select the correct ones, but if you are still unsure, our advice is this: when in doubt, leave it out! You can always go back and add packages later.

Modern distributions have a very nifty feature, the so-called *dependency tracking*. Some packages work only when some other packages are installed (e.g., a graphics viewer might need special graphics libraries to import files). With dependency tracking, the installation program can inform you about those dependencies and will let you automatically select the package you want along with all the ones it depends on. Unless you are very sure about what you are doing, you should always accept this offer, or the package might not work afterwards.

Installation programs can help you make your selection and avoid mistakes in other ways. For example, the installation program might refuse to start the installation when you deselect a package that is absolutely crucial for even the most minimal system to boot (like the basic directory structure). Or, it might check for mutual exclusions, such as cases in which you can only have one package or the other, but not both.

Some distributions like SuSE come with a large book that among other things lists all the packages together with short descriptions. It might be a good idea to at least skim those description to see what's in store for you, or you might be surprised when you select the packages and are offered the twenty-fifth text editor.

Creating the Boot Floppy or Installing LILO

Every distribution provides some means of booting your new Linux system after you have installed the software. In many cases, the installation procedure suggests you create a boot floppy, which contains a Linux kernel configured to use your newly created root filesystem. In order to boot Linux, you could boot from this floppy; control is transferred to your hard drive after you boot. On other distributions, this boot floppy is the installation floppy itself.

Many distributions give you the option of installing LILO on your hard drive. LILO is a program that resides on your drive's master boot record. It boots a number of operating systems, including MS-DOS and Linux, and allows you to select which to boot at startup time.

In order for LILO to be installed successfully, it needs to know a good deal of information about your drive configuration: for example, which partitions contain which operating systems, how to boot each operating system, and so on. Many distributions, when installing LILO, attempt to "guess" at the appropriate parameters for your configuration. Although it's not often, the automated LILO installation provided by some distributions can fail and leave your master boot record in shambles (although it's very doubtful that any damage to the actual data on your hard drive will take place). In particular, if you use OS/2's Boot Manager, you should *not* install LILO using the automated procedure; there are special instructions for using LILO with the Boot Manager, which will be covered in Chapter 5, *Essential System Management.*

Chapter 5

In many cases, it is best to use a boot floppy until you have a chance to configure LILO yourself, by hand. If you're feeling exceptionally trustworthy, though, you can go ahead with the automated LILO installation if it is provided with your distribution.

In the section "Using LILO" in Chapter 5, we'll cover in detail how to configure and install LILO for your particular setup.

If everything goes well, then congratulations! You have just installed Linux on your system. Go have a cup of tea or something; you deserve it.

In case you did run into any trouble, the section "Running Into Trouble," later in this chapter, describes the most common sticking points for Linux installations, and how to get around them.

Additional Installation Procedures

Some distributions of Linux provide a number of additional installation procedures, allowing you to configure various software packages, such as TCP/IP networking, the X Window System, and so on. If you are provided with these configuration options during installation, you may wish to read ahead in this book for more information on how to configure this software. Otherwise, you should put off these installation procedures until you have a complete understanding of how to configure the software.

It's up to you; if all else fails, just go with the flow and see what happens. It's doubtful that anything you do incorrectly now cannot be undone in the future (knock on wood).

Post-Installation Procedures

After you have completed installing the Linux software, you should be able to reboot the system, log in as **root**, and begin exploring the system. (Each distribution has a different method for doing this; follow the instructions given by the distribution.)

Before you strike out on your own, however, there are some tasks you should do now that may save you a lot of grief later. Some of these tasks are trivial if you have the right hardware and Linux distribution; others may involve a little research on your part, and you may decide to postpone them.

Creating a User Account

In order to start using your system, you need to create a user account for yourself. Eventually, if you plan to have other users on your system, you'll create user accounts for them as well. But before you begin to explore you need at least one account.

Why is this? Every Linux system has several preinstalled accounts, such as **root**. The root account, however, is intended exclusively for administrative purposes. As **root** you have all kinds of privileges and can access all files on your system.

However, using **root** can be dangerous, especially if you're new to Linux. Because there are no restrictions on what **root** can do, it's all too easy to mistype a command, inadvertently delete files, damage your filesystem, and so on. You should log in as **root** only when you need to perform system-administration tasks, such as fixing configuration files, installing new software, and so on. See the section "Running the System" in Chapter 5 for details.

Chapter 5

For normal usage, you should create a standard user account. Unix systems have built-in security that prevents users from deleting other users' files and corrupting important resources, such as system configuration files. As a regular user, you'll be protecting yourself from your own mistakes. This is especially true for users who don't have Unix system-administration experience.

Many Linux distributions provide tools for creating new accounts. These programs are usually called *useradd* or *adduser*. As **root**, invoking one of these commands should present you with a usage summary for the command, and creating a new account should be fairly self-explanatory.

Most modern distributions provide a generic system administration tool for various tasks, one of which is creating a new user account.

Again other distributions, like SuSE Linux or Caldera Open Linux, integrate system installation and system administration in one tool: *yast* on SuSE Linux or *lisa* on Caldera Open Linux.

If all else fails, you can create an account by hand. Usually, all that is required to create an account is:

1. Edit the file */etc/passwd* to add the new user.

2. Optionally edit the file */etc/shadow* to specify "shadow password" attributes for the new user.

3. Create the user's home directory.

4. Copy skeleton configuration files (such as *.bashrc*) to the new user's home directory. These can sometimes be found in the directory */etc/skel.*

Chapter 5

We don't want to go into great detail here: the particulars of creating a new user account can be found in virtually every book on Unix system administration (see the Bibliography for suggested reading). We also talk about creating users in the section "Managing User Accounts" in Chapter 5. With luck, there will be a tool provided to take care of these details for you.

Keep in mind that to set or change the password on the new account, you use the *passwd* command. For example, to change the password for the user **duck**, issue the following command:

```
# passwd duck
```

This will prompt you to set or change the password for duck. If you execute the *passwd* command as **root**, it will not prompt you for the original password. In this way, if you have forgotten your old password, but can still log in as **root**, you can reset it.

Getting Online Help

Linux provides online help in the form of manual pages—or "man pages" for short. Throughout this book, we'll be directing you to look at the manual pages for particular commands to get more information. Manual pages describe programs and applications on the system in detail, and it's important for you to learn how to access this online documentation in case you get into a bind.

To get online help for a particular command, use the *man* command. For example, to get information on the *passwd* command, type the following command:

```
$ man passwd
```

This should present you with the manual page for *passwd*.

Usually, manual pages are provided as an optional package with most distributions, so they won't be available unless you have opted to install them. However, we very strongly advise you to install the manual pages, you will feel lost many times without them.

In addition, certain manual pages may be missing or incomplete on your system. It depends on how complete your distribution is and how up-to-date the manual pages are.

Chapter 4

Linux manual pages also document system calls, library functions, configuration file formats, and kernel internals. In the section "Manual Pages" in Chapter 4, *Basic Unix Commands and Concepts*, we'll describe their use in more detail.

Besides traditional manual pages, there are also so-called info pages. These can be read either with the text editor Emacs, the command *info* or one of many graphical info readers available.

Many distributions also provide documentation in HTML format that you can read with any Web browser like Netscape Navigator but also with the text editor Emacs.

Finally, there are documentation files that are simply plain text. You can read these with any text editor or simply with the command *more.*

If you cannot find documentation for a certain command, you can also try running it with either the *–h* or *– –* option. Most commands then provide a brief summary of their usage.

Editing /etc/fstab

In order to ensure that all of your Linux filesystems will be available when you reboot the system, you may need to edit the file */etc/fstab*, which describes your filesystems. Many distributions automatically generate the */etc/fstab* file for you during installation, so all may be well. However, if you have additional filesystems that were not used during the installation process, you may need to add them to */etc/fstab* in order to make them available. Swap partitions should be included in */etc/fstab* as well.

In order to access a filesystem, it must be *mounted* on your system. Mounting a filesystem associates that filesystem with a particular directory. For example, the root filesystem is mounted on /, the */usr* filesystem on */usr*, and so on. (If you did not create a separate filesystem for */usr*, all files under */usr* will be stored on the root filesystem.)

Chapter 6

We don't want to smother you with technical details here, but it is important to understand how to make your filesystems available before exploring the system. For more details on mounting filesystems, see the section "Mounting Filesystems" in Chapter 6, or any book on Unix system administration.

The root filesystem is automatically mounted on / when you boot Linux. However, your other filesystems must be mounted individually. Usually, this is accomplished by the command:

```
# mount -av
```

in one of the system startup files in */etc/rc.d* or wherever your distribution stores its configuration files. This tells the *mount* command to mount any filesystems listed in the file */etc/fstab*. Therefore, in order to have your filesystems mounted automatically at boot time, you need to include them in */etc/fstab*. (Of course, you could always mount the filesystems by hand, using the *mount* command after booting, but this is unnecessary work.)

Here is a sample */etc/fstab* file. In this example, the root filesystem is on */dev/hda1*, the */home* filesystem is on */dev/hdb2*, and the swap partition is on */dev/hdb1*:

```
# /etc/fstab
# device        directory     type    options
#
/dev/hda1       /             ext2    defaults
/dev/hdb2       /home         ext2    defaults
/dev/hdb1       none          swap    sw
/proc           /proc         proc    defaults
```

The lines beginning with the "#" character are comments. Also, you'll notice an additional entry for */proc*. */proc* is a "virtual filesystem" used to gather process information by commands such as *ps*.

As you can see, */etc/fstab* consists of a series of lines. The first field of each line is the device name of the partition, such as */dev/hda1*. The second field is the *mount point*—the directory where the filesystem is mounted. The third field is the type; Linux *ext2fs* filesystems should use `ext2` for this field. `swap` should be used for swap partitions. The fourth field is for mounting options. You should use `defaults` in this field for filesystems and `sw` for swap partitions.

Using this example as a model, you should be able to add entries for any filesystems not already listed in the */etc/fstab* file.

How do we add entries to the file? The easiest way is to edit the file, as **root**, using an editor such as *vi* or Emacs. We won't get into the use of text editors here—*vi* and Emacs are both covered at the beginning of Chapter 9, *Editors, Text Tools, Graphics, and Printing*.

Chapter 9

After editing the file, you'll need to issue the command:

```
# /bin/mount -a
```

or reboot for the changes to take effect.

If you're stuck at this point, don't be alarmed. We suggest that Unix novices do some reading on basic Unix usage and system administration. Most of the remainder of this book is going to assume familiarity with these basics, so don't say we didn't warn you.

Shutting Down the System

Chapter 5

You should never reboot or shut down your Linux system by pressing the reset switch or simply turning off the power. As with most Unix systems, Linux caches disk writes in memory. Therefore, if you suddenly reboot the system without shutting down "cleanly," you can corrupt the data on your drives. Note, however, that the "Vulcan nerve pinch" (pressing Ctrl-Alt-Del in unison) is generally safe: the kernel traps the key sequence and initiates a clean shutdown of the system (as described in the section "init, inittab, and rc files" in Chapter 5. Your system configuration might reserve the Ctrl-Alt-Del for the system administrator so that normal users cannot shut down the network server that the whole department depends upon. To set permissions for this keystroke combination, create a file called */etc/shutdown.allow* that lists the names of all the users that are allowed to shut down the machine.

The easiest way to shut down the system is with the *shutdown* command. As an example, to shutdown and reboot the system immediately, use the following command as **root**:

```
# shutdown -r now
```

This will cleanly reboot your system. The manual page for *shutdown* describes the other available command-line arguments. Instead of now, you can also specify when the system should be shut down. Most distributions also provide *halt*, which calls *shutdown now*. On some distributions, there is also *poweroff* which actually shuts the computer down and turns it off. Whether it works depends on the hardware (which must support APM), not on Linux.

Running Into Trouble

Almost everyone runs into some kind of snag or hangup when attempting to install Linux the first time. Most of the time, the problem is caused by a simple misunderstanding. Sometimes, however, it can be something more serious, such as an oversight by one of the developers or a bug.

This section will describe some of the most common installation problems and how to solve them. If your installation appears to be successful, but you received unexpected error messages during the installation, these are described here as well.

Problems with Booting the Installation Media

When attempting to boot the installation media for the first time, you may encounter a number of problems. Note that the following problems are *not* related to booting your newly installed Linux system. See the section "Problems After Installing Linux" for information on these kinds of pitfalls.

Floppy or media error occurs when attempting to boot.

The most popular cause for this kind of problem is a corrupt boot floppy. Either the floppy is physically damaged, in which case you should recreate the disk with a brand new floppy, or the data on the floppy is bad, in which case you should verify that you downloaded and transferred the data to the floppy correctly. In many cases, simply recreating the boot floppy will solve your problems. Retrace your steps and try again.

If you received your boot floppy from a mail-order vendor or some other distributor, instead of downloading and creating it yourself, contact the distributor and ask for a new boot floppy—but only after verifying that this is indeed the problem.

System "hangs" during boot or after booting.

After the installation media boots, you see a number of messages from the kernel itself, indicating which devices were detected and configured. After this, you are usually presented with a login prompt, allowing you to proceed with installation (some distributions instead drop you right into an installation program of some kind). The system may appear to "hang" during several of these steps. Be patient; loading software from floppy is very slow. In many cases, the system has not hung at all, but is merely taking a long time. Verify that there is no drive or system activity for at least several minutes before assuming that system is hung.

The proper boot sequence is:

1. After booting from the LILO prompt, the system must load the kernel image from floppy. This may take several seconds; you know things are going well if the floppy drive light is still on.

2. While the kernel boots, SCSI devices must be probed for. If you do not have any SCSI devices installed, the system will "hang" for up to 15 seconds while the SCSI probe continues; this usually occurs after the line:

   ```
   lp_init: lp1 exists (0), using polling driver
   ```

   appears on your screen.

3. After the kernel is finished booting, control is transferred to the system bootup files on the floppy. Finally, you will be presented with a login prompt, or be dropped into an installation program. If you are presented with a login prompt such as:

   ```
   Linux login:
   ```

   you should then log in (usually as **root** or **install**—this varies with each distribution). After entering the username, the system may pause for 20 seconds or more while the installation program or shell is being loaded from floppy. Again, the floppy drive light should be on. Don't assume the system is hung.

Each of the preceding activities may cause a delay that makes you think the system has stopped. However, it is possible that the system actually may "hang" while booting, which can be due to several causes. First of all, you may not have enough available RAM to boot the installation media. (See the following item for information on disabling the ramdisk to free up memory.)

Chapter 1

Hardware incompatibility causes many system hangs. The section "Hardware Requirements" in Chapter 1, *Introduction to Linux*, presents an overview of supported hardware under Linux. Even if your hardware is supported, you may run into problems with incompatible hardware configurations that are causing the system to hang. See the next section, "Hardware Problems," for a discussion of hardware incompatibilities:

System reports out-of-memory errors while attempting to boot or install the software.
This problem relates to the amount of RAM you have available. On systems with 4 MB of RAM or less, you may run into trouble booting the installation media or installing the software itself. This is because many distributions use a "ramdisk," which is a filesystem loaded directly into RAM, for operations while using the installation media. The entire image of the installation boot floppy, for example, may be loaded into a ramdisk, which may require more than 1 MB of RAM.

The solution to this problem is to disable the ramdisk option when booting the install media. Each release has a different procedure for doing this; on the SLS release, for example, you type `floppy` at the LILO prompt when booting the *a1* disk. See your distribution's documentation for details.

You may not see an "out of memory" error when attempting to boot or install the software; instead, the system may unexpectedly hang or fail to boot. If your system hangs, and none of the explanations in the previous section seem to be the cause, try disabling the ramdisk.

Keep in mind that Linux itself requires at least 4 MB of RAM to run at all; almost all current distributions of Linux require 8 MB or more.

The system reports an error, such as "Permission denied" or "File not found" while booting.
This is an indication that your installation boot media is corrupt. If you attempt to boot from the installation media (and you're sure you're doing everything correctly), you should not see any errors such as this. Contact the distributor of your Linux software and find out about the problem, and perhaps obtain another copy of the boot media if necessary. If you downloaded the boot disk yourself, try recreating the boot disk, and see if this solves your problem.

The system reports the error "VFS: Unable to mount root" when booting.
This error message means that the root filesystem (found on the boot media itself) could not be found. This means that either your boot media is corrupt or that you are not booting the system correctly.

For example, many CD-ROM distributions require you to have the CD-ROM in the drive when booting. Also be sure that the CD-ROM drive is on, and check for any activity. It's also possible the system is not locating your CD-ROM drive at boot time; see the next section, "Hardware Problems," for more information.

If you're sure you are booting the system correctly, then your boot media may indeed be corrupt. This is an uncommon problem, so try other solutions before attempting to use another boot floppy or tape.

Hardware Problems

The most common problem encountered when attempting to install or use Linux is an incompatibility with hardware. Even if all your hardware is supported by Linux, a misconfiguration or hardware conflict can sometimes cause strange results: your devices may not be detected at boot time, or the system may hang.

It is important to isolate these hardware problems if you suspect they may be the source of your trouble. In the following sections, we describe some common hardware problems and how to resolve them.

Isolating hardware problems

If you experience a problem you believe is hardware-related, the first thing to do is attempt to isolate the problem. This means eliminating all possible variables and (usually) taking the system apart, piece-by-piece, until the offending piece of hardware is isolated.

This is not as frightening as it may sound. Basically, you should remove all nonessential hardware from your system (after turning the power off), and then determine which device is actually causing the trouble—possibly by reinserting each device, one at a time. This means you should remove all hardware other than the floppy and video controllers, and, of course, the keyboard. Even innocent-looking devices, such as mouse controllers, can wreak unknown havoc on your peace of mind unless you consider them nonessential.

For example, let's say the system hangs during the Ethernet board detection sequence at boot time. You might hypothesize that there is a conflict or problem with the Ethernet board in your machine. The quick and easy way to find out is to pull the Ethernet board and try booting again. If everything goes well when you reboot, then you know that either the Ethernet board is not supported by Linux (see the section "Hardware Requirements" in Chapter 1 for a list of compatible boards), or there is an address or IRQ conflict with the board. In addition, some badly designed network boards (mostly NE2000 clones) can hang the entire system when they auto-probed. If this appears to be the case for you, your best bet is to remove the network board from the system during the installation and put it back in later, or pass the appropriate kernel parameters during boot-up so that

Chapter 1

auto-probing of the network board can be avoided. The most permanent fix is to dump that card and get a new one from another vendor that designs its hardware more carefully.

"Address or IRQ conflict?" What on earth does that mean? All devices in your machine use an *interrupt request line*, or IRQ, to tell the system they need something done on their behalf. You can think of the IRQ as a cord the device tugs when it needs the system to take care of some pending request. If more than one device is tugging on the same cord, the kernel won't be able to determine which device it needs to service. Instant mayhem.

Therefore, be sure all your installed devices are using unique IRQ lines. In general, the IRQ for a device can be set by jumpers on the card; see the documentation for the particular device for details. Some devices do not require an IRQ at all, but it is suggested you configure them to use one if possible (the Seagate ST01 and ST02 SCSI controllers being good examples).

In some cases, the kernel provided on your installation media is configured to use a certain IRQ for certain devices. For example, on some distributions of Linux, the kernel is preconfigured to use IRQ 5 for the TMC-950 SCSI controller, the Mitsumi CD-ROM controller, and the busmouse driver. If you want to use two or more of these devices, you'll need first to install Linux with only one of these devices enabled, then recompile the kernel in order to change the default IRQ for one of them. (See the section "Building a New Kernel" in Chapter 7, *Upgrading Software and the Kernel*, for information on recompiling the kernel.)

Chapter 7

Another area where hardware conflicts can arise is with *direct memory access* (DMA) channels, I/O addresses, and shared memory addresses. All these terms describe mechanisms through which the system interfaces with hardware devices. Some Ethernet boards, for example, use a shared memory address as well as an IRQ to interface with the system. If any of these are in conflict with other devices, the system may behave unexpectedly. You should be able to change the DMA channel, I/O, or shared memory addresses for your various devices with jumper settings. (Unfortunately, some devices don't allow you to change these settings.)

The documentation for your various hardware devices should specify the IRQ, DMA channel, I/O address, or shared memory address the devices use, and how to configure them. Again, the simple way to get around these problems is to temporarily disable the conflicting devices until you have time to determine the cause of the problem.

Table 3-2 is a list of IRQ and DMA channels used by various "standard" devices found on most systems. Almost all systems have some of these devices, so you should avoid setting the IRQ or DMA of other devices to these values.

Table 3–2: Common Device Settings

Device	I/O address	IRQ	DMA
ttyS0 (*COM1*)	3f8	4	n/a
ttyS1 (*COM2*)	2f8	3	n/a
ttyS2 (*COM3*)	3e8	4	n/a
ttyS3 (*COM4*)	2e8	3	n/a
lp0 (*LPT1*)	378 – 37f	7	n/a
lp1 (*LPT2*)	278 – 27f	5	n/a
fd0, fd1 (floppies 1 and 2)	3f0 – 3f7	6	2
fd2, fd3 (floppies 3 and 4)	370 – 377	10	3

Problems recognizing hard drive or controller

When Linux boots, you see a series of messages on your screen such as the following:

```
Console: colour EGA+ 80x25, 8 virtual consoles
Serial driver version 3.96 with no serial options enabled
tty00 at 0x03f8 (irq = 4) is a 16450
tty03 at 0x02e8 (irq = 3) is a 16550A
lp_init: lp1 exists (0), using polling driver
...
```

Here, the kernel is detecting the various hardware devices present on your system. At some point, you should see the line:

```
Partition check:
```

followed by a list of recognized partitions, for example:

```
Partition check:
  hda: hda1 hda2
  hdb: hdb1 hdb2 hdb3
```

If, for some reason, your drives or partitions are not recognized, you will not be able to access them in any way.

There are several conditions that can cause this to happen:

Hard drive or controller not supported
> If you are using a hard drive controller (IDE, SCSI, or otherwise) not supported by Linux, the kernel will not recognize your partitions at boot time.

Drive or controller improperly configured
> Even if your controller is supported by Linux, it may not be configured correctly. (This is a problem particularly for SCSI controllers; most non-SCSI controllers should work fine without additional configuration.)

Refer to the documentation for your hard drive and controller for information on solving these kinds of problems. In particular, many hard drives will need to have a jumper set if they are to be used as a "slave" drive (e.g., as the second hard drive). The acid test for this kind of condition is to boot up MS-DOS or some other operating system known to work with your drive and controller. If you can access the drive and controller from another operating system, then it is not a problem with your hardware configuration.

See the previous section, "Isolating hardware problems," for information on resolving possible device conflicts and the following section, "Problems with SCSI controllers and devices," for information on configuring SCSI devices.

Controller properly configured, but not detected

Some BIOS-less SCSI controllers require the user to specify information about the controller at boot time. The following section, "Problems with SCSI controllers and devices," describes how to force hardware detection for these controllers.

Hard drive geometry not recognized

Some systems, such as the IBM PS/ValuePoint, do not store hard-drive geometry information in the CMOS memory where Linux expects to find it. Also, certain SCSI controllers need to be told where to find drive geometry in order for Linux to recognize the layout of your drive.

Most distributions provide a boot option to specify the drive geometry. In general, when booting the installation media, you can specify the drive geometry at the LILO boot prompt with a command such as:

```
boot: linux hd=cylinders,heads,sectors
```

where *cylinders*, *heads*, and *sectors* correspond to the number of cylinders, heads, and sectors per track for your hard drive.

After installing the Linux software, you can install LILO, allowing you to boot from the hard drive. At that time, you can specify the drive geometry to the LILO installation procedure, making it unnecessary to enter the drive geometry each time you boot. See the section "Using LILO" in Chapter 5 for more about LILO.

Chapter 5

Problems with SCSI controllers and devices

Presented here are some of the most common problems with SCSI controllers and devices, such as CD-ROMs, hard drives, and tape drives. If you are having problems getting Linux to recognize your drive or controller, read on. Let us again emphasize that most distributions use a modularized kernel and that you might have to load a module supporting your hardware during an early phase of the installation process. This might also be done automatically for you.

[69] SCSI
HOWTO

The Linux SCSI HOWTO contains much useful information on SCSI devices in addition to that listed here. SCSIs can be particularly tricky to configure at times.

It might be economizing on the false end, for example, if you use cheap cables, especially if you use wide SCSI. Cheap cables are a major source of problems and can cause all kinds of failures, as well as major headaches. If you use SCSI, use proper cabling.

Here are common problems and possible solutions:

A SCSI device is detected at all possible IDs.
> This problem occurs when the system straps the device to the same address as the controller. You need to change the jumper settings so that the drive uses a different address from the controller itself.

Linux reports sense errors, even if the devices are known to be error-free.
> This can be caused by bad cables or by bad termination. If your SCSI bus is not terminated at both ends, you may have errors accessing SCSI devices. When in doubt, always check your cables. In addition to disconnected cables, bad-quality cables are a not-so-uncommon source of troubles.

SCSI devices report timeout errors.
> This is usually caused by a conflict with IRQ, DMA, or device addresses. Also, check that interrupts are enabled correctly on your controller.

SCSI controllers using BIOS are not detected.
> Detection of controllers using BIOS will fail if the BIOS is disabled, or if your controller's "signature" is not recognized by the kernel. See the Linux SCSI HOWTO for more information about this.

Controllers using memory-mapped I/O do not work.
> This happens when the memory-mapped I/O ports are incorrectly cached. Either mark the board's address space as uncacheable in the XCMOS settings, or disable cache altogether.

When partitioning, you get a warning "cylinders > 1024," or you are unable to boot from a partition using cylinders numbered above 1023.
> BIOS limits the number of cylinders to 1024, and any partition using cylinders numbered above this won't be accessible from the BIOS. As far as Linux is concerned, this affects only booting; once the system has booted, you should be able to access the partition. Your options are to either boot Linux from a boot floppy, or boot from a partition using cylinders numbered below 1024. See the section "Creating the Boot Floppy or Installing LILO" earlier in this chapter.

CD-ROM drive or other removable media devices are not recognized at boot time.
> Try booting with a CD-ROM (or disk) in the drive. This is necessary for some devices.

If your SCSI controller is not recognized, you may need to force hardware detection at boot time. This is particularly important for SCSI controllers without BIOS. Most distributions allow you to specify the controller IRQ and shared memory address when booting the installation media. For example, if you are using a TMC-8xx controller, you may be able to enter:

```
boot: linux tmx8xx=interrupt,memory-address
```

at the LILO boot prompt, where *interrupt* is the IRQ of controller, and *memory-address* is the shared memory address. Whether you can do this depends on the distribution of Linux you are using; consult your documentation for details.

Problems Installing the Software

Installing the Linux software should be trouble free if you're lucky. The only problems you might experience would be related to corrupt installation media or lack of space on your Linux filesystems. Here is a list of common problems:

System reports "Read error, file not found," or other errors while attempting to install the software.
> This is indicative of a problem with your installation media. If you are installing from floppy, keep in mind that floppies are quite susceptible to media errors of this type. Be sure to use brand-new, newly formatted floppies. If you have a Windows partition on your drive, many Linux distributions allow you to install the software from the hard drive. This may be faster and more reliable than using floppies.

> If you are using a CD-ROM, be sure to check the disk for scratches, dust, or other problems that might cause media errors.

> The cause of the problem may also be that the media is in the incorrect format. For example, if using floppies, many Linux distributions require floppies to be formatted in high-density MS-DOS format. (The boot floppy is the exception; it is not in MS-DOS format in most cases.) If all else fails, either obtain a new set of floppies, or recreate the floppies (using new ones) if you downloaded the software yourself.

System reports errors such as "tar: read error" or "gzip: not in gzip format."
> This problem is usually caused by corrupt files on the installation media itself. In other words, your floppy may be error-free, but the data on the floppy is in some way corrupted. For example, if you downloaded the Linux software using text mode, rather than binary mode, your files will be corrupt and unreadable by the installation software. When using FTP, just issue the *binary* command to set that mode before you request a file transfer.

System reports errors such as "device full" while installing.

This is a clear-cut sign you have run out of space when installing the software. If the disk fills up, not all distributions can clearly recover, so aborting the installation won't give you a working system.

The solution is usually to recreate your filesystems with the *mke2fs* command, which will delete the partially installed software. You can then attempt to reinstall the software, this time selecting a smaller amount of software to install. In other cases, you may need to start completely from scratch, and rethink your partition and filesystem sizes.

System reports errors such as "read_intr: 0x10" while accessing the hard drive.

This is usually an indication of bad blocks on your drive. However, if you receive these errors while using *mkswap* or *mke2fs*, the system may be having trouble accessing your drive. This can either be a hardware problem (see the section "Hardware Problems" earlier in this chapter), or it might be a case of poorly specified geometry. If you used the option:

```
hd=cylinders,heads,sectors
```

at boot time to force detection of your drive geometry and incorrectly specified the geometry, you could receive this error. This can also happen if your drive geometry is incorrectly specified in the system CMOS.

System reports errors such as "file not found" or "permission denied."

This problem can occur if not all of the necessary files are present on the installation media or if there is a permissions problem with the installation software. For example, some distributions of Linux have been known to have bugs in the installation software itself; these are usually fixed rapidly and are quite infrequent. If you suspect that the distribution software contains bugs, and you're sure that you have not done anything wrong, contact the maintainer of the distribution to report the bug.

If you have other strange errors when installing Linux (especially if you downloaded the software yourself), be sure you actually obtained all of the necessary files when downloading.

For example, some people use the FTP command:

```
mget *.*
```

when downloading the Linux software via FTP. This will download only those files that contain a "." in their filenames; if there are any files without the "." you will miss them. The correct command to use in this case is:

```
mget *
```

The best advice is to retrace your steps when something goes wrong. You may think that you have done everything correctly, when in fact you forgot a small but important step somewhere along the way. In many cases, just attempting to re-download or reinstall the Linux software can solve the problem. Don't beat your head against the wall any longer than you have to!

Also, if Linux unexpectedly hangs during installation, there may be a hardware problem of some kind. See the section "Hardware Problems" for hints.

Problems After Installing Linux

You've spent an entire afternoon installing Linux. In order to make space for it, you wiped your Windows and OS/2 partitions and tearfully deleted your copies of SimCity 2000 and Railroad Tycoon 2. You reboot the system and nothing happens. Or, even worse, *something* happens, but it's not what should happen. What do you do?

In the section "Problems with Booting the Installation Media," earlier in this chapter, we covered the most common problems that can occur when booting the Linux installation media; many of those problems may apply here. In addition, you may be victim to one of the following maladies.

Problems booting Linux from floppy

If you are using a floppy to boot Linux, you may need to specify the location of your Linux root partition at boot time. This is especially true if you are using the original installation floppy itself and not a custom boot floppy created during installation.

While booting the floppy, hold down the Shift or Control key. This should present you with a boot menu; press Tab to see a list of available options. For example, many distributions allow you to boot from a floppy by entering:

```
boot: linux root=partition
```

at the boot menu, where *partition* is the name of the Linux root partition, such as */dev/hda2*. SuSE Linux offers a menu entry early in the installation program that boots your newly created Linux system from the installation boot floppy. Consult the documentation for your distribution for details.

Problems booting Linux from the hard drive

If you opted to install LILO instead of creating a boot floppy, you should be able to boot Linux from the hard drive. However, the automated LILO installation procedure used by many distributions is not always perfect. It may make incorrect assumptions about your partition layout, in which case you need to reinstall LILO

Chapter 5

to get everything right. Installing LILO is covered in the section "Using LILO" in Chapter 5.

Here are some common problems:

System reports "Drive not bootable–Please insert system disk."
You will get this error message if the hard drive's master boot record is corrupt in some way. In most cases, it's harmless, and everything else on your drive is still intact. There are several ways around this:

- While partitioning your drive using *fdisk*, you may have deleted the partition that was marked as "active." MS-DOS and other operating systems attempt to boot the "active" partition at boot time (Linux, in general, pays no attention to whether the partition is "active," but the Master Boot Records installed by some distributions like Debian do). You may be able to boot MS-DOS from floppy and run FDISK to set the active flag on your MS-DOS partition, and all will be well.

  Another command to try (with MS-DOS 5.0 and higher) is:

  ```
  FDISK /MBR
  ```

  This command will attempt to rebuild the hard drive master boot record for booting MS-DOS, overwriting LILO. If you no longer have MS-DOS on your hard drive, you'll need to boot Linux from floppy and attempt to install LILO later.

- If you created an MS-DOS partition using Linux's version of *fdisk*, or vice versa, you may get this error. You should create MS-DOS partitions only by using MS-DOS's version of FDISK. (The same applies to operating systems other than MS-DOS.) The best solution here is either to start from scratch and repartition the drive correctly, or to merely delete and recreate the offending partitions using the correct version of *fdisk*.

- The LILO installation procedure may have failed. In this case, you should boot either from your Linux boot floppy (if you have one), or from the original installation media. Either of these should provide options for specifying the Linux root partition to use when booting. At boot time, hold down the Shift or Control key and press Tab from the boot menu for a list of options.

When you boot the system from the hard drive, MS-DOS (or another operating system) starts instead of Linux.
First of all, be sure you actually installed LILO when installing the Linux software. If not, the system will still boot MS-DOS (or whatever other operating system you may have) when you attempt to boot from the hard drive. In order to boot Linux from the hard drive, you need to install LILO (see the section "Using LILO" in Chapter 5).

Chapter 5

On the other hand, if you *did* install LILO, and another operating system boots instead of Linux, then you have LILO configured to boot that other operating system by default. While the system is booting, hold down the Shift or Control key and press Tab at the boot prompt. This should present you with a list of possible operating systems to boot; select the appropriate option (usually just linux) to boot Linux.

If you wish to select Linux as the default operating system to boot, you will need to reinstall LILO.

It also may be possible that you attempted to install LILO, but the installation procedure failed in some way. See the previous item on installation.

Problems logging in

After booting Linux, you should be presented with a login prompt:

```
Linux login:
```

At this point, either the distribution's documentation or the system itself will tell you what to do. For many distributions, you simply log in as **root**, with no password. Other possible usernames to try are **guest** or **test**.

Most Linux distributions ask you for an initial root password. Hopefully, you have remembered what you typed in during installation; you will need it again now. If your distribution does not ask you for a root password during installation, you can try using an empty password.

If you simply can't log in, consult your distribution's documentation; the username and password to use may be buried in there somewhere. The username and password may have been given to you during the installation procedure, or they may be printed on the login banner.

One possible cause of this password impasse may be a problem with installing the Linux login and initialization files. If this is the case, you may need to reinstall (at least parts of) the Linux software, or boot your installation media and attempt to fix the problem by hand.

Problems using the system

Chapter 4

If login is successful, you should be presented with a shell prompt (such as # or $) and can happily roam around your system. The next step in this case is to try the procedures in Chapter 4. However, there are some initial problems with using the system that sometimes creep up.

The most common initial configuration problem is incorrect file or directory permissions. This can cause the error message:

```
Shell-init: permission denied
```

to be printed after logging in. (In fact, any time you see the message permission denied, you can be fairly certain it is a problem with file permissions.)

In many cases, it's a simple matter of using the *chmod* command to fix the permissions of the appropriate files or directories. For example, some distributions of Linux once used the incorrect file mode 0644 for the root directory (/). The fix was to issue the command:

```
# chmod 755 /
```

Chapter 4

as **root**. (File permissions are covered by the section "File Ownership and Permissions" in Chapter 4.) However, in order to issue this command, you needed to boot from the installation media and mount your Linux root filesystem by hand—a hairy task for most newcomers.

Chapter 1
Chapter 5

As you use the system, you may run into places where file and directory permissions are incorrect, or software does not work as configured. Welcome to the world of Linux! While most distributions are quite trouble-free, you can't expect them to be perfect. We don't want to cover all of those problems here. Instead, throughout the book we help you to solve many of these configuration problems by teaching you how to find them and fix them yourself. In Chapter 1, we discussed this philosophy in some detail. In Chapter 5, we give hints for fixing many of these common configuration problems.

CHAPTER FOUR

BASIC UNIX COMMANDS AND CONCEPTS

I f you've come to Linux from MS-DOS or another non-Unix operating system, you have a steep learning curve ahead of you. We might as well be candid on this point. Unix is a world all its own.

In this chapter, we're going to introduce the rudiments of Unix for those readers who have never had exposure to this operating system. If you are coming from MS-DOS, Microsoft Windows, or other environments, the information in this chapter will be absolutely vital to you. Unlike other operating systems, Unix is not at all intuitive. Many of the commands have seemingly odd names or syntax, the reasons for which usually date back many years to the early days of this system. And, although many of the commands may appear to be similar to their MS-DOS counterparts, there are important differences.

There are dozens of other books that cover basic Unix usage. You should be able to go to the computer section of any chain bookstore and find at least three or four of them on the shelf. (A few we like are listed in the Bibliography.) However, most of these books cover Unix from the point of view of someone sitting down at a workstation or terminal connected to a large mainframe, not someone who is running their own Unix system on a personal computer.

Also, these books often dwell upon the more mundane aspects of Unix: boring text-manipulation commands, such as *awk*, *tr*, and *sed*, most of which you will never need unless you get into doing some serious Unix trickery. In fact, many Unix books talk about the original *ed* line editor, which has long been made obsolete by *vi* and Emacs. Therefore, although many of the Unix books available today contain a great deal of useful information, many of them contain pages upon pages of humdrum material you couldn't probably care less about at this point.

Instead of getting into the dark mesh of text processing, shell syntax, and other issues, in this chapter we strive to cover the basic commands needed to get you up to speed with the system if you're coming from a non-Unix environment. This chapter is far from complete; a real beginner's Unix tutorial would take an entire book. It's our hope that this chapter will give you enough to keep you going in your adventures with Linux, and that you'll invest in one of the aforementioned Unix books once you have a need to do so. We'll give you enough Unix background to make your terminal usable, keep track of jobs, and enter essential commands.

Chapter 5

Chapter 5, *Essential System Management*, contains material on system administration and maintenance. This is by far the most important chapter for anyone running his own Linux system. If you are completely new to Unix, the material found in Chapter 5 should be easy to follow given the tutorial here.

Chapter 9

One big job we don't cover in this chapter is how to edit files. It's one of the first things you need to learn on any operating system. The two most popular editors for Linux, *vi* and Emacs, are discussed at the beginning of Chapter 9, *Editors, Text Tools, Graphics, and Printing*.

Logging In

Let's assume that your installation went completely smoothly, and you are facing the following prompt on your screen:

```
Linux login:
```

Many Linux users are not so lucky; they have to perform some heavy tinkering when the system is still in a raw state or in single-user mode. But for now, we'll talk about logging into a functioning Linux system.

Logging in, of course, distinguishes one user from another. It lets several people work on the same system at once and makes sure that you are the only person to have access to your files.

You may have installed Linux at home and be thinking right now, "Big deal. No one else shares this system with me, and I'd just as soon not have to log in." But logging in under your personal account also provides a certain degree of protection: your account won't have the ability to destroy or remove important system files. The system administration account (covered in the next chapter) is used for such touchy matters.

If you connect your computer to the Internet, even via a modem, make sure you set non-trivial passwords on all of your accounts. Use punctuation and strings that don't represent real words or names.

You were probably asked to set up a login account for yourself when you installed Linux. If you have such an account, type the name you chose at the `Linux login:` prompt. If you don't have an account yet, type `root` because that account is certain to exist. Some distributions may also set up an account called **install** or some other name for fooling around when you first install the system.

After you choose your account, you see:

```
Password:
```

and you need to enter the correct password. The terminal turns off the normal echoing of characters you enter for this operation, so that nobody looking at the screen can read your password. If the prompt does not appear, you should add a password to protect yourself from other people's tampering; we'll go into this later.

By the way, both the name and the password are case-sensitive. Make sure the Caps Lock key is not set, because typing ROOT instead of root will not work.

When you have successfully logged in, you will see a prompt. If you're **root**, this may be a simple:

```
#
```

For other users, the prompt is usually a dollar sign. The prompt may also contain the name you assigned to your system or the directory you're in currently. Whatever appears here, you are now ready to enter commands. We say that you are at the "shell level" here and that the prompt you see is the "shell prompt." This is because you are running a program called the shell that handles your commands. Right now we can ignore the shell, but later in this chapter we'll find that it does a number of useful things for us.

As we show commands in this chapter, we'll show the prompt simply as $. So if you see:

```
$ pwd
```

it means that the shell prints $ and that pwd is what you're supposed to enter.

Setting a Password

If you don't already have a password, we recommend you set one. Just enter the command *passwd*. The command will prompt you for a password and then ask you to enter it a second time to make sure you enter it without typos.

There are standard guidelines for choosing passwords so that they're hard for other people to guess. Some systems even check your password and reject any that don't meet the minimal criteria. For instance, it is often said that you should have at least six characters in the password. Furthermore, you should mix uppercase and lowercase characters or include characters other than letters and digits.

To change your password, just enter the *passwd* command again. It prompts you for your old password (to make sure you're you) and then lets you change it.

Virtual Consoles

As a multiprocessing system, Linux gives you a number of interesting ways to do several things at once. You can start a long software installation and then switch to reading mail or compiling a program simultaneously. This should be a major part of Linux's appeal to MS-DOS users (although the latest Microsoft Windows has finally come to grips with multiprocessing, too).

Most Linux users, when they want this asynchronous access, will employ the X Window System. But before you get X running, you can do something similar through virtual consoles. This feature appears on a few other versions of Unix, but is not universally available.

To try out virtual consoles, hold down the left Alt key and press one of the function keys, F1 through F8. As you press each function key, you see a totally new screen complete with a login prompt. You can log in to different virtual consoles just as if you were two different people, and you can switch between them to carry out different activities. You can even run a complete X session in each console. The X Window System will use the virtual console 7 by default. So if you start X and then switch to one of the text-based virtual consoles, you can go back again to X by typing Alt-F7. If you discover that the Alt + function key combination brings up an X menu or some other fuction instead of switching virtual consoles, use Ctrl + Alt + function key.

In earlier versions of Linux (until kernel 1.1.54), the number of available virtual consoles was fixed, but could be changed by patching, recompiling and reinstalling the kernel; the default was 8. Nowadays, the Linux kernel creates virtual consoles as needed on the fly. However, this does not mean that you can simply go to virtual console 13 and log in there. You can log in only on virtual consoles where a getty process is running (see the next chapter for more information on this).

Popular Commands

The number of commands on a typical Unix system is enough to fill a few hundred reference pages. And you can add new commands too. The commands we'll tell you about here are just enough to navigate and to see what you have on the system.

Directories

Like MS-DOS, and virtually every modern computer system, Unix files are organized into a hierarchical directory structure. Unix imposes no rules about where files have to be, but conventions have grown up over the years. Thus, on Linux you'll find a directory called */home* where each user's files are placed. Each user has a subdirectory under */home*. So if your login name is **mdw**, your personal files are located in */home/mdw*. This is called your home directory. You can, of course, create more subdirectories under it.

As you can see, the components of a directory are separated by slashes. The term *pathname* is often used to refer to this slash-separated list.

What directory is */home* in? The directory named */* of course. This is called the root directory. We have already mentioned it when setting up file systems.

When you log in, the system puts you in your home directory. To verify this, use the "print working directory" or *pwd* command:

```
$ pwd
/home/mdw
```

The system confirms that you're in */home/mdw*.

You certainly won't have much fun if you have to stay in one directory all the time. Now try using another command, *cd*, to move to another directory:

```
$ cd /usr/bin
$ pwd
/usr/bin
$ cd
```

Where are we now? A *cd* with no arguments returns us to our home directory. By the way, the home directory is often represented by a tilde (~). So the string *~/programs* means that *programs* is located right under your home directory.

While we're thinking about it, let's make a directory called *~/programs*. From your home directory, you can enter either:

```
$ mkdir programs
```

or the full pathname:

```
$ mkdir /home/mdw/programs
```

Now change to that directory:

```
$ cd programs
$ pwd
/home/mdw/programs
```

The special character sequence .. refers to "the directory just above the current one." So you can move back up to your home directory by typing the following:

```
$ cd ..
```

The opposite of *mkdir* is *rmdir*, which removes directories:

```
$ rmdir programs
```

Chapter 9

Similarly, the *rm* command deletes files. We won't show it here, because we haven't yet shown how to create a file. You generally use the *vi* or Emacs editor for that (see Chapter 9), but some of the commands later in this chapter will create files too. With the *−r* (recursive) option, *rm* deletes a whole directory and all its contents. (Use with care!)

Listing Files

Enter *ls* to see what is in a directory. Issued without an argument, the *ls* command shows the contents of the current directory. You can include an argument to see a different directory:

```
$ ls /home
```

Some systems have a fancy *ls* that displays special files—such as directories and executable files—in bold, or even in different colors. If you want to change the default colors, edit the file */etc/DIR_COLORS*, or create a copy of it in your home directory named *.dir_colors* and edit that.

Like most Unix commands, *ls* can be controlled with options that start with a hyphen (−). Make sure you type a space before the hyphen. One useful option for *ls* is *−a* for "all," which will reveal to you riches that you never imagined in your home directory:

```
$ cd
$ ls −a
.                       .bashrc              .fvwmrc
..                      .emacs               .xinitrc
.bash_history           .exrc
```

The single dot refers to the current directory, and the double dot refers to the directory right above it. But what are those other files beginning with a dot? They are called hidden files. Putting a dot in front of their names keeps them from being shown during a normal *ls* command. Many programs employ hidden files for user options—things about their default behavior that you want to change. For instance, you can put commands in the file *.Xdefaults* to alter how programs using the X Window System operate. So most of the time you can forget these files exist, but when you're configuring your system you'll find them very important. We'll list some of them later.

Another useful *ls* option is *−l* for "long." It shows extra information about the files. Figure 4-1 shows typical output and what each field means.

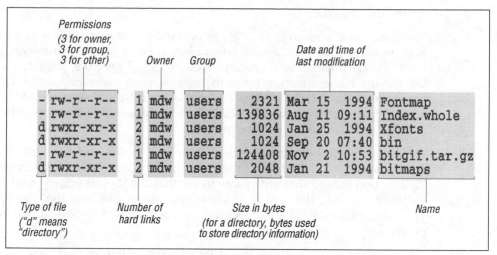

Figure 4–1: Output of ls –l

We'll discuss the permissions, owner, and group fields later in this chapter, in the section "File Ownership and Permissions." The *ls* command also shows the size of each file and when it was last modified.

Viewing Files, More or Less

One way to look at a file is to invoke an editor, such as:

```
$ emacs .bashrc
```

But if you just want to scan a file quickly, rather than edit it, other commands are quicker. The simplest is the strangely named *cat* command (named after the verb *concatenate*, because you can also use it to concatenate several files into one):

```
$ cat .bashrc
```

But a long file will scroll by too fast for you to see it, so most people use the *more* command instead:

```
$ more .bashrc
```

This prints a screenfull at a time and waits for you to press the space bar before printing more. *more* has a lot of powerful options. For instance, you can search for a string in the file: press the slash key (/), type the string, and press Return.

A popular variation on the *more* command is called *less*. It has even more powerful features; for instance, you can mark a particular place in a file and return there later.

Symbolic Links

Sometimes you want to keep a file in one place and pretend it is in another. This is done most often by a system administrator, not a user. For instance, you might keep several versions of a program around, called *prog.0.9*, *prog.1.1*, and so on, but use the name *prog* to refer to the version you're currently using. Or you may have a file installed in one partition because you have disk space for it there, but the program that uses the file needs it to be in a different partition because the pathname is hard-coded into the program.

Unix provides *links* to handle these situations. In this section, we'll examine the *symbolic link*, which is the most flexible and popular type. A symbolic link is a kind of dummy file that just points to another file. If you edit or read or execute the symbolic link, the system is smart enough to give you the real file instead. Symbolic links work a lot like shortcuts under Windows 95/98, but are much more powerful.

Let's take the *prog* example. You want to create a link named *prog* that points to the actual file, which is named *prog.1.1*. Enter the command:

```
$ ln -s prog.1.1 prog
```

Now you've created a new file named *prog* that is kind of a dummy file; if you run it, you're really running *prog.1.1*. Let's look at what *ls -l* has to say about the file:

```
$ ls -l prog
lrwxrwxrwx   2 mdw        users          8 Nov 17 14:35 prog -> prog.1.1
```

The 1 at the beginning of the line shows that the file is a link, and the little -> indicates the real file the link points to.

Symbolic links are really simple, once you get used to the idea of one file pointing to another. You'll encounter links all the time when installing software packages.

Shells

As we said before, logging in to the system puts you into a shell (or a graphical interface if your system is configured to use a display manager). So does opening an *xterm* window in X. The shell interprets and executes all your commands. Let's look a bit at different shells before we keep going, because they're going to affect some of the material coming up.

If it seems confusing that Unix offers many different shells, just accept it as an effect of evolution. Believe us, you wouldn't want to be stuck using the very first shell developed for Unix, the Bourne shell. While it was a very powerful user interface for its day (the mid-1970s), it lacked a lot of useful features for interactive use—including the ones shown in this section. So other shells have been developed over time, and you can now choose the one that best suits your way of working.

Some of the shells available on Linux are:

bash
> Bourne Again shell. The most commonly used (and most powerful) shell on Linux. POSIX-compliant, compatible with Bourne shell, created and distributed by the GNU project (Free Software Foundation). Offers command-line editing, history substitution, and Bourne Shell compatibility.

csh
> C shell. Developed at Berkeley. Mostly compatible with the Bourne shell for interactive use, but has a very different interface for programming. Does not offer command-line editing, although it does have a sophisticated alternative called history substitution.

ksh
> Korn shell. Perhaps the most popular on Unix systems generally, and the first to introduce modern shell techniques (including some borrowed from the C shell) into the Bourne shell. Compatible with Bourne shell. Offers command-line editing.

sh Bourne shell. The original shell. Does not offer command-line editing.

tcsh
> Enhanced C shell. Offers command-line editing.

zsh
> Z shell. The newest of the shells. Compatible with Bourne shell. Offers command-line editing.

Try the following command to find out what your shell is. It prints out the full pathname where the shell is located. Don't forget to type the dollar sign:

```
$ echo $SHELL
```

You are probably running *bash*, the Bourne Again Shell. If you're running something else, this might be a good time to change to *bash*. It's powerful, POSIX-compliant, well-supported, and very popular on Linux. Use the *chsh* command to change your shell:

```
$ chsh
Enter password: Type your password here—this is for security's sake
Changing the login shell for kalle
Enter the new value, or press return for the default

        Login Shell [/bin/sh]:/bin/bash
```

Before a user can choose a particular shell, that shell must be installed and the system administrator must make it available by entering it in */etc/shells*.

There are a couple of ways to conceptualize the differences between shells. One is to distinguish Bourne-compatible shells from *csh*-compatible shells. This will be of interest to you when you start to program with the shell, also known as writing shell scripts. The Bourne shell and C shell have different programming constructs. Most people now agree that Bourne-compatible shells are better, and there are many Unix utilities that recognize only the Bourne shell.

Another way to categorize shells is to identify those that offer command-line editing (all the newer ones) versus those that do not. *sh* and *csh* lack this useful feature.

When you combine the two criteria—being compatible with the Bourne shell and offering command-line editing—your best choice comes down to *bash*, *ksh*, or *zsh*. Try out several shells before you make your choice; it helps to know more than one, in case someday you find yourself on a system that limits your choice of shells.

Useful Keys and How to Get Them to Work

When you type a command, pressing the Backspace key should remove the last character. Ctrl-U should delete the whole line.* When you have finished entering a command, and it is executing, Ctrl-C should abort it, and Ctrl-Z should suspend it. (When you want to resume the program, enter *fg* for "foreground.")

If any of these keys fail to work, your terminal is not configured correctly for some reason. You can fix it through the *stty* command. Use the syntax:

```
stty function key
```

where `function` is what you want to do, and `key` is the key that you press. Specify a control key by putting a circumflex (^) in front of the key.

Here is a set of sample commands to set up the functions described earlier:

```
$ stty erase ^H
$ stty kill ^U
$ stty intr ^C
$ stty susp ^Z
```

The first control key shown, ^H, represents the ASCII code generated by the Backspace key.

By the way, you can generate a listing of your current terminal settings by entering *stty −a*. But that doesn't mean you can understand the output: *stty* is a complicated command with many uses, some of which require a lot of knowledge about terminals.

---

* Ctrl-U means hold down the Control key and press u.

Typing Shortcuts

If you've been following along this tutorial at the terminal, you may be tired of typing the same things over and over again. It can be particularly annoying when you make a mistake and have to start over again. Here is where the shell really makes life easier. It doesn't make Unix as simple as a point-and-click interface, but it can help you work really fast in a command environment.

This section discusses command-line editing. The tips here work if your shell is *bash*, *ksh*, *tcsh*, or *zsh*. Command-line editing treats the last fifty or so lines you typed as a buffer in an editor. You can move around these lines and change them the way you'd edit a document. Every time you press the Return key, the shell executes the current line.

Word Completion

First, let's try something simple that can save you a lot of time. Type the following, without pressing the Return key:

```
$ cd /usr/inc
```

Now press the Tab key. The shell will add `lude` to complete the name of the directory */usr/include*. Now you can press the Return key, and the command will execute.

The criteria for specifying a filename is "minimal completion." Type just enough characters to distinguish a name from all the others in that directory. The shell can find the name and complete it—up to and including a slash, if the name is a directory.

You can use completion on commands too. For instance, if you type:

```
$ ema
```

and press the Tab key, the shell will add the `cs` to make `emacs` (unless some other command in your path begins with `ema`).

What if there are multiple files that match what you've typed? If they all start with the same characters, the shell completes the word up to the point where names differ. Beyond that, most shells do nothing. *bash* has a neat enhancement: if you press the Tab key twice, it displays all the possible completions. For instance, if you enter:

```
$ cd /usr/l
```

and press the Tab key twice, *bash* prints something like:

```
lib        local
```

Moving Around Among Commands

Press the up arrow, and the command you typed previously appears. The up arrow takes you back through the command history, while the down arrow takes you forward. If you want to change a character on the current line, use the left or right arrow keys.

As an example, suppose you tried to execute:

```
$ mroe .bashrc
bash: mroe: command not found
```

Of course, you typed mroe instead of more. To correct the command, call it back by pressing the up arrow. Then press the left arrow until the cursor lies over the o in mroe. You could use the Backspace key to remove the o and r and retype them correctly. But here's an even neater shortcut: just press Ctrl-T. It will reverse o and r, and you can then press the Return key to execute the command.

Many other key combinations exist for command-line editing. But the basics shown here will help you quite a bit. If you learn the Emacs editor, you will find that most keys work the same way in the shell. And if you're a *vi* fan, you can set up your shell so that it uses *vi* key bindings instead of Emacs bindings. To do this in *bash*, *ksh*, or *zsh*, enter the command:

```
$ export VISUAL=vi
```

In *tcsh* enter:

```
$ setenv VISUAL vi
```

Filename Expansion

Another way to save time in your commands is to use special characters to abbreviate filenames. You can specify many files at once by using these characters. This feature of the shell is sometimes called "globbing."

MS-DOS provides a few crude features of this type. You can use a question mark to mean "any character" and an asterisk to mean "any string of characters." Unix provides these wildcards too, but in a more robust and rigorous way.

Let's say you have a directory containing the following C source files:

```
$ ls
inv1jig.c    inv2jig.c    inv3jig.c    invinitjig.c    invpar.c
```

To list the three files containing digits in their names, you could enter:

```
$ ls inv?jig.c
inv1jig.c    inv2jig.c    inv3jig.c
```

The shell looks for a single character to replace the question mark. Thus, it displays *inv1jig.c*, *inv2jig.c*, and *inv3jig.c*, but not *invinitjig.c* because that name contains too many characters.

If you're not interested in the second file, you can specify the ones you want using brackets:

```
$ ls inv[13]jig.c
inv1jig.c   inv3jig.c
```

If any single character within the brackets matches a file, that file is displayed. You can also put a range of characters in the brackets:

```
$ ls inv[1-3]jig.c
inv1jig.c   inv2jig.c   inv3jig.c
```

Now we're back to displaying all three files. The hyphen means "match any character from 1 through 3, inclusive." You could ask for any numeric character by specifying 0-9, and any alphabetic character by specifying [a-zA-Z]. In the latter case, two ranges are required because the shell is case-sensitive. The order used, by the way, is that of the ASCII character set.

Suppose you want to see the init file, too. Now you can use an asterisk, because you want to match any number of characters between the inv and the jig:

```
$ ls inv*jig.c
inv1jig.c   inv2jig.c   inv3jig.c   invinitjig.c
```

The asterisk actually means "zero or more characters," so if a file named *invjig.c* existed, it would be shown, too.

Unlike MS-DOS, the Unix shells let you combine special characters and normal characters any way you want. Let's say you want to look for any source (*.c*) or object (*.o*) file that contains a digit. The resulting pattern combines all the expansions we've studied in this section:

```
$ ls *[0-9]*.[co]
```

Filename expansion is very useful in shell scripts (programs), where you don't always know exactly how many files exist. For instance, you might want to process multiple log files named *log001*, *log002*, and so on. No matter how many there are, the expression *log** will match them all.

One final warning: filename expansions are not the same as regular expressions, which are used by many utilities to specify groups of strings. Regular expressions are beyond the scope of this book, but are described by many books that explain Unix utilities. A taste of regular expressions appears in Chapter 13, *Programming Languages.*

Chapter 13

Saving Your Output

System administrators (and other human beings too) see a lot of critical messages fly by on the computer screen. It's often important to save these messages so you can scrutinize them later, or (all too often) send them to a friend who can figure out what went wrong. So, in this section, we'll explain a little bit about redirection, a powerful feature provided by Unix shells. If you come from MS-DOS, you have probably seen a similar, but more limited, type of redirection.

If you put a greater-than sign (>) and a filename after any command, the output of the command will be sent to that file. For instance, to capture the output of *ls*, you can enter:

```
$ ls /usr/bin > ~/Binaries
```

A listing of */usr/bin* will be stored in your home directory in a file named *Binaries*. If *Binaries* had already existed, the > would wipe out what was there and replace it with the output of the *ls* command. Overwriting a current file is a common user error. If your shell is *csh* or *tcsh*, you can prevent overwriting with the command:

```
$ set noclobber
```

And in *bash* you can achieve the same effect by entering:

```
$ noclobber=1          It doesn't have to be 1; any value will have the same effect.
```

Another (and perhaps more useful) way to prevent overwriting is to append new output. For instance, having saved a listing of */usr/bin*, suppose we now want to add the contents of */bin* to that file. We can append it to the end of the *Binaries* file by specifying two greater-than signs:

```
$ ls /bin >> ~/Binaries
```

You will find the technique of output redirection very useful when you are running a utility many times and saving the output for troubleshooting.

Most Unix programs have two output streams. One is called the standard output, and the other is the standard error. If you're a C programmer you'll recognize these: the standard error is the file named *stderr* to which you print messages.

The > character does not redirect the standard error. It's useful when you want to save legitimate output without mucking up a file with error messages. But what if the error messages are what you want to save? This is quite common during troubleshooting. The solution is to use a greater-than sign followed by an ampersand. (This construct works in almost every modern UNIX shell.) It redirects both the standard output and the standard error. For instance:

```
$ gcc invinitjig.c >& error-msg
```

This command saves all the messages from the *gcc* compiler in a file named *error-msg*. (Of course, the object code is not saved there. It's stored in *invinitjig.o* as always.) On the Bourne shell and *bash* you can also say it slightly differently:

```
$ gcc invinitjig.c &> error-msg
```

Now let's get really fancy. Suppose you want to save the error messages but not the regular output—the standard error but not the standard output. In the Bourne-compatible shells you can do this by entering the following:

```
$ gcc invinitjig.c 2> error-msg
```

The shell arbitrarily assigns the number 1 to the standard output and the number 2 to the standard error. So the above command saves only the standard error.

Finally, suppose you want to throw away the standard output—keep it from appearing on your screen. The solution is to redirect it to a special file called */dev/ null*. (You've heard people say things like "Send your criticisms to /dev/null"? Well, this is where the phrase came from.) The */dev* directory is where Unix systems store special files that refer to terminals, tape drives, and other devices. But */dev/null* is unique; it's a place you can send things so that they disappear into a black hole. For example, the following command saves the standard error and throws away the standard output:

```
$ gcc invinitjig.c 2>error-msg >/dev/null
```

So now you should be able to isolate exactly the output you want.

In case you've wondered whether the less-than sign (<) means anything to the shell: yes, it does. It causes commands to take their input from a file. But most commands allow you to specify input files on their command lines anyway, so this "input redirection" is rarely necessary.

Sometimes you want one utility to operate on the output of another utility. For instance, you can use the *sort* command to put the output of other commands into a more useful order. A crude way to do this would be to save output from one command in a file, and then run *sort* on it. For instance:

```
$ du > du_output
$ sort -n du_output
```

Unix provides a much more succinct and efficient way to do this using a *pipe*. Just place a vertical bar between the first command and the second:

```
$ du | sort -n
```

The shell sends all the input from the *du* program to the *sort* program.

In the previous example, *du* stands for "disk usage" and shows how many blocks each file occupies under the current directory. Normally, its output is in a somewhat random order:

```
$ du
10          ./zoneinfo/Australia
13          ./zoneinfo/US
9           ./zoneinfo/Canada
4           ./zoneinfo/Mexico
5           ./zoneinfo/Brazil
3           ./zoneinfo/Chile
20          ./zoneinfo/SystemV
118         ./zoneinfo
298         ./ghostscript/doc
183         ./ghostscript/examples
3289        ./ghostscript/fonts
   .
   .
   .
```

So we have decided to run it through *sort* with the *-n* and *-r* options. The *-n* option means "sort in numerical order" instead of the default ASCII sort, and the *-r* option means "reverse the usual order" so that the highest number appears first. The result is output that quickly shows you which directories and files hog the most space:

```
$ du | sort -rn
34368       .
16005       ./emacs
16003       ./emacs/20.4
13326       ./emacs/20.4/lisp
4039        ./ghostscript
3289        ./ghostscript/fonts
   .
   .
   .
```

Since there are so many files, we had better use a second pipe to send output through the *more* command (one of the more common uses of pipes):

```
$ du | sort -rn | more
34368       .
16005       ./emacs
16003       ./emacs/20.4
13326       ./emacs/20.4/lisp
4039        ./ghostscript
3289        ./ghostscript/fonts
   .
   .
   .
```

What Is a Command?

We've said that Unix offers a huge number of commands and that you can add new ones. This makes it radically different from most operating systems, which contain a strictly limited table of commands. So what are Unix commands, and how are they stored? On Unix, a command is simply a file. For instance, the *ls* command is a binary file located in the directory *bin*. So, instead of *ls*, you could enter the full pathname, also known as the *absolute pathname*:

```
$ /bin/ls
```

This makes Unix very flexible and powerful. To provide a new utility, a system administrator can simply install it in a standard directory where commands are located. There can also be different versions of a command—for instance, you can offer a new version of a utility for testing in one place while leaving the old version in another place, and users can choose the one they want.

Here's a common problem: sometimes you enter a command that you expect to be on the system, but you receive a message such as "Not found." The problem may be that the command is located in a directory that your shell is not searching. The list of directories where your shell looks for commands is called your path. Enter the following to see what your path is (remember the dollar sign!):

```
$ echo $PATH
/usr/local/bin:/usr/bin:/usr/X11R6/bin:/bin:/usr/lib/java/bin:\
/usr/games:/usr/bin/TeX:.
```

This takes a little careful eyeballing. The output is a series of pathnames separated by colons. The first pathname, for this particular user, is */usr/local/bin*. The second is */usr/bin*, and so on. So if two versions of a command exist, one in */usr/local/bin* and the other in */usr/bin*, the one in */usr/local/bin* will execute. The last pathname in this example is simply a dot; it refers to the current directory. Unlike MS-DOS, Unix does not look automatically in your current directory. You have to tell it to explicitly, as shown here. Some people think it's a bad idea to look in the current directory, for security reasons. (An intruder who gets into your account might copy a malicious program to one of your working directories.) However, this mostly applies to root, normal users generally do not need to worry about this.

If a command is not found, you have to figure out where it is on the system and add that directory to your path. The manual page should tell you where it is. Let's say you find it in */usr/sbin*, where a number of system administration commands are installed. You realize you need access to these system administration commands, so you enter the following (note that the first PATH doesn't have a dollar sign, but the second one does):

```
$ export PATH=$PATH:/usr/sbin
```

This command adds */usr/sbin*, but makes it the last directory that is searched. The command is saying, "Make my path equal to the old path plus */usr/sbin*."

The previous command works for some shells but not others. It's fine for most Linux users, who are working in a Bourne-compatible shell like *bash*. But if you use *csh* or *tcsh* you need to issue the following command instead:

```
set path = ( $PATH /usr/sbin )
```

Finally, there are a few commands that are not files; *cd* is one. Most of these commands affect the shell itself, and therefore have to be understood and executed by the shell. Because they are part of the shell, they are called built-in commands.

Putting a Command in the Background

Before the X Window System, which made it easy to run multiple programs at once, Unix users took advantage of Unix's multitasking features by simply putting an ampersand at the end of commands, as shown in this example:

```
$ gcc invinitjig.c &
[1] 21457
```

The ampersand puts the command into the background, meaning that the shell prompt comes back, and you can continue to execute other commands while the *gcc* command is compiling your program. The [1] is a job number that is assigned to your command. The 21457 is a process ID, which we'll discuss later. Job numbers are assigned to background commands in order and therefore are easier to remember and type than process IDs.

Of course, multitasking does not come for free. The more commands you put into the background, the slower your system runs as it tries to interleave their execution.

You wouldn't want to put a command in the background if it requires user input. If you do so, you see an error message like:

```
Stopped (tty input)
```

You can solve this problem by bringing the job back into the foreground through the *fg* command. If you have many commands in the background, you can choose one of them by its job number or its process ID. For our long-lived *gcc* command, the following commands are equivalent:

```
$ fg %1
$ fg 21457
```

Don't forget the percent sign on the job number; that's what distinguishes job numbers from process IDs.

To get rid of a command in the background, issue a *kill* command:

```
$ kill %1
```

Manual Pages

The most empowering information you can get is how to conduct your own research. Following this precept, we'll now tell you about the online help system that comes built in to Unix systems. It is called manual pages, or man pages for short.

Actually, manual pages are not quite the boon they ought to be. This is because they are short and take a lot of Unix background for granted. Each one focuses on a particular command and rarely helps you decide why you should use that command. Still, they are critical. Commands can vary slightly on different Unix systems, and the manual pages are the most reliable way to find out what your system does. The Linux Documentation Project deserves a lot of credit for the incredible number of hours they have put into creating manual pages. To find out about a command, enter a command like:

```
$ man ls
```

Manual pages are divided into different sections depending on what they are for. User commands are in section 1, Unix system calls in section 2, and so on. The sections that will interest you most are 1, 5 (file formats), and 8 (system administration commands). When you view man pages online, the section numbers are conceptual; you can optionally specify them when searching for a command:

```
$ man 1 ls
```

But if you consult a hard-copy manual, you'll find it divided into actual sections according to the numbering scheme. Sometimes an entry in two different sections can have the same name. (For instance, *chmod* is both a command and a system call.) So you will sometimes see the name of a manual page followed by the section number in parentheses, as in *ls(1)*.

There is one situation in which you will need the section number on the command line: when there are several manual pages for the same keyword (e.g., one for a command with that name and one for a system function with the same name). Suppose you want to look up a library call, but the *man* shows you the command because its default search order looks for the command first. In order to see the manual page for the library call, you need to give its section number.

Look near the top of a manual page. The first heading is NAME. Under it is a brief one-line description of the item. These descriptions can be valuable if you're not quite sure what you're looking for. Think of a word related to what you want, and specify it in an *apropos* command:

```
$ apropos edit
```

The previous command shows all the manual pages that have something to do with editing. It's a very simple algorithm: *apropos* simply prints out all the NAME lines that contain the string you ask for.

Chapter 11

An X Window System application, *xman*, also helps you browse manual pages. It is described in the section "xman: A Point-and-Click Interface to Manual Pages" in Chapter 11, *Customizing Your X Environment*.

Like commands, manual pages are sometimes installed in strange places. For instance, you may install some site-specific programs in the directory */usr/local*, and put their manual pages in */usr/local/man*. The *man* command will not automatically look in */usr/local/man*, so when you ask for a manual page you may get the message "No manual entry." Fix this by specifying all the top *man* directories in a variable called MANPATH. For example (you have to put in the actual directories where the manual pages are on your system):

```
$ export MANPATH=/usr/man:/usr/local/man
```

The syntax is like PATH, described earlier in this chapter. Each two directories are separated by a colon. If your shell is *csh* or *tcsh*, you need to say:

```
$ setenv MANPATH /usr/man:/usr/local/man
```

Have you read some manual pages and still found yourself confused? They're not meant to be introductions to new topics. Get yourself a good beginner's book about Unix, and come back to manual pages gradually as you become more comfortable on the system; then they'll be irreplaceable.

Manual pages are not the only source of information on Unix systems. Programs from the GNU project often have Info pages that you read with the program *info*. For example, to read the Info pages for the command *find*, you would enter:

```
info find
```

The *info* program is arcane and has lots of navigation features; to learn it, your best bet will be to type Ctrl-H in the *info* program and read through the help screen. Fortunately, there are also programs that let you read Info pages more easily, notably *tkinfo* and *kdehelp*. These commands use the X Window System to present a graphical interface. You can also read Info pages from Emacs (see the section "The Emacs Editor" in Chapter 9) or use the command *pinfo* available on some Linux distributions that works more like the Lynx web browser.

Chapter 16

In recent times, more and more documentation is provided in the form of HTML pages. You can read those with any web browser (see Chapter 16, *The World Wide Web and Electronic Mail*). For example, in Netscape Navigator, you select "Open Page . . ." from the "File" menu and press the "Choose File" button, which opens an ordinary file selection dialog where you can select your documentation file.

File Ownership and Permissions

Ownership and permissions are central to security. It's important to get them right, even when you're the only user, because odd things can happen if you don't. For the files that users create and use daily, these things usually work without much thought (although it's still useful to know the concepts). For system administration, matters are not so easy. Assign the wrong ownership or permission, and you might get into a frustrating bind like not being able to read your mail. In general, the message:

```
Permission denied
```

means that someone has assigned an ownership or permission that restricts access more than you want.

What Permissions Mean

Permissions refer to the ways in which someone can use a file. There are three such permissions under Unix:

- *Read* permission means you can look at the file's contents.

- *Write* permission means you can change or delete the file.

- *Execute* permission means you can run the file as a program.

When each file is created, the system assigns some default permissions that work most of the time. For instance, it gives you both read and write permission, but most of the world has only read permission. If you have a reason to be paranoid, you can set things up so that other people have no permissions at all.

Additionally, most utilities know how to assign permissions. For instance, when the compiler creates an executable program, it automatically assigns executable permission. When you check a file out of the revision control system (RCS) without locking it, you get only read permission (because you're not expected to change the file), but if you lock the file, you get read and write permission (you're expected to edit it and check it back in). We'll discuss RCS in the section "Revision Control Tools—RCS" in Chapter 14, *Tools for Programmers*.

Chapter 14

There are times when defaults don't work, though. For instance, if you create a shell script or Perl program, you'll have to assign executable permission yourself so that you can run it. We'll show how to do that later in this section, after we get through the basic concepts.

Permissions have different meanings for a directory:

- Read permission means you can list the contents of that directory.

- Write permission means you can add or remove files in that directory.

- Execute permission means you can list information about the files in that directory.

Don't worry about the difference between read and execute permission for directories; basically, they go together. Assign both, or neither.

Chapter 7

Note that, if you allow people to add files to a directory, you are also letting them remove files. The two privileges go together when you assign write permission. However, there is a way you can let users share a directory and keep them from deleting each other's files. See the section "Upgrading Other Software" in Chapter 7, *Upgrading Software and the Kernel*.

There are more files on Unix systems than the plain files and directories we've talked about so far. These are special files (devices), sockets, symbolic links, and so forth—each type observing its own rules regarding permissions. But you don't need to know the details on each type.

Owners and Groups

Now, who gets these permissions? To allow people to work together, Unix has three levels of permission: owner, group, and other. The "other" covers everybody who has access to the system and who isn't the owner or a member of the group.

The idea behind having groups is to give a set of users, like a team of programmers, access to a file. For instance, a programmer creating source code may reserve write permission to herself, but allow members of her group to have read access through a group permission. As for "other," it might have no permission at all. (You think your source code is *that* good?)

Chapter 5

Each file has an owner and a group. The owner is generally the user who created the file. Each user also belongs to a default group, and that group is assigned to every file the user creates. You can create many groups, though, and assign each user to multiple groups. By changing the group assigned to a file, you can give access to any collection of people you want. We'll discuss groups more when we get to the section "The Group File" in Chapter 5.

Now we have all the elements of our security system: three permissions (read, write, execute) and three levels (user, group, other). Let's looks at some typical files and see what permissions are assigned.

Figure 4-2 shows a typical executable program. We generated this output by executing *ls* with the *−l* option.

Two useful facts stand right out: the owner of the file is an author of this book and your faithful guide, **mdw**, while the group is **lib** (perhaps a group created for programmers working on libraries). But the key information about permissions is encrypted in the set of letters on the left side of the display.

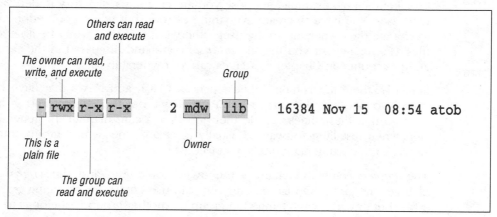

Figure 4-2: *Displaying ownership and permissions*

The first character is a hyphen, indicating a plain file. The next three bits apply to the owner; as we would expect, **mdw** has all three permissions. The next three bits apply to members of the group: they can read the file (not too useful for a binary file) and execute it, but they can't write to it because the field that should contain a w contains a hyphen instead. And the last three bits apply to "other"; they have the same permissions in this case as the group.

As another exercise, here is a file checked out of RCS for editing:

```
-rw-r--r--   2 mdw      lib          878 Aug  7 19:28 tools.tex
```

The only difference between this file and that shown in Figure 4-2 is that the x bits in this case have been replaced by hyphens. No one needs to have execute permission because the file is not meant to be executed; it's just text.

One more example—a typical directory:

```
drwxr-xr-x   2 mdw      lib          512 Jul 17 18:23 perl
```

The left-most bit is now a d, to show that this is a directory. The executable bits are back, because you want people to see the contents of the directory.

Files can be in some obscure states that aren't covered here; see the *ls* manual page for gory details. But now it's time to see how you can change ownership and permissions.

Changing the Owner, Group, and Permissions

As we said, most of the time you can get by with the default security the system gives you. But there are always exceptions, particularly for system administrators.

Chapter 5

To take a simple example, suppose you are creating a directory under */home* for a new user. You have to create everything as **root**, but when you're done you have to change the ownership to the user; otherwise, that user won't be able to use the files! (Fortunately, if you use the *adduser* command discussed in the section "Creating Accounts" in Chapter 5, it takes care of ownership for you.)

Similarly, there are certain utilities such as UUCP and News that have their own users. No one ever logs in as **UUCP** or **News**, but those users and groups must exist so that the utilities can do their job in a secure manner. In general, the last step when installing software is usually to change the owner, group, and permissions as the documentation tells you to do.

The *chown* command changes the owner of a file, and the *chgrp* command changes the group. On Linux, only **root** can use *chown* for changing ownership of a file, but any user can change the group to another group he belongs to.

So after installing some software named *sampsoft*, you might change both the owner and the group to **bin** by executing:

```
# chown bin sampsoft
# chgrp bin sampsoft
```

You could also do this in one step by using the dot notation:

```
# chown bin.bin sampsoft
```

The syntax for changing permissions is more complicated. The permissions can also be called the file's "mode," and the command that changes permissions is *chmod*. Let's start our exploration of this command through a simple example; say you've written a neat program in Perl or Tcl named *header*, and you want to be able to execute it. You would type the following command:

```
$ chmod +x header
```

The plus sign means "add a permission," and the **x** indicates which permission to add.

If you want to remove execute permission, use a minus sign in place of a plus:

```
$ chmod -x header
```

This command assigns permissions to all levels—user, group, and other. Let's say that you are secretly into software hoarding and don't want anybody to use the command but yourself. (No, that's too cruel; let's say instead that you think the script is buggy and want to protect other people from hurting themselves until you've exercised it.) You can assign execute permission just to yourself through the command:

```
$ chmod u+x header
```

Whatever goes before the plus sign is the level of permission, and whatever goes after is the type of permission. User permission (for yourself) is u, group permission is g, and other is o. So, to assign permission to both yourself and the file's group, enter:

```
$ chmod ug+x header
```

You can also assign multiple types of permissions:

```
$ chmod ug+rwx header
```

There are a few more shortcuts you can learn from the *chmod* manual page in order to impress someone looking over your shoulder, but they don't offer any functionality besides what we've shown you.

As arcane as the syntax of the mode argument may seem, there's another syntax that is even more complicated. We have to describe it though, for several reasons. First of all, there are several situations that cannot be covered by the syntax, called *symbolic mode,* that we've just shown. Second, people often use the other syntax, called *absolute mode,* in their documentation. Third, there are times you may actually find the absolute mode more convenient.

To understand absolute mode, you have to think in terms of bits and octal notation. Don't worry, it's not too hard. A typical mode contains three characters, corresponding to the three levels of permission (user, group, and other). These levels are illustrated in Figure 4-3. Within each level, there are three bits corresponding to read, write, and execute permission.

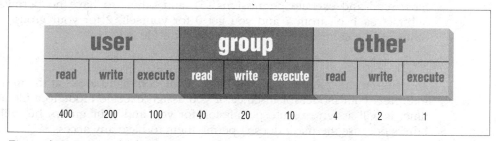

Figure 4-3: Bits in absolute mode

Let's say you want to give yourself read permission and no permission to anybody else. You want to specify just the bit represented by the number 400. So the *chmod* command would be:

```
$ chmod 400 header
```

To give read permission to everybody, choose the correct bit from each level: 400 for yourself, 40 for your group, and 4 for other. The full command is:

```
$ chmod 444 header
```

This is like using a mode +r, except that it simultaneously removes any write or execute permission. (To be precise, it's just like a mode of =r, which we didn't mention earlier. The equal sign means "assign these rights and no others.")

To give read and execute permission to everybody, you have to add up the read and execute bits. 400 plus 100 is 500, for instance.

So the corresponding command is:

```
$ chmod 555 header
```

which is the same as =rx. To give someone full access, you would specify that digit as a 7—the sum of 4, 2, and 1.

One final trick: how to set the default mode that is assigned to each file you create (with a text editor, the > redirection operator, and so on). You do so by executing a *umask* command, or putting one in your shell's start-up file. This file could be called *.bashrc*, *.cshrc*, or something else depending on the shell you use (we'll discuss startup files in the next section).

The *umask* command takes an argument like the absolute mode in *chmod*, but the meaning of the bits is inverted. You have to determine the access you want to grant for user, group, and other, and subtract each digit from 7. That gives you a three-digit mask.

For instance, say you want yourself to have all permissions (7), your group to have read and execute permissions (5), and others to have no permissions (0). Subtract each bit from 7 and you get 0 for yourself, 2 for your group, and 7 for other. So the command to put in your start-up file is:

```
umask 027
```

A strange technique, but it works. The *chmod* command looks at the mask when it interprets your mode; for instance, if you assign execute mode to a file at creation time, it will assign execute permission for you and your group, but will exclude others because the mask doesn't permit them to have any access.

Startup Files

Configuration is a strong element of Unix. This probably stems from two traits commonly found in hackers: they want total control over their environment, and they strive to minimize the number of keystrokes and other hand movements they have to perform. So all the major utilities on Unix—editors, mailers, debuggers, X Window System clients—provide files that let you override their default behaviors in a bewildering number of ways. Many of these files have names ending in *rc* which means *resource configuration*.

Startup files are usually in your home directory. Their names begin with a period, which keeps the *ls* command from displaying them under normal circumstances. None of the files are required; all the affected programs are smart enough to use defaults when the file does not exist. But everyone finds it useful to have the startup files. Here are some common ones:

.bashrc

> For the *bash* shell. The file is a shell script, which means it can contain commands and other programming constructs. Here's a very short startup file that might have been placed in your home directory by the tool that created your account:

```
PS1='\u$'        # The prompt contains the user's login name.

HISTSIZE=50      # Save 50 commands for when the user presses the up arrow.

# All the directories to search for commands.
PATH=/usr/local/bin:/usr/bin:/bin:/usr/bin/X11

# To prevent the user from accidentally ending a login session,
# disable Ctrl-D as a way to exit.
IGNOREEOF=1

stty erase "^H"        # Make sure the backspace key erases.
```

.bash_profile

> For the *bash* shell. Another shell script. The difference between this script and *.bashrc* is that *.bash_profile* runs only when you log in. It was originally designed so you could separate interactive shells from those run by background processors like *cron* (discussed in Chapter 8, *Other Administrative Tasks*). But it is not too useful on modern computers with the X Window System, because when you open a new *xterm* window, only *.bashrc* runs. If you start up a window with the command *xterm –ls*, it will run *.bash_profile*, too.

Chapter 8

.cshrc

> For the C shell or *tcsh*. The file is a shell script using C shell constructs.

.login

> For the C shell or *tcsh*. The file is a shell script, using C shell constructs. Like *.bash_profile* in the *bash* shell, this runs only when you log in. Here are some commands you might find in *.cshrc* or *.login*:

```
set prompt='% '        # Simple % for prompt.

set history=50 # Save 50 commands for when the user presses the up arrow.

# All the directories to search for commands.
set path=(/usr/local/bin /usr/bin /bin /usr/bin/X11)

# To prevent the user from accidentally ending a login session,
```

```
# disable Ctrl-D as a way to exit.
set ignoreeof

stty erase "^H"          # Make sure the backspace key erases.
```

Chapter 9

.emacs

For the Emacs editor. Consists of LISP functions. See the section "Tailoring Emacs" in Chapter 9.

.exrc

For the *vi* editor (also known as *ex*). Each line is an editor command. See the section "Extending vi" in Chapter 9.

Chapter 10

.fvwm2rc

For the *fvwm2* window manager. Consists of special commands interpreted by *fvwm2*. A sample file is shown in the section "Configuring fvwm" in Chapter 10, *Installing the X Window System*.

.twmrc

For the *twm* window manager. Consists of special commands interpreted by *twm*.

.newsrc

For news readers. Contains a list of all newsgroups offered at the site.

.Xdefaults

For programs using the X Window System. Each line specifies a resource (usually the name of a program and some property of that program) along with the value that resource should take. This file is described in the section "The X Resource Database" in Chapter 10.

.xinitrc

For the X Window System. Consists of shell commands that run whenever you log into an X session. See the section "Basics of X Customization" in Chapter 10 for details on using this file.

Important Directories

You already know about */home*, where user files are stored. As a system administrator and programmer, several other directories will be important to you. Here are a few, along with their contents:

/bin

The most essential Unix commands, such as *ls*.

/usr/bin

Other commands. The distinction between */bin* and */usr/bin* is arbitrary; it was a convenient way to split up commands on early Unix systems that had small disks.

/usr/sbin
> Commands used by the superuser for system administration.

/boot
> Location where the kernel and other files used during booting are sometimes stored.

/etc
> Files used by subsystems such as networking, NFS, and mail. Typically, these contain tables of network services, disks to mount, and so on.

/var
> Administrative files, such as log files, used by various utilities.

/var/spool
> Temporary storage for files being printed, sent by UUCP, and so on.

/usr/lib
> Standard libraries, such as *libc.a*. When you link a program, the linker always searches here for the libraries specified in *–l* options.

/usr/lib/X11
> The X Window System distribution. Contains the libraries used by X clients, as well as fonts, sample resources files, and other important parts of the X package. This directory is usually a symbolic link to */usr/X11R6/lib/X11*.

/usr/include
> Standard location of include files used in C programs, such as *<stdio.h>*.

/usr/src
> Location of sources to programs built on the system.

/usr/local
> Programs and data files that have been added locally by the system administrator.

/etc/skel
> Sample startup files you can place in home directories for new users.

Programs That Serve You

We're including this section because you should start to be interested in what's running on your system behind your back.

Many modern computer activities are too complex for the system simply to look at a file or some other static resource. Sometimes these activities need to interact with another running process.

For instance, take FTP, which you may have used to download some Linux-related documents or software. When you FTP to another system, another program has to be running on that system to accept your connection and interpret your commands. So there's a program running on that system called *ftpd*. The *d* in the name stands for *daemon*, which is a quaint Unix term for a server that runs in the background all the time. Most daemons handle network activities.

You've probably heard of the buzzword *client/server* enough to make you sick, but here it is in action—it has been in action for years on Unix.

Daemons start up when the system is booted. To see how they get started, look in the */etc/inittab* and */etc/inetd.conf* files, as well as distribution-specific configuration files. We won't go into their formats here. But each line in these files lists a program that runs when the system starts. You can find the distribution-specific files either by checking the documentation that came with your system or by looking for pathnames that occur more often than others in */etc/inittab*. Those normally indicate the directory tree where your distribution stores its system startup-files.

To give an example of how your system uses */etc/inittab*, look at one or more lines with the string `getty` or `agetty`. This is the program that listens at a terminal (tty) waiting for a user to log in. It's the program that displays the `login :` prompt we talked about at the beginning of this chapter.

The */etc/inetd.conf* file represents a more complicated way of running programs— another level of indirection. The idea behind */etc/inetd.conf* is that it would waste a lot of system resources if a dozen or more daemons were spinning idly, waiting for a request to come over the network. So, instead, the system starts up a single daemon named *inetd*. This daemon listens for connections from clients on other machines, and when an incoming connection is made, starts up the appropriate daemon to handle it. For example, when an incoming FTP connection is made, *inetd* starts up the FTP daemon (*ftpd*) to manage the connection. In this way, the only network daemons running are those actually in use.

In the next section, we'll show you how to see which daemons are running on your system. There's a daemon for every service offered by the system to other systems on a network: *fingerd* to handle remote *finger* requests, *rwhod* to handle *rwho* requests, and so on. A few daemons also handle nonnetworking services, such as *kerneld*, which handles the automatic loading of modules into the kernel.

Processes

At the heart of Unix lies the concept of a process. Understanding this concept will help you keep control of your login session as a user. If you are also a system administrator, the concept is even more important.

A process is an independently running program that has its own set of resources. For instance, we showed in an earlier section how you could direct the output of a program to a file while your shell continued to direct output to your screen. The reason that the shell and the other program can send output to different places is that they are separate processes.

On Unix, the finite resources of the system, like the memory and the disks, are managed by one all-powerful program called the kernel. Everything else on the system is a process.

Thus, before you log in, your terminal is monitored by a *getty* process. After you log in, the *getty* process dies (a new one is started by the kernel when you log out) and your terminal is managed by your shell, which is a different process. The shell then creates a new process each time you enter a command. The creation of a new process is called *forking*, because one process splits into two.

If you are using the X Window System, each process starts up one or more windows. Thus, the window in which you are typing commands is owned by an *xterm* process. That process forks a shell to run within the window. And that shell forks yet more processes as you enter commands.

To see the processes you are running, enter the command *ps*. Figure 4-4 shows some typical output and what each field means. You may be surprised how many processes you are running, especially if you are using X. One of the processes is the *ps* command itself, which of course dies as soon as the output is displayed.

```
$   ps
    PID      TTY      STAT      TIME      COMMAND
    1663     pp3      S         0:01      -bash
    1672     pp3      T         0:07      emacs
    1676     pp3      R         0:00      ps
```

PID   – *Process ID (used to kill a process)*   TIME   – *CPU time used so far*
TTY   – *Controlling terminal*   COMMAND – *Command running*
STAT – *State*

Figure 4-4: Output of ps command

The first field in the *ps* output is a unique identifier for the process. If you have a runaway process that you can't get rid of through Ctrl-C or other means, you can kill it by going to a different virtual console or X window and entering:

```
$ kill process-id
```

The TTY field shows which terminal the process is running on, if any. (Everything run from a shell uses a terminal, of course, but background daemons don't have a terminal.)

The STAT field shows what state the process is in. The shell is currently suspended, so this field shows an S. An Emacs editing session is running, but it's suspended using Ctrl-Z. This is shown by the T in its STAT field. The last process shown is the *ps* that is generating all this input; its state, of course, is R because it is running.

The TIME field shows how much CPU time the processes have used. Since both *bash* and Emacs are interactive, they actually don't use much of the CPU.

You aren't restricted to seeing your own processes. Look for a minute at all the processes on the system. The *a* option stands for all processes, while the *x* option includes processes that have no controlling terminal (such as daemons started at runtime):

$ **ps ax | more**

Now you can see the daemons that we mentioned in the previous section.

And here, with a breathtaking view of the entire Unix system at work, we end this chapter (the lines are cut off at column 76; if you want to see the command lines in their full glory, add the option *-w* to the *ps* command):

```
kalle@tigger: > ps aux
      USER    PID  %CPU %MEM    VSZ    RSS  TT STAT  START     TIME COMMAND
at            724   0.0  0.2    824    348   ?  S    Mar 18    0:00 /usr/sbin/
bin           703   0.0  0.2    832    316   ?  S    Mar 18    0:00 /usr/sbin/
kalle         181   0.0  0.6   1512    856   1  S    Mar 18    0:00 -bash
kalle         230   0.0  0.4   1396    596   1  S    Mar 18    0:00 sh /usr/X1
kalle         231   0.0  0.1    808    256   1  S    Mar 18    0:00 tee /home/
kalle         234   0.0  0.4   1952    624   1  S    Mar 18    0:00 xinit /hom
kalle         238   0.0  0.4   1396    616   1  S    Mar 18    0:00 sh /home/k
kalle         242   0.0  3.8   6744   4876   1  S    Mar 18    0:43 kwm
kalle         246   0.0  3.3   6552   4272   1  S    Mar 18    4:48 /usr/local
kalle         255   0.0  0.0      0      0   1  Z    Mar 18    0:00 kaudioserv
kalle         256   0.0  3.0   6208   3844   1  S    Mar 18    0:02 kwmsound
kalle         257   0.0  5.1   8892   6596   1  S    Mar 18    0:11 kfm
kalle         258   0.0  3.3   6292   4320   1  S    Mar 18    0:02 krootwm
kalle         259   0.0  4.6   7848   5988   1  S    Mar 18    0:37 kpanel
kalle         260   0.0  3.6   6764   4688   1  S    Mar 18    0:06 kbgndwm
kalle         273   0.0  3.6   6732   4668   1  S    Mar 18    0:08 kvt -resto
kalle         274   0.0  3.6   6732   4668   1  S    Mar 18    0:11 kvt -resto
kalle         276   0.0  0.6   1536    892  p0  S    Mar 18    0:00 bash
kalle         277   0.0  0.6   1512    864  p1  S    Mar 18    0:00 bash
kalle       11752   0.1  9.8  14056  12604   1  S    Mar 20    3:35 xemacs
kalle       18738   0.2 16.4  26164  21088   1  S    01:14     1:03 netscape
kalle       18739   0.0  2.6  14816   3392   1  S    01:14     0:00 (dns helpe
kalle       29744   0.0  0.3    904    428  p0  R    09:24     0:00 ps -auxw
root            1   0.0  0.2    820    292   ?  S    Mar 18    0:06 init [2]
```

```
root       2  0.0  0.0     0     0  ?  SW   Mar 18   0:00 kflushd
root       3  0.0  0.0     0     0  ?  SW<  Mar 18   0:00 kswapd
root       8  0.0  0.2   804   264  ?  S    Mar 18   0:02 update (bd
root      55  0.0  0.2   816   328  ?  S    Mar 18   0:00 /sbin/kern
root      78  0.0  0.0     0     0  ?  Z    Mar 18   0:00 request-ro
root      96  0.0  0.3   832   408  ?  S    Mar 18   0:00 /usr/sbin/
root      98  0.0  0.3   932   448  ?  S    Mar 18   0:00 /usr/sbin/
root     167  0.0  0.2   824   288  ?  S    Mar 18   0:00 /usr/bin/g
root     182  0.0  0.6  1508   856  2  S    Mar 18   0:00 -bash
root     183  0.0  0.2   808   288  3  S    Mar 18   0:00 /sbin/ming
root     184  0.0  0.2   808   284  4  S    Mar 18   0:00 /sbin/ming
root     185  0.0  0.2   808   284  5  S    Mar 18   0:00 /sbin/ming
root     186  0.0  0.2   808   284  6  S    Mar 18   0:00 /sbin/ming
root     235  0.3 11.8 25292 15196  ?  S    Mar 18  19:19 /usr/X11R6
root     682  0.0  0.4  1076   556  ?  S    Mar 18   0:00 /usr/sbin/
root     684  0.0  0.3   948   484  ?  S    Mar 18   0:00 /usr/sbin/
root     707  0.0  0.3   860   440  ?  S    Mar 18   0:00 /usr/sbin/
root     709  0.0  0.3   896   452  ?  S    Mar 18   0:00 /usr/sbin/
root     712  0.0  0.5  1212   668  ?  S    Mar 18   0:00 /usr/sbin/
root     727  0.0  0.2   840   356  ?  S    Mar 18   0:00 /usr/sbin/
root     733  0.0  0.2   820   304  ?  S    Mar 18   0:00 /usr/sbin/
root     737  0.0  0.2   836   316  ?  S    Mar 18   0:00 /usr/sbin/
root     745  0.0  0.5  1204   708  ?  S    Mar 18   0:00 sendmail:
root     752  0.0  0.4  1772   592  ?  S    Mar 18   0:00 /opt/appli
wwwrun   718  0.0  0.5  1212   668  ?  S    Mar 18   0:00 /usr/sbin/
wwwrun   719  0.0  0.5  1212   652  ?  S    Mar 18   0:00 /usr/sbin/
wwwrun   720  0.0  0.5  1212   644  ?  S    Mar 18   0:00 /usr/sbin/
wwwrun   721  0.0  0.5  1212   644  ?  S    Mar 18   0:00 /usr/sbin/
wwwrun   722  0.0  0.5  1212   644  ?  S    Mar 18   0:00 /usr/sbin/
```

CHAPTER FIVE

ESSENTIAL SYSTEM MANAGEMENT

If you're running your own Linux system, one of the first tasks at hand is to learn the ropes of system administration. You won't be able to get by for long without having to perform some kind of system maintenance, software upgrade, or mere tweaking necessary to keep things in running order.

Running a Linux system is not unlike riding and taking care of a motorcycle.* Many motorcycle hobbyists prefer caring for their own equipment—routinely cleaning the points, replacing worn-out parts, and so forth. Linux gives you the opportunity to experience the same kind of "hands-on" maintenance with a complex operating system.

While a passionate administrator can spend any amount of time tuning it for performance, you really have to perform administration only when a major change occurs: you install a new disk, a new user comes on the system, or a power failure causes the system to go down unexpectedly. We discuss all these situations over the next four chapters.

Linux is surprisingly accessible, in all respects—from the more mundane tasks of upgrading shared libraries to the more esoteric, such as mucking about with the kernel. Because all the source code is available, and the body of Linux developers and users has traditionally been of the hackish breed, systems maintenance is not only a part of daily life but also a great learning experience. Trust us: there's nothing like telling your friends how you upgraded from X11R6.1 to X11R6.3 in less than half an hour, and all the while you were recompiling the kernel to support

---

* At least one author attests a strong correspondence between Linux system administration and Robert Pirsig's *Zen and the Art of Motorcycle Maintenance*. Does Linux have the Buddha nature?

the ISO 9660 filesystem. (They may have no idea what you're talking about, in which case you can give them a copy of this book.)

In the next few chapters, we explore your Linux system from the mechanic's point of view—showing you what's under the hood, as it were—and explain how to take care of it all, including software upgrades, managing users, filesystems, and other resources, taking backups, and what to do in emergencies. If you've never used a Unix system before, we'll also take you for a test drive and show you the basics of running and using the system.

Once you put the right entries in startup files, your Linux system will, for the most part, run itself. As long as you're happy with the system configuration and the software that's running on it, very little work will be necessary on your part. However, we'd like to encourage Linux users to experiment with their system and customize it to taste. Very little about Linux is carved in stone, and if something doesn't work the way that you'd like it to, you should be able to change that. For instance, if you'd rather read blinking green text on a cyan background, rather than the traditional white-on-black, we'll show you how to configure that. (As long as you promise not to let anyone know who told you.)

It should be noted that many Linux systems include fancy tools to simplify many system administration tasks. These include YaST on SuSE systems, LISA on Caldera systems, and the *control-panel* or *linuxconf* on Red Hat systems. These tools can do everything from managing user accounts to creating filesystems to doing your laundry. These utilities can either make your life easier or more difficult, depending on how you look at them. In these chapters, we present the "guts" of system administration, demonstrating the tools that should be available on any Linux system and indeed nearly all Unix systems. These are the core of the system administrator's toolbox: the metaphorical hammer, screwdriver, and socket wrench that you can rely on to get the job done. If you'd rather use the 40-hp circular saw, feel free, but it's always nice to know how to use the hand tools in case the power goes out. Good follow-up books, should you wish to investigate more topics in Unix system administration, include the *Unix System Administration Handbook* and *Essential System Administration*.

[56] Unix
Sys. Admin
[57] Essential
Sys. Admin

Running the System

Being the system administrator for any Unix system requires a certain degree of responsibility and care. This is equally true for Linux, even if you're the only user on your system.

Many of the system administrator's tasks are done by logging into the **root** account. This account has special properties on Unix systems; specifically, the usual file permissions and other security mechanisms simply don't apply to **root**. That is, **root** can access and modify any file on the system—no matter who it belongs to. Whereas normal users can't damage the system (say, by corrupting filesystems or touching other users' files), **root** has no such restrictions.

Why does the Unix system have security in the first place? The most obvious reason for this is to allow users to choose how they wish their own files to be accessed. By changing file-permission bits (with the *chmod* command), users can specify that certain files should only be readable, writable, or executable by certain groups of other users or no other users at all. Permissions help ensure privacy and integrity of data; you wouldn't want other users to read your personal mailbox, for example, or to edit the source code for an important program behind your back.

The Unix security mechanisms also prevent users from damaging the system. The system restricts access to many of the raw device files (accessed via */dev*—more on this in the section "Device Files" in Chapter 6, *Managing Filesystems, Swap, and Devices*) corresponding to hardware, such as your hard drives. If normal users could read and write directly to the disk-drive device, they could wreak all kinds of havoc: say, completely overwriting the contents of the drive. Instead, the system requires normal users to access the drives via the filesystem—where security is enforced via the file permission bits described previously.

Chapter 6

It is important to note that not all kinds of "damage" that can be caused are necessarily malevolent. System security is more a means to protect users from their own natural mistakes and misunderstandings rather than to enforce a police state on the system. And, in fact, on many systems security is rather lax; Unix security is designed to foster the sharing of data between groups of users who may be, say, cooperating on a project. The system allows users to be assigned to groups, and file permissions may be set for an entire group. For instance, one development project might have free read and write permission to a series of files, while at the same time other users are prevented from modifying those files. With your own personal files, you get to decide how public or private the access permissions should be.

The Unix security mechanism also prevents normal users from performing certain actions, such as calling certain system calls within a program. For example, there is a system call that causes the system to halt, called by programs such as *shutdown* (more on this later in the chapter) to reboot the system. If normal users could call this function within their programs, they could accidentally (or purposefully) halt the system at any time.

In many cases, you have to bypass Unix security mechanisms in order to perform system maintenance or upgrades. This is what the **root** account is for. Because no such restrictions apply to **root**, it is easy for a knowledgeable system administrator to get work done without worrying about the usual file permissions or other limitations. The usual way to log in as **root** is with the *su* command. *su* allows you to assume the identification of another user—for example:

```
su andy
```

will prompt you for the password for **andy**, and if it is correct will set your user ID to that of **andy**. A superuser often wants to temporarily assume a regular user's identity to correct a problem with that user's files or some similar reason. Without a username argument, *su* will prompt you for the **root** password, validating your user ID as **root**. Once you are finished using the **root** account, you log out in the usual way and return to your own mortal identity.

Why not simply log in as **root** from the usual login prompt? As we'll see, this is desirable in some instances, but most of the time it's best to use *su* after logging in as yourself. On a system with many users, use of *su* records a message such as:

```
Nov  1 19:28:50 loomer su: mdw on /dev/ttyp1
```

in the system logs, such as */var/log/messages* (we'll talk more about these files later). This message indicates that the user **mdw** successfully issued a *su* command, in this case for **root**. If you were to log in directly as **root**, no such message would appear in the logs; you wouldn't be able to tell which user was mucking about with the **root** account. This is important if there are multiple administrators on the machine: it is often desirable to find out who used *su* and when.

The **root** account can be considered a magic wand—both a useful and potentially dangerous tool. Fumbling the magic words you invoke while holding this wand can wreak unspeakable damage on your system. For example, the simple eight-character sequence `rm -rf /` will delete every file on your system, if executed as **root**, and if you're not paying attention. Does this problem seem far-fetched? Not at all. You might be trying to delete an old directory, such as */usr/src/oldp*, and accidently slip in a space after the first slash, producing the following:

```
rm -rf / usr/src/oldp
```

Another common mistake is to confuse the arguments for commands such as *dd*, a command often used to copy large chunks of data from one place to another. For instance, in order to save the first 1024 bytes of data from the device */dev/hda* (which contains the boot record and partition table for that drive), one might use the command:

```
dd if=/dev/hda of=/tmp/stuff bs=1k count=1
```

However, if we reverse `if` and `of` in this command, something quite different happens: the contents of */tmp/stuff* are written to the top of */dev/hda*. If */tmp/stuff* contains garbage or incorrect data, you've just succeeded in hosing your partition table and possibly a filesystem superblock. Welcome to the wonderful world of system administration!

The point here is that you should sit on your hands before executing any command as **root**. Stare at the command for a minute before pressing Enter and make sure it makes sense. If you're not sure of the arguments and syntax of the command, quickly check the manual pages or try the command in a safe environment before firing it off. Otherwise you'll learn these lessons the hard way; mistakes made as **root** can be disastrous.

In many cases, the prompt for the **root** account differs from that for normal users. Classically, the **root** prompt contains a hash mark (#), while normal user prompts contain $ or %. (Of course, use of this convention is up to you; it is utilized on many Unix systems, however.) Although the prompt may remind you that you are wielding the **root** magic wand, it is not uncommon for users to forget this or accidentally enter a command in the wrong window or virtual console.

Like any powerful tool, the **root** account can also be abused. It is important, as the system administrator, to protect the root password, and if you give it out at all, to give it only to those users whom you trust (or who can be held responsible for their actions on the system). If you're the only user of your Linux system, this certainly doesn't apply—unless, of course, your system is connected to a network or allows dial-in login access.

The primary benefit of not sharing the **root** account with other users is not so much that the potential for abuse is diminished, although this is certainly the case. Even more important is that if you're the one person with the ability to use the **root** account, you have complete knowledge of how the system is configured. If anyone were able to, say, modify important system files (as we'll talk about in this chapter), the system configuration could be changed behind your back, and your assumptions about how things work would be incorrect. Having one system administrator act as the arbiter for the system configuration means that one person always knows what's going on.

Also, allowing other people to have the root password means that it's more likely someone will eventually make a mistake using the **root** account. Although each person with knowledge of the root password may be trusted, anybody can make mistakes. If you're the only system administrator, you have only yourself to blame for making the inevitable human mistakes as **root**.

That being said, let's dive into the actual tasks of system administration under Linux. Buckle your seatbelt.

Booting the System

There are several ways of booting Linux on your system. The most common methods involve booting from the hard drive or using a boot floppy. In many cases, the installation procedure will have configured one or both of these for you; in any case, it's important to understand how to configure booting for yourself.

Using a Boot Floppy

Chapter 7

Traditionally, a Linux boot floppy simply contains a kernel image, which is loaded into memory when the floppy is booted on the system.* The kernel image is usually compressed, using the same algorithm as the *gzip* compression program (more on this in the section "Building the Kernel" in Chapter 7, *Upgrading Software and the Kernel*). Compression allows the kernel, which may be a megabyte or more in size, to require only a few hundred kilobytes of disk space. Part of the kernel code is not compressed: this part contains the routines necessary to uncompress the kernel from the disk image and load it into memory. Therefore, the kernel actually "bootstraps" itself at boot time by uncompressing into memory.

A number of parameters are stored in the kernel image. Among these parameters is the name of the device to use as the root filesystem once the kernel boots. Another parameter is the text mode to use for the system console. All of these parameters may be modified using the *rdev* command, which we'll discuss later in the section.

Chapter 6

After the kernel has started, it attempts to mount a filesystem on the root device hard-coded in the kernel image itself. This will serve as the root filesystem—that is, the filesystem on /. The section "Managing Filesystems" in Chapter 6 discusses filesystems in more detail; all that you need to know for now is that the kernel image must contain the name of your root filesystem device. If the kernel can't mount a filesystem on this device, it gives up, issuing a kernel "panic" message. (Essentially, a *kernel panic* is a fatal error signaled by the kernel itself. A panic will occur whenever the kernel is terminally confused and can't continue with execution. For example, if there is a bug in the kernel itself, a panic might occur when it attempts to access memory that doesn't exist. We'll talk about kernel panics more in the section "What to Do in an Emergency" in Chapter 8, *Other Administrative Tasks.*)

Chapter 8

The root device stored in the kernel image is that of your root filesystem on the hard drive. This means that once the kernel boots, it mounts a hard-drive partition as the root filesystem, and all control transfers to the hard drive. Once the kernel is loaded into memory, it stays there—the boot floppy need not be accessed again (until you reboot the system, of course).

Many Linux distributions create a boot floppy for you in this way when installing the system. Using a boot floppy is an easy way to boot Linux if you don't want to bother booting from the hard drive. (For example, OS/2's or Windows NT's boot managers are somewhat difficult to configure for booting Linux. We'll talk about this in the next section.) Once the kernel has booted from the floppy, you are free to use the floppy drive for other purposes.

---

* A Linux boot floppy may instead contain a LILO boot record, which causes the system to boot a kernel from the hard drive. We'll discuss this in the next section, when we talk about LILO.

Given a kernel image, you can create your own boot floppy. On many Linux systems, the kernel itself is stored in the file */boot/vmlinuz*.[*] This is not a universal convention, however; other Linux systems store the kernel in */vmlinuz* or */vmlinux*, others in a file such as */Image*. (If you have multiple kernel images, you can use LILO to select which one to boot. See the next section.) Note that newly installed Linux systems may not have a kernel image on the hard drive if a boot floppy was created for you. In any case, you can build your own kernel. It's usually a good idea to do this anyway; you can "customize" the kernel to only include those drivers for your particular hardware. See the section "Building the Kernel" in Chapter 7 for details.

Chapter 7

All right. Let's say that you have a kernel image in the file */boot/vmlinuz*. To create a boot floppy, the first step is to use *rdev* to set the root device to that of your Linux root filesystem. (If you built the kernel yourself, this should be already set to the correct value, but it can't hurt to check with *rdev*.) We discussed how to create the root device in the sections "Drives and Partitions Under Linux" and "Creating Linux Partitions" in Chapter 3, *Installation and Initial Configuration*.

Chapter 3

As **root**, use *rdev –h* to print a usage message. As you will see, there are many supported options, allowing you to specify the root device (our task here), the swap device, ramdisk size, and so on. For the most part, you needn't concern yourself with these options now.

If we use the command *rdev /boot/vmlinuz*, the root device encoded in the kernel found in */boot/vmlinuz* will be printed:

```
courgette:/# rdev /boot/vmlinuz
Root device /dev/hda1
```

If this is incorrect, and the Linux root filesystem is actually on */dev/hda3*, we should use the following command:

```
courgette:/# rdev /boot/vmlinuz /dev/hda3
courgette:/#
```

rdev is the strong, silent type; nothing is printed when you set the root device, so run *rdev /boot/vmlinuz* again to check that it is set correctly.

Now you're ready to create the boot floppy. For best results, use a brand-new, formatted floppy. You can format the floppy under MS-DOS or using *fdformat* under

---

[*] Why the silly filename? On many Unix systems, the kernel is stored in a file named */vmunix* where *vm* stands for "virtual memory." Naturally, Linux has to be different and names its kernel images *vmlinux*, and places them in the directory */boot* to get them out of the root directory. The name *vmlinuz* was adopted to differentiate compressed kernel images from uncompressed images. Actually, the name and location of the kernel don't matter a bit, as long as you have either a boot floppy containing a kernel or LILO knows how to find the kernel image.

Chapter 6

Linux;* this will lay down the sector and track information so that the system can auto-detect the size of the floppy. (See the section "Managing Filesystems" in Chapter 6 for more on using floppies.)

To create the boot floppy, use *dd* to copy the kernel image to it, as in:

```
courgette:/# dd if=/boot/vmlinuz of=/dev/fd0 bs=8192
```

If you're interested in *dd*, the manual page will be illustrative; in brief, this copies the input file (*if* option) named */boot/vmlinuz* to the output file (*of* option) named */dev/fd0* (the first floppy device), using a block size (*bs*) of 8192 bytes. Of course, the plebian *cp* can be used as well, but we Unix sysadmins love to use cryptic commands to complete relatively simple tasks. That's what separates us from mortal users.

Your boot floppy should now be ready to go. You can shut down the system (see the section "Shutting Down the System" later in this chapter) and boot with the floppy, and if all goes well, your Linux system should boot as it usually does. It might be a good idea to make an extra boot floppy as a spare, and in the section "What to Do in an Emergency" in Chapter 8, we describe methods by which boot floppies can be used to recover from disaster.

Chapter 8

Using LILO

LILO is a general-purpose boot manager that can boot whatever operating systems you have installed on your machine, including Linux. There are dozens of ways to configure LILO. Here, we're going to discuss the two most common methods: installing LILO on the master boot record of your hard drive and installing LILO as a secondary boot loader for Linux only.

LILO is the most common way to boot Linux from the hard drive. (By the expression "boot from the hard drive," we mean that the kernel itself is stored on the hard drive and no boot floppy is required, but remember that even when you use a boot floppy, control is transferred to the hard drive once the kernel is loaded into memory.) If LILO is installed on your drive's master boot record, or MBR, it is the first code to run when the hard drive is booted. LILO can then boot other operating systems—such as Linux or MS-DOS—and allow you to select between them at boot time.

However, both OS/2 and Windows NT have boot managers of their own that occupy the MBR. If you are using one of these systems, in order to boot Linux from the hard drive, you may have to install LILO as the "secondary" boot loader for Linux only. In this case, LILO is installed on the boot record for just your Linux root partition, and the boot manager software (for OS/2 or Windows NT) takes care of executing LILO from there when you wish to boot Linux.

---

* The Debian distribution doesn't have an *fdformat* command; use the aptly named *super-format* instead.

As we'll see, however, both the OS/2 and Windows NT boot managers are some-what uncooperative when it comes to booting LILO. This is a poor design deci-sion, and if you must absolutely use one of these boot managers, it might be easier to boot Linux from floppy instead. Read on.

Use of LILO with Windows 95/98, on the other hand, is quite simple. You simply configure LILO to boot Windows 95/98 as you would configure it to boot MS-DOS (see the next section). However, if you install Windows 95/98 after installing LILO, you need to reinstall LILO (as the Windows 95/98 installation procedure over-writes the MBR of your primary hard drive). Just be sure you have a Linux boot floppy on hand so you can boot Linux and rerun LILO.

Before proceeding you should note that a number of Linux distributions are capa-ble of configuring and installing LILO when you first install the Linux software. However, it's often best to configure LILO yourself, just to ensure that everything is done correctly.

The /etc/lilo.conf file

The first step in configuring LILO is to set up the LILO configuration file, which is often stored in */etc/lilo.conf.* (On other systems, the file may be found in */boot/ lilo.conf* or */etc/lilo/config.*)

We are going to walk through a sample *lilo.conf* file. You can use this file as a base for your own *lilo.conf* and edit it for your own system.

The first section of this file sets up some basic parameters:

```
boot = /dev/hda
compact
install = /boot/boot.b
map = /boot/map
```

The `boot` line sets the name of the device where LILO should install itself in the boot record. In this case, we want to install LILO in the master boot record of */dev/ hda*, the first non-SCSI hard drive. If you're booting from a SCSI hard drive, use a device name such as */dev/sda* instead. If you give a partition device name (such as */dev/hda2*), instead of a drive device, LILO will be installed as a secondary boot loader on the named partition. (Debian users should always do this.) We'll talk about this in more detail later.

The `compact` line tells LILO to perform some optimization; always use this unless you are seriously hacking on your LILO configuration.* Likewise, always use the `install` and `map` lines as shown. `install` names the file containing the boot sec-tor to use on the MBR, and `map` specifies the "map file" that LILO creates when installed. These files should be in the directory */boot*, although on other systems

---

* In some cases, you will need the `linear` option, which should not be used together with `compact`. See the LILO documentation for more information.

they may be found in */etc/lilo. /boot/map* won't be created until you install LILO for the first time.

Now, for each operating system you wish LILO to boot, add a stanza to */etc/lilo.conf.* For example, a Linux stanza might look like this:

```
# Stanza for Linux with root partition on /dev/hda2.
   image = /boot/vmlinuz   # Location of kernel
   label = linux           # Name of OS (for the LILO boot menu)
   root = /dev/hda2        # Location of root partition
   vga = ask               # Ask for VGA text mode at boot time
```

The `image` line specifies the name of the kernel image. Subfields include `label`, which gives this stanza a name to use with the LILO boot menu (more on this later); `root`, which specifies the Linux root partition; and `vga`, which specifies the VGA text mode to use for the system console.

Valid modes for `vga` are `normal` (for standard 80x25 display), `extended` (for extended text mode, usually 132x44 or 132x60), `ask` (to be prompted for a mode at boot time), or an integer (such as 1, 2, or 3). The integer corresponds to the number of the mode you select when using `ask`. The exact text modes available depend on your video card; use `vga = ask` to get a list.

If you have multiple Linux kernels you wish to boot—for example, if you're doing some kernel debugging—you can add an `image` stanza for each one. The only required subfield of the `image` stanza is `label`. If you don't specify **root** or `vga`, the defaults coded into the kernel image itself using *rdev* will be used. If you do specify **root** or `vga`, these override the values you may have set using *rdev*. Therefore, if you are booting Linux using LILO, there's no need to use *rdev*; the LILO configuration file sets these boot parameters for you.

A stanza for booting MS-DOS or Windows 95/98 would look like the following:

```
# Stanza for MSDOS/Win 95/Win 98 partition on /dev/hda1.
   other = /dev/hda1    # Location of partition
   table = /dev/hda     # Location of partition table for /dev/hda2
   label = msdos        # Name of OS (for boot menu)
```

You would use an identical stanza to boot OS/2 from LILO (using a different `label` line, of course).

If you wish to boot an MS-DOS or Windows 95/98 partition located on the second drive, you should add the line:

```
   loader = /boot/any_d.b
```

to the MS-DOS `other` stanza. For OS/2 partitions on the second drive, add the line:

```
   loader = /boot/os2_d.b
```

There are many more options available for LILO configuration. The LILO distribution itself (found on most Linux FTP sites and distributions) includes an extensive manual describing them all. The previous examples should suffice for most systems, however.

Once you have your */etc/lilo.conf* ready, you can run the command:

```
/sbin/lilo
```

as **root**. This should display information such as the following:

```
courgette:/# /sbin/lilo
Added linux
Added msdos
courgette:/#
```

Using the *−v* option with *lilo* prints more diagnostic information should something go wrong; also, using the *−C* option allows you to specify a configuration file other than */etc/lilo.conf.*

Once this is done, you're ready to shut down your system (again, see the section "Shutting Down the System" later in this chapter for details), reboot, and try it out. The first operating system stanza listed in */etc/lilo.conf* will be booted by default. To select one of the other kernels or operating systems listed in */etc/lilo.conf*, hold down the Shift or Control key or simply press the Scroll Lock key while the system boots. This should present you with a LILO boot prompt:

```
boot:
```

Here, you can press Tab to get a list of available boot options:

```
boot: tab-key
linux msdos
```

These are the names given with `label` lines in */etc/lilo.conf.* Enter the appropriate label, and that operating system will boot. In this case, entering `msdos` causes MS-DOS to boot from */dev/hda1*, as we specified in the *lilo.conf* file.

Using LILO as a secondary boot loader

If you're using the OS/2 or Windows NT boot manager, installing the Debian distribution of Linux, or don't want LILO to inhabit the master boot record of your drive, you can configure LILO as a secondary boot loader, which will live on the boot record of just your Linux root partition.

To do this, simply change the `boot = ...` line of */etc/lilo.conf* to the name of the Linux root partition. For example:

```
boot = /dev/hda2
```

will install LILO on the boot record of */dev/hda2*, to boot Linux only. Note that this works only for primary partitions on the hard drive (not extended or logical partitions). This restriction applies to the Debian distribution, however, where the MBR can boot an operating system from a boot sector in an extended (but not logical) partition. In order to boot Linux in this way, the Linux root partition should be marked as "active" in the partition table. This can be done using *fdisk* under Linux or MS-DOS. When booting the system, the BIOS will read the boot record of the first "active" partition to start Linux.

If you are using OS/2's or Windows NT's boot manager, you should install LILO in this way, and then tell the boot manager to boot another operating system from that partition on your hard drive. The method for doing this depends on the boot manager in question; see your documentation for details.

LILO is known to work with OS/2's Boot Manager, but getting things to work well is not always easy. The problem is that OS/2 Boot Manager won't even recognize your partitions created with Linux *fdisk*. The way around this problem is to use OS/2's *fdisk* to give the Linux partitions (created using Linux *fdisk*) a name. Another workaround is to create the Linux partitions using OS/2's *fdisk* and format them (say, as an MS-DOS FAT partition) first. Now OS/2 will recognize the partitions, and you can use the Linux *fdisk* command to set the types of the partitions to `Linux native` and `Linux swap`, as described in the section "Creating Linux Partitions" in Chapter 3. You can then install Linux on these partitions and install LILO on the boot record of your Linux root partition. Hopefully, all will be well.

Chapter 3

Why are we telling you this now? Because OS/2's Boot Manager is broken with respect to booting operating systems it doesn't know about. Instead of using OS/2 Boot Manager, you can install LILO on the MBR of your drive and have it boot OS/2, using an `other` stanza in the */etc/lilo.conf* file as you would with MS-DOS. Another option is to simply boot Linux from floppy—or, even better, not to use OS/2 at all. But let's not get carried away.

Specifying boot time options

When you first installed Linux, more than likely you booted either from a floppy or a CD-ROM, which gave you the now-familiar LILO boot prompt. At this prompt you can enter several boot time options, such as:

`hd=cylinders,heads,sectors`

to specify the hard-drive geometry. Each time you boot Linux, it may be necessary to specify these parameters in order for your hardware to be detected correctly, as described in the section "Booting Linux" in Chapter 3. If you are using LILO to boot Linux from the hard drive, you can specify these parameters in */etc/lilo.conf* instead of entering them at the boot prompt each time. To the Linux stanza of the *lilo.conf* file, just add a line such as:

```
append = "hd=683,16,38"
```

This causes the system to behave as though hd=683,16,38 were entered at the LILO boot prompt. If you wish to specify multiple boot options, you can do so with a single append line, as in:

```
append = "hd=683,16,38 hd=64,32,202"
```

In this case, we specify the geometry for the first and second hard drives, respectively.

Note that you need to use such boot options only if the kernel doesn't detect your hardware at boot time. You should already know if this is necessary, based on your experiences with installing Linux; in general, you should have to use an append line in *lilo.conf* only if you had to specify these boot options when first booting the Linux installation media.

There are a number of other boot-time options available. Most of them deal with hardware detection, which has already been discussed in Chapter 3. However, the following additional options may also be useful to you:

single

Chapter 8

> Boot the system in single-user mode; skip all of the system configuration and start a root shell on the console. See the section "What to Do in an Emergency" in Chapter 8 for hints on using this.

root=*partition*

> Mounts the named *partition* as the Linux root filesystem. This overrides any value given in */etc/lilo.conf.*

Chapter 6

ro Mounts the root filesystem as read-only. This is usually done in order to run *fsck*; see the section "Checking and Repairing Filesystems" in Chapter 6.

ramdisk=*size*

> Specifies a size, in bytes, for the ramdisk device. This overrides any value in */etc/lilo.conf.* Most users need not worry about using the ramdisk; it's useful primarily for installation.

vga=*mode*

> Sets the VGA display mode. This overrides any value in */etc/lilo.conf.* Valid modes are normal, extended, ask, or an integer. This option is equivalent to the vga = values used in *lilo.conf*; see the section "The /etc/lilo.conf file" earlier in this chapter.

mem=*size*

> Tells the kernel how much RAM you have. If you have 64 MB or less, the kernel can get this information from the BIOS, but if you use an older kernel and you have more, you will have to tell the kernel the exact amount, or it will only use the first 64 MB. For example, if you have 128 MB, specify mem=128m. Fortunately, this is no longer necessary with newer kernels.

Any of these options can be entered by hand at the LILO boot prompt or specified with the `append` option in */etc/lilo.conf.*

LILO includes complete documentation that describes all of the configuration options available. On many Linux systems this documentation can be found in */usr/src/lilo*; on Debian systems, it is in */usr/doc/lilo/Manual.txt.gz.* If you can't seem to find anything, grab the LILO distribution from one of the Linux archive sites, or ask your Linux vendor to provide the sources and documentation for LILO. This documentation includes a manual that describes all the concepts of booting and using LILO in detail, as well as a *README* file that contains excerpts from this manual, formatted as plain text.

Removing LILO

If you have LILO installed on your MBR, the easiest way to remove it is to use MS-DOS FDISK. The command:

```
FDISK /MBR
```

runs FDISK and overwrites the MBR with a valid MS-DOS boot record.

LILO saves backup copies of your original boot record in the files */boot/boot.0300* (for IDE drives) and */boot/boot.0800* (for SCSI drives). These files contain the MBR of the drive before LILO was installed. You can use the *dd* command to replace the boot record on the drive with this backup copy. For example:

```
dd if=/boot/boot.0300 of=/dev/hda bs=446 count=1
```

copies the first 446 bytes of the file */boot/boot.0300* to */dev/hda.* Even though the files are 512 bytes in size, only the first 446 bytes should be copied back to the MBR.

Be very careful when using this command! This is one of those cases where blindly executing commands you find in a book can cause real trouble if you're not sure what you're doing. Only use this method as a last resort and only if you're certain that the files */boot/boot.0300* or */boot/boot.0800* contain the boot record you want. Many distributions of Linux come installed with bogus versions of these two files; you might need to delete them before you install LILO.

The LILO documentation contains further hints for removing LILO and debugging your LILO configuration.

System Startup and Initialization

In this section, we're going to talk about exactly what happens when the system boots. Understanding this process and the files involved is important for performing various kinds of system configuration.

Kernel Boot Messages

The first step is booting the kernel. As described in the previous section, this can be done from floppy or hard drive. As the kernel loads into memory, it will print messages to the system console, but usually also saves them in the system log files as well. As **root**, you can always check the file */var/log/messages* (which contains kernel messages emitted during runtime as well). The command *dmesg* prints out the last lines of the kernel message ring buffer; directly after booting, naturally, you will get the boot messages, such as (not necessarily the same, and not necessarily in the same order):

```
Console: 16 point font, 480 scans
Console: colour VGA+ 80x30, 1 virtual console (max 63)
pcibios_init : BIOS32 Service Directory structure at 0x000fb1d0
pcibios_init : BIOS32 Service Directory entry at 0xfb5a0
pcibios_init : PCI BIOS revision 2.00 entry at 0xfb5d0
Probing PCI hardware.
Calibrating delay loop.. ok - 36.04 BogoMIPS
Memory: 14984k/16384k available (552k kernel code, 384k reserved,\
464k data)
Swansea University Computer Society NET3.035 for Linux 2.0
NET3: Unix domain sockets 0.13 for Linux NET3.035.
Swansea University Computer Society TCP/IP for NET3.034
IP Protocols: ICMP, UDP, TCP
VFS: Diskquotas version dquot_5.6.0 initialized
Checking 386/387 coupling... Ok, fpu using exception 16 error\
reporting.
Checking 'hlt' instruction... Ok.
Intel Pentium with F0 0F bug - workaround enabled.
alias mapping IDT readonly ...  ... done
Linux version 2.0.35 (root@rabbit) (gcc version egcs-2.90.29\
980515 (egcs-1.0.3 release)) #3 Fri Nov 13 15:07:45 CET 1998
Starting kswapd v 1.4.2.2
Serial driver version 4.13 with no serial options enabled
tty00 at 0x03f8 (irq = 4) is a 16550A
tty01 at 0x02f8 (irq = 3) is a 16550A
APM BIOS not found.
Real Time Clock Driver v1.09
Configuring Adaptec (SCSI-ID 7) at IO:330, IRQ 11, DMA priority 5
scsi0 : Adaptec 1542
scsi : 1 host.
  Vendor: IBM       Model: DORS-32160     Rev: WA0A
  Type:   Direct-Access                   ANSI SCSI revision: 02
Detected scsi disk sda at scsi0, channel 0, id 0, lun 0
  Vendor: SANYO     Model: CRD-254S       Rev: 1.05
  Type:   CD-ROM                          ANSI SCSI revision: 02
Detected scsi CD-ROM sr0 at scsi0, channel 0, id 4, lun 0
scsi : detected 1 SCSI cdrom 1 SCSI disk total.
SCSI device sda: hdwr sector= 512 bytes. Sectors= 4226725 [2063 MB]\
[2.1 GB]
Partition check:
```

```
sda: sda1 sda2 sda3
VFS: Mounted root (ext2 filesystem) readonly.
Adding Swap: 130748k swap-space (priority -1)
lp1 at 0x0378, (polling)
3c59x.c:v0.99E 5/12/98 Donald Becker http://cesdis.gsfc.nasa.gov/\
linux/drivers/vortex.html
eth0: 3Com 3c905B Cyclone 100baseTx at 0x6000, 00:10:4b:45:1d:53,\
IRQ 12
  8K byte-wide RAM 5:3 Rx:Tx split, 10baseT interface.
  Enabling bus-master transmits and whole-frame receives.
ISDN subsystem Rev: 1.44/1.41/1.47/1.28/none loaded
HiSax: Driver for Siemens chip set ISDN cards
HiSax: Version 2.1
HiSax: Revisions 1.15/1.10/1.10/1.30/1.8
HiSax: Total 1 card defined
HiSax: Card 1 Protocol EDSS1 Id=teles (0)
HiSax: Teles IO driver Rev. 1.11
HiSax: Teles 16.3 config irq:5 isac:980  cfg:d80
HiSax: hscx A:180  hscx B:580
Teles3: HSCX version A: V2.1  B: V2.1
Teles3: ISAC 2086/2186 V1.1
HiSax: DSS1 Rev. 1.16
HiSax: 2 channels added
HiSax: module installed
inserting floppy driver for 2.0.35
Floppy drive(s): fd0 is 1.44M
FDC 0 is an 8272A
```

These messages are all printed by the kernel itself, as each device driver is initialized. The exact messages printed depend on what drivers are compiled into your kernel and what hardware you have on your system. Here's a quick rundown on what they mean.

First, the kernel reports which console font it has picked and which console type it has detected; note that this involves only the text mode being used by the kernel, not the capabilities of your video card. (An SVGA video card is reported as VGA+ as far as the console text mode is concerned.)

Next, the kernel gathers information about the PCI bus and checks for any PCI cards present in the system.

The next message printed is the "BogoMips" calculation for your processor. This is an utterly bogus (hence the name) measurement of processor speed, which is used to obtain optimal performance in delay loops for several device drivers. The kernel also prints information on the system memory:

```
Memory: 14984k/16384k available (552k kernel code, 384k reserved, 464k data)
```

Here, we see that 14984k of RAM are available for the system to use. This means the kernel itself is using 1400k.

The networking code in the kernel is then initialized and the CPU type checked. You can see from the line:

```
Intel Pentium with F0 0F bug - workaround enabled.
```

that the Linux kernel is even clever enough to detect the infamous Pentium bug and provide a workaround. The line:

```
Linux version 2.0.35 (root@rabbit) (gcc version egcs-2.90.29 980515\
(egcs-1.0.3 release)) #3 Fri Nov 13 15:07:45 CET 1998
```

tells you the version number of the kernel and who has compiled it on which machine (in this case, it was **root** on the machine **rabbit** and which compiler was used). The serial device driver is then initialized, which prints information on each detected serial port. A line such as:

```
tty00 at 0x03f8 (irq = 4) is a 16550A
```

means that the first serial device (*/dev/tty00*, or COM1) was detected at address 0x03f8, IRQ 4, using 16550A UART functions. Next comes configuration and checking for a SCSI host adapter. The kernel prints out information about all SCSI devices found. The line:

```
Adding Swap: 130748k swap-space (priority -1)
```

tells you how much swap space the kernel has found. Among the further tasks performed during a typical boot are finding and configuring a parallel port (1p1), detecting and configuring the network card, and finally setting up the ISDN subsystem. The last thing it reports is the detection of the floppy disk driver. Depending on your hardware, other messages will be printed in addition to those given in the example. For example, parallel port and SCSI drivers will be initialized at this point, if you have them.

init, inittab, and rc files

Once the device drivers are initialized, the kernel executes the program *init*, which is found in */etc*, */bin*, or */sbin* (it's */sbin/init* on most systems). *init* is a general-purpose program that spawns new processes and restarts certain programs when they exit. For example, each virtual console has a *getty* process running on it, started by *init*. When you exit from a login session on one of the virtual consoles, the *getty* process exits, and *init* starts a new one, allowing you to log in again.

init is also responsible for running a number of programs and scripts when the system boots. Everything *init* does is controlled by the file */etc/inittab*. Each line in this file is of the format:

code:runlevels:action:command

code is a unique one- or two-character sequence used to identify this entry in the file. Several of the entries must have a particular *code* to work correctly; more on this later.

runlevels is the list of "runlevels" in which this entry should be executed. A runlevel is a number or letter that specifies the current system state, as far as *init* is concerned. For example, when the system runlevel is changed to 3, all entries in */etc/inittab* containing 3 in the *runlevels* field will be executed. Runlevels are a useful way to group entries in */etc/inittab* together. For example, you might want to say that runlevel 1 executes only the bare minimum of configuration scripts, runlevel 2 executes everything in runlevel 1 plus networking configuration, runlevel 3 executes everything in levels 1 and 2 plus dial-in login access, and so on. Today, the Red Hat distribution is set up so that runlevel 5 automatically starts the X Window System graphical interface. The SuSE distribution does it at runlevel 3, and the Debian distribution does so at runlevel 2—provided you have installed X.

For the most part, you don't need to concern yourself with runlevels. When the system boots, it enters the default runlevel (set in */etc/inittab*, as we will soon show). On most systems, this default is runlevel 2 or 3. After we discuss normal booting, we'll show you how to enter another runlevel that you will sometimes need to use—runlevel 1, or single-user mode.

Let's take a look at a sample */etc/inittab* file:

```
# Set the default runlevel to three
id:3:initdefault:

# Execute /etc/rc.d/rc.sysinit when the system boots
si:S:sysinit:/etc/rc.d/rc.sysinit

# Run /etc/rc.d/rc with the runlevel as an argument
10:0:wait:/etc/rc.d/rc 0
11:1:wait:/etc/rc.d/rc 1
12:2:wait:/etc/rc.d/rc 2
13:3:wait:/etc/rc.d/rc 3
14:4:wait:/etc/rc.d/rc 4
15:5:wait:/etc/rc.d/rc 5
16:6:wait:/etc/rc.d/rc 6

# Executed when we press ctrl-alt-delete
ca::ctrlaltdel:/sbin/shutdown -t3 -rf now

# Start agetty for virtual consoles 1 through 6
c1:12345:respawn:/sbin/agetty 38400 tty1
c2:12345:respawn:/sbin/agetty 38400 tty2
c3:45:respawn:/sbin/agetty 38400 tty3
c4:45:respawn:/sbin/agetty 38400 tty4
c5:45:respawn:/sbin/agetty 38400 tty5
c6:45:respawn:/sbin/agetty 38400 tty6
```

Fields are separated by colons. The last field is the most recognizable: it is the command that *init* executes for this entry. The first field is an arbitrary identifier (it doesn't matter what it is so long as it's unique in the file) while the second indicates what runlevels cause the command to be invoked. The third field tells *init* how to handle this entry; for example, whether to execute the given command once or to respawn the command whenever it exits.

The exact contents of */etc/inittab* depend on your system and the distribution of Linux you have installed.

In our sample file, we see first that the default runlevel is set to 3. The `action` field for this entry is `initdefault`, which causes the given `runlevel` to be set to the default. That's the runlevel normally used whenever the system boots. You can override the default with any level you want by running *init* manually (which you might do when debugging your configuration) and passing in the desired runlevel as an argument. For instance, the following command shuts down all current processes and starts runlevel 5 (warn all your users to log off before doing this!):

```
tigger# init 5
```

LILO can also boot in single-user mode (usually runlevel 1)—see the section "Specifying boot time options" earlier in this chapter.

The next entry tells *init* to execute the script */etc/rc.d/rc.sysinit* when the system boots. (The `action` field is `sysinit`, which specifies that this entry should be executed when *init* is first started at system boot.) This file is simply a shell script containing commands to handle basic system initialization; for example, swapping is enabled, filesystems are checked and mounted, and the system clock is synchronized with the CMOS clock. You can take a look at this file on your system; we'll be talking more about the commands contained therein in Chapter 6; see the sections "Managing Filesystems" and "Managing Swap Space." On other distributions, this file might be elsewhere, for example, on SuSE it is */sbin/init.d/boot*.

Next, we see that the system executes the script */etc/rc.d/rc* when it enters any of the runlevels 0 through 6, with the appropriate runlevel as an argument. *rc* is a generic startup script that executes other scripts as appropriate for that runlevel. The `action` field here is `wait`, which tells *init* to execute the given `command`, and to wait for it to complete execution before doing anything else.

rc files

Linux stores startup commands in files with *rc* in the name, using an old Unix convention. The commands do all the things necessary to have a fully functioning system, like starting the servers or daemons mentioned in Chapter 4, *Basic Unix Commands and Concepts*. Thanks to these commands, the system comes up ready with logging facilities, mail, a web server, or whatever you installed and asked it to run. As explained in the previous section, the files are invoked from */etc/inittab*. The commands are standard shell commands, and you can simply read the various *rc* files to see what they do.

In this section, we describe the structure of the *rc* files, so you understand where everything starts and can start or stop servers manually in the rare case that they don't do what you want them to do. We'll use Red Hat as our model, but once you get the idea of what to look for, you can find the corresponding files on any Linux distribution.

On Red Hat, the top-level *rc* script is */etc/rc.d/rc*. The path is slightly different in other distributions (*/etc/init.d/rc* on Debian, for instance) but the contents are similar. In the previous section, you could see how the */etc/inittab* invokes the script under a variety of circumstances with different numbers from 0 to 6 as arguments. The numbers correspond to runlevels, and each one causes the *rc* files to invoke a different set of scripts. So our next step is to find the scripts corresponding to each runlevel.

On Red Hat, scripts for each runlevel are stored in the directory */etc/rc.d/rcN.d* where *N* is the runlevel being started. Thus, for runlevel 3, scripts in */etc/rc.d/rc3.d* would be used. Again, slightly different conventions are the rule in other distributions. On Debian, for instance, the directory for each runlevel is */etc/rcN.d/*.

Take a look in one of those directories; you will see a number of filenames of the form *Snnxxxx* or *Knnxxxx* where *nn* is a number from 00 to 99, and *xxxx* is the name of some system service. The scripts whose names begin with K are executed by */etc/rc.d/rc* first to kill any existing services, then the scripts whose names begin with S are executed to start new services.

The numbers *nn* in the names are used to enforce an ordering on the scripts as they are executed: scripts with lower numbers are executed before those with higher numbers. The name *xxxx* is simply used to help you identify which system service the script corresponds to. This naming convention might seem odd, but it makes it easy to add or remove scripts from these directories and have them automatically executed at the appropriate time by */etc/rc.d/rc*. For customizing startup scripts, you'll find it convenient to use a graphical runlevel editor, such as *ksysv*, in the KDE (see "The K Development Environment" in Chapter 11, *Customizing Your X Environment*).

Chapter 11

For example, the script to initialize networking might be called *S10network*, while the script to stop the system logging daemon might be called *K70syslog*. If these files are placed in the appropriate */etc/rc.d/rcN.d* directories, */etc/rc.d/rc* will run them, in numerical order, at system startup or shutdown time. If the default runlevel of your system is 3, look in */etc/rc.d/rc3.d* to see which scripts are executed when the system boots normally.

Because the same services are started or stopped at different runlevels, the Red Hat distribution uses symbolic links instead of repeating the same script in multiple places. Thus, each S or K file is a symbolic link that points to a central directory that stores startup or shutdown scripts for all services. On Red Hat, this central directory is */etc/rc.d/init.d*, while on SuSE and Debian, it is */etc/init.d*. On Debian, the directory contains a script called *skeleton* that you can adapt to start and stop any new daemons you might write.

Knowing the location of a startup or shutdown script is useful in case you don't want to completely reboot or enter a different runlevel, but need to start or stop a particular service. Look in the *init.d* directory for a script of the appropriate name and execute it, passing the parameter `start` or `stop`. For example, on SuSE, if you want the Apache web server to be running but your system is in a runlevel that does not include Apache, just enter the following:

```
tigger# /sbin/init.d/apache start
```

Another important system configuration script is */etc/rc.d/rc.local*, which is executed after the other system-initialization scripts are run. (How is this accomplished? Generally, a symbolic link to *rc.local* is made in each */etc/rc.d/rcN.d* directory with the name *S99local*. Since 99 is the largest numerical order any of the S scripts can have, it is executed last. *Voila!*) You can edit *rc.local* to accomplish any peculiar or otherwise out-of-place system commands at boot time, or if you're not sure where else they should be executed. Debian doesn't have an equivalent of *rc.local* script, but nothing stops you from adding it and invoking it from *rc* if you're used to having it.

The next entry, labeled `ca`, is executed when the key combination Ctrl-Alt-Del is pressed on the console. This key combination produces an interrupt that usually reboots the system. Under Linux, this interrupt is caught and sent to *init*, which executes the entry with the `action` field of `ctrlaltdel`. The command shown here, */sbin/shutdown –t3 –rf now*, will do a "safe" reboot of the system. (See the section "Shutting Down the System" later in this chapter.) This way we protect the system from sudden reboot when Ctrl-Alt-Del is pressed.

Finally, the *inittab* file includes entries that execute */sbin/agetty* for the first six virtual consoles. *agetty* is one of the several *getty* variants available for Linux. These programs permit logins on terminals; without them the terminal would be effectively dead and would not respond when a user walked up and pressed a key or mouse button. The various *getty* commands open a terminal device (such as a virtual console, or a serial line), set various parameters for the terminal driver, and execute */bin/login* to initiate a login session on that terminal. Therefore, to allow logins on a given virtual console, you must be running *getty* or *agetty* on it. *agetty* is the version used on a number of Linux systems, but others use *getty*, which has a slightly different syntax. See the manual pages for *getty* and *agetty* on your system.

agetty takes two arguments: a baud rate and a device name. The port names for Linux virtual consoles are */dev/tty1*, */dev/tty2*, and so forth. *agetty* assumes the given device name is relative to */dev*. The baud rate for virtual consoles should generally be 38400.

Note that the `action` field for each *agetty* entry is `respawn`. This means that *init* should restart the command given in the entry when the *agetty* process dies, which is every time a user logs out.

Now you should be familiar with *init*, but the various files and commands in */etc/rc.d*, which do all of the work, remain a mystery. We can't delve into these files without more background on other system administration tasks, such as managing filesystems. We'll lead you through these tasks in the next few chapters, and eventually all should be clear.

Single-User Mode

Most of the time, you operate the system in multiuser mode so that users can log in. But there is a special state called *single-user mode*, where Unix is running but there is no login prompt. When you're in single-user mode, you're basically superuser (**root**). You may have to enter this mode during installation if something goes wrong. Single-user mode is important for certain routine system administration tasks, like checking corrupted filesystems. (This is not fun; try not to corrupt your filesystem. For instance, always shut down the system through a *shutdown* command before you turn off the power. This is described in the section "Shutting Down the System" later in this chapter.)

Chapter 8

Under single-user mode, the system is nearly useless; very little configuration is done, filesystems are unmounted, and so on. This is necessary for recovering from certain kinds of system problems; see the section "What to Do in an Emergency" in Chapter 8 for details.

Note that Unix is still a multiprocessing system, even in single-user mode. You can run multiple programs at once. Servers can run in the background, so that special functions, such as the network, can operate. But if your system supports more than one terminal, only the console can be used. And the X Window System cannot run.

Shutting Down the System

Fortunately, shutting down the Linux system is much simpler than booting and startup. However, it's not just a matter of hitting the reset switch. Linux, like all Unix systems, buffers disk reads and writes in memory. This means disk writes are delayed until absolutely necessary, and multiple reads on the same disk block are served directly from RAM. This greatly increases performance as disks are extremely slow relative to the CPU.

The problem is that if the system were to be suddenly powered down or rebooted, the buffers in memory would not be written to disk, and data could be lost or corrupted. */sbin/update* is a program started from */etc/rc.d/rc.sysinit* on most systems; it flushes dirty buffers (ones that have been changed since they were read from the disk) back to disk every five seconds to prevent serious damage from occurring should the system crash. However, to be completely safe, the system needs to undergo a "safe" shutdown before rebooting. This will not only ensure that disk buffers are properly synchronized, but also allow all running processes to exit cleanly.

shutdown is the general, all-purpose command used to halt or reboot the system. As **root**, you can issue the command:

```
/sbin/shutdown -r +10
```

to cause the system to reboot in ten minutes. The *−r* switch indicates the system should be rebooted after shutdown, and +10 is the amount of time to wait (in minutes) until shutting down. The system will print a warning message to all active terminals, counting down until the shutdown time. You can add your own warning message by including it on the command line, as in:

```
/sbin/shutdown -r +10 "Rebooting to try new kernel"
```

You can also specify an absolute time to shutdown, as in:

```
/sbin/shutdown -r 13:00
```

to reboot at 1:00 pm. Likewise, you can say:

```
/sbin/shutdown -r now
```

to reboot immediately (after the safe shutdown process).

Using the *−h* switch, instead of *−r*, will cause the system to simply be halted after shutdown; you can then turn off the system power without fear of losing data. If you specify neither *−h* nor *−r*, the system will go into single-user mode.

As we saw in the section "init, inittab, and rc files," you can have *init* catch the Ctrl-Alt-Del key sequence and execute a *shutdown* command in response to it. If you're used to rebooting your system in this way it might be good idea to check that your */etc/inittab* contains a `ctrlaltdel` entry. Note that you should never reboot your Linux system by pressing the system power switch or the reboot switch on the front panel of your machine. Unless the system is flat-out hung (a rare occurrence), you should always use *shutdown*. The great thing about a multiprocessing system is that one program may hang, but you can almost always switch to another window or virtual console to recover.

shutdown provides a number of other options. The *−c* switch will cancel a currently running *shutdown*. (Of course, you can kill the process by hand using *kill*, but *shutdown −c* might be easier.) The *−k* switch will print the warning messages but not actually shut down the system. See the manual page for *shutdown* if you're interested in the gory details.

shutdown(8)

The /proc filesystem

Unix systems have come a long way with respect to providing uniform interfaces to different parts of the system; as you will learn in the next chapter, hardware is represented in Linux in the form of a special type of file. There is, however, a special filesystem called the */proc* filesystem that goes even one step further: it unifies files and processes.

From the user's or the system administrator's point of view, the */proc* filesystem looks just like any other filesystem; you can navigate around it with the *cd* command, list directory contents with the *ls* command and view file contents with the *cat* command. However, none of these files and directories occupy any space on your hard disk. The kernel traps accesses to the */proc* filesystem and generates directory and file contents on the fly. In other words, whenever you list or directory or view file contents in the */proc* filesystem, the kernel dynamically generates the contents you want to see.

To make this less abstract, let's see some examples. The following example displays the list of files in the top-level directory of the */proc* filesystem:

```
tigger # ls /proc
1          184        25472      8          8525       kmsg
130        185        25475      82         8526       ksyms
134        186        25497      8484       8593       loadavg
136        187        25498      8485       963        locks
139        2          25499      8488       965        meminfo
143        24924      25500      8489       9654       modules
144        25441      25515      8492       968        mounts
145        25442      25549      8496       97         net
146        25445      25550      8507       99         pci
147        25446      26019      8508       cmdline    scsi
148        25449      26662      8510       cpuinfo    self
151        25451      26663      8511       devices    stat
163        25462      270        8512       dma        sys
168        25463      3          8520       filesystems uptime
172        25464      4484       8522       interrupts version
180        25465      4639       8523       ioports
182        25466      55         8524       kcore
```

The numbers will be different on your system, but the general organization will be the same. All those numbers are directories that represent one of the processes running on your system each. For example, let's look at the information about the process with the ID 172:

```
tigger # ls /proc/172
cmdline   environ   fd        mem       stat      status
cwd       exe       maps      root      statm
```

You see a number of files that each contain information about this process. For example, the *cmdline* file shows the command line with which this process was started. *status* gives information about the internal state of the process and *cwd* links to the current working directory of this process.

Probably you'll find the hardware information even more interesting than the process information. All the information that the kernel has gathered about your hardware is collected in the */proc* filesystem, even though it can be difficult to find the information you are looking for.

Let's start by checking your machine's memory. This is represented by the file */proc/meminfo*:

```
tigger # cat /proc/meminfo
         total:     used:     free:  shared: buffers:  cached:
Mem:  130957312 128684032  2273280 37888000  3198976 20615168
Swap: 133885952 64434176 69451776
MemTotal:     127888 kB
MemFree:        2220 kB
MemShared:     37000 kB
Buffers:        3124 kB
Cached:        20132 kB
SwapTotal:    130748 kB
SwapFree:      67824 kB
```

If you then try the command *free*, you can see that that is exactly the same information, only the numbers are reformatted a bit. *free* does nothing more than read */proc/meminfo* and rearrange the output a bit.

Most tools on your system that report information about your hardware do it this way. The */proc* filesystem is a portable and easy way to get at this information. The information is especially useful if you want to add new hardware to your system. For example, most hardware boards need a few I/O addresses to communicate with the CPU and the operating system. If you configured two boards to use the same I/O addresses, disaster is about to happen. You can avoid this by checking which I/O addresses the kernel has already detected as being in use:

```
tigger # more /proc/ioports
0000-001f : dma1
0020-003f : pic1
0040-005f : timer
0060-006f : keyboard
0080-009f : dma page reg
00a0-00bf : pic2
00c0-00df : dma2
00f0-00ff : npu
01f0-01f7 : ide0
0220-022f : soundblaster
02e8-02ef : serial(auto)
0388-038b : OPL3/OPL2
03c0-03df : vga+
03f0-03f5 : floppy
03f6-03f6 : ide0
```

```
03f7-03f7 : floppy DIR
03f8-03ff : serial(auto)
0530-0533 : WSS config
0534-0537 : MSS audio codec
e000-e0be : aic7xxx
e400-e41f : eth0
```

Now you can look for IO addresses that are free. Of course, the kernel can show IO addresses only for boards that it has detected and recognized, but in a correctly configured system, this should be the case for all boards.

You can use the */proc* filesystem for the other information that you might need for configuring new hardware as well: */proc/interrupts* lists the occupied interrupt lines (IRQs) and */proc/dma* lists the DMA (direct memory access) channels in use.

Managing User Accounts

Even if you're the only actual human being who uses your Linux system, understanding how to manage user accounts is important—even more so if your system hosts multiple users.

User accounts serve a number of purposes on Unix systems. Most prominently, they give the system a way to distinguish between different people who use the system for reasons of identification and security. Each user has a personal account with a separate username and password. As discussed in the section "File Ownership and Permissions" in Chapter 4, users may set permissions on their files, allowing or restricting access to them by other users. Each file on the system is "owned" by a particular user, who may set the permissions for that file. User accounts are used to authenticate access to the system; only those people with accounts may access the machine. Also, accounts are used to identify users, keep system logs, tag electronic mail messages with the name of the sender, and so forth.

Chapter 4

Apart from personal accounts, there are users on the system that provide administrative functions. As we've seen, the system administrator uses the **root** account to perform maintenance—but usually not for personal system use. Such accounts are accessed using the *su* command, allowing another account to be accessed after logging in through a personal account.

Other accounts on the system may not be set aside for human interaction at all. These accounts are generally used by system daemons, which must access files on the system through a specific user ID other than **root** or one of the personal user accounts. For example, if you configure your system to receive a newsfeed from another site, the news daemon must store news articles in a spool directory that anyone can access, but only one user (the news daemon) can write to. No human being is associated with the **news** account; it is an "imaginary" user set aside for the news daemon only.

One of the permissions bits that can be set on executables is the *setuid* bit, which causes the program to be executed with the permissions of the owner of that file.

For example, if the news daemon were owned by the user **news**, and the setuid bit set on the executable, it would run as if by the user **news**. **news** would have write access to the news spool directory, and all other users would have read access to the articles stored there. This is a security feature. News programs can give users just the right amount of access to the news spool directory, but no one can just play around there.

As the system administrator, it is your job to create and manage accounts for all users (real and virtual) on your machine. This is actually a painless, hands-off task in most cases, but it's important to understand how it works.

The passwd File

Every account on the system has an entry in the file */etc/passwd*. This file contains entries, one line per user, that specify several attributes for each account, such as the username, real name, and so forth.

Each entry in this file is of the format:

```
username:password:uid:gid:gecos:homedir:shell
```

The following list explains each of these fields:

username

> A unique character string, identifying the account. For personal accounts, this is the name the user logs in with. On most systems it is limited to eight alphanumeric characters—for example, **larry** or **kirsten**.

password

> An encrypted representation of the user's password. This field is set using the *passwd* program to set the account's password; it uses a one-way encryption scheme that is difficult (but not impossible) to break. You don't set this by hand; the *passwd* program does it for you. Note, however, that if the first character of the *passwd* field is * (an asterisk), the account is "disabled"; the system will not allow logins as this user. See the section "Creating Accounts" later in this chapter.

uid

> The user ID, a unique integer the system uses to identify the account. The system uses the *uid* field internally when dealing with process and file permissions; it's easier and more compact to deal with integers than byte strings. Therefore, both the *uid* and the *username* identify a particular account: the *uid* is more important to the system, while *username* is more convenient for humans.

gid

The group ID, an integer referring to the user's default group, found in the file */etc/group*. See the section "The Group File" that follows.

gecos

Miscellaneous information about the user, such as the user's real name, and optional "location information" such as the user's office address or phone number. Such programs as *mail* and *finger* use this information to identify users on the system; we'll talk more about it later. By the way, *gecos* is a historical name dating back to the 1970s; it stands for *General Electric Comprehensive Operating System*. GECOS has nothing to do with Unix, except that this field was originally added to */etc/passwd* to provide compatibility with some of its services.

homedir

The user's home directory, for his personal use; more on this later. When the user first logs in, her shell finds its current working directory in the named *homedir*.

shell

The name of the program to run when the user logs in; in most cases, this is the full pathname of a shell, such as */bin/bash* or */bin/tcsh*.

Many of these fields are optional; the only required fields are *username*, *uid*, *gid*, and *homedir*. Most user accounts have all fields filled in, but "imaginary" or administrative accounts may use only a few.

Here are two sample entries you might find in */etc/passwd*:

```
root:ZxPsI9ZjiVd9Y:0:0:The root of all evil:/root:/bin/bash
aclark:BjDf5hBysDsii:104:50:Anna Clark:/home/aclark:/bin/bash
```

The first entry is for the **root** account. First of all, notice that the uid of **root** is zero. This is what makes **root root**: the system knows that uid 0 is "special" and that it does not have the usual security restrictions. The gid of **root** is also zip, which is mostly a convention. Many of the files on the system are owned by **root** and the **root** group, which have a uid and gid of zero, respectively. More on groups in a minute.

On many systems, **root** uses the home directory */root*, or just */*. This is not usually relevant, because you most often use *su* to access **root** from your own account. Also, it is tradition to use a Bourne-shell variant (in this case */bin/bash*) for the **root** account, although you can use C shell if you like. (Shells are discussed in the section "Shells" in Chapter 4.) Be careful, though: Bourne shells and C shells have differing syntax, and switching between them when using **root** can be confusing and lead to mistakes.

Chapter 4

The second entry is for an actual human being, username **aclark**. In this case, the *uid* is 104. The *uid* field can technically be any unique integer; on many systems, it's customary to have user accounts numbered 100 and above and administrative accounts in the sub-100 range. The gid is 50, which just means that **aclark** is in whatever group is numbered 50 in the */etc/group* file. Hang on to your horses; groups are covered in section "The Group File" later in this chapter.

Home directories are often found in */home*, and named for the username of their owner. This is, for the most part, a useful convention that avoids confusion when finding a particular user's home directory, but you can technically place a home directory anywhere. You should, however, observe the directory layout used on your system.

Note that as the system administrator, it's not usually necessary to modify the */etc/passwd* file directly. There are several programs available that can help you create and maintain user accounts; see the section "Creating Accounts" that follows.

Shadow Passwords

To some extent, it is a security risk to let everybody with access to the system view the encrypted passwords in */etc/passwd*. Special crack programs are available that try a huge number of possible passwords and check whether the encrypted version of those passwords is equal to a specified one.

To overcome this potential security risk, shadow passwords have been invented. When shadow passwords are used, the password field in */etc/passwd* contains only an x or a *, which can never occur in the encrypted version of a password. Instead, a second file called */etc/shadow* is used. This file contains entries that look very similar to those in */etc/passwd*, but contain the real encrypted password in the password field. */etc/shadow* is readable only by **root**, so that normal users do not have access to the encrypted passwords. The other fields in */etc/shadow*, except the username and the password are present as well, but normally contain bogus values or are empty.

Note that in order to use shadow passwords, you need special versions of the programs that access or modify user information like *passwd* or *login*. Nowadays, most distributions come with shadow passwords already set up so that this should not be a problem for you.

There are two tools for converting "normal" user entries to shadow entries and back. *pwconv* takes the */etc/passwd* file, looks for entries that are not yet present in */etc/shadow*, generates shadow entries for those and merges them with the entries already present in */etc/shadow*.

Debian users should use "shadowconfig on" instead to ensure that shadow passwords are enabled on their systems.

pwunconv is rarely used, because it gives you less security instead of more. It works like *pwconv*, but generates traditional */etc/passwd* entries that work without */etc/shadow* counterparts.

PAM and Other Authentication Methods

You might think that having two means of user authentication, */etc/passwd* and */etc/shadow*, is already enough choice, but you are wrong in this case. There are a number of other authentification methods with strange names like Kerberos authentication (so named after the dog from Greek mythology that guards the entrance to Hell). While we think that shadow passwords provide enough security for almost all cases, it all depends on how much security you really need and how paranoid you want to be.

The problem with all those authentication methods is that you cannot simply switch from one to another, because you always need a set of programs like *login* and *passwd* that go with those tools. To overcome this problem, the Pluggable Authentification Methods (*PAM*) system has been invented. Once you have a *PAM*-enabled set of tools, you can change the authentification method of your system by reconfiguring PAM. The tools will automatically get the code necessary to perform the required authentication procedures from dynamically loaded shared libraries.

Setting up and using PAM is beyond the scope of this book, but you can get all the information you need from *http://www.de.kernel.org/pub/linux/libs/pam/*.

The Group File

User groups are a convenient way to logically organize sets of user accounts and allow users to share files within their group or groups. Each file on the system has both a user and a group owner associated with it. Using *ls –l*, you can see the owner and group for a particular file, as in:

```
rutabaga% ls -l boiler.tex
-rwxrw-r--    1 mdw        megabozo      10316 Oct  6 20:19 boiler.tex
rutabaga%
```

This file is owned by the user **mdw** and belongs to the **megabozo** group. We can see from the file permissions that **mdw** has read, write, and execute access to the file; that anyone in the **megabozo** group has read and write access; and that all other users have read access only.

This doesn't mean that **mdw** is in the **megabozo** group; it simply means the file may be accessed, as shown by the permissions bits, by anyone in the **megabozo** group (which may or may not include **mdw**).

Chapter 4

This way files can be shared among groups of users, and permissions can be specified separately for the owner of the file, the group to which the file belongs, and everyone else. An introduction to permissions appears in the section "File Ownership and Permissions" in Chapter 4.

Every user is assigned to at least one group, which you specify in the *gid* field of the */etc/passwd* file. However, a user can be a member of multiple groups. The file

/etc/group contains a one-line entry for each group on the system, very similar in nature to */etc/passwd*. The format of this file is:

```
groupname:password:gid:members
```

Here, `groupname` is a character string identifying the group; it is the group name printed when using commands such as *ls –l*.

`password` is an optional password associated with the group, which allows users not in this group to access the group with the *newgrp* command. Read on for information on this.

`gid` is the group ID used by the system to refer to the group; it is the number used in the `gid` field of */etc/passwd* to specify a user's default group.

`members` is a comma-separated list of usernames (with no whitespace in between), identifying those users who are members of this group, but who have a different `gid` in */etc/passwd*. That is, this list need not contain those users who have this group set as their "default" group in */etc/passwd*; it's only for users who are additional members of the group.

For example, */etc/group* might contain the following entries:

```
root:*:0:
bin:*:1:root,daemon
users:*:50:
bozo:*:51:linus,mdw
megabozo:*:52:kibo
```

The first entries, for the groups **root** and **bin**, are administrative groups, similar in nature to the "imaginary" accounts used on the system. Many files are owned by groups such as **root** and **bin**. The other groups are for user accounts. Like user IDs, the group ID values for user groups are often placed in ranges above 50 or 100.

The `password` field of the *group* file is something of a curiosity. It isn't used much, but in conjunction with the *newgrp* program it allows users who aren't members of a particular group to assume that group ID if they have the password. For example, using the command:

```
rutabaga% newgrp bozo
Password: password for group bozo
rutabaga%
```

starts a new shell with the group ID of **bozo**. If the `password` field is blank, or the first character is an asterisk, you receive a `permission denied` error if you attempt to *newgrp* to that group.

However, the `password` field of the *group* file is seldom used and is really not necessary. (In fact, most systems don't provide tools to set the password for a group; you could use *passwd* to set the password for a dummy user with the same name as the group in */etc/passwd* and copy the encrypted *password* field to */etc/group*.) Instead, you can make a user a member of multiple groups simply by including the username in the *members* field for each additional group. In the previous example, the users **linus** and **mdw** are members of the **bozo** group, as well as whatever group they are assigned to in the */etc/passwd* file. If we wanted to add **linus** to the **megabozo** group as well, we'd change the last line of the previous example to:

```
megabozo:*:52:kibo,linus
```

The command *groups* tells you which groups you belong to, as in:

```
rutabaga% groups
users bozo
```

Giving a list of usernames to *groups* lists the groups each user in the list belongs to.

When you log in, you are automatically assigned to the group ID given in */etc/passwd*, as well as any additional groups for which you're listed in */etc/group*. This means you have "group access" to any files on the system with a group ID contained in your list of groups. In this case, the group permission bits (set with *chmod g+...*) for those files apply to you. (Unless you're the owner, in which case the owner permission bits apply, instead.)

Now that you know the ins and outs of groups, how should you assign groups on your system? This is really a matter of style and depends on how your system will be used. For systems with just one or a handful of users, it's easiest to have a single group (called, say, **users**) to which all personal user accounts belong. Note that all the system groups—those groups contained within */etc/group* when the system is first installed—should probably be left alone. Various daemons and programs may depend upon them.

If you have a number of users on your machine, there are several ways to organize groups. For example, an educational institution may have separate groups for **students**, **faculty**, and **staff**. A software company might have different groups for each design team. On other systems, each user is placed into a separate group, named identically to the username. This keeps each pigeon in its own hole, so to speak, and allows users to share files with a particular group. However, adding a user to an additional group usually requires the system administrator to intervene (by editing */etc/group*; Debian has the utility *gpasswd*). It's really up to you.

Another situation where groups are often used is special hardware groups. Let's say that you have a scanner that is accessed via */dev/scanner*. If you do not want to give everybody access to the scanner, you could create a special group called **scanner**, assign */dev/scanner* to this group, make this special file readable for the group and nonreadable for everybody else, and add everybody who is allowed to use the scanner to the **scanner** group in the */etc/groups* file.

Creating Accounts

Creating a user account requires several steps: adding an entry to */etc/passwd*, creating the user's home directory, and setting up the user's default configuration files (such as *.bashrc*) in her home directory. Luckily, you don't have to perform these steps manually; nearly all Linux systems include a program called *adduser* to do this for you.*

Running *adduser* as **root** should work as follows. Just enter the requested information at the prompts; many of the prompts have reasonable defaults you can select by pressing Enter:

```
Adding a new user. The username should not exceed 8 characters
in length, or you many run into problems later.

Enter login name for new account (^C to quit): norbert

Editing information for new user [norbert]

Full Name: Norbert Ebersol
GID [100]: 117

Checking for an available UID after 500
First unused uid is 501

UID [501]: (enter)
Home Directory [/home/norbert]: (enter)
Shell [/bin/bash]: (enter)
Password [norbert]: (norbert's password)

Information for new user [norbert]:
Home directory: [/home/norbert] Shell: [/bin/bash]
Password: [(norbert's password)] uid: [501] gid: [117]

Is this correct? [y/N]: y

Adding login [norbert] and making directory [/home/norbert]
Adding the files from the /etc/skel directory:
./.emacs -> /home/norbert/./.emacs
./.kermrc -> /home/norbert/./.kermrc
./.bashrc -> /home/norbert/./.bashrc
```

There should be no surprises here; just enter the information as requested or choose the defaults. Note that *adduser* uses 100 as the default group ID, and looks

---

* Note that some Linux systems, such as Red Hat or SuSE, use a different set of tools for account creation and deletion. If the sequence of inputs in this section does not work for you, check the documentation for your distribution. (Red Hat allows accounts to be managed through the *control-panel* tool, and SuSE does it via *YaST*; Debian includes a non-interactive "adduser" script that automatically sets up users based on the configuration file */etc/adduser.conf*). In addition, there are graphical user management programs like *kuser* from KDE (see The K Desktop Environment in Chapter 11).

for the first unused user ID after 500 (500 is used as the minimum on SuSE and Red Hat, Debian uses 1000). It should be safe to go along with these defaults; in the previous example we used a group ID of 117 and the default user ID of 501.

After the account is created, the files from */etc/skel* are copied to the user's home directory. */etc/skel* contains the "skeleton" files for a new account; they are the default configuration files (such as *.emacs* and *.bashrc*) for the new user. Feel free to place other files here if your new user accounts should have them.

After this is done, the new account is ready to roll; **norbert** can log in, using the password set using *adduser*. To guarantee security, new users should always change their own passwords, using *passwd*, immediately after logging in for the first time.

root can set the password for any user on the system. For example, the command:

```
passwd norbert
```

prompts for a new password for **norbert**, without asking for the original password. Note, however, that you must know the **root** password in order to change it. If you forget the **root** password entirely, you can boot Linux into a root shell, in single-user mode, or from an "emergency floppy," and clear the `password` field of the */etc/passwd* entry for **root**. See the section "What to Do in an Emergency" in Chapter 8.

Chapter 8

Some Linux systems provide the command-line–driven *useradd* instead of *adduser*. This program requires you to provide all relevant information as command-line arguments. If you can't locate *adduser* and are stuck with *useradd*, see the manual pages, which should help you out.

Deleting and Disabling Accounts

Deleting a user account is much easier than creating one; this is the well-known concept of entropy at work. To delete an account, you must remove the user's entry in */etc/passwd*, remove any references to the user in */etc/group*, and delete the user's home directory, as well as any additional files created or owned by the user. For example, if the user has an incoming mailbox in */var/spool/mail*, it must be deleted as well.

The command *userdel* (the yin to *useradd*'s yang) deletes an account and the account's home directory. For example:

```
userdel -r norbert
```

will remove the recently created account for **norbert**. The *–r* option forces the home directory to be removed as well. Other files associated with the user—for example, the incoming mailbox, *crontab* files, and so forth—must be removed by hand. Usually these are quite insignificant and can be left around. By the end of this chapter, you should know where these files are, if they exist. A quick way to find the files associated with a particular user is through the command:

```
find / -user username -ls
```

This will give an *ls –l* listing of each file owned by *username*. Of course, to use this, the account associated with *username* must still have an entry in */etc/passwd*. If you deleted the account, use the *–uid num* argument instead, where *num* is the numeric user ID of the dearly departed user.

Temporarily (or not-so-temporarily) disabling a user account, for whatever reason, is even simpler. You can either remove the user's entry in */etc/passwd* (leaving the home directory and other files intact), or add an asterisk to the first character of the *password* field of the */etc/passwd* entry, as so:

```
aclark:*BjDf5hBysDsii:104:50:Anna Clark:/home/aclark:/bin/bash
```

This will disallow logins to the account in question.

Modifying User Accounts

Modifying attributes of user accounts and groups is usually a simple matter of editing */etc/passwd* and */etc/group*. Many systems provide commands such as *usermod* and *groupmod* to do just this; it's often easier to edit the files by hand.

To change a user's password, use the *passwd* command, which will prompt for a password, encrypt it, and store the encrypted password in the */etc/passwd* file.

If you need to change the user ID of an existing account, you can do this by editing the *uid* field of */etc/passwd* directly. However, you should also *chown* the files owned by the user to that of the new uid. For example:

```
chown -R aclark /home/aclark
```

will set the ownership for all files in the home directory used by **aclark** back to **aclark**, if you changed the uid for this account. If *ls –l* prints a numeric user ID, instead of a username, this means there is no username associated with the uid owning the files. Use *chown* to fix this.

## CHAPTER SIX

MANAGING FILESYSTEMS, SWAP, AND DEVICES

Y ou probably created filesystems and swap space when you first installed Linux (most distributions help you do the basics). Here is a chance to fine-tune these resources. Most of the time, you do these things shortly after installing your operating system, before you start loading up your disks with fun stuff. But occasionally you will want to change a running system, in order to add a new device or perhaps upgrade the swap space when you upgrade your RAM.

Managing Filesystems

To Unix systems, a filesystem is some device (such as a hard drive, floppy, or CD-ROM) that is formatted to store files. Filesystems can be found on hard drives, floppies, CD-ROMs, and other storage media that permit random access. (Note: a tape allows only sequential access, and therefore can't contain a filesystem per se.)

The exact format and means by which files are stored is not important; the system provides a common interface for all *filesystem types* it recognizes. Under Linux, filesystem types include the Second Extended filesystem, or *ext2fs*, which you probably use to store Linux files; the MS-DOS filesystem, which allows files on MS-DOS partitions and floppies to be accessed under Linux; and several others, including the ISO 9660 filesystem used by CD-ROM.

Each of these filesystem types has a very different underlying format for storing data. However, when you access any filesystem under Linux, the system presents the data as files arranged into a hierarchy of directories, along with owner and group IDs, permissions bits, and the other characteristics you're familiar with.

In fact, information on file ownership, permissions, and so forth is provided only by filesystem types that are meant to be used for storing Linux files. For filesystem types that don't store this information, the kernel drivers used to access these filesystems "fake" the information. For example, the MS-DOS filesystem has no concept of file ownership; therefore, all files are presented as if they were owned by **root**. This way, above a certain level, all filesystem types look alike, and each file has certain attributes associated with it. Whether or not these data are actually used in the underlying filesystem is another matter altogether.

As the system administrator, you need to know how to create filesystems should you want to store Linux files on a floppy or add additional filesystems to your hard drives. You also need to know how to use the various tools to check and maintain filesystems should data corruption occur. Also, you must know the commands and files used to access filesystems, for example, those on floppy or CD-ROM.

Filesystem Types

Table 6-1 lists the filesystem types supported by the Linux kernel as of Version 2.2.2. New filesystem types are always being added to the system, and experimental drivers for several filesystems not listed here are available. To find out what filesystem types your kernel supports, look at the kernel source tree, in the directory */usr/src/linux/fs*. You can select which filesystem types to support when building your kernel; see the section "Building the Kernel" in Chapter 7, *Upgrading Software and the Kernel*.

Chapter 7

Table 6-1: Linux Filesystem Types

Filesystem	Type	Description
Second Extended filesystem	*ext2*	Most common Linux filesystem
Minix filesystem	*minix*	Original Minix filesystem; rarely used
ROM filesystem	*romfs*	A tiny read-only filesystem, mainly used for ramdisks
Network File System (NFS)	*NFS*	Allows access to remote files on network
UMSDOS filesystem	*umsdos*	Installs Linux on an MS-DOS partition
DOS-FAT filesystem	*msdos*	Accesses MS-DOS files
VFAT filesystem	*vfat*	Accesses Windows 95/98 files
NT filesystem	*ntfs*	Accesses Windows NT files
HPFS filesystem	*hpfs*	OS/2 filesystem
/proc filesystem	*proc*	Provides process information for *ps*
ISO 9660 filesystem	*iso9660*	Used by most CD-ROMs

Table 6–1: Linux Filesystem Types (continued)

Filesystem	Type	Description
Joliet filesystem	*iso9660*	An extension to the ISO 9660 filesystem that can handle Unicode filenames
Xenix filesystem	*xenix*	Accesses files from Xenix
System V filesystem	*sysv*	Accesses files from System V variants
Coherent filesystem	*coherent*	Accesses files from Coherent
UFS filesystem	*ufs*	Accesses files from UFS filesystems, like those on SunOS or BSD
ADFS filesystem	*adfs*	Accesses files from Acorn partitions
AFFS filesystem	*affs*	Accesses files from standard AmigaOS filesystem partitions
Apple Mac filesystem	*hfs*	Accesses files from Apple Macintosh
QNX4 filesystem	*qnx4*	Accesses files from a QNX4 partitions
Novell filesystem	*ncpfs*	Accesses files from a Novell server
SMB filesystem	*smbfs*	Accesses files from a Windows for Workgroups or Windows NT server

Each filesystem type has its own attributes and limitations; for example, the MS-DOS filesystem restricts filenames to eight characters plus a three-character extension and should be used only to access existing MS-DOS floppies or partitions. For most of your work with Linux, you'll use the Second Extended filesystem, which was developed primarily for Linux and supports 256-character filenames, a 4-terabyte maximum filesystem size, and a slew of other goodies. Earlier Linux systems used the Extended filesystem (no longer supported) and the Minix filesystem. (The Minix filesystem was originally used for several reasons. First of all, Linux was originally cross-compiled under Minix. Also, Linus was quite familiar with the Minix filesystem, and it was straightforward to implement in the original kernels.) The Xia filesystem is no longer supported.

You will rarely need the ROM filesystem, which is very small, does not support write operations, and is meant to be used in ramdisks at system configuration, startup time, or even in EPROMS.

The UMSDOS filesystem is used to install Linux under a private directory of an existing MS-DOS partition. This is a good way for new users to try out Linux without repartitioning. The DOS-FAT filesystem, on the other hand, is used to access MS-DOS files directly. Files on partitions created with Windows 95 or 98 can be accessed via the VFAT filesystem, while the NTFS filesystem lets you access Windows NT filesystems. The HPFS filesystem is used to access the OS/2 filesystem.

With the CVF-FAT extension to the DOS-FAT filesystem, it is possible to access partitions that have been compressed with DoubleSpace/DriveSpace from Microsoft or Stacker from Stac. See the file *Documentation/filesystems/fat_cvf.txt* in the Linux kernel sources for further details.

Chapter 5

/proc is a virtual filesystem; that is, no actual disk space is associated with it. See the */proc* filesystem in Chapter 5, *Essential System Management.*[*]

The ISO 9660 filesystem (previously known as the High Sierra Filesystem and abbreviated *hsfs* on other Unix systems), is used by most CD-ROMs. Like MS-DOS, this filesystem type restricts filename length and stores only limited information about each file. However, most CD-ROMs provide the Rock Ridge Extensions to ISO 9660, which allow the kernel filesystem driver to assign long filenames, ownerships, and permissions to each file. The net result is that accessing an ISO 9660 CD-ROM under MS-DOS gives you 8.3-format filenames, but under Linux gives you the "true," complete filenames.

In addition, Linux now supports the Microsoft Joliet extensions to ISO 9660 which can handle long filenames made up of Unicode characters. This is not widely used now but may become valuable in the future, because Unicode has been accepted internationally as the standard for encoding characters of scripts world-wide.

Next, we have four filesystem types corresponding to other Unix variants found on the personal computer: UFS, Xenix, System V, and Coherent. (The latter three are actually handled by the same kernel driver, with slightly different parameters for each). If you have filesystems created under one of these formats, you'll be able to access the files from Linux.

Finally, there is a slew of filesystems for accessing data on partitions; these are created by operating systems other than the DOS and Unix families. Those filesystems support the Acorn Disk Filing System (ADFS), the AmigaOS filesystems (no floppy disk support except on Amigas), the Apple Mac HFS, and the QNX4 filesystem. Most of the specialized filesystems are useful only on certain hardware architectures; for instance, you won't have hard disks formatted with the Amiga FFS filesystem in an Intel machine. If you need one of those drivers, please read the information that comes with them; some are only in an experimental state.

---

[*] Note that the */proc* filesystem under Linux is not the same format as the */proc* filesystem under SVR4 (say, Solaris 2.x). Under SVR4, each running process has a single "file" entry in */proc*, which can be opened and treated with certain *ioctl()* calls to obtain process information. On the contrary, Linux provides most of its information in */proc* through *read()* and *write()* requests.

Mounting Filesystems

In order to access any filesystem under Linux, you must mount it on a certain directory. This makes the files on the filesystem appear as though they reside in the given directory, allowing you to access them.

The *mount* command is used to do this and usually must be executed as root. (As we'll see later, ordinary users can use *mount* if the device is listed in the */etc/fstab* file.) The format of this command is:

```
mount -t type device mount-point
```

where *type* is the type name of the filesystem as given in Table 6-1, *device* is the physical device where the filesystem resides (the device file in */dev*), and *mount-point* is the directory on which to mount the filesystem. You have to create the directory before issuing *mount*.

For example, if you have a Second Extended filesystem on the partition */dev/hda2*, and wish to mount it on the directory */mnt*, use the command:

```
mount -t ext2 /dev/hda2 /mnt
```

If all goes well you should be able to access the filesystem under */mnt*. Likewise, to mount a floppy that was created on a Windows system and therefore is in DOS format, you use the command:

```
mount -t msdos /dev/fd0 /mnt
```

This makes the files available on an MS-DOS format floppy under */mnt*.

There are many options to the *mount* command, which can be specified with the −*o* switch. For example, the MS-DOS and ISO 9660 filesystems support "auto-conversion" of text files from MS-DOS format (which contain CR-LF at the end of each line), to Unix format (which contain merely a newline at the end of each line). Using a command such as:

```
mount -o conv=auto -t msdos /dev/fd0 /mnt
```

turns on this conversion for files that don't have a filename extension that could be associated with a binary file (such as *.exe*, *.bin*, and so forth).

One common option to mount is −*o ro* (or, equivalently, −*r*), which mounts the filesystem as read-only. All write access to such a filesystem is met with a "permission denied" error. Mounting a filesystem as read-only is necessary for media like CD-ROMs that are nonwritable. You can successfully mount a CD-ROM without the −*r* option, but you'll get the annoying warning message:

```
mount: block device /dev/cdrom is write-protected, mounting read-only
```

Use a command such as:

```
mount -t iso9660 -r /dev/cdrom /mnt
```

instead. This is also necessary if you are trying to mount a floppy that has the write-protect tab in place.

The *mount* manual page lists all available mounting options. Not all are of immediate interest, but you might have a need for some of them, someday.

The inverse of mounting a filesystem is, naturally, unmounting it. Unmounting a filesystem has two effects: it synchronizes the system's buffers with the actual contents of the filesystem on disk, and it makes the filesystem no longer available from its mount point. You are then free to mount another filesystem on that mount point.

Unmounting is done with the *umount* command (note that the first "n" is missing from the word "unmount"), as in:

```
umount /dev/fd0
```

to unmount the filesystem on */dev/fd0*. Similarly, to unmount whatever filesystem is currently mounted on a particular directory, use a command such as:

```
umount /mnt
```

It is important to note that removable media, including floppies and CD-ROMs, should not be removed from the drive or swapped for another disk while mounted. This causes the system's information on the device to be out of sync with what's actually there and could lead to no end of trouble. Whenever you want to switch a floppy or CD-ROM, unmount it first, using the *umount* command, and then remount the device.

Reads and writes to filesystems on floppies are buffered in memory as they are for hard drives. This means that when you read or write data to a floppy, there may not be any immediate drive activity. The system handles I/O on the floppy asynchronously and reads or writes data only when absolutely necessary. So if you copy a small file to a floppy, but the drive light doesn't come on, don't panic; the data will be written eventually. You can use the *sync* command to force the system to write all filesystem buffers to disk, causing a physical write of any buffered data. Unmounting a filesystem makes this happen as well.

If you wish to allow mortal users to mount and unmount certain devices, you have two options. The first option is to include the **user** option for the device in */etc/fstab* (described later in this section). This allows any user to use the *mount* and *umount* command for a given device. Another option is to use one of the mount frontends available for Linux. These programs run setuid **root** and allow ordinary users to mount certain devices. In general, you wouldn't want normal users mounting and unmounting a hard drive partition, but use of CD-ROM and floppy drives might be more lenient on your system.

There are quite a few things that can go wrong when attempting to mount a filesystem. Unfortunately, the *mount* command will give you the same error message in response to a number of problems:

```
mount: wrong fs type, /dev/cdrom already mounted, /mnt busy, or other error
```

wrong fs type is simple enough: this means that you may have specified the wrong type to *mount*. If you don't specify a type, *mount* tries to guess the filesystem type from the superblock (this only works for *minix*, *ext*, *ext2*, *xia* and *iso9660*). If *mount* still cannot determine the type of the filesystem, it tries all the types for which drivers are included in the kernel (as listed in */proc/filesystems*). If this still does not lead to success, *mount* fails. `device` already `mounted` means just that: the device is already mounted on another directory. You can find out what devices are mounted, and where, using the *mount* command with no arguments:

```
rutabaga# mount
/dev/hda2 on / type ext2 (rw)
/dev/hda3 on /msdos type msdos (rw)
/dev/cdrom on /cdrom type iso9660 (ro)
/proc on /proc type proc (rw,none)
```

Here, we see two hard-drive partitions, one of type *ext2* and the other of type *msdos*, a CD-ROM mounted on */cdrom*, and the */proc* filesystem. The last field of each line (for example, (rw)) lists the options under which the filesystem is mounted. More on these soon. Note that the CD-ROM device is mounted in */cdrom*. If you use your CD-ROM often, it's convenient to create the directory */cdrom* and mount the device there. */mnt* is generally used to temporarily mount filesystems such as floppies.

The error *mount-point* busy is rather odd. Essentially, it means there is some activity taking place under *mount-point* that prevents you from mounting a filesystem there. Usually, this means that there is an open file under this directory, or some process has its current working directory beneath *mount-point*. When using *mount*, be sure your root shell is not within *mount-point*; do a *cd /* to get to the top-level directory. Or, another filesystem could be mounted with the same *mount-point*. Use *mount* with no arguments to find out.

Of course, other error isn't very helpful. There are several other cases in which *mount* could fail. If the filesystem in question has data or media errors of some kind, *mount* may report it is unable to read the filesystem's *superblock*, which is (under Unix-like filesystems) the portion of the filesystem that stores information on the files and attributes for the filesystem as a whole. If you attempt to mount a CD-ROM or floppy, and there's no CD-ROM or floppy in the drive, you will receive an error message such as:

```
mount: /dev/cdrom is not a valid block device
```

Floppies are especially prone to physical defects (more so than you might initially think), and CD-ROMs suffer from dust, scratches, and fingerprints, as well as being inserted upside-down—that kind of thing. (If you attempt to mount your Stan Rogers CD as ISO 9660 format, you will likely run into similar problems.)

Also, be sure the mount point you're trying to use (such as */mnt*) exists. If not, you can simply create it with the *mkdir* command.

If you have problems mounting or accessing a filesystem, data on the filesystem may be corrupt. There are several tools that help repair certain filesystem types under Linux; see "Checking and Repairing Filesystems" later in this chapter.

The system automatically mounts several filesystems when the system boots. This is handled by the file */etc/fstab*, which includes an entry for each filesystem that should be mounted at boot time. Each line in this file is of the format:

```
device mount-point type options
```

Here, `device`, `mount-point`, and `type` are equivalent to their meanings in the *mount* command, and `options` is a comma-separated list of options to use with the *–o* switch to *mount*.

A sample */etc/fstab* is shown here:

```
# device         directory        type      options
/dev/hda2        /                ext2      defaults
/dev/hda3        /msdos           msdos     defaults
/dev/cdrom       /cdrom           iso9660   ro
/proc            /proc            proc      none

/dev/hda1        none             swap      sw
```

The last line of this file specifies a swap partition. This is described in the section "Managing Swap Space." later in this chapter.

mount(8)

The *mount* manual page lists the possible values for `options`; if you wish to specify more than one option, you can list them with separating commas and no whitespace, as in:

```
/dev/cdrom        /cdrom           iso9660   ro,user
```

The **user** option allows users other than **root** to mount the filesystem. If this option is present, a user can execute a command such as:

```
mount /cdrom
```

to mount the device. Note that if you specify only a device or mount point (not both) to *mount*, it looks up the device or mount point in */etc/fstab* and mounts the device with the parameters given there. This allows you to mount devices listed in */etc/fstab* with ease.

The option `defaults` should be used for most filesystems; it enables a number of other options, such as `rw` (read-write access), `async` (buffer I/O to the filesystem in memory asynchronously), and so forth. Unless you have a specific need to modify one of these parameters, use `defaults` for most filesystems, and `ro` for read-only devices such as CD-ROMs. Another potentially useful option is `umask` that lets you set the default mask for the permission bits, something that is especially useful with some foreign filesystems.

The command *mount −a* will mount all filesystems listed in */etc/fstab*. This command is executed at boot time by one of the scripts found in */etc/rc.d*, such as *rc.sysinit* (or wherever your distribution stores its configuration files). This way, all filesystems listed in */etc/fstab* will be available when the system starts up; your hard drive partitions, CD-ROM drive, and so on will all be mounted.

There is an exception to this: the *root filesystem*. The root filesystem, mounted on */*, usually contains the file */etc/fstab* as well as the scripts in */etc/rc.d*. In order for these to be available, the kernel itself must mount the root filesystem directly at boot time. The device containing the root filesystem is coded into the kernel image and can be altered using the *rdev* command (see "Using a Boot Floppy" in Chapter 5). While the system boots, the kernel attempts to mount this device as the root filesystem, trying several filesystem types in succession (first Minix, then Extended, and so forth). If at boot time, the kernel prints an error message such as:

Chapter 5

```
VFS: Unable to mount root fs
```

one of the following has happened:

- The root device coded into the kernel is incorrect.

Chapter 7

- The kernel does not have support compiled in for the filesystem type of the root device. (See "Building the Kernel" in Chapter 7 for more details. This is usually relevant only if you build your own kernel.)

- The root device is corrupt in some way.

In any of these cases, the kernel can't proceed and panics. See "What to Do in an Emergency" in Chapter 8, *Other Administrative Tasks*, for clues on what to do in this situation. If filesystem corruption is the problem, this can usually be repaired; see "Checking and Repairing Filesystems" later in this chapter.

Chapter 8

A filesystem does not need to be listed in */etc/fstab* in order to be mounted, but it does need to be listed there in order to be mounted "automatically" by *mount −a*, or to use the `user` mount option.

Automounting Devices

If you need to access a lot of different filesystems, especially networked ones, you might be interested in a fairly new addition to the Linux kernel: the *automounter*. This is a combination of kernel functionality, a daemon, and some configuration files that automatically detect when somebody wants to access a certain filesystem and mounts the filesystem transparently. When the filesystem is not used for some time, the automounter automatically unmounts it in order to save resources like memory and network throughput.

Chapter 7

If you want to use the automounter, you first need to turn this feature on when building your kernel. (See "Building the Kernel" in Chapter 7 for more details.) You will also need to enable the NFS option.

Next, you need to start the *automount* daemon. Since this feature is quite new, your distribution might not yet have it. Look for the directory */usr/lib/autofs*, if it is not there, you will need to get the *autofs* package from your friendly Linux archive and compile and install it according to the instruction.

You can automount filesystems wherever you like, but for simplicity's sake, we will assume here that you want to automount all filesystems below one directory which we will call */automount* here. If you want your automount points to be scattered over your filesystem, you will need to use multiple *automount* daemons.

If you have compiled the *autofs* package yourself, it might be a good idea to start by copying the sample configuration files that you can find in *sample* directory, and adapt them to your needs. To do this, copy the files *sample/auto.master* and *sample/auto.misc* into the */etc* directory, and the file *sample/rc.autofs* under the name *autofs* wherever your distribution stores its boot scripts. We'll assume here that you use */sbin/init.d*.

The first configuration file to edit is */etc/auto.master*. This lists all the directories (the so-called *mount points*) below which the automounter should mount partitions. Since we have decided to use only one partition in this chapter's example, we will need to make only one entry here. The file could look like this:

```
/automount      /etc/auto.misc
```

This file consists of lines with two entries each, separated by whitespace. The first entry specifies the mount point, and the second entry names a so-called *map file* that specifies how and where to mount the devices or partitions to be automounted. You need one such map file for each mount point.

In our case, the file */etc/auto.misc* looks like the following:

```
cd              -fstype=iso9660,ro      :/dev/scd0
floppy          -fstype=auto            :/dev/fd0
```

Again, this file consists of one-line entries that each specify one particular device or partition to be automounted. The lines have two mandatory and one optional field, separated by whitespaces. The first value is mandatory and specifies the directory, onto which the device or partition of this entry is automounted. This value is appended to the mount point so that the CD-ROM will be automounted onto */automount/cd*.

The second value is optional and specifies flags to be used for the *mount* operation. These are equivalent to those for the *mount* command itself, with the exception that the type is specified with the option *-fstype=* instead of *-T*.

Finally, the third value specifies the partition or device to be mounted. In our case, we specify the first SCSI CD-ROM drive and the first floppy drive, respectively. The colon in front of the entry is mandatory; it separates the host part from the device/directory part, just as with *mount*. Since those two devices are on a local machine, there is nothing to the left of the colon. If we wanted to automount the directory *sources* from the NFS server sourcemaster, we would specify something like:

```
sources     -fstype=nfs,soft     sourcemaster:/sources
```

After editing the configuration files to reflect your system, you can start the automount daemon by issuing (replace the path with the path that suits your system):

```
tigger# /sbin/init.d/autofs start
```

Since this command is very taciturn, you should check whether the automounter has really started. One way to do this is to issue:

```
tigger# /sbin/init.d/autofs status
```

but it is difficult to determine from the output whether the automounter is really running. Your best bet, therefore, is to check whether the *automount* process exists:

```
tigger# ps -aux | grep automount
```

If this command shows the automount process, everything should be all right. If it doesn't, you need to check your configuration files again. It could also be the case that the necessary kernel support is not available: either the automount support is not in your kernel, or you have compiled it as a module but not installed this module. If the latter is the case, you can fix the problem by issuing:

```
tigger# modprobe autofs
```

When your automounter works to your satisfaction, you might want to put the *modprobe* call as well as the *autofs* call in one of your system's startup configuration files like */etc/rc.local*, */sbin/init.d/boot.local* or whatever your distribution uses.

If everything is correctly set up, all you need to do is access some directory below the mount point, and the automounter will mount the appropriate device or partition for you. For example, if you type:

```
tigger$ ls /automount/cd
```

the automounter will automatically mount the CD-ROM, so that *ls* can list its contents. The only difference between normal and automounting is that with automounting you will notice is a slight delay, before the output comes.

In order to conserve resources, the automounter unmounts a partition or device if it has not been accessed for a certain amount of time (the default is five minutes).

The automounter supports a number of advanced options; for example, you do not need to read the map table from a file but can also access system databases or even have the automounter run a program and use this program's output as the mapping data. See the man pages for *autofs* and *automount* for further details.

autofs(5)
automount(8)

Creating Filesystems

A filesystem can be created using the *mkfs* command. Creating a filesystem is analogous to "formatting" a partition or floppy, allowing it to store files.

Each filesystem type has its own *mkfs* command associated with it—for example, MS-DOS filesystems may be created using *mkfs.msdos*, Second Extended filesystems using *mkfs.ext2*, and so on. The program *mkfs* itself is a frontend that creates a filesystem of any type by executing the appropriate version of *mkfs* for that type.*

When you installed Linux, you may have created filesystems by hand using a command such as *mke2fs*. (If not, then the installation software created the filesystems for you.) In fact, *mke2fs* is equivalent to *mkfs.ext2*. The programs are the same (and on many systems, one is a symbolic link to the other), but the *mkfs.fs-type* filename makes it easier for *mkfs* to execute the appropriate filesystem-type specific program. If you don't have the *mkfs* frontend, you can use *mke2fs* or *mkfs.ext2* directly.

Assuming that you're using the *mkfs* frontend, a filesystem can be created using this command:

```
mkfs -t type device blocks
```

where `type` is the type of filesystem to create, given in Table 6-1, `device` is the device on which to create the filesystem (such as */dev/fd0* for a floppy), and `blocks` is the size of the filesystem, in 1024-byte blocks.

---

* Under Linux the *mkfs* command historically created a Minix filesystem. On newer Linux systems, *mkfs* is a frontend for any filesystem type, and Minix filesystems are created using *mkfs.minix*.

For example, to create an *ext2* filesystem on a floppy, you use this command:

```
mkfs -t ext2 /dev/fd0 1440
```

Here, `blocks` is 1440, which specifies a 1.44-MB, high-density 3.5-inch floppy. You could create an MS-DOS floppy using *-t msdos* instead.

We can now mount the floppy, as described in the previous section, copy files to it, and so forth. Remember to unmount the floppy before removing it from the drive.

Creating a filesystem deletes all data on the corresponding physical device (floppy, hard-drive partition, whatever). *mkfs* usually does not prompt you before creating a filesystem, so be absolutely sure you know what you're doing.

Chapter 3

Creating a filesystem on a hard-drive partition is done exactly as shown earlier, except that you would use the partition name, such as */dev/hda2*, as the `device`. Don't try to create a filesystem on a device, such as */dev/hda*. This refers to the entire drive, not just a single partition on the drive. You can create partitions using *fdisk*, as described in the section "Creating Linux Partitions" in Chapter 3, *Installation and Initial Configuration.*

You should be especially careful when creating filesystems on hard-drive partitions. Be absolutely sure that the `device` and `size` arguments are correct. If you enter the wrong `device`, you could end up destroying the data on your current filesystems, and if you specify the wrong `size`, you could overwrite data on other partitions. Be sure that `size` corresponds to the partition size as reported by Linux *fdisk.*

When creating filesystems on floppies, it's usually best to do a low-level format first. This lays down the sector and track information on the floppy so that its size can be automatically detected using the devices */dev/fd0* or */dev/fd1*. One way to do a low-level format is with the MS-DOS FORMAT command; another way is with the Linux program *fdformat.** For example, to format the floppy in the first floppy drive, use the command:

```
rutabaga# fdformat /dev/fd0
Double-sided, 80 tracks, 18 sec/track. Total capacity 1440 kB.
Formatting ... done
Verifying ... done
```

Using the *-n* option with *fdformat* will skip the verification step.

Each filesystem-specific version of *mkfs* supports several options you might find useful. Most types support the *-c* option, which causes the physical media to be checked for bad blocks while creating the filesystem. If bad blocks are found, they are marked and avoided when writing data to the filesystem. In order to use these type-specific options, include them after the *-t type* option to *mkfs*, as follows:

---

* Debian users should use *superformat* instead.

```
mkfs -t type -c device blocks
```

To determine what options are available, see the manual page for the type-specific version of *mkfs*. (For example, for the Second Extended filesystem, see *mke2fs*.)

You may not have all available type-specific versions of *mkfs* installed. If this is the case, *mkfs* will fail when you try to create a filesystem of a type for which you have no *mkfs.type*. Many filesystem types supported by Linux have a corresponding *mkfs.type* available, somewhere.

If you run into trouble using *mkfs*, it's possible that Linux is having problems accessing the physical device. In the case of a floppy, this might just mean a bad floppy. In the case of a hard drive, it could be more serious; for example, the disk device driver in the kernel might be having problems reading your drive. This could be a hardware problem or a simple matter of your drive geometry being specified incorrectly. See the manual pages for the various versions of *mkfs*, and read the sections in Chapter 3 on troubleshooting installation problems. They apply equally here.*

Chapter 3

Checking and Repairing Filesystems

It is sometimes necessary to check your Linux filesystems for consistency and repair them if there are any errors or lost data. Such errors commonly result from a system crash or loss of power, where the kernel isn't able to sync the filesystem buffer cache with the contents of the disk. In most cases, such errors are relatively minor. However, if the system were to crash while writing a large file, that file may be lost and the blocks associated with it marked as "in use," when in fact there is no file entry corresponding to them. In other cases, errors can be caused by accidentally writing data directly to the hard-drive device (such as */dev/hda*), or one of the partitions.

The program *fsck* is used to check filesystems and correct any problems. Like *mkfs*, *fsck* is a frontend for a filesystem-type–specific *fsck.type*, such as *fsck.ext2* for Second Extended filesystems. (As with *mkfs.ext2*, *fsck.ext2* is a symbolic link to *e2fsck*, either of which you could execute directly if the *fsck* frontend is not installed.)

Use of *fsck* is quite simple; the format of the command is:

```
fsck -t type device
```

where *type* is the type of filesystem to repair, as given in Table 6-1, and *device* is the device (drive partition or floppy) on which the filesystem resides.

For example, to check an *ext2* filesystem on */dev/hda2*, you use:

---

* Also, the procedure for making an ISO9660 filesystem for a CD-ROM is more complicated than simply formatting a filesystem and copying files. See the CD-Writing HOWTO for more details.

```
rutabaga# fsck -t ext2 /dev/hda2
Parallelizing fsck version 1.06 (7-Oct-96)
e2fsck 1.06, 7-Oct-96 for EXT2 FS 0.5b, 95/08/09
/dev/hda2 is mounted.  Do you really want to continue (y/n)? yes

/dev/hda2 was not cleanly unmounted, check forced.
Pass 1: Checking inodes, blocks, and sizes
Pass 2: Checking directory structure
Pass 3: Checking directory connectivity
Pass 4: Check reference counts.
Pass 5: Checking group summary information.

Free blocks count wrong for group 3 (3331, counted=3396).  FIXED
Free blocks count wrong for group 4 (1983, counted=2597).  FIXED
Free blocks count wrong (29643, counted=30341).  FIXED
Inode bitmap differences: -8280.  FIXED
Free inodes count wrong for group #4 (1405, counted=1406).  FIXED
Free inodes count wrong (34522, counted=34523).  FIXED

/dev/hda2: ***** FILE SYSTEM WAS MODIFIED *****
/dev/hda2: ***** REBOOT LINUX *****
/dev/hda2: 13285/47808 files, 160875/191216 blocks
```

First of all, note that the system asks for confirmation before checking a mounted filesystem. If any errors are found and corrected while using *fsck*, you'll have to reboot the system if the filesystem is mounted. This is because the changes made by *fsck* may not be propagated back to the system's internal knowledge of the filesystem layout. In general, it's not a good idea to check mounted filesystems.

As we can see, several problems were found and corrected, and because this filesystem was mounted, the system informed us that the machine should be rebooted.

How can you check filesystems without mounting them? With the exception of the root filesystem, you can simply *umount* any filesystems before running *fsck* on them. The root filesystem, however, can't be unmounted while running the system. One way to check your root filesystem while it's unmounted is to use a boot/root floppy combination, such as the installation floppies used by your Linux distribution. This way, the root filesystem is contained on a floppy, and the root filesystem (on your hard drive) remains unmounted, and you can check the hard-drive root filesystem from there. See "What to Do in an Emergency" in Chapter 8 for more details about this.

Chapter 8

Another way to check the root filesystem is to mount it read-only. This can be done using the option ro from the LILO boot prompt (see the section "Specifying boot time options" in Chapter 5). However, other parts of your system configuration (for example, the programs executed by */etc/init* at boot time) may require write access to the root filesystem, so you can't boot the system normally or these programs will fail. To boot the system with the root filesystem mounted as read-only you might want to boot the system into single-user mode as well (using the

Chapter 5

boot option `single`). This prevents additional system configuration at boot time; you can then check the root filesystem and reboot the system normally.

To cause the root filesystem to be mounted read-only, you can either use the `ro` boot option, or use *rdev* to set the read-only flag in the kernel image itself.

Many Linux systems automatically check the filesystems at boot time. This is usually done by executing *fsck* from */etc/rc.d/rc.sysinit*. When this is done, the system usually mounts the root filesystem initially as read-only, runs *fsck* to check it, and then runs the command:

```
mount -w -o remount /
```

The *–o remount* option causes the given filesystem to be remounted with the new parameters; in this case, the *–w* option (equivalent to *–o rw*) causes the filesystem to be mounted read-write. The net result is that the root filesystem is remounted with read-write access.

When *fsck* is executed at boot time, it checks all filesystems other than root before they are mounted. Once *fsck* completes, the other filesystems are mounted using *mount*. Check out the files in */etc/rc.d*, especially *rc.sysinit* (if present on your system), to see how this is done. If you want to disable this feature on your system, comment out the lines in the appropriate */etc/rc.d* file that execute *fsck*.

There are several options you can pass to the type-specific *fsck*. Most types support the options *–a*, which automatically confirms any prompts that *fsck.type* may display; *–c*, which does bad-block checking, as with *mkfs*; and *–v*, which prints verbose information during the check operation. These options should be given after the *–t type* argument to *fsck*, as in:

```
fsck -t type -v device
```

to run *fsck* with verbose output.

See the manual pages for *fsck* and *e2fsck* for more information.

Not all filesystem types supported by Linux have a *fsck* variant available. To check and repair MS-DOS filesystems, you should use a tool under MS-DOS, such as the Norton Utilities, to accomplish this task. You should be able to find versions of *fsck* for the Second Extended filesystem, Minix filesystem, and Xia filesystem at least.

Chapter 8

In the section "What to Do in an Emergency" in Chapter 8, we provide additional information on checking filesystems and recovering from disaster. *fsck* will by no means catch and repair every error to your filesystems, but most common problems should be handled. If you delete an important file, there is currently no easy way to recover it—*fsck* can't do that for you. There is work underway to provide an "undelete" utility in the Second extended filesystem. Be sure to keep backups, or use *rm –i*, which always prompts you before deleting a file.

Managing Swap Space

Swap space is a generic term for disk storage used to increase the amount of apparent memory available on the system. Under Linux, swap space is used to implement *paging*, a process whereby memory pages (a page is 4096 bytes on Intel systems; this value can differ on other architectures) are written out to disk when physical memory is low and read back into physical memory when needed. The process by which paging works is rather involved, but it is optimized for certain cases. The virtual memory subsystem under Linux allows memory pages to be shared between running programs. For example, if you have multiple copies of Emacs running simultaneously, there is only one copy of the Emacs code actually in memory. Also, text pages (those pages containing program code, not data) are usually read-only, and therefore not written to disk when swapped out. Those pages are instead freed directly from main memory and read from the original executable file when they are accessed again.

Of course, swap space cannot completely make up for a lack of physical RAM. Disk access is much slower than RAM access, by several orders of magnitude. Therefore, swap is useful primarily as a means to run a number of programs simultaneously that would not otherwise fit into physical RAM; if you are switching between these programs rapidly you'll notice a lag as pages are swapped to and from disk.

At any rate, Linux supports swap space in two forms: as a separate disk partition or a file somewhere on your existing Linux filesystems. You can have up to 16 swap areas, with each swap area being a disk file or partition up to 128 MB in size (again, these values can differ on non-Intel systems). You math whizzes out there will realize that this allows up to 2 GB of swap space. (If anyone has actually attempted to use this much swap, the authors would love to hear about it, whether you're a math whiz or not.)

Note that using a swap partition can yield better performance, because the disk blocks are guaranteed to be contiguous. In the case of a swap file, however, the disk blocks may be scattered around the filesystem, which can be a serious performance hit in some cases. Many people use a swap file when they must add additional swap space temporarily—for example, if the system is thrashing because of lack of physical RAM and swap. Swap files are a good way to add swap on demand.

Chapter 3

Nearly all Linux systems utilize swap space of some kind—usually a single swap partition. In Chapter 3, we explained how to create a swap partition on your system during the Linux installation procedure. In this section we describe how to add and remove swap files and partitions. If you already have swap space and are happy with it, this section may not be of interest to you.

How much swap space do you have? The *free* command reports information on system-memory usage:

```
rutabaga% free
           total       used       free     shared    buffers     cached
Mem:      127888     126744       1144      27640       1884      51988
-/+ buffers:          72872      55016
Swap:     130748      23916     106832
```

All the numbers here are reported in 1024-byte blocks. Here, we see a system with 127,888 blocks (about 127 MB) of physical RAM, with 126,744 (about 126 MB) currently in use. Note that your system actually has more physical RAM than that given in the "total" column; this number does not include the memory used by the kernel for its own sundry needs.

The "shared" column lists the amount of physical memory shared between multiple processes. Here, we see that about 27 MB of pages are being shared, which means that memory is being utilized well. The "buffers" column shows the amount of memory being used by the kernel buffer cache. The buffer cache (described briefly in the previous section) is used to speed up disk operations, by allowing disk reads and writes to be serviced directly from memory. The buffer cache size will increase or decrease as memory usage on the system changes; this memory is reclaimed if it is needed by applications. Therefore, although we see that 126 MB of system memory is in use, not all (but most) of it is being used by application programs. The "cache" column indicates how many memory pages the kernel has cached for faster access later.

Since the memory used for buffers and cache can easily be reclaimed for use by applications, the second line (-/+ buffers/cache) provides an indication of the memory actually used by applications (the "used" column) or available to applications (the "free" column). The sum of the memory used by buffers and cache reported in the first line is subtracted from the total used memory and added to the total free memory to give the two figures on the second line.

In the third line, we see the total amount of swap, 130,748 blocks (about 128 MB). In this case, only very little of the swap is being used; there is plenty of physical RAM available. If additional applications were started, larger parts of the buffer cache memory would be used to host them. Swap space is generally used as a last resort when the system can't reclaim physical memory in other ways.

Note that the amount of swap reported by *free* is somewhat less than the total size of your swap partitions and files. This is because several blocks of each swap area must be used to store a map of how each page in the swap area is being utilized. This overhead should be rather small; only a few kilobytes per swap area.

If you're considering creating a swap file, the *df* command gives you information on the amount of space remaining on your various filesystems. This command prints a list of filesystems, showing each one's size and what percentage is currently occupied.

Creating Swap Space

Chapter 3

The first step in adding additional swap is to create a file or partition to host the swap area. If you wish to create an additional swap partition, you can create the partition using the *fdisk* utility, as described in the section "Creating Linux Partitions" in Chapter 3.

To create a swap file, you'll need to open a file and write bytes to it equaling the amount of swap you wish to add. One easy way to do this is with the *dd* command. For example, to create an 8-MB swap file, you can use the command:

```
dd if=/dev/zero of=/swap bs=1024 count=8192
```

This will write 8192 blocks (8 MB) of data from */dev/zero* to the file */swap*. (*/dev/zero* is a special device in which read operations always return null bytes. It's something like the inverse of */dev/null*.) After creating a file of this size, it's a good idea to use the *sync* command to sync the filesystems in case of a system crash.

Chapter 3

Once you have created the swap file or partition, you can use the *mkswap* command to "format" the swap area. As described in the section "Creating Swap Space" in Chapter 3, the format of the *mkswap* command is:

```
mkswap -c device size
```

where `device` is the name of the swap partition or file, and `size` is the size of the swap area in blocks (again, one block is equal to one kilobyte). You normally do not need to specify this when creating a swap area, because *mkswap* can detect the partition size on its own. The *−c* switch is optional and causes the swap area to be checked for bad blocks as it is formatted.

For example, for the swap file created in the previous example, you would use the command:

```
mkswap -c /swap 8192
```

If the swap area is a partition, you would substitute the name of the partition (such as */dev/hda3*) and the size of the partition, also in blocks.

After running *mkswap* on a swap file, use the *sync* command to ensure the format information has been physically written to the new swap file. Running *sync* is not necessary when formatting a swap partition.

Enabling the Swap Space

In order for the new swap space to be utilized, you must enable it with the *swapon* command. For example, after creating the previous swap file and running *mkswap* and *sync*, we could use the command:

```
swapon /swap
```

This adds the new swap area to the total amount of available swap; use the *free* command to verify that this is indeed the case. If you are using a new swap partition, you can enable it with a command such as:

```
swapon /dev/hda3
```

if */dev/hda3* is the name of the swap partition.

If you are using a swap file (and not a swap partition), you need to change its permissions first, like:

```
chmod 0600 /swap
```

Like filesystems, swap areas are automatically enabled at boot time using the *swapon −a* command from one of the system startup files (usually in */etc/rc.d/rc.sysinit*). This command looks in the file */etc/fstab*, which, as you'll remember from the section "Mounting Filesystems," includes information on filesystems and swap areas. All entries in */etc/fstab* with the `options` field set to sw are enabled by *swapon −a*.

Therefore, if */etc/fstab* contains the entries:

```
# device      directory    type    options
/dev/hda3     none         swap    sw
/swap         none         swap    sw
```

then the two swap areas */dev/hda3* and */swap* will be enabled at boot time. For each new swap area, you should add an entry to */etc/fstab*.

Disabling Swap Space

As is usually the case, undoing a task is easier than doing it. To disable swap space, simply use the command:

```
swapoff device
```

where `device` is the name of the swap partition or file that you wish to disable. For example, to disable swapping on the device */dev/hda3*, use the command:

```
swapoff /dev/hda3
```

If you wish to disable a swap file, you can simply remove the file, using *rm, after* using *swapoff.* Don't remove a swap file before disabling it; this can cause disaster.

If you have disabled a swap partition using *swapoff,* you are free to reuse that partition as you see fit: remove it using *fdisk,* or do whatever.

Also, if there is a corresponding entry for the swap area in */etc/fstab*, remove it. Otherwise, you'll get errors when you next reboot the system and the swap area can't be found.

Device Files

Device files allow user programs to access hardware devices on the system through the kernel. They are not "files" per se, but look like files from the program's point of view: you can read from them, write to them, *mmap()* onto them, and so forth. When you access such a device "file," the kernel recognizes the I/O request and passes it a device driver, which performs some operation, such as reading data from a serial port, or sending data to a sound card.

Device files (although inappropriately named, we will continue to use this term) provide a convenient way to access system resources without requiring the applications programmer to know how the underlying device works. Under Linux, as with most Unix systems, device drivers themselves are part of the kernel. In the section "Building the Kernel" in Chapter 7 , we show you how to build your own kernel, including only those device drivers for the hardware on your system.

Chapter 7

Device files are located in the directory */dev* on nearly all Unix-like systems. Each device on the system should have a corresponding entry in */dev*. For example, */dev/ttyS0* corresponds to the first serial port, known as COM1 under MS-DOS; */dev/hda2* corresponds to the second partition on the first IDE drive. In fact, there should be entries in */dev* for devices you do not have. The device files are generally created during system installation and include every possible device driver. They don't necessarily correspond to the actual hardware on your system.

There are a number of pseudo-devices in */dev* that don't correspond to any actual peripheral. For example, */dev/null* acts as a byte sink; any write request to */dev/null* will succeed, but the data written will be ignored. Similarly, we've already demonstrated the use of */dev/zero* to create a swap file; any read request on */dev/zero* simply returns null bytes.

When using *ls –l* to list device files in */dev*, you'll see something like the following:

```
brw-rw----   1 root     disk      3,   0 May 19 1994 /dev/hda
```

This is */dev/hda*, which corresponds to the first IDE drive. First of all, note that the first letter of the permissions field is b, which means this is a block device file. (Recall that normal files have a – in this first column, directories a d, and so on.) Device files are denoted either by b, for block devices, or c, for character devices. A block device is usually a peripheral such as a hard drive: data is read and written to the device as entire blocks (where the block size is determined by the device; it may not be 1024 bytes as we usually call "blocks" under Linux), and the device may be accessed randomly. In contrast, character devices are usually read or written sequentially, and I/O may be done as single bytes. An example of a character device is a serial port.

Also, note that the size field in the *ls −l* listing is replaced by two numbers, separated by a comma. The first value is the *major device number* and the second is the *minor device number*. When a device file is accessed by a program, the kernel receives the I/O request in terms of the major and minor numbers of the device. The major number generally specifies a particular driver within the kernel, and the minor number specifies a particular device handled by that driver. For example, all serial port devices have the same major number, but different minor numbers. The kernel uses the major number to redirect an I/O request to the appropriate driver, and the driver uses the minor number to figure out which specific device to access. In some cases, minor numbers can also be used for accessing specific functions of a device.

The naming convention used by files in */dev* is, to put it bluntly, a complete mess. Because the kernel itself doesn't care what filenames are used in */dev* (it cares only about the major and minor numbers), the distribution maintainers, applications programmers, and device driver writers are free to choose names for a device file. Often, the person writing a device driver will suggest a name for the device, and later the name will be changed to accommodate other, similar devices. This can cause confusion and inconsistency as the system develops; hopefully, you won't encounter this problem unless you're working with newer device drivers—those that are under testing.

Chapter 7

At any rate, the device files included in your original distribution should be accurate for the kernel version and device drivers included with that distribution. When you upgrade your kernel, or add additional device drivers (see the section "Building a New Kernel" in Chapter 7), you may need to add a device file using the *mknod* command. The format of this command is:

```
mknod -m permissions name type major minor
```

where:

- *name* is the full pathname of the device to create, such as */dev/rft0*.

- *type* is either c for a character device or b for a block device.

- *major* is the major number of the device.

- *minor* is the minor number of the device.

- *−m permissions* is an optional argument that sets the permission bits of the new device file to *permissions*.

For example, let's say you're adding a new device driver to the kernel, and the documentation says that you need to create the block device */dev/bogus*, major number 42, minor number 0. You would use the command:

```
mknod /dev/bogus b 42 0
```

Making devices is even easier with the shell script */dev/MAKEDEV* that comes with many distributions—you specify only the kind of device you want, and *MAKEDEV* finds out the major and minor numbers for you.

If you don't specify the `-m permissions` argument, the new device is given the permissions for a newly created file, modified by your current umask—usually 0644. To set the permissions for */dev/bogus* to 0666 instead, we use:

```
mknod -m 666 /dev/bogus b 42 0
```

You can also use *chmod* to set the permissions for a device file after creation.

Chapter 4

Why are device permissions important? Like any file, the permissions for a device file control who may access the raw device and how. As we saw in the previous example, the device file for */dev/hda* has permissions 0660, which means that only the owner and users in the file's group (here, the group **disk** is used) may read and write directly to this device. (Permissions are introduced in "File Ownership and Permissions" in Chapter 4, *Basic Unix Commands and Concepts*.)

In general, you don't want to give any user direct read and write access to certain devices—especially those devices corresponding to disk drives and partitions. Otherwise, anyone could, say, run *mkfs* on a drive partition and completely destroy all data on the system.

In the case of drives and partitions, write access is required to corrupt data in this way, but read access is a also breach of security; given read access to a raw device file corresponding to a disk partition, a user could peek in on other user's files. Likewise, the device file */dev/mem* corresponds to the system's physical memory (it's generally used only for extreme debugging purposes). Given read access, clever users could spy on other users' passwords, including the one belonging to **root**, as they are entered at login time.

Be sure that the permissions for any device you add to the system correspond to how the device can and should be accessed by users. Devices such as serial ports, sound cards, and virtual consoles are generally safe for mortals to have access to, but most other devices on the system should be limited to use by **root** (and programs running setuid as **root**).

Many files found in */dev* are actually symbolic links (created using *ln -s*, in the usual way) to another device file. These links make it easier to access certain devices by using a more common name. For example, if you have a serial mouse, that mouse might be accessed through one of the device files */dev/ttyS0*, */dev/ttyS1*, */dev/ttyS2*, or */dev/ttyS3*, depending on which serial port the mouse is attached to. Many people create a link named */dev/mouse* to the appropriate serial device, as in:

```
ln -s /dev/ttyS2 /dev/mouse
```

In this way, we can access the mouse from */dev/mouse*, instead of having to remember which serial port it is on. This convention is also used for devices such as */dev/cdrom* and */dev/modem*. These files are usually symbolic links to a device file in */dev* corresponding to the actual CD-ROM or modem device.

To remove a device file, just use *rm*, as in:

```
rm /dev/bogus
```

Removing a device file does not remove the corresponding device driver from memory or from the kernel; it simply leaves you with no means to talk to a particular device driver. Similarly, adding a device file does not add a device driver to the system; in fact, you can add device files for drivers that don't even exist. Device files simply provide a "hook" into a particular device driver should such a driver exist in the kernel.

CHAPTER SEVEN
UPGRADING SOFTWARE AND THE KERNEL

In this chapter, we'll show you how to upgrade software on your system, including rebuilding and installing a new operating system kernel. Although most Linux distributions provide some automated means to install, remove, and upgrade specific software packages on your system, it is often necessary to install software by hand. The kernel is the operating system itself. It is a set of routines and data that is loaded by the system at boot time and controls everything on the system: software access to hardware devices, scheduling of user processes, memory management, and more. Building your own kernel is often beneficial, as you can select which features you want included in the operating system.

Installing and upgrading free software is usually more complicated than installing commercial products. Even when you have precompiled binaries available, you may have to uncompress them and unpack them from an archive file. You may also have to create symbolic links or set environment variables so that the binaries know where to look for the resources they use. In other cases, you'll need to compile the software yourself from sources.

Another common Linux activity is building the kernel. This is an important task for several reasons. First of all, you may find yourself in a position where you need to upgrade your current kernel to a newer version, to pick up new features or hardware support. Secondly building the kernel yourself allows you to select which features you do (and do not) want included in the compiled kernel.

Why is the ability to select features a win for you? All kernel code and data is "locked down" in memory; that is, it cannot be swapped out to disk. For example, if you use a kernel image with drivers for hardware you do not have or use, the memory consumed by those hardware drivers cannot be reclaimed for use by user applications. Customizing the kernel allows you to trim it down for your needs.

Archive and Compression Utilities

When installing or upgrading software on Unix systems, the first things you need to be familiar with are the tools used for compressing and archiving files. There are dozens of such utilities available. Some of these (such as *tar* and *compress*) date back to the earliest days of Unix; others (such as *gzip*) are relative newcomers. The main goal of these utilities is to archive files (that is, to pack many files together into a single file for easy transportation or backup) and to compress files (to reduce the amount of disk space required to store a particular file or set of files).

In this section, we're going to discuss the most common file formats and utilities you're likely to run into. For instance, a near-universal convention in the Unix world is to transport files or software as a *tar* archive, compressed using *compress* or *gzip*. In order to create or unpack these files yourself, you'll need to know the tools of the trade. The tools are most often used when installing new software or creating backups—the subject of the following two sections in this chapter.

Using gzip and bzip2

gzip is a fast and efficient compression program distributed by the GNU project. The basic function of *gzip* is to take a file, compress it, save the compressed version as *filename.gz*, and remove the original, uncompressed file. The original file is removed only if *gzip* is successful; it is very difficult to accidentally delete a file in this manner. Of course, being GNU software, *gzip* has more options than you want to think about, and many aspects of its behavior can be modified using command-line options.

First, let's say that we have a large file named *garbage.txt*:

```
rutabaga% ls -l garbage.txt
-rw-r--r--   1 mdw        hack         312996 Nov 17 21:44 garbage.txt
```

To compress this file using *gzip*, we simply use the command:

```
gzip garbage.txt
```

This replaces *garbage.txt* with the compressed file *garbage.txt.gz*. What we end up with is the following:

```
rutabaga% gzip garbage.txt
rutabaga% ls -l garbage.txt.gz
-rw-r--r--   1 mdw        hack         103441 Nov 17 21:44 garbage.txt.gz
```

Note that *garbage.txt* is removed when *gzip* completes.

You can give *gzip* a list of filenames; it compresses each file in the list, storing each with a *.gz* extension. (Unlike the *zip* program for Unix and MS-DOS systems, *gzip* will not, by default, compress several files into a single *.gz* archive. That's what *tar* is for; see the next section.)

How efficiently a file is compressed depends upon its format and contents. For example, many graphics file formats (such as GIF and JPEG) are already well compressed, and *gzip* will have little or no effect upon such files. Files that compress well usually include plain-text files, and binary files such as executables and libraries. You can get information on a gzipped file using *gzip –l*. For example:

```
rutabaga% gzip -l garbage.txt.gz
compressed   uncompr. ratio uncompressed_name
   103115    312996  67.0% garbage.txt
```

To get our original file back from the compressed version, we use *gunzip*, as in:

```
gunzip garbage.txt.gz
```

After doing this, we get:

```
rutabaga% gunzip garbage.txt.gz
rutabaga% ls -l garbage.txt
-rw-r--r--   1 mdw        hack       312996 Nov 17 21:44 garbage.txt
```

which is identical to the original file. Note that when you *gunzip* a file, the compressed version is removed once the uncompression is complete.

gzip stores the name of the original, uncompressed file in the compressed version. This way, if the compressed filename (including the *.gz* extension) is too long for the filesystem type (say, you're compressing a file on an MS-DOS filesystem with 8.3 filenames), the original filename can be restored using *gunzip* even if the compressed file had a truncated name. To uncompress a file to its original filename, use the *–N* option with *gunzip*. To see the value of this option, consider the following sequence of commands:

```
rutabaga% gzip garbage.txt
rutabaga% mv garbage.txt.gz rubbish.txt.gz
```

If we were to *gunzip rubbish.txt.gz* at this point, the uncompressed file would be named *rubbish.txt*, after the new (compressed) filename. However, with the *–N* option, we get:

```
rutabaga% gunzip -N rubbish.txt.gz
rutabaga% ls -l garbage.txt
-rw-r--r--   1 mdw        hack       312996 Nov 17 21:44 garbage.txt
```

gzip and *gunzip* can also compress or uncompress data from standard input and output. If *gzip* is given no filenames to compress, it attempts to compress data read from standard input. Likewise, if you use the *–c* option with *gunzip*, it writes uncompressed data to standard output. For example, you could pipe the output of a command to *gzip* to compress the output stream and save it to a file in one step, as in:

```
rutabaga% ls -laR $HOME | gzip > filelist.gz
```

This will produce a recursive directory listing of your home directory and save it in the compressed file *filelist.gz*. You can display the contents of this file with the command:

```
rutabaga% gunzip -c filelist.gz | more
```

This will uncompress *filelist.gz* and pipe the output to the *more* command. When you use *gunzip –c*, the file on disk remains compressed.

The *zcat* command is identical to *gunzip –c*. You can think of this as a version of *cat* for compressed files. Linux even has a version of the pager *less* for compressed files, called *zless*.

When compressing files, you can use one of the options *–1*, *–2*, through *–9* to specify the speed and quality of the compression used. *–1* (also *--fast*) specifies the fastest method, which compresses the files less compactly, while *–9* (also *--best*) uses the slowest, but best compression method. If you don't specify one of these options the default is *–6*. None of these options has any bearing on how you use *gunzip*; *gunzip* will be able to uncompress the file no matter what speed option you use.

gzip is relatively new in the Unix world. The compression programs used on most Unix systems are *compress* and *uncompress*, which were included in the original Berkeley versions of Unix. *compress* and *uncompress* are very much like *gzip* and *gunzip*, respectively; *compress* saves compressed files as *filename.Z* as opposed to *filename.gz*, and uses a slightly less efficient compression algorithm.

However, the free software community has been moving to *gzip* for several reasons. First of all, *gzip* works better. Second there has been a patent dispute over the compression algorithm used by *compress*—the results of which could prevent third parties from implementing the *compress* algorithm on their own. Because of this, the Free Software Foundation urged a move to *gzip*, which at least the Linux community has embraced. *gzip* has been ported to many architectures, and many others are following suit. Happily, *gunzip* is able to uncompress the *.Z* format files produced by *compress*.

Another compression/decompression program has also emerged to take the lead from *gzip*. *bzip2* is the new kid on the block and sports even better compression (on the average about 10-20 percent better than *gzip*), at the expense of longer compression times. You cannot use *bunzip2* to uncompress files compressed with *gzip* and vice versa, and since you cannot expect everybody to have *bunzip2* installed on their machine, you might want to confine yourself to *gzip* for the time being if you want to send the compressed file to somebody else. However, it pays to have *bzip2* installed, because more and more FTP servers now provide *bzip2*-compressed packages in order to conserve disk space and bandwidth. You can recognize *bzip2*-compressed files from their typical *.bz2* file name extension.

bzip2 (1)

While the command-line options of *bzip2* are not exactly the same as those of *gzip*, those that have been described in this section are. For more information, see the *bzip2* manual page.

The bottom line is that you should use *gzip/gunzip* or *bzip2/bunzip2* for your compression needs. If you encounter a file with the extension *.Z*, it was probably produced by *compress*, and *gunzip* can uncompress it for you.

Earlier versions of *gzip* used *.z* (lowercase) instead of *.gz* as the compressed-file-name extension. Because of the potential confusion with *.Z*, this was changed. At any rate, *gunzip* retains backwards-compatibility with a number of filename extensions and file types.

Using tar

tar is a general-purpose archiving utility capable of packing many files into a single archive file, retaining information, such as file permissions and ownership. The name *tar* stands for *tape archive*, because the tool was originally used to archive files as backups on tape. However, use of *tar* is not at all restricted to making tape backups, as we'll see.

The format of the *tar* command is:

```
tar functionoptions files...
```

where *function* is a single letter indicating the operation to perform, *options* is a list of (single-letter) options to that function, and *files* is the list of files to pack or unpack in an archive. (Note that *function* is not separated from *options* by any space.)

function can be one of:

c   To create a new archive

x   To extract files from an archive

t   To list the contents of an archive

r   To append files to the end of an archive

u   To update files that are newer than those in the archive

d   To compare files in the archive to those in the filesystem

You'll rarely use most of these functions; the more commonly used are c, x, and t.

The most common *options* are:

v   To print verbose information when packing or unpacking archives *k*   To keep any existing files when extracting—that is, to not overwrite any existing files which are contained within the tar file

f `filename`
    To specify that the tar file to be read or written is `filename`

z   To specify that the data to be written to the tar file should be compressed or that the data in the tar file is compressed with *gzip*

v   To make *tar* show the files it is archiving or restoring—it is good practice to use this so that you can see what actually happens (unless, of course, you are writing shell scripts)

There are others, which we will cover later in this section.

Although the *tar* syntax might appear complex at first, in practice it's quite simple. For example, say we have a directory named *mt*, containing these files:

```
rutabaga% ls -l mt
total 37
-rw-r--r--   1 root      root          24 Sep 21  1993 Makefile
-rw-r--r--   1 root      root         847 Sep 21  1993 README
-rwxr-xr-x   1 root      root        9220 Nov 16 19:03 mt
-rw-r--r--   1 root      root        2775 Aug  7  1993 mt.1
-rw-r--r--   1 root      root        6421 Aug  7  1993 mt.c
-rw-r--r--   1 root      root        3948 Nov 16 19:02 mt.o
-rw-r--r--   1 root      root       11204 Sep  5  1993 st_info.txt
```

We wish to pack the contents of this directory into a single *tar* archive. To do this, we use the command:

```
tar cf mt.tar mt
```

The first argument to *tar* is the `function` (here, c, for create) followed by any `options`. Here, we use the one option *f mt.tar*, to specify that the resulting tar archive be named *mt.tar*. The last argument is the name of the file or files to archive; in this case, we give the name of a directory, so *tar* packs all files in that directory into the archive.

Note that the first argument to *tar* must be a function letter followed by a list of options. Because of this, there's no reason to use a hyphen (-) to precede the options as many Unix commands require. *tar* allows you to use a hyphen, as in:

```
tar -cf mt.tar mt
```

but it's really not necessary. In some versions of *tar*, the first letter must be the `function`, as in c, t, or x. In other versions, the order of letters does not matter.

The function letters as described here follow the so-called "old option style." There is also a newer "short option style" where you precede the function options with a hyphen, and a "long option style," where you use long option names with two hyphens. See the Info page for *tar* for more details if you are interested.

It is often a good idea to use the v option with *tar*; this lists each file as it is archived. For example:

```
rutabaga% tar cvf mt.tar mt
mt/
mt/st_info.txt
mt/README
mt/mt.1
mt/Makefile
mt/mt.c
mt/mt.o
mt/mt
```

If you use v multiple times, additional information will be printed, as in:

```
rutabaga% tar cvvf mt.tar mt
drwxr-xr-x root/root          0 Nov 16 19:03 1994 mt/
-rw-r--r-- root/root      11204 Sep  5 13:10 1993 mt/st_info.txt
-rw-r--r-- root/root        847 Sep 21 16:37 1993 mt/README
-rw-r--r-- root/root       2775 Aug  7 09:50 1993 mt/mt.1
-rw-r--r-- root/root         24 Sep 21 16:03 1993 mt/Makefile
-rw-r--r-- root/root       6421 Aug  7 09:50 1993 mt/mt.c
-rw-r--r-- root/root       3948 Nov 16 19:02 1994 mt/mt.o
-rwxr-xr-x root/root       9220 Nov 16 19:03 1994 mt/mt
```

This is especially useful as it lets you verify that *tar* is doing the right thing.

Chapter 8

In some versions of *tar*, f must be the last letter in the list of options. This is because *tar* expects the f option to be followed by a filename—the name of the tar file to read from or write to. If you don't specify f *filename* at all, *tar* assumes for historical reasons that it should use the device */dev/rmt0* (that is, the first tape drive). In the section "Making Backups," in Chapter 8, *Other Administrative Tasks*, we'll talk about using *tar* in conjunction with a tape drive to make backups.

Now, we can give the file *mt.tar* to other people, and they can extract it on their own system. To do this, they would use the command:

```
tar xvf mt.tar
```

This creates the subdirectory *mt* and places all the original files into it, with the same permissions as found on the original system. The new files will be owned by the user running the *tar xvf* (you) unless you are running as **root**, in which case the original owner is preserved. The x option stands for "extract." The *v* option is used again here to list each file as it is extracted. This produces:

```
courgette% tar xvf mt.tar
mt/
mt/st_info.txt
mt/README
mt/mt.1
mt/Makefile
mt/mt.c
```

```
mt/mt.o
mt/mt
```

We can see that *tar* saves the pathname of each file relative to the location where the tar file was originally created. That is, when we created the archive using *tar cf mt.tar mt*, the only input filename we specified was *mt*, the name of the directory containing the files. Therefore, *tar* stores the directory itself and all of the files below that directory in the tar file. When we extract the tar file, the directory *mt* is created and the files placed into it, which is the exact inverse of what was done to create the archive.

By default, *tar* extracts all tar files relative to the current directory where you execute *tar*. For example, if you were to pack up the contents of your */bin* directory with the command:

```
tar cvf bin.tar /bin
```

tar would give the warning:

```
tar: Removing leading / from absolute path names in the archive.
```

What this means is that the files are stored in the archive within the subdirectory *bin*. When this tar file is extracted, the directory *bin* is created in the working directory of *tar*—not as */bin* on the system where the extraction is being done. This is very important and is meant to prevent terrible mistakes when extracting tar files. Otherwise, extracting a tar file packed as, say, */bin*, would trash the contents of your */bin* directory when you extracted it. If you really wanted to extract such a tar file into */bin*, you would extract it from the root directory, */*. You can override this behavior using the *P* option when packing tar files, but it's not recommended you do so.

Another way to create the tar file *mt.tar* would have been to *cd* into the *mt* directory itself, and use a command such as:

```
tar cvf mt.tar *
```

This way the *mt* subdirectory would not be stored in the tar file; when extracted, the files would be placed directly in your current working directory. One fine point of *tar* etiquette is to always pack tar files so that they contain a subdirectory, as we did in the first example with *tar cvf mt.tar mt*. Therefore, when the archive is extracted, the subdirectory is also created and any files placed there. This way you can ensure that the files won't be placed directly in your current working directory; they will be tucked out of the way and prevent confusion. This also saves the person doing the extraction the trouble of having to create a separate directory (should they wish to do so) to unpack the tar file. Of course, there are plenty of situations where you wouldn't want to do this. So much for etiquette.

When creating archives, you can, of course, give *tar* a list of files or directories to pack into the archive. In the first example, we have given *tar* the single directory *mt*, but in the previous paragraph we used the wildcard *, which the shell expands into the list of filenames in the current directory.

Before extracting a tar file, it's usually a good idea to take a look at its table of contents to determine how it was packed. This way you can determine whether you do need to create a subdirectory yourself where you can unpack the archive. A command such as:

```
tar tvf tarfile
```

lists the table of contents for the named `tarfile`. Note that when using the t function, only one v is required to get the long file listing, as in this example:

```
courgette% tar tvf mt.tar
drwxr-xr-x root/root         0 Nov 16 19:03 1994 mt/
-rw-r--r-- root/root     11204 Sep  5 13:10 1993 mt/st_info.txt
-rw-r--r-- root/root       847 Sep 21 16:37 1993 mt/README
-rw-r--r-- root/root      2775 Aug  7 09:50 1993 mt/mt.1
-rw-r--r-- root/root        24 Sep 21 16:03 1993 mt/Makefile
-rw-r--r-- root/root      6421 Aug  7 09:50 1993 mt/mt.c
-rw-r--r-- root/root      3948 Nov 16 19:02 1994 mt/mt.o
-rwxr-xr-x root/root      9220 Nov 16 19:03 1994 mt/mt
```

No extraction is being done here; we're just displaying the archive's table of contents. We can see from the filenames that this file was packed with all files in the subdirectory *mt*, so that when we extract the tar file, the directory *mt* will be created, and the files placed there.

You can also extract individual files from a tar archive. To do this, use the command:

```
tar xvf tarfile files
```

where `files` is the list of files to extract. As we've seen, if you don't specify any `files`, *tar* extracts the entire archive.

When specifying individual files to extract, you must give the full pathname as it is stored in the tar file. For example, if we wanted to grab just the file *mt.c* from the previous archive *mt.tar*, we'd use the command:

```
tar xvf mt.tar mt/mt.c
```

This would create the subdirectory *mt* and place the file *mt.c* within it.

tar has many more options than those mentioned here. These are the features that you're likely to use most of the time, but GNU *tar*, in particular, has extensions that make it ideal for creating backups and the like. See the *tar* manual page and the following section for more information.

Using tar with gzip

tar does not compress the data stored in its archives in any way. If you are creating a tar file from three 200K files, you'll end up with an archive of about 600K. It is common practice to compress tar archives with *gzip* (or the older *compress* program). You could create a gzipped tar file using the commands:

```
tar cvf tarfile files...
gzip -9 tarfile
```

But that's so cumbersome, and requires you to have enough space to store the uncompressed *tar* file before you *gzip* it.

A much trickier way to accomplish the same task is to use an interesting feature of *tar* that allows you to write an archive to standard output. If you specify – as the tar file to read or write, the data will be read from or written to standard input or output. For example, we can create a gzipped tar file using the command:

```
tar cvf - files... | gzip -9 > tarfile.tar.gz
```

Here, *tar* creates an archive from the named `files` and writes it to standard output; next, *gzip* reads the data from standard input, compresses it, and writes the result to its own standard output; finally, we redirect the gzipped tar file to *tarfile.tar.gz*.

We could extract such a tar file using the command:

```
gunzip -9c tarfile.tar.gz | tar xvf -
```

gunzip uncompresses the named archive file, writes the result to standard output, which is read by *tar* on standard input and extracted. Isn't Unix fun?

Of course, both of these commands are rather cumbersome to type. Luckily, the GNU version of *tar* provides the *z* option which automatically creates or extracts gzipped archives. (We saved the discussion of this option until now, so you'd truly appreciate its convenience.) For example, we could use the commands:

```
tar cvzf tarfile.tar.gz files...
```

and:

```
tar xvzf tarfile.tar.gz
```

to create and extract gzipped tar files. Note that you should name the files created in this way with the *.tar.gz* filename extensions (or the equally often used *.tgz*, which also works on systems with limited filename capabilities), to make their format obvious. The *z* option works just as well with other tar functions such as t.

Only the GNU version of *tar* supports the *z* option; if you are using *tar* on another Unix system, you may have to use one of the longer commands to accomplish the same tasks. Nearly all Linux systems use GNU *tar*.

When you want to use *tar* in conjunction with *bzip2*, you need to tell *tar* about your compression program preferences like this:

```
tar cvf tarfile.tar.bz2 --use-compress-program=bzip2 files...
```

or, shorter:

```
tar cvf tarfile.tar.bz2 --use=bzip2 files...
```

or, shorter still:

```
tar cvIf tarfile.tar.bz2 files
```

The latter version only works with newer versions of GNU *tar* that supports the *I* option.

Keeping this in mind, you could write short shell scripts or aliases to handle cookbook tar file creation and extraction for you. Under *bash*, you could include the following functions in your *.bashrc*:

```
tarc () { tar czvf $1.tar.gz $1 }
tarx () { tar xzvf $1 }
tart () { tar tzvf $1 }
```

With these functions, to create a gzipped tar file from a single directory, you could use the command:

```
tarc directory
```

The resulting archive file would be named *directory.tar.gz*. (Be sure that there's no trailing slash on the directory name; otherwise the archive will be created as *.tar.gz* within the given directory.) To list the table of contents of a gzipped tar file, just use:

```
tart file.tar.gz
```

Or, to extract such an archive, use:

```
tarx file.tar.gz
```

tar Tricks

Because *tar* saves the ownership and permissions of files in the archive and retains the full directory structure, as well as symbolic and hard links, using *tar* is an excellent way to copy or move an entire directory tree from one place to another on the same system (or even between different systems, as we'll see). Using the – syntax described earlier, you can write a tar file to standard output, which is read and extracted on standard input elsewhere.

For example, say that we have a directory containing two subdirectories: *from-stuff* and *to-stuff*. *from-stuff* contains an entire tree of files, symbolic links, and so forth—something that is difficult to mirror precisely using a recursive *cp*. In order to mirror the entire tree beneath *from-stuff* to *to-stuff*, we could use the commands:

```
cd from-stuff
tar cf - . | (cd ../to-stuff; tar xvf -)
```

Simple and elegant, right? We start in the directory *from-stuff* and create a tar file of the current directory, which is written to standard output. This archive is read by a subshell (the commands contained within parentheses); the subshell does a *cd* to the target directory, *../to-stuff* (relative to *from-stuff*, that is), and then runs *tar xvf*, reading from standard input. No tar file is ever written to disk; the data is sent entirely via pipe from one *tar* process to another. The second *tar* process has the *v* option that prints each file as it's extracted; in this way, we can verify that the command is working as expected.

In fact, you could transfer directory trees from one machine to another (via the network) using this trick; just include an appropriate *rsh* command within the subshell on the right side of the pipe. The remote shell would execute *tar* to read the archive on its standard input. (Actually, GNU *tar* has facilities to read or write tar files automatically from other machines over the network; see the *tar* manual page for details.)

tar(1)

Upgrading Software

Linux is a fast-moving target. Because of the cooperative nature of the project, new software is always becoming available, and programs are constantly being updated with newer versions. This is especially true of the Linux kernel, which has many groups of people working on it. During the development process, it's not uncommon for a new kernel patch to be released on a nightly basis. While other parts of the system may not be as dynamic, the same principles apply.

With this constant development, how can you possibly hope to stay on top of the most recent versions of your system software? The short answer is, you can't. While there are people out there who have a need to stay current with, say, the nightly kernel patch release, for the most part, there's no reason to bother upgrading your software this often. In this section, we're going to talk about why and when to upgrade and show you how to upgrade several important parts of the system.

When should you upgrade? In general, you should consider upgrading a portion of your system only when you have a demonstrated *need* to upgrade. For example, if you hear of a new release of some application that fixes important bugs (that is, those bugs that actually affect your personal use of the application), you might want to consider upgrading that application. If the new version of the program provides new features you might find useful, or has a performance boost over your present version, it's also a good idea to upgrade. When your machine is somehow connected to the Internet, another good reason for upgrading would be plugging in a security hole that has been recently reported. However, upgrading just for the sake of having the newest version of a particular program is probably silly.

Upgrading can sometimes be a painful thing to do. For example, you might want to upgrade a program that requires the newest versions of the compiler, libraries, and other software in order to run. Upgrading this program will also require you to upgrade several other parts of the system, which can be a time-consuming process. On the other hand, this can be seen as an argument for keeping your software up to date; if your compiler and libraries are current, upgrading the program in question won't be a problem.

Chapter 1

How can you find out about new versions of Linux software? The best way is to watch the Usenet newsgroup *comp.os.linux.announce* (see the section "Usenet Newsgroups" in Chapter 1, *Introduction to Linux*) where announcements of new software releases and other important information are posted. If you have Internet access, you can then download the software via FTP and install it on your system. Another good source to learn about new Linux software is the web site *http://www.freshmeat.net.*

If you don't have access to Usenet or the Internet, the best way to keep in touch with recent developments is to pay for a CD-ROM subscription. Here you receive an updated copy of the various Linux FTP sites, on CD-ROM, every couple of months. This service is available from a number of Linux vendors. It's a good thing to have, even if you have Internet access.

This brings us to another issue: what's the best upgrade method? Some people feel it's easier to completely upgrade the system by reinstalling everything from scratch whenever a new version of their favorite distribution is released. This way you don't have to worry about various versions of the software working together. For those without Internet access, this may indeed be the easiest method; if you receive a new CD-ROM only once every two months, a great deal of your software may be out of date.

It's our opinion, however, that reinstallation is not a good upgrade plan at all. Most of the current Linux distributions are not meant to be upgraded in this way, and a complete reinstallation may be complex or time-consuming. Also, if you plan to upgrade in this manner, you generally lose all your modifications and customizations to the system, and you'll have to make backups of your user's home directories and any other important files that would be deleted during a reinstallation. Many novices choose this upgrade path because it's the easiest to follow. In actuality, not much changes from release to release, so a complete reinstallation is usually unnecessary and can be avoided with a little upgrading know-how.

In this section, we'll show you how to upgrade various pieces of your system individually. We'll show you how to upgrade your system libraries and compiler, as well as give you a generic method for installing new software. In the following section, we'll talk about building a new kernel.

Upgrading Libraries

Most of the programs on a Linux system are compiled to use shared libraries. These libraries contain useful functions common to many programs. Instead of storing a copy of these routines in each program that calls them, the libraries are contained in files on the system that are read by all programs at run-time. That is, when a program is executed, the code from the program file itself is read, followed by any routines from the shared library files. This saves a great deal of disk space; only one copy of the library routines is stored on disk.

In some instances, it's necessary to compile a program to have its own copy of the library routines (usually for debugging) instead of using the routines from the shared libraries. We say that programs built in this way are *statically linked*, while programs built to use shared libraries are *dynamically linked*.

Therefore, dynamically linked executables depend upon the presence of the shared libraries on disk. Shared libraries are implemented in such a way that the programs compiled to use them generally don't depend on the version of the available libraries. This means that you can upgrade your shared libraries, and all programs that are built to use those libraries will automatically use the new routines. (There is an exception: if major changes are made to a library, the old programs won't work with the new library. You'll know this is the case because the major version number is different; we'll explain more later. In this case, you keep both the old and new libraries around. All your old executables will continue to use the old libraries, and any new programs that are compiled will use the new libraries.)

When you build a program to use shared libraries, a piece of code is added to the program that causes it to execute *ld.so*, the dynamic linker, when the program is started. *ld.so* is responsible for finding the shared libraries the program needs and loading the routines into memory. Dynamically linked programs are also linked against "stub" routines, which simply take the place of the actual shared library routines in the executable. *ld.so* replaces the stub routine with the code from the libraries when the program is executed.

The *ldd* command can be used to list the shared libraries on which a given executable depends. For example:

```
rutabaga% ldd /usr/bin/X11/xterm
        libXaw.so.6 => /usr/X11R6/lib/libXaw.so.6.0
        libXt.so.6 => /usr/X11R6/lib/libXt.so.6.0
        libX11.so.6 => /usr/X11R6/lib/libX11.so.6.0
        libc.so.5 => /lib/libc.so.5.0.9
```

Here, we see that the *xterm* program depends on the four shared libraries *libXaw*, *libXt*, *libX11*, and *libc*. (The first three are related to the X Window System, and the last is the standard C library.) We also see the version numbers of the libraries for which the program was compiled (that is, the version of the stub routines used), and the name of the file which contains each shared library. This is the file that *ld.so* will find when the program is executed.

In order to use a shared library, the version of the stub routines (in the executable) must be compatible with the version of the shared libraries. Basically, a library is compatible if its major version number matches that of the stub routines. The major version number is the part before the first period in the version number; in 6.0, the major number is 6. This way, if a program was compiled with version 6.0 of the stub routines, shared library versions 6.1, 6.2, and so forth could be used by the executable. In the section "More Fun with Libraries" in Chapter 13, *Programming Languages*, we describe how to use shared libraries with your own programs.

Chapter 13

The file */etc/ld.so.conf* contains a list of directories that *ld.so* searches to find shared library files. An example of such a file is:

```
/usr/lib
/usr/local/lib
/usr/X11R6/lib
```

ld.so always looks in */lib* and */usr/lib*, regardless of the contents of *ld.so.conf*. Usually, there's no reason to modify this file, and the environment variable `LD_LIBRARY_PATH` can add additional directories to this search path (e.g., if you have your own private shared libraries that shouldn't be used systemwide). However, if you do add entries to */etc/ld.so.conf* or upgrade or install additional libraries on your system, be sure to use the *ldconfig* command which will regenerate the shared library cache in */etc/ld.so.cache* from the *ld.so* search path. This cache is used by *ld.so* to find libraries quickly at runtime without actually having to search the directories on its path. For more information, check the manual pages for *ld.so* and *ldconfig*.

Now that you understand how shared libraries are used, let's move on to upgrading them. The two libraries that are most commonly updated are *libc* (the standard C library) and *libm* (the math library). For each shared library, there are two separate files:

library.a
> This is the static version of the library. When a program is statically linked, routines are copied from this file directly into the executable, so the executable contains its own copy of the library routines.

library.so.version
> This is the shared library image itself. When a program is dynamically linked, the stub routines from this file are copied into the executable, allowing *ld.so* to locate the shared library at runtime. When the program is executed, *ld.so* copies routines from the shared library into memory for use by the program. If a program is dynamically linked, the *library.a* file is not used for this library.

For the *libc* library, you'll have files such as *libc.a* and *libc.so.5.2.18*. The *.a* files are generally kept in */usr/lib*, while *.so* files are kept in */lib*. When you compile a program, either the *.a* or the *.so* file is used for linking, and the compiler looks in */lib* and */usr/lib* (as well as a variety of other places) by default. If you have your own libraries, you can keep these files anywhere, and control where the linker looks with the −*L* option to the compiler. See the section "More Fun with Libraries" in Chapter 13 for details.

Chapter 13

The shared library image, *library.so.version*, is kept in */lib* for most systemwide libraries. Shared library images can be found in any of the directories that *ld.so* searches at runtime; these include */lib*, */usr/lib*, and the files listed in *ld.so.conf.* See the *ld.so* manual page for details.

If you look in */lib*, you'll see a collection of files such as the following:

```
lrwxrwxrwx  1 root    root        14 Oct 23 13:25 libc.so.5 -> libc.so.5.2.18
-rwxr-xr-x  1 root    root    623620 Oct 23 13:24 libc.so.5.2.18
lrwxrwxrwx  1 root    root        15 Oct 17 22:17 libvga.so.1 ->\
libvga.so.1.2.10
-rwxr-xr-x  1 root    root    128004 Oct 17 22:17 libvga.so.1.2.10
```

Here, we see the shared library images for two libraries—*libc* and *libvga*. Note that each image has a symbolic link to it, named *library.so.major*, where `major` is the major version number of the library. The minor number is omitted because *ld.so* searches for a library only by its major version number. When *ld.so* sees a program that has been compiled with the stubs for version 5.2.18 of *libc*, it looks for a file called *libc.so.5* in its search path. Here, */lib/libc.so.5* is a symbolic link to */lib/libc.so.5.2.18*, the actual version of the library we have installed.

When you upgrade a library, you must replace the *.a* and *.so.version* files corresponding to the library. Replacing *.a* file is easy: just copy over it with the new versions. However, you must use some caution when replacing the shared library image, *.so.version*; most of the programs on the system depend on those images, so you can't simply delete them or rename them. To put this another way, the symbolic link *library.so.major* must *always* point to a valid library image. To accomplish this, first copy the new image file to */lib*, and then change the symbolic link to point to the new file in one step, using *ln −sf.* This is demonstrated in the following example.

Let's say you're upgrading from Version 5.2.18 of the *libc* library to Version 5.4.47. You should have the files *libc.a* and *libc.so.5.4.47.* First, copy the *.a* file to the appropriate location, overwriting the old version:

```
rutabaga# cp libc.a /usr/lib
```

Now, copy the new image file to */lib* (or wherever the library image should be):

```
rutabaga# cp libc.so.5.4.47 /lib
```

Now, if you use the command *ls –l /lib/libc** you should see something like:

```
lrwxrwxrwx  1 root   root        14 Oct 23 13:25 libc.so.5 -> libc.so.5.2.18
-rwxr-xr-x  1 root   root    623620 Oct 23 13:24 libc.so.5.2.18
-rwxr-xr-x  1 root   root    720310 Nov 16 11:02 libc.so.5.4.47
```

To update the symbolic link to point to the new library, use the command:

```
rutabaga# ln –sf /lib/libc.so.5.4.47 /lib/libc.so.5
```

This gives you:

```
lrwxrwxrwx  1 root   root        14 Oct 23 13:25 libc.so.5 ->\
/lib/libc.so.5.4.47
-rwxr-xr-x  1 root   root    623620 Oct 23 13:24 libc.so.5.2.18
-rwxr-xr-x  1 root   root    720310 Nov 16 11:02 libc.so.5.4.47
```

Now you can safely remove the old image file, *libc.so.5.2.18*. You must use *ln –sf* to replace the symbolic link in one step, especially when updating libraries, such as *libc*. If you were to remove the symbolic link first, and then attempt to use *ln –s* to add it again, more than likely *ln* would not be able to execute because the symbolic link is gone, and as far as *ld.so* is concerned, the *libc* library can't be found. Once the link is gone, nearly all the programs on your system will be unable to execute. Be very careful when updating shared library images.

Whenever you upgrade or add a library to the system, it's not a bad idea to run *ldconfig* to regenerate the library cache used by *ld.so*. In some cases, a new library may not be recognized by *ld.so* until you run *ldconfig*.

The Linux community is currently moving from the old *libc* version 5 to the new so-called *glibc2*, also called *libc6*. In principle, this is not different from any other incompatible library update, but in practice this brings all kinds of problems because exchanging the C library in an incompatible manner affects each and every program on the system. While the new *glibc2* has several advantages— among other things it is thread-safe, meaning that it makes it a lot easier to write programs that do more than one thing at a time—many people consider it still unstable. In addition, you cannot run programs compiled for one version with the other library version. If you want to run a program for which you do not have the sources, you will have to install the C library version that this program needs. Fortunately, it is possible to have both versions on your system, albeit with some problems. Those distributions that have already switched to *glibc2* usually provide an installed package named something like "libc5 compatibility"; install this package if you want to be able to run software compiled with the old C library.

One question remains: where can you obtain the new versions of libraries? Several of the basic system libraries (*libc*, *libm*, and so on) can be downloaded from the directory */pub/Linux/GCC* on *ftp://metalab.unc.edu*. It contains the Linux versions of the *gcc* compiler, libraries, include files, and other utilities. Each file there should have a *README* or *release* file that describes what to do and how to install it. Other libraries are maintained and archived separately. At any rate, all libraries you install should include the *.a* and *.so.version* files, as well as a set of include files for use with the compiler.

Upgrading the Compiler

One other important part of the system to keep up to date is the C compiler and related utilities. These include *gcc* (the GNU C and C++ compiler itself), the linker, the assembler, the C preprocessor, and various include files and libraries used by the compiler itself. All are included in the Linux *gcc* distribution. Usually, a new version of *gcc* is released along with new versions of the *libc* library and include files, and each requires the other.

You can find the current *gcc* release for Linux on the various FTP archives, including */pub/Linux/GCC* on *ftp://metalab.unc.edu*. The release notes there should tell you what to do. Usually, upgrading the compiler is a simple matter of unpacking several tar files as **root**, and possibly removing some additional files. If you don't have Internet access, you can obtain the newest compiler from CD-ROM archives of the FTP sites, as described earlier.

To find out what version of *gcc* you have, use the command:

```
gcc -v
```

This should tell you something like:

```
Reading specs from /usr/lib/gcc-lib/i486-linux/2.8.1/specs
gcc version 2.8.1
```

Note that *gcc* itself is just a front-end to the actual compiler and code-generation tools found under:

```
/usr/lib/gcc-lib/machine/version
```

Chapter 13

gcc (usually in */usr/bin*) can be used with multiple versions of the compiler proper, with the *−V* option. In the section "Programming with gcc" in Chapter 13, we describe the use of *gcc* in detail.

If you are developing software in C++, it might also be a good idea to use *egcs*, a new version of *gcc* that is much more robust than *gcc* itself and supports most of the modern C++ features. Unfortunately, *egcs*, older versions of *gcc* (up to version 2.7.2), and newer versions of *gcc* (from version 2.8.0) all use different and incompatible object file formats, which means that you should recompile all your C++ libraries and applications if you migrate from one compiler to another. The Free Software Foundation has announced recently that *egcs* will become its default compiler, thus replacing *gcc*, so these considerations might be obsolete soon.

Upgrading Other Software

Of course, you'll have to periodically upgrade other pieces of your system. As discussed in the previous section, it's usually easier and best to upgrade only those applications you need to upgrade. For example, if you never use Emacs on your system, why bother keeping up-to-date with the most recent version of Emacs? For that matter, you may not need to stay completely current with oft-used applications. If something works for you, there's little need to upgrade.

In order to upgrade other applications, you'll have to obtain the newest release of the software. This is usually available as a gzipped or compressed tar file. Such a package could come in several forms. The most common are *binary distributions*, where the binaries and related files are archived and ready to unpack on your system, and *source distributions*, where the source code (or portions of the source code) for the software is provided, and you have to issue commands to compile and install it on your system.

Shared libraries make distributing software in binary form easy; as long as you have a version of the libraries installed that is compatible with the library stubs used to build the program, you're set. However, in many cases, it is easier (and a good idea) to release a program as source. Not only does this make the source code available to you for inspection and further development, it allows you to build the application specifically for your system, with your own libraries. Many programs allow you to specify certain options at compile-time, such as selectively including various features in the program when built. This kind of customization isn't possible if you get prebuilt binaries.

There's also a security issue at play when installing binaries without source code. Although on Unix systems viruses are nearly unheard of,* it's not difficult to write a "trojan horse," a program that appears to do something useful, but in actuality causes damage to the system. For example, someone could write an application that includes the "feature" of deleting all files in the home directory of the user executing the program. Because the program would be running with the permissions of the user executing it, the program itself has the ability to do this kind of damage. (Of course, the Unix security mechanism prevents damage being done to other users' files or to any important system files owned by **root**.)

While having source won't necessarily prevent this from happening (do you read the source code for every program you compile on your system?), at least it gives you a way to verify what the program is really doing. A programmer would have to make a certain effort to prevent such a trojan horse from being discovered, but if you install binaries blindly, you are setting yourself up for trouble.

---

* A "virus" in the classic sense is a program that attaches to a "host," which runs when the host is executed. On Unix systems, this usually requires root privileges to do any harm, and if programmers could obtain such privileges, they probably wouldn't bother with a virus.

At any rate, dealing with source and binary distributions of software is quite simple. If the package is released as a tar file, first use the *tar t* option to determine how the files have been archived. In the case of binary distributions, you may be able to unpack the tar file directly on your system, say from / or */usr*. When doing this, be sure to delete any old versions of the program and its support files (those that aren't overwritten by the new tar file). If the old executable comes before the new one on your path, you'll continue to run the old version unless you remove it.

Many distributions now use a special packaging system that makes installing and uninstalling software a lot easier. There are several packaging systems available, but most distributions, including Red Hat, SuSE, and Caldera use the RPM system, which we will cover in the next section. The Debian distribution uses its own *.deb* system not covered here.

Source distributions are a bit trickier. First, you must unpack the sources into a directory of their own. Most systems use */usr/src* for just this. Because you usually don't have to be **root** to build a software package (you will usually require **root** permissions to install the program once compiled!), it might be a good idea to make */usr/src* writable by all users, with the command:

```
chmod 1777 /usr/src
```

This allows any user to create subdirectories of */usr/src* and place files there. The first 1 in the mode is the "sticky" bit, which prevents users from deleting each other's subdirectories.

You can now create a subdirectory under */usr/src* and unpack the tar file there, or you can unpack the tar file directly from */usr/src* if the archive contains a subdirectory of its own.

Once the sources are available, the next step is to read any *README* files or installation notes included with the sources. Nearly all packages include such documentation. The basic method used to build most programs is:

Chapter 13

1. Check the *Makefile*. This file contains instructions for *make*, which controls the compiler to build programs. Many applications require you to edit minor aspects of the *Makefile* for your own system; this should be self-explanatory. The installation notes will tell you if you have to do this. If you need more help with the *Makefile*, read the section "Makefiles" in Chapter 13. If there is no *Makefile* in the package, you might have to generate it first. See item 3 for how to do this.

2. Possibly edit other files associated with the program. Some applications require you to edit a file named *config.h*; again, this will be explained in the installation instructions.

3. Possibly run a configuration script. Such a script is used to determine what facilities are available on your system, which is necessary to build more complex applications.

   Specifically, when the sources do not contain a *Makefile* in the top-level directory, but instead a file called *Makefile.in* and a file called *configure*, the package has been built with the Autoconf system. In this (more and more common case), you run the configuration script like this:

   ```
   ./configure
   ```

   The `./` should be used so that the local *configure* is run, and not another *configure* program that might accidentally be in your path. Some packages let you pass options to *configure* that often enable or disable specific features of the package. Once the *configure* script has run, you can proceed with the next step.

4. Run *make*. Generally, this executes the appropriate compilation commands as given in the *Makefile*. In many cases you'll have to give a "target" to *make*, as in *make all* or *make install*. These are two common targets; the former is usually not necessary but can be used to build all targets listed in a *Makefile* (e.g., if the package includes several programs, but only one is compiled by default); the latter is often used to install the executables and support files on the system after compilation. For this reason, *make install* is usually run as **root**.

Chapter 13

You might have problems compiling or installing new software on your system, especially if the program in question hasn't been tested under Linux, or depends on other software you don't have installed. In Chapter 13, we talk about the compiler, *make*, and related tools in detail.

Most software packages include manual pages and other files, in addition to the source and executables. The installation script (if there is one) will place these files in the appropriate location. In the case of manual pages, you'll find files with names such as *foobar.1* or *foobar.man*. These files are usually *nroff* source files, which are formatted to produce the human-readable pages displayed by the *man* command. If the manual page source has a numeric extension, such as *.1*, copy it to the directory */usr/man/man1*, where *1* is the number used in the filename extension. (This corresponds to the manual "section" number; for most user programs, it is 1.) If the file has an extension such as *.man*, it usually suffices to copy the file to */usr/man/man1*, renaming the *.man* extension to *.1*.

Using RPM

RPM, the Red Hat Package Manager, is a tool that automates the installation of software binaries and remembers what files are needed so that you can be assured the software will run properly. Despite the name, RPM is not Red Hat–specific, but is used in many other distributions nowadays, including SuSE and Caldera. Using RPM makes installing and uninstalling software a lot easier.

The basic idea of RPM is that you have a database of packages and the files that belong to a package. When you install a new package, the information about this package is recorded in the database. Then, when you want to uninstall the package, for every file of the package, RPM checks whether there are other packages installed using this file, too. If this is the case, the file in question is not deleted.

In addition, RPM tracks dependencies. Each package can be dependent on one or more other packages. When you install a package, RPM checks whether the packages the new package is dependent on are already installed. If not, it informs you about the dependency and refuses to install the package.

The dependencies are also used for removing packages: when you want to uninstall a package that other packages are still dependent upon, RPM tells you about this, too, and refuses to execute the task.

The increased convenience of using RPM packages comes at a price, however: First, as a developer, it is significantly more difficult to make a RPM package than to simply pack everything in a *tar* archive. And second, it is not possible to retrieve just one file from a RPM package; you have to install everything or nothing.

If you already have an RPM system, installing RPM packages is very easy. Let's say that you have a RPM package called *SuperFrob-4.i386.rpm* (RPM package always have the extension *.rpm*; the *i386* indicates that this is a binary package compiled for Intel machines). You could then install it with:

```
tigger # rpm -i SuperFrob-4.i386.rpm
```

Instead of *-i*, you can also use the long-named version of this option; choose whatever you like better:

```
tigger # rpm --install SuperFrob-4.i386.rpm
```

If everything goes well, there will be no output. If you want RPM to be more verbose, you can try:

```
tigger # rpm -ivh SuperFrob-4.i386.rpm
```

This prints the name of the package plus a number of hash marks, so that you can see how the installation progresses.

If the package you want to install needs another package that is not yet installed, you will get something like the following:

```
tigger # rpm -i SuperFrob-4.i386.rpm
failed dependencies:
        frobnik-2 is needed by SuperFrob-4
```

If you see this, you have to hunt for the package *frobnik-2* and install this first. Of course, this package can itself be dependent on other packages again.

If you want to update a package, use the *-U* or *--update* option (which is just the *-i* option combined with a few more implied options):

```
tigger # rpm -U SuperFrob-5.i386.rpm
```

Uninstalling a package is done with the *-e* or *—erase* option. In this case, you do not specify the package file (you might not have that around any longer), but the package name and version number:

```
tigger # rpm -e SuperFrob-5
```

Besides the options described so far that alter the state of your system, the *-q* option provides various kinds of informations about everything that is recorded in the RPM database as well as package files. Here are some useful things you can do with *-q*:

- Find out the version number of an installed package:

  ```
  tigger# rpm -q SuperFrob
  SuperFrob-5
  ```

- Get a list of all installed packages:

  ```
  tigger# rpm -qa
  SuperFrob-5
  OmniFrob-3
  ...
  libc-5.4.47-1
  ```

- Find out to which package a file belongs:

  ```
  tigger# rpm -qf /usr/bin/dothefrob
  SuperFrob-5
  tigger# rpm -qf /home/kalle/.xinitrc
  file /home/kalle/.xinitrc is not owned by any package
  ```

- Display information about the specified package:

  ```
  tigger# rpm -qi rpm
  Name         : rpm              Distribution: SuSE Linux 5.2 (i386)
  Version      : 2.4.12           Vendor: SuSE GmbH, Fuerth, Germany
  Release      : 3                Build Date: Tue Mar 10 01:35:47 1998
  Install date: Fri Sep 25 18:43:41 1998 Build Host: Pascal.fs100.suse.d
  Group        :                  Source RPM: rpm-2.4.12-3.src.rpm
  Size         : 1163708
  Packager     : feedback@suse.de
  Summary      : rpm - Red Hat Package Manager
  Description :
  rpm (Red Hat Package Manager) is the main tool for managing software
  packages of the SuSE Linux distribution. rpm can be used to install
  ```

and remove software packages; with rpm it's easy to update packages.
rpm keep track of all these manipulations in a central database. This
way it is possible to get an overview of all installed packages; rpm
also supports database queries.

- Show the files that will be installed for the specified package file:

```
tigger# rpm -qpl SuperFrob-5.i386.rpm
/usr/bin/dothefrob
/usr/bin/frobhelper
/usr/doc/SuperFrob/Installation
/usr/doc/SuperFrob/README
/usr/man/man1/dothefrob.1
```

rpm (8)

What we've just finished showing are the basic modes of operation, which are supplemented by a large number of additional options. You can check those in the manual page for the *rpm* command.

If you are faced with a RPM package that you want to install, but have a system like Slackware or Debian that is not based on RPM, things get a little bit more difficult.

You can either use the fairly self-explanatory command *alien* that can convert between various package formats and comes with most distributions, or you can build the RPM database from scratch.

The first thing you have to do in this latter case is to get the *rpm* program itself. You can download it from *http://www.rpm.org*. Follow the installation instructions to build and install it; if you have the C compiler *gcc* installed on your system, there should be no problems with this.

The next task is to initialize the RPM database. Distributions that come with RPM do the initialization automatically, but on other systems you will have to issue the command:

```
tigger # rpm --initdb
```

This command creates several files in the directory */var/lib/rpm*. The directory */var/lib* should already exist; if it doesn't, create it with the *mkdir* command first.

Now you can install RPM packages the normal way, but since you have not installed the basic parts of the system like the C library with RPM, you will get errors like the following:

```
tigger # rpm -i SuperFrob-4.i386.rpm
failed dependencies:
        libm.so.5 is needed by SuperFrob-4
        libdl.so.1 is needed by SuperFrob-4
        libc.so.5 is needed by SuperFrob-4
```

because those files are not recorded in the RPM database. Of course, you really do have those files on your system; otherwise most programs wouldn't run. For RPM to work, you must tell it not to care about any dependencies. You do this by specifying the command-line option *--nodeps*:

```
tigger # rpm -i --nodeps SuperFrob-4.i386.rpm
```

Now, RPM will install the package without complaining.

With this information, you should be able to administer your RPM-based system. If you want to know more, read the manual page for the *rpm* command or check out *http://www.rpm.org*.

Building a New Kernel

Rebuilding the kernel sounds like a pastime for hackers, but it is an important skill for any system administrator. First, you should rebuild the kernel on your system to eliminate the device drivers you don't need. This reduces the amount of memory used by the kernel itself, as described in the section "Managing Swap Space," in Chapter 6, *Managing Filesystems, Swap, and Devices*, the kernel is always present in memory, and the memory it uses cannot be reclaimed for use by programs if necessary.

Chapter 6

You also need to occasionally upgrade your kernel to a newer version. As with any piece of your system, if you know of important bug fixes or new features in a kernel release, you may want to upgrade to pick them up. Those people who are actively developing kernel code will also need to keep their kernel up to date in case changes are made to the code they are working on. Sometimes, it is necessary to upgrade your kernel to use a new version of the compiler or libraries. Some applications (such as the X Window System) require a certain kernel version to run.

You can find out what kernel version you are running through the command *uname –a*. This should produce something like:

```
rutabaga% uname -a
Linux tigger 2.0.35 #4 Wed Sep 30 12:44:16 CEST 1998 i586
```

uname(1)

Here, we see a machine running Version 2.0.35 of the kernel, which was last compiled on September 30. We see other information as well, such as the hostname of the machine, the number of times this kernel has been compiled (four), and the fact that the machine is a Pentium or equivalent (as denoted by i586). The manual page for *uname* can tell you more.

The Linux kernel is a many-tentacled beast. Many groups of people work on different pieces of it, and some parts of the code are a patchwork of ideas meeting different design goals. Overall, however, the kernel code is clean and uniform, and those interested in exploring its innards should have little trouble doing so. However, because of the great amount of development going on with the kernel, new releases are made very rapidly—sometimes daily! The chief reason for this is that nearly all device drivers are contained within the kernel code, and every time someone updates a driver, a new release is necessary. As the Linux community moves towards loadable device drivers, the maintainers of those drivers can release them independently of the main kernel, alleviating the necessity of such rapid updates.

Currently, Linus Torvalds maintains the "official" kernel release. Although the General Public License allows anyone to modify and rerelease the kernel under the same copyright, Linus's maintenance of an "official" kernel is a helpful convention that keeps version numbers uniform and allows everyone to be on equal footing when talking about kernel revisions. In order for a bug fix or new feature to be included in the kernel, all one must do is send it to Linus, who will usually incorporate the change as long as it doesn't break anything.

Kernel version numbers follow the convention:

`major.minor.patchlevel`

major is the major version number, which rarely changes, *minor* is the minor version number, which indicates the current "strain" of the kernel release, and *patchlevel* is the number of the patch to the current kernel version. Some examples of kernel versions are 2.0.36, (patch level 36 of kernel Version 2.0), and 2.1.52 (patch level 52 of kernel Version 2.1).

By convention, even-numbered kernel versions (2.0, 2.2, and so on) are "stable" releases, patches that contain only bug fixes and no new features. Odd-numbered kernel versions (2.1, 2.3, and so on) are "development" releases, patches that contain whatever new code developers wish to add and bug fixes for that code. When a development kernel matures to the point where it is stable enough for wide use, it is renamed with the next highest (even) minor version number, and the development cycle begins again.

For example, kernel Versions 2.0 and 2.1 were worked on concurrently. Patches made to 2.0 were bug fixes—meant only to correct problems in the existing code. Patches to 2.1 included bug fixes as well as a great deal of new code—new device drivers, new features, and so on. When kernel Version 2.1 was stable enough, it was renamed to 2.2; a copy was made and named Version 2.3. Development continued with Versions 2.2 and 2.3. 2.2 would be the new "stable" kernel while 2.3 was a development kernel for new features.

Note that this version-numbering convention applies only to Linus's official kernel release and only to kernel versions after 1.0. Prior to 1.0 (this is now ancient history), there was only one "current" kernel version and patches were consistently made to it. The kernel development community has found that having two concurrent kernel versions allows those who want to experiment to use the development kernel, and those who need a reliable platform to stick with the stable kernel. In this way, if the development kernel is seriously broken by new code, it shouldn't affect those who are running the newest stable kernel. The general rule is that you should use development kernels if you want to be on the leading edge of new features and are willing to risk problems with your system. Use the development kernels at your own risk.

If you are interested in how the kernel versions so far have evolved, check out *http://ps.cus.mist.ac.uk/~rhw/kernel.versions.html.*

On your system, the kernel sources most probably live in */usr/src/linux* (unless you use the Debian distribution, where you can find the kernel sources in */usr/src/ kernel-source-versionsnumber*). If you are going to rebuild your kernel only from the current sources, you don't need to obtain any files or apply any patches. If you wish to upgrade your kernel to a new version, you need to follow the instructions in the following section.

Obtaining Kernel Sources

The official kernel is released as a gzipped tar file, containing the sources along with a series of patch files—one per patch level. The tar file contains the source for the unpatched revision; for example, there is a tar file containing the sources for kernel Version 1.1 with no patches applied. Each subsequent patch level is released as a patch file (produced using *diff*), which can be applied using the *patch* program. In the section "Patching Files" in Chapter 14, *Tools for Programmers*, we describe the use of *patch* in detail.

Chapter 14

Let's say you're upgrading to kernel Version 1.1 patch level 15. You'll need the sources for 1.1 (the file might be named *v1.1.0.tar.gz*) and the patches for patch levels 1 through 15. These files would be named *patch1*, *patch2*, and so forth. (You need *all* of the patch files up to the version you're upgrading to. Usually, these patch files are rather small, and are gzipped on the archive sites.) All these files can be found in the *kernel* directory of the Linux FTP archive sites; for example, on *ftp://ftp.kernel.org*, the directory containing the 2.2 sources and patches is */pub/linux/kernel/v2.2*. You will find the kernel sources here as tar archives, both compressed with *gzip* and *bzip2*.

If you are already at some patch level of the kernel (such as 2.1 patch level 15) and want to upgrade to a newer patch level, you can simply apply the patches from the version you have up to the version you'd like to upgrade to. If you're upgrading from, say, 2.1 patch level 15 to 2.1 patch level 19, you need the patch files for 2.1.16 to 2.1.19 inclusive.

Unpacking the sources

First, you need to unpack the source tar file from */usr/src*. You do this with commands such as:

```
rutabaga# cd /usr/src
rutabaga# mv linux linux.old
rutabaga# tar xzf v1.1.0.tar.gz
```

This saves your old kernel source tree as */usr/src/linux.old* and creates */usr/src/linux*, containing the new sources. Note that the tar file containing the sources includes the *linux* subdirectory.

You should keep your current kernel sources in the directory */usr/src/linux*, because there are two symbolic links—*/usr/include/linux* and */usr/include/asm*—that point into the current kernel source tree to provide certain header files when compiling programs. (You should always have your kernel sources available so that programs using these include files can be compiled.) If you want to keep several kernel source trees around, be sure that */usr/src/linux* points to the most recent one.

Applying patches

If you are applying any patch files, you use the *patch* program. Let's say that you have the files *patch1.gz* through *patch15.gz*, which are gzipped. These patches should be applied from */usr/src*. That doesn't mean the patch files themselves should be located there, but rather that *patch* should be executed from */usr/src*. For each patch file, use the command:

```
gunzip -c patchfile | patch -p0
```

from */usr/src*. The *–p0* option tells *patch* it shouldn't strip any part of the filenames contained within the patch file.

You must apply each patch in numerical order by patch level. This is very important. Note that using a wildcard such as *patch** will not work because the * wildcard uses ASCII order, not numeric order. (Otherwise you'd get *patch1* followed by *patch10* and *patch11*, as opposed to *patch2* and *patch3*.) It is best to run the previous command for each patch file in succession, by hand. This way you can ensure you're doing things in the right order.

You shouldn't encounter problems when patching your source tree in this way unless you try to apply patches out of order or apply a patch more than once. Check the *patch* manual page if you do encounter trouble. If all else fails, remove the new kernel source tree and start over from the original tar file.

To double-check that the patches were applied successfully, use the commands:

```
find /usr/src/linux -follow -name "*.rej" -print
find /usr/src/linux -follow -name "*#" -print
```

This lists any files that are "rejected" portions of the patch process. If any such files exist, they contain sections of the patch file that could not be applied for some reason. Look into these, and if there's any doubt start over from scratch. You cannot expect your kernel to compile or work correctly if the patch process did not complete successfully and without rejections.

Building the Kernel

Whether or not you've upgraded your kernel sources, you're ready to build a new kernel. The primary reason to do this is either to simply upgrade or to trim down your current kernel, excluding unneeded device drivers.

There are six steps to building the kernel, and they should be quite painless. All of these steps are described in more detail in the following pages.

1. Run *make config*, which asks you various questions about which drivers you wish to include. You could also use the more comfortable variants *make menuconfig* or (only when you are running the X Window System) *make xconfig*.

2. Run *make dep* to gather dependencies for each source file and include them in the various makefiles.

3. If you have built a kernel from this source tree before, run *make clean* to clear out old object files and force a complete rebuild.

4. Run *make zImage* to build the kernel itself.

5. Go have a coffee (or two, depending on the speed of your machine and amount of available memory).

6. Install the new kernel image, either on a boot floppy or via LILO.

All these commands are executed from */usr/src/linux*, except for Step 5, which you can do anywhere.

There is a *README* included in the kernel sources, which should be located at */usr/src/linux/README* on your system. Read it. It contains up-to-date notes on kernel compilation, which may be more current than the information presented here. Be sure to follow the steps described there, using the descriptions given later in this section as a guide.

The first step is to run *make config*. This executes a script that asks you a set of yes/no questions about which drivers to include in the kernel. There are defaults for each question, but be careful: the defaults probably don't correspond to what you want. (When several options are available, the default will be shown as a capital letter, as in [Y/n].) Your answers to each question will become the default the next time you build the kernel from this source tree.

Simply answer each question, either by pressing Enter for the default, or pressing y or n (followed by Enter). Not all of the questions have a yes/no answer; you may be asked to enter a number or some other value. A number of the configuration questions allow an answer of m in addition to y or n. This option allows the corresponding kernel feature to be compiled as a loadable kernel module, as opposed to building it into the kernel image itself. Loadable modules, covered in the following section, "Loadable Device Drivers," allow portions of the kernel (such as device drivers) to be loaded and unloaded as needed on a running system. If you are unsure about an option, type ? at the prompt; for most options, a message will be shown that tells you more about the option.

An alternative to running *make config* is *make xconfig*, which compiles and runs an X-Window-based kernel configuration program. In order for this to work, you must have the X Window System running, have the appropriate X11 and Tcl/Tk libraries installed, and so forth. Instead of asking a series of questions, the X-based configuration utility allows you to use checkboxes to select which kernel options you want to enable. The system remembers your configuration options each time you run *make config*, so if you're only adding or removing a few features from your kernel, you need not reenter all the options.

Also available is make menuconfig, which uses the text-based *curses* library, providing a similar menu-based kernel configuration if you don't have X installed. *make menuconfig* and *make xconfig* are much more comfortable than *make config*, especially because you can go back to an option and change your mind until you save your configuration.

The following is part of a session with *make config*. When using *make menuconfig* or *make xconfig*, you will encounter the same options, only presented more user-friendly:

```
*
* Code maturity level options
*
Prompt for development and/or incomplete code/drivers\
(CONFIG_EXPERIMENTAL) [N/y/?]
*
* Processor type and features
*
Processor family (386, 486/Cx486, 586/K5/5x86/6x86,Pentium/K6/TSC,\
PPro/6x86MX) [PPro/6x86MX]
   defined CONFIG_M686
Math emulation (CONFIG_MATH_EMULATION) [N/y/?]
MTRR (Memory Type Range Register) support (CONFIG_MTRR) [N/y/?]
Symmetric multi-processing support (CONFIG_SMP) [Y/n/?]
*
* Loadable module support
*
Enable loadable module support (CONFIG_MODULES) [Y/n/?]
Set version information on all symbols for modules\
(CONFIG_MODVERSIONS) [N/y/?]
Kernel module loader (CONFIG_KMOD) [N/y/?]
*
* General setup
*
```

```
Networking support (CONFIG_NET) [Y/n/?]
The linux kernel is now hopefully configured for your setup.
Check the top-level Makefile for additional configuration,
and do a 'make dep ; make clean' if you want to be sure all
the files are correctly re-made
```

If you understand the hardware present on your machine, the questions should be straightforward. The following questions are found in the kernel configuration for version 2.2. If you have applied other patches, additional questions might appear. The same is true for later versions of the kernel. Note that in the following list we don't show all of the kernel configuration options; there are simply too many of them, and most are self-explanatory. We have highlighted only those that may require further explanation. Remember that if you're not sure how to answer a particular question, the default answer is often the best choice. When in doubt, it is also a good idea to type ? and check the help message.

It should be noted here that not all Linux device drivers are actually built into the kernel. Instead, some drivers are available only as loadable modules, distributed separately from the kernel sources. (As mentioned earlier, some drivers can be either built into the kernel or compiled as modules.) One notable kernel driver available only as a module is the "floppy tape" driver for QIC-117 tape drives that connect to the floppy controller.

If you can't find support for your favorite hardware device in the list presented by *make config*, it's quite possible that the driver is available as a module or a separate kernel patch. Scour the FTP sites and archive CD-ROMs if you can't find what you're looking for. In the section "Loadable Device Drivers" later in this chapter, kernel modules are covered in detail.

`Prompt for development and/or incomplete code/drivers`
 Answer yes for this item if you want to try new features that aren't considered stable enough by the developers. You do not want this option unless you want to help test new features.

`Processor family (386, 486/Cx486, 586/K5/5x86/6x86,`
`Pentium/K6/TSC, PPro/6x86MX)`
 Here, you have to specify the CPU type that you have. The kernel will then be compiled with optimizations especially geared towards your machine. Note that if you specify a higher processor here than you actually have, the kernel might not work. Also, the Pentium II MMX is a 686, not a 586 chip.

`Math emulation`
 Answer no if you have a Pentium or better. Answer yes to this item if you do not have a floating-point coprocessor in your machine. This is necessary for the kernel to emulate the presence of a math coprocessor.

MTRR (Memory Type Range Register) support

This enables special support for a feature present only on Pentium II and Pentium Pro systems. If you do not have these CPUs, you do not need this option, but it will not hurt you if you do (it will only make your kernel larger).

Symmetric multi-processing support

This enables kernel support for more than one CPU. If your machine has more than one CPU, say yes here; if not, say no.

Enable loadable module support

This enables the support for dynamically loading additional modules. You definitely want to enable this.

Set version information on all symbols for modules

This is a special option that makes it possible to use a module compiled for one kernel version with another kernel version. There are a number of problems attached to this; say no here unless you know exactly what you are doing.

Kernel module loader

If you enable this option, you can—with the help of a program called *kerneld*, described later—automatically load and unload dynamically loadable modules as needed.

Networking support

Answer yes to this option if you want any sort of networking support in your kernel (including TCP/IP, SLIP, PPP, NFS, and so on).

PCI support

Enable this option if your motherboard includes the PCI bus and you have PCI-bus devices installed in your system. The PCI BIOS is used to detect and enable PCI devices; kernel support for it is necessary for use of any PCI devices in your system.

System V IPC

Answering yes to this option includes kernel support for System V interprocess communication (IPC) functions, such as *msgrcv* and *msgsnd*. Some programs ported from System V require this; you should answer yes unless you have a strong aversion to these features.

Sysctl support

This option instructs the kernel to provide a way to change kernel parameters on-the-fly, without rebooting. It is good idea to enable this unless you have very limited memory, because this option makes the kernel 8 KB larger.

Kernel support for ELF binaries

Enabling this option allows your system to execute Linux binaries stored in Executable and Linkable Format (ELF) format. ELF is a standard format for executables, object files, and system libraries. Such standards are required for the operating system to cooperate with tools such as compilers and linkers. Most current Linux systems store binaries in ELF format, so you should answer yes to this question. Very old Linux systems use the *a.out* format for binaries.

Parallel port support

Enable this option if you have a parallel port in your system and want to access it from Linux. Linux can use the parallel port not only for printers, but also for PLIP (a networking protocol for parallel lines), ZIP drives, scanners, and other things. In most cases, you will need an additional driver to attach a device to the parallel port.

Plug and Play support

Enable this if you have an ISA Plug-and-Play card in your system. This option does not apply to PCI cards, which are plug and play by nature.

Normal floppy disk support

Answer yes to this option unless you don't want support for floppy drives (this can save some memory on systems where floppy support isn't required).

Enhanced IDE/MFM/RLL disk/cdrom/tape/floppy support

Answer yes to this option unless you don't need MFM/RLL/IDE drive support. After answering yes, you will be prompted for types of devices (hard disks, CD-ROM drives, tape drives, and floppy drives) you want to access over the IDE driver. If you have no IDE hardware (only SCSI), it may be safe to disable this option.

XT harddisk support

Answer yes to this only if you have an older XT disk controller and plan to use it with your Linux system.

Parallel port IDE device support

This option enables support for IDE devices that are attached to the parallel port, such as portable CD-ROM drives.

Networking options

If you previously selected networking support, you will be asked a series of questions about which networking options you want enabled in your kernel. Unless you have special networking needs (in which case you'll know how to answer the questions appropriately), answering the defaults for these questions should suffice. A number of the questions are esoteric in nature (such as IP: Disable Path MTU Discovery) and you should select the defaults for these in almost all cases.

SCSI support

If you have a SCSI controller of any kind, answer yes to this option. You will be asked a series of questions about the specific SCSI devices on your system; be sure you know what type of hardware you have installed. All of these questions deal with specific SCSI controller chips and boards; if you aren't sure what sort of SCSI controller you have, check the hardware documentation or consult the Linux HOWTO documents.

You will also be asked if you want support for SCSI disks, tapes, CD-ROMs, and other devices; be sure to enable the options appropriate for your hardware.

If you don't have any SCSI hardware, you should answer no to this option; it greatly reduces the size of your kernel.

Network device support

This is a series of questions about the specific networking controllers Linux supports. If you plan to use an Ethernet card (or some other networking controller), be sure to enable the options for your hardware. As with SCSI devices, you should consult your hardware documentation or the Linux HOWTO documents (such as the Ethernet HOWTO) to determine which driver is appropriate for your network controller.

Amateur Radio support

This option enables basic support for networking over public radio frequencies like CB. If you have the equipment to use the feature, enable this option and read the AX25 and the HAM HOWTO.

ISDN subsystem

If you have ISDN hardware in your system, enable this option and select the ISDN hardware driver suitable for your hardware. You will most probably also want to select Support synchronous PPP (see PPP over ISDN).

Old CD-ROM drivers

This is a series of questions dealing with the specific CD-ROM drivers supported by the kernel, such as the Sony CDU31A/33A, Mitsumi, or SoundBlaster Pro CD-ROM, and so on. If you have a SCSI or IDE CD-ROM controller (and have selected support for it earlier), you need not enable any of these options. Some CD-ROM drives have their own interface boards, and these options enable drivers for them.

Character devices

Linux supports a number of special "character" devices, such as serial and parallel port controllers, QIC-02 tape drives, and mice with their own proprietary interfaces (not mice that connect to the serial port, such as the Microsoft serial mouse). This section also includes the joystick support and the "Video for Linux" drivers that support video and frame-grabbing hardware. Be sure to enable the options corresponding to your hardware.

Filesystems

This is a series of questions for each filesystem type supported by the kernel. As discussed in the section "Managing Filesystems," in Chapter 6, there are a number of filesystem types supported by the system, and you can pick and choose which to include in the kernel. Nearly all systems should include support for the Second Extended and */proc* filesystems. You should include support for the MS-DOS filesystem if you want to access your MS-DOS files directly from Linux, and the ISO 9660 filesystem to access files on a CD-ROM (most of which are encoded in this way).

Console drivers

Make sure that you select at least VGA text console in this section, or you won't be able to use your Linux system from the console.

Sound card support

Answering yes to this option presents you with several questions about your sound card, which drivers you wish to have installed, and other details, such as the IRQ and address of the sound hardware.

Kernel hacking

This section contains options that are useful only if you plan on hacking the Linux kernel yourself. If you do not want to do this, answer no.

After running *make config* or its equivalent, you'll be asked to edit "the top-level Makefile," which means */usr/src/linux/Makefile*. In most cases, it's not necessary to do this. If you wanted to alter some of the compilation options for the kernel, or change the default root device or SVGA mode, you could edit the makefile to accomplish this. Setting the root device and SVGA mode can easily be done by running *rdev* on a compiled kernel image, as we saw in the section "Using a Boot Floppy" in Chapter 5, *Essential System Management*.

Chapter 5

The next step is to run *make dep*. This issues a series of commands that walk through the directory tree and gather dependencies for source files, adding information to the various makefiles for them. (If you really want to know what's going on here: *make dep* adds rules for the makefile so that certain code will be recompiled if, say, a header file included by a source file changes.) This step should take five or ten minutes at most to complete.

If you wish to force a complete recompilation of the kernel, you should issue *make clean* at this point. This removes all object files produced from a previous build from this source tree. If you have never built the kernel from this tree, you're probably safe skipping this step (although it can't hurt). If you are tweaking minor parts of the kernel, you might want to avoid this step so that only those files that have changed will be recompiled. At any rate, running *make clean* simply ensures the entire kernel will be recompiled "from scratch," and if you're in any doubt, use this command to be on the safe side.

Now you're ready to compile the kernel. This is done with the command *make zImage*. It is best to build your kernel on a lightly loaded system, with most of your memory free for the compilation. If other users are accessing the system, or if you're trying to run any large applications yourself (such as the X Window System, or another compilation), the build may slow to a crawl. The key here is memory. A slower processor completes the kernel compilation just as rapidly as a faster one, given enough RAM for the task.

The kernel compilation can take anywhere from a few minutes to many hours, depending on your hardware. There is a great deal of code—well over 10 MB—in the entire kernel, so this should come as no surprise. Slower systems with 4 MB (or less) of RAM can expect to take several hours for a complete rebuild; faster machines with more memory can complete in less than half an hour. Your mileage will most assuredly vary.

If any errors or warnings occur while compiling, you cannot expect the resulting kernel to work correctly; in most cases, the build will halt if an error occurs. Such errors can be the result of incorrectly applying patches, problems with the *make config* and *make dep* steps, or actual bugs in the code. In the "stock" kernels, this latter case is rare, but is more common if you're working with development code or new drivers under testing. If you have any doubt, remove the kernel source tree altogether and start over.

When the compilation is complete, you will be left with the file *zImage* in the directory */usr/src/linux/arch/i386/boot*. (Of course, if you're attempting to build Linux on a platform other than the Intel x86, the kernel image will be found in the corresponding subdirectory under *arch*.) The kernel is so named because it is the executable image of the kernel, and it has been internally compressed using the *gzip* algorithm. When the kernel boots, it uncompresses itself into memory: don't attempt to use *gzip* or *gunzip* on *zImage* yourself! The kernel requires much less disk space when compressed in this way, allowing kernel images to fit on a floppy.

If you pick too much kernel functionality, it can happen that you get a `kernel too big` error at the end of the kernel compilation. This happens rarely, because you only need a very limited amount of hardware support for one machine, but it can happen. In this case, you have two options: Compile some kernel functionality as modules (see the next section, "Loadable Device Drivers") or use *make bzImage* instead of *make zImage*. This will create a kernel that loads itself into high memory but works only with not-so-old Intel machines. You will then find the kernel image in the same directory but with the name *bzImage*. Don't worry if it took you a lot of time to compile the kernel before. Most of the time spent during the first compile was creating object files that remain on your system and are still usable. So running *make bzImage* will pick up most of the compiled objects from the earlier run, and this build should go much faster.

Chapter 5

You should now run *rdev* on the new kernel image to verify that the root filesystem device, console SVGA mode, and other parameters have been set correctly. This is described in the section "Using a Boot Floppy" in Chapter 5.

With your new kernel in hand, you're ready to configure it for booting. This involves either placing the kernel image on a boot floppy, or configuring LILO to boot the kernel from the hard drive. These topics are discussed in the section "Booting the System" in Chapter 5. To use the new kernel, configure it for booting in one of these ways, and reboot the system.

Loadable Device Drivers

Traditionally, device drivers have been included as part of the kernel. There are several reasons for this. First of all, nearly all device drivers require the special hardware access provided by being part of the kernel code. Such hardware access can't be obtained easily through a user program. Also, device drivers are much easier to implement as part of the kernel; such drivers would have complete access to the data structures and other routines in the kernel and could call them freely.

There are several problems with a conglomerate kernel containing all drivers in this way. First of all, it requires the system administrator to rebuild the kernel in order to selectively include device drivers, as we saw in the previous section. Also, this mechanism lends itself to sloppy programming on the part of the driver writers: there's nothing stopping a programmer from writing code that is not completely modular—code which, for example, directly accesses data private to other parts of the kernel. The cooperative nature of the Linux kernel development compounds this problem, and not all parts of the code are as neatly contained as they should be. This can make it more difficult to maintain and debug the code.

In an effort to move away from this paradigm, the Linux kernel supports loadable device drivers—device drivers that are added to or removed from memory at runtime, with a series of commands. Such drivers are still part of the kernel, but they are compiled separately and enabled only when loaded. Loadable device drivers, or *modules*, are generally loaded into memory using commands in one of the boot-time *rc* scripts.

Modules provide a cleaner interface for writing drivers. To some extent, they require the code to be somewhat modular and to follow a certain coding convention. (Note that this doesn't actually prevent a programmer from abusing the convention and writing nonmodular code. Once the module has been loaded, it is just as free to wreak havoc as if it were compiled directly into the kernel.) Using modules makes drivers easier to debug; you can simply unload a module, recompile it, and reload it without having to reboot the system or rebuild the kernel as a whole. Modules can be used for other parts of the kernel, such as filesystem types, in addition to device drivers.

Most device drivers, and a lot of other kernel functionality under Linux, are implemented as modules. One of the most popular is the floppy tape driver (or *ftape* driver), for tape drives that connect to the floppy controller, such as the Colorado Memory Jumbo 120/250 models. If you plan to use this driver on your system, it is good to know how to build, load, and unload modules. While nobody stops you from compiling this module statically into your kernel, a tape drive is something that you need only rarely (normally once a day or so), and its driver shouldn't occupy value RAM during the times it is not needed. See the Linux Ftape HOWTO for more about these devices and supported hardware.

[87] Ftape HOWTO

The first thing you'll need is the *modules* package, which contains the commands used to load and unload modules from the kernel. On the FTP archive sites, this is usually found as *modules.tar.gz* in the directory where the kernel sources are kept. This package contains the sources to the commands *insmod*, *modprobe*, *rmmod*, and *lsmod*. Most Linux distributions include these commands (found in *sbin*). If you already have these commands installed, you probably don't need to get the *modules* package. However, it can't hurt to get the package and rebuild these commands, to be sure that you have the most up-to-date version.

To rebuild these commands, unpack *modules.tar.gz* (say, in a subdirectory of */usr/ src*). Follow the installation instructions contained there; usually all you have to do is execute *make* followed by *make install* (as **root**). The three commands will now be installed in */sbin* and ready to use.

A module is simply a single object file containing all of the code for the driver. For example, the *ftape* module might be called *ftape.o*. On many systems, the modules themselves are stored in a directory tree below */lib/modules/kernelversion*, where you can find different directories for the various types of modules. For example, the modules compiled for the 2.2.2 kernel would be below */lib/modules/2.2.2*. You might already have a number of modules on your system; check the appropriate directory.

Modules can be either in the kernel source or external. The former is the case for those device drivers, filesystems, and other functionality that are used most often and that are maintained as part of the official kernel sources. Using these modules is very easy: during the *make config*, *make menuconfig*, or *make xconfig* step, type m to build a feature as a module. Repeat this for everything you want to compile as a module. Then, after the *make zImage* step, execute the commands *make modules* and *make modules_install*. This will compile the modules and install them in */lib/modules/kernelversion*. It is a good idea (for reasons to be explained later in this section) to run the command *depmod -a* afterwards to correct module dependencies.

New modules that are not yet integrated into the official kernel sources, or those that are simply too esoteric to be put into the kernel sources (e.g., a device driver for some custom-built hardware that is not publicly available), can be available as stand-alone, external modules. Unpack the archive of this module, compile it according to the instructions that are hopefully included, and copy the resulting module file to the appropriate subdirectory of */lib/modules/kernelversion*. Some modules might also have an install script, or allow you to issue the command *make install* to perform the last step.

Once you have a compiled module (either from the kernel sources or external), you can load it using the command:

```
insmod module
```

where *module* is the name of the module object file. For example:

```
insmod /lib/modules/2.2.2/char/ftape.o
```

installs the *ftape* driver if it is found in that file.

Once a module is installed, it may display some information to the console (as well as to the system logs), indicating that it is initialized. For example, the *ftape* driver might display the following:

```
ftape v1.14 29/10/94 (c) 1993, 1994 Bas Laarhoven (bas@vimec.nl)
  QIC-117 driver for QIC-40 and QIC-80 tape drives
[000] kernel-interface.c (init_module) - installing QIC-117 ftape\
driver....
[001] kernel-interface.c (init_module) - 3 tape_buffers @ 001B8000.
[002]  calibr.c (time_inb) - inb() duration: 1436 nsec.
[003]  calibr.c (calibrate) - TC for 'udelay()' = 2944 nsec (at 2049\
counts).
[004]  calibr.c (calibrate) - TC for 'fdc_wait()' = 2857 nsec (at 2049\
counts).
```

The exact messages printed depend on the module, of course. Each module should come with ample documentation describing just what it does and how to debug it if there are problems.

It is likely that *insmod* will tell you it could not load the module into the kernel because there were "symbols missing." This means that the module you want to load needs functionality from another part of the kernel that is neither compiled into the kernel nor contained in a module already loaded. You could now try to find out which module contains those functions, load that module first with *insmod*, and try again. You will eventually succeed with this method, but it can be cumbersome, and this would not be Linux if there weren't a better way.

You first need a module database in the file */lib/modules/kernelversion/modules.dep*. You can create this database by calling:

```
depmod -a
```

This goes through all the modules you have and records whether they need any other modules. With this database in place, you can simply replace the *insmod* command with the *modprobe* command, which checks the module database and loads any other modules that might be needed before loading the requested module. For example, our *modules.dep* file contains—among others—the following line:

```
/lib/modules/2.0.35/misc/hisax.o:    /lib/modules/2.0.35/misc/isdn.o
```

This means that in order to load the *hisax* module (a device driver for a number of ISDN boards), the *isdn* module must be loaded. If we now load the *hisax* module with *modprobe* (this example is slightly simplified, because the *hisax* module needs additional parameters):

```
modprobe hisax
```

modprobe will detect the dependency and load the *isdn* module.

Some modules need so-called module parameters. For example, a device driver might need to be assigned an interrupt request line (IRQ). You can pass those parameters in the form *parametername=parametervalue* with both the *insmod* and the *modprobe* command. In the following example, several parametes are passed to the *hisax* module:

```
tigger # modprobe hisax type=3 protocol=2 io=0x280 irq=10
```

The documentation for each module should tell you which parameters the module supports.

One caveat about modules if you use the Debian distribution: Debian uses a file */etc/modules* where the modules are listed that should be loaded at boot time. If a module that you do not want keeps reappearing, check whether it is listed here.

You can list the drivers that are loaded with the command *lsmod*, as in:

```
rutabaga% lsmod
Module:         #pages:         Used by
ftape              40
```

The memory usage of the module is displayed as well; under Linux, a page is 4 KB. The *ftape* driver here is using 160 KB of memory. If the other modules are dependent on this module, they are shown in the third column.

A module can be unloaded from memory using the *rmmod* command. For example:

```
rmmod ftape
```

The argument to *rmmod* is the name of the driver as it appears in the *lsmod* listing.

Once you have modules working to your satisfaction, you can include the appropriate *insmod* commands in one of the *rc* scripts executed at boot time. One of your *rc* scripts might already include a place where *insmod* commands can be added, depending on your distribution.

One feature of the current module support is that you must rebuild a module any time you upgrade your kernel to a new version or patch level. (Rebuilding your kernel, but keeping the same kernel version, doesn't require you to do this.) This is done to ensure that the module is compatible with the kernel version you're using. If you attempt to load a module with a newer or older kernel than it was compiled for, *insmod* will complain and not allow the module to be loaded. When rebuilding a module, you must be running the kernel under which it will be used. Therefore, when upgrading your kernel, upgrade and reboot the new kernel first, then rebuild your modules and load them. There is an option that allows you to keep your modules when switching kernels, but there are a number of problems associated with it, and we recommend against using it.

Loading Modules Automatically

The so-called kernel daemon *kerneld* is an especially useful feature. With the help of this daemon, the kernel can load needed device drivers and other modules automatically and without manual intervention from the system administrator. If the modules are not needed after a period of time (60 seconds), they are automatically unloaded as well.

In order to use *kerneld*, you need to turn on support for it during kernel configuration, and you also need the System V IPC option. *kerneld* must be started from one of the system startup files; newer distributions are doing this automatically.

Modules that need other modules must be correctly listed into */lib/modules/kernelversion/modules.dep*, and there must be aliases for the major and minor number in */etc/conf.modules*. See the documentation from the *modules* package for further information.

If a module has not been loaded manually with *insmod* or *modprobe*, but loaded automatically from *kerneld*, the module is listed with the addition (autoclean) in the *lsmod* output. This tells you that *kerneld* will remove the module if it has not been used for more than one minute.

One last word about *kerneld*: In the latest kernels, *kerneld* is obsolete, because there is a new kernel feature called *kmod* that does the same (by running a separate kernel thread that loads the modules on demand). Still, running *kerneld* does not hurt.

CHAPTER EIGHT

OTHER ADMINISTRATIVE TASKS

Af ter reading the previous three chapters, you now have all the skills you need to start using your system. But don't ignore this chapter for long. Some of the activities, such as making backup tapes, are important habits to develop. You may also find it useful to have access to files and programs on MS-DOS and Windows. Finally, we'll help you handle events that you hope will never happen, but sometimes do—system panics and corruption.

Making Backups

Making backups of your system is an important way to protect yourself from data corruption or loss in case you have problems with your hardware, or you make a mistake such as deleting important files inadvertently. During your experiences with Linux, you're likely to make quite a few customizations to the system that can't be restored by simply reinstalling from your original installation media. However, if you happen to have your original Linux floppies or CD-ROM handy, it may not be necessary to back up your entire system. Your original installation media already serves as an excellent backup.

Under Linux, as with any Unix-like system, you can make mistakes while logged in as **root** that would make it impossible to boot the system or log in. Many newcomers approach such a problem by reinstalling the system entirely from backup, or worse, from scratch. This is seldom, if ever, necessary. In the section "What to Do in an Emergency," we'll talk about what to do in these cases.

Chapter 6

If you do experience data loss, it is sometimes possible to recover that data using the filesystem maintenance tools described in the section "Checking and Repairing Filesystems" in Chapter 6, *Managing Filesystems, Swap, and Devices*. Unlike some other operating systems, however, it's generally not possible to "undelete" a file that has been removed by *rm* or overwritten by a careless *cp* or *mv* command (for example, copying one file over another destroys the file you're copying to). In these extreme cases, backups are key to recovering from problems.

Backups are usually made to tape or floppy. Neither medium is 100 percent reliable, although tape is more dependable than floppy in the long term. There are many tools available that help you to make backups. In the simplest case, you can use a combination of *gzip* and *tar* to back up files from your hard drive to floppy or tape. This is the best method to use when you make only occasional backups, no more often than, say, once a month.

If you have numerous users on your system or you make frequent changes to the system configuration, it makes more sense to employ an incremental backup scheme. Under such a scheme, you would take a "full backup" of the system only about once a month. Then, every week, you would back up only those files that changed in the last week. Likewise, each night, you could back up just those files that changed over the previous 24 hours. There are several tools to aid you in this type of backup.

The idea behind an incremental backup is that it is more efficient to take backups in small steps; you use fewer floppies or tapes, and the weekly and nightly backups are shorter and easier to run. With this method, you have a backup that is at most a day old. If you were to, say, accidentally delete your entire system, you would restore it from backup in the following manner:

1. Restore from the most recent monthly backup. Say, if you wiped the system on July 17th, you would restore the July 1 full backup. Your system now reflects the state of files when the July 1 backup was made.

2. Restore from each of the weekly backups made so far this month. In our case, we could restore from the two weekly backups from July 7th and 14th. Restoring each weekly backup updates all of the files that changed during that week.

3. Restore from each of the daily backups during the last week, that is, since the last weekly backup. In this case, we would restore the daily backups from July 15th and 16th. The system now looks as it did when the daily backup was taken on July 16th; no more than a day's worth of files have been lost.

Depending on the size of your system, the full monthly backup might require 2 GB or more of backup storage—often not more than one tape using today's tape media, but quite a few ZIP disks. However, the weekly and daily backups would generally require much less storage space. Depending on how your system is used, you might decide to take the weekly backup on Sunday night and not bother with daily backups for the weekend.

One important characteristic that backups should (usually) have is the ability to select individual files from the backup for restoration. This way, if you accidentally delete a single file or group of files, you can simply restore those files without having to do a full system restoration. Depending on how you take backups, however, this task will be either very easy or painfully difficult.

In this section, we're going to talk about the use of *tar*, *gzip*, and a few related tools for making backups to floppy and tape. We'll even cover the use of floppy and tape drives in the bargain. These tools allow you to take backups more or less "by hand"; you can automate the process by writing shell scripts and even schedule your backups to run automatically during the night using *cron*. All you have to do is flip tapes. There are other software packages that provide a nice menu-driven interface for creating backups, restoring specific files from backup, and so forth. Many of these packages are, in fact, nice frontends to *tar* and *gzip*. You can decide for yourself what kind of backup system suits you best.

Simple Backups

The simplest means of taking a backup is to use *tar* to archive all the files on the system or only those files in a set of specific directories. Before you do this, however, you need to decide what files to back up. Do you need to back up every file on the system? This is rarely necessary, especially if you have your original installation disks or CD-ROM. If you have made important changes to the system, but everything else is as just the way it was found on your installation media, you could get by only archiving those files you have made changes to. Over time, however, it is difficult to keep track of such changes.

Chapter 10

In general, you will be making changes to the system configuration files in */etc*. There are other configuration files as well, and it can't hurt to archive directories, such as */usr/lib*, */usr/X11R6/lib/X11* (which contains the XFree86 configuration files, as we'll see in the section "Installing XFree86" in Chapter 10, *Installing the X Window System*).

You should also back up your kernel sources (if you have upgraded or built your own kernel); these are found in */usr/src/linux*.

During your Linux adventures it's a good idea to keep notes on what features of the system you've made changes to so you can make intelligent choices when taking backups. If you're truly paranoid, go ahead and back up the whole system: that can't hurt, but the cost of backup media might.

Chapter 16

Of course, you should also back up the home directories for each user on the system; these are generally found in */home*. If you have your system configured to receive electronic mail (see the section "The smail Mail Transport Agent" in Chapter 16, *The World Wide Web and Electronic Mail*), you might want to back up the incoming mail files for each user. Many people tend to keep old and "important" electronic mail in their incoming mail spool, and it's not difficult to accidentally corrupt one of these files through a mailer error or other mistake. These files are usually found in */var/spool/mail*.

Backing up to tape

Chapter 7

Assuming you know what files or directories to back up, you're ready to roll. The *tar* command can be used directly, as we saw in the section "Using tar" in Chapter 7, *Upgrading Software and the Kernel*, to make a backup. For example, the command:

```
tar cvf /dev/rft0 /usr/src /etc /home
```

archives all of the files from */usr/src*, */etc*, and */home* to */dev/rft0*. */dev/rft0* is the first "floppy-tape" device—that is, for the type of tape drive that hangs off of the floppy controller. Many popular tape drives for the PC use this interface. If you have a SCSI tape drive, the device names are */dev/st0*, */dev/st1*, and so on, based on the drive number. Those tape drives with another type of interface have their own device names; you can determine these by looking at the documentation for the device driver in the kernel.

You can then read the archive back from the tape using a command such as:

```
tar xvf /dev/rft0
```

This is exactly as if you were dealing with a tar file on disk, as seen in the section "Archive and Compression Utilities" in Chapter 7.

When you use the tape drive, the tape is seen as a stream that may be read from or written to in one direction only. Once *tar* is done, the tape device will be closed, and the tape will rewind. You don't create a filesystem on a tape, nor do you mount it or attempt to access the data on it as files. You simply treat the tape device itself as a single "file" to create or extract archives from.

Be sure your tapes are formatted before you use them. This ensures that the beginning-of-tape marker and bad-blocks information has been written to the tape. At the time of this writing, no tools exist for formatting QIC-80 tapes (those used with floppy tape drivers) under Linux; you'll have to format tapes under MS-DOS or use preformatted tapes.

Creating one tar file per tape might be wasteful if the archive requires but a fraction of the capacity of the tape. In order to place more than one file on a tape, you must first prevent the tape from rewinding after each use, and you must have a way to position the tape to the next "file marker," both for tar file creation and for extraction.

The way to do this is to use the nonrewinding tape devices, which are named */dev/nrft0*, */dev/nrft1*, and so on for floppy-tape drivers, and */dev/nrst0*, */dev/nrst1*, and so on for SCSI tapes. When this device is used for reading or writing, the tape will not be rewound when the device is closed (that is, once *tar* has completed). You can then use *tar* again to add another archive to the tape. The two tar files on the tape won't have anything to do with each other. Of course, if you later overwrite the first tar file, you may overwrite the second file or leave an undesirable gap between the first and second files (which may be interpreted as garbage). In general, don't attempt to replace just one file on a tape that has multiple files on it.

Using the nonrewinding tape device, you can add as many files to the tape as space permits. In order to rewind the tape after use, use the *mt* command. *mt* is a general-purpose command that performs a number of functions with the tape drive.

For example, the command:

```
mt /dev/nrft0 rewind
```

rewinds the tape in the first floppy-tape device. (In this case, you can use the corresponding rewinding tape device as well; however, the tape will rewind just as a side effect of the tape device being closed.)

Similarly, the command:

```
mt /dev/nrft0 reten
```

retensions the tape by winding it to the end and then rewinding it.

When reading files on a multiple-file tape, you must use the nonrewinding tape device with *tar* and the *mt* command to position the tape to the appropriate file.

For example, to skip to the next file on the tape, use the command:

```
mt /dev/nrft0 fsf 1
```

This skips over one file on the tape. Similarly, to skip over two files, use:

```
mt /dev/nrft0 fsf 2
```

mt(1)

Be sure to use the appropriate nonrewinding tape device with *mt*. Note that this command does not move to "file number two" on the tape; it skips over the next two files based on the current tape position. Just use *mt* to rewind the tape if you're not sure where the tape is currently positioned. You can also skip back; see the *mt* manual page for a complete list of options.

You need to use *mt* every time you read a multifile tape. Using *tar* twice in succession to read two archive files usually won't work; this is because *tar* doesn't recognize the file marker placed on the tape between files. Once the first *tar* finishes, the tape is positioned at the beginning of the file marker. Using *tar* immediately will give you an error message, because *tar* will attempt to read the file marker. After reading one file from a tape, just use:

```
mt device fsf 1
```

to move to the next file.

Backing up to floppy

Just as we saw in the last section, the command:

```
tar cvf /dev/fd0 /usr/src /etc /home
```

makes a backup of */usr/src*, */etc*, and */home* to */dev/fd0*, the first floppy device. You can then read the backup using a command such as:

```
tar xvf /dev/fd0
```

Because floppies have a rather limited storage capacity, GNU *tar* allows you to create a "multivolume" archive. (This feature applies to tapes, as well, but is far more useful in the case of floppies.) With this feature, *tar* prompts you to insert a new volume after reading or writing each floppy. To use this feature, simply provide the M option to *tar*, as in:

```
tar cvMf /dev/fd0 /usr/src /etc /home
```

Be sure to label your floppies well, and don't get them out of order when attempting to restore the archive.

One caveat of this feature is that it doesn't support the automatic *gzip* compression provided by the z option (as seen in the previous section). However, there are various reasons why you may not want to compress your backups created with *tar*, as discussed later. At any rate, you can create your own multivolume backups using *tar* and *gzip* in conjunction with a program that reads and writes data to a sequence of floppies (or tapes), prompting for each in succession. One such program is *backflops*, available on several Linux distributions and on the FTP archive sites. A do-it-yourself way to accomplish the same thing would be to write the backup archive to a disk file and use *dd* or a similar command to write the archive as individual chunks to each floppy. If you're brave enough to try this, you can figure it out for yourself.

To gzip, or not to gzip?

There are good arguments both for and against compression of *tar* archives when making backups. The overall problem is that neither *tar* nor *gzip* is particularly fault-tolerant, no matter how convenient they are. Although compression using *gzip* can greatly reduce the amount of backup media required to store an archive, compressing entire *tar* files as they are written to floppy or tape makes the backup prone to complete loss if one block of the archive is corrupted, say, through a media error (not uncommon in the case of floppies and tapes). Most compression algorithms, *gzip* included, depend on the coherency of data across many bytes in order to achieve compression. If any data within a compressed archive is corrupt, *gunzip* may not be able to uncompress the file at all, making it completely unreadable to *tar*.

This is much worse than if the tar file were uncompressed on the tape. Although *tar* doesn't provide much protection against data corruption within an archive, if there is minimal corruption within a tar file, you can usually recover most of the archived files with little trouble, or at least those files up until the corruption occurs. Although far from perfect, it's better than losing your entire backup.

A better solution would be to use an archiving tool other than *tar* to make backups. There are several options available. *cpio* is an archiving utility that packs files together, similar in fashion to *tar*. However, because of the simpler storage method used by *cpio*, it recovers cleanly from data corruption in an archive. (It still doesn't handle errors well on gzipped files.)

The best solution may be to use a tool such as *afio*. *afio* supports multivolume backups and is similar in some respects to *cpio*. However, *afio* includes compression and is more reliable because each individual file is compressed. This means that if data on an archive is corrupted, the damage can be isolated to individual files, instead of to the entire backup.

These tools should be available with your Linux distribution, as well as from all of the Internet-based Linux archives. A number of other backup utilities, with varying degrees of popularity and usability, have been developed or ported for Linux. If you're serious about backups, you should look into them.* Among those programs are the freely available are *taper* and *tob*, as well as commercial programs like *ARKEIA* and *Perfect Backup*.

Incremental Backups

Incremental backups, as described earlier in this chapter, are a good way to keep your system backups up to date. For example, you can take nightly backups of only those files that changed in the last 24 hours, weekly backups of all files that changed in the last week, and monthly backups of the entire system.

You can create incremental backups using the tools mentioned above: *tar*, *gzip*, *cpio*, and so on. The first step in creating an incremental backup is to produce a list of files that changed since a certain amount of time ago. This is easily done with the *find* command.† If you use a special backup program, you will most likely not have to do this, but set some option somewhere that you want to do an incremental backup.

---

* Of course, this section was written after the author took the first backup of his Linux system in nearly four years of use!

† If you're not familiar with *find*, become so soon. *find* is a great way to locate files across many directories that have certain filenames, permissions, or modification times. *find* can even execute a program for each file that it locates. In short, *find* is your friend, and all good system administrators know how to use it well.

For example, to produce a list of all files that were modified in the last 24 hours, we can use the command:

```
find / -mtime -1 \! -type d -print > /tmp/filelist.daily
```

The first argument to *find* is the directory to start from—here, /, the root directory. The *–mtime –1* option tells *find* to locate all files that changed in the last 24 hours.

The \! *–type d* is complicated (and optional), but it cuts some unnecessary stuff from your output. It tells *find* to exclude directories from the resulting file list. The ! is a negation operator (meaning here, "exclude files of type d"), but put a back-slash in front of it because otherwise the shell interprets it as a special character.

The *–print* causes all filenames matching the search to be printed to standard output. We redirect standard output to a file for later use. Likewise, to locate all files that changed in the last week, use:

```
find / -mtime -7 -print > /tmp/filelist.weekly
```

Note that if you use *find* in this way, it traverses all mounted filesystems. If you have a CD-ROM mounted, for example, *find* attempts to locate all files on the CD-ROM as well (which you probably do not wish to backup). The *–prune* option can be used to exclude certain directories from the walk performed by *find* across the system; or, you can use *find* multiple times with a first argument other than /. See the manual page for *find* for details.

find(1)

Now you have produced a list of files to back up. Previously, when using *tar*, we have specified the files to archive on the command line. However, this list of files may be too long for a single command line (which is usually limited to around 2048 characters), and the list itself is contained within a file.

You can use the *–T* option with *tar* to specify a file containing a list of files for *tar* to back up. In order to use this option, you have to use an alternate syntax to *tar* in which all options are specified explicitly with dashes. For example, to back up the files listed in */tmp/filelist.daily* to the device */dev/rft0*, use the command:

```
tar -cv -T /tmp/filelist.daily -f /dev/rft0
```

You can now write a short shell script that automatically produces the list of files and backs them up using *tar*. You can use *cron* to execute the script nightly at a certain time; all you have to do is make sure there's a tape in the drive. You can write similar scripts for your weekly and monthly backups. *cron* is covered in the next section.

Scheduling Jobs Using cron

The original purpose of the computer was to automate routine tasks. If you must back up your disk at 1:00 A.M. every day, why should you have to enter the commands manually each time—particularly if it means getting out of bed? You should be able to tell the computer to do it and then forget about it. On Unix systems, *cron* exists to perform this automating function. Briefly, you use *cron* by running the *crontab* command and entering lines in a special format recognized by *cron*. Each line specifies a command to run and when to run it.

Behind your back, *crontab* saves your commands in a file bearing your username in the */var/spool/cron/crontabs* directory. (For instance, the *crontab* file for user mdw would be called */var/spool/cron/crontabs/mdw*.) A daemon called *crond* reads this file regularly and executes the commands at the proper times. One of the *rc* files on your system starts up *crond* when the system boots. There actually is no command named *cron*, only the *crontab* utility and the *crond* daemon.

On some systems, use of *cron* is limited to the **root** user. In any case, let's look at a useful command you might want to run as **root** and show how you'd specify it as a *crontab* entry. Suppose that every day you'd like to clean old files out of the */tmp* directory, which is supposed to serve as temporary storage for files created by lots of utilities.

Most systems remove the contents of */tmp* when the system reboots, but if you keep it up for a long time, you may find it useful to use *cron* to check for old files (say, files that haven't been accessed in the past three days). The command you want to enter is:

```
ls -l filename
```

But how do you know which `filename` to specify? You have to place the command inside a *find* command, which lists all files beneath a directory and performs the operation you specify on each one.

We've already seen the *find* command in the section "Incremental Backups." Here, we'll specify */tmp* as the directory to search, and use the *–atime* option to find files whose last access time is more than three days in the past. The *–exec* option means "execute the following command on every file we find":

```
find /tmp \! -type d -atime +3 -exec ls -l {} \;
```

The command we are asking *find* to execute is *ls –l*, which simply shows details about the files. (Many people use a similar *crontab* entry to remove files, but this is hard to do without leaving a security hole.) The funny string { } is just a way of saying "Do it to each file you find, according to the previous selection material." The string \; tells *find* that the *–exec* option is finished.

Now we have a command that looks for old files on */tmp*. We still have to say how often it runs. The format used by *crontab* consists of six fields:

```
minute   hour   day   month   dayofweek   command
```

Fill the fields as follows:

1. Minute (specify from 0 to 59)

2. Hour (specify from 0 to 23)

3. Day of the month (specify from 1 to 31)

4. Month (specify from 1 to 12, or a name such as `jan`, `feb`, and so on)

5. Day of the week (specify from 0 to 6 where 0 is Sunday, or a name such as `mon`, `tue`, and so on)

6. Command (can be multiple words)

Figure 8-1 shows a *cron* entry with all the fields filled in. The command is a shell script, run with the Bourne shell *sh*. But the entry is not too realistic: the script runs only when all the conditions in the first five fields are true. That is, it has to run on a Sunday that falls on the 15th day of either January or July—not a common occurrence! So this is not a particularly useful example.

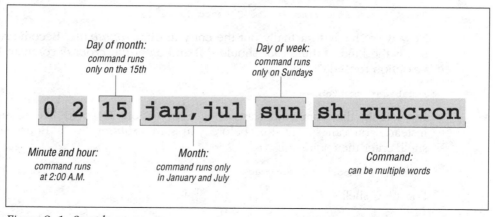

Figure 8-1: Sample cron entry

If you want a command to run every day at 1:00 A.M., specify the minute as 0 and the hour as 1. The other three fields should be asterisks, which mean "every day and month at the given time." The complete line in *crontab* is:

```
0 1 * * * find /tmp -atime 3 -exec ls -l {} \;
```

Since there are a lot of fancy things you can do with the time fields, let's play with this command a bit more. Suppose you want to run the command just on the first day of each month. You would keep the first two fields, but add a 1 in the third field:

```
0 1 1 * * find /tmp -atime 3 -exec ls -l {} \;
```

To do it once a week on Monday, restore the third field to an asterisk but specify either 1 or mon as the fifth field:

```
0 1 * * mon find /tmp -atime 3 -exec ls -l {} \;
```

To get even more sophisticated, there are ways to specify multiple times in each field. Here, a comma means "run on the 1st and 15th day" of each month:

```
0 1 1,15 * * find /tmp -atime 3 -exec ls -l {} \;
```

while a hyphen means "run every day from the 1st through the 15th, inclusive":

```
0 1 1-15 * * find /tmp -atime 3 -exec ls -l {} \;
```

and a slash followed by a 5 means "run every fifth day" which comes out to the 1st, 6th, 11th, and so on:

```
0 1 */5 * * find /tmp -atime 3 -exec ls -l {} \;
```

Now we're ready to actually put the entry in our *crontab* file. Become **root** (since this is the kind of thing **root** should do) and enter the *crontab* command with the *−e* option for "edit":

```
rutabaga# crontab -e
```

By default, this command starts a *vi* edit session. If you'd like to use Emacs instead, you can specify this before you start *crontab*. For a Bourne-compliant shell, enter the command:

```
rutabaga# export VISUAL=emacs
```

For the C shell:

```
rutabaga# setenv VISUAL emacs
```

The environment variable EDITOR also works in place of VISUAL for some versions of *crontab*. Enter a line or two beginning with hash marks (#) to serve as comments explaining what you're doing, then put in your *crontab* entry:

```
# List files on /tmp that are 3 or more days old.  Runs at 1:00 AM
# each morning.
0 1 * * * find /tmp -atime 3 -exec ls -l {} \;
```

When you exit *vi*, the commands are saved. Look at your *crontab* entry by entering:

```
rutabaga# crontab -l
```

We have not yet talked about a critical aspect of our *crontab* entry: where does the output go? By default, *cron* saves up the standard output and standard error and sends them to the user as a mail message. In this example, the mail goes to **root**, but that should automatically be directed to you as the system administrator. Make sure the following line appears in */usr/lib/aliases* (*/etc/aliases* on Debian):

```
root: your-account-name
```

In a moment, we'll show what to do if you want output saved in a file instead of being mailed to you.

Here's another example of a common type of command used in *crontab* files. It performs a tape backup of a directory. We assume that someone has put a tape in the drive before the command runs. First, an *mt* command makes sure the tape in the */dev/rft0* device is rewound to the beginning. Then a *tar* command transfers all the files from the directory */src* to the tape. A semicolon is used to separate the commands; that is standard shell syntax:

```
# back up the /src directory once every two months.
0 2 1 */2 * mt -f /dev/rft0 rewind; tar cf /dev/rft0 /src
```

The first two fields ensure that the command runs at 2:00 A.M., and the third field specifies the first day of the month. The fourth field specifies every two months. We could achieve the same effect, in a possibly more readable manner, by entering:

```
0 2 1 jan,mar,may,jul,sep,nov * mt -f /dev/rft0 rewind; \
        tar cf /dev/rft0 /src
```

The section "Making Backups" explains how to do backups on a regular basis.

The following example uses *mailq* every two days to test whether there is any mail stuck in the mail queue, and sends the mail administrator the results by mail. If there is mail stuck in the mail queue, the report includes details about addressing and delivery problems, but otherwise the message is empty:

```
0 6 */2 * * mailq -v | \
        mail -s "Tested Mail Queue for Stuck Email" postmaster
```

Probably you don't want to receive a mail message every day when everything is going normally. In the examples we've used so far, the commands do not produce any output unless they encounter errors. But you may want to get into the habit of redirecting the standard output to */dev/null*, or sending it to a log file like this (note the use of two > signs so that we don't wipe out previous output):

```
0 1 * * * find /tmp -atime 3 -exec ls -l {} \; >> /home/mdw/log
```

In this entry, we redirect the standard output, but allow the standard error to be sent as a mail message. This can be a nice feature, because we'll get a mail message if anything goes wrong. If you want to make sure you don't receive mail under any circumstances, redirect both the standard output and the standard error to a file:

```
0 1 * * * find /tmp -atime 3 -exec ls -l {} \; >> /home/mdw/log 2>&1
```

When you save output in a log file, you get the problem of a file that grows continuously. You may want another *cron* entry that runs once a week or so, just to remove the file.

Only Bourne shell commands can be used in *crontab* entries. That means you can't use any of the convenient extensions recognized by *bash* and other modern shells, such as aliases or the use of ~ to mean "my home directory." You can use $HOME, however; *cron* recognizes the $USER, $HOME, and $SHELL environment variables. Each command runs with your home directory as its current directory.

Some people like to specify absolute path names for commands, like */usr/bin/find* and */bin/rm*, in *crontab* entries. This ensures that the right command is always found, instead of relying on the path being set correctly.

If a command gets too long and complicated to put on a single line, write a shell script and invoke it from *cron*. Make sure the script is executable (use *chmod +x*) or execute it by using a shell like:

```
0 1 * * * sh runcron
```

As a system administrator, you often have to create *crontab* files for dummy users, such as **news** or UUCP. Running all utilities as **root** would be overkill and possibly dangerous, so these special users exist instead.

The choice of a user also affects file ownership: a *crontab* file for **news** should run files owned by **news**, and so on. In general, make sure utilities are owned by the user in whose name you create the *crontab* file.

As **root**, you can edit other users' *crontab* files by using:

```
tigger # crontab -u user -e
```

Chapter 4

Also, think about who is going to use the output files you create. If a file is created by a *cron* entry running as **news**, you may have trouble reading the file later as another user. You may have to use *chown* or *chmod* in your *cron* script to make sure the file is usable later. These commands are discussed in the section "Changing the Owner, Group, and Permissions" in Chapter 4, *Basic Unix Commands and Concepts.*

Since you can't log in as **news**, you can edit **news**'s crontab file as **root** using the command:

```
rutabaga# crontab -e -u news
```

Managing System Logs

The *syslogd* utility logs various kinds of system activity, such as debugging output from *sendmail* and warnings printed by the kernel. *syslogd* runs as a daemon and is usually started in one of the *rc* files at boot time.

The file */etc/syslog.conf* is used to control where *syslogd* records information. Such a file might look like the following:

```
*.info;*.notice     /var/log/messages
mail.debug          /var/log/maillog
*.warn              /var/log/syslog
kern.emerg          /dev/console
```

The first field of each line lists the kinds of messages that should be logged, and the second field lists the location where they should be logged. The first field is of the format:

```
facility.level [; facility.level ... ]
```

where `facility` is the system application or facility generating the message, and `level` is the severity of the message.

For example, `facility` can be `mail` (for the mail daemon), `kern` (for the kernel), `user` (for user programs), or `auth` (for authentication programs such as *login* or *su*). An asterisk in this field specifies all facilities.

`level` can be (in increasing severity): `debug`, `info`, `notice`, `warning`, `err`, `crit`, `alert`, or `emerg`.

In the previous */etc/syslog.conf*, we see that all messages of severity `info` and `notice` are logged to */var/log/messages*, all `debug` messages from the mail daemon are logged to */var/log/maillog*, and all `warn` messages are logged to */var/log/syslog*. Also, any `emerg` warnings from the kernel are sent to the console (which is the current virtual console, or an *xterm* started with the −*C* option).

The messages logged by *syslogd* usually include the date, an indication of what process or facility delivered the message, and the message itself—all on one line. For example, a kernel error message indicating a problem with data on an *ext2fs* filesystem might appear in the log files as:

```
Dec  1 21:03:35 loomer kernel: EXT2-fs error (device 3/2):
  ext2_check_blocks_bit map: Wrong free blocks count in super block,
  stored = 27202, counted = 27853
```

Similarly, if an *su* to the root account succeeds, you might see a log message such as:

```
Dec 11 15:31:51 loomer su: mdw on /dev/ttyp3
```

Log files can be important in tracking down system problems. If a log file grows too large, you can delete it using *rm*; it will be recreated when *syslogd* starts up again.

Your system probably comes equipped with a running *syslogd* and an */etc/syslog.conf* that does the right thing. However, it's important to know where your log files are and what programs they represent. If you need to log many messages (say, debugging messages from the kernel, which can be very verbose) you can edit *syslog.conf* and tell *syslogd* to reread its configuration file with the command:

```
kill -HUP `cat /var/run/syslog.pid`
```

Note the use of backquotes to obtain the process ID of *syslogd*, contained in */var/run/syslog.pid*.

Other system logs might be available as well. These include:

/var/log/wtmp

This file contains binary data indicating the login times and duration for each user on the system; it is used by the *last* command to generate a listing of user logins. The output of *last* might look like:

```
mdw       tty3               Sun Dec 11 15:25    still logged in
mdw       tty3               Sun Dec 11 15:24 - 15:25  (00:00)
mdw       tty1               Sun Dec 11 11:46    still logged in
reboot    ~                  Sun Dec 11 06:46
```

A record is also logged in */var/log/wtmp* when the system is rebooted.

/var/run/utmp

This is another binary file that contains information on users currently logged into the system. Commands, such as *who*, *w*, and *finger*, use this file to produce information on who is logged in. For example, the *w* command might print:

```
  3:58pm  up  4:12,  5 users,  load average: 0.01, 0.02, 0.00
User      tty        login@  idle   JCPU   PCPU  what
mdw       ttyp3     11:46am   14                 -
mdw       ttyp2     11:46am            1         w
mdw       ttyp4     11:46am                      kermit
mdw       ttyp0     11:46am   14                 bash
```

w(1)

We see the login times for each user (in this case, one user logged in many times), as well as the command currently being used. The *w* manual page describes all of the fields displayed.

/var/log/lastlog

This file is similar to *wtmp*, but is used by different programs (such as *finger*, to determine when a user was last logged in.)

Note that the format of the *wtmp* and *utmp* files differs from system to system. Some programs may be compiled to expect one format and others another format. For this reason, commands that use the files may produce confusing or inaccurate information—especially if the files become corrupted by a program that writes information to them in the wrong format.

Logfiles can get quite large, and if you do not have the necessary hard disk space, you have to do something about your partitions being filled too fast. Of course, you can delete the log files from time to time, but you may not want to do this, since the log files also contain information that can be valuable in crisis situations.

One option is to copy the log files from time to time to another file and compress this file. The log file itself starts at 0 again. Here is a short shell script that does this for the log file */var/log/messages*:

```
mv /var/log/messages /var/log/messages-backup
cp /dev/null /var/log/messages

CURDATE=`date +"%m%d%y"`

mv /var/log/messages-backup /var/log/messages-$CURDATE
gzip /var/log/messages-$CURDATE
```

First, we move the log file to a different name and then truncate the original file to 0 bytes by copying to it from */dev/null*. We do this so that further logging can be done without problems while the next steps are done. Then, we compute a date string for the current date that is used as a suffix for the filename, rename the backup file, and finally compress it with *gzip*.

You might want to run this small script from *cron*, but as it is presented here, it should not be run more than once a day—otherwise the compressed backup copy will be overwritten, because the filename reflects the date but not the time of day. If you want to run this script more often, you must use additional numbers to distinguish between the various copies.

There are many more improvements that could be made here. For example, you might want to check the size of the log file first and only copy and compress it if this size exceeds a certain limit.

Even though this is already an improvement, your partition containing the log files will eventually get filled. You can solve this problem by keeping only a certain number of compressed log files (say, 10) around. When you have created as many log files as you want to have, you delete the oldest, and overwrite it with the next one to be copied. This principle is also called *log rotation*. Some distributions have scripts like *savelog* or *logrotate* that can do this automatically.

To finish this discussion, it should be noted that most recent distributions like SuSE, Debian, and Red Hat already have built-in *cron* scripts that manage your log files and are much more sophisticated than the small one presented here.

Managing Print Services

Linux has a fairly complicated printing system, compared to the printing services most personal computers use. It allows many users to print documents at the same time, and each user can send documents from one or more applications without waiting for the previous document to finish printing. The printing system processes the files to be printed correctly on different kinds of printers connected to the computer in different ways. If you print on a network, files can be created on one host and printed out on a printer controlled by another host.

The whole process happens without much fuss, when you press the Print button in an application or issue a command, such as *lpr*, to print a document. That document does not go directly to the printer, though, because it might already be busy. Instead, the document is stored in a temporary file in a directory called the printer spool directory. As the word "spool" suggests, the documents get taken out of the directory one by one as the printer becomes free. Each printer has its own spool directory.

When Linux starts, it sets up a printer daemon (an independently running process) called *lpd*. This process waits around checking each spool directory for files that should be printed. When the process finds a file, it makes a copy of itself. The new *lpd* takes control of the print spool where the file was placed and queues it for printing. It won't send the next file to that printer until the last file has finished printing. The master *lpd* starts an *lpd* for each spooling directory on the system when a file is sent to it, so there may be as many *lpd* daemons running as the number of active spooling directories plus the master *lpd*. Each subordinate *lpd* stays around until its spool directory is empty.

Your Linux installation process associates the printer port on your system to a device named in the */dev* directory. You must then link that device name to the convenient printer names you use in your commands; that's the role of the printer capability file called */etc/printcap*.

Another key task in printer management is to make sure you have filters in place for *lpd* to use when formatting documents for printing. These filters are also specified in the */etc/printcap* file, and we'll talk a lot about them in this section.

There are several printer-support packages for Linux. Most distributions use the BSD-derived package that contains the *lpd* printer daemon. These packages include a set of utilities and manpage documents to support traditional Unix-style printing on Linux. The BSD printing system doesn't have as many administrative tools or user controls as, for example, the System V Unix printer-management system (which uses the *lpsched* daemon), but each user controls the files that she sends to the printer. This section describes installation and configuration of the BSD printer-support package. (The various printing utilities are described in the section "Printing" in Chapter 9, *Editors, Text Tools, Graphics, and Printing.*)

Chapter 9

Some Linux distributions provide a printer-management tool that simplifies printer installation and management through a graphical user interface. These tools are documented by the vendor that supplies them. They manage printing by controlling the same tools and files we are about to describe, but with less fine control. They can save you a lot of trouble in getting started, but they don't always get things right. If you want to correct an installation set up through these tools or want to improve on their performance, you still should work through the procedures in this section.

Checking Printer Hardware

Before you set up printer services, be sure the printing devices are online. If you also use another operating system, such as OS/2, Coherent, or MS-DOS, you can exercise the hardware to ensure that it is connected properly and working before loading Linux. Successfully printing a document from another operating system immediately eliminates one major source of woe and headscratching. Similarly, if you are going to use printer services on a network, your system should be on the network and all protocols functioning before proceeding.

You install printer services as the **root** user, with superuser privileges. The superuser is the only user besides the *lpd* print daemon able to write directly to a printer by directing output to the corresponding output device. Other users cannot send output directly to the printer and must instead use the printer utilities to handle printing tasks.

Before you get started, you can abuse your root privileges to verify that your system's assigned device files actually have a valid link to the physical device. Just send a brief ASCII test file directly to the printer by redirection. For instance, if you have a printer on your first parallel port, its device name is probably either */dev/ lp0* or */dev/lp1*, depending on your installation. The following command outputs some text suited for testing a printer setup, which you can redirect to your printer. (If you have an early PostScript printer, you may need instead to send it a small PostScrip test file to prevent it from getting confused.)

```
lptest > /dev/lp1
```

The *lptest* utility is designed to conveniently exercise an ASCII printer or terminal to make sure it is working correctly. It sends a prepared file composed of the 96 ASCII characters in a sequence that creates a "ripple" or "barber-pole" output effect. The default output of *lptest* on Linux is 16,000 characters arrayed in 79-character lines, long enough to require more than one page to print. If you run *lptest* with no arguments, it prints the standard output to your screen, and you can see what should be sent to the printer. The *lptest* command allows you to trim the width of the output column and to limit the number of output lines. For example, to display an output 35 characters wide, limited to six lines, you would enter:

```
lptest 35 6
```

The output should look much like this:

```
!"#$%&'()*+,-./0123456789:;<=>?@ABC
"#$%&'()*+,-./0123456789:;<=>?@ABCD
#$%&'()*+,-./0123456789:;<=>?@ABCDE
$%&'()*+,-./0123456789:;<=>?@ABCDEF
%&'()*+,-./0123456789:;<=>?@ABCDEFG
&'()*+,-./0123456789:;<=>?@ABCDEFGH
```

This output is short enough that you can see the result of redirecting it to your printer without wasting a lot of paper and long enough to identify many obvious problems with printing.

Of course, you can also use the *cat* command to direct a file to the printer. To send a PostScript test file to a PostScript printer, for example, type:

```
cat testfile.ps > /dev/lp1
```

If you have a serial printer, try directing output to the serial port to which it is connected. For the first serial port (COM1: in MS-DOS) try something like:

```
lptest > /dev/ttys0
```

or:

```
lptest > /dev/ttyS0
```

Make sure you send to the correct serial port; don't try to output the file to a serial mouse, for example. If your serial printer is on the second serial port, for example, it is addressed as */dev/ttyS1* or */dev/ttys1*.

If you have a page printer that buffers a partial page, after it stops printing you may need to take the printer offline and press the Form Feed button to get it to print the last partial page. Don't forget to put the printer back online afterward. (If your printer does buffer partial pages, you want Linux to send the formfeed character to the printer, either by forcing it through the */etc/printcap* entry for the printer or by having the printer filter append it to the end of the file. We'll discuss these options later.)

If your little test resulted in "laddered" text (text that looks something like the following example) and then continued off the page, the printer did not insert a carriage return at the end of each line:

```
!"#$%&'()*+,-./0123456789:;<=>?@ABC
                          "#$%&'()*+,-./0123456789:;<=>?@ABCD
                                                   #$
```

You might be able to figure out what went wrong here. Text files in Unix use just a newline (also known as a linefeed, ASCII code 10) to terminate each line. MS-DOS uses both a newline and a carriage return. Your printer was therefore set up to use MS-DOS–style line endings with both newline and carriage-return characters at the end of each line. In order to print a text file from Unix, you can install a printer filter to accommodate the Unix newline, or you can reconfigure your printer to properly return to the start of the line on receipt of a newline character. Often this is simply a matter of setting a dip switch. Check your printer manual. (Be careful about changing your printer characteristics if you use multiple operating systems.)

Laddering won't be an issue if you have a printer using a page-description language such as PostScript (the universally used page-layout language from Adobe), and you always filter plain text into that output form before printing. Filtering is described later in this chapter.

Gathering Resources

OK, you have your printer hardware set up and connected. You should collect hardcopy of your resource documents (at least the manpages for the print utilities and files described here, and the Printing HOWTO file). Also, it is useful to have the technical specifications for your printer. Often these are no longer provided when you buy your printer, but you can usually download the information you need from an FTP site or BBS operated by the printer manufacturer. While you are retrieving such information, look around and see if there is documentation (such as a description of printer error messages and their meanings) that can help you troubleshoot and manage your printer. Most printer manufacturers also offer a technical manual for the printer that you can buy. This may or may not be the same volume as the service manual.

For example, on the Hewlett Packard FTP site, *ftp://boi.external.hp.com*, you can retrieve printer technical data sheets; product specs; port-configuration information; PostScript, PCL, and HP-GL files for testing your printers (and filters); descriptions of printer control sequences you can pass to the printer to control its behavior; and documents telling how you can integrate *lpd*-based printing services with HP's JetAdmin package (and thereby with Netware-networked printers as well).

Now, before starting, take a deep breath; be patient with yourself. Printer services configuration is a skill that takes time to develop. If you have sufficiently standard equipment and successfully use one of the new-fangled printer management utilities to quickly and efficiently install and configure printer services, celebrate! Then note that you can probably fine-tune the installation for better performance by applying the procedures we describe next and perhaps by using filters and utilities written specifically to support all the features of your printer model. If you decide to revise a successful printer installation, make sure you take notes on the changes you make so you can find your way back if your changes don't do what you expected.

Choosing Printer Software

In order to print from Linux, you need to install the BSD print system. This provides basic tools, but it does not support modern printers. Indeed, it was designed to support line printers and devices common to the computer rooms of the '60s and '70s. In order to support modern printers, powerful supplemental packages provide the features most users think of as essential. (The *ftp://metalab.unc.edu* FTP site and its mirrors archive the packages we mention here.)

Chapter 9

In this section, we discuss some important packages to support modern print services. We assume your system will have at least the *groff* formatter, the Ghostscript page-formatting package, and the *GNU Enscript* filter packages, which are described in Chapter 9. Most Linux distributions already include these as well as other formatting and printing utilities. If yours does not, you can retrieve them from the usual Linux FTP sites or take them from the CD-ROM of another distribution.

It matters where you get formatting and filtering packages. If you receive Ghostscript from a European distribution, for example, it probably defaults to an A4 paper format rather than the 8.5x11-inch paper format kept in U.S. binary archives. In either case, the default can easily be overridden through an *lpr* option passed to the filter. Alternatively, you can build the tools from source.

The trend in printer technology is away from character-oriented output and toward adoption of a page-description language (PDL) that provides sophisticated graphics and font control. By far the most popular of the PDLs is PostScript, which has been widely adopted in the Unix and Internet communities. A major reason for its acceptance is Ghostscript, a PostScript implementation copyrighted by Aladdin Enterprises. A version is also distributed under the GNU Public License through the Free Software Foundation, along with a large font library, that can be used with either version or other PostScript interpreters.

Ghostscript implements almost all the instructions of the PostScript language and supports viewer utilities, such as Ghostview, that allow PostScript documents to be displayed in X windows. Similarly, excellent filters are readily available that convert PostScript output into other printing languages, such as Hewlett-Packard's PCL, and into forms printable as raster output on inkjet, dot matrix, and laser printers. Ghostscript is indispensable if you do any kind of printing besides character-based output and is easily extensible. The Ghostscript package supports Adobe type 1 and 3 PostScript fonts and provides a number of utilities for graphic format conversion and filtering. It can even generate PDF files, i.e., files that conform to the Adobe Portable Document Format specification.

Ghostscript may be insufficient to use by itself, however, because it doesn't provide printer control to switch between PostScript and text modes. Although Ghostscript does provide a filter that provides this capability (and more), the *nenscript* filter meets the tests of simplicity, flexibility, and reliability for most systems, so we document it here.

A typical Linux formatting and printing system might primarily use *groff* to format, creating PostScript output that is then processed by Ghostscript for printing and display. Often there will be parallel printing systems installed that perform document formatting to suit preferences of various users or accommodate files received in different typesetting formats.

Checking Print Utilities

You probably also want to install the TEX formatting package. Even if you do not install the full TEX distribution, you should at least install the *xdvi* utility, in order to view TEX output and Texinfo files in an X window. Other filters can process DVI output into forms such as PostScript (*dvips*) or PCL (*dvilj*) if you have an aversion to the Ghostscript package or need to use native printer fonts for efficient data transfer and rapid printing.

The Lout package is also worthy of consideration as an efficient and compact package to format documents for PostScript output. It supports Level 2 PostScript and the Adobe Structuring Conventions, takes comparatively little memory, and comes with good enough documentation to learn quickly. Lout doesn't create an intermediate output form; it goes directly from markup input to PostScript output.

To support graphics work and X Window System utilities, you probably want to install other tools, some of which probably come with your distribution. A collection of current versions of the most popular print support packages for Linux can be found at the *ftp://metalab.unc.edu* Linux archive, in */pub/Linux/system/printing*. The *netpbm* and *pbmplus* packages support a large variety of graphic file format conversions. (Such formats have to be converted to PostScript before you try to print them.) The Ghostview package provides display tools to view PostScript files in an X Window System environment, and also provides PostScript and PDF support for other packages, such as your Web browser.

Chapter 9

The ImageMagick package, described in Chapter 9, deserves special mention. It lets you display a large number of graphic formats in an X window. (It uses Ghostview and Ghostscript when it needs to display a PostScript image.) Most of the graphics files you can print you can also display using ImageMagick.

A "magic" filter package may also save you much grief in configuring and supporting different document output formats. We will discuss the APSfilter magic filter package (not in great depth) but you may prefer the Magic-Filter package instead. Both are available at the *ftp://metalab.unc.edu* FTP archive. For more on magic filters, see the section "Magic Filters: APSfilter and Alternatives" later in this chapter.

If you want to support fax devices, the *tiffg3* utility can be used with Ghostscript to output Group III fax format files. To control a Class 1 or Class 2 faxmodem on your Linux host, you can use the efax package, which is provided in many distributions, or you can install and configure the more capable, but more complex, FlexFax package.

There are additional tools to support double-sided printing on laser printers and packages that convert PostScript to less common printer-control languages to support Canon and IBM Proprinter devices, for example. There is a package to support printing in Chinese on laser printers and bitmap devices. Most of these packages don't directly affect management of print services so we don't describe them in detail here, but this is a good time to install them if you wish to use them.

For the benefit of your users, make sure that all the manual pages for the packages you install are prepared properly when you complete your installations. Then run */sbin/mkwhatis* (*/usr/bin/mandb* on Debian) to build the manual page index file that facilitates locating information online. Some packages, such as Ghostscript, also provide additional documention that you can print or make available on the system for reference. (Linux distributions tend to omit these documents, but you can FTP them from the sites where the software packages are developed and maintained. The GNU archives of the Free Software Foundation, for example, are accessed by anonymous FTP at *ftp://GNU.ai.mit.edu.*)

Filter selection and use is described "Print Filters" section later in this chapter.

Setting Up the Printcap File

The essence of printer configuration is creating correct entries in the printer capabilities file, */etc/printcap*. A simple printcap entry for an HP Laserjet 4MP laser printer attached to the first (bidirectional) parallel port on an ISA bus PC might look something like this:*

```
ljet|lp|ps|Postscript|600dpi 20MB memory|local|LPT1:\
    :lp=/dev/lp0:rw:\
    :sd=/var/spool/lpd/ljet4:mx#0:mc#0:pl#72:pw#85:\
    :lf=/var/log/lpd-errs:if=/usr/local/cap/ljet4:
```

Don't be scared. After reading the following sections, you will find yourself browsing printcap files with ease.

 The */etc/printcap* file should accommodate every printer and printer port or address—serial, parallel, SCSI, USB, or networked—your system will use. Make

---

* In this chapter, we use ljet4 in several examples. Be aware that the HP Laserjet 4 model is available in several versions. Some Laserjet 4 models are PCL5 printers only, and others use PostScript. Unless you are aware that such things can happen, you can find it very frustrating trying to debug a printer filter that is expecting, for example, PostScript, when Ghostscript is passing it PCL5 input.

sure it reflects any change in hardware. And as always, be aware that some hardware changes should be performed only when power to your system is shut off.

Printcap file format rules

The printcap file format rules, briefly, are:

- A comment line begins with a pound sign (#).

- Each "line" of the printcap file defines a printer. A line that ends with a backslash character (\) is continued on the next line. Be very careful that no space or tab character follows the backslash character on the line. Traditionally, a continuation line is indented for readability. Multiple printer definitions can use the same actual printer, applying the same or different filters.

- Fields in the line are separated by colon characters (:); fields can be empty. However, a printcap line entry cannot be an empty field.

- Traditionally, the first field in the entry has no preceding colon.

- The first field of the entry line contains names for the printer, each separated by a vertical bar character (|). In the earlier example entry, this portion is the name field:

```
ljet|lp|ps|Postscript|600dpi 20MB memory|local|LPT1
```

Printer naming is discussed in detail in the next section. You should create a subdirectory of */var/spool/lpd* with the same name as the first printer ID listed in each printcap entry. However, the actual print spool that is used is assigned by the sd variable for the printcap entry; if the sd variable doesn't point to the actual print spool directory, any file sent to that printer definition will vanish.

- There must be at least a default printer entry in printcap. If a printer is named lp, that printer is used as the default system printer. Do not confuse the lp default printer name with the **lp** local printer variable, which is described next. We recommend you use **lp** as an alias (one of the names after the | characters) rather than the primary printer name (the first in the list), so you can switch the default printer without difficulty.

- Each local printer must have an **lp** variable set. In the previous example, the variable was set by this segment of the printcap entry:

```
lp=/dev/lp0
```

- For compulsive and sometimes practical reasons, some administrators recommend that the entries of the printcap file be kept in alphabetical order.

Printer names

Most printer entries traditionally begin with a short printer name entry in the first field, at least one fuller printer name, and one longer explanatory entry. Thus, both ljet and PostScript are names for the printer whose nameline is:

```
ljet|lp|ps|Postscript|600dpi 20MB memory|local|LPT1:
```

Documents can be output to any printer named in a nameline in */etc/printcap*.

You might name your printers after the model (hp, epson) or the type of printer (ps, pcl) or its specific modes. The DeskJet 540, for example, is a printer that should have two definitions in the printcap file, one for black print and another for color. The filters you use to support it are likely to be those for DeskJet 500 or 550C. For simple administration, you can assign printer names that are the names of a filter or filter parameter used for a specific device. Thus, if you have one LaserJet 4 and will use the ljet4 filter only for it, **ljet4** is one logical name for the printer. Similarly, a dot-matrix printer might be named **72dpi** when accessed via its low-resolution printer definition line, and have the name **144dpi** when accessed in a higher resolution.

If you use a printer administration utility that comes with your Linux distribution, you may have to follow certain arbitrary rules in preparing your printcap entries in order to get the tools working. For example, if you use Red Hat's printer manager utility provided on the administrator's desktop, you may need to make sure that **hp** is the first name of the first active printer entry in the printcap file. This means that when you need to switch default printers, you need to move the new default printer to the top entry of the list and then remove the **hp** name from the old default printer and prepend it as the first name of the new default printer. In order to prevent confusion in use of the spool queues, you should just leave the */var/spool/lpd/lp* directory set up and create a new directory with the actual name of the spool directory that corresponds to the name by which you actually will address the printer. Thus, if you want to send your files to print on a printer named **moa**, you will need to create a directory named */var/spool/lpd/moa*, with appropriate permissions, and specify that directory as the printer spool for that printer. Setting up printer directories is described in the next section.

The rest of the printcap variables

The printcap file provides a number of variables that you can define. Some are fairly universal, and others are specific to the implemented features of *lpd*. Most variables are provided to specify page parameters, files and directories, filters, communication channel settings, and remote access control. Any time you prepare a printcap file on a new system, read the printcap manual page to make sure you use the correct variable names. Variables set in a printcap entry that are not recognized are passed through to the filter for processing.

The printcap variables described here are listed in roughly their order of importance. Some variables are boolean, and are considered set if they are present. Others are set with the assignment operator (=) or numeric value operator (#) and a value; the variable preceedes the operator and the string or number follows the operator. Examples of the variables described in the following list are included in the contrived sample */etc/printcap* file that follows. The printcap manual page has a more complete listing of variables recognized by *lpd*:

sd   Specifies the spool directory used by the printer. Spool directories should all be in the same directory tree (on a fast hard disk), which is usually */var/spool*. Spool files are defined even for remote printers. Each spool file should have one of the names assigned to the printer it serves.

lp   Assigns a local printer device, typically connected through parallel port, serial port, or SCSI interface. The lp variable must be assigned to a device file in the */dev* directory, which may be a link to a physical device. The lp variable must be assigned if there is a local printer. This variable should not be assigned if the rp variable is assigned (that is, the print spool manager is on another host).* If lp assigns a serial device, the baud rate must be specified with the br variable.

lf   Specifies the log file for storing error messages. All printers should have this variable set and normally use the same error log file. Error entries include the name of the printer and can reveal problems with the user's printer environment, the host configuration, the communications channel that is used, and sometimes the printer hardware itself.

rw   This variable should be specified if the printer is able to send data back to the host through the specified device file. The rw variable tells *lpd* that the device should be opened for both reading and writing. This can be useful for serial or SCSI PostScript printers, for example, because they may return fairly useful error messages to *lpd*, which stores them in the error log.

mx   Specifies the maximum size of a print job in the spool. A value of zero sets no limit (the default, mx#0), and any other value sets the maximum file size in blocks. Most of the time you don't want to set a limit, but you could, for example, set a value slightly smaller than the expected minimum space available on a disk.

if   Specifies an input filter to use. If you do not specify an input (if) or output (of) filter, the system uses the default */usr/sbin/lpf* filter. For some MS DOS–style character printers, this is sufficient. Other useful filters are provided in the formatting utilities, and there are some flexible "magic filter" packages

---

* A special case arises where the printer to be addressed is a true networked printer (that is, it has its own IP address). In that instance, the lp variable assigns the name of a dummy file that is used for setting a temporary lock on the file when the networked printer is in use. The documentation for the networked printer should describe the procedure for setting up and managing print services to access it.

that will determine (usually correctly) the filtering to apply from the content of the data file passed to it. See the section "Print Filters" that follows.

of Specifies an "output" filter to use. When you assign the of variable and don't assign the if variable, the system uses the filter once when the device is opened. All queued jobs are then sent without reapplying the filter until the queue is exhausted (and *lpd* removes the lock file from the spool directory). This is not normally useful, but it could serve such purposes as sending faxes to a faxmodem for dialed connection over a telephone line.

When you assign both the if and of variables, the if-specified filter normally processes the file, but the of-specified filter prints a banner page before the input filter is applied. Using both input and output filters effectively on the same print queue is notoriously difficult.

br Specifies the data-transfer rate (baud rate) for a serial port. You must supply this value if the printer is accessed via serial port. A pound sign precedes a numeric value that expresses the data-transfer rate in bits per second (not truly the baud rate, which is an effective rate of flow as opposed to the maximum rate of flow). The specified rate should not exceed any hardware limits. For example, if your serial port is capable of a 57.6 Kbps rate and the printer can process 28.8 Kbps, the assigned rate should not exceed that lower limit (perhaps br#19200). Supported bps values are the usual multiples for serial communications: 300, 600, 1200, 2400, 4800, 9600, and so on. A number of additional data conditioning values may be set if you do assign a br value, but most of them aren't useful for typical Linux installations. The default behavior is probably acceptable for your printing purposes, but if you intend to print via serial port, study the br, fc, fs, xc, and xs variables in the printcap manual page.

pl Specifies the page length as the number of lines using the default font characters for character devices (and printers that can use a character mode). An example is pl#66 for an 11-inch page at six lines per inch. This value allows space for cropping and accommodates limits of some other devices, such as inkjet printers that cannot print to the bottom of the sheet or the edge of the paper. Normally used in conjunction with the pw variable.

pw Specifies the width of the page supported, in characters, using the default font characters for character devices. pw is set like the pl variable; for example, pw#85 for 10 characters per inch with an 8.5-inch printable page width.

px Specifies the number of pixels to use on the X axis for a bitmap image file sent to a raster device.

py Specifies the number of pixels to use on the Y axis for a bitmap image file sent to a raster device.

sh Suppresses printing of a header or banner page. In most cases, you should set this.

rp Specifies the name of a remote printer to use. This variable cannot be set if the lp variable is set for the same printer. The printer handling is performed by the remote host assigned in the rm variable, which is required when rp is set. Usually, the only variables set along with these are spooling and error recording. See the example that follows.

rm Specifies a remote host that controls the remote printer you print to. The specified host ID assigned by rm should be one that is known to the network services as installed (set up in */etc/hosts* or known through NIS, for example).

rs Restricts access to local printers to those users with an account on the system.

rg Specifies a restricted group that can use the printer. For example, to reserve a defined printer for superuser, enter rg=root.

sf Suppresses the formfeed sent to the printer by default at the end of a print file.

ff Assigns the formfeed character or string the device should use. The default is Ctrl-L (equivalent to ff='\f'), which is usual for most devices.

fo Sends a formfeed character to the device before sending the file.

mc Specifies the maximum number of copies you can print. Values are the same as for the mx variable; usually you want to allow unlimited copies (mc#0), which is the default.

sc Suppresses multiple copies (equivalent to mc#1).

Example 8-1 contains a sample printcap file that shows off many of the variables discussed in the previous list.

Example 8-1: Sample /etc/printcap file

```
# Fare well, sweet prints.
hp|bat|west|spigot|berkeley|TI MicroLaser Turbo:\
     :mx#0:rp=lp:\
     :lp=:sd=/var/spool/lpd:rm=spigot.berk.ora.com:\
     :lf=/var/log/lpd-errs:
# To the print room
kiwi|810|rint|Big Apple|Apple 810 via EtherTalk:\
     :lp=/var/spool/lpd/kiwi:sh:\
     :sd=/var/spool/lpd/kiwi:pl#72:pw#85:mx#0:\
     :lf=/var/log/lpd-errs:if=/usr/local/cap/kiwi:
```

Example 8-1: Sample /etc/printcap file (continued)

```
# big bird--agapornis via shielded serial access
samoa|S|PostScript|secure|QMS 1725 by serial adapter:\
        :lp=dev/tty01:br#38400:rw:xc#0:xs#0400040:sh:\
        :sd=/var/spool/lpd/samoa:pl#72:pw#85:mx#0:mc#0:\
        :lf=/var/log/lpd-errs:if=/usr/local/cap/samoa:
# agapornis via printer room subnet (standard access)
moa|ps|QMS 1725 via Ethernet:\
        :lp=/var/spool/lpd/moa/moa:rm=agapornis:rp=samoa:\
        :sd=/var/spool/lpd/moa:mx#0:sh:\
        :lf=/var/log/lpd-errs:if=/usr/local/cap/samoa:
```

Configuring Ghostscript

Ghostscript is included in standard Linux packages; it is an essential utility in an X Window System environment and is useful even if you don't run X. Ghostscript can provide graphics output to a standard VGA display even where no window manager is running and can also process and create PostScript-formatted files without a graphics display. You can examine what devices Ghostscript is configured to recognize and format for on your system by entering Ghostscript in interactive mode. If you enter:

```
$ gs
```

Ghostscript should load in interactive mode and await your instructions:

```
GS>
```

You can then query the devices that Ghostscript is configured to recognize, and Ghostscript will display them:

```
GS> devicenames ==
[/pkm /sj48 /la75plus /t4693d2 /pjxl300 /cdj500 /mgr8 /tifflzw /ppm
/okiibm /la70 /iwlo /ljet3d /pjxl /cdjcolor /mgrgray8 /tiffg32d /pnm
/oce9050 /declj250 /bjc600 /ljet2p /st800 /stcolor /png256 /mgrgray2
/tiffcrle /pgnm /m8510 /lbp8 /bj200 /pdfwrite /pjetxl /eps9high
/pnggray /bitcmyk /faxg32d /pgm /jetp3852 /epson /lp2563 /paintjet
/appledmp /x11cmyk /pcx24b /bit /dfaxlow /pbm /cp50 /tek4696 /lj4dith
/djet500c /x11 /pcx16 /tiff24nc /pkmraw /ccr /ln03 /t4693d4 /deskjet
/cdj550 /pcxmono /tiffpack /ppmraw /r4081 /la75 /nullpage /ljet4 /iwlq
/cdjmono /mgr4 /tiffg4 /pnmraw /oki182 /la50 /iwhi /ljet3 /cdj850
/cdeskjet /png16m /mgrgray4 /tiffg3 /pgnmraw /necp6 /lips3 /epsonc
/laserjet /x11mono /png16 /mgrmono /faxg4 /pgmraw /imagen /bjc800
/bj10e /pj /eps9mid /x11alpha /pngmono /bitrgb /faxg3 /pbmraw /ibmpro
/ap3250 /ljetplus /dnj650c /pcx256 /psmono /dfaxhigh /xes /lj250
/t4693d8 /djet500 /miff24 /pcxgray /tiff12nc]
GS> quit
$
```

If you are·not using X, and Ghostscript fails to initialize when you try to invoke it, complaining that it cannot open an X display, then the first device Ghostscript loaded in its build file was the X Window System device; Ghostscript uses the first device as its default device. You can work around this problem by specifying some other device that Ghostscript will have installed, for example, `gs -sDE-VICE=epson`. You can guard against the problem in the future by setting a global GS_DEVICE environment variable to some other device on your system that can be opened by Ghostscript.

If you have such an unusual output device that the default Ghostscript installation does not support it, you need to rebuild Ghostscript to support the device, or else process your output files through a filter that converts it to a form usable by your output device. Ghostscript comes with makefiles and is easy to build if you follow the Ghostscript documentation that comes with the distribution.

The more graphics utilities, X window managers, games, and applications you use, the more likely you will need to reinstall Ghostscript to suit your requirements. Read the Ghostscript documentation before running the makefile that comes with the package. (This requires that you have *gcc* installed on your system.)

You can define the GSDIR environment variable to locate the path of the *ghostscript* command, and to set GS_LIB variables if you need to build Ghostscript utilities and add them to your installation. For example:

```
export GSDIR=/usr/bin
export GS_LIB=/usr/lib/ghostscript:/usr/local/lib/fonts:/usr/X11R6/fonts
```

Set the GS_LIB_DEFAULTS variable before you make a new build of Ghostscript; see the *gs* manual page.

The Ghostscript package also contains some PostScript programs that provide useful print-support functions, including some sophisticated printing capabilities we do not document here. The *gs_init.ps* file, in particular, affects the general behavior of Ghostscript. Additional scripts (filters, shell scripts, and so on) can be found in */usr/lib/ghostscript* or */usr/local/lib/ghostscript*. You may find it useful to examine the *ps2epsi.ps* utility, which converts PostScript into encapsulated PostScript, and the *ps2ascii.ps* utility, which converts PostScript files into plain text.

Print Filters

Every document passes through a filter before going to the printer, thanks to the `if` variable in the printcap file. A print filter can be found in a Linux distribution, acquired from the printer's vendor, found on the Net, or even made yourself from scratch or by cobbling together existing filters and shell utilities.

An input filter can also be used to restrict use of a printer to a specific user or group, or users with accounts on a particular host. Typical `if`-assigned filters are executable shell scripts that process the text file, but they can be any program that can take the input data stream and process it for output to a printer.

It is increasingly common for commercial Linux distributions to build a filter interactively. While you can usually improve on such a filter, it can help to use one as a starting point. The Red Hat distribution, for example, created the following shell-script filter (named */var/spool/lpd/ljet4/filter*)* on one of our systems from information provided to it in the printer manager window and from default assumptions. The */etc/printcap* was modified to specify the use of this filter, which proved to be perfectly functional on our system:

```
#!/bin/sh

DEVICE=ljet4
RESOLUTION=600x600
PAPERSIZE=letter
SENDEOF=

nenscript -TUS -ZB -p- |
if [ "$DEVICE" = "PostScript" ]; then
        cat -
else
        gs -q -sDEVICE=$DEVICE \
                -r$RESOLUTION \
                -sPAPERSIZE=$PAPERSIZE \
                -dNOPAUSE \
                -dSAFER \
                -sOutputFile=- -
fi

if [ "$SENDEOF" != "" ]; then
        printf ""
fi

exit 0
```

There's nothing exotic about this filter. First it sets some variables that appear later as arguments in the Ghostscript command. The script passes output through *nenscript* and passes PostScript files to the *gs* Ghostscript utility. (In this particular case, the automatically generated filter will never invoke *gs* because DEVICE never equals "PostScript" in the `if` test.) If your printer doesn't eject the final pages of output, you can force it to by setting the SENDEOF variable near the top of the file. For example:

```
SENDEOF='\f'
```

will cause a formfeed to be sent to the printer when it reaches the end of a file.

---

* Putting a filter in a printer's spool directory is a convenient technique for a printer management program to use when setting up your printer system. You may prefer to keep all your print filters and graphics conversion filters in the same directory (following the Unix tradition), such as */usr/sbin* or */var/spool/lpd/filters*. Of course, in that case, each filter you create must be uniquely named.

You might modify such a script and substitute a filter specifically designed for a LaserJet 4 printer, such as the actual ljet4 filter package, for example, and accommodate printing of TEX DVI files by filtering them through *dvips* and feeding them to Ghostscript. There is an elementary discussion of how to create a filter in the Linux Printing HOWTO.

[82] Printing HOWTO

If you use a character printer that expects a carriage return at the end of each line, it will be unhappy with Linux, which follows Unix fashion in terminating a line with a linefeed, but no carriage return. To force correct treatment of newlines on these printers, the filter has to insert the carriage return. This can be done by writing the processing into the filter, or, alternatively, by using a filter that already has the capacity of inserting the character.

Some printer vendors provide filters and utilities for their printers, especially where the usual solutions are likely to be inadequate to take advantage of the printer's capabilities. For example, Hewlett-Packard provides a JetAdmin package with filters to use with their TCP/IP network-addressed LaserJet printers.

The default filter that comes with the BSD print-management package is */usr/sbin/ lpf.* This filter is undocumented and probably best ignored, unless you wish to retrieve the C source and trace through the program to learn its capabilities. (The full BSD source for this can be found in the lpr-secure package in the printing directory from *ftp://metalab.unc.edu.*)

Most of the print-filtering needs you have were long ago resolved, and there are filters out there to meet your needs. By running:

```
apropos filter
```

you can probably identify several print filters installed on your host.

Changing filters is simple. You need only change the */etc/printcap* input filter specification (if) to specify the filter you want, and then kill and restart *lpd*, which you can do using the *lpc* utility. Enter (as root):

```
lpc restart all
```

The *lpc* utility reports any *lpd* processes it kills, then it restarts *lpd*. If there are files in a print spool waiting to print, *lpd* also reports that an *lpd* daemon for that printer has been started. The *lpc* printer control utility is described later in this chapter, in the section "Controlling Printer Services with lpc."

Study the manual page for a filter and then pass some test files through before adopting a strange print filter. We have found that filters don't always perform "as advertised" in their manual page; often the document is obsolete or the filter was compiled by someone using different configuration parameters than the document assumes. There is no substitute for testing all the things you expect the filter to do before adopting it. Two good filtering packages, *nenscript* and APSfilter, are discussed in the next section.

The nenscript Filter

The *nenscript* filter is a typical modern filter for Linux. You should find it in */usr/bin/nenscript* if it was provided in your Linux distribution. Otherwise, it may be installed in */usr/local/bin. nenscript* controls headers, footers, rotation of text, and so on, and produces PostScript output conforming to the Adobe Structuring Conventions from plain ASCII input (by calling Ghostscript). It sends output to the printer specified by the user's NENSCRIPT environment variable, if set, or the user's PRINTER environment variable otherwise. If neither variable is set, *nenscript* uses the default printer that *lpr* wants to use.

If *nenscript* is called using the −Z option, it is supposed to pass PostScript files through without altering them. *nenscript* examines the input file, and if the first two characters in the input file are %!, *nenscript* suppresses formatting. Since this output "type-checking" is primitive, it is easily fooled. Obviously if the first two characters happen to be something other than %!, perhaps because a formfeed is the first character, for example, the file will not be recognized as PostScript even if it is. This can easily happen if some filter processing takes place before the file passes through to *nenscript*. Of course, a file can also have %! as the first characters and not be PostScript (or could be nonconforming PostScript) and may not therefore be handled properly if passed to a PostScript printer. There are smarter filters for this type of checking, including Magic-Filter or APSfilter, but *nenscript* may easily meet your needs, especially if you print only to a PostScript printer.

If you use the *nenscript* filter for a PostScript printer on your system, therefore, you could specify the −Z option in the NENSCRIPT environment variable for all user shells by default, in order to pass through the PostScript received by the filter.

There are other comparable filters. The *nenscript* filter emulates the traditional Unix enscript filter. A shell script provided in the *nenscript* package invokes *nenscript* configured to behave as though it were another (similar) traditional Unix filter, *pstext*.

To use *nenscript* to filter your print files, make sure *nenscript* is installed in an appropriate path, and then set the printers for which you want *nenscript* to filter to point to a filter that invokes the *nenscript* filter. You may find that the printcap entry can point directly to the *nenscript* filter if you set a system-wide default NENSCRIPT variable to control its options, or you can create a simple processing filter that calls *nenscript*, much like the sample configuration file shown earlier. Verify file and directory ownerships and permissions after you have altered the printcap file and set up filters.

Magic Filters: APSfilter and Alternatives

The most versatile filters are the so-called "magic" filters. A magic filter examines the contents of a file passed to it, and filters the output for printing based on the what it learns from the format of the information. If it sees the file is DVI routed to a PostScript printer, for instance, it will apply another filter (perhaps *dvips*) to convert the data into PostScript for printing. This is very convenient, but on occasion, the filter can make a mistake. If that happens, the user can resubmit the file with command-line options that specify which filtering to perform, or the user can preprocess the file by piping it through the needed filtering before passing it to *lpr* for routine print processing. There are some good magic filter packages, including APSfilter (which we have chosen to describe here) Magic-Filter, and the *gslp.ps* filter provided with complete Ghostscript packages.

Some Linux distributions, regrettably, omit Ghostscript's supplemental utilities or documents, but you can always retrieve a complete Ghostscript distribution via FTP from the GNU archive site (*ftp://ftp.gnu.org/gnu/*) or one of its mirrors. You can get the APSfilter package from the *ftp://metalab.unc.edu* FTP site in the */pub/ Linux/system/printing* directory. The primary FTP site for the Magic-Filter package is the *ftp://tsx-11.mit.edu* Linux archive. The Ghostscript filter, *gslp.ps*, is written in the PostScript language and can be used only with Ghostscript or another interpretor compatible with Adobe PostScript.

The APSfilter package for Linux is a port of a package developed for FreeBSD. For that reason, there are a few precautions to take in order to ensure that things configure properly when you install the APSfilter package. On a Linux host, it is probably best to install the APSfilter package in */usr/lib/apsfilter*. The package comes from *ftp://metalab.unc.edu* as a gzipped, tarred file. To unpack the package, put it in the */usr/lib/apsfilter* directory and enter:

```
gunzip apsfilter*gz
```

This results in a tar file. As of this writing, the tar file does not install correctly if you simply use the *tar* command on it in the *apsfilter* directory. Instead, from the *apsfilter* directory, use this command:

```
tar -vxf apsfilter*.tar -C /usr/lib
```

Now the APSfilter package unpacks within subdirectories of the *apsfilter* directory.

Change to the *apsfilter* directory. Before you run the *SETUP* command, you want to make sure you have all the filters you might want to use with APSfilter installed and configured. The */usr/lib/apsfilter/FAQ* file tells you of some of the more important and useful packages.

Before you run the installation, read the *INSTALL* document to make sure there aren't any surprises. Then run *./SETUP*. It tests for the presence and location of graphics utilities and other filters APSfilter uses to convert files into a form printable on your printer.

The *SETUP* script lets you know if the filter installed correctly. It can be run again if you wish to install more than one printer or more than one mode for a single printer. For example, if you install a Deskjet 540 printer, you probably will want to use the dj500 definition for the black cartridge and the dj550c definition for the CMYK color cartridge. APSfilter uses very long directory names for its spool directories. If you don't like that, you can rename the spool directories and change the corresponding directory fields in the corresponding */etc/printcap* entry. Be sure not to shorten the name of the filter used; that path is critical. We don't recommend you undertake to make things pretty until you are satisfied that things are working.

Before you try your new setup, you need to restart the print daemon:

```
/usr/sbin/lpc restart all
```

APSfilter sets systemwide variables for printer definitions in the */etc/apsfilterrc* file; reading it can be informative. Common print problems are probably the usual file ownership or permission problems, so don't forget to check that out. Then, read the *FAQ* and *TROUBLESHOOTING* files in the */usr/lib/apsfilter* directory.

If your APSfilter installation didn't work, you can always return to the configuration you had before you installed it by copying the */etc/printcap.orig* file that APSfilter saved for you back to */etc/printcap*.

APSfilter names its printers sequentially, from lp1 up. Don't be confused; that has nothing to do with the actual physical device assigned to the printer. Again, you can change those names.

APSfilter allows you to loosen restrictions so individual users can set up their own *.apsfilterr* file in their home directories. The default is to not allow it, which is a bit more secure.

The latest version of Magic-Filter (at the time of this writing, Version 1.2) is remarkably easy to install and makes a clean alternative to APSfilter. However, the installation doesn't do any hand-holding. Though there is a useful manual page, there isn't much information to walk you through setting up the alternate processing that the Magic-Filter utility should do for most printing devices. In particular, if you have a versatile printer that outputs in multiple modes (PostScript, PCL5, text, and so on), you may find it worth your while to install and use this package.

BSD Print System Elements: Files, Directories, and Utilities

The print-management system requires you to create directories that match the printcap printer names in order to spool files for printing. It also requires you to create other files for controlling the print process itself. You must set up directories and files with the correct ownership and privileges, and the printer utilities themselves also need correct permissions.

Setting up printer directories

Your Linux installation created a standard spool directory. Ideally, this is on a fast-access disk drive. The basic spool directory (*/var/spool*) is normally used for managing mail, news, and UUCP communications as well as for holding printer files. We recommend you follow this practice, which is a Linux standard. Some utilities or filters you get may expect to find */usr/spool/lpd* as the printer spool path. You will have to make corrections if you find this condition. You can, of course, create */usr/spool* and link it to */var/spool*, but that is a good idea only if */usr* and */var* are on the same disk drive.

You must create your own printer spool directories. The */var/spool/lpd* directory is the standard path for each printer subdirectory. Each printer subdirectory name must be used as a printer name in the first field in a corresponding */etc/printcap* entry. For example, */var/spool/lpd/moa* is appropriate for a printer with `moa` in a name field of the printcap entry. In turn, the */etc/printcap* entry for this printer should have an `sd` variable set to point to the spooling directory (`sd=/var/spool/lpd/moa`, for example).

You shouldn't use `lp` as the actual spool directory name unless you never expect to have more than one printer on your system or network, because `lp` is the default printer. (If your default printer is somewhere else on the network, your files will still get spooled to */var/spool/lpd/lp* first, before your *lpd* forwards them to the print daemon on the remote host to print.) You may have a printer-management utility that automatically creates an `lp` spool directory, but you can always edit the printcap file to point to any directory you wish.

The spool directory name should be the first name listed in the associated */etc/printcap* entry for the printer to make identification easy. The printcap entry will then be associated with the names under which *lpq* and *lpc* utilities report print queue status.

File, directory, and utility privileges

The most common problem in establishing print services is with file and directory permissions. Table 8-1 lists the important files, directories, and utilities that comprise BSD print management on Linux. Installed locations may vary according to your Linux distribution. The ownerships and permissions given in the following table are recommended for the files and directories of the printing system. (Additional filters and nonstandard spool paths may be specified in */etc/printcap*). Different permissions may still work, but if you have permissions problems, this is where you can straighten them out. An asterisk in the first column of Table 8-1 indicates that many files can exist with the names of different printers.

Table 8–1: BSD's Files, Directories, and Utilities for Printing

Directory or File	Permissions	Owner/Group	Description
/dev/ttys1	`crwsr-----`	root/lp	Typical serial port printing device
/dev/lp1	`crws------`	root/lp	Typical parallel port device (not bidirectional)
/usr/bin/lpc	`-rwsrwsr-x`	root/lp	Controls print-spooling services
/usr/bin/lpr	`-rwsrwsr-x`	root/lp	Receives print file, assigns processing data, and spools both
/usr/bin/lpq	`-rwsrwsr-x`	root/lp	Reports on spooled files with user and print queue data
/usr/bin/lprm	`-rwsrwsr-`	root/lp	Removes print jobs from spool
/usr/bin/tunelp	`-rwsr-sr-`	root/lp	Tests print services to improve them
/usr/bin/lptest	`-rwxr-xr-x`	root/root	Outputs an ASCII file for printer and display testing
/usr/sbin/lpd	`-rwsr-s---`	root/lp	Daemon manages printing using printcap data and data passed by *lpr*
/usr/sbin/lpf	`-rwxr-xr-x`	root/lp	Primitive BSD text print filter
/usr/sbin/pac	`-rwxr-r-`	root/root	BSD utility reports on printer activity and usage by user ID
/var/spool/	`drwxr-sr-x`	root/daemon	Basic system location for temporary files
/var/spool/lpd	`-rws-s-x`	root/lp	Standard path for the print-spooling system
/var/spool/lpd/*	`drwxr-sr-x`	root/lp	Spooling subdirectories for each defined printer
/var/spool/lpd/*/filter	`-rwxr-xr-x`	root/lp	Filters created by Red Hat printer-management utility for each print spool
/var/spool/lpd/lpd.lock	`-rw-rw----`	root/lp	*lpd* queue control lock
/var/spool/lpd/*/.seq	`-rw-rw----`	lp/lp	Sequence file *lpd* uses to order spooled files
/var/spool/lpd/*/lock	`-rw-------`	root/lp	*lpd* writes lock to prevent sending next file until printer is ready

Table 8–1: BSD's Files, Directories, and Utilities for Printing (continued)

Directory or File	Permissions	Owner/Group	Description
/var/spool/lpd//status*	-rw-------	lp/lp	*lpd* stores latest printer status report here
/var/log/lp-acct	-rw-------	root/root	Accounting record file, from which *pac* extracts and formats print data[a]
/var/log/lpd-errs	-rw-rw-r--	root/lp	Standard BSD log file for *lpd* errors

[a] This file remains empty if system accounting is not installed, unless you configure Ghostscript to perform its limited reporting there and make the file writable by all.

The usual Linux printer-management utilities set the print files with **root** ownership and **lp** group privilege. Traditionally, BSD distributions have used **root** ownership and **daemon** group privilege. You can use either group privilege, but if you use both **daemon** and **lp** privileges with different utilities and files, you will have problems. Be particularly careful about this if you add utilities from other packages to your services.

Let's say you (as **root**) need to create the printer-spooling directory, */var/spool/lpd*. You execute the command:

```
mkdir /var/spool/lpd
```

Assuming your */var/spool* was created with the usual permissions, the new *lpd* directory has permissions of `drwxrwxr-x`, which is too permissive. If you enter the command:

```
chmod 755 /var/spool/lpd
```

the permissions are changed to `drwxr-xr-x`. This is close, but not what you want. You need to set the setuid bit, so **lp** can setuid **root**:

```
chmod +s /var/spool/lpd
```

This results in `drwsr-sr-x`, which is what you want. However, the group should be **lp**, not **root**, so you need to fix that:

```
chgrp lp /var/spool/lpd
```

Create the spool directories needed for each printer as subdirectories of the */var/spool/lpd* directory in the same way, and then use *touch* to create a *.seq* file in each print directory:

```
touch .seq
```

Exercising the Printer Daemon

The *lpd* daemon consults */etc/printcap* and then sends files to printers by directing them to a device file in the */dev* directory. Most printers on Linux boxes are serial (usually addressed through devices named */dev/ttys0*, */dev/ttys1*, and so on, or */dev/ttyS0*, */dev/ttyS1*, and so on.) or parallel (*/dev/lp0*, */dev/lp1*, or */dev/lp2*, depending on the physical addresses the ports use). The port assignments are described in the section "Printer System Troubleshooting." A common mistake when configuring print services is to use the wrong port.

You can link a virtual device, */dev/fax* for example, to an actual device you can use by creating a symbolic link. For example:

```
ln -s /dev/ttys1 /dev/fax
```

This allows users to set up scripts and filters that address */dev/fax*, while you move the physical device (a faxmodem, for example) around simply by removing */dev/ fax* and then creating it again with a link to the new device.

The BSD printer daemon is notorious for dying or just becoming inert. To be fair, this seems to be less common than it was some years ago, but it still happens. When it does, just kill the old daemon and start a new one. If *lpd* isn't fairly reliable, though, there is a cause somewhere. There could be something wrong with a user's environment or the specified command-line options used with *lpr* or a faulty filter that sends setup data to the printer in a form the printer doesn't like. However, you have every reason to expect to have a "pretty good" printing package installation. If you are having problems, check out "Printer System Troubleshooting."

OK, let's see if you have a working print system. After making all these changes, you can be sure that *lpd* doesn't know what is going on. So run the *ps* command and find the ID of the *lpd* process. Then enter:

```
kill -9 processid
```

to kill the process you specified.* You should now have no print daemon running. Just enter */usr/sbin/lpd* to start the print daemon.

Now, while watching the activity LEDs on your printer front panel (if there are any), send a file to the printer (still acting with superuser privilege):

```
lptest | lpr
```

The *lptest* ASCII barber pole should begin printing to your default printer, as configured in your */etc/printcap* file. If it doesn't, you have a configuration problem that has nothing to do with privileges.

---

* You may prefer to use *lpc* to perform this task. Also, if your root desktop has a printer-manager tool, you can probably click on the lpd button to kill and restart the print daemon.

Did the printer show any activity? Does your default printer have a spool directory? Does the directory have a *.seq* file? Check */var/log/lpd-errs* and see if anything was stored in it. Use the *lpc* command and get a report on the status of the print daemon and the print spool.

If everything else looks good, make sure the printer is using the port you expected by sending a file directly to the port—for example:

```
# lptest > /dev/lp1
```

To test for a serial printer:

```
# lptest > /dev/ttys1
```

and so on. If none of these worked, reexamine your */etc/printcap* file. Is your entry properly formed? Are there no blank spaces or tabs following the continuation character (\) on your entry line? Is the printer queue correctly specified? Does the name `lp` appear as one of the printer names of the name field? Is the first name in the name field the same name as the spool directory it uses?

Let's assume you got through this first little test unscathed, and you now have several pages of lovely barber-pole printout in your printer tray. Next comes the real challenge. Can you print as a regular user? Log in (or run *su*) to become a normal system user. Now, try the same experiment. If it works, congratulations, you've got a printer! If it doesn't, you have a problem, but it is probably a file or directory ownership or permissions problem. You know what you have to do about that. Become **root** again, look at the manual pages for *chgrp*, *chmod*, and *chown*, and go down the list of files and directories to find your problem and fix it. Repeat until Joe User can print.

Controlling Printer Services with lpc

The *lpc* utility is provided to manage printer queues and requires root privilege to perform most of its functions. *lpc* reports on all print queues and their attending *lpd* daemons. You can also specify reports on a specific printer or printing system user. To get a status report on all printers and users, type:

```
$ lpc status
ibis:
        queuing is enabled
        printing is enabled
        no entries
        no daemon present
crow:
        queuing is enabled
        printing is enabled
        1 entry in spool area
        crow is ready and printing
```

```
ada:
        queuing is disabled
        printing is disabled
        no entries
        no daemon present
```

Queuing can be enabled within *lpc* through the *enable* command and disabled using its *disable* command. The *disable* command works by setting a group execute permission on the lock file in the print spool directory.

Printing can be enabled in *lpc* using its *start* command and disabled using its *stop* command. Jobs held in a print queue when a printer is stopped will remain there until printing is restarted. The *stop* command functions by setting a lock file in the printer spool directory and killing the print daemon for that queue, but it allows the currently printing job to complete. The *abort* command works like *stop*, but halts any printing job immediately, too. (Since the job did not complete, *lpr* retains it and starts over again when the queue is restarted.)

The *down* command functions as though both a *disable* and a *stop* command were issued, and the *up* command does the reverse, issuing *enable* and *start* commands.

You could also limit the display to one printer:

```
$ lpc status crow
crow:
        queuing is enabled
        printing is enabled
        1 entry in spool area
        crow is ready and printing
```

The status-reporting feature is useful for anyone, and *lpc* allows all users to use it. The real work for *lpc* usually involves solving a printing crisis. Sometimes a print daemon dies, and printing jobs back up. Sometimes a printer runs out of ink or paper, or even fails. Jobs in the print spools have to be suspended or moved to another spool where they can be printed. Someone may simply have an urgent printing task that needs to be moved to the top of the queue.

The *lpc* command is a classic Unix command: tight-lipped and forbidding. When you simply enter the *lpc* command, all you get back is a prompt:

```
lpc>
```

The command is interactive and waiting for your instructions. You can get help by entering `help` or a question mark at the *lpc* prompt. *lpc* responds and gives you a new prompt. For example, entering a question mark displays:

```
#  lpc
lpc> ?
Commands may be abbreviated.  Commands are:
abort    enable  disable help    restart status  topq    ?
clean    exit    down    quit    start   stop    up
lpc>
```

You can get additional help by asking for help about a specific command. For example, to learn more about restarting a stalled print queue, type:

```
lpc> help restart
restart          kill (if possible) and restart a spooling daemon
lpc>
```

The *lpc* help message does not offer online help about the secondary arguments you can specify in some places. The manual page will offer you some guidance. Most of the commands accept *all* or a print spool name as a secondary argument.

The *lpc topq* command recognizes a print spool name as the first argument and printer job numbers or user IDs as following arguments. The arguments are used to reorder the print queue. For example, to move job 237 to the top of the **ada** print queue, followed by all jobs owned by **bckeller** in the queue, enter:

```
lpc> topq ada 237 bckeller
```

The *lpd* daemon will start job 237 as soon as the current job is finished and will put any files in the queue owned by **bckeller** before the rest of the print spool. If you were very impatient, you could use the *abort* and *clean* commands to kill and purge the currently printing job, then use *topq* to put the job you want at the top of the queue, before using *restart* to create a new *lpd* and restart the queue.

When you use the *stop* command to stop a print spool (or all print spools) you can broadcast a message to all system users at the same time. For example:

```
lpc> stop ada "Printer Ada taken down to replace toner cartridge."
```

If you do major surgery on the print spools—stopping queues and moving files around—it is wise to use *lpc*'s *clean* command. This minimizes the risk that some loose end will cause an *lpd* daemon to stall:

```
lpc> clean
```

Then get a new status report and restart or start all stopped print spools before exiting. There is a difference between aborting a process, stopping a process, and bringing a print queue down. If you bring a print queue down (*lpc down ada* for example) you will find you cannot get *lpd* to serve the print spool again until you restore services with an *lpc up ada* command. Similarly, if you stop a queue, you have to start or restart it.

Follow up after you clear print spool problems using *lpc*. Further status reports will let you know promptly whether the problems were actually solved.

You should not wait for disaster to become familiar with *lpc* commands, because printing jobs can pass through a Linux spool very fast, especially when a printer has lots of memory to buffer jobs sent to it. Study the manual page and work with *lpc* enough to be comfortable with the control it gives you over print spools and *lpd* daemons.

You can abbreviate subcommands unless it makes them ambiguous. For instance, in the following command, h stands for *help*:

```
lpc> h topq
```

To exit from *lpc*, enter the command:

```
lpc> quit
```

or:

```
lpc> exit
```

Printer Optimization

For performance improvement, you can first try to maximize the physical tuning of the system. You should try to determine the maximum data flow rates you can sustain to the printers you install. Don't specify a faster rate of communication than can be supported unless your printer is going to return flow control signals to the print daemon. That is, you must have bidirectional communications (and the printer must return the necessary signals) or else you must limit your transmission speeds so that data doesn't get lost en route to the printer. You may have to experiment with this to wring the best possible performance from printers limited by restricted bandwidth.

Old PC serial and parallel cards just don't have the throughput available with later cards. Newer serial cards have faster I/O processors. Newer parallel ports are typically faster and meet the EPP standard to support bidirectional communications, which may allow *lpd* to control data flow to the printer better. A significant performance improvement may be only a few dollars away.

If your printer is just plain slow and cannot buffer print jobs, there isn't much to be gained from optimizing the data-transfer rate, of course, but it may still be useful for you to use interrupt-driven flow control instead of port polling if your hardware permits.

You can try out various printer optimizations using the *tunelp* utility. Read the manual page carefully before attempting this. If a tuning procedure fails, you may need to turn the printer off and back on to reset it. Also, don't forget to use *lpc* to restart the *lpd* daemon after each change to the configuration. Back up your working setup before monkeying around with *tunelp*.

An excellent first use for *tunelp* is to cause a print job to abort on receiving a printer error and to notify you. (The default is not to abort.) Setting this up can shorten the test cycle. To cause abort on printer error, enter as **root**:

```
tunelp -aon
```

If you use a parallel port printer, and your parallel port supports interrupt-driven printing, you can use *tunelp* to accellerate printer access:

```
tunelp /dev/lp1 -i7
```

This example switches the port controlled by interrupt 7 to use interrupt-driven printing. If an attempt to print after this change is made fails, you should reset the port and switch back to noninterrupt driven polling:

```
tunelp /dev/lp1 -r -i0
```

If you don't know the interrupt this device uses, you can query with *tunelp -q on*, and the IRQ setting will be displayed.

You can probably speed up printing a bit by reducing the pause the driver takes when it cannot send a character to the printer after a certain number of tries. For example, a fast laser printer might happily accommodate very brief pauses and not require many attempts to transmit. To try putting a character 10 times before pausing (the default is 250 attempts) and set the pause to .01, type:

```
tunelp /dev/lp1 -c10 -t1
```

The *−t* takes a numeric value that represents a multiple of .01 seconds. The default pause is .1 seconds.

Note that if you find the optimal transfer rate for plain-text files, it is likely to be less efficient for graphics files, which are generally processed more slowly.

When you finish tuning your printing system, you may want to reset the printer abort flag to prevent the process from aborting on receipt of printer error:

```
tunelp -aoff
```

The *tunelp* utility will continue to be developed in subsequent releases of Linux. Check the manual page to see the capabilities of your release.

Printer System Troubleshooting

When you have a printer problem, first resort to *lpc* to generate a status report. The print daemons should be alive and well, and no error should be returned. You can also check the contents of the */var/spool/lpd/printername/status* file and see if there is an error message from the printer stored there. Check the */var/log/ lpd-errs* file for any errors reported by *lpd*. If you are using Ghostscript, and its reporting features are active, use */sbin/pac* on Ghostscript's log file to get a report that may reveal errors Ghostscript generated. (As long as Linux system accounting isn't available, you might as well use */var/log/lp-acct* to store these reports. You'll have to make the file writable by all to do this.)

Look at that *lpc* status report again. Do files get to the print spool? Do they leave the spool? Are the necessary supporting files for *lpd* present (*.seq*, *lock*, and so on). If *lpc status* reported a printer named " : " there is a malformed */etc/printcap* line; the last character on a continuation line must be the backslash, not a space or tab.

Sometimes the */etc/printcap* file is set up wrong, and it makes *lpd* misroute a file. To test for that condition, prepare a file for print but save it to a file instead of spooling it to the printer. Examine the file. Is it in the form you expect? Try a couple of sanity checks:

- If as **root** you send the file directly to the device (for example, `cat file-name.ps > /dev/lp1`) does it print? If so, it means the problem lies in your software configuration, not in the hardware.

- Can you view your PostScript file using Ghostview? If so, you know that the format of the file is correct but the printer or filter is not interpreting it properly.

If you are testing a text file, try preparing it and routing it to a display, passing it through a utility such as *less*, and examine the result. A custom filter can also misroute a file.

Sometimes it is difficult to figure out where a printing problem originates. Printer configuration problems can be masked (or introduced) by having defaults overridden, for example. You may have to start by looking at an individual user's printing habits and then work forward. Individual users can set environment variables in their shell startup files to specify the printer they want to use as a default, and the behavior of formatters and print filters. Default system values are often overridden by environment variables, and they in turn are overridden by option arguments passed to *lpr* on the command line or by another utility.

When a print job terminates abnormally, it may be necessary to clear the lock file for the spool before *lpd* will send another file to print from that spool (*/var/spool/lpd/printername/lock*). The *lpd* daemon creates the lock file and changes it on completion. You can use *lpc* to stop the print daemon and then clean up the spool before starting it again.

Some problems derive from the data-transfer process. A printer may drop characters or be unable to keep up with the data flow you are attempting to provide, especially if the printer is old and slow or if the cable is unusually long. One possible symptom of data-transfer problems is when the printer can handle plain text readily, but pauses and thrashes when trying to print graphic files. If you suspect some problem of this nature, try increasing the pause the system takes before attempting to resend data and slowing the wait loop. The *tunelp* utility lets you control this conveniently:

```
tunelp -t200 -w5
```

This command tells *lpd* to pause 2 seconds between attempts. The *−w* option sets the number of loops for the busy loop counter to read between strobe signals. Normally *−w* is set to 0. For more information on *tunelp*, see the section "Printer Optimization."

If *lpd* never seems to run on your system, perhaps it isn't started up when the system boots. If this is the case, append a */etc/lpd* line to the end of your */etc/rc.d/ rc.local* file. Most Linux distributions start *lpd* these days as part of the default installation.

Some problems may never occur unless you use another package that presents conflicts by attempting to address the same devices. For example, UUCP utilities address a serial port using a */dev/ttyS** device driver. However, UUCP is a daemon with greater privileges than **lp**, and (although it shouldn't) it can leave the device set with a privilege level *lpd* cannot write to.

The Linux distribution of the BSD print package is usually installed with **lp** group permissions. On traditional BSD print-management installations, *lpd* is owned by **daemon** and has **daemon** group privileges. (There's no special **lp** group to support printing.) If you think there are subtle problems relating to device access collisions by processes owned by different daemons, you can change all print utilities group privileges to **daemon** and, of course, change directory and file-access privileges as well. That would restore the traditional BSD configuration. A better solution would be to find the problem devices and change their ownership to **lp**, since UUCP will still be able to use devices **lp** owns. Be aware that a serial port address can be reached by a number of virtual devices linked to the actual device; you have to correctly set the ownership of the real port.

Occasionally, a user believes his print job is going to the "wrong" printer. This is usually an environment variable problem. Double-check your */etc/printcap*, but also check the user's environment variables. For example, a user may have a GS_DEVICE variable set that Ghostscript uses as the default printer. If Ghostscript processing precedes *nenscript* processing, for example, the Ghostscript printer assignment could be passed to *nenscript*, overriding a NENSCRIPT or PRINTER device specification. This can also cause strange results if one parameter is over-ridden while others stay as before, so that, for example, a filter performs some special page layout for one printer, but the file goes to another.

Older PostScript printers may simply ignore ASCII files sent to them. If a user complains about disappearing output, maybe the file isn't getting passed through *nenscript* for PostScript encapsulation, or (very rarely) maybe *nenscript* was fooled into thinking it is already PostScript.

A multimode printer that knows when to switch modes (between PCL and plain text, for example) may still fail to eject the page and start the next file on the new page when one file of the same type is queued immediately following another of the same type. If this occurs, you can force the filter to add a formfeed at the end of each document (see the sample filter in the earlier section "Print Filters") at the cost of sometimes printing unnecessary blank pages.

Parallel port printer addressing can be confusing. On an XT bus system, the first parallel port is addressed as */dev/lp0* at 0x3bc. On the usual ISA bus system, the first parallel port device is */dev/lp1* at 0x378, which is the second parallel port on an XT system (still the */dev/lp1* device). The usual second parallel port on an ISA bus system is */dev/lp2*, as you would expect, at 0x278. However, there are some unusual configurations out there, such as systems with three parallel ports (if installed correctly these will be addressed as */dev/lp0*, */dev/lp1*, and */dev/lp2*). IRQ assignments may also be unusual and present a problem if you are trying to set up interrupt-driven printing.

If all else fails, review the initial installation procedure, making sure the hardware is actually connected and functional by booting another operating system if possible, testing devices as **root** user, and so on.

Setting Terminal Attributes

setterm is a program that sets various characteristics of your terminal (say, each virtual console), such as the keyboard repeat rate, tab stops, and text colors.

Most people use this command to change the colors for each virtual console. In this way, you can tell which virtual console you're currently looking at based on the text color.

For example, to change the color of the current terminal to white text on a blue background, use the command:

```
$ setterm -foreground white -background blue
```

Some programs and actions cause the terminal attributes to be reset to their default values. In order to store the current set of attributes as the default, use:

```
$ setterm -store
```

setterm(1)

setterm provides many options (most of which you will probably never use). See the *setterm* manual page or use *setterm −help* for more information.

What to Do in an Emergency

It's not difficult to make a simple mistake as **root** that can cause real problems on your system, such as not being able to log in or losing important files. This is especially true for novice system administrators who are beginning to explore the system. Nearly all new system admins learn their lessons the hard way, by being forced to recover from a real emergency. In this section, we'll give you some hints about what to do when the inevitable happens.

You should always be aware of preventative measures that reduce the impact of such emergencies. For example, take backups of all important system files, if not the entire system. If you happen to have a Linux distribution on CD-ROM, the CD-ROM itself acts as a wonderful backup for most files (as long as you have a way to access the CD-ROM in a tight situation—more on this later). Backups are vital to recovering from many problems; don't let the many weeks of hard work configuring your Linux system go to waste.

Also, be sure to keep notes on your system configuration, such as your partition table entries, partition sizes and types, and filesystems. If you were to trash your partition table somehow, fixing the problem might be a simple matter of rerunning *fdisk*, but this only helps as long as you can remember what your partition table used to look like. (True story: one of the authors once did this by booting a blank floppy, and had *no* record of the partition table contents. Needless to say, some guesswork was necessary to restore the partition table to its previous state!)

Of course, for any of these measures to work, you'll need a way to boot the system and access your files, or recover from backups, in an emergency. This is best accomplished with an "emergency disk," or "root disk." Such a disk contains a small root filesystem with the basics required to run a Linux system from floppy— just the essential commands and system files, as well as tools to repair problems. Such a disk is used by booting a kernel from another floppy (see the section "Using a Boot Floppy" in Chapter 5, *Essential System Management*) and telling the kernel to use the emergency disk as the root filesystem.

Chapter 5

Most distributions of Linux include such a boot/root floppy combination as the original installation floppies. The installation disks usually contain a small Linux system that can be used to install the software as well as perform basic system maintenance. Some systems include both the kernel and root filesystem on one floppy, but this severely limits the number of files that can be stored on the emergency disk. How useful these disks are as a maintenance tool depends on whether they contain the tools (such as *fsck*, *fdisk*, a small editor such as *vi*, and so on) necessary for problem recovery. Some distributions have such an elaborate installation process, the installation floppies don't have room for much else.

At any rate, you can create such a root floppy yourself. Being able to do this from scratch requires an intimate knowledge of what's required to boot and use a Linux system, and exactly what can be trimmed down and cut out. For example, you could dispose of the startup programs *init*, *getty*, and *login*, as long as you know how to rig things so that the kernel starts a shell on the console instead of using a real boot procedure. (One way to do this is to have */etc/init* be a symbolic link to */sbin/bash*, all on the floppy filesystem.)

While we can't cover all of the details here, the first step in creating an emergency floppy is to use *mkfs* to create a filesystem on a floppy (see the section "Creating

Chapter 6

Filesystems" in Chapter 6). You then mount the floppy and place whatever files on it that you'll need, including appropriate entries in */dev* (most of which can be copied from */dev* on your hard drive root filesystem). You'll also need a boot floppy, which merely contains a kernel. The kernel should have its root device set to */dev/fd0*, using *rdev*. This is covered in the section "Using a Boot Floppy" in Chapter 5. You'll also have to decide if you want the root floppy filesystem loaded into a ramdisk (which can be set using *rdev* as well). If you have more than 4 MB of RAM, this is a good idea because it can free up the floppy drive to be used for, say, mounting another floppy containing additional tools. If you have two floppy drives, you can do this without using a ramdisk. If you feel that setting up an emergency floppy is too hard for you now after reading all this, you might also want to try some of the scripts available that do it for you. But whatever you do, be sure to try the emergency floppy *before* disaster happens!

At any rate, the best place to start is your installation floppies. If those floppies don't contain all of the tools you need, create a filesystem on a separate floppy and place the missing programs on it. If you load the root filesystem from floppy into a ramdisk, or have a second floppy drive, you can mount the other floppy to access your maintenance tools.

What tools do you need? In the following sections, we'll talk about common emergencies and how to recover from them; this should guide you to what programs would be required for various situations.

Repairing Filesystems

Chapter 6

As discussed in the section "Checking and Repairing Filesystems" in Chapter 6, you can use *fsck* to recover from several kinds of filesystem corruption. Most of these filesystem problems are relatively minor, however, and can be repaired by booting your system in the usual way and running *fsck* from the hard drive. However, it is usually better to check and repair your root filesystem while it is unmounted. In this case, it's easier to run *fsck* from an emergency floppy.

There are no differences between running *fsck* from floppy and from the hard drive; the syntax is exactly the same as described earlier in the chapter. However, remember that *fsck* is usually a frontend to tools such as *fsck.ext2*. On other systems, you'll need to use *e2fsck* (for Second Extended Filesystems).

It is possible to corrupt a filesystem so that it cannot be mounted. This is usually the result of damage to the filesystem's *superblock*, which stores information about the filesystem as a whole. If the superblock is corrupted, the system won't be able to access the filesystem at all, and any attempt to mount it will fail (probably with an error to the effect of "can't read superblock").

Because of the importance of the superblock, the filesystem keeps backup copies of it at intervals on the filesystem. Second Extended Filesystems are divided into "block groups," where each group has, by default, 8192 blocks. Therefore, there are backup copies of the superblock at block offsets 8193, 16385 (that's 8192 × 2 + 1), 24577, and so on. If you use the *ext2* filesystem, check that the filesystem has 8192-block groups with the following command:

```
dumpe2fs device | more
```

(Of course, this works only when the master superblock is intact.) This command will print a great deal of information about the filesystem, and you should see something like:

```
Blocks per group:        8192
```

If another offset is given, use it for computing offsets to the superblock copies, as mentioned earlier.

If you can't mount a filesystem because of superblock problems, chances are that *fsck* (or *e2fsck*) will fail as well. You can tell *e2fsck* to use one of the superblock copies, instead, to repair the filesystem. The command is:

```
e2fsck -f -b offset device
```

where `offset` is the block offset to a superblock copy; usually, this is 8193. The –*f* switch is used to force a check of the filesystem; when using superblock backups, the filesystem may appear "clean," in which case no check is needed. –*f* overrides this. For example, to repair the filesystem on */dev/hda2* with a bad superblock, we can say:

```
e2fsck -f -b 8193 /dev/hda2
```

Superblock copies save the day. The previous commands can be executed from an emergency floppy system and will hopefully allow you to mount your filesystems again.

Accessing Damaged Files

Chapter 6

You might need to access the files on your hard-drive filesystems when booting from an emergency floppy. In order to do this, simply use the *mount* command as described in the section "Mounting Filesystems" in Chapter 6, mounting your filesystems under a directory such as */mnt*. (This directory must exist on the root filesystem contained on the floppy.) For example:

```
mount -t ext2 /dev/hda2 /mnt
```

will allow us to access the files on the Second Extended filesystem stored on */dev/hda2* in the directory */mnt*. You can then access the files directly and even execute programs from your hard-drive filesystems. For example, if you wish to execute *vi* from the hard drive, normally found in */usr/bin/vi*, you would use the command:

```
/mnt/usr/bin/vi filename
```

You could even place subdirectories of */mnt* on your path to make this easier.

Be sure to unmount your hard-drive filesystems before rebooting the system. If your emergency disks don't have the ability to do a clean shutdown, unmount your filesystems explicitly with *umount*, to be safe.

One problem that is easily fixed by doing this is forgetting the root password or trashing the contents of */etc/passwd*. In either case, it might be impossible to log in to the system or *su* to **root**. To repair this problem, boot from your emergency disks, mount your root filesystem under */mnt*, and edit */mnt/etc/passwd*. (It might be a good idea to keep a backup copy of this file somewhere in case you delete it accidentally.) For example, to clear the root password altogether, change the entry for **root** to:

```
root::0:0:The root of all evil:/:/bin/bash
```

Now **root** will have no password; you can reboot the system from hard drive and use the *passwd* command to reset it.

Another common problem is corrupt links to system shared libraries. The shared library images in */lib* are generally accessed through symbolic links, such as */lib/libc.so.5*, which point to the actual library, */lib/libc.so.version*. If this link is removed or is pointing to the wrong place, many commands on the system won't run. You can fix this problem by mounting your hard-drive filesystems and re-linking the library with a command such as:

```
cd /mnt/lib; ln -sf libc.so.5.4.47 libc.so.5
```

to force the *libc.so.5* link to point to *libc.so.5.4.47*. Remember that symbolic links use the pathname given on the *ln* command line. For this reason, the command:

```
ln -sf /mnt/lib/libc.so.5.4.47 /mnt/lib/libc.so.5
```

won't do the right thing; *libc.so.5* will point to */mnt/lib/libc.so.5.4.47*. When you boot from the hard drive, */mnt/lib* can't be accessed, and the library won't be located. The first command works because the symbolic link points to a file in the same directory.

Restoring Files from Backup

If you have deleted important system files, it might be necessary to restore backups while booting from an emergency disk. For this reason, it's important to be sure your emergency disk has the tools you need to restore backups; this includes programs such as *tar* and *gzip*, as well as the drivers necessary to access the backup device. For instance, if your backups are made using the floppy tape device driver, be sure that the *ftape* module and *insmod* command are available on your emergency disk. See the section "Loadable Device Drivers" in Chapter 7 for more about this.

Chapter 7

All that's required to restore backups to your hard-drive filesystems is to mount those filesystems, as described earlier, and unpack the contents of the archives over those filesystems (using the appropriate *tar* and *gzip* commands, for example; see the section "Making Backups") earlier in this chapter. Remember that every time you restore a backup you will be overwriting other system files; be sure you're doing everything correctly and not make the situation worse. With most archiving programs, you can extract individual files from the archive.

Likewise, if you want to use your original CD-ROM to restore files, be sure the kernel used on your emergency disks has the drivers necessary to access the CD-ROM drive. You can then mount the CD-ROM (remember the *mount* flags *−r −t iso9660*) and copy files from there.

The filesystems on your emergency disks should also contain important system files; if you have deleted one of these from your system, it's easy to copy the lost file from the emergency disk to your hard-drive filesystem.

## CHAPTER NINE

EDITORS, TEXT TOOLS, GRAPHICS, AND PRINTING

In the next few chapters, we'll introduce a number of popular applications for Linux. We'll start here with text editing, which underlies nearly every activity on the system. (You need an editor to create a file of more than trivial size, whether it is a program to be compiled, a configuration file for your system, or a mail message to send to a friend.) On a related topic, we'll show you some text formatters that can make attractive documents and utilities that manage printing.

Editing Files Using *vi*

In this section, we're going to cover the use of the *vi* (pronounced "vee-eye") text editor. *vi* was the first real screen-based editor for Unix systems. It is also simple, small, and sleek. If you're a system administrator, learning *vi* can be invaluable; in many cases, larger editors, such as Emacs, won't be available in emergency situations (for instance, when booting Linux from a maintenance disk).

vi is based on the same principles as many other Unix applications: that each program should provide a small, specific function and be able to interact with other programs. For example, *vi* doesn't include its own spellchecker, or paragraph filler, but those features are provided by other programs that are easy to fire off from within *vi*. Therefore, *vi* itself is a bit limited, but is able to interact with other applications to provide virtually any functionality you might want.

At first, *vi* may appear to be somewhat complex and unwieldy. However, its single-letter commands are fast and powerful once you've learned them. In the next section, we're going to describe Emacs, a more flexible editor (really an integrated work environment) with an easier learning curve. Do keep in mind that knowing *vi* may be essential to you if you are in a situation where Emacs is not available, so we encourage you to learn the basics, as odd as they may seem. It should also be added that there are now a number of *vi* clones available that are much more comfortable to use than the original *vi*. These include *vim* (*vi* improved) and *nvi* (new *vi*). Chances are that your distribution has things set up so that when starting *vi*, you actually start one of those. We'll stick to the basics here, though so that you can use the information presented here no matter which version of *vi* you use. You can find coverage of the newer versions in the book *Learning the vi Editor* by Linda Lamb and Arnold Robbins.

Starting vi

Let's fire up *vi* and edit a file. The syntax for *vi* is:

```
vi filename
```

For example:

```
eggplant$ vi test
```

will edit the file *test*. Your screen should look like this:

```
_
~
~
~
~
"test" [New file]
```

The column of ~ characters indicates that you are at the end of the file.

Inserting Text and Moving Around

While using *vi*, at any one time you are in one of three modes of operation. These modes are known as *command mode, edit mode*, and *ex mode*.

After starting *vi*, you are in command mode. This mode allows you to use a number of (usually single-letter) commands to modify text, as we'll see soon. Text is actually inserted and modified within edit mode. To begin inserting text, press i (which will place you into edit mode) and begin typing:

```
Now is the time for all good men to come to the aid of the party.
~
~
~
~
```

While inserting text, you may type as many lines as you wish (pressing the Enter key after each, of course), and you may correct mistakes using the Backspace key. To end edit mode and return to command mode, press the Esc key).

While in command mode, you can use the arrow keys to move around the file. Alternatively, you may use h, j, k, and 1, which move the cursor left, down, up, and right, respectively.

There are several ways to insert text other than using the i command. The a command (for "append") inserts text *after* the current cursor position. For example, use the left arrow key to move the cursor between the words good and men:

```
Now is the time for all good_men to come to the aid of the party.
~
~
~
~
~
```

Press a, type wo, and then press Esc to return to command mode:

```
Now is the time for all good women to come to the aid of the party.
~
~
~
~
~
```

To open a line below the current one and begin inserting text, use the o command. Press o and type another line or two:

```
Now is the time for all good women to come to the aid of the party.
Afterwards, we'll go out for pizza and beer._
~
~
~
~
```

Remember that at any time you're either in command mode (where commands such as i, a, or o are valid) or in edit mode (where you're inserting text, followed by Esc to return to command mode). If you're not sure which mode you're in, press Esc. This takes you out of edit mode, if you are in it, and does nothing except beep if you're already in command mode.

Deleting Text and Undoing Changes

From command mode, the x command deletes the character under the cursor. If you press x five times, you end up with the following:

```
Now is the time for all good women to come to the aid of the party.
Afterwards, we'll go out for pizza and_
~
~
~
~
```

Now press a and insert some text, followed by Esc:

```
Now is the time for all good women to come to the aid of the party.
Afterwards, we'll go out for pizza and Diet Coke.
~
~
~
~
```

You can delete entire lines using the command *dd* (that is, press d twice in a row).
If your cursor is on the second line, *dd* will produce the following:

```
Now is the time for all good women to come to the aid of the party.
~
~
~
~
~
```

Text that is deleted may be reinserted using the *p* command (for "put"). Pressing p
now will return the deleted line to the buffer after the current line. Using P
(uppercase) instead will insert the text before the current line. By default, *p* and *P*
insert text from the "undo buffer"; you can also yank and replace text from other
buffers, as we'll see later.

The u command undoes the latest change (in this case, pressing u after dd is
equivalent to p). If you inserted a large amount of text using the *i* command,
pressing u immediately after returning to command mode would undo it.

To delete the word beneath the cursor, use the dw command. Place the cursor on
the word Diet and type dw:

```
Now is the time for all good women to come to the aid of the party.
Afterwards, we'll go out for pizza and Coke.
~
~
~
~
```

Changing Text

You can replace text using the R command, which overwrites the text beginning at the cursor. Place the cursor on the first letter in pizza, press R, and type:

```
Now is the time for all good women to come to the aid of the party.
Afterwards, we'll go out for burgers and fries.
~
~
~
~
```

The r command replaces the single character under the cursor. r does not place you in insert mode per se, so there is no reason to use Esc to return to command mode.

The ~ command changes the case of the letter under the cursor from upper to lowercase, and vice versa. If you place the cursor on the o in Now in the previous example, and repeatedly press ~, you end up with the following:

```
NOW IS THE TIME FOR ALL GOOD WOMEN TO COME TO THE AID OF THE PARTY.
Afterwards, we'll go out for burgers and fries.
~
~
~
~
```

Another useful command for changing words is the cw command, which lets you simply type in the new word and—after pressing Ecs—removes anything that might be left over from the original word.

Moving Commands

You already know how to use the arrow keys to move around the document. In addition, the w command moves the cursor to the beginning of the next word; b moves it to the beginning of the current word. The 0 (that's a zero) command moves the cursor to the beginning of the current line, and the $ command moves it to the end of the line.

When editing large files, you'll want to move forward or backward through the file a screen at a time. Pressing Ctrl-F moves the cursor one screen. forward, and Ctrl-B moves it a screen backward.

In order to move the cursor to the end of the file, type G. You can also move to an arbitrary line: the command 10G would move the cursor to line 10 in the file. To move to the beginning of the file, use 1G.

Typing / followed by a pattern and the Enter key causes you to jump to the first occurrence of that pattern in the text following the cursor. For example, placing the cursor on the first line of text in our example, and typing /burg moves the cursor to the beginning of the word "burgers." Using ? instead of / searches backward through the file.

ed(1)

The pattern following a / or ? command is actually a *regular expression*. Regular expressions are a powerful way to specify patterns for search and replace operations and are used by many Unix utilites. (The manual page for *ed* describes regular expressions in some detail.) Using regular expressions, you could, for example, search for the next uppercase letter, using the command:

```
/[A-Z]
```

Therefore, if the pattern you're searching for is not a static string, regular expressions can be used to specify just what you want.

You can couple moving commands with other commands, such as deletion. For example, the command d$ will delete everything from the cursor to the end of the line; dG will delete everything from the cursor to the end of the file.

Saving Files and Quitting vi

Most of the commands dealing with files within *vi* are invoked from ex mode. You enter ex mode when you press the : key from command mode. This places the cursor on the last line of the display, allowing you to enter various extended-p commands.

For example, to write the file being edited, use the command :w. Typing : causes you to enter *ex* mode, and typing w followed by the Enter key completes the command. The command :wq writes the file and exits *vi*. (The command ZZ—from command mode, without the ":"—is equivalent to :wq.

To quit *vi* without saving changes to the file, use the command :q!. Using :q alone will quit *vi*, but only if modifications to the file have been saved. The ! in :q! means to quit *vi*—and that you really mean it.

Editing Another File

To edit another file, use the :e command. For example, to stop editing *test*, and edit the file *foo* instead, use the command shown at the bottom of the following box:

```
NOW IS THE TIME FOR ALL GOOD WOMEN TO COME TO THE AID OF THE PARTY.
Afterwards, we'll go out for burgers and fries.
~
~
~
~
:e foo_
```

If you use :e without writing the file first, you'll get the error message:

```
No write since last change (:edit! overrides)
```

At this point, you can use :w to save the original file, and then use :e, or you can use the command :e! foo, which tells *vi* to edit the new file without saving changes to the original.

Including Other Files

If you use the :r command, you can include the contents of another file in the *vi* buffer. For example, the command:

```
:r foo.txt
```

inserts the contents of the file *foo.txt* after the current line.

Running Shell Commands

The :! command allows you to enter the name of a command, which is executed within *vi*. For example, the command:

```
:! ls -F
```

executes the *ls* command and displays the results on your screen.

The :r ! command is similar to :!, but includes the standard output of the command in the buffer. The command:

```
:r! ls -F
```

produces the following:

```
NOW IS THE TIME FOR ALL GOOD WOMEN TO COME TO THE AID OF THE PARTY.
Afterwards, we'll go out for burgers and fries.
letters/
misc/
papers/
~
```

If you need to execute a series of shell commands, it's often easier to use the suspend key (usually Ctrl-Z), provided you're using a shell that supports job control, such as *tcsh* or *bash*.

Global Searching and Replacing

There are many more features of *vi* than are documented here; most of these features are simply implemented through combinations of the simple features we've seen. Here are one or two other tidbits most *vi* users find useful.

The command:

`:[x,y]s/pattern/replacement/flags`

searches for *pattern* between lines *x* and *y* in the buffer, and replaces instances of *pattern* with the *replacement* text. *pattern* is a regular expression; *replacement* is literal text but can contain several special characters to refer to elements in the original *pattern*. The following command replaces the first occurrence of `weeble` with `wobble` on lines 1 through 10 inclusive:

`:1,10s/weeble/wobble`

Instead of giving line-number specification, you can use the `%` symbol to refer to the entire file. Other special symbols can be used in place of *x* and *y*. `$` refers to the last line of the file. Leave *x* or *y* blank to refer to the current line.

Among the *flags* you can use are `g` to replace all instances of *pattern* on each line, and `c` to ask for confirmation for each replacement. In most instances, you will want to use the `g` flag, unless you want to replace only the first occurrence of *pattern* on each line.

You can also use *marks* to refer to lines. Marks are just single-letter names that are given to cursor locations within the document. Moving the cursor to a location in the file and typing `ma` will set the mark `a` at that point. (Marks may be named any of the letters a–z or A–Z.) You can move the cursor directly to the mark `a` with the command `` `a `` (with a backquote). Using a regular single quote (as in `'a`) will move the cursor to the beginning of the line that the mark `a` is on.

Marks allow you to "remember" cursor locations that denote a region of text. For example, if you want to search and replace a block of text, you can move the cursor to the beginning of the text, set a mark, move the cursor to the end of the text, and use the command:

```
:`a,.s/weeble/wobble
```

where `a refers to the line containing mark a, and . refers to the current line.

Moving Text, and Using Registers

One way to copy and move text is to delete it (using the d or dd commands) and then replace it with the P command, as described earlier. For example, if you want to delete the 10 lines, starting with the line that contains the cursor, and paste them somewhere else, just use the command 10dd (to delete 10 lines), move the cursor to the new location for the text, and type p. You can copy text in this way as well: typing 10dd followed by P (at the same cursor location) deletes the text and immediately replaces it. You can then paste the text elsewhere by moving the cursor and using p multiple times.

Similar to dd is the yy command, which "yanks" text without deleting it. You use p to paste the yanked text as with dd. The deletion and yank commands can be used on more general regions than lines. Recall that the d command deletes text through a move command; for example, d$ deletes text from the cursor to the end of the line. Similarly, y$ yanks text from the cursor to the end of the line.

Let's say you want to yank (or delete) a region of text. This can be done with marks as well. Move the cursor to the beginning of the text to be yanked and set a mark, as in ma. Move the cursor to the end of the text to be yanked and use the command y`a. This yanks text from the cursor position to the mark a. (Remember that the command `a moves the cursor to the mark a.) Using d instead of y deletes the text from the cursor to the mark.

The most convenient way to cut, copy, and paste portions of text within *vi* is to use registers. A register is just a named temporary storage space for text you wish to copy between locations, cut and paste within the document, and so forth.

Registers are given single letter names; any of the characters a–z or A–Z are valid. The " command (a quotation mark) specifies a register; it is followed by the name of the register, as in "a for register a. The lower-case letters and their upper-case counterparts refer to the same registers: using the lower-case letter overwrites the previous contents of the register and using the upper-case letter appends to it.

For instance, if we move the cursor to the first line in our example:

```
NOW IS THE TIME FOR ALL GOOD WOMEN TO COME TO THE AID OF THE PARTY.
Afterwards, we'll go out for burgers and fries.
~
~
~
~
```

and use the command `"ayy`, the current line is yanked into the register a. We can then move the cursor to the second line, and use the command `"ap` to paste the text from register a after the current line:

```
NOW IS THE TIME FOR ALL GOOD WOMEN TO COME TO THE AID OF THE PARTY.
Afterwards, we'll go out for burgers and fries.
NOW IS THE TIME FOR ALL GOOD WOMEN TO COME TO THE AID OF THE PARTY.
~
~
~
```

Similarly, the command `"ay`a` yanks text from the cursor to mark a into register a. Note that there is no correspondence between mark and register names!

Using registers allows you copy text between files. Just copy the text to a register, use the `:e` command to edit a new file and paste the text from the register.

Extending *vi*

vi is extensible in many ways. Most of the commands we've introduced can be generalized to arbitrary regions of text. As we've already seen, commands such as d and y operate on the text from the cursor to a move operation, such as $ or G. (dG deletes text from the cursor to the end of the file.) Many other commands operate on text through a move command in the same way. Using marks you can operate on any region of text.

As we mentioned before, *vi* is just a text editor; it doesn't have facilities for spellchecking text, compiling programs, and other such features. However, *vi* executes other programs, which you can use to extend the editor. The command:

:x,y! command

executes the named *command* with the text on lines *x* through *y* as standard input, and replaces the lines with the standard output of the command. As with the s (search and replace) command, other specifications such as % and $ can be used for the line numbers.

Chapter 13

For example, let's say you want to prepend a quote character (>) to all of the lines in a region of text. One way to do this is to write a short shell or Perl script (see Chapter 13, *Programming Languages*) that reads lines of input and outputs those same lines with the quote character prepended. (Or use a *sed* command; there are many alternatives.) You can then send lines of text through this filter, which replaces them with the quoted text within *vi*. If the script is called *quote* just use a command such as

```
:'a,.!quote
```

which quotes the region of text between the cursor location and the mark a.

Be familiar with the various ex commands that are available. The `:set` command allows you to set various options; for example, `:set ai` turns on auto indentation of text. (`:set noai` turns it off.)

You can specify *ex* commands (such as `:set`) to execute when starting up *vi* in the file *.exrc* in your home directory. (The name of this file can be changed with the `EXINIT` environment variable.) For example, your *.exrc* file might contain:

```
set ai
```

to turn on autoindentation. You don't need the `:` before ex commands in this file.

[15]
Learning vi

There are a number of good tutorials and references for *vi* available—both online as well as in print. *Learning the vi Editor* is a good place to look for more information. If you have Internet access, the *comp.editors* archives for *vi* contain a number of reference and tutorial documents, as well as interesting *vi* hacks. *ftp://alf.uib.no: /pub/vi* is the archive home site; it is mirrored at *cs.uwp.edu* and elsewhere.

The Emacs Editor

Text editors are among the most important applications in the Unix world. They are used so often that many people spend more time within an editor than anywhere else on their Unix system. The same holds true for Linux.

The choice of an editor can be a religious one. Many editors exist, but the Unix community has arranged itself into two major groups: the Emacs camp and the *vi* camp. Because of its somewhat nonintuitive user interface, many people (newcomers and seasoned users alike) prefer Emacs over *vi*. However, long-time users of *vi* (and single-finger typists) use it more efficiently than a more complex editor such as Emacs.

If *vi* is one end of the text-editor spectrum, Emacs is the other; they are widely different in their design and philosophy. Emacs is partly the brainchild of Richard Stallman, founder of the Free Software Foundation and author of much of the GNU software.

Emacs is a very large system with more features than any single Unix application to date (some people would even go so far as not to call it an editor but an "integrated environment"). It contains its own LISP language engine you can use to write extensions for the editor. (Many of the functions within Emacs are written in Emacs LISP). Emacs includes extensions for everything from compiling and

[14] Learning
GNU Emacs

debugging programs to reading and sending electronic mail to X Window System support and more. Emacs also includes its own online tutorial and documentation. The book *Learning GNU Emacs* by Debra Cameron, Bill Rosenblatt, and Eric Raymond, is a popular guide to the editor.

Most Linux distributions include two variants of Emacs. GNU Emacs is the original version, which is still being developed, but development seems to have slowed down. XEmacs is larger, slightly slower, but much more user-friendly and better integrated with the X Window System (even though you can also use it from the command line, despite its name). If you are not tight on memory and have a reasonably fast computer, we suggest using XEmacs. We will not cover the differences here, though; the discussion in this section applies to both.

Firing It Up

GNU Emacs is simply invoked as:

```
$ emacs options
```

likewise, XEmacs is invoked as

```
$ xemacs options
```

Most of the time, you don't need options. You can specify filenames on the command line, but it's more straightforward to read them in after starting the program.

In Emacs lingo, `C-x` means Ctrl-X, and `M-p` is equivalent to Alt-P. As you might guess, `C-M-p` means Ctrl-Alt-P.

Using these conventions, press `C-x` followed by `C-f` to read in a file or create a new one. The keystrokes display a prompt at the bottom of your screen showing your current working directory. You can create a buffer now to hold what will end up to be the content of a new file; let's call the file *wibble.txt*. We now see the following:

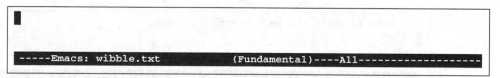

```
-----Emacs: wibble.txt        (Fundamental)----All------------------
```

The mode line at the bottom indicates the name of the file as well as the type of buffer you're in (which here is Fundamental). Emacs supports many kinds of editing modes; Fundamental is the default for plain-text files, but other modes exist for editing C and TEX source, modifying directories, and so on. Each mode has certain key bindings and commands associated with it, as we'll see soon. Emacs typically determines the mode of the buffer based on the filename extension.

To the right of the buffer type is the word All, which means that you are currently looking at the entire file (which is empty). Typically, you will see a percentage, which represents how far into the file you are.

Chapter 11

If you're running Emacs under the X Window System, a new window will be created for the editor with a menu bar at the top, scrollbars, and other goodies. In the section "Emacs," in Chapter 11, *Customizing Your X Environment*, we discuss Emacs's special features when used within X.

Simple Editing Commands

Emacs is more straightforward than *vi* when it comes to basic text editing. The arrow keys should move the cursor around the buffer; if they don't (in case Emacs is not configured for your terminal), use the keys C-p (previous line), C-n (next line), C-f (forward character), and C-b (backward character).

If you find using the Alt key uncomfortable, press Esc and then p. Pressing and releasing Esc is equivalent to holding down Alt.

Already we must take the first aside on our tour of Emacs. Literally every command and key within Emacs is customizable. That is, with a "default" Emacs configuration, C-p maps to the internal function *previous-line*, which moves the cursor (also called "point") to the previous line. However, you can easily rebind different keys to these functions, or write new functions and bind keys to them, and so forth. Unless otherwise stated, the keys we introduce here work for the default Emacs configuration. Later we'll show you how to customize the keys for your own use.

Back to editing: using the arrow keys or one of the equivalents moves the cursor around the current buffer. Just start typing text, and it is inserted at the current cursor location. Pressing the Backspace or Delete key should delete text at the cursor. If it doesn't, we'll show how to fix it in the section "Tailoring Emacs" later in this chapter. Now begin to type:

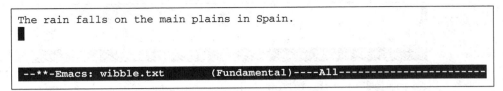

The keys C-a and C-e move the cursor to the beginning and end of the current line, respectively. C-v moves forward a page; M-v moves back a page. There are many more basic editing commands, but we'll allow the Emacs online documentation (discussed shortly) to fill those in.

In order to get out of Emacs, use the command C-x C-c. This is the first of the extended commands we've seen; many Emacs commands require several keys. C-x alone is a "prefix" to other keys. In this case, pressing C-x followed by C-c quits Emacs, first asking for confirmation if you want to quit without saving changes to the buffer.

You can use C-x C-s to save the current file, and C-x C-f to "find" another file to edit. For example, typing C-x C-f presents you with a prompt such as:

```
Find file: /home/loomer/mdw/
```

where the current directory is displayed. After this, type the name of the file to find. Pressing the Tab key will do filename completion similar to that used in *bash* and *tcsh*. For example, entering:

```
Find file: /home/loomer/mdw/.bash
```

and pressing Tab opens another buffer, showing all possible completions, as so:

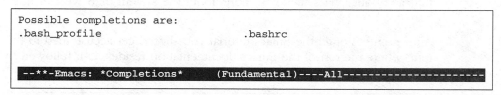

After you complete the filename, the *Completions* buffer goes away and the new file is displayed for editing. This is one example of how Emacs uses temporary buffers to present information.

Emacs allows you to use multiple buffers when editing text; each buffer may contain a different file you're editing. When you load a file with C-x C-f, a new buffer is created to edit the file, but the original buffer isn't deleted.

You can switch to another buffer using the C-x b command, which asks you for the name of the buffer (usually the name of the file within the buffer). For example, pressing C-x b presents the prompt:

```
Switch to buffer: (default wibble.txt)
```

The default buffer is the previous one visited. Press Enter to switch to the default buffer, or type another buffer name. Using C-x C-b will present a buffer list (in a buffer of its own), as so:

```
MR Buffer        Size    Mode          File
-- ------        ----    ----          ----
.  wibble.txt    44      Fundamental   /home/loomer/mdw/wibble.txt
   .bashrc       1763    Fundamental   /home/loomer/mdw/.bashrc
   *scratch*     0       Lisp Interaction
*  *Buffer List* 265     Buffer Menu
```

Popping up the buffer menu splits the Emacs screen into two "windows," which you can switch between using C-x o. More than two concurrent windows are possible as well. In order to view just one window at a time, switch to the appropriate one and press C-x 1. This hides all of the other windows, but you can switch to them later using the C-x b command just described. Using C-x k actually deletes a buffer from Emacs's memory.

Tutorial and Online Help

[13] GNU
Emacs manual

Already Emacs looks a bit complex; that is simply because it's such a flexible system. Before we go any further, it is instructive to introduce Emacs's built-in online help and tutorial. This documentation has also been published in book form.

Using the C-h command gives you a list of help options on the last line of the display. Pressing C-h again describes what they are. In particular, C-h followed by t drops you into the Emacs tutorial. It should be self-explanatory, and an interactive tutorial about Emacs tells you more about the system than we can hope to cover here.

After going through the Emacs tutorial you should get accustomed to the Info system, where the rest of the Emacs documentation resides. C-h followed by i enters the Info reader. A mythical Info page might look like this:

```
File: intercal.info,  Node: Top,  Next: Instructions,  Up: (dir)


   This file documents the Intercal interpreter for Linux.


   * Menu:

   * Instructions::        How to read this manual.
   * Overview::            Preliminary information.
   * Examples::            Example Intercal programs and bugs.
   * Concept Index::       Index of concepts.
```

As you see, text is presented along with a menu to other "nodes." Pressing m and then entering a node name from the menu will allow you to read that note. You can read nodes sequentially by pressing the space bar, which jumps to the next node in the document (indicated by the information line at the top of the buffer). Here, the next node is Instructions, which is the first node in the menu.

Each node also has a link to the parent node (Up), which here is (dir), meaning the Info page directory. Pressing u takes you to the parent node. In addition, each node has a link to the previous node, if it exists (in this case, it does not). The p command moves to the previous node. The l command returns you to the node most recently visited.

Within the Info reader, pressing ? gives you a list of commands and pressing h presents you with a short tutorial on using the system. Since you're running Info within Emacs, you can use Emacs commands as well (such as C-x b to switch to another buffer).

If you think that the Info system is arcane and obsolete, please keep in my mind that it was designed to work on all kinds of systems, including those lacking graphics or powerful processing capabilities.

Other online help is available within Emacs. Pressing C-h C-h gives you a list of help options. One of these is C-h k, after which you press a key, and documentation about the function that is bound to that key appears.

Deleting, Copying, and Moving Text

There are various ways to move and duplicate blocks of text within Emacs. These methods involve use of the *mark*, which is simply a "remembered" cursor location you can set using various commands. The block of text between the current cursor location (*point*) and the mark is called the *region*.

The mark can be set using the key C-@ (or C-Space on most systems). Moving the cursor to a location and pressing C-@ sets the mark at that position. You can now move the cursor to another location within the document, and the region is defined as the text between mark and point.

Many Emacs commands operate on the region. The most important of these commands deal with deleting and yanking text. The command C-w deletes the current region and saves it in the *kill ring*. The kill ring is a list of text blocks that have been deleted. You can then paste (*yank*) the text at another location, using the C-y command. (Note that the semantics of the term *yank* differ between *vi* and Emacs. In *vi*, "yanking" text is equivalent to adding it to the undo register without deleting it, while in Emacs, "yank" means to paste text.) Using the kill ring, you can paste not only the most recently deleted block of text but also blocks of text that were deleted previously.

For example, type the following text into an Emacs buffer:

```
The rain falls on the main plains in Spain.
Here is a line that we wish to move.
She sells Bourne shells by the sea shore.
█


--**-Emacs: wibble.txt          (Fundamental)----All------------------
```

Now, move the cursor to the beginning of the second line ("Here is a line..."), and set the mark with C-@. Move to the end of the line (with C-e), and delete the region, using C-w. The buffer should now look like the following:

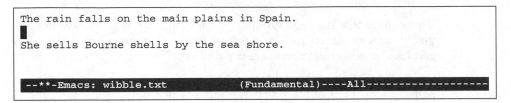

In order to yank the text just deleted, move the cursor to the end of the buffer, and press C-y. The line should be pasted at the new location:

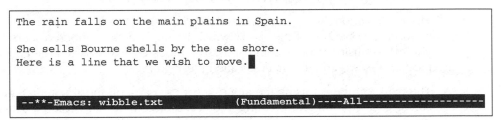

Pressing C-y repeatedly will insert the text multiple times.

You can copy text in a similar fashion. Using M-w instead of C-w will copy the region into the kill ring without deleting it. (Remember that M- means holding down the Alt key or pressing Esc before the w.)

Text that is deleted using other kill commands, such as C-k, is also added to the kill ring. This means that you don't need to set the mark and use C-w to move a block of text; any deletion command will do.

In order to recover previously deleted blocks of text (which are saved on the kill ring), use the command M-y after yanking with C-y. M-y replaces the yanked text with the previous block from the kill ring. Pressing M-y repeatedly cycles through the contents of the kill ring. This feature is useful if you wish to move or copy multiple blocks of text.

Emacs also provides a more general *register* mechanism, similar to that found in *vi*. Among other things, you can use this feature to save text you want to paste in later. A register has a one-character name; let's use a for this example:

1. At the beginning of the text you want to save, set the mark by pressing the Control key and space bar together (or if that doesn't work, press C-@).

2. Move point (the cursor) to the end of the region you want to save.

3. Press C-x x followed by the name of the register (a in this case).

4. When you want to paste the text somewhere, press C-x g followed by the name of the register, a.

Searching and Replacing

The most common way to search for a string within Emacs is to press C-s. This starts what is called an *incremental search*. You then start entering the characters you are looking for. Each time you press a character, Emacs searches forward for a string matching everything you've typed so far. If you make a mistake, just press the Delete key and continue typing the right characters. If the string cannot be found, Emacs beeps. If you find an occurrence, but you want to keep searching for another one, press C-s again.

You can also search backward this way using the C-r key. Several other types of searches exist, including a regular expression search that you can invoke by pressing M-C-s. This lets you search for something like jo.*n, which matches names like John, Joan, and Johann. (By default, searches are not case sensitive.)

To replace a string, enter M-%. You are prompted for the string that is currently in the buffer, and then the one you want to replace it with. Emacs displays each place in the buffer where the string is and asks you if you want to replace this occurrence. Press the space bar to replace the string, the Delete key to skip this string, or a period to stop the search.

If you know you want to replace all occurrences of a string that follow your current place in the buffer, without being queried for each one, enter M-x *string*. (The M-x key allows you to enter the name of an Emacs function and execute it, without use of a key binding. Many Emacs functions are available only via M-x, unless you bind them to keys yourself.) A regular expression can be replaced by entering M-x *regexp*.

Macros

The name Emacs comes partly from "macros," and in fact they are a simple but powerful feature that makes Emacs a pleasure to use. If you plan on doing anything frequently and repetitively, just press C-x (, perform the operation once, and then press C-x). The two C-x commands with the opening and closing parentheses remember all the keys you pressed. Then you can execute the commands over and over again by pressing C-x e.

Here's a trivial example you can try on any text file; it capitalizes the first word of each line.

1. Press C-x (to begin the macro.

2. Press C-a to put point at the beginning of the current line. It's important to know where you are each time a macro executes. By pressing C-a you are making sure the macro will always go to the beginning of the line, which is where you want to be.

3. Press M-c to make the first letter of the first word a capital letter.

4. Press C-a again to return to the beginning of the line and C-n or the down arrow to go to the beginning of the following line. This ensures that the macro will start execution at the right place next time.

5. Press C-x) to end the macro.

6. Press C-x e repeatedly to capitalize the following lines. Or press C-u several times, followed by C-x e. The repeated uses of C-u are prefix keys, causing the following command to execute many times. If you get to the end of the document while the macro is still executing, no harm is done; Emacs just beeps and stops executing the macro.

Running Commands and Programming Within Emacs

Emacs provides interfaces for many programs, which you can run within an Emacs buffer. For example, Emacs modes exist for reading and sending electronic mail, reading Usenet news, compiling programs, and interacting with the shell. In this section, we'll introduce some of these features.

To send electronic mail from within Emacs, press C-x m. This opens up a buffer that allows you to compose and send an email message:

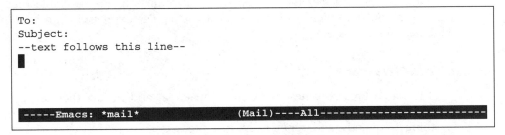

Simply enter your message within this buffer and use C-c C-s to send it. You can also insert text from other buffers, extend the interface with your own Emacs LISP functions, and so on.

RMAIL is Emacs's interface for reading electronic mail. Many users prefer it to other mail readers, because Emacs can be used directly as the editor for both sending and reading mail. To start RMAIL, use the command M-x rmail.

When you run RMAIL, Emacs converts messages in your incoming mailbox to a special format it uses to keep track of messages, and mail will be moved to the file *RMAIL* in your home directory. Therefore, be careful! Your incoming mail file will be converted to RMAIL format, and to convert it back (in case you don't want to use RMAIL as your mail reader), you need to use the M-x unrmail function.

When you start RMAIL, a buffer is created, displaying the first message in your inbox. The n and p commands can be used to display the previous and next messages. (As with all Emacs modes, using C-h m gives you a summary of the available keys.) While you're viewing a message, the r key replies to that message, opening a mail buffer (as described earlier) with the header fields initialized. While in the mail buffer you can use C-c C-y to insert the original message.

Within RMAIL, the h command displays a summary of the messages in your mailbox:

```
  11   17-Feb                   johnsonm@metalab   Re: Which release?

  12   25-Feb                             schar   Vision Group meeting
  13   26-Feb               okir@monad.swb.de    Re: Spaces in .ms?
  14   26-Feb            wirzeniu@cc.helsinki.fi  Re: LDP
--%%-Emacs:  RMAIL-summary      (RMAIL Summary)----50%--------------------
```

Several M-x commands are available in summary mode for sorting the list, and so forth. RMAIL commands such as n, p, and r may be used as well.

Similar to the RMAIL mail interface is GNUS, the Emacs-based newsreader, which you can start with the M-x gnus command. After startup (and a bit of chewing on your *.newsrc* file), a list of newsgroups will be presented, along with a count of unread articles for each:

```
    10: comp.os.linux.development
     0: cucs.system
    32: alt.fan.warlord
   195: alt.folklore.urban
--- GNUS: List of Newsgroups       (Newsgroup {cloyd.cs})--6%--------------
```

Using the arrow keys, you can select a newsgroup to read. Press the space bar to begin reading articles from that group. Two buffers will be displayed, one containing a list of articles and the other displaying the current article. Using n and p moves to the next and previous articles, f and F follows up to the current article (either with or without including the current article), and r and R replies to the article via electronic mail. There are many other GNUS commands; use C-h m for a list. If you're used to a newsreader such as *rn*, GNUS will be somewhat familiar.

Emacs provides a number of modes for editing various types of files. For example, there is C mode for editing C source code, and TEX mode for editing (surprise) TEX source. Each of these modes boast features that make editing the appropriate type of file easier.

For example, within C mode, you can use the command M-x compile, which, by default, runs *make –k* in the current directory and redirect errors to another buffer. For example, the compilation buffer may contain:

```
cd /home/loomer/mdw/pgmseq/
make -k
gcc -O -O2 -I. -I../include -c stream_load.c -o stream_load.o
stream_load.c:217: syntax error before 'struct'
stream_load.c:217: parse error before 'struct'
```

You can move the cursor to a line containing an error message, press C-c C-c, and the cursor will jump to that line in the corresponding source buffer (opening a buffer for the appropriate source file if one does not already exist). Now you can edit and compile programs entirely within Emacs.

Chapter 14

Emacs also provides a complete interface to the *gdb* debugger, which is described in the section "Using Emacs with gdb" in Chapter 14, *Tools for Programmers*.

Usually, Emacs selects the appropriate mode for the buffer based on the filename extension. For example, editing a file with the extension *.c* in the filename automatically selects C mode for that buffer.

Shell mode is one of the most popular Emacs extensions. Shell mode allows you to interact with the shell in an Emacs buffer, using the command M-x shell. Editing shell command lines and using command history can be done with standard Emacs commands. You can also run single shell commands from Emacs using M-!. If you use M-| instead, the contents of the current region is piped to the given shell command as standard input. This is a general interface for running subprograms from within Emacs.

Tailoring Emacs

The Emacs online documentation should be sufficient to get you on track to learning more about the system and growing accustomed to it. However, sometimes it is hard to locate some of the most helpful hints for getting started. Here we'll present a run-down on certain customization options many Emacs users choose to employ to make life easier.

The Emacs personal customization file is *.emacs*, which should reside in your home directory. This file should contain code, written in Emacs LISP, which runs or defines functions to customize your Emacs environment. (If you've never written LISP before, don't worry; most customizations using it are quite simple.)

One of the most common things users customize are key bindings. For instance, if you use Emacs to read your mail, you can bind the key C-c r to execute the rmail function. Put this in your *.emacs* file:

```
; Provide quick way to read mail.
(global-set-key "\C-cr" 'rmail)
```

Comments in Emacs LISP start with a semicolon. The command that follows runs the command *global-set-key*. Now you don't have to type in the long sequence M-x rmail every time you get that little message "Mail" in your mode line. Just press the two characters C-c r. This works anywhere in Emacs—no matter what mode your buffer is in—because it is global.

A customization that you might want to use is making the text mode the default mode and turning on the "auto-fill" minor mode (which makes text automatically wrap if it is too long for one line) like this:

```
; Make text mode the default, with auto-fill
(setq default-major-mode 'text-mode)
(add-hook 'text-mode-hook 'turn-on-auto-fill)
```

You don't always want your key mappings to be global. As you use TEX mode, C mode, and other modes defined by Emacs, you'll find useful things you'd like to do only in a single mode. Here, we define a simple LISP function to insert some characters into C code, and then bind the function to a key for our convenience:

```
(defun start-if-block()
   (interactive)
   (insert "if () {\n}\n")
   (backward-char 6)
)
```

We start the function by declaring it "interactive" so that we can invoke it (otherwise, it would be used only internally by other functions). Then we use the *insert* function to put the following characters into our C buffer:

```
if () {
}
```

Strings in Emacs can contain standard C escape characters. Here we've used \n for a newline.

Now we have a template for an if block. To put on the ribbon and the bow, our function also moves backward six characters so that point is within the parentheses, and we can immediately start typing an expression.

Our whole goal was to make it easy to insert these characters, so now let's bind our function to a key:

```
(define-key c-mode-map "\C-ci" 'start-if-block)
```

The *define-key* function binds a key to a function. By specifying `c-mode-map`, we indicate that the key works only in C mode. There is also a `tex-mode-map` for TEX mode, a `lisp-mode-map` that you will want to know about if you play with your *.emacs* file a lot, and so on.

If you're interested in writing your own Emacs LISP functions, you should read the Info pages for *elisp*, which should be available on your system.

Now here's an important customization you may need. On many terminals the Backspace key sends the character `C-h`, which is the Emacs help key. To fix this, you should change the internal table Emacs uses to interpret keys as follows:

```
(keyboard-translate ?\C-h ?\C-?)
```

Pretty cryptic code. `\C-h` is recognizable as the Control key pressed with `h`, which happens to produce the same ASCII code (8) as the Backspace key. `\C-?` represents the Delete key (ASCII code 127). Don't confuse this question mark with the question marks that precede each backslash. `?\C-h` means "the ASCII code corresponding to `\C-h`." You could just as well specify 8 directly.

So now, both Backspace and `C-h` will delete. You've lost your help key. Therefore, another good customization would be to bind another key to `C-h`. Let's use `C-\`, which isn't used often for anything else. You have to double the backslash when you specify it as a key:

```
(keyboard-translate ?\C-\\ ?\C-h)
```

xmodmap(1)

On the X Window System, there is a way to change the code sent by your Backspace key using the *xmodmap* command, but we'll have to leave it up to you to do your own research. It is not a completely portable solution (so we can't show you an example guaranteed to work), and it may be too sweeping for your taste (it also changes the meaning of the Backspace key in your *xterm* shell and everywhere else).

There are other key bindings you may want to use. For example, you may prefer to use the keys `C-f` and `C-b` to scroll forward (or backward) a page at a time, as in *vi*. In your *.emacs* file you might include the following lines:

```
(global-set-key "\C-f" 'scroll-up)
(global-set-key "\C-b" 'scroll-down)
```

Again, we have to issue a caveat: be careful not to redefine keys that have other important uses. (One way to find out is to use `C-h k` to tell you what a key does in the current mode. You should also consider that the key may have definitions in other modes.) In particular, you'll lose access to a lot of functions if you rebind the *prefix keys* that start commands, such as `C-x` and `C-c`.

You can create your own prefix keys, if you really want to extend your current mode with lots of new commands. Use something like:

```
(global-unset-key "\C-d")
(global-set-key "\C-d\C-f" 'my-function)
```

First, we must unbind the `C-d` key (which simply deletes the character under the cursor), in order to use it as a prefix for other keys. Now, pressing `C-d C-f` will execute *my-function*.

You may also prefer to use another mode besides `Fundamental` or `Text` for editing "vanilla" files. `Indented Text` mode, for example, automatically indents lines of text relative to the previous line (as with the `:set ai` function in *vi*). To turn on this mode by default, use:

```
; Default mode for editing text
(setq default-major-mode 'indented-text-mode)
```

You should also rebind the Enter key to indent the next line of text:

```
(define-key indented-text-mode-map "\C-m" 'newline-and-indent)
```

Emacs also provides "minor" modes, which are modes you use along with major modes. For example, `Overwrite` mode is a minor mode that causes text to overwrite that in the buffer, instead of inserting it. To bind the key `C-r` to toggle overwrite mode, use the command:

```
; Toggle overwrite mode.
(global-set-key "\C-r" 'overwrite-mode)
```

Another minor mode is `Autofill`, which automatically wraps lines as you type them. That is, instead of pressing the Enter key at the end of each line of text, you may continue typing and Emacs automatically breaks the line for you. To enable `Autofill` mode, use the commands:

```
(setq text-mode-hook 'turn-on-auto-fill)
(setq fill-column 72)
```

This turns on `Autofill` mode whenever you enter `Text` mode (through the *text-mode-hook* function). It also sets the point at which to break lines at 72 characters.

Text and Document Processing

In the first chapter, we briefly mentioned various text processing systems available for Linux and how they differ from word processing systems that you may be familiar with. While most word processors allow the user to enter text in a WYSISYG environment, text processing systems have the user enter source text using a text-formatting language, which can be modified with any text editor. (In fact, Emacs provides special modes for editing various types of text-formatting languages.) Then, the source is processed into a printable (or viewable) document using the text processor itself. Finally, you process the output and send it to a file or to a viewer application for display, or you hand it off to a printer daemon to queue for printing to a local or remote device.

In this section, we'll talk first about three of the most popular text processing systems for Linux: TEX, *groff*, and Texinfo. At the end, we include a discussion about the available options if you would rather like to use a WYSIMWYG (what-you-see-is-maybe-what-you-get) word processor like those that predominate on Windows and Macintosh.

TEX and LATEX

TEX is a professional text-processing system for all kinds of documents, articles, and books—especially those that contain a great deal of mathematics. It is a somewhat "low-level" text-processing language, because it describes to the system how to lay out text on the page, how it should be spaced, and so on. TEX doesn't concern itself directly with higher-level elements of text such as chapters, sections, footnotes, and so forth (those things that you, the writer, care about the most). For this reason, TEX is known as a functional text-formatting language (referring to the actual physical layout of text on a page) rather than a logical one (referring to logical elements, such as chapters and sections). TEX was designed by Donald E. Knuth, one of the world's foremost experts in programming. One of Knuth's motives for developing TEX was to produce a typesetting system powerful enough to handle the mathematics formatting needs for his series of computer science textbooks. Knuth ended up taking an eight-year detour to finish TEX; most would agree the result was well worth the wait.

Of course, TEX is very extensible, and it is possible to write macros for TEX that allow writers to concern themselves primarily with the logical, rather then the physical, format of the document. In fact, a number of such macro packages have been developed—the most popular of which is LATEX, a set of extensions for TEX designed by Leslie Lamport. LATEX commands are concerned mostly with logical structure, but because LATEX is just a set of macros on top of TEX, you can use plain TEX commands as well. LATEX greatly simplifies the use of TEX, hiding most of the low-level functional features from the writer.

In order to write well-structured documents using TEX, you would either have to decide on a prebuilt macro package, such as LATEX, or develop your own (or use a combination of the two). In *The TEXbook*, Knuth presents his own set of macros that he used for production of the book. As you might expect, they include commands for beginning new chapters, sections, and the like—somewhat similar to their LATEX counterparts. In this section, we'll concentrate on the use of LATEX, which provides support for many types of documents: technical articles, manuals, books, letters, and so on. As with plain TEX, LATEX is extensible as well.

Learning the ropes

If you're never used a text-formatting system before, there are a number of new concepts you should be aware of. As we said, text processing systems start with a source document, which you enter with a plain-text editor, such as Emacs. The source is written in a text-formatting language, which includes the text you wish to appear in your document, as well as commands that tell the text processor how to format it. In the first chapter we gave a simple example of what the LATEX language looks like and what kind of output it produces.

So, without further ado, let's dive in and see how to write a simple document, and format it, from start to finish. As a demonstration, we'll show how to use LATEX to write a short business letter. Sit down at your favorite text editor, and enter the following text into a file (without the line numbers, of course). Call it *letter.tex*:

```
1   \documentclass{letter}
2   \address{755 Chmod Way \\ Apt 0x7F \\
3           Pipeline, N.M. 09915}
4   \signature{Boomer Petway}
5
6   \begin{document}
7   \begin{letter}{O'Reilly and Associates, Inc. \\
8               103 Morris Street Suite A \\
9               Sebastopol, C.A. 95472}
10
11  \opening{Dear Mr. O'Reilly,}
12
13  I would like to comment on the \LaTeX\ example as presented in
14  Chapter~9 of {\em Running Linux}. Although it was a valiant effort,
15  I find that the example falls somewhat short of what
16  one might expect in a discussion of text-formatting systems.
17  In a future edition of the book, I suggest that you replace
18  the example with one that is more instructive.
19
20  \closing{Thank you,}
21
22  \end{letter}
23  \end{document}
```

This is a complete LATEX document for the business letter that we wish to send. As you can see, it contains the actual text of the letter, with a number of commands (using backslashes and braces) thrown in. Let's walk through it.

Line 1 uses the `documentclass` command to specify the class of document that we're producing (which is a `letter`). Commands in LATEX begin with a backslash and are followed by the actual command name, which is in this case `document-class`. Following the command name are any arguments, enclosed in braces. LATEX supports several document classes, such as `article`, `report`, and `book`, and you can define your own. Specifying the document class defines global macros for use within the TEX document, such as the `address` and `signature` commands used on lines 2-4. As you might guess, the `address` and `signature` commands specify your own address and name in the letter. The double-backslashes (\\) that appear in the `address` generate line breaks in the resulting output of the address.

A word about how LaTeX processes input: as with most text formatting systems, whitespace, line breaks, and other such features in the input source are not passed literally into the output. Therefore, you can break lines more or less wherever you please; when formatting paragraphs, LaTeX will fit the lines back together again. Of course, there are exceptions: blank lines in the input begin new paragraphs, and there are commands to force LaTeX to treat the source text literally.

On line 6, the command \begin{document} is used to signify the beginning of the document as a whole. Everything enclosed within the \begin{document} and \end{document} on line 22 is considered part of the text to be formatted; anything before \begin{document} is called the *preamble* and defines formatting parameters before the actual body.

On lines 7-9, \begin{letter} begins the actual letter. This is required because you may have many letters within a single source file, and a \begin{letter} is needed for each. This command takes as an argument the address of the intended recipient; as with the address command, double-backslashes signify line breaks in the address.

Line 11 uses the opening command to open the letter. Following on lines 12-18 is the actual body of the letter. As straightforward as it may seem, there are a few tricks hidden in the body as well. On line 13 the LaTeX command generates the LaTeX logo. You'll notice that a backslash follows the LaTeX command as well as preceding it; the trailing backslash is used to force a space after the word "LaTeX." This is because TeX ignores spaces after command invocations; the command must be followed by a backslash and a space. (Otherwise, "LaTeX is fun" would appear as "LaTeXis fun.")

There are two quirks of note on line 14. First of all, there is a tilde (~) present between Chapter and 9, which causes a space to appear between the two words, but prevents a line break between them in the output (that is, to prevent Chapter from being on the end of a line, and 9 to be on the beginning of the next). You need only use the tilde to generate a space between two words that should be stuck together on the same line, as in Chapter~9 and Mr.~Jones. (In retrospect, we could have used the tilde in the \begin{letter} and opening commands, although it's doubtful TeX would break a line anywhere within the address or the opening.)

The second thing to take note of on line 14 is the use of \em to generate *emphasized text* in the output. LaTeX supports various other fonts, including **boldface** (\bf), and typewriter (\tt).

Line 19 uses the closing command to close off the letter. This also has the effect of appending the signature used on line 4 after the closing in the output. Lines 21–22 use the commands \end{letter} and \end{document} to end the letter and document environments begun on lines 6 and 7.

You'll notice that none of the commands in the LATEX source has anything to do with setting up margins, line spacing, or other functional issues of text formatting. That's all taken care of by the LATEX macros on top of the TEX engine. LATEX provides reasonable defaults for these parameters; if you wanted to change any of these formatting options, you could use other LATEX commands (or lower-level TEX commands) to modify them.

We don't expect you to understand all of the intricacies of using LATEX from such a limited example, although this should give you an idea of how a living, breathing LATEX document looks. Now, let's format the document in order to print it out.

Formatting and printing

Believe it or not, the command used to format LATEX source files into something printable is *latex*. After editing and saving the previous example, *letter.tex*, you should be able to use the command:

```
eggplant$ latex letter
This is TeX, Version 3.14159 (C version 6.1)
(letter.tex
LaTeX2e <1996/12/01>
Babel <v3.6h> and hyphenation patterns for american, german, loaded.
(/usr/lib/teTeX/texmf/tex/latex/base/letter.cls
Document Class: letter 1997/01/07 v1.2w Standard LaTeX document class
(/usr/lib/teTeX/texmf/tex/latex/base/size10.clo))
No file letter.aux.
[1] (letter.aux) )
Output written on letter.dvi (1 page, 1128 bytes).
Transcript written on letter.log.
eggplant$
```

latex assumes the extension *.tex* for source files. Here, LATEX has processed the source *letter.tex* and saved the results in the file *letter.dvi*. This is a "device-independent" file that generates printable output on a variety of printers. Various tools exist for converting *.dvi* files to PostScript, HP LaserJet, and other formats, as we'll see shortly.

Instead of immediately printing your letter, you may wish to preview it to be sure that everything looks right. If you're running the X Window System, you can use the *xdvi* command to preview *.dvi* files on your screen. What about printing the letter? First, you need to convert the *.dvi* to something your printer can handle. dvi drivers exist for many printer types. Almost all the program names begin with the three characters *dvi*, as in *dvips*, *dvilj*, and so forth. If your system doesn't have one you need, you have to get the appropriate driver from the TEX archives if you have Internet access. See the FAQ for *comp.text.tex* for details.

If you're lucky enough to have a PostScript printer, you can use *dvips* to generate PostScript from the *.dvi*:

```
eggplant$ dvips -o letter.ps letter.dvi
```

You can then print the PostScript using *lpr*. Or, to do this in one step:

```
eggplant$ dvips letter.dvi | lpr
```

In addition, *dvilj* will print *.dvi* files on HP LaserJet printers, and *eps* will print *.dvi* files on Epson-compatible printers.

If you can't find a DVI driver for your printer, you might be able to use Ghostscript to convert PostScript (produced by *dvips*) into something you can print. Although some of Ghostscript's fonts are less than optimal, it does allow you to use Adobe fonts (which you can obtain for MS-DOS and use with Ghostscript under Linux). Ghostscript also provides an SVGA preview mode you can use if you're not running X. At any rate, after you manage to format and print the example letter, it should end up looking something like that in Figure 9-1.

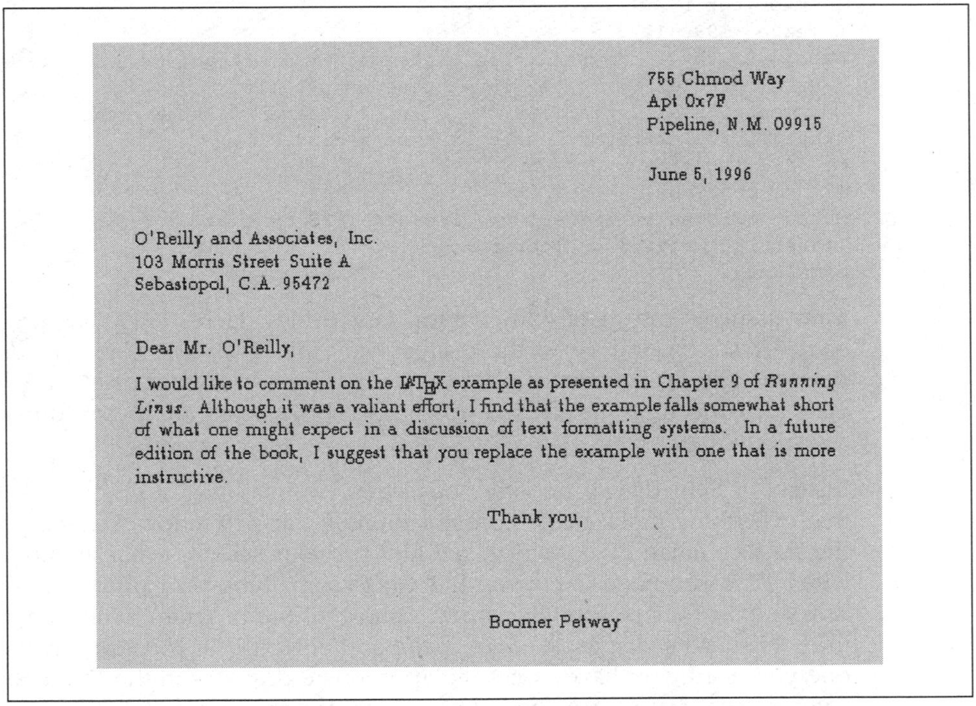

> 755 Chmod Way
> Apt 0x7F
> Pipeline, N.M. 09915
>
> June 5, 1996
>
> O'Reilly and Associates, Inc.
> 103 Morris Street Suite A
> Sebastopol, C.A. 95472
>
> Dear Mr. O'Reilly,
>
> I would like to comment on the LaTeX example as presented in Chapter 9 of *Running Linux*. Although it was a valiant effort, I find that the example falls somewhat short of what one might expect in a discussion of text formatting systems. In a future edition of the book, I suggest that you replace the example with one that is more instructive.
>
> Thank you,
>
> Boomer Petway

Figure 9-1: Sample output from a LaTeX file

Further reading

[19] LaTeX
[18] TeXbook

If LaTeX seems right for your document-processing needs, and you have been able to get at least this initial example working and printed out, we suggest checking into Leslie Lamport's *LaTeX User's Guide and Reference Manual*, which includes everything you need to know about LaTeX for formatting letters, articles, books, and more. If you're interested in hacking or want to know more about the underlying workings of TeX (which can be invaluable), Donald Knuth's *The TeXbook* is the definitive guide to the system.

comp.text.tex is the Usenet newsgroup for questions and information about these systems, although information found there assumes you have access to TeX and LaTeX documentation of some kind, such as the manuals mentioned earlier.

groff

Parallel to TeX, growing independently, were *troff* and *nroff*, two text processing systems developed at Bell Labs for the original implementation of Unix (in fact, the development of Unix was spurred, in part, to support such a text-processing system). The first version of this text processor was called *roff* (for "runoff"); later came *nroff* and *troff*, which generated output for a particular typesetter in use at the time (*nroff* was written for fixed-pitch printers (such as dot matrix printers), *troff* for proportional space devices—initially typesetters). Later versions of *nroff* and *troff* became the standard text processor on Unix systems everywhere. *groff* is GNU's implementation of *nroff* and *troff* that is used on Linux systems. It includes several extended features and drivers for a number of printing devices.

groff is capable of producing documents, articles, and books, much in the same vein as TeX. However, *groff* (as well as the original *nroff*) has one intrinsic feature that is absent from TeX and variants: the ability to produce plain-ASCII output. While TeX is great for producing documents to be printed, *groff* is able to produce plain ASCII to be viewed online (or printed directly as plain text on even the simplest of printers). If you're going to be producing documentation to be viewed online as well as in printed form, *groff* may be the way to go (although there are other alternatives as well—Texinfo, which is discussed later, is one).

groff also has the benefit of being much smaller than TeX; it requires fewer support files and executables than even a minimal TeX distribution.

One special application of *groff* is to format Unix manual pages. If you're a Unix programmer, you'll eventually need to write and produce manual pages of some kind. In this section, we'll introduce the use of *groff* through the writing of a short manual page.

As with TeX, *groff* uses a particular text-formatting language to describe how to process the text. This language is slightly more cryptic than TeX but is also less verbose. In addition, *groff* provides several macro packages that are used on top of the basic *groff* formatter; these macro packages are tailored to a particular type of document. For example, the mgs macros are an ideal choice for writing articles and papers, while the man macros are used for manual pages.

Writing a manual page

Writing manual pages with *groff* is actually quite simple. In order for your manual page to look like other manual pages, you need to follow several conventions in the source, which are presented in the following example. In this example, we'll write a manual page for a mythical command *coffee*, which controls your net-worked coffee machine in various ways.

Enter the following source with your text editor, and save the result as *coffee.man*:

```
1   .TH COFFEE 1 "23 March 94"
2   .SH NAME
3   coffee \- Control remote coffee machine
4   .SH SYNOPSIS
5   \fBcoffee\fP [ -h | -b ] [ -t \fItype\fP ] \fIamount\fP
6   .SH DESCRIPTION
7   \fIcoffee\fP queues a request to the remote coffee machine at the
8   device \fB/dev/cf0\fR. The required \fIamount\fP argument specifies
9   the number of cups, generally between 0 and 15 on ISO standard
10  coffee machines.
11  .SS Options
12  .TP
13  \fB-h\fP
14  Brew hot coffee. Cold is the default.
15  .TP
16  \fB-b\fP
17  Burn coffee. Especially useful when executing \fIcoffee\fP on behalf
18  of your boss.
19  .TP
20  \fB-t \fItype\fR
21  Specify the type of coffee to brew, where \fItype\fP is one of
22  \fBcolombian\fP, \fBregular\fP, or \fBdecaf\fP.
23  .SH FILES
24  .TP
25  \fI/dev/cf0\fR
26  The remote coffee machine device
27  .SH "SEE ALSO"
28  milk(5), sugar(5)
29  .SH BUGS
30  May require human intervention if coffee supply is exhausted.
```

Don't let the amount of obscurity in this source file frighten you. It helps to know that the character sequences \fB, \fI, and \fR are used to change the font to boldface, italics, and roman type, respectively. \fP resets the font to the one previously selected.

Other *groff* requests appear on lines beginning with a dot (.). On line 1, we see that the .TH request sets the title of the manual page to COFFEE and the manual section to 1. (Manual section 1 is used for user commands, section 2 for system calls, and so forth.) The .TH request also sets the date of the last manual page revision.

On line 2, the .SH request starts a section entitled NAME. Note that almost all Unix manual pages use the section progression NAME, SYNOPSIS, DESCRIPTION, FILES, SEE ALSO, NOTES, AUTHOR, and BUGS, with extra optional sections as needed. This is just a convention used when writing manual pages and isn't enforced by the software at all.

Line 3 gives the name of the command and a short description, after a dash (\-). You should use this format for the NAME section so that your manual page can be added to the *whatis* database used by the *man –k* and *apropos* commands.

On lines 4–5, we give the synopsis of the command syntax for *coffee*. Note that italic type \fI...\fP is used to denote parameters on the command line, and that optional arguments are enclosed in square brackets.

Lines 6–10 give a brief description of the command. Italic type generally denotes commands, filenames, and user options. On line 11, a subsection named Options is started with the .SS request. Following this on lines 11-22 is a list of options, presented using a tagged list. Each item in the tagged list is marked with the .TP request; the line *after* .TP is the tag, after which follows the item text itself. For example, the source on lines 12-14:

```
.TP
\fB-h\fP
Brew hot coffee. Cold is the default.
```

will appear as the following in the output:

```
-h        Brew hot coffee. Cold is the default.
```

You should document each command-line option for your program in this way.

Lines 23–26 make up the FILES section of the manual page, which describes any files the command might use to do its work. A tagged list using the .TP request is used for this as well.

On lines 27–28, the SEE ALSO section is given, which provides cross references to other manual pages of note. Notice that the string "SEE ALSO" following the .SH request on line 27 is in quotation marks; this is because .SH uses the first whitespace-delimited argument as the section title. Therefore any section titles that are more than one word need to be enclosed in quotation marks to make up a single argument. Finally, on lines 29–30, the BUGS section is presented.

Formatting and installing the manual page

In order to format this manual page and view it on your screen, use the command:

```
eggplant$ groff -Tascii -man coffee.man | more
```

The *-Tascii* option tells *groff* to produce plain-ASCII output; *-man* tells *groff* to use the manual-page macro set. If all goes well, the manual page should be displayed as:

```
COFFEE(1)                                                           COFFEE(1)


NAME
       coffee - Control remote coffee machine

SYNOPSIS
       coffee [ -h | -b ] [ -t type ] amount

DESCRIPTION
       coffee  queues  a  request to the remote coffee machine at
       the device /dev/cf0. The required amount  argument  speci-
       fies the number of cups, generally between 0 and 12 on ISO
       standard coffee machines.

   Options
       -h     Brew hot coffee. Cold is the default.

       -b     Burn coffee. Especially useful when executing  cof-
              fee on behalf of your boss.

       -t type
              Specify  the  type of coffee to brew, where type is
              one of colombian, regular, or decaf.

FILES
       /dev/cf0
              The remote coffee machine device

SEE ALSO
       milk(5), sugar(5)

BUGS
       May  require  human  intervention  if  coffee  supply   is
       exhausted.
```

As mentioned before, *groff* is capable of producing other types of output. Using the *-Tps* option in place of *-Tascii* produces PostScript output that you can save to a file, view with Ghostview, or print on a PostScript printer. *-Tdvi* produces device-independent *.dvi* output similar to that produced by TEX.

If you wish to make the manual page available for others to view on your system, you need to install the *groff* source in a directory that is present on the users' MAN-PATH. The location for standard manual pages is */usr/man*. The source for section 1 manual pages should therefore go in */usr/man/man1*. The command:

```
eggplant$ cp coffee.man /usr/man/man1/coffee.1
```

installs this manual page in */usr/man* for all to use (note the use of the *.1* filename extension, instead of *.man*). When *man coffee* is subsequently invoked, the manual page will be automatically reformatted, and the viewable text saved in */usr/man/cat1/coffee.1.gz*.

Chapter 4

If you can't copy manual page sources directly to */usr/man*, you can create your own manual page directory tree and add it to your MANPATH. See the section "Manual Pages" in Chapter 4, *Basic Unix Commands and Concepts*.

Texinfo

Texinfo is a text-formatting system used by the GNU project to produce both online documentation in the form of hypertext Info pages, and printed manuals through TEX from a single-source file. By providing Texinfo source, users can convert the documentation to Info files, HTML, DVI, PostScript, PDF or plain text.

Texinfo is documented completely through its own Info pages, which are readable within Emacs (using the C-h i command) or a separate Info reader, such as *info*. If the GNU Info pages are installed in your system, complete Texinfo documentation is contained therein. Just as you'll find yourself using *groff* to write a manual page, you'll use Texinfo to write an Info document.

Writing the Texinfo source

In this section, we're going to present a simple Texinfo source file—chunks at a time—and describe what each chunk does as we go along.

Our Texinfo source file will be called *vacuum.texi*. As usual, you can enter the source using a plain-text editor:

```
\input texinfo @c -*-texinfo-*-
@c %**start of header
@setfilename vacuum.info
@settitle The Empty Info File
@setchapternewpage odd
@c %**end of header
```

This is the header of the Texinfo source. The first line is a TEX command used to input the Texinfo macros when producing printed documentation. Commands in Texinfo begin with the at-sign, @. The @c command begins a comment; here, the comment -*-texinfo-*- is a tag that tells Emacs this is a Texinfo source file, so that Emacs can set the proper major mode. (Major modes were discussed earlier, in the section "Tailoring Emacs.")

The comments `@c %**start of header` and `@c %**end of header` are used to denote the Texinfo header. This is required if you wish to format just a portion of the Texinfo file. The `@setfilename` command specifies the filename to use for the resulting Info file, `@settitle` sets the title of the document, and `@setchapternewpage odd` tells Texinfo to start new chapters on an odd-numbered page. These are just cookbook routines that should be used for all Texinfo files.

The next section of the source file sets up the title page, which is used when formatting the document using TEX. These commands should be self-explanatory:

```
@titlepage
@title Vacuum
@subtitle The Empty Info File
@author by Tab U. Larasa
@end titlepage
```

Now we move on to the body of the Texinfo source. The Info file is divided into nodes, where each node is somewhat like a "page" in the document. Each node has links to the next, previous, and parent nodes, and can be linked to other nodes as cross references. You can think of each node as a chapter or section within the document with a menu to nodes below it. For example, a chapter-level node has a menu that lists the sections within the chapter. Each section node points to the chapter-level node as its parent. Each section also points to the previous and next section, if they exist. This is a little complicated, but will become clear when you see it in action.

Each node is given a short name. The topmost node is called Top. The `@node` command is used to start a node; it takes as arguments the node name, the name of the next node, the previous node, and the parent node. As noted earlier, the next and previous nodes should be nodes on the same hierarchical level. The parent node is the node above the current one in the node tree (e.g., the parent of Section 2.1 in a document is Chapter 2). A sample node hierarchy is depicted in Figure 9-2.

Here is the source for the Top node:

```
@c     Node, Next, Previous, Up
@node Top ,      ,           , (dir)

@ifinfo
This Info file is a close approximation to a vacuum. It documents
absolutely nothing.
@end ifinfo

@menu
* Overview::            Overview of Vacuum
* Invoking::            How to use the Vacuum
```

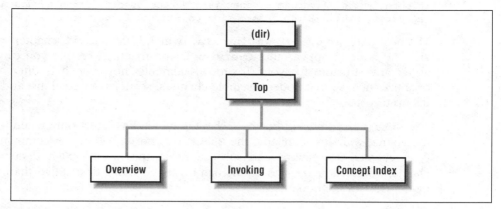

Figure 9-2: Hierarchy of nodes in Texinfo

```
* Concept Index::             Index of concepts
@end menu
```

The `@node` command is preceded by a comment to remind us of the order of the arguments to `@node`. Here, `Top` has no previous or next node, so they are left blank. The parent node for `Top` is `(dir)`, which denotes the systemwide Info page directory. Supposedly your Info file will be linked into the system's Info page tree, so you want the `Top` node to have a link back to the overall directory.

Following the `@node` command is an abstract for the overall document, enclosed in an `@ifinfo`...`@end ifinfo` pair. These commands are used because the actual text of the `Top` node should appear only in the Info file, not the TEX-generated printed document.

The `@menu`...`@end menu` commands demarcate the node's menu. Each menu entry includes a node name followed by a short description of the node. In this case, the menu points to the nodes `Overview`, `Invoking`, and `Concept Index`, the source for which appears later in the file. These three nodes are the three "chapters" in our document.

We continue with the `Overview` node, which is the first "chapter":

```
@c    Node,     Next,     Previous, Up
@node Overview, Invoking,         , Top
@chapter Overview of @code{vacuum}

@cindex Nothingness
@cindex Overview
@cindex Vacuum cleaners

A @code{vacuum} is a space entirely devoid of all matter. That means no
air, no empty beer cans, no dust, no nothing. Vacuums are usually found
```

```
in outer space. A vacuum cleaner is a device used to clean a vacuum.
See @xref{Invoking} for information on running @code{vacuum}.
```

The next node for `Overview` is `Invoking`, which is the second "chapter" node and also the node to appear after `Overview` in the menu. Note that you can use just about any structure for your Texinfo documents; however, it is often useful to organize them so that nodes resemble chapters, sections, subsections, and so forth. It's up to you.

The `@chapter` command begins a chapter, which has effect only when formatting the source with TEX. Similarly, the `@section` and `@subsection` commands begin (you guessed it) sections and subsections in the resulting TEX document. The chapter (or section or subsection) name can be more descriptive than the brief name used for the node itself.

You'll notice that the `@code...` command is used in the chapter name. This is just one way to specify text to be emphasized in some way. `@code` should be used for the names of commands, as well as source code that appears in a program. This causes the text within the `@code...` to be printed in constant-width type in the TEX output, and enclosed in quotes (like `'this'`) in the Info file.

Following this are three `@cindex` commands, which produce entries in the concept index at the end of the document. After this appears the actual text of the node. Again, `@code` marks the name of the `vacuum` "command."

The `@xref` command produces a cross reference to another node, which the reader can follow with the `f` command in the Info reader. `@xref` can also make cross references between other Texinfo documents. See the Texinfo documentation for a complete discussion.

Our next node is `Invoking`:

```
@node Invoking, Concept Index, Overview, Top
@chapter Running @code{vacuum}

@cindex Running @code{vacuum}
@code{vacuum} is executed as follows:

@example
vacuum @var{options} @dots{}
@end example
```

Here, `@example...@end example` sets off an example. Within the example, `@var` denotes a metavariable, a placeholder for a string provided by the user (in this case, the options given to the *vacuum* command). `@dots{}` produces an ellipsis. The example will appear as:

```
vacuum options ...
```

in the TEX-formatted document, and as:

```
vacuum OPTIONS ...
```

in the Info file. Commands such as `@code` and `@var` provide emphasis that can be represented in different ways in the TEX and Info outputs.

Continuing the `Invoking` node, we have:

```
@cindex Options
@cindex Arguments
The following options are supported:

@cindex Getting help
@table @samp
@item -help
Print a summary of options.

@item -version
Print the version number for @code{vacuum}.

@cindex Empty vacuums
@item -empty
Produce a particularly empty vacuum. This is the default.
@end table
```

Here, we have a table of the options *vacuum* supposedly supports. The command `@table @samp` begins a two-column table (which ends up looking more like a tagged list), where each item is emphasized using the `@samp` command. `@samp` is similar to `@code` and `@var`, except that it's meant to be used for literal input, such as command-line options.

A normal Texinfo document would contain nodes for examples, information on reporting bugs, and much more, but for brevity we're going to wrap up this example with the final node, `Concept Index`. This is an index of concepts presented in the document and is produced automatically with the `@printindex` command:

```
@node Concept Index, , Invoking, Top
@unnumbered Concept Index

@printindex cp
```

Here, `@printindex cp` tells the formatter to include the concept index at this point. There are other types of indices as well, such as a function index, command index, and so forth. All are generated with variants on the `@cindex` and `@printindex` commands.

The final three lines of our Texinfo source are:

```
@shortcontents
@contents
@bye
```

This instructs the formatter to produce a "summary" table of contents (@shortcontents), a full table of contents (@contents), and to end formatting (@bye). @shortcontents produces a brief table of contents that lists only chapters and appendices. In reality, only long manuals would require @shortcontents in addition to @contents.

Formatting Texinfo

To produce an Info file from the Texinfo source, use the *makeinfo* command. (This command, along with the other programs used to process Texinfo, are included in the Texinfo software distribution, which is sometimes bundled with Emacs.) The command:

```
eggplant$ makeinfo vacuum.texi
```

produces *vacuum.info* from *vacuum.texi*. *makeinfo* uses the output filename specified by the @setfilename in the source; you can change this using the *−o* option.

If the resulting Info file is large, *makeinfo* splits it into a series of files named *vacuum.info-1*, *vacuum.info-2*, and so on, where *vacuum.info* will be the top-level file that points to the various split files. As long as all of the *vacuum.info* files are in the same directory, the Info reader should be able to find them.

You can also use the Emacs commands M-x makeinfo-region and M-x makeinfo-buffer to generate Info from the Texinfo source.

The Info file can now be viewed from within Emacs, using the C-h i command. Within Emacs Info mode, you'll need to use the g command and specify the complete path to your Info file, as in:

```
Goto node: (/home/loomer/mdw/info/vacuum.info)Top
```

This is because Emacs usually looks for Info files only within its own Info directory (which may be */usr/local/emacs/info* on your system).

Another alternative is to use the Emacs-independent Info reader, *info*. The command:

```
eggplant$ info -f vacuum.info
```

invokes *info*, reading your new Info file.

If you wish to install the new Info page for all users on your system, you must add a link to it in the *dir* file in the Emacs *info* directory. The Texinfo documentation describes how to do this in detail.

To produce a printed document from the source, you need to have TEX installed on your system. The Texinfo software comes with a TEX macro file, *texinfo.tex*, which includes all of the macros used by Texinfo for TEX formatting. If installed correctly, *texinfo.tex* should be in the TEX *inputs* directory on your system where TEX can find it. If not, you can copy *texinfo.tex* to the directory where your Texinfo files reside.

First, process the Texinfo file using TEX:

```
eggplant$ tex vacuum.texi
```

This produces a slew of files in your directory, some of which are associated with TEX, others to generate the index. The *texindex* command (which is included in the Texinfo package) reformats the index into something TEX can use. The next command to issue is therefore:

```
eggplant$ texindex vacuum.??
```

Using the ?? wildcard runs *texindex* on all files in the directory with two-letter extensions; these are the files produced by Texinfo for generating the index.

Finally, you need to reformat the Texinfo file using TEX, which clears up cross references and includes the index:

```
eggplant$ tex vacuum.texi
```

This should leave you with *vacuum.dvi*, a device-independent file you can now view with *xdvi* or convert into something printable. See the section "TEX and LATEX" earlier in the chapter for a discussion of how to print *.dvi* files.

As usual, there's much more to learn about this system. Texinfo has a complete set of Info pages of its own, which should be available in your Info reader. Or, now that you know the basics, you could format the Texinfo documentation sources yourself using TEX. The *.texi* sources for the Texinfo documentation are found in the Texinfo source distribution.

Word Processors

If you insist on a popular WYSIWYG word-processing system, there are now quite a number of options available. Lately, it was even rumoured that Microsoft is going to port their office suite to Linux, but whether this is true remains to be seen. A Microsoft suite is not really needed any longer anyway, because you can get quite good word processors.

One of the most powerful and popular word processors in the United States, Corel WordPerfect, has been ported and is available from its current owner, Corel Inc. (see Figure 9-3). Many people have grown to like WordPerfect and will be delighted to hear that their word processor of choice is available for Linux.

Another option is to use ApplixWare by Applix, Inc. ApplixWare (see Figure 9-4) is an office suite that is commercially made but inexpensive for Linux. It includes not only a word processor, but also a spreadsheet, a drawing program, a mail

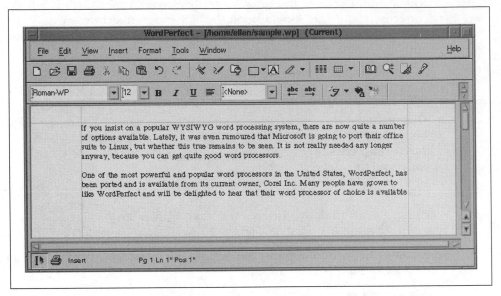

Figure 9–3: WordPerfect for Linux

program, and other smaller tools. In some respects, ApplixWare behaves differently from word processors like Microsoft Word or WordPerfect, but once you get used to it, it can be quite useful and handy. Especially noteworthy is its support for importing and exporting FrameMaker documents.

The German software company Star Division is making its office productivity suite StarOffice available for free for private use on all supported platforms (which include Linux, Solaris, Windows, OS/2, and the Macintosh). If you don't mind the annoying registration procedure and the long download, you can get StarOffice from the Star Division web site at *http://www.stardivision.com*. SuSE Linux and Caldera OpenLinux already include StarOffice, so you can avoid the massive download if you already have a SuSE or Caldera distribution.

All those programs have one feature in common that many consider a key requirement for doing office-type work on Linux: they can import Microsoft Word documents quite well. While you may well decide, as a new Linux enthusiast, that you won't accept documents sent to you in proprietary formats, sometimes they come from your boss, and you can't refuse to read them just because you are running Linux. In this case, it is good to know that there are Linux-based solutions available.

The LyX package (also available as KLyX with a more modern user interface) is another alternative. It provides a decent WYSIWYG X user interface that works with window managers from standard Linux distributions and uses the LaTeX and TeX packages in order to format the text for printing. If you can live with the

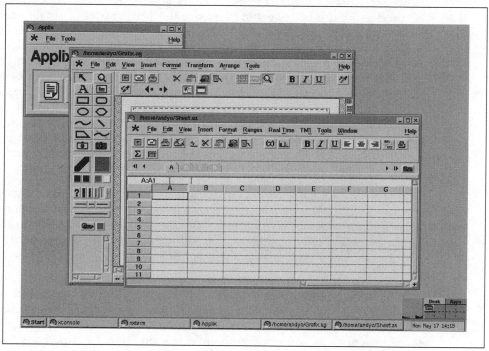

Figure 9–4: ApplixWare for Linux

formatting limits of the LATEX package (most of us can), you may find that LyX/KLyX is an excellent solution. LyX/KLyX does not know how to display some of the powerful formatting features that TEX provides, so if you are a TEX power user, this isn't for you. LyX/KLyX isn't part of most Linux distributions; to try it you will have to get it from a Linux archive.

Graphics

Many people are fascinated by computer graphics. Computers are being used to create photo-realistic images of surreal scenes or fractally generated images of mountain ridges with lakes and valleys; to change images by bending, polishing, aging them; or to make any other manipulations.

Linux does not need to step shyly aside when it comes to graphics. It can do just about anything that other computing environments can do, and in some areas, like dealing with many graphics files at the same time, it even excels. The X Window System, described in the next chapter, forms a very good base for bitmapped graphics, while hardware support will eventually arrive for 3D graphics conforming to the OpenGL standard.

However, working with graphics on Linux is often different from what you might be used to from other operating systems; the Unix model of small, interoperating tools is in effect here, too. This philosophy is be illustrated most clearly with the suite of graphics manipulation programs *ImageMagick* that we will describe here. ImageMagick is a collection of tools that operate on graphics files and are started from the command line or from shell scripts. Imagine that you have two thousand files of one file format that you want to reduce to 256 colors, slant, and convert to another file format. On Linux, this is only a few lines in a shell script. Now imagine doing this on Windows: Click on the File menu, click on the Open menu entry, select a file, select an operation, specify the parameters for the operation in a dialog, click OK, choose save from the menu, select a filename, and then click OK. Now repeat for next 1999 files. Can you say RSI?*

Graphics can not only be drawn but also programmed. There are tools like the ray-tracer POVRAY presented in this chapter where you specify the graphics to be generated by a suite of commands, often in a full-blown graphics-programming language. While this is perhaps more difficult than drawing the desired graphics with the mouse, it is also infinitely more flexible once you have mastered how to use it.

Now, not everybody wants to work with graphics from the command line. Part of the appeal of working with computer graphics is the immediate feedback when working with graphics programs, and Linux can provide these, too, even though those programs are currently in the minority on Linux (and perhaps will continue to be).

In this section, we will talk about some of the options for using and working with graphics on your Linux system. Most of the programs discussed here require the X Window System, which we'll show you how to install and configure in later chapters.

The programs we are covering here are:

ImageMagick
 A number of command-line tools for image manipulation

GIMP
 A graphical image manipulation program

POVRAY
 A famous ray-tracer

There are many more graphics programs available for Linux, including 3D modelers and video players. Scouring some Linux archives will reveal a wealth of good software to you.

---

* Repetitive Strain Injury—a malady that comes from typing too much. The better-known carpal tunnel syndrome is one form of RSI.

ImageMagick

ImageMagick is a suite of programs that convert and manipulate graphics files from the command line. It is also well suited for batch conversions, that is, converting many files at once. In addition, ImageMagick includes PerlMagick, a binding that lets you invoke the ImageMagick utilities from the Perl programming language. It comes with most Linux distributions; if yours does not have it, you can get it from *ftp://ftp.x.org/contrib/applications/ImageMagick*.

ImageMagick consists of a library and a number of utilities:

display

display (1)

> *display* is a graphical frontend to many of the functions provided by ImageMagick. It is very useful if you want to experiment with the effects of a function before you go and batch-convert hundreds of images with these effects. *display* can load many different graphics file formats and display them on the X Window System. You can start *display* and pass it one or more file-names on the command line, or load a file from the menu provided. If you have started *display* and do not see a menu, click the image displayed with the left mouse button. Figure 9-5 shows *display* in action. *display* features a huge number of command-line switches. See the manual page for details.

Figure 9-5: ImageMagick in action

import

import is a small program to capture either one window or the whole server into a file; that is, it allows you to make screenshots. For example, to make a screenshot of your whole screen and save it as *myscreen.xpm* in the graphics file format XPM, you would execute:

```
tigger$ import -window root myscreen.xpm
```

When you hear the first beep, the screen capture begins, and when the second one sounds, capturing is finished and the image data is in the process of being saved to the file you specified.

If you want to capture the contents of only one window, the easiest way is to start *import* without the *-window* option:

```
tigger$ import mywindow.xpm
```

The cursor then turns into a crossbar, which prompts you to click on any window. This window's contents are then captured and saved to the specified file.

image (1)

Like all ImageMagick programs, *import* has many command-line options; check the manual page.

montage

montage is a very useful little tool with a functionality rarely found elsewhere. It takes a number of images and puts them together as one large image in a tiled manner. There are lots of options for changing how the images are exactly tiled and put together.

montage (1)

In order to tile all your JPEG images in the current directory and create the image all.jpg out of it, you could call:

```
tigger$ montage *.jpg all.jpg
```

By default, there will be a label with the filename below each image. You can remove this by saying:

```
tigger$ montage +frame *.jpg all.jpg
```

convert

In a way, *convert* is the heart of the ImageMagick suite. It convert an amazing number of graphics formats. For example, let's assume that you want to port a GUI program from Windows to Linux. You have a large number of toolbar icons in Windows BMP format and want to convert those to XPM. This could be done with:

```
for i in *.bmp
do
convert $i xpm:'basename $i .bmp'.xpm
done
```

convert (1)

convert will happily chug through all the images and convert them. If you want to do other things to the images, just add the necessary switches, e.g., -despeckle for removing speckles from the images.

mogrify

mogrify (1)

mogrify is like *convert*, but it overwrites the original images and is meant more for applying filter functions than for converting file formats (even though you can easily change the file format by using the switch -format).

identify

identify outputs information about the images passed on the command line. For example:

```
tigger$ identify tux.gif
tux.gif 257x303+0+0 DirectClass 10968b GIF 1s
```

identify (1)

This tells you, among other things, that *tux.gif* is a GIF file 257 pixels wide and 303 pixels high. If this is not enough information for you, try the *-verbose* switch!

combine

combine (1)

As its name indicates, *combine* combines several images into one. You can for example put color-separated images together or put a logo on top of a larger image.

xtp

xtp (1)

Like the *ftp* program, *xtp* downloads files from a remote site or uploads them to a remote site. But unlike *ftp*, it does not need interactive input (in order to get this with *ftp*, you would have to edit its configuration file). *xtp* can be very favorably combined with the other tools from ImageMagick suite to automatically manipulate images on remote servers.

To sum up, the programs from the ImageMagick suite are an extremely versatile means to manipulate graphics files. It takes some time to familiarize yourself with all the command-line options in order to know what is available.

The GIMP

The GIMP (which expands to either GNU Image Manipulation Program or General Image Manipulation Program and is often written with the definite article) specializes in image-manipulation like the ImageMagick package described in the last section. But while ImageMagick's strength is batch processing, GIMP does everything via its GUI. The GIMP is often cited as one of the most impressive and successful products for Linux (and other Unix versions). People who use image-manipulation programs professionally have said that while GIMP can feel a little bit awkward to use, it is functionally comparable to its commercial competitor from the Windows and Macintosh world, Adobe Photoshop. Some people even have called it "the free alternative to Photoshop."

GIMP draws its power from an amazing number of plug-ins that are available for it. Thus, in order to be able to use a newly written image manipulation filter or file format import filter, you only need to install the plug-in, restart GIMP, and you are ready to go.

In addition, GIMP uses a clever tiling mechanism that allows you to load arbitrarily large images into it; GIMP will keep in memory only the part that is currently being used or visible. And if these features are not enough, GIMP also has its own scripting language called *script-fu*.

GIMP comes with most Linux distributions on the market today and can be run simply by entering the command *gimp* in a shell after starting X. If your distribution does not have GIMP, you can get the source code from *www.gimp.org*. If you plan to do more work with GIMP, you should check this web site anyway, because it also contains the documentation and sample images that show off what you can do with GIMP. A screenshot showing the toolbar, dialog boxes, and a work area is shown in Figure 9-6.

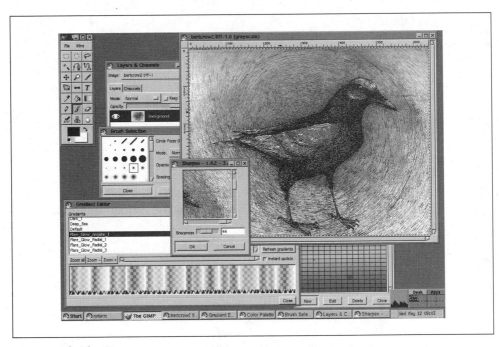

Figure 9–6: The Gimp

POVRAY

While ImageMagick and GIMP are mainly for manipulating existing images, POVRAY (the first three letters stand for "Persistence Of Vision") is a program for automatically creating new images. It is a so-called ray-tracer; a program that computes a scene from some information about which objects should be in the scene, what their physical and optical properties are, where the light is coming from, and where the spectator is standing. You describe this to POVRAY in a programming language of its own.

This brief description should already indicate that using POVRAY is not something you learn in one afternoon. If you are interested in this program, you can download it from *http://www.povray.org*, which is also the first source for all kind of POVRAY resources like sample files, documentation, and so on. Since we could not give you even a crash course into using POVRAY here, we'll refrain from attempting this futile task.

Printing

The *lpr* command prints a document on Linux. You might not always invoke this command directly—you may just press a Print button on some glitzy drag-and-drop graphical interface—but ultimately, printing is handled by *lpr* and the other print-management utilities we'll describe here.

If you want to print a program listing, you might enter:

```
lpr myprogram.c
```

Input is also often piped to *lpr* from another command, as we will see later. *lpr* starts the printing process by storing the data temporarily to a directory called a print spool. Other parts of the print management system, which we showed you how to set up in the section "Managing Print Services" in Chapter 8, *Other Administrative Tasks*, remove files from the print queue in the correct order, process the file for printing, and control the flow of data to the printer.

Chapter 8

There is at least one print spool for each printer on the system.* By default, *lpr* looks for a printer named lp. But if you need to specify a printer of a different name, just include a *–P* option.

For example, to send your document to a printer named nene, enter:

```
lpr -Pnene myprogram.c
```

If you forget the name of a printer, you can look at the names of the spool directories under the */var/spool/lpd* directory or at the */etc/printcap* file entries to see all the names recognized for each printer.

---

* A printer that can be used in different modes of operation, such as for printing faxes as well as letters, may have a separate print spool for each purpose.

If you want to use a particular printer for most of your printing needs, you can also set it in the PRINTER environment variable. So, assuming that you are using the *bash* shell, you could make nene your personal default printer by putting this command in your *.bashrc* file:

```
export PRINTER=nene
```

The *−P* option in *lpr* overrides the PRINTER variable.

Once you know how to print a file, the next problem you might face is finding out what is happening if your file doesn't instantly print as you expect. You can find out the status of files in the print queue by using the *lpq* command. To find out the status of files sent to your default printer (the PRINTER environment variable applies to all the commands discussed in this section), enter:

```
$ lpq
nene is ready and printing
Rank    Owner     Job  Files                    Total Size
active  lovelace  020  (standard input)         776708 bytes
1st     parcifal  024  (standard input)        2297842 bytes
1st     lark      023  (standard input)          10411 bytes
```

You see that the printer is running, but there are large jobs queued ahead of yours (if you are **lark**). If you just can't wait, you might decide to remove the job from the print queue. You can use the job number of the printing task that *lpq* reported to remove the printing job:

```
$ lprm 23
023 dequeued
023 dequeued
```

The spooled print file identified as job 023 is discarded, along with an associated file that contains instructions for formatting the file.

You can narrow the *lpq* report by asking about a specific print job by task ID (rarely used), by printer, or by user ID. For example, to get a report that identifies spooled files sent to a printer named ada you would enter:

```
$ lpq ada
ada is ready and printing
Rank    Owner     Job  Files            Total Size
active  lovelace  788  standard input   16713 bytes
1st     lark      796  standard input   70750 bytes
```

If you are the **root** user, you can kill all pending printing tasks by entering the command:

```
lprm -
```

If you are not the **root** user, issuing that command kills only the printing tasks you own. This restriction also holds true if you specify a printer:

```
lprm ada
```

If you are **root**, the `ada` print queue is emptied. If you are a normal user, only the print files you own are removed from the specified print spool. The *lprm* utility reports on the tasks it kills.

The **root** user can kill all the print tasks issued by any user, by specifying:

```
lprm username
```

If you issue *lprm* with no argument, it deletes the currently active print jobs that you own. This is equivalent to entering:

```
lprm yourusername
```

If you want to see whether a printer is down, you can use the *lpc* command:

```
/usr/sbin/lpc status ada
```

Chapter 8

See the section "Controlling Printer Services with lpc" in Chapter 8 for details. The *lpc* utility is usually installed in the */sbin* or */usr/sbin* directory.

Now for some more examples of common printing tasks and filters you can use.

To get a quick hardcopy printout of the printcap manual page, enter:

```
man printcap | col -b | lpr
```

The *man* command finds, formats, and outputs the printcap manual page in an enriched ASCII output that uses backspaces to overstrike and underline characters (in place of italics) for highlighting. The output is piped through *col*, a Unix text filter, where *-b* specifies stripping the "backspace" instructions embedded in the man page which results in simple text strings, still maintaining the layout of the formatted man page. The output of *col* is piped to *lpr*, which spools the text in a spool directory.

If you want to simulate underlining, you could instead use a filter designed originally for formatting print to a text display:

```
man printcap | colcrt | lpr
```

Suppose you want to print the fully enriched man page with highlighting and all. You might use a command like this:

```
groff -man -Tps /usr/man/man5/printcap.5 | lpr
```

The *groff* command applies the `man` macros to the file specified, creating PostScript output (specified by *−Tps*); output is passed to *lpr*, which spools it, and *lpd* applies the default print-processing instructions from the */etc/printcap* file.

Most Linux installations use BSD-style print utilities developed for the Berkeley Software Distribution of Unix. If you find utilities named *lp*, *lpstat*, *cancel*, and *lpadmin*, your Linux host has a System V–based print system. You need to read the manual pages and perhaps other documentation for that package. There are other printing systems that could be installed on your system, such as the PLP package, but we only document the usual Linux BSD-based print-management utilities here. We also describe how to use some of the other commonly installed print support utilities for Linux, such as filters that prepare documents in special ways to print on your printers.

The BSD-style print-management system is traditionally called "lp" after the line printers that were the standard print devices of the era in which the package was developed.* In the Linux community, the BSD print management package is more commonly usually called "the lpr package." Of course, the *lpr* command is only one tool in the package.

What Happens to a File After It's Put on the Queue

Only the **root** user has the ability to access printers directly, without using the printing system. (That's not a wise thing to do, by the way.) Linux doesn't grant system users the ability to address various physical devices directly, because crippling conflicts could result, and also because it's just too much work for them to bother with. Instead, utilities call background system processes to schedule your printing among other tasks, convert source file data to print to a specific printer using its printer language and protocols, set print resolution and format the pages, and add (or know not to add) header and footer data and page numbering. Linux configures itself to handle its physical devices when it is booted, including setting up ports and protocols to handle printing.

The print-management system is controlled by *lpd*, the "line printer daemon," which has necessary privileges to access printers for you. Once the print management system is installed, *lpd* is started every time the Linux system is initialized (booted). The */etc/printcap* file provides the control information *lpd* needs to manage the files you print.

Here's what the printer-management system is actually doing when you enter a printing command. When called, *lpr* checks whether you have a PRINTER environment variable set. If you do, *lpr* loads the print options stored there as instructions to process the print file it is receiving. Next, *lpr* applies any option parameters you gave it or that are passed to it by a program that preprocessed the file. Last, *lpr*

---

* Don't be misled if you hear someone use the term *lp*, which is a confusing misnomer. There is no *lp* utility in the BSD print-management package, but there is one in the later-developed System V print package. It is still possible that your BSD package allows you to use an *lp* command in order to print, though. Some systems use a shell script (filter) named *lp* to convert *lp* command options into *lpr* command options, and pass them on to *lpr*. This is solely for the convenience of users that are familiar with the System V *lp* command.

sends the file to the spool directory for the printer that will be used, along with another temporary file that stores the processing specifications for *lpd* to apply. Then *lpr* notifies *lpd* that there is a print file spooled. If *lpr* receives an option it doesn't understand, it passes the option on to the print filter, which we'll discuss shortly.

When *lpd* finds a job in the print spool, it reads the processing specifications (which tell it how to pass the print file through filters and direct the output to a device) and completes the printing task, erasing the print file and processing file when the printer has received all of the processed print file.

All Unix printing systems process a file through at least one filter to prepare it for output. This filter processes the file using any of the usual options that Unix print utilities pass to it.

Appropriate filters are set up by the administrator and specified in the printcap file to meet your usual printing needs. If you want to do any special processing, you give your processing instructions as options to the print commands. Your instructions enter the printer management system through the *lpr* command (directly on the command line or passed indirectly by some other command). The *lpr* command spools the print file in the correct print spool directory and stores the related processing instructions in an associated file in the same print spool.

When it is time to print your file, the *lpd* daemon reads any special processing directions for the print file, which may override default processing directions set in the */etc/printcap* file. When *lpd* passes your file to the correct filter for the printer you are using, it also passes along any instructions it did not act on. The filter then further processes the file itself according to the instructions or calls yet other filters to perform the processing it could not. The file is then passed on to the printer by *lpd*. You can see that this hidden filter provides most actual control of print formatting.

If you have special printing requirements, you need to learn the options to pass to the filter that control print formatting. The standard options are discussed in the *lpr* manual page. Additional filter options are documented in the filter package that is used. Later we discuss a couple of filters that are probably on your system. We can't possibly describe how to use all the filters and filter packages available to you for use with Linux. You should read the manual pages for the filters on your system to learn how to get the output you want.

A well-configured printcap file uses the printer's name to determine what kind of filtering to apply. For example, if your printer can automatically format and print an HTML (World Wide Web) document, you may be able to tell *lpr* to print to the html printer:

```
lpr -Phtml ~/homepage.html
```

This printer could actually be the same printer you use for PostScript, for example, but by specifying a printer named html you cause *lpd* to use a different printcap definition that processes the file through an HTML filter into a graphic format the printer understands.

Since the system administrator controls the contents of */etc/printcap*, you are not at liberty to simply exchange one filtering process for another. You do have a lot of control on the command line and through environment variables that affect your typesetting tools, filter parameters, and printer selection. When necessary, you can filter files before submitting them to the printer management system. For example, if you receive email with an attached graphic that you cannot display or print, you might save the file to disk and then use one of the many graphic conversion utilities available for Linux to convert it (filter it) into a printable form, before passing the file to *lpr*.

Much depends on the cleverness of the filter. If an option is passed through *lpr* and the filter but is never interpreted, it may end up passed through to the printer, either before or after the actual print file. This may have no effect. In some cases, a printer configuration command is deliberately passed to the printer this way. More typically a passed option prints extra pages, probably with stray characters on them; usually this is harmless. If you observe such behavior, make sure you aren't causing the problem yourself with environment variables, badly formed commands, or unsupported options. If it wasn't your fault, the administrator should try to trace the problem to save paper and time.

Some filters automatically apply the PRINTER environment variable if you set it. You should know that the equivalent printer variable for a System V print system is LPDEST, and some print filters you acquire may expect or accept that variable. You may even work on a mixed network with accounts on different systems where one uses BSD print management and another uses System V. If you are a belt-and-suspenders kind of person, you can set both LPDEST and PRINTER in your shell initialization file.

Problems using a print filter may affect other users on a multiuser system. Report any difficulties to the print-system administrator.

nenscript

The *nenscript* utility is a flexible filter that provides good formatted output for PostScript printers, even from ASCII text files. It isn't a basic Linux utility, but it is included in a number of Linux distributions and can be retrieved from the usual Linux FTP sites. While you can invoke *nenscript* to send a prepared file to the printer, it usually is specified in the */etc/printcap* file as a pass-through filter that takes text from the standard input and sends it to the standard output.

Suppose you are printing out a C program and want line numbering and a printout on green-striped fanfold paper (not the same format you'd want when printing those graphics you downloaded from the Internet on your nifty PostScript printer). You need to have the program processed, and then insert the line numbers in front of the lines. The solution is to process the file through a filter such as the *nenscript* utility (if you have it installed). After doing its own processing, *nenscript* passes the file to *lpr* for spooling and printing to your trusty tractor-feed printer (named `dino` here):

```
nenscript -B -L66 -N -Pdino myprogram.c
```

The *nenscript* filter numbers each line of the file passed through it when you specify the *–N* option. The *–B* option suppresses the usual header information from being printed on each page, and the *–L66* option specifies formatting at 66 lines per page. The *nenscript* filter just passes the *–Pdino* option through to *lpr*, which interprets it and directs the output to `dino`'s print spool directory for printing.

When called on the command line, *nenscript* automatically passes output to *lpr* unless you specify standard output by supplying the *–p* option. You don't need to pipe or redirect *nenscript* output to *lpr* explicitly.*

Suppose you are going to print a lot of program listings today. For convenience, you can set an environment variable for *nenscript* to specially process and print your listings each time:

```
export NENSCRIPT=" -B -L66 -N -Pdino"
```

Now, to print your listing correctly, all you need enter is:

```
nenscript myprogram.c
```

nenscript optionally sends output to a file, which is often useful for preparing PostScript files on Linux hosts that don't actually have a PostScript printer available. For example, to convert a text file to a PostScript file, formatted for two-column printing on A4 pages in 6-point Courier font, for instance, you would type:

```
nenscript -2 -fCourier6 -TA4 -pdocument.ps document.txt
```

The *–2* option overrides the one-column default, and the *–fCourier6* option overrides the 7-point Courier default for two-column output. (The one-column default is Courier10; *nenscript* always uses Courier font when converting plain text into PostScript.) The *–TA4* argument specifies European standard A4 paper format. If *nenscript* was compiled using the US_VERSION variable, the default paper format is 8.5 x 11 inches (if you're not using the US_VERSION environment variable, you can specify this size through *–TUS*). The *–p* option specifies that the output should be stored to *document.ps*, and the filename specified with no option is the input to *nenscript*. If no filename had been specified, *nenscript* would have taken standard input as the filename.

---

* The *nenscript* utility could also be the usual filter that the printcap file specifies for use with your printer. It won't hurt for the file to go through a properly designed filter more than once. A filter passes a processing instruction on only when it does not perform the processing itself. As a filter executes an instruction, it discards the processing option. You needn't worry that your file will end up with two sets of line numbers on the page.

As another example, to print the *nenscript* manual page as basic text on a PostScript printer, enter:

```
man nenscript | col -b | nenscript
```

The *man* command retrieves and formats the manual page and formats it for text display. The *col -b* command strips the backspace instructions for highlighting and underlining, leaving plain text that is piped to the *nenscript* filter. This turns the plain text into simple PostScript with some "pretty printing" that applies headers, footers, page numbering, and the like. Finally, the file is passed to *lpr*, which spools the file. The file passes once more through the filter specified in the print-cap file, which could be a "dummy" filter that simply passes the text through. Or the filter could do additional things, such as attaching a formfeed character to the end of the print file.

If you specify the −*Z* option with *nenscript*, it attempts to detect PostScript files passed to it and passes them through unaltered.

If a PostScript file is passed to *nenscript* and is taken for a text file (probably because *nenscript* was not called with the -*Z* option) *nenscript* will encapsulate it and pass it through to print. This can result in the PostScript code being printed out literally. Even a small PostScript file can use up a lot of paper in this way.

Suppose the *lpd* daemon already applies *nenscript* to process files sent to the printer. The file should still process correctly if it does, but intervening filtering could cause the second pass through *nenscript* to encapsulate the PostScript source. It would be safer to set the NENSCRIPT variable. When the *nenscript* filter is applied by */etc/printcap* to a print file, the options set in your NENSCRIPT environment variable are used, but are overridden by explicit options passed through *lpr* from a command line or another utility.

Note that you could specify the default printer to use either in PRINTER or as a -*P* argument stored to NENSCRIPT. If you set NENSCRIPT to specify a printer to use, that printer will be used every time NENSCRIPT filters one of your files. We recommend that you set PRINTER rather than -*P* in NENSCRIPT, so that you can change the printer specification and have it filtered appropriately.

## CHAPTER TEN

INSTALLING THE X WINDOW SYSTEM

We come now to the X Window System—one of the most powerful and important software packages available for Linux. If you've ever used X on a Unix system before, you're in luck; running X under Linux is almost no different from Unix systems. And, if you've never had the occasion to use it before, never fear: salvation is at hand.

It's difficult to describe the X Window System in a nutshell. X is a complete windowing graphics interface for Unix systems. It provides a huge number of options to both the programmer and the user. For instance, there are at least half a dozen *window managers* available for X, each one offering a different interface for manipulating windows. By customizing the attributes of the window manager, you have complete control over how windows are placed on the screen, the colors and borders used to decorate them, and so forth.

X was originally developed by Project Athena at MIT and Digital Equipment Corporation. The current version of X is Version 11 revision 6 (X11R6), which was first released in April 1994. Since the release of Version 11, X has virtually taken over as the de facto standard for Unix graphical environments. It is now developed and distributed by The Open Group, an association that is composed of many large computer manufacturers.

Despite its commercial use, the X Window System remains distributable under a liberal license from the X Consortium. As such, a complete implementation of X is freely available for Linux systems. XFree86, an implementation of X, originally for i386 Unix systems, is the version most often used by Linux. Today, this version supports not only Intel-based systems, but also Alpha AXP, MicroSPARC, PowerPC, and other architectures. Further architectures will follow. XFree86 is based on X386-1.2, which was part of the official X11R5 sources, but is no longer maintained and is therefore outdated. The current versions now have only a very little part in common with their ancestors. Support for innumerable graphics boards and many other operating systems (including Linux) has been added—and XFree86 implements the latest version X11R6.3.

In this chapter, we will tell you how to install and configure the X Window System, and in the next chapter, we will explore how to use X.

Linux distributions automatically install X (if you ask them to). If you're lucky, you won't need this chapter at all. But a large percentage of users aren't lucky—the distribution doesn't recognize some graphics hardware, writes a file to the wrong location so the X server can't start up, or has some other problem. One of the big advantages of this book is that we take you down to the depths of X configuration so you can get it running no matter what your distribution does. You may not need to read this chapter, but if you do need it, you'll appreciate everything that's here.

X Concepts

X is based on a client-server model in which the X *server* is a program that runs on your system and handles all access to the graphics hardware. An X *client* is an applications program that communicates with the server, sending it requests such as "draw a line" or "pay attention to keyboard input." The X server takes care of servicing these requests by drawing a line on the display or sending user input (via the keyboard, mouse, or whatever) to the client application. Examples of X clients are *xterm* (which emulates a terminal within a window) or *xman* (an X-based manual-page reader).

It is important to note that X is a network-oriented graphics system. That is, X clients can run either locally (on the same system that the server is running) or remotely (on a system somewhere on a TCP/IP network). The X server listens to both local and remote network sockets for requests from clients. This feature is obviously quite powerful. If you have a connection to a TCP/IP network, you can log in to another system over the network and run an X application there, directing it to display on your local X server.

Further advantages of X are security (if the user so desires), the modular separation of functions, and the support for many different architectures. All this makes the X Window System technically superior by far to all other window systems.

The X Window System makes a distinction between application behavior and *window management*. Clients running under X are displayed within one or more *windows* on your screen. However, how windows are manipulated (placed on the display, resized, and so forth) and how they are decorated (the appearance of the window frames) is not controlled by the X server. Instead, it is handled by another X client called a *window manager* that runs concurrently with the other X clients. Your choice of window manager will decide to some extent how X as a whole looks and feels. Most window managers are utterly flexible and configurable; the user can select the look of the window decoration, the focus policy, the meaning of the mouse buttons when the mouse is on the background part of the screen rather than on an application window, and many other things by editing the configuration files of the window manager. More modern systems even let you configure those aspects over a graphical user interface.

In order to fully understand the concept of window managers, you need to know that the window manager does not affect the presentation of the window created by the client. The window manager is only in charge of painting the window decoration, that is, the frame and the buttons that let you close, move, and resize windows.

There can be only one window manager on any X server. Theoretically, it is even possible to completely do away with window managers, but then you would not be able to move windows around the screen; put a hidden window on top; or minimize, maximize, or resize windows unless the programs themselves provide this functionality.

Hardware Requirements

As of XFree86 Version 3.3.3.1, released in January 1999, the video chipsets listed in this section are supported. The documentation included with your video adaptor should specify the chipset used. If you are in the market for a new video card, or are buying a new machine that comes with a video card, have the vendor find out exactly what the make, model, and chipset of the video card is. This may require the vendor to call technical support on your behalf; vendors usually will be happy to do this. Many PC hardware vendors will state that the video card is a "standard SVGA card" that "should work" on your system. Explain that your software (mention Linux and XFree86!) does not support all video chipsets and that you must have detailed information.

A good source for finding out whether your graphics board is supported and which X server it needs is *http://www.xfree86.org/cardlist.html*.

You can also determine your video card chipset by running the *SuperProbe* program included with the XFree86 distribution. This is covered in more detail later.

The following accelerated and nonaccelerated SVGA chipsets are supported:

- 3DLabs GLINT 500TX, GLINT MX, Permedia, Permedia 2, Permedia 2v

- 8514/A (and true clones)

- Alliance AP6422, AT24

- ATI 18800, 18800-1, 28800-2, 28800-4, 28800-5, 28800-6, 68800-3, 68800-6, 68800AX, 68800LX, 88800GX-C, 88800GX-D, 88800GX-E, 88800GX-F, 88800CX, 264CT, 264ET, 264VT, 264GT, 264VT-B, 264VT3, 264GT-B, 264GT3 (includes the Mach8, Mach32, Mach64, 3D Rage, 3D Rage II and 3D Rage Pro)

- ARK Logic ARK1000PV, ARK2000PV, ARK1000VL, ARK2000MT

- Avance Logic ALG2101, ALG2228, ALG2301, ALG2302, ALG2308, ALF2401

- Chips and Technology 65520, 65525, 65530, 65535, 65540, 65545, 65546, 65548, 65550, 65554, 65555, 68554, 69000, 64200, 64300

- Cirrus Logic CLGD5420, CLGD5422, CLGD5424, CLGD5426, CLGD5428, CLGD5429, CLGD5430, CLGD5434, CLGD6205, CLGD6215, CLGD6225, CLGD6235, GLGD6410, CLGD6412, CLGD6420, CLGD6440, CLGD7541, CLGD7543, CLGD7548, CLGD7555

- Compaq AVGA

- Cyrix MediaGX, MediaGXm

- Digital Equipment Corporation TGA

- Epson SPC8110

- Genoa GVGA

- IBM XGA-2

- IIT AGX-014, AGX-015, AGX-016

- Matrox MGA2064W (Millenium), MGA1064SG (Mystique and Mystique 220), MGA2164W (Millenium II PCI and AGP), G100, G200

- MX MX68000, MX680010

- NCR 77C22, 77C22E, 77C22E+

- NeoMagic 2200, 2160, 2097, 2093, 2090, 2070

- Number Nine I128 (series I, II, and IV), Revolution 3D (T2R)

- NVidia/SGS Thomson NV1, STG2000, Riva 128, Riva TNT

- OAK OTI067, OTI077, OTI087

- RealTek RTG3106

- Rendition V1000, V2x00

- S3 86C911, 86C924, 86C801, 86C805, 86C805i, 86C928, 86C864, 86C964, 86C732, 86C764, 86C765, 86C767, 86C775, 86C785, 86C868, 86C968, 86C325, 86C357, 86C375, 86C385, 86C988, 86CM65, 86C260

- SiS 86C201, 86C202, 86C205, 86C215, 86C225, 5597, 5598, 6326

- Trident TVGA8800CS, TVGA8900B, TVGA8900C, TVGA8900CL, TVGA9000, TVGA9000i, TVGA9100B, TVGA9200CXR, Cyber9320, TVGA9400CXi, TVGA9420, TGUI9420DGi, TGUI9430DGi, TGUI9440AGi, TGUI9660XGi, TGUI9680, ProVidia 9682, ProVidia 9685, Cyber 9382, Cyber 9385, Cyber 9388, 3DImage975, 3DImage985, Cyber 9397, Cyber 9520

- Tseng ET3000, ET4000AX, ET4000/W32, ET4000/W32i, ET4000/W32p, ET6000, ET6100

- Video 7/Headland Technologies HT216-32

- Weitek P9000, P9100

- Western Digital WD90C00, WD90C10, WD90C11, WD90C24, WD90C30, WD90C31, WD90C33, WD90C24A

- Western Digital/Paradise PVGA1

Video cards using these chipsets are normally supported on all bus types, including the PCI and AGP.

All of these chipsets are supported in 256-color mode, some are supported in mono- and 16-color modes, and some are supported on higher color depths.

The monochrome server also supports generic VGA cards, using 64k of video memory in a single bank, the Hercules monochrome card, the Hyundai HGC1280, the Sigma LaserView, the Visa, and the Apollo monochrome cards.

The VGA16 server supports memory banking with the ET4000, Trident, ATI, NCR, OAK and Cirrus 6420 chipsets, allowing virtual display sizes up to about 1600x1200 (with 1 MB of video memory). The maximum display size for other chipsets and X servers varies, but you can get 1024x768 with most modern chipsets, often more (this also depends on the amount of video memory available and the color mode that you choose).

This list will undoubtedly expand as time passes. The release notes for the current version of XFree86 should contain the complete list of supported video chipsets. Please also always see the *README* file for your particular chipset.

Besides those chipsets, there is also support for the framebuffer device in the 2.2 kernel series via the **FBDev** server; this kernel has unaccelerated support for several chipsets for which there is not yet a dedicated server; it also supports acceleration on some hardware. If your graphics board is supported by any of the "ordinary" servers, you should use one of those, not the framebuffer server.

One problem faced by the XFree86 developers is that some video card manufacturers use nonstandard mechanisms for determining clock frequencies used to drive the card. Some of these manufacturers either don't release specifications describing how to program the card or require developers to sign a nondisclosure statement to obtain the information. This would obviously restrict the free distribution of the XFree86 software, something that the XFree86 development team is not willing to do.

The suggested minimum setup for XFree86 under Linux is a 486 machine with at least 16 MB of RAM and a video card with a chipset listed earlier. For optimal performance, we suggest using an accelerated card, such as an S3-chipset card. You should check the documentation for XFree86 and verify that your particular card is supported before taking the plunge and purchasing expensive hardware. Benchmark ratings comparisons for various video cards under XFree86 are posted to the Usenet newsgroups *comp.windows.x.i386unix* and *comp.os.linux.misc* regularly.

As a side note, one author's (Kalle's) personal Linux system is an AMD K6-2 with 128 MB of RAM and is equipped with a PCI Permedia II chipset card with 8 MB of DRAM. This setup is already a lot faster with respect to display speed than many workstations. XFree86 on a Linux system with an accelerated SVGA card will give you much greater performance than that found on commercial Unix workstations (which often employ simple frame buffers for graphics and provide accelerated graphics hardware only as a high-priced add-on).

Your machine will need at least 8 MB of physical RAM, and 16 MB of virtual RAM (for example, 8 MB physical and 8 MB swap). Remember that the more physical RAM you have, the less the system will swap to and from disk when memory is low. Because swapping is inherently slow (disks are very slow compared to memory), having 8 MB of RAM or more is necessary to run XFree86 comfortably. A system with 8 MB of physical RAM could run *much* more slowly (up to 10 times more slowly) than one with 16 MB or more.

Installing XFree86

The Linux binary distribution of XFree86 can be found on a number of FTP sites. On *ftp://ftp.xfree86.org*, it is found in the directory */pub/XFree86/3.3.3.1/binaries*; there you will find systems for Intel, m68k, PPC, and Alpha AXP in subdirectories. (At the time of this writing, the current version is 3.3.3.1; newer versions are released periodically).

It's quite likely you obtained XFree86 as part of a Linux distribution, in which case downloading the software separately is not necessary. If you are downloading XFree86 directly, the following tables list the files in the XFree86-3.3.3.1 distribution.

One of the following servers is required (not all of those are available for all platforms, but all are available for Intel systems):

File	Description
X8514.tgz	Server for 8514-based boards
XAGX.tgz	Server for AGX-based boards
XMa32.tgz	Server for Mach32-based boards
XMa64.tgz	Server for Mach64-based boards
XMa8.tgz	Server for Mach8-based boards
XMono.tgz	Server for monochrome video modes
XP9K.tgz	Server for P9000-based boards
XS3.tgz	Server for S3-based boards
XSVGA.tgz	Server for Super VGA-based boards
XVG16.tgz	Server for VGA/EGA-based boards (needed for XF86Setup)
XW32.tgz	Server for ET4000/W32-based boards
X3DL.tgz	Server for boards with 3Dlabs chipsets
XI128.tgz	Server for I128-based boards

All of the following files are required:

File	Description
Xbin.tgz	The rest of the X11R6 binaries
Xcfg.tgz	Configuration files for *xdm* and *xinit*
Xdoc.tgz	Documentation
Xlib.tgz	Shared X libraries and support files
Xfnts.tgz	Basic fonts
Xman.tgz	Manual pages
Xset.tgz	Configuration utility XF86Setup
XVG16.tgz	VGA server; needed by configuration utility
XF86Setup	
preinst.sh	Pre-installation script
postinst.sh	Post-installation script
extract	Extraction utility

The following files are optional:

File	Description
Xlkit.tgz	Server link kit for customization
Xf100.tgz	100-dpi screen fonts
Xfscl.tgz	Scaled fonts (Speedo, Type1)

File	Description
Xfcyr.tgz	Cyrillic fonts
Xfnon.tgz	Other fonts (Chinese, Japanese, Korean, and Hebrew)
Xfsrv.tgz	Font server and configuration files
Xprog.tgz	X header files, configuration files, and libraries needed at compilation time
Xnest.tgz	Nested X server
Xvfb.tgz	X server that uses a virtual framebuffer
Xprt.tgz	X Print server
Xps.tgz	PostScript version of the documentation
Xhtml.tgz	HTML version of the documentation
Xjdoc.tgz	Japanese version of some documentation
Xjhtm.tgz	Japanese HTML version of the documentation

The XFree86 directory should contain *README* files and installation notes for the current version.

Obtain these files and save them in the directory */var/tmp* (you can use any other directory; just change the pathname accordingly in the following examples), and create the directory */usr/X11R6* as **root**. Copy the three files *preinst.sh*, *postinst.sh* and *extract* to */var/tmp*. Change to the directory */usr/X11R6* and run:

```
sh /var/tmp/preinst.sh
```

Next, make sure the *extract* utility that you downloaded is executable:

```
chmod 755 extract
```

Now unpack the binaries by typing:

```
/var/tmp/extract /var/tmp/X*.tgz
```

Finally, run the post-installation script:

```
sh /var/tmp/postinst.sh
```

You need to make sure that */usr/X11R6/bin* is on your path. This can be done by editing your system default */etc/profile* or */etc/csh.login* (based on the shell that you or other users on your system, use). Or you can simply add the directory to your personal path by modifying */etc/.bashrc* or */etc/.cshrc*, based on your shell.

You also need to make sure that */usr/X11R6/lib* can be located by *ld.so*, the run-time linker. To do this, add the line:

```
/usr/X11R6/lib
```

to the file */etc/ld.so.conf*, and run */sbin/ldconfig* as **root**.

Configuring XFree86

Setting up XFree86 is not difficult in most cases. However, if you happen to be using hardware for which drivers are under development, or wish to obtain the best performance or resolution from an accelerated graphics card, configuring XFree86 can be somewhat time-consuming.

In this section, we describe how to create and edit the *XF86Config* file, which configures the XFree86 server. In many cases, it is best to start out with a "basic" XFree86 configuration—one that uses a low resolution. A good choice is 640x480, which should be supported on all video cards and monitor types. Once you have XFree86 working at a lower, standard resolution, you can tweak the configuration to exploit the capabilities of your video hardware. The idea is that you want to make sure XFree86 works at least minimally on your system and that something isn't wrong with your installation before attempting the sometimes difficult task of setting up XFree86 for real use. With current hardware, you should easily be able to get up to 1024x768 pixels.

But before you start to write a *XF86Config* file yourself, try one of the configuration programs that are available. In many cases, you can avoid going through the hassle that will be described on the next pages. Some programs that may help you are:

XF86Setup

> This graphical configuration program is provided by the XFree86 team themselves. It starts up a VGA X server with 16 colors (which is quite sure to run on just about any display hardware) and then lets you select your graphics board, your monitor type, your mouse type, and other options. At the end, it tries to start up a server as configured, and if you are satisfied, it offers to write the configuration file for you. We have found this program to be very useful and reliable in many cases.

ConfigXF86

> This is a text-based program that asks you a number of questions and then generates a configuration file from your answers. It is by no means as comfortable to use as *XF86Setup* (and is slightly outdated), but it has been reported to work in cases where *XF86Setup* has failed.

Distribution-specific configuration tools

> Some distributions also have their own configuration tools. For example, SuSE has *SaX* and Red Hat has *Xconfigurator*. Caldera OpenLinux now even configures the mouse and the video board automatically during installation.

If one of these tools is able to configure your X server for you, you should use it and save yourself a lot of trouble. However, if all of the tools fail or if you really want to fine-tune your X server, you will have to know how to edit the *XF86Config* file yourself.

In addition to the information here, you should read the following documentation:

- The XFree86 documentation in */usr/X11R6/lib/X11/doc* (contained within the *Xdoc* package). You should especially see the file *README.Config*, which is an XFree86 configuration tutorial.

- The *README* file for your video chipset, if one exists, in the directory */usr/X11R6/lib/X11/doc*. These *README* files have names such as *README.Cirrus* and *README.S3*.

- The manual page for *XFree86*.

- The manual page for *XF86Config*.

- The manual page for the particular server that you are using (such as *XF86_SVGA* or *XF86_S3*).

The main configuration file you need to create is */usr/X11R6/lib/X11/XF86Config* (some distributions put this in */etc/XF86Config* or */etc/X11* instead). This file contains information on your mouse, video card parameters, and so on. The file *XF86Config.eg* is provided with the XFree86 distribution as an example. Copy this file to *XF86Config* and edit it as a starting point.

The *XF86Config* manual page explains the format of this file in detail. Read this manual page now if you have not done so already.

We are going to present a sample *XF86Config* file, piece by piece. This file may not look exactly like the sample file included in the XFree86 distribution, but the structure is the same.

The *XF86Config* file format may change with each version of XFree86; this information is only valid for XFree86 Version 3.3.3.1.

Also, you should not simply copy the configuration file listed here to your own system and attempt to use it. Attempting to use a configuration file that doesn't correspond to your hardware could drive the monitor at a frequency that is too high for it; there have been reports of monitors (especially fixed-frequency monitors) being damaged or destroyed by using an incorrectly configured *XF86Config* file. The bottom line is this: make absolutely sure your *XF86Config* file corresponds to your hardware before you attempt to use it.

Each section of the *XF86Config* file is surrounded by the pair of lines `Section "section-name"`...`EndSection`. The first part of the *XF86Config* file is `Files`, which looks like this:

```
Section "Files"
    RgbPath      "/usr/X11R6/lib/X11/rgb"
    FontPath     "/usr/X11R6/lib/X11/fonts/misc/"
    FontPath     "/usr/X11R6/lib/X11/fonts/75dpi/"
EndSection
```

The RgbPath line sets the path to the X11R6 RGB color database, and each Font-Path line sets the path to a directory containing X11 fonts. In general, you shouldn't have to modify these lines; just be sure there is a FontPath entry for each font type you have installed (i.e., for each directory in */usr/X11R6/lib/X11/fonts*). If you add the string :unscaled to a FontPath, the fonts from this directory will not be scaled. This is often an improvement because fonts that are vastly scaled look ugly. In addition to FontPath and RgbPath, you can also add a ModulePath to this section, to point to a directory with dynamically loaded modules. Those modules are currently used for some special input devices, as well as the PEX and XIE extensions.

The next section is ServerFlags, which specifies several global flags for the server. In general this section is empty:

```
Section "ServerFlags"
# Uncomment this to cause a core dump at the spot where a signal is
# received.  This may leave the console in an unusable state, but may
# provide a better stack trace in the core dump to aid in debugging
#    NoTrapSignals
# Uncomment this to disable the <Crtl><Alt><BS> server abort sequence
#    DontZap
EndSection
```

Here, we have all lines within the section commented out.

The next section is Keyboard:

```
Section "Keyboard"
    Protocol    "Standard"
    AutoRepeat  500 5
    ServerNumLock
EndSection
```

Other options are available as well: see the *XF86Config* file if you wish to modify the keyboard configuration. The previous example should work for most systems with U.S. keyboards. If you have another keyboard, you will have to add additional lines. For example, the following works for a standard German keyboard:

```
XkbRules        "xfree86"
XkbModel        "pc102"
XkbLayout       "de"
XkbVariants     ""
XkbOptions      ""
```

The next section is Pointer, which specifies parameters for the mouse device:

```
Section "Pointer"

    Protocol    "MouseSystems"
    Device      "/dev/mouse"
```

```
# Baudrate and SampleRate are only for some Logitech mice
#    BaudRate    9600
#    SampleRate 150

# Emulate3Buttons is an option for 2-button Microsoft mice
#    Emulate3Buttons

# ChordMiddle is an option for some 3-button Logitech mice
#    ChordMiddle

EndSection
```

The only options you should concern yourself with now are `Protocol` and `Device`. `Protocol` specifies the mouse *protocol* your mouse uses (not the make or brand of mouse). Valid types for `Protocol` (under Linux—there are other options available for other operating systems) are:

- `BusMouse`

- `Logitech`

- `Microsoft`

- `MMSeries`

- `Mouseman`

- `MouseManPlusPS/2`

- `MouseSystems`

- `PS/2`

- `MMHitTab`

- `GlidePoint`

- `GlidePointPS/2`

- `IntelliMouse`

- `IMPS/2`

- `NetMousePS/2`

- `NetScrollPS/2`

- `SysMouse`

- `ThinkingMouse`

- `ThinkingMousePS/2`

- `Xqueue`

`BusMouse` should be used for the Logitech busmouse. Note that older Logitech mice that are not bus mice should use `Logitech`, but newer Logitech mice that are not bus mice use either the `Microsoft` or the `Mouseman` protocol. This is a case where the protocol doesn't necessarily have anything to do with the make of the mouse.

If you have a modern serial mouse, you could also try to specify `Auto`, which will try to autoselect a mouse driver.

It is easy to check whether you have selected the correct mouse driver once you have started up X; when you move your mouse, the mouse pointer on the screen should follow this movement. If it does this, your setup is very likely to be correct. If it doesn't, try another driver, and also check whether the device you specified is correct.

`Device` specifies the device file where the mouse can be accessed. On most Linux systems, this is */dev/mouse*. */dev/mouse* is usually a link to the appropriate serial port (such as */dev/ttyS0*) for serial mice or to the appropriate busmouse device for busmice. At any rate, be sure that the device file listed in `Device` exists.

The next section is `Monitor`, which specifies the characteristics of your monitor. As with other sections in the *XF86Config* file, there may be more than one `Monitor` section. This is useful if you have multiple monitors connected to a system, or use the same *XF86Config* file under multiple hardware configurations. In general though, you will need only a single `Monitor` section:

```
Section "Monitor"

    Identifier  "CTX 5468 NI"

    # These values are for a CTX 5468NI only! Don't attempt to use
    # them with your monitor (unless you have this model)

    HorizSync    30-38,47-50
    VertRefresh  50-90

    # Modes: Name        dotclock  horiz             vert

    ModeLine "640x480"   25        640 664 760 800   480 491 493 525
    ModeLine "800x600"   36        800 824 896 1024  600 601 603 625
    ModeLine "1024x768"  65        1024 1088 1200 1328 768 783 789 818

EndSection
```

The `Identifier` line is used to give an arbitrary name to the `Monitor` entry. This can be any string; you will use it to refer to the `Monitor` entry later in the *XF86Config* file.

`HorizSync` specifies the valid horizontal sync frequencies for your monitor in kHz. If you have a multisync monitor, this can be a range of values (or several comma-separated ranges), as seen in the `Monitor` section. If you have a fixed-frequency monitor, this will be a list of discrete values, such as:

```
HorizSync     31.5, 35.2, 37.9, 35.5, 48.95
```

Your monitor manual should list these values in the technical specifications section. If you do not have this information, you should contact either the manufacturer or the vendor of your monitor to obtain it. There are other sources of information, as well; they are listed later.

You should be careful with those settings. While the settings `VertRefresh` and `HorizSync` (described next) help to make sure that your monitor will not be destroyed by wrong settings, you won't be very happy with your X setup if you get these values wrong. Unsteady pictures, flickering, or just plain snow can result.

`VertRefresh` specifies the valid vertical refresh rates (or vertical synchronization frequencies) for your monitor in Hz. Like `HorizSync`, this can be a range or a list of discrete values; your monitor manual should list them.

`HorizSync` and `VertRefresh` are used only to double-check that the monitor resolutions you specify are in valid ranges. This reduces the chance that you will damage your monitor by attempting to drive it at a frequency for which it wasn't designed.

The `ModeLine` directive is used to specify a single resolution mode for your monitor. The format of `ModeLine` is:

`ModeLine` *name dot-clock horiz-values vert-values*

name is an arbitrary string, which you will use to refer to the resolution mode later in the file. *dot-clock* is the driving clock frequency or *dot clock* associated with the resolution mode. A dot clock is usually specified in MHz and is the rate at which the video card must send pixels to the monitor at this resolution. *horiz-values* and *vert-values* are four numbers each; they specify when the electron gun of the monitor should fire and when the horizontal and vertical sync pulses fire during a sweep across the screen.

How can you determine the `ModeLine` values for your monitor? The file *Video-Modes.doc*, included with the XFree86 distribution, describes in detail how to determine these values for each resolution mode your monitor supports. First of all, `clock` must correspond to one of the dot-clock values that your video card can produce. Later in the *XF86Config* file, you will specify these clocks; you can use only video modes that have a `clock` value supported by your video card.

Two files included in the XFree86 distribution may include `ModeLine` data for your monitor. These files are *modeDB.txt* and *Monitors*, both of which are found in */usr/X11R6/lib/X11/doc*.

You should start with `ModeLine` values for the VESA standard monitor timings, which most monitors support. *modeDB.txt* includes timing values for VESA standard resolutions. In that file, you will see entries such as:

```
# 640x480@60Hz Non-Interlaced mode
# Horizontal Sync = 31.5kHz
# Timing: H=(0.95us, 3.81us, 1.59us), V=(0.35ms, 0.064ms, 1.02ms)
#
# name       clock   horizontal timing    vertical timing     flags
  "640x480"  25.175  640  664  760  800    480  491  493  525
```

This is a VESA standard timing for a 640x480 video mode. It uses a dot clock of 25.175, which your video card must support to use this mode (more on this later).

To include this entry in the *XF86Config* file, you'd use the line:

```
ModeLine "640x480" 25.175  640 664 760 800  480 491 493 525
```

Note that the *name* argument to `ModeLine` (in this case "640x480") is an arbitrary string; the convention is to name the mode after the resolution, but *name* can technically be anything descriptive that describes the mode to you.

For each `ModeLine` used, the server checks that the specifications for the mode fall within the range of values specified with `HorizSync` and `VertRefresh`. If they do not, the server will complain when you attempt to start up X (more on this later).

If the VESA standard timings do not work for you (you'll know after trying to use them later when the screen is unsteady, flickers, or shows snow), the files *mode-DB.txt* and *Monitors* include specific mode values for many monitor types. You can create `ModeLine` entries from the values found in those two files as well. Be sure to use values only for your specific model. Note that many 14- and 15-inch monitors cannot support higher-resolution modes and often can support resolutions of 1024x768 at low dot clocks only or not at all. This means that if you can't find high-resolution modes for your monitor in these files, your monitor probably does not support those resolution modes.

If you are completely at a loss, and can't find working `ModeLine` values for your monitor, you can follow the instructions in the *VideoModes.doc* file included in the XFree86 distribution to generate `ModeLine` values from the specifications listed in your monitor's manual. While your mileage will certainly vary when attempting to generate `ModeLine` values by hand, this is a good place to look if you can't find the values you need. *VideoModes.doc* also describes the format of the `ModeLine` directive and other aspects of the XFree86 server in gory detail.

Lastly, if you do obtain `ModeLine` values that are almost, but not quite, right, it may be possible to simply modify the values slightly to obtain the desired result. For example, if while running XFree86 the image on the monitor shifts slightly or seems to "roll," you can follow the instructions in the *VideoModes.doc* file to try to fix these values. Also, be sure to check the knobs and controls on the monitor itself! In many cases it is necessary to change the horizontal or vertical size of the display after starting up XFree86 in order for the image to be centered and of the appropriate size. Having these controls on the front of the monitor can certainly make life easier. Another option is to use the program *xvidtune* (see the manual page for how to use it) that can help you to get all the numbers for the `modeline`, lets you try your changes, and even allows you to undo them if you did something wrong.

xvidtune (1)

You shouldn't use monitor timing values or `ModeLine` values for monitors other than the model you own. If you attempt to drive the monitor at a frequency for which it was not designed, you can damage or even destroy it.

The next section of the *XF86Config* file is `Device`, which specifies parameters for your video card. Here is an example:

```
Section "Device"
        Identifier "#9 GXE 64"

        # Nothing yet; we fill in these values later.

EndSection
```

This section defines properties for a particular video card. `Identifier` is an arbitrary string describing the card; you will use this string to refer to the card later.

Initially, you don't need to include anything in the `Device` section, except for `Identifier`. This is because we will be using the X server itself to probe for the properties of the video card and entering them into the `Device` section later. The XFree86 server is capable of probing for the video-card chipset, clocks, RAMDAC (one of the chips on the video board), and amount of video RAM on the board.

Before we do this, however, we need to finish writing the *XF86Config* file. The next section is `Screen`, which specifies the monitor/video card combination to use for a particular server:

```
Section "Screen"
    Driver      "Accel"
    Device      "#9 GXE 64"
    Monitor     "CTX 5468 NI"
    Subsection "Display"
        Depth       16
        Modes       "1024x768" "800x600" "640x480"
        ViewPort    0 0
        Virtual     1024 768
    EndSubsection
EndSection
```

The `Driver` line specifies the X server you will be using. The possible values for `Driver` are:

Accel

> For the *XF86_S3*, *XF86_S3V*, *XF86_Mach64*, *XF86_Mach32*, *XF86_Mach8*, *XF86_8514*, *XF86_P9000*, *XF86_AGX*, *XF86_I128*, *XF86_TGA*, and *XF86_W32* servers

SVGA

> For the *XF86_SVGA* server

VGA16

> For the *XF86_VGA16* server

VGA2

> For the *XF86_Mono* server

Mono

> For the non-VGA monochrome drivers in the *XF86_Mono* and *XF86_VGA16* servers

Be sure that */usr/X11R6/bin/X* is a symbolic link to your server; you might have to create this link yourself if you install XFree86 for the first time. Make a link with a command like the following:

```
ln -s /usr/X11R6/bin/XF86_SVGA /usr/X11R6/bin/X
```

Of course, you have to replace the first pathname with that of another server binary if you don't use the SVGA server.

The Device line specifies the Identifier from the Device section. Earlier, we created a Device section with the line:

```
Identifier "#9 GXE 64"
```

Therefore, we use "#9 GXE 64" on the Device line here.

Similarly, the Monitor line specifies the name of the Monitor section to be used with this server. Here, "CTX 5468 NI" is the Identifier used in the Monitor section described earlier.

Subsection "Display" defines several properties of the XFree86 server corresponding to your monitor/video-card combination. The *XF86Config* file describes all these options in detail; most of them are icing on the cake and are not necessary to get the system working.

The options you should know about are:

DefaultColorDepth

> Specifies the color depth to use in case the X server supports several color depths.

Depth

Defines the number of color planes—the number of bits per pixel. Usually, Depth is set to 8. For the VGA16 server, you would use a depth of 4, and for the monochrome server a depth of 1. If you are using an accelerated video card or one of the better SVGA cards with enough memory to support more bits per pixel, you can set Depth to 16, 24, or 32. If you have problems with depths higher than 8, set it back to 8 and attempt to debug the problem later.

Modes

Lists of video mode names that have been defined using the ModeLine directive in the Monitor section. In the previous section, we used ModeLines named "1024x768", "800x600", and "640x480", so we use a Modes line of:

```
Modes    "1024x768" "800x600" "640x480"
```

The first mode listed on this line will be the default when XFree86 starts up. After XFree86 is running, you can switch between the modes listed here using Ctrl-Alt with the plus or minus on the numeric keypad.

It might be best, when initially configuring XFree86, to use lower resolution video modes, such as 640x480, which tend to work on most systems. Once you have the basic configuration working, you can modify *XF86Config* to support higher resolutions.

Virtual

Sets the virtual desktop size. XFree86 has the ability to use any additional memory on your video card to extend the size of your desktop. When you move the mouse pointer to the edge of the display, the desktop scrolls, bringing the additional space into view. Therefore, even if you are running at a lower video resolution, such as 800x600, you can set Virtual to the total resolution your video card can support. A 1 MB video card can support 1024x768 at a depth of 8 bits per pixel, while a 2 MB card can support 1280x1024 at depth 8, or 1024x768 at depth 16. Of course, the entire area will not be visible at once, but it can still be used.

The Virtual option is a nice way to utilize the memory of your video card, but it is rather limited. If you want to use a true virtual desktop, we suggest using a window manager like *kwm* or *fvwm2* instead. Both allow you to have rather large virtual desktops (implemented by such software techniques as hiding windows instead of actually storing the entire desktop in video memory at once). See the next chapter for more details about this; most Linux systems use *kwm*, which is a part of the K Development Environment, by default.

ViewPort

If you are using the Virtual option described earlier, ViewPort sets the coordinates of the upper-left corner of the virtual desktop when XFree86 starts up. ViewPort 0 0 is often used, putting the screen at the top left corner of the desktop; if this is unspecified, the desktop is centered on the virtual desktop display (which may be undesirable to you).

Many other options for this section exist; see the *XF86Config* manual page for a complete description. In practice, these other options are not necessary to get XFree86 working initially.

Filling in Video Card Information

Your *XF86Config* file is now ready to go with the exception of complete information on the video card. What we're going to do is use the X server to probe for the rest of this information and fill it into *XF86Config*.

Instead of probing for this information with the X server, you can find the *XF86Config* values for many cards in the files *modeDB.txt*, *AccelCards*, and *Devices*. These files are all in */usr/X11R6/lib/X11/doc*. In addition, there are various *README* files for certain chipsets. You should look in these files for information on your video card, and use that information (the clock values, chipset type, and any options) in the *XF86Config* file. Unfortunately, some manufacturers put out a graphics board with a new chipset without changing the board's name. If any information is missing, you can probe for it as described here.

In these examples, we will demonstrate configuration for a #9 GXE 64 video card, which uses the XF86_S3 chipset. This card happens to be the one that used by one of the authors, but the discussion here applies to any video card.

The first thing to do is to determine the video chipset used on the card. Running *SuperProbe* (found in */usr/X11R6/bin*) will tell you this information, but you need to know the chipset name as it is known to the X server.

To do this, run the command:

```
# X -showconfig
```

This lists the chipset names known to your X server. (The manual pages for each X server list these as well.) For example, with the accelerated XF86_S3 server, we obtain:

```
XFree86 Version 3.3.3.1 / X Window System
(protocol Version 11, revision 0, vendor release 6000)
Release Date: March 2 1998
        If the server is older than 6-12 months, or if your card is newer
        than the above date, look for a newer version before reporting
        problems.  (see http://www.XFree86.Org/FAQ)
Operating System: Linux 2.0.33 i686 [ELF]
Configured drivers:
  S3: accelerated server for S3 graphics adaptors (Patchlevel 0)
      newmmio, mmio_928, s3_generic
```

The valid chipset names for this server are newmmio, mmio_928, and s3_generic. The XF86_S3 manual page describes these chipsets and which video cards use them. In the case of the #9 GXE 64 video card, mmio_928 is appropriate.

If you don't know which chipset to use, the X server can probe it for you. To do this, run the command:

```
# X -probeonly > /tmp/x.out 2>&1
```

if you use *bash* as your shell. If you use *csh*, try:

```
% X -probeonly >& /tmp/x.out
```

You should run this command while the system is unloaded, that is, while no other activity is occurring on the system. This command also probes for your video-card dot clocks (as seen later), and system load can throw off this calculation.

The output from this command (in */tmp/x.out*) should contain lines such as the following:

```
XFree86 Version 3.3.3.1 / X Window System
(protocol Version 11, revision 0, vendor release 6000)
Operating System: Linux

Configured drivers:
   S3: accelerated server for S3 graphics adaptors (Patchlevel 0)
        newmmio, mmio_928, s3_generic
        .
        .
        .
(--) S3: card type: 386/486 localbus
(--) S3: chipset:   864 rev. 0
(--) S3: chipset driver: mmio_928
```

Here, we see that the three valid chipsets for this server (XF86_S3) are `newmmio`, `mmio_928` and `s3_generic`. The server probed for and found a video card using the `mmio_928` chipset driver.

In the `Device` section of the *XF86Config* file, add a `Chipset` line containing the name of the chipset you determined earlier. For example:

```
Section "Device"
        # We already had Identifier here...
        Identifier "#9 GXE 64"
        # Add this line:
        Chipset "mmio_928"
EndSection
```

Now we need to determine which dot clocks are made available by the video card. First, you should look into the files (*modeDB.txt* and so forth) mentioned at the beginning of this section and see if your card's clocks are listed there. The dot clocks will usually be a list of 8 or 16 values, all of which are in MHz. For example, when looking at *mode-DB.txt*, we see an entry for the Cardinal ET4000 video board, which looks like this:

```
# chip     RAM    virtual   clocks    default-mode  flags
  ET4000   1024   1024 768   25  28  38  36  40  45  32   0  "1024x768"
```

As we can see, the dot clocks for this card are 25, 28, 38, 36, 40, 45, 32, and 0 MHz.

In the Devices section of the *XF86Config* file, you should add a Clocks line containing the list of dot clocks for your card. For example, for the clocks in this example, we would add the line:

```
Clocks 25 28 38 36 40 45 32 0
```

to the Devices section of the file, after Chipset. The order of the clocks is important! Don't re-sort the list of clocks or remove duplicates.

If you cannot find the dot clocks associated with your card, the X server can probe for these as well. Using the *X −probeonly* command described earlier, the output should contain lines that look like the following:

```
(--) S3: clocks:  25.18  28.32  38.02  36.15  40.33  45.32  32.00  00.00
```

We could then add a Clocks line containing all of these values, as printed. You can use more than one Clocks line in *XF86Config* if all the values (sometimes there are more than eight clock values printed) don't fit onto one line. Again, be sure to keep the list of clocks in the order that they are printed.

Be sure there is no Clocks line (or that it is commented out) in the Devices section of the file when using *X −probeonly* to probe for the clocks. If there is a Clocks line present, the server will not probe for the clocks; it will use the values given in *XF86Config*.

Note that some accelerated video boards use a programmable clock chip. (See the XF86_Accel manual page for details; this generally applies to S3, AGX, and XGA-2 boards.) This chip essentially allows the X server to tell the card which dot clocks to use. If this is the case, you may not find a list of dot clocks for the card in any of the files mentioned earlier. Or the list of dot clocks printed when using *X −probeonly* will contain only one or two discrete clock values, with the rest being duplicates or zero.

For boards that use a programmable clock chip, you would use a ClockChip line, instead of a Clocks line, in your *XF86Config* file. ClockChip gives the name of the clock chip as used by the video card. But in most cases, the X server can detect your clock chip automatically and find the correct entry itself.

If you are not so lucky, the manual pages for each server describe the possible values for your server. For example, in the file *README.S3*, we see that several S3-864 video cards use an ICD2061A clock chip, and that we should use the line:

```
ClockChip "icd2061a"
```

instead of `Clocks` in the *XF86Config* file. As with `Clocks`, this line should go in the `Devices` section after `Chipset`.

Similarly, some accelerated cards require you to specify the RAMDAC chip type in the *XF86Config* file, using a `Ramdac` line. The XF86_Accel manual page describes this option. Usually, the X server will correctly probe for the RAMDAC.

Some video card types require you to specify several options in the `Devices` section of *XF86Config*. These options will be described in the manual page for your server, as well as in the various files (such as *README.cirrus* or *README.S3*). These options are enabled using the `Option` line. For example, the #9 GXE 64 card requires the option:

```
Option "number_nine"
```

Usually, the X server works without these options, but they are necessary to obtain the best performance. There are too many such options to list here, and they each depend on the particular video card being used. If you must use one of these options, fear not: the X server manual pages and various files in */usr/X11R6/lib/X11/doc* will tell you what they are.

So when you're finished, you should end up with a `Devices` section that looks something like this:

```
Section "Device"
        # Device section for the #9 GXE 64 only !
        Identifier "#9 GXE 64"
        Chipset "mmio_928"
        ClockChip "icd2061a"
        Option "number_nine"
EndSection
```

This `Device` entry is valid only for a particular video card, the #9 GXE 64; it is given here only as an example. Most video cards require a `Clocks` line, instead of `ClockChip`.

There are other options you can include in the `Devices` entry. Check the X server manual pages for the gritty details, but the explanation in this section should suffice for most systems.

Running XFree86

With your *XF86Config* file configured, you're ready to fire up the X server and give it a spin. First, be sure that */usr/X11R6/bin* is on your path.

The command to start up XFree86 is:

```
startx
```

This is a frontend to *xinit* (in case you're used to using *xinit* on other Unix systems). You can still use *xinit*, which gives you precise control about what exactly is started but requires you to start all needed programs manually.

This command starts the X server and runs the commands found in the file *.xinitrc* in your home directory. *.xinitrc* is just a shell script containing X clients to run. If this file does not exist, the system default */usr/X11R6/lib/X11/xinit/xinitrc* will be used.

You can change the initial display when starting up the X Window System by providing a different *.xinitrc* in your home directory. The next chapter tells you what you can put in this file.

[11] X User
Guide

If you are new to the X Window System environment, we strongly suggest picking up a book such as *The X Window System User's Guide* by Valerie Quercia and Tim O'Reilly.

Running Into Trouble

Often, something will not be quite right when you initially fire up the X server. This is almost always caused by a problem in your *XF86Config* file. Usually, the monitor timing values are off or the video-card dot clocks are set incorrectly. If your display seems to roll, or the edges are fuzzy, this is a clear indication that the monitor timing values or dot clocks are wrong. Also be sure you are correctly specifying your video card chipset, as well as other options for the `Device` section of *XF86Config*. Be absolutely certain that you are using the right X server and that */usr/X11R6/bin/X* is a symbolic link to this server.

If all else fails, try to start X "bare"; that is, use a command such as:

```
X > /tmp/x.out 2>&1
```

You can then kill the X server (using the Ctrl-Alt-Backspace key combination) and examine the contents of */tmp/x.out*. The X server reports any warnings or errors—for example, if your video card doesn't have a dot clock corresponding to a mode supported by your monitor. This output can be very helpful in diagnosing all kinds of problems. Examine it closely if your X server does not start up at all, does not provide the resolutions you wanted, or shows a flaky, snowy, or otherwise insufficient picture. Even if everything works to your satisfaction, you might want to check this file for interesting information that the X server has found out about your hardware. The lines starting with (`**`) contain data that you provided yourself in the configuration file, while lines starting with (`--`) contain data that the X server has found out itself.

The file *VideoModes.doc* included in the XFree86 distribution contains many hints for tweaking the values in your *XF86Config* file.

Remember that you can use Ctrl-Alt with the plus or minus on the numeric keypad to switch between the video modes listed on the Modes line of the Screen section of *XF86Config*. If the highest-resolution mode doesn't look right, try switching to lower resolutions. This lets you know, at least, that the configurations for those lower resolutions in your X configuration are working correctly.

Also, check the vertical and horizontal size/hold knobs on your monitor. In many cases it is necessary to adjust these when starting up X. For example, if the display seems to be shifted slightly to one side, you can usually correct this using the monitor controls.

The Usenet newsgroup *comp.windows.x.i386unix* is devoted to discussions about XFree86. It might be a good idea to watch that newsgroup for postings relating to your video configuration; you might run across someone with the same problems as your own. If this fails, please contact your Linux distributor; their support staff should be able to help you as well.

## CHAPTER ELEVEN

CUSTOMIZING YOUR X ENVIRONMENT

In the last chapter, you learned how to set up the X Window System so that it recognizes your graphics board and your monitor. While this is clearly necessary, it is of course only one half of the story. In this chapter, we will tell you the other half: customizing your X environment. Unlike the hardware setup that you normally do only once for a particular computer, you might want to change your work environment from time to time because your work habits have changed, because new and better environments are available, or simply because the old one has become boring for you. Some of these environments are quite sophisticated. For examples they let you start up a program with all the options you want at the press of a key or the click of a mouse, they let you drag file icons onto a printer to have text printed, and they can do lots of other fancy things.

Today, many distributions more or less automatically configure your X server for you and put you into a graphical environment from the start. However, if things go wrong during installation and you want to fine-tune your X server (in order to achieve a higher resolution, for example) or if you simply want to use another windowing environment than the one your distribution vendor has selected as the default, we'll tell you what to do.

We will first tell you the basics of configuring X, including what happens at startup, what X resources are, and how you can use them. In principle, this is already enough to configure X for use, but if you are anything more than a Spartan, you demand more from your work environment. We will therefore tell you how to configure a work environment based on the *fvwm* window manager first. For a long time, *fvwm* was the favorite window manager among Linux users, and only recently other window managers and desktop environments have taken the lead.

Until recently, the problem with using X on Unix systems in general and Linux in particular was that nothing was integrated. You would use a window manager and a number of X applications, but they would all look different, behave differently, and operate in a manner that was not integrated. For example, drag-and-drop—ubiquitous on Windows or the Macintosh—was hardly heard of on Linux, and if it was, it was difficult to find two applications that could interact together with drag-and-drop.

A relatively new category of software, the so-called desktop environments, has accepted the challenge to produce a state-of-the-art Unix GUI and tries to provide an integrated, consistent desktop where all programs have the same look-and-feel, behave the same, and even provide the same menus in all applications (to the extent where this is possible).

Currently, there are two main desktop environments available for Linux, the K Desktop Environment and GNOME. KDE is a little bit older and much more advanced with respect to functionality and stability. It aims at making people coming from other computing environments feel at home, as well as providing long-term Unix users a more productive and friendly work-environment. GNOME, on the other hand, has put a lot of work into the visual aspects of a desktop environment with colorful icons and the like, but it is still lacking stability and a number of features. Therefore, we will cover KDE here.

The Red Hat, SuSE, and Caldera releases include both KDE and GNOME, while Debian includes only GNOME. You can also find more about GNOME at *http://www.gnome.org*. Appendix B reprints an article describing the design of that desktop.

Basics of X Customization

Before running X applications, it's a good idea to learn the rudiments of X customization, so that you're not forced to live with the (often unappealing) default configuration used on many systems.

xinit

You run X with the *startx* command. This is a frontend (passing in reasonable options) for *xinit*, the program responsible for starting the X server and running various X clients that you specify. *xinit* (via *startx*) executes the shell script *.xinitrc* in your home directory. This script merely contains commands that you wish to run when starting X, such as *xterm*, *xclock*, and so on. If you don't have a *.xinitrc* file, the system default */usr/lib/X11/xinit/xinitrc* is used instead.

Here, we'll present a sample *.xinitrc* file and explain what it does. You could use this as your own *.xinitrc* or copy the system default *xinitrc* as a starting point:

```
 1  #!/bin/sh
 2  # Sample .xinitrc shell script
 3
 4  # Start xterms
 5  xterm -geometry 80x40+10+100 -fg black -bg white &
 6  xterm -geometry -20+10 -fn 7x13bold -fg darkslategray -bg white &
 7  xterm -geometry -20-30 -fn 7x13bold -fg black -bg white &
 8
 9  # Other useful X clients
10  oclock -geometry 70x70+5+5 &
11  xload -geometry 85x60+85+5 &
12  xbiff -geometry +200+5 &
13  xsetroot -solid darkslateblue &
14
15  # Start the window manager
16  exec fvwm2
```

This should be quite straightforward, even if you're not familiar with X. The first two lines simply identify the shell script. Lines 5–7 start up three *xterm* clients (recall that *xterm* is a terminal-emulator client). Other clients are started on lines 10–13, and on line 16 the window manager, *fvwm*, is started.

Running *startx* with this particular *.xinitrc* in place gives you something that looks like Figure 11-1.*

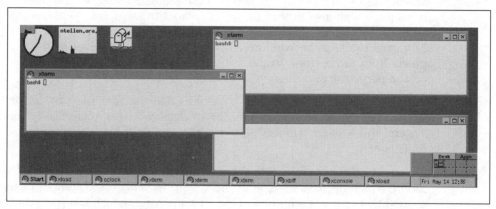

Figure 11–1: Screen created by sample .xinitrc file

Let's look at this in more detail. On line 5, we see that *xterm* is started with several options, *–geometry*, *–fg*, and *–bg*. Most X clients support these standard options, among others.

---

* All right, so it's not a work of art, but we needed something simple that would work correctly on most displays!

The *–geometry* option allows you to specify the size and position of the window on the display. The geometry specification has the format:

```
xsizexysize+xoffset+yoffset
```

In this case, the option *–geometry 80x40+10+100* puts the window at the location (10,100) on the screen (where (0,0) is the top-left corner), making it 80 characters wide by 40 characters high. Note that *xterm* measures the size of the window in *characters*, not pixels. The actual size of the window in pixels is determined by the font that is used.

The *–fg* and *–bg* arguments allow you to specify the foreground (text) and background colors for the *xterm* window, respectively. The colors used here are a rather boring black and white, but this should work on color and monochrome displays alike. Under X, colors are usually specified by name, although you can provide your own RGB values if you prefer. The list of color names (and corresponding RGB values) is given in the file */usr/lib/X11/rgb.txt.* Running *xcolors* will display these colors, along with their names.

Line 6 runs another *xterm,* although the arguments are slightly different:

```
xterm -geometry -20+10 -fn 7x13bold -fg darkslategray -bg white &
```

First of all, the geometry specification is just -20+10. Without size parameters, *xterm* will use the default, which is usually 80x25. Also, we see that the xoffset is prefixed with a -, instead of +. This places the window 20 pixels from the *right* edge of the screen. Likewise, a geometry specification of -20-30 (as used on line 7) means to place the window 20 pixels from the right edge of the screen and 30 pixels from the bottom. In this way, the placement of windows is less dependent on the particular resolution you're using.

The *–fn* option on lines 6 and 7 specifies that the font used by *xterm* should be 7x13bold. Using the command *xlsfonts* displays a complete list of fonts on your system; the X client *xfontsel* allows you to select fonts interactively—more about fonts later.

On line 10 we start an *oclock* client, which is a simple analog clock. Line 11 starts *xload,* which displays a graph of the system *load average* (number of running processes) that changes with time. Line 12 starts *xbiff,* which just lets you know when mail is waiting to be read. Finally, on line 13 we do away with the bland grey X background and replace it with a flashy darkslateblue. (Fear not; there is more fun to be had with X decor than this example shows.)

You'll notice that each of the X clients started on lines 6–13 is executed in the background (the ampersand on the end of each line forces this). If you forget to put each client in the background, *xinit* executes the first *xterm,* waits for it to exit (usually, after you log out), executes the next *xterm,* and so on. The ampersands cause each client to start up concurrently.

What about line 16? Here, we start *fvwm* (Version 2), a window manager used on many Linux systems. As mentioned before, the window manager is responsible for decorating the windows, allowing you to place them with the mouse, and so forth. However, it is started with the command:

```
exec fvwm2
```

This causes the *fvwm2* process to replace the *xinit* process. This way, once you kill *fvwm*,* the X server shuts down. This is equivalent to, but more succinct than, using the Ctrl-Alt-Backspace key combination.

In general, you should put an ampersand after each X client started from *.xinitrc*, and *exec* the window manager at the end of the file. Of course, there are other ways of doing this, but many users employ this technique.

[11] X User
Guide

If you read the manual pages for *xterm* and the other X clients, you'll see many more command-line options than those described here. As we said, virtually everything about X is configurable. *fvwm* (Version 2) uses a configuration file of its own, *.fvwm2rc*, described in its manual page. (If you have no *.fvwm2rc* file, the system default */usr/lib/X11/fvwm2/system.fvwmrc* is used instead.) The manual pages, as well as books on using X (such as *X Window System User's Guide* by Valerie Quercia and Tim O'Reilly), provide more information on configuring individual clients.

The X Resource Database

Depending on which environment you use, you can't use X for long without running into X resources; they are mentioned in virtually every manual page. X resources provide a more flexible and powerful way to configure X clients than using command-line options such as *–geometry* and *–fg*. They allow you to specify defaults for entire classes of clients; for example, we could set the default font for all invocations of *xterm* to 7x13bold, instead of specifying it on each command line.

Recently, X resources have fallen out of favor with X developers. While they are really very flexible, they are not particularly easy to work with and feel more like a relic of ancient times. A growing number of programs are therefore customized not by X resources but instead via comfortable configuration dialog boxes. However, it still pays to know about X resources because you will come across them for a long time to come.

Using X resources requires two steps. First, you must create a file containing your X resource defaults. Typically, this file is called *.Xdefaults* and lives in your home

---

* If you have experimented with *fvwm*, you'll notice that pressing the first mouse button while the cursor is on the background causes a menu to pop up. Selecting the Quit fvwm option from this menu causes *fvwm* to exit.

directory. Second, you need to use *xrdb* to load the X resources into the server, which makes them available for use. In general, you run *xrdb* from your *.xinitrc* before starting any clients.

As a simple example, let's take the various command-line options used by the clients in the earlier sample *.xinitrc* and specify them as X resources instead. Afterwards, we'll show you what kinds of changes need to be made to *.xinitrc* to make use of the resources.

First a few words about resources and how they work. Each X application is part of a certain *application class*. For example, *xterm* is a member of the XTerm class. *xclock* and *oclock* are both members of the Clock class. Setting resources for the Clock class affects all applications that are part of that class; because *xclock* (a square analog clock) and *oclock* (an oval analog clock) are similar, they belong to the same class and share the same resources. Most applications are members of their own exclusive class; *xload* is the only member of the XLoad class. However, if another *xload*-like application were to be written, it might be part of the XLoad class as well. Placing X clients into application classes allows you to set resources for all applications in that class. (The manual page for each X client specifies the application class the client belongs to.)

Standard X clients employ resources such as foreground, background, geometry, and font. Also, many X clients have specific resources of their own; for example, *xterm* defines the resource logFile, which allows you to specify a file in which to log the terminal session. Again, the manual pages for X clients specify which resources are available.

Moreover, resources themselves are arranged into a hierarchy of classes. For instance, the background resource is a member of the Background class. Resource classes allow many separate resources to be members of the same class, for which you can set resource values for the class as a whole. For example, the background resource usually determines the primary background color of a window. However, if an application window has several panels or regions, you may wish to set the background for each panel separately. There might be resources such as background1, background2, and so on, for each panel, but they would all be members of the Background resource class. Setting the resource value for the Background class sets the value for all resources in that class.

In general, you won't need to concern yourself with the differences between resource classes and the resources within that class. In most cases, it's easier to set resource values for an entire class (such as Background) instead of individual resources in that class.

Now, let's look at how resource values are set in the X resource database. A complete resource specification is of the form:*

```
(ApplicationClass|applicationName)*(ResourceClass|resourceName) : value
```

The vertical bar means "choose one or the other." Let's say you want to set the background color of an *xterm* window. The *complete* resource specification might be:

```
xterm*background: darkslategray
```

However, this sets only a particular background resource (not all of the resources that might be in the `Background` class) and only for the *xterm* client when it is invoked as *xterm* (more on this later). Therefore, we might want to use resource classes instead:

```
XTerm*Background: darkslategray
```

This resource specification will apply to *all xterm* clients, and all `Background`-class resources used by *xterm*.

Now, let's look at translating the options given in the earlier *.xinitrc* file into application resources. Create a file in your home directory, called *.Xdefaults*. For the previous sample *.xinitrc*, it should contain:

```
1  Clock*Geometry:        70x70+5+5
2  XLoad*Geometry:        85x50+85+5
3  XBiff*Geometry:         +200+5
4
5  ! Defaults for all xterm clients
6  XTerm*Foreground:      white
7  XTerm*Background:      black
8
9  ! Specific xterms
10 xterm-1*Geometry:      80x40+10+110
11
12 xterm-2*Geometry:      -20+10
13 xterm-2*Font:          7x13bold
14 xterm-2*Background:    darkslategray
15
16 xterm-3*Geometry:      80x25-20-30
17 xterm-3*Font:          7x13bold
```

Lines 1–3 set the `Geometry` resource class for the `Clock`, `XLoad`, and `XBiff` application classes. On lines 6–7, we set the `Foreground` and `Background` resource classes for the `XTerm` class as whole. All *xterm* clients will use these values for `Foreground` and `Background` by default.

---

* Actually, resource specifications have a more complex syntax than this, and the rules used to determine resource and value bindings are somewhat involved. For simplification, we are presenting a reasonable model for application resource settings—and we direct curious readers to a good book on using X like the *X Window System User's Guide*.

On lines 10–17, we set resources specific to each invocation of *xterm*. This is necessary because not all of the *xterm*s are alike; they each have different geometry specifications, for example. In this case, we have named the individual *xterm* invocations xterm-1, xterm-2, and xterm-3. As you can see, we set the Geometry resource for each on lines 10, 12, and 16. Also, we set the Font class for xterm-2 and xterm-3. And we set the Background class to darkslategray for xterm-2.

X resource binding rules work so that certain bindings have precedence over others. In this case, setting a resource for a specific invocation of *xterm* (as in xterm-2*Background on line 14) has precedence over the resource setting for the XTerm class as a whole (XTerm*Background on line 7). In general, bindings for an application or resource class have *lower* precedence than bindings for particular instances of that class. In this way, you can set defaults for the class as a whole but override those defaults for particular instances of the class.

Now, let's look at the changes required to *.xinitrc* to use the X resources defined here. First, we need to add an *xrdb* command, which loads the application resources into the server. And, we can get rid of the various command-line options that the resources have replaced. To wit:

```
#!/bin/sh
# Sample .xinitrc shell script

# Load resources
xrdb -load $HOME/.Xdefaults

# Start xterms
xterm -name "xterm-1" &
xterm -name "xterm-2" &
xterm -name "xterm-3" &

# Other useful X clients
oclock &
xload &
xbiff &
xsetroot -solid darkslateblue &

# Start the window manager
exec fvwm2
```

As you see, the *–name* argument given to the three instances of *xterm* lets us specify the application name that *xterm* uses for locating X resources. Most X clients don't support a *–name* argument; the name used is usually the one which it was invoked with. However, because many users run several *xterm*s at once, it is helpful to distinguish between them when setting resources.

Now, you should be able to modify your X environment to some degree. Of course, knowing how to configure X depends partly on being familiar with the many X clients out there, as well as the window manager (and how to configure it). The rest of this section will present various X applications for Linux. We'll also look at a particular window manager, *fvwm*, in detail.

The fvwm Window Manager

Your choice of window manager determines, to a large extent, the look and feel of your X environment. Many window managers also provide menus, which allow you to start other X applications using the mouse, and a virtual desktop, which increases your overall desktop space considerably.

fvwm is a virtual desktop window manager used by many Linux users. It is based partially on the code for *twm*, a classic window manager included with the MIT X11 distribution. However, *fvwm* has been trimmed down and requires about half the memory used by *twm*—welcome news for Linux systems with 8 MB or less of physical RAM. *fvwm* provides many features not available in other window managers, and for this reason (as well as the fact it was developed specifically for Linux), we are covering it here.

Unlike *twm* and some other window managers, *fvwm* undergoes constant development. This means that some of the features described here may not be present in the same form in newer versions of the software. Refer to the manual page for *fvwm* to verify that the features presented here are available. We will cover Version 2 of *fvwm* here.

fvwm2 (1)

Among the features offered by *fvwm* are:

- A simple virtual desktop, which provides a *pager* (an overall birds-eye view of the desktop) and automatic desktop scrolling when the pointer reaches the screen boundary.

- A keyboard equivalent for almost every mouse-based feature; this is helpful when using X on laptops without a mouse or trackball, or for people with RSI or other physical problems making use of the mouse difficult.

- Support for color icons using the XPM libraries.

- A programming interface for extensions, allowing you to add new features to *fvwm*. One extension included in the *fvwm* distribution is a button box that stays put on your root window. You can bind commands to each button, allowing you to point and click to start applications.

- Fully configurable desktop menus, which appear when you press the mouse buttons.

- A Motif-like 3D look and feel for window frames. In fact, *fvwm* includes options to make it compatible with the Motif window manager (*mwm*).

Among the most powerful *fvwm* features is the *virtual desktop*, which allows you to place windows on an area much larger than the actual size of the visible display. Using the mouse, you can switch (page) between areas of the virtual desktop. For example, when you move the mouse pointer to the right edge of the display, the desktop will shift a screen to the left, bringing new windows into view. This way you can place windows across an area larger than your screen, viewing only a portion of the virtual desktop at one time.

A sample desktop using *fvwm* was shown in Figure 11-1 in the section "xinit." Each window is given a decorative frame, provided by *fvwm*, with configurable titlebar buttons. Later in this section, we'll describe how to customize these to your liking.

The pager, in the top-right corner of the display, gives a bird's-eye view of the entire virtual desktop. The pager can also move windows around the virtual desktop and select the portion of the desktop currently in view.

Configuring fvwm

In order to customize *fvwm*, you'll need to create a configuration file, *.fvwm2rc*, in your home directory. In this section, we're going to present a number of features of *fvwm* and describe how to enable them from *.fvwm2rc*.

We must warn you that the syntax of some of the options has changed between different versions of *fvwm*; check them against the manual page if you have problems. You may wish to use the system default *.fvwm2rc* file (usually found in */usr/lib/X11/fvwm2/system.fvwmrc*) as a starting point.

The most basic *fvwm* customizations deal with colors and fonts used for window frames and menus. For example, you might include the following in your *.fvwm2rc*:

```
# Set up colors
Style "*"            Color White/Midnightblue
HilightColor         White Red
WindowFont           -adobe-helvetica-bold-r-normal-*-*-120-*
```

Some commands depend on which window has the *focus*, which means that it is receiving input. (Normally you just click with the mouse in a window to make it the one in focus.) Unfocused windows, menus, and the pager use the color that has been set with `Style "*" Color`, while the window with the focus uses the color that was set with `HilightColor`. The foreground color is generally used for text (in the window title, and so forth) and the background is used for the window frame itself. Be artistic! `WindowFont` names the font used by window titlebars.

Note that none of these options sets the colors used inside windows, because these are controlled by the application (client). The options apply only to window frames and menus, because those are managed by *fvwm*.

To get a list of all the colors defined on your system, enter the command:

```
eggplant$ showrgb | more
```

Most *fvwm* users also make use of the virtual desktop. In order to configure it, you should include lines such as the following in *.fvwm2rc*:

```
# Configure virtual desktop
DeskTopSize     3x3
AddToFunc       InitFunction "I" Module FvwmPager 0 0
Style           "FvwmPager" Sticky, NoTitle, WindowListSkip
*FvwmPagerGeometry -10 -10
EdgeScroll      100 100
```

We want the size of the desktop (`DeskTopSize`) to be three screens wide by three screens high. The line starting with `AddToFunc` says that when starting *fvwm*, the pager should be started, too. The `Style` line determines that the pager is to be shown in each virtual desktop (`Sticky`), that it should not have a window titlebar (`NoTitle`), and that it should not be shown in the window list (`WindowListSkip`). In addition, we place the pager in the bottom right corner of the screen. The pager window provides a view onto the full virtual desktop; clicking with the mouse in the pager window makes the corresponding part of the desktop visible on the screen. In Version 1 of fvwm, the pager was a fixed part of the window manager, but Version 2 makes the pager a module of its own. That's also why the pager is no longer configured via *fvwm* options like `Pager` as in earlier versions, but via the settings for the module `FvwmPager`. A module is an add-on to the window manager that cannot run standalone. Frequently used modules, like the pager, are shipped with *fvwm2*.

`EdgeScroll` specifies the percentage by which the desktop should scroll when the pointer reaches the edge of the screen. Using `EdgeScroll 100 100` causes the desktop to shift by an entire screen when we move the mouse cursor to the edge; this gives the appearance of switching from one screen to an entirely different one. This way you can place windows across the entire virtual desktop and wander around the desktop using only the mouse.

The `Style` command sets a whole slew of attributes for windows on your screen. For instance, to specify that the *xbiff* always stays on top of other windows on the display, use the command:

```
Style "XBiff" StaysOnTop
```

Now, no other window is allowed to obscure *xbiff*. Besides `StaysOnTop`, other popular options to `Style` include:

NoTitle

> Prevents a window from having a decorative title on the top with its name. This option is often used for small windows like *xclock* and *xbiff*, especially if you don't expect to move or resize them.

NoBorder

> Prevents a window from having a border.

Sticky

> Makes a window stay in the same place on the screen when you shift the virtual desktop.

BoundaryWidth

> Sets the width in pixels of frames placed around windows by *fvwm*. The default used by *fvwm* is six pixels, which is quite wide.

Arguments to Style may be window titles or application-class names. Older versions of *fvwm* don't have the Style command. Instead, they offer a variety of commands named StaysOnTop, NoTitle, and so on. You use them like this:

```
StaysOnTop XBiff
```

There are various *.fvwm2rc* commands dealing with icons. As with other window managers, *fvwm* allows you to iconify a window; this replaces the window with a small icon containing the name of the window and possibly a picture depicting the type of window. *fvwm* supports both *bitmaps* and color *pixmaps* for icons. A bitmap allows only one bit for each pixel it displays and therefore is limited to one background and one foreground color (although you can get a mixture or gray by alternating pixels, a process called dithering). A pixmap, on the other hand, has several bits per pixel and can therefore support a large number of colors:

```
IconFont    -adobe-helvetica-medium-r-*-*-*-120-*
IconPath    /usr/include/X11/bitmaps/:/usr/include/X11/xfm/bitmaps
PixmapPath  /usr/include/X11/pixmaps/:/usr/include/X11/xfm/pixmaps

Style IconBox    700 0 1080 50
Style "*" Icon unknown.xpm
Style "XTerm" Icon xterm.xpm
Style "Emacs" Icon emacs.xpm
```

IconFont specifies the font to use for icons. IconPath and PixmapPath specify colon-separated pathnames where icon images can be found; if you keep images in several directories, separate their pathnames with colons. IconPath specifies locations for bitmaps (XBM), and PixmapPath specifies locations for color pixmaps (XPM).

Style IconBox defines a region of the screen where icons should be placed. You can specify more than one IconBox: up to four, if you wish. In this case, icons should be placed in an invisible box defined by the top-left corner at location (700,0) and bottom-right corner at (1080,50).

Following `Style IconBox` are several `Style` commands that bind icon images to windows. In this case, we want all `XTerm` windows to use *xterm.xpm*, and Emacs to use *emacs.xpm*. The name of the icon file can either be a full pathname, or a pathname relative to either `IconPath` or `PixmapPath`. The command:

```
Style "*" Icon unknown.xpm
```

sets the default icon to *unknown.xpm*.

If your *fvwm* does not support the `Style` command, use commands such as:

```
Icon "" unknown.xpm
Icon "XTerm" xterm.xpm
Icon "Emacs" emacs.xpm
```

More Customizations

Most *fvwm* users include at least the previous options in the *.fvwm2rc* file. However, *fvwm* also provides the ability to configure the desktop menus, functions executed by the window titlebar buttons, and so on. Here, we'll introduce several of those features.

First, let's configure *fvwm* pop-up menus, which appear when pressing the mouse buttons on the root window. You can use these menus to execute commands, manipulate windows, and so on. Note that some distributions, like Debian and SuSE, can automatically update your window manager menus with the installed packages on the system:

```
AddToMenu xclients "Xclients" Title
+ "Netscape"    Exec netscape
+ "xterm"            Exec xterm
+ "emacs"            Exec emacs -w
+ ""                 Nop
+ "eggplant"    Exec xterm -e rlogin eggplant &
+ "papaya"      Exec xterm -e rlogin papaya &
+ ""                 Nop
+ "screensaver" Exec xscreensaver-command -activate &
+ "xcalc"       Exec xcalc &
+ "xman"        Exec xman &
+ "xlock"       Exec xlock -mode rotor &
EndPopup
```

The menu is defined with the command `AddToMenu`. There is no command for terminating a menu definition; the menu entries do not even have to be on subsequent lines. Each menu gets a name with which it can be referenced later (in this case `xclients`).

The format of the menu is relatively self-explanatory. The title is already set in the `AddToMenu` line; `Nop` causes a separator line to appear in the menu. The `Exec` function causes a command to be executed when the menu item is chosen; the arguments to Exec determine which command is executed. The leftmost argument of each command line is the name of the item as it appears in the menu (such as "Netscape"); the remaining arguments specify the command to be executed.

We define a second menu, *fvwm*, which uses the *fvwm* window-manipulation functions:

```
AddToMenu fvwm "Window Ops" Title
+ "Move Window"            Move
+ "Resize Window"       Resize
+ "Raise Window"        Raise
+ "Lower Window"        Lower
+ "Iconify Window"      Iconify
+ "Stick Window"        Stick
+ ""                          Nop
+ "Xclients"            Popup Xclients
+ ""                          Nop
+ "Destroy Window"   Destroy
+ "Delete Window"    Delete
+ ""                 Nop
+ "Load Xdefaults"   Exec xrdb -load $HOME/.Xdefaults
+ "Restart Fvwm"     Restart fvwm2
+ "Start twm"        Restart twm
+ "Quit Fvwm"
EndPopup
```

Each of the built-in functions Move, Resize, Lower, and so on are described in the *fvwm2* manual page. One function of note is Popup, which allows a previously defined pop-up menu to be used as a submenu of the current menu. Here, we include the xclients menu defined as a submenu.

Also included here are commands for restarting *fvwm* or starting another window manager (*twm*) in place of *fvwm*.

fvwm also allows you to modify the function of the mouse buttons in various contexts. The Mouse command is used for this, and takes the form:

```
Mouse button context modifiers function
```

button is 1, 2, 3, or 0 (where 0 means "any button"). *context* specifies the region in which the mouse binding takes effect; *context* may be:

- R for the root window

- W for an application window

- S for a window frame

- F for a window frame corner

- T for a window titlebar

- I for an icon window

- A digit from 0–9, specifying a particular titlebar button (described later)

- A for any context (except titlebar buttons)

- Any combination of these

For example, a *context* of TSIF specifies window titlebars, frames, and frame corners, as well as icon windows.

Using a digit from 0 through 9 in *context* binds the function to a window titlebar button. By default, there are two such buttons—one on the left edge of the titlebar, and one on the right. Binding mouse functions to other buttons causes them to be visible. Left titlebar buttons are given odd numbers (1, 3, 5, 7, and 9), and right titlebar buttons are given even numbers (2, 4, 6, 8, 0). Figure 11-2 shows a window with all buttons visible, with their corresponding numbers. Unless you bind mouse functions to each button, most of them will be invisible.

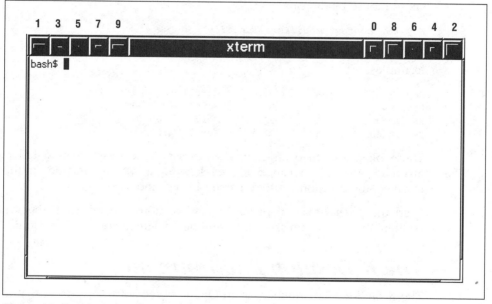

Figure 11–2: Buttons on fvwm titlebar

modifiers specifies various key combinations to be used in conjunction with a mouse-button click. Valid *modifiers* are C for control, M for meta, S for shift, N for none, or A for any of the above. For example, setting *modifiers* to C means that the Control key must be pressed while the mouse button is clicked.

Here are some examples of mouse bindings:

```
# Button         Context Modifi  Function
Mouse 1          R       N       PopUp "Fvwm"
Mouse 2          R       N       PopUp "Xclients"
Mouse 3          R       N       WindowList
```

These lines bind each mouse button to one of the pop-up menus *fvwm* or xclients, defined previously, or the WindowList command, which is a pop-up menu containing entries for each window on the display:

```
# Window titlebar buttons
Mouse 1          1       N       Popup "Fvwm"
Mouse 1          3       N       Iconify
Mouse 1          4       N       Destroy
Mouse 1          2       N       Resize
```

Here we bind titlebar buttons 1, 3, 4, and 2 (two buttons on each side of the title-bar) to various functions. The left-most titlebar button pops up the *fvwm* menu, the second-left button iconifies the window, and so on. The *fvwm2* manual page lists all the available functions, such as Resize, Move, and RaiseLower.

You can also specify key bindings with the Key command. They are similar in syntax to mouse bindings:

```
Key key context modifiers function
```

with *context* and *modifiers* having the meanings given earlier. Here are some examples:

```
Key Up           A       C       Scroll +0    -100
Key Down         A       C       Scroll +0    +100
Key Left         A       C       Scroll -100 0
Key Right        A       C       Scroll +100 +0
```

These bindings cause Ctrl-*arrowkey* to scroll the desktop by a full page in the given direction. You can bind any key to an *fvwm* function in this way; for instance, the function keys are named F1, F2, and so on.

Read the *fvwm2* manual page. As new versions are released, the syntax of the configuration file changes slightly, and new features are added periodically.

The K Desktop Environment

The K Desktop Environment is an Open Source software project that aims at providing a consistent, user-friendly, contemporary desktop for Unix and hence Linux systems. Since its inception in October 1996, it has made amazing progress. This is partly due to the choice of a very high-quality GUI toolkit, Qt, as well as the consequent choice of using C++ and its object-oriented features for the implementation.

It should be noted up front that KDE is *not* a window manager like *fvwm*, but a whole desktop system that can be used with any other window manager. However, it also comes with its own window manager called *kwm*, which will give best results and is therefore what we will cover here.

In the section about configuring the *fvwm* window manager, you have seen that configuring Linux desktops usually means learning the syntax of configuration files and editing those files, something that long-term Linux users take for granted but that often rebuffs new users. The KDE team has therefore made it one of its goals that everything that is configurable in KDE (and about everything is) should be configurable via GUI dialogs. You can still edit configuration files, if you prefer, but you don't need to, and even the most experienced users usually admit that in order to do simple things like change the background color of the desktop, it's faster to click a few buttons than to read the manual page, find the syntax for specifying the background color, open the configuration file, edit it, and restart the window manager.

Besides easy configuration, KDE sports a few other features that were previously unheard of on Linux. For example, it provides a full Internet integration of the desktop. It comes with a file manager that doubles as a web browser, and browsing files on some FTP site is just the same as browsing your local hard disk. You can drag and drop icons that represent Internet locations to your desktop and thus easily find them again later. In addition, almost all KDE application are able to open and save files in remote locations.

Drag-and-drop, commonplace on Windows or the Macintosh, is also central to KDE. For example, to open a file in the text editor, you just grab its icon in the file manager window and drop it onto the editor window. This works no matter where the file is located; if it is on a remote server, KDE automatically downloads the file for you before opening it in the text editor or whichever application you choose to open it with.

While manual pages are very well suited to give programmers instant access to terse information about system libraries, they are not really very well suited for end-user documentation. KDE therefore uses standard HTML files and comes with a fast help viewer. The viewer also knows how to display manual page and Info files so that you can access all the documentation on your system from one application. In addition, most KDE applications support context-sensitive help.

For a few releases, the X Window System has supported a feature called session management. This is a capability that lets you leave your X environment (for example, because you want to turn off or reboot your computer), and when you return to X, all the applications that you had opened reappear at the same positions and in the same configuration. Unfortunately, this very user-friendly feature was rarely supported by X applications. KDE uses it extensively. KDE provides a session manager that handles session management, and all KDE applications are written to behave properly with that feature.

It should be mentioned that KDE is not just another window manager. KDE contains a window manager, *kwm*, and a very good one at that, but that is only one part of KDE. Some of the others are the file manager, the web browser, the panel, a pager, the control center for configuring your desktop, and many, many more. If you want to, you can even run KDE with another window manager, but you might lose some of the integration features.

You might be thinking, "Well, this all sounds very nice, but I have a couple of normal X applications that I want to run." In this case, you will be delighted to hear that you can continue to do that. Yes, you can run all X applications on a KDE desktop, and KDE even provides some means to integrate them as far as possible into the overall desktop. For example, if you so desire, KDE can try to reconfigure your other X applications to use the same colors as the overall desktop so that you get a nice consistent environment. Of course, non-KDE applications will not support some of KDE's advanced features like drag-and-drop or session management, but you can continue to use the programs you have grown accustomed to until someone releases KDE applications that address the same needs (or perhaps KDE versions of your favorite programs themselves).

The current development version of KDE, as well as the upcoming KDE office suite (see *http://koffice.kde.org*), is heavily based on CORBA, which among other things enables embedding of office components running on different machines into each other.

KDE is in continuing development, but every few months the KDE team releases a so-called official release that is considered very stable and suitable for end users. These releases are made available in both source and binary packages in various package formats, often specifically adapted for the most common Linux distributions. If you don't mind fiddling around with KDE and can stand an occasional bug, you can also live on the bleeding edge and download daily snapshots of KDE, but this is not for the faint at heart.

Installing KDE

Most Linux distributions come with KDE nowadays, but if yours doesn't, or you want to use a newer version of KDE, you can download it from the Internet. *http://www.kde.org* is your one-stop shop for everything KDE related, including documentation, screenshots, and download locations. *ftp://ftp.kde.org* is the KDE project's FTP site, but it is often overloaded, so you might be better off trying a mirror instead.

KDE consists of a number of packages. These include:

kdesupport
> This package contains third-party libraries that are not part of KDE itself but that are used by KDE. It is recommended that you install this package to make sure that you have the correct versions of all the libraries installed.

kdelibs

This package contains the KDE libraries. They contain the basic application frame, a number of GUI widgets, the configuration system, the HTML display system, and many other things. Without this package, nothing in KDE will run.

kdebase

In this package, you will find the basic KDE applications that make a desktop a KDE desktop, including the file manager/web browser, the window manager, and the panel. You definitely need this package if you want to use KDE.

kdegames

A number of games, including card games, action games, and strategy games. Everybody will probably want to install these but only to get acquainted with the system, of course.

kdegraphics

A number of graphics-related programs like a dvi viewer, a PostScript viewer, and an icon editor.

kdeutils

This package contains some productivity tools like text editors, a calculator, printer managers, and an address-book program.

kdemultimedia

As the name implies, this package contains multimedia programs, including a CD player, a MIDI player and—of all things—a Karaoke player.

kdenetwork

Here, you will find programs for use with the Internet, including a mail reader, a news reader, and some network management tools.

kdeadmin

This package contains some programs for the system administrator, including a user manager, a runlevel editor, and a backup program.

korganizer

This package contains only one application: a full-featured personal information manager that even supports synchronization with Palm Pilots.

In addition to the packages mentioned here, which are officially provided by the KDE team, there are literally hundreds of other KDE programs available. See *http://www.kde.org/applications.html* for a list of applications that are currently available.

Once you have selected which packages to install, you can go on and actually install them. How you do that depends on which Linux distribution you use and whether you install a binary package or compile KDE yourself from the source code. If your distribution contains KDE, you will also be able to install KDE during your system installation.

Once the software is loaded onto your hard disk, there are only a few steps left to do. First, you have to make sure that the directory containing the KDE applications is in your PATH environment variable. The default location of the executable KDE programs is *opt/kde/bin*, but if you have chosen to install KDE to another location, you will have to insert your path here. You can add this directory to your PATH variable by issuing:

```
export PATH=/opt/kde/bin:$PATH
```

To make this permanent, either add this line to your configuration file *.bashrc* in your home directory or to the system-wide configuration file */etc/profile*.

Next, do the same with the directory containing the KDE libraries (by default */opt/kde/lib*) and the environment variable LD_LIBRARY_PATH:

```
export LD_LIBRARY_PATH=/opt/kde/lib:$LD_LIBRARY_PATH
```

Now you are almost done, but you still need to tell X that you want to run the KDE desktop when X starts. This is done in the file *.xinitrc* in your home directory. Make a backup copy first. Then remove everything in this file and insert the single line:

```
startkde
```

startkde is a tiny shell script provided with KDE that simply starts up the KDE window manager *kwm* and a number of basic applications.

Using KDE

Using KDE is quite easy. Most things are very intuitive, so you can often simply guess what to do. We will, however, give you some hints for what you can do with KDE here, to encourage you to start further explorations into your KDE desktop.

When you start KDE for the first time, it looks like Figure 11-3. Along the lower border of the screen, you see the so-called *panel*. The panel serves several purposes, including fast access to installed applications. Along the upper border, you can see the *taskbar*. This bar shows all open windows and can be used for quickly accessing any window currently on the desktop. In addition, KDE opens a file manager window when started for the first time.

KDE provides a number of workspaces that are accessible via the buttons in the middle of the panel, labeled One to Four by default. Try clicking on those buttons. You can see how the file manager window is visible only while you are on workspace One, while the panel and the taskbar are always visible. Now go to workspace Two and start a calculator by clicking on the calculator icon on the panel. When the panel appears, change workspaces again. You will see that the calculator is visible only while you are on workspace Two. When you are on any

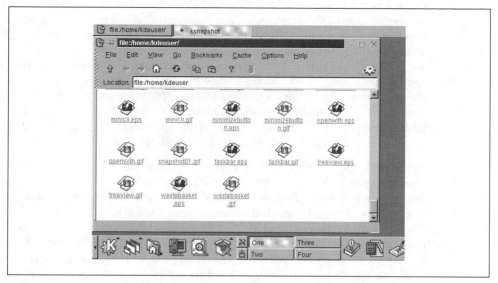

Figure 11–3: The KDE desktop at first startup

other workspace, click on the calculator label in the taskbar. This will immediately bring you back to the workspace where your calculator is shown.

To try another nifty feature, push the small button in the title bar of the calculator window that looks like a push pin. Now change workspaces again. You will see that the calculator window is now visible on every workspace—it has been "pinned down" to the background of the desktop, so to speak.

If you grow tired of the calculator window on every workspace, simply click on the pin again, and if you want to get rid of the window as a whole, click on the button with the little x on it in the upper-right corner.

There are lots of things that you can do with windows in KDE, but we'll take you now on a short exploration trip to the so-called *K menu*. You open the K menu by clicking on the icon with the gear-and-K symbol to the far left of the panel. Besides some options for configuring the K menu and the panel itself, you will find all installed KDE applications here, grouped into submenus. To start one of those applications, simply select the menu entry.

We have promised that you can run old X applications on your KDE desktop. You can do that either by opening a terminal window and typing the application name on the command line, or by pressing Ctrl-F2 and entering the application name in the small command line that appears in the middle of the screen. But you can also integrate non-KDE applications into the K menu and the panel, that is, showing them as icons that you can click on to run the associated programs, even though this requires a little bit more work.

Depending on how you have installed KDE, it may well be that there is already a submenu Non-KDE programs in your K menu that contains a number of non-KDE applications. If you don't have this, run the application *Appfinder* that you can find in the System submenu. This is a tool that searches your system for a number of applications that it has in its database and integrates each one into the KDE desktop by generating a so-called *.kdelnk* file for it. If the program that you want to integrate into KDE is not included in the *Appfinder*'s database, you will have to write such a *.kdelnk* file yourself, but as always in KDE, there are dialogs for doing this where you just have to fill in the required information. See the KDE documentation at *http://www.kde.org/documentation/index.html*.

By default, the panel already contains a number of icons to start the most often-used programs, but you can easily add your own. To do this, open the K menu again, but this time, first open the submenu Panel and then the submenu Add Application. Probably much to your surprise, something that looks like a copy of the K menu pops up. Find the application whose icon you want to add to the panel and select it, just as if you wanted to start it. KDE will then add the icon for this application to the panel. You can even add full submenus to the panel by selecting the first menu entry in a submenu in the Add Application tree. The icon will then have a small black arrow in it, which indicates that clicking on the icon opens a menu instead of starting an application.

There is only limited space on the panel, so you might need to remove some icons of programs that you do not often use. Just click with the right mouse button on the icon and select Remove. In general, you can get at a lot of functionality in KDE by clicking the right mouse button!

Next, we will show you how to configure your KDE desktop to your tastes. As promised, we will not edit any configuration files to do this.

Configuration is done in the KDE Control Center, which you can start from the K menu. All the configuration options are grouped at different levels. When you start up the control center, you will see the top-level groups. By clicking on the plus signs, you can open a group to see the entries in this group.

As an example, we will now change the background color to something else. To do this, open the Desktop group and choose Background. After a short time, the configuration window for configuring the background will appear (see Figure 11-4).

By default, the background is configured to have one single color. If you want to leave it at that and just change this color, click on the color field below the One Color button. A color selection dialog pops up where you can select a color to your tastes. When you close the color selection dialog, the new color is displayed in the monitor in the upper right corner of the configuration window. When you configure KDE, you often see such monitors that allow you to preview your choice. However, you also have the option to see what your choice looks like when in full use. Simply click on the Apply button at the lower border of the

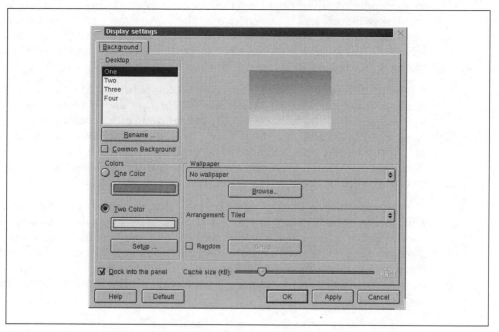

Figure 11–4: Configuring the background of the KDE desktop

configuration window, and your change is automatically applied. There is no need to restart the desktop.

If you think that a single color is boring, maybe you want a gradient where one color is slowly morphed into another. In this case, select the Two Colors button and select a second color; KDE will compute the gradient and display it in the monitor.

You also have the option of using a background image. If that is what you want, go to the Wallpaper area of the configuration dialog. You can either select one of the wallpapers that come with KDE, which contains some very stylish ones, by choosing from the drop-down list, or you can select any graphics file of your own.

There are more things you can do with the background, but we'll leave it at that for now and look at something else: Configuring styles and colors of the windows.

With normal window managers, you can configure the color of the window decorations, but not of the window contents. With KDE, this is different. Since KDE is an integrated desktop, color and other settings apply both to the window decorations painted by the window manager and to the window contents painted by the applications. We'll now set off to configure a little bit of the appearance.

In the control center, open the Desktop group, and choose Colors. You'll see a preview window and a selection list where you can pick a color scheme. KDE does not work by configuring individual colors, but by defining so-called color schemes. This is because it does not make sense to change only one color; all colors must fit together to achieve a pleasing and eye-friendly look.

While KDE lets you create your own color schemes, doing so is a task that requires some knowledge about color psychology and human vision. we'd therefore suggest that you pick one of the predefined color schemes. Check in the preview monitor whether you like what you see. Now comes the fun part: click on the Apply button and watch how all running applications flicker a bit and suddenly change colors—without having to restart them. While Windows users tend to take this for granted, it was never seen before on Unix before KDE.

The same feature applies to other settings. For example, open the Desktop group and choose Style. Here, you can select "Windows 95" style. If this is selected, all user interface elements are drawn according to the Windows standard; if it is not selected, they are drawn according to the Motif standard common on Unix. You can change this setting by clicking Apply and watch your running applications change their style. The same goes, by the way, for the fonts that you can select on the Font page.

There are many more things to configure in KDE, but we cannot go through all the options here, otherwise there would not be much space left for other topics in this book. But there's one more thing that we'd like to show you. You will especially like this if English is not your native language or if you frequently converse in another language.

Go to the Language page in the Desktop group (see Figure 11-5). Here, you can select the language in which your KDE desktop and the KDE applications should be running. Currently, KDE lets you choose from more than thirty languages.

You might be wondering why you can select more than one language. The reason is that the KDE programs are translated by volunteers, and not all the applications are translated at the same time. Thus, a particular application might not be available in the language that you have chosen as your primary language. In this case, the secondary language is chosen automatically for that application, and if there is no translation available for this application, the tertiary language is chosen. If all else fails, English is chosen, which always exists.

There is much more to say about using the KDE desktop, but we'll let you explore it yourself. Besides the obvious and intuitive features, there are also those that are not so obvious but very useful nevertheless, so be sure to check the documentation at *http://www.kde.org/documentation/index.html*.

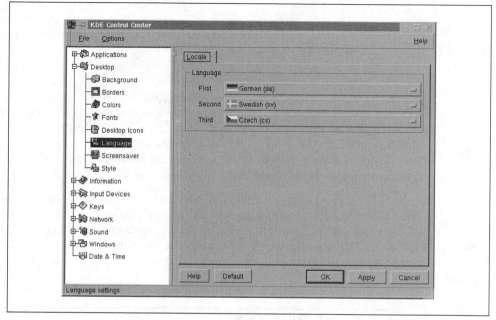

Figure 11–5: Configuring the language of the KDE desktop

X Applications

There are thousands of programs available for X. They range from basic utilities (such as *xterm* and *xclock*, already discussed) to editors to programming aids to games to multimedia applications. The most we can provide here is a tiny slice of the software available for X. In this section, we'll present those applications that all X users should know how to use. These aren't necessarily the most exciting programs out there, but they should certainly be part of your toolbox. Note that if you are using a desktop environment such as KDE, described in the last section, it may have tools of its own that do the same things as the ones described here, but work better with the desktop. The general techniques described here usually apply to the desktop tools as well.

[11] X User Guide

A more comprehensive explanation of X applications can be found in *X Window System User's Guide*.

xterm: Your Home Base

Let's start our exploration of X applications with the workhorse that you'll be spending most of your time with—*xterm*. This is simply a window that contains a Unix shell. It displays a prompt, accepts commands, and scrolls like a terminal.

NOTE   If you use KDE, you can also use KDE's own terminal emulator *kvt*,
              which provides more or less the same features as *xterm*, but can be
              configured via a user-friendly GUI.

Perhaps you are struck by the irony of buying a high-resolution color monitor, installing several megabytes of graphics software, and then being confronted by an emulation of an old VT100 terminal. But Linux is simply not a point-and-click operating system. There are plenty of nice graphical applications, but a lot of the time you'll want to manipulate text, and a command-line interface still offers the most powerful tools for doing that.

So let's take look at an *xterm* window. Figure 11-6 shows one where we've already entered a few commands. By the way, if you've read the section "Basics of X Customization" earlier in this chapter, you may enjoy browsing some of the files in */usr/lib/X11/app-defaults*; they show the default behavior of X applications when you don't specify your own preferences.

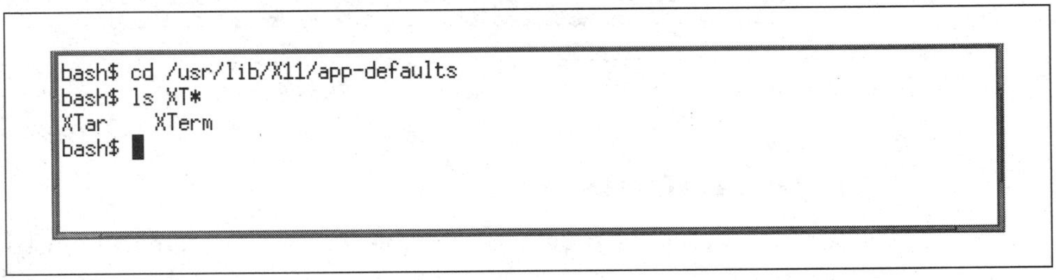

```
bash$ cd /usr/lib/X11/app-defaults
bash$ ls XT*
XTar    XTerm
bash$ ▌
```

Figure 11–6: xterm window

Starting up xterm

Maybe first we should explain how we created the *xterm* window. You can reproduce it through the command:

eggplant$ **xterm -geometry 80x25-20-30 -fn 7x13bold -sb -name xterm-3**

where the options mean:

–geometry 80x25-20-30
    The window is 80 characters wide and 25 characters high, located 20 pixels from the right edge of the screen and 30 pixels from the bottom edge.

—fn 7x13bold

> Text appears in a medium-sized bold font. (A large, but limited, set of fonts are available; we'll show you how to look at them later, in the section "Choosing Fonts.")

—sb

> A scrollbar is displayed.

—name xterm-3

> The string `xterm-3` appears in the titlebar at the top of the window, and on the icon when you iconify the window.

But you don't want to go to the trouble of entering this long command every time you start an *xterm*. What we did (as you can see in the earlier section "Basics of X Customization") was put the following options in our *.Xdefaults* file:

```
! Defaults for all xterm clients
XTerm*scrollBar:        true

! Specific xterms
xterm-3*Geometry:       80x25-20-30

xterm-3*Font:           7x13bold
```

and when we logged in, our *.xinitrc* file issued the command:

```
xterm -name "xterm-3" &
```

which created the window. As you saw in the section "The fvwm Window Manager" earlier in this chapter, you can easily set up a menu, mouse button, function key, and so on, to start the *xterm*.

To close a window, type `exit` or press Ctrl-D. If this capability seems dangerous to you (because you could lose your window by pressing Ctrl-D accidentally), start up the *xterm* with the *—ls* option, which stands for login shell. Now you have to enter *logout* to close the window. (The option has some other consequences, too. In the *bash* shell, it causes your ~/.bash_profile file to run. In the C shell, it causes your ~/.login file to run.)

Cutting and Pasting Selections

Actually, *xterm* offers a good deal more than a VT100 terminal. One of its features is a powerful cut-and-paste capability.

Take another look at Figure 11-6. Let's say we didn't really want the *app-defaults* directory; we wanted to look at the fonts in */usr/lib/X11/fonts* instead. (This is actually not too interesting; it was an arbitrary choice.)

First, we'll choose the part of the *cd* command that interests us. Put the mouse just to the left of the c in cd. Press the left mouse button, and drag the mouse until it highlights the slash following X11. The result is shown in Figure 11-7.

Did you include too many characters or too few? That's all right; just hold down the Shift key and press the left mouse button anywhere in the highlighted area. Now you can make the highlighted area bigger or smaller.

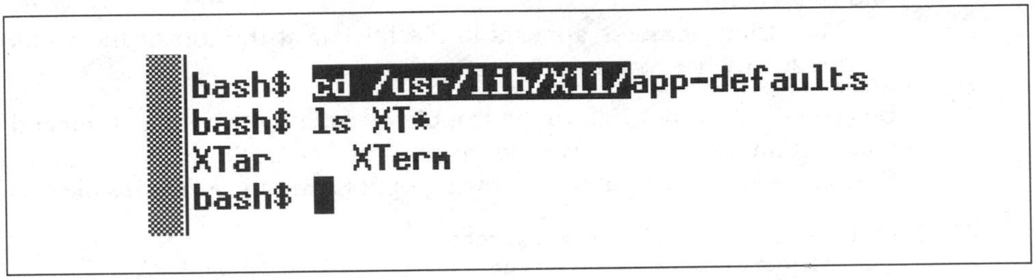

```
bash$ cd /usr/lib/X11/app-defaults
bash$ ls XT*
XTar     XTerm
bash$ █
```

Figure 11-7: Selected text in xterm

When the highlighted area covers just the right number of characters, click the middle button. *xterm* pastes in what you've selected on the next command line. See the result in Figure 11-8.

```
bash$ cd /usr/lib/X11/app-defaults
bash$ ls XT*
XTar     XTerm
bash$ cd /usr/lib/X11/█
```

Figure 11-8: xterm window after text is pasted

Now you can type in the remainder of the directory name *fonts* and press the Enter key to execute the command.

You can select anything you want in the window—output as well as input. To select whole words instead of characters, double-click the left mouse button. To select whole lines, triple-click it. You can select multiple lines too. Selecting multiple lines is not useful when you're entering commands but is convenient if you're using the *vi* editor and want to cut and paste a lot of text between windows.

Be careful: if a long line wraps around, you will end up with a newline in the selection even though you didn't press the Enter key when you entered the line.

Scrolling

Eventually, as you type along in your *xterm*, previous commands will scroll off the top of the window. That's why we specified a scrollbar when we started the *xterm*. Using it is pretty simple (as it ought to be with any point-and-click tool), but there are a few neat tricks. By the way, the techniques you learn here should work in most applications that offer scrollbars. An X application is free to act any way the programmer designed it to, but most developers use the same conventions as *xterm*.

First, let's get a lot of text into our window. Issuing one of the following commands should suffice:

```
eggplant$ ls /bin
eggplant$ ls /usr/bin
eggplant$ cat ~/.*
```

Of course, the output will go streaming by too fast for you to see it. Now we can go back and look at it. If you examine the scrollbar area on the left side of the window, you'll see a little dark area near the bottom. Its size indicates how much of the output you can currently see, and its position shows you where you are (at the end).

Place the mouse in the scrollbar area near the bottom, and press the right mouse button. This moves you one whole page upward; what used to be at the top of the screen is now at the bottom. If you click near the top of the screen, you move back by just a couple lines. If you click near the middle, you move back half a window at a time. Notice that the scrollbar moves up as you click the button.

To go back down, click the left mouse button. Again, clicking near the top moves you just a couple lines, while clicking near the bottom moves you a full window's length.

When you have a really big buffer of saved material, you may want to go to the beginning or end really fast; that's what the middle mouse button is good for. Click anywhere in the scrollbar area, and you'll go to that part of the buffer. Therefore, click at the top to go to the beginning, and at the bottom to go to the end. Or click right on the scrollbar itself, hold down the button, and drag the scrollbar where you want to go.

Chapter 4

If you're a keyboard kind of person, you don't need to use the mouse to scroll. You can also hold down the Shift key and press the Page Up key to scroll backward, or the Page Down key to scroll forward. By the way, the keys work the same in a virtual console (see the section "Virtual Consoles" in Chapter 4, *Basic Unix Commands and Concepts*).

You'll find that *xterm* does not save much output by default. To increase the number of lines that are saved, use the *–sl number* option or put an entry like the following in your *.Xdefaults* file:

```
XTerm*saveLines:          400
```

Choosing Fonts

Think your fonts are ugly or too small? There are plenty of others to choose from. Virtually every X application lets you choose the font used to display each kind of text (menus, and so on). You just have to know what their names are and what they look like.

A desktop, as described earlier in this chapter, gives you a simple and intuitive way to choose a font. If you're not using a desktop, you can at least view fonts using the *xfontsel* and *xfd* utilities. But after you find a font you like, you must copy it into *.Xdefaults* or do whatever else you have to to configure an application.

Fonts on the X Window System have incredibly long names. A typical one is:

```
-misc-fixed-bold-r-normal--13-100-100-100-c-70-iso8859-1
```

The hyphens divide the fonts into fields. For now, what interests us most is the field following the eleventh hyphen, where we see c in this example.

For *xterm* and many other applications, what you need is a *monospaced font*. That means a font where every character takes up the same amount of space, as opposed to *proportional fonts*, where an m is wider than an i. Proportional fonts are great for displaying the output of a text processor like TEX, but they look horrible when used in a program that's not designed to handle the variety of spacing. When the eleventh field of the font name is c or m, it represents a monospaced font.

Other fields can also help you make a choice. The third field tells you whether the font is medium (which means normal weight) or bold. The seventh field, which says 13 in this example, gives you the size (actually the height of the largest character in pixels).

Now let's see whether our system has a font with the size and style we want. Start the utility *xfontsel* from a command line in an *xterm* window. It loads all the fonts on your system and displays a screen where you make your selection. You can also restrict the fonts to ones of particular interest, but the syntax of the command is rather daunting because any field you don't specify explicitly must be specified as an asterisk:

```
eggplant$ xfontsel -pattern -*-*-bold-*-*-*-18-*-*-*-m-*-*
```

A typical *xfontsel* display looks like Figure 11-9.

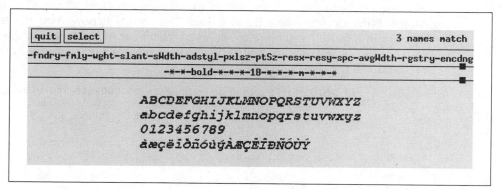

Figure 11-9: xfontsel to show fonts

Each of the strings such as wght and slant represents a part of the font name. The font name in our earlier example has a weight of bold and a slant of r which stands for roman. The eleventh field is spc, but we want to be c or m. So, put your mouse on the spc field, press the left mouse button to display a menu, and select either c or m from the menu. You can then try other fields (to select a size, choose from the ptSz menu) and view a font matching your specification.

An older way of checking available fonts is to use the *xlsfonts* command. Just as *ls* lists files, *xlsfonts* lists fonts. But if you enter the command without arguments, the volume of output will overwhelm you. It's better to figure out what types of fonts you need and just look at those.

In *xlsfonts*, you specify a font through the *–fn* option and use an asterisk to match an arbitrary set of characters. If we want to match the third and eleventh fields exactly, and don't care what the other fields are, we enter:

```
eggplant$ xlsfonts -fn -*-*-bold-*-*-*-*-*-*-*-m-*-*
```

This tells *xlsfonts* that the first and second fields can be anything. But the third must be bold. The eleventh is also specified; it's an m. What we'll see is a list of monospaced bold fonts. If none exist, we'll get the message: g:

```
xlsfonts: pattern "-*-*-bold-*-*-*-*-*-*-*-m-*-*" unmatched
```

Now replace the m with a c and look for the rest of the monospaced fonts.

Actually, you don't have to use such complicated names. In our examples earlier in the chapter, we specified the short name 7x13bold. That kind of name is called an *alias*; it represents another name of the longer type. To see a short list of monospaced fonts using these aliases, enter:

```
eggplant$ xlsfonts *x*
```

We've gone through a fair amount of trouble already, and all we have is a list of names. What do fonts actually look like? The *xfontsel* shows you the letters and digits from a font. If you want to see every character in the font, use the *xfd* command, which stands for "X font display." It displays a grid with one rectangle for each character:

```
eggplant$ xfd -fn -misc-fixed-bold-r-normal--13-100-100-100-c-70-iso8859-1
```

When you find a font you like, cast it in concrete by putting it in your *.Xdefaults* file:

```
XTerm*Font:        7x13bold
```

Clocks

How can your screen be complete if it is unadorned by a little clock that tells you how much time you are wasting on customizing the screen's appearance? You can have a clock just the way you want it, square or round, analog or digital, big or small. You can even make it chime.

The *.xinit* file shown earlier in this chapter contains a line that starts *oclock*:

```
oclock -geometry 70x70+5+5 &
```

Refer to Figure 11-1 to see what this clock looks like. You may prefer the square outline of the *xclock* program:

```
xclock -geometry 150x150+5+5 &
```

Or perhaps a tiny digital clock at the bottom of your screen:

```
xclock -digital -geometry +10-10
```

oclock allows you to scatter more colors about, while *xclock* gives you more control over other aspects of the clock; see the manual pages for more information. To get a beep every half hour, invoke *xclock* with the *–chime* option.

Emacs

The X features in Emacs are getting spiffier and spiffier. They include pull-down menus, different typefaces for different parts of your window, and a complete integration of cut-and-paste functions with the X environment.

NOTE   Most distributions nowadays also carry XEmacs, a version of Emacs that integrates even better into the X Window System and has a much nicer and more user-friendly appearance. You might want to try it out. Most of the concepts here apply to XEmacs, too.

Let's start by defining some nice colors for different parts of the Emacs window. Try this command:

```
eggplant$ emacs  -bg ivory  -fg slateblue  -ms orangered  -cr brown
```

You are setting the background color, foreground color, mouse color, and cursor color respectively. The cursor is the little rectangle that appears in the window, representing what's called "point" in Emacs—the place where you type in text. We'll return to colors soon.

When you start Emacs, the menu bar on top and the scrollbar on the right side of the window stand out. See Figure 11-10.

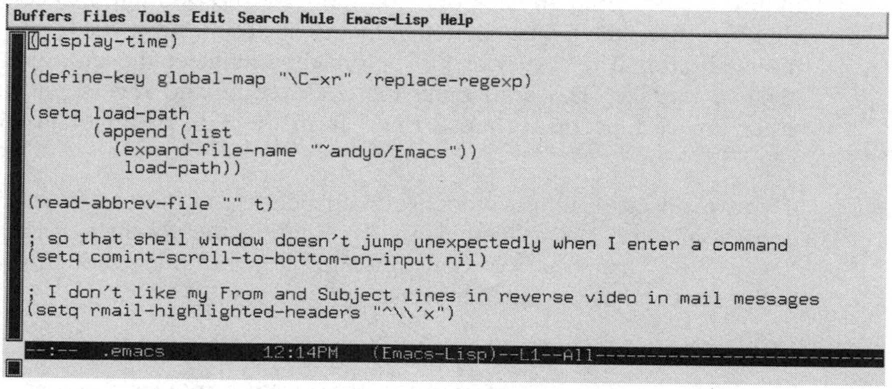

Figure 11-10: Emacs window

The scrollbar works just like the *xterm* scrollbar. The menu bar offers a lot of common functions. Some editing modes, like C and TEX, have their own pull-down menus. The menus are not documented, so you will just have to experiment and try to figure out which Emacs functions they correspond to.

When you want to use a function that doesn't have a simple key sequence—or you've forgotten the sequence—the menus come in handy. For instance, if you rarely use a regular expression search (a quite powerful feature, well worth studying), the easiest way to invoke it is to pull down the Edit menu and choose Regexp Search.

Another useful menu item is Choose Next Paste on the Edit menu. This offers something you can't get any other way: a list of all the pieces of text you've cut recently. In other words, it shows you the kill ring. You can choose the text you want to paste in next, and the next time you press C-y, it's put into your buffer.

If you get tired of the scrollbar and the menu, put the following LISP code in your *.emacs* file to make them go away:

```
(if (getenv "DISPLAY")
    (progn (menu-bar-mode -1)
           (scroll-bar-mode -1))
   )
```

The mouse is the next X feature with interesting possibilities. You can cut and paste text much the same way as in *xterm*. And you can do this between windows; if you see some output in an *xterm* you'd like to put in a file, you can copy it from the *xterm* and paste it into your Emacs buffer. Moreover, any text you cut the normal way (such as through C-w) goes into the same selection as text you cut with the mouse. So you can cut a few words from your Emacs buffer and paste them into an *xterm*.

The right mouse button works a little unusually. If you select text with the left mouse button, you can click once on the right mouse button to copy it. A second click on the right mouse button removes it. To paste it back, press the middle mouse button. The text goes just before the character the mouse is currently on. Make a mistake? That's all right; the undo command reverses it just as for any other Emacs function. (Choose Undo from the Edit menu or just press the C-_ key.)

If you really love mouse work, you can define the buttons to execute any functions you want, just as with keys. Try putting the following command in your *.emacs* file. When you hold down the Shift key and press the left mouse button, a buffer for composing a mail message appears:

```
(define-key global-map [S-mouse-1] 'mail)
```

We don't recommend you redefine the existing mouse functions, but the Shift, Control, and Meta keys offer plenty of unused possibilities. Combine S-, C-, and M- any way you want in your definitions:

```
(define-key global-map [S-C-mouse-1] 'mail)
```

Now let's play around a bit with windows. Emacs has had windows of its own for decades, of course, long before the X Window System existed. So an Emacs window is not the same as an X window. What X considers a window, Emacs calls a *frame*.

How would you like to edit in two frames at once? Press C-x 5 2, and another frame appears. The new frame is simply another view onto the same editing session. You can edit different buffers in the two frames, but anything you do in one frame is reflected to the corresponding buffer in the other. When you exit Emacs by pressing C-x C-c, both frames disappear; if you want to close just one frame, press C-x 5 0.

To end our exploration of Emacs on the X Window System, we'll look at the exciting things you can do with colors. You can change these during an Emacs session, which makes it easy to play around with different possibilities. Press `M-x`, then type `set-background-color` and press the Enter key. At the prompt, type `ivory` or whatever other color you've chosen. (Remember, Emacs uses the convention `M-x` where we use Meta-x or Alt-x in the rest of the book.)

Be careful to make the foreground and background different enough so that you can see the text! In addition to `set-background-color`, Emacs offers `set-fore-ground-color`, `set-cursor-color`, and `set-mouse-color`.

These settings may seem idle play, but now they show their true colors when you let Emacs highlight different parts of your buffer in different ways. For instance, when you are programming in C or LISP, you can display strings, comments, func-tion names, and keywords in different colors.

To set up color coding, you have to set `font-lock` mode. The easiest way to do this is in your *.emacs* start-up file; add lines like the following:

```
(require 'font-lock)
(setq global-font-lock-mode t)
(setq font-lock-maximum-decoration t)
```

These rather complicated commands tell each major mode to set the font lock whenever you open a buffer in that mode. So whenever you edit a file ending with the suffix *.c*, for instance, you automatically set the font lock.

Next, you want to play with the font faces, which are the different kinds of text defined by Emacs. Press `M-x` and enter the command `list-faces-display`. You'll see a list like the following:

```
              bold abcdefghijklmnopqrstuvwxyz ABCDEFGHIJKLMNOPQRSTUVWXYZ
       bold-italic abcdefghijklmnopqrstuvwxyz ABCDEFGHIJKLMNOPQRSTUVWXYZ
           default abcdefghijklmnopqrstuvwxyz ABCDEFGHIJKLMNOPQRSTUVWXYZ
         highlight abcdefghijklmnopqrstuvwxyz ABCDEFGHIJKLMNOPQRSTUVWXYZ
            italic abcdefghijklmnopqrstuvwxyz ABCDEFGHIJKLMNOPQRSTUVWXYZ
          modeline abcdefghijklmnopqrstuvwxyz ABCDEFGHIJKLMNOPQRSTUVWXYZ
            region abcdefghijklmnopqrstuvwxyz ABCDEFGHIJKLMNOPQRSTUVWXYZ
 secondary-selection abcdefghijklmnopqrstuvwxyz ABCDEFGHIJKLMNOPQRSTUVWXYZ
         underline abcdefghijklmnopqrstuvwxyz ABCDEFGHIJKLMNOPQRSTUVWXYZ
```

You can now set the background and foreground of each face interactively. Here is an example:

1. Enter `M-x set-face-background`.

2. Type `modeline` at the first prompt.

3. Type `lemonchiffon` at the second prompt.

You see the results immediately. Then set the foreground:

1. Enter `M-x set-face-foreground`.

2. Type `modeline` at the first prompt.

3. Type `green` at the second prompt.

No, that probably doesn't offer enough contrast for you to read the words. So do it again and use the color `maroon`. That looks better.

Find a buffer with C or LISP code in it and try setting each of the other faces. Faces are assigned rather arbitrarily to elements of the code. As you add colors, new dimensions will be revealed in your code. For instance, in C or C++ mode:

- Comments and preprocessor keywords appear in *italic*.

- Strings and include filenames appear in underline.

- Function names and defined variables appear in **bold-italic**.

It probably looks best to reserve the bolder colors for short, rarely seen pieces of text.

When you find a set of colors you like, hard-wire them into your *.emacs* file by using the LISP functions that correspond to the commands you've been experimenting with. Here's a sample set:

```
(set-background-color "ivory")
(set-foreground-color "slateblue")
(set-cursor-color "brown")
(set-mouse-color "orangered")
(set-face-foreground 'bold "black")
(set-face-background 'bold "lightpink")
(set-face-foreground 'bold-italic "red")
(set-face-background 'bold-italic "wheat")
(set-face-foreground 'italic "darkolivegreen")
(set-face-background 'modeline "lemonchiffon")
(set-face-foreground 'modeline "maroon")
(set-face-foreground 'underline "violet")
```

You can also set colors in your *.Xdefaults* file, but that takes a little more effort, so we won't bother to explain it here.

Ghostview: Displaying PostScript

Adobe PostScript, as a standard in its own right, has become one of the most popular formats for exchanging documents in the computer world. Many academics distribute papers in PostScript format. The Linux Documentation Project offers its manuals in PostScript form, among others. This format is useful for people who lack the time to format LaTeX input, or who have immense network bandwidth for transferring files. When you create documents of your own using *groff* or TeX, you'll want to view them on a screen before you use up precious paper resources by printing them.

Ghostview, a GNU application, offers a pleasant environment for viewing PostScript on the X Window System. It's very simple; invoke it with the name of the file to be displayed, for instance:

```
eggplant$ ghostview article.ps
```

The Ghostview window is huge; it can easily take up most of your screen. The first page of the document is displayed with a vertical scrollbar on the right and a horizontal one on the bottom. Menu options appear on the left side of the window, and page numbers just to their right.

Like most X applications, Ghostview offers both menu options and keys (accelerators) for common functions. Thus, to view the next page, you can pull down the Page menu and choose the Next option. Or you can just press the space bar.

To go back to the previous page, choose Previous from the Page menu. To go to any page you want, press the middle mouse button on its number in the number column. To exit, choose Quit from the File menu or just press q.

Documents from different countries often use different page sizes. The Ghostview default is the standard U.S. letter size (this can be overridden by comments in the PostScript file). You can specify a different size on the command line:

```
eggplant$ ghostview -a3 article.ps
```

or in your *.Xdefaults* file:

```
Ghostview*pageMedia:            A3
```

Finally, you can also choose a different size at runtime from the Media menu.

Ghostview lets you enlarge or reduce the size of the page, a useful feature for checking the details of your formatting work. (But be warned that fonts on the screen are different from the fonts on a printer, and therefore the exact layout of characters in Ghostview will not be the same as that in the hard copy.) To zoom in on a small part of the page, press any mouse button on it. (The right mouse button enlarges the most; the left mouse button the least.)

You can also change the default size for displaying the whole document by using the Magstep menu. The higher the number you choose, the more the document is enlarged. Negative numbers reduce the size of the document.

To print a page, choose Print from the File menu or press p anywhere in the window. You are prompted to make sure that you've chosen the right printer; you can erase what is shown there and enter a different name. The name shown comes from your environment. So, if your printer is named **doorway**, you should have issued a shell command in your startup file like:

```
export PRINTER=doorway
```

You can also print several pages. Select individual ones by clicking on their numbers with the middle mouse button. Or select the first page with the left mouse button, and the last page with the right mouse button; the whole range of pages will be printed when you press **p**.

NOTE   KDE comes with its own version of Ghostview, called *kghostview*, which is really just Ghostview with a more user-friendly interface and a nicer appearance. You can run *kghostview* even if you do not plan to run the rest of KDE.

Another option would be to use *gv*, which has become quite popular lately.

---

xman: A Point-and-Click Interface to Manual Pages

Manual pages, read through the *man* command, are the ultimate authority on a Unix system. Other books can describe a significant percentage of any given command's functions—and often describe them in a more readable fashion—but only the manual page has all the details. See the section "Manual Pages" in Chapter 4 for basic information.

Chapter 4

Now there's a simple X interface to manual pages: the *xman* command. As befits a tool that displays documents, it contains a pretty good description of itself. In order to see this documentation clearly, start up the program with a large page size:

```
eggplant$ xman -pagesize 650x600
```

What you see first is a tiny box with three buttons. Click on the Manual Page button to bring up the main screen, where you'll do most of your work.

Now you see the *xman* documentation. You'll have plenty of time to read this; for now, just pull down the Options menu and choose Search, or press Ctrl-S. (You can also display the options menu by holding down the Control key and pressing the left mouse button.) In the box that pops up, type in a command or function you'd like to read about, then press the Enter key. The contents of the main window are replaced by the corresponding manual page.

If you don't know what to look for, try pulling down the Sections menu or pressing the Control key along with the middle button. Choose a section from the menu that appears. You'll see a long list of manual pages. Click the left button on one of them, and the document will be displayed.

Chapter 4

Another time-honored way to look for information is through the *apropos* command (discussed already in the section "Manual Pages" in Chapter 4). Press Ctrl-S again, type in a word about a subject you're interested in, and press the Apropos button. If any manual pages match that word, their names will be displayed along with short descriptions. Unfortunately, you can't call up their manual pages by clicking on them; that little convenience was left out of *xman*. You have to press Ctrl-S and type in the page that looks interesting.

Within a manual page, scrolling is easy. Use the space bar or f to move down a page, b to move up. You can also use the scrollbar, just as in *xterm*.

Now you can read the documentation! Press the Help button on the small window that appeared when you started *xterm*. To exit the program, press Ctrl-Q or the Quit button, or choose Quit from the Options menu.

If you think that *xman* is still too bare-bones and not much of an improvement over the command-line *man* command, you can try one of its more advanced companions. For example, *tkman* has a much nicer user interface and features advanced navigation possibilities. The KDE help system, *kdehelp*, can display manual and info pages in addition to its own HTML pages and thus unifies the three major documentation formats on Linux.

## CHAPTER TWELVE

WINDOWS COMPATIBILITY AND SAMBA

Linux is a remarkably effective operating system that normally replaces MS-DOS/Windows. However, there are always those of us who want to have their cake and eat it, too. We want to continue to use other operating systems as well as Linux, or at least to exchange files directly with them. Linux satisfies such yearnings with internal enhancements that allow it to access foreign filesystems and act on their files, with compatibility utilities that allow it to invoke MS-DOS to run DOS applications, or with a utility that allows Linux to run Xenix binaries without recompiling. The most outstanding tool for getting Linux and Windows to cooperate is Samba, which we'll discuss in enough depth to help you get a basic, functional server running.

Samba is the package that lets you access Unix files and printers from Windows, and it is one of the most famous Open Source programs of all. People have found that Unix servers running Samba can—depending on the circumstances—serve Windows computers faster than even Windows servers can! In addition, Samba has proven to be very stable and reliable.

We use the term Windows somewhat generically in this chapter to refer to any of the DOS-based operating systems coming from Microsoft or those compatible with them, like MS-DOS, PC-DOS, and DR-DOS/Novell DOS (all with or without Windows 3.x running on top of them), as well as the various Windows versions themselves, no matter whether they build upon a separate DOS installation like the venerable Windows 3.x or whether they have a DOS kernel built in like Windows 95 and Windows 98. It should be added that Windows NT/2000 is a completely different animal; many of the things described here will not work with these, or will work differently. Your mileage may vary.

Some of these utilities work well, while others are perhaps "not ready for prime time." These tools allow many who otherwise couldn't find out about Linux to try it out without first abandoning their reliable working platform or without buying a second computer to play with.

You should be a little skeptical of some dreams of compatibility though. Just because something can be done, doesn't mean it is a great idea. As a practical matter, you might find, for example, that you need twice the disk storage in order to support two operating systems and their associated files and applications programs, plus file conversion and graphic-format conversion tools, and so on. You may find that hardware tuned for one OS won't be tuned for the other, and you will have to choose where to spend your cash.

If you find yourself stuck with a piece of hardware that you would like to use because of its Windows support (like a USB device), but for which there are no Linux drivers yet, do not despair. The desire to have everything will probably continue to drive Linux developers, so we confidently expect that for each hardware device that is supported on Windows, there will at one point or other be a driver for Linux, too. For example, there is already work going on with respect to USB devices; see *http://video.komm.hdk-berlin.de/~rasca/uusbd-utils/* for more information.

Chapter 5

One of the first and foremost things you probably want to do with Linux and Windows is install both of them on your computer and decide at boot time which of the two you want to boot. The section "Booting the System" in Chapter 5, *Essential System Management*, tells you what to do in order to get a multiboot system.

The next thing you will want to do is share files between Windows and Linux, a topic which we will explore in the next section. You will find out that this works smoothly for most cases nowadays, if you know the tricks of the trade.

Finally, we cover tools that let you (at least partly) run some of your DOS and Windows programs on Linux. We will be leaving the highway here and follow quite stony roads, but as always, those offer the most exciting sights.

Sharing Files

When you install both Windows and Linux on your computer, you will often wish you could access files on one operating system that you saved with the other operating system. While there are few, if any, ways to get at your Linux files from Windows on the same machine, it is surprisingly easy to access your Windows files from Linux. Linux can read and write files on the traditional FAT filesystem and the newer VFAT filesystem, which was introduced with Windows 95 and supports long filenames. It can read (and eventually will be able to write to) the NTFS filesystem of Windows NT.

In some cases, it can be even easier to access your files over the network using Samba. If you run Linux on one machine and a version of Windows with built-in networking, like Windows for Workgroups or the newer Windows versions 95/98 and NT, you will probably be able to exchange files between the two machines.

Getting at your data is only half the match, though. You must also be able to make sense out of it. You might be surprised to hear that you can have problems even with the simplest file format, raw text—let alone more elaborate file formats like those saved by graphics programs or word processors.

Mounting DOS, VFAT, and NTFS Partitions

Chapter 6

If you have already read the section "Mounting Filesystems" in Chapter 6, *Managing Filesystems, Swap, and Devices*, you know by now that you access partitions on local hard disks by "mounting" them into your directory hierarchy. In order to be able to read and write to a specific filesystem, the Linux kernel needs to have support for this filesystem.

Chapter 7

In the section "Building a New Kernel" in Chapter 7, *Upgrading Software and the Kernel*, you learned how to build your own kernel. In order to be able to access DOS (used by MS-DOS and Windows 3.x) and VFAT (used by Windows 95 and Windows 98) partitions, you need to enable DOS FAT fs support in the filesystems section during kernel configuration. After you say yes to that option, you can choose MSDOS fs support and VFAT (Windows-95) fs support. The first lets you mount FAT partitions and the second lets you mount VFAT partitions. VFAT support is relatively recent; it appeared first in kernel Version 2.0.34, but really became stable only with recent kernel versions.

While Linux is running, you can then mount a Windows partition like any other type of partition. If, for example, the third partition on your first SCSI hard disk contains your Windows 98 installation, you can make those files accessible with the following command, which must be executed as **root**:

```
mount -t vfat /dev/sda3 /mnt/windows98
```

The */dev/sda3* option specifies the disk drive corresponding to the Windows 98 disk, while the */mnt/windows98* option can be changed to any directory you've created for the purpose of accessing the files. But how do you know that you need—in this case—*/dev/sda3*? If you're familiar with the arcane naming conventions for Linux filesystems (shown in Table 3-1), you'll know that *sda3* is the third partition on the first SCSI hard disk, but you'll find life easier if you write down the partitions while you are creating them with *fdisk*.

Of course, you are free to choose other mount points than */mnt/windows98*. If you want to mount a FAT partition, you do the same, but replace vfat with msdos in the previous command.

mount (8)

Both the `msdos` and the `vfat` filesystem driver support a number of options that can be specified with the -o option of the *mount* command, but in most cases, you will not need them. The man page tells you all the options. There are, however, two options that might be useful for you: *check* and *conv*.

The option *check* determines whether the kernel should accept filenames that are not permissible on MS-DOS and what it should do with them. Obviously, this applies only to creating and renaming files. You can specify three values for *check*: `relaxed` lets you do just about everything with the filename. If it does not fit into the 8.3 convention of MS-DOS files, the filename will be truncated accordingly. `normal`, the default, will also truncate the filenames as needed, but not accept special characters like * and ? that are not allowed in MS-DOS filenames. Finally, `strict` forbids both long filenames and the special characters. In order to make Linux more restrictive with respect to filenames on the partition mounted above, the *mount* command could be used as follows:

```
mount -o check=strict -t msdos /dev/sda5 /mnt/dos
```

Obviously, the restrictions of the filename length do not apply to `vfat` filesystems.

The second option that is potentially useful, but not quite ready for most users is *conv*. Windows and Unix systems have different conventions for how a line end is marked in text files. Windows uses both a carriage return and a linefeed character, while Unix only uses the linefeed. While this does not make the files completely illegible on the other system, it can still be a bother. To tell the kernel to perform the conversion between Windows and Unix text file styles automatically, you need to pass the *mount* command the option *conv*. *conv* has three possible values: `binary`, the default, does not perform any conversion; `text` converts every file; and `auto` tries to guess whether the file in question is a text file or a binary file. Auto does this by looking at the filename extension. If this extension is included in the list of "known binary extensions," it is not converted, otherwise it will be converted.

It is not advisable to use *text*, because this will invariable damage any binary files, including graphics files and files written by word processors, spreadsheets and other programs. Likewise, *auto* can be dangerous, because the extension-based detection mechanism is not very sophisticated. So we'd suggest you don't use the option. Stick with *binary* (the default) and convert your files on an as-needed basis.

If you want to access files on a Windows NT partition that carries an NTFS filesystem, you need another driver. Activate the option `NTFS filesystem support` during the kernel configuration. This lets you mount NTFS partitions by specifying the file system type `ntfs`. Note, however, that the current NTFS driver supports just read-only access. There is an alpha version of a driver available that supports writing as well, and so far, it has worked for us quite nicely, but *we do not advise using this without backing up your NTFS partition first!*

Using Samba to Mount Directories from Windows Systems on Your Network

So far, we have covered how to access Windows partitions on the same machine. In this section, we will extend this discussion to partitions (which in this context are often called shares) that reside on other servers. In Windows versions, starting with Windows for Workgroups, you can make directories or printers accessible for other computers. The protocol used for this feature is called SMB (Server Message Block). With the SMB support in Linux, you can access these directories from Linux. Note that the Windows machines must be configured to use TCP/IP in addition to or instead of the native Windows protocol NETBEUI, because the Linux SMB support does not include NETBEUI. Of course, your Linux machine must be set up for TCP/IP networking as well; see Chapter 15, *TCP/IP and PPP*, to learn how to do that. For now, we will assume that a TCP/IP connection can be established between your Linux and your Windows computer.

Chapter 15

In this section, we cover sharing in one direction: how to access files on Windows systems from Linux. The next section will show you how to do the reverse, and make selected files on your Linux system available to people on Windows systems.

In order to get SMB support running, you have to follow these steps:

1. Compile support for SMB into your kernel.

2. Install Samba (described in the next section) and create at least a minimal configuration file.

3. Mount the services with the *smbmount* command.

Let's go through these steps one at a time. The first one is easy: In the `filesystems/Network File Systems` section during kernel configuration, select `SMB file system support (to mount WfW shares etc.)`. Compile and install your kernel, or install and load the module. If you plan to mount shares from a Windows 95 server, you should also select `SMB Win95 bug work-around`, which works around in bug in showing directories on a Windows 95 share. You don't need this if you are accessing shares only on a Windows 98 or Windows NT machine and should leave it off in this case because it slows down directory reading.

Next, you will need to install the Samba package. This package is meant for providing (not accessing) SMB shares, but its package contains one utility program and one configuration file you will need. If you do not have it on your machine (check whether the file */etc/smb.conf* exists), please read the next section to learn how to get it.

You will learn about how to write the configuration file */etc/smb.conf* in the next section, but for our purposes here, it suffices to have the following content:

```
[global]
socket options = TCP_NODELAY
```

There may be other configuration parameters in the [global] section; this parameter does not need to be the first. If you already have a *smb.conf*, there can be other socket options too. Don't let yourself be bothered by that; just make sure that you have the TCP_NODELAY option, as this speeds up directory reading a lot.

The last thing to do is to mount the partition (which in the Windows world is called a *share*). Unlike the partition types described in the last section and unlike the Network File System, you do not use the familiar *mount* command, but a special command from the Samba package called *smbmount*. This is because SMB shares have a different addressing scheme. Accordingly, you use *smbumount* for unmounting an SMB share.

If you are lucky, using *smbmount* can be quite easy. The general format is:

```
smbmount options servicename mount_point
```

where *mount_point* specifies a directory just as in the *mount* command. *servicename* follows more or less the Windows naming conventions, except that it replaces the backslashes with slashes. For example, if you want to mount a SMB share from the computer called **winloser** that is exported under the name *mydocs* onto the directory */windocs*, you could use the following command:

```
tigger# smbmount //winloser/mydocs/ /windocs
```

You can also specify a directory below the exported root if you want to mount only a part of the share. For example, suppose we didn't want to share everything in the *mydocs* directory of the previous example, but just a subdirectory under it called *htmldocs*. We could say:

```
tigger# smbmount //winloser/mydocs/htmldocs /windocs
```

If a password is needed to access the share, *smbmount* will ask you for it.

As we previously wrote, if you are lucky, the preceding steps could be everything you need. But if you are unlucky, things could get messy here. If you do not know much about how Windows computers handle networking, you might want to seek help from the person who has set up the Windows machine where the files that you are trying to access are.

The most common problem is that in the SMB protocol, machines can have two different hostnames: the normal hostname and a NetBIOS name. While having two names might not be a good idea anyway, you will not be able to simply mount a SMB share with the previous commands if the two differ. If you know the NetBIOS name, you can pass it with the *−s* option:

```
tigger#smbmount -s nbname //winloser/mydocs/ /windocs
```

Another thing to try is to tell *smbmount* about the IP address of the machine exporting the SMB share. This is done with the −I option (see Chapter 15 to learn about IP addresses). If the server has the IP address 192.168.0.5, you could try the following command:

```
tiger# smbmount -I 192.168.0.5 //winloser/mydocs/ /windocs
```

smb-
mount (8)

Please see the manual page for *smbmount* for further tricks to try.

One problem with the *smbmount* command is that is does not really tell you what went wrong. For hints on what the problem is, try the utility program *smbclient*, which also comes from the Samba package. *smbclient* lets you copy files to and from a SMB share and list its directory contents, and it has the advantage of providing a little more detailed error messages. See the manual page for *smbclient* for further details. If you can access a SMB share with *smbclient*, but not with *smbmount*, it is very likely that either SMB support is not available in the kernel or that the mount point cannot be accessed, that is, that the problem has nothing to do with the network.

smbclient (1)

Using Samba to Serve SMB Shares

You probably want to access Linux files from Windows, in addition to accessing Windows files from Linux as we did in the previous section. For instance, a safe and popular networking strategy is to locate user's critical files in Unix home directories and serve them up to the users on their PCs.

A warning before you plunge into the wonderful world of Samba: NetBIOS, the underlying protocol for SMB, is quite complex, and because Samba has to deal with all those complexities, it provides a huge number of configuration options. Thus, if you are really serious about serving a department of 50 employees that use all kinds of Windows and perhaps even OS/2 machines, you are well advised to read the Samba documentation thoroughly and perhaps even read a good book about Samba.

That being said, I can reassure you that for the not-so-complex cases, setting up Samba is surprisingly easy, both as a file and as a print server. In addition, there is a small tool that helps you check your configuration file for errors.

Setting up Samba involves the following steps:

1. Compile and install the Samba programs if they are not already present on your system.

2. Write the Samba configuration file *smb.conf* and check it for correctness.

3. Start the two Samba daemons *smbd* and *nmdb*.

If you successfully set up your system, the directories you select will appear in the browse lists of the Windows users on your local network—normally accessed by clicking on the Network Neighborhood icon on Windows. The users on those systems will be able to read and write files according to your security settings just as they do on their local systems.

Installing Samba

Most Linux distributions nowadays contain Samba, and you can install it simply by choosing an option when installing Linux. If your distribution doesn't have Samba, you can get it from *ftp://ftp.samba.org*. It comes with installation instructions. Follow those instructions and build the package. During the configuration, you will have to decide where the configuration file *smb.conf* should reside. We will assume here that you pick */etc/smb.conf*. If you choose a different location, you will have to substitute that location in the following description.

The next step is to create a *smb.conf* file that is suitable for your system. There are graphical configuration tools available for Samba, including the nifty, web-based SWAT (Samba Web Administration Tool), but as always, it's good to know what goes on under the hood in case the graphical configuration tools get things wrong.

Samba comes with several sample configuration files that you can simply take and adapt to your situation. But it is not difficult to write one from scratch, either. In this section, we will assume that you want to provide your unfortunate Windows colleagues with the home directories of your machine, your printers, and a CD-ROM drive mounted on */cdrom*—a quite common setup.

The format of the *smb.conf* file is like the one used by Windows 3.x: there are entries of the type:

```
key = value
```

which are put into groups. A group starts with a line like the following:

```
[groupname]
```

Each directory or printer you share is called a service in Windows networking terminology. You can specify each service as a separate group name, but we'll show you some ways to simplify the configuration file and support lots of services in a few lines. One special group called [global] contains parameters that apply to all services. While Samba literally understands hundreds of parameters (keys), it is very likely that you will need to use only a few of them, because most of them have reasonable defaults. If you are curious which keys are available or are looking for a special parameter, you can check the manual page *smb.conf*.

smb.conf (5)

For starters, we will now create a minimal *smb.conf* that looks as follows:

```
workgroup = your workgroup

[homes]
guest ok = no
read only = no
```

This does not do much yet, but it serves two purposes: You can check your Samba installation, and you can get used to a test tool called *testparm* that is used to check the validity of your *smb.conf* file.

We assume here that you have already started the Samba daemons as described later. If your distribution contains Samba, and you have opted to install it during the installation, this might already have been done for you.

You can now test your Samba installation by issuing a command like the following (replace TIGGER with the hostname of your computer in capitals):

```
tigger# nmblookup TIGGER
Added interface ip=192.168.0.3 bcast=192.168.0.255 nmask=255.255.255.0
Sending queries to 192.168.0.255
192.168.0.3 TIGGER
```

You should get an output similar to the previous example. If you don't get it, here are some things to check:

- Check whether Samba can find your *smb.conf* file. If you installed Samba during the installation of your Linux system, you should check the documentation of your distribution for the location where the Samba package is looking for its configuration file. A common place is */etc/smb.conf,* but others are possible as well. If you have compiled Samba yourself, you might have specified during the configuration where Samba should look for *smb.conf* and hopefully remember this location now. If you did not make any changes to the setup files while building and installing Samba, the configuration file is being searched for in */usr/local/samba/lib/smb.conf.*

- Check whether *smbd* and (more important for this test) *nmbd* are in fact running.

- Samba might not have autodetected the network interface to use. Try adding a line like:

  ```
  interfaces = your IP address
  ```

  to your *smb.conf* file to tell Samba explicitly which interface to use.

- *nmbd* might not be able to find out the NetBIOS name (which by default is the hostname in capitals). You can try stopping your *nmbd* and restarting it with the option -n, followed by the NetBIOS name.

Once you see a successful result from the *nmblookup* command, you can start to explore what you get from the sample *smb.conf* file we shipped. Short as it is, it's sophisticated enough to let Samba serve home directories. Check the service with the command *smbclient*, which is like a small FTP client for SMB servers. Try the following (replacing TIGGER with your hostname in capitals and kalle with your user name):

```
tigger$ smbclient \\\\TIGGER\\kalle
Added interface ip=192.168.0.3 bcast=192.168.0.255 nmask=255.255.255.0
Server time is Thu Mar 11 23:49:53 1999
Timezone is UTC+1.0
Password:
Domain=[THE TIGERS] OS=[Unix] Server=[Samba 1.9.16p10]
smb: \>
```

Samba asks for your password and then "logs you in" to your home directory. Since that's probably where you issued the *smbclient* command from anyway, you have not gained much, but now you know that your Samba installation really works, and you can continue tuning your installation.

The program *testparm*, checks your *smb.conf* for errors and inconsistencies. A run should look roughly as follows:

```
tigger$ testparm
Load smb config files from /etc/smb.conf
Processing section "[homes]"
Loaded services file OK.
Press enter to see a dump of your service definitions
```

testparm tells you where it is looking for the configuration file, which services it has found, and whether it has found any errors in the configuration file. If it does not report Loaded services file OK., it will tell you the errors so that you can correct them and try again.

After succeeding in reading the configuration file, *testparm* offers to show you all service definitions. This is a lengthy list of all services defined together with all their parameters, not only the parameters you specified, but also those that are defaulted. Since the output can be very, very long, we won't bother repeating it here, but it can be very useful for you to check whether the parameters are really as you expect them to be.

Configuring Samba

Now that you have a rudimentary Samba installation, we can look at a more full-blown *smb.conf*:

```
[global]
   workgroup = The tigers
   guest account = nobody
   keep alive = 30
   printing = bsd
   printcap name = /etc/printcap
   load printers = yes
   print command = /usr/bin/lpr -r -P%p %s
   lpq command = /usr/bin/lpq -P%p
   lprm command = /usr/bin/lprm -P%p %j
   preserve case = yes
   short preserve case = yes
```

```
       case sensitive = no

[homes]
   comment = Home directory
   browseable = yes
   read only = no
   create mode = 0750

[usr]
   comment = /usr
   browseable = yes
   read only = no
   create mode = 0750
   directory = /usr

[cdrom]
   comment = Linux CD-ROM
   path = /cdrom
   read only = yes
   locking = no

[printers]
   comment = All Printers
   browseable = yes
   printable = yes
   public = no
   read only = yes
   create mode = 0700
   directory = /tmp
```

We will not cover every single line here, but go through everything that is important for you to set up your own Samba server.

First, you need to know that there are three sections that are special: [global], [homes], and [printers]. Samba treats those sections slightly differently from the others. The section [global] contains parameters that apply to all services. For example, workgroup specifies the workgroup the Samba server is supposed to be in. If you have Windows networking experience, you might already know that in Windows networking, all computers belong to a certain workgroup and can access services only from computers in the same workgroup. Therefore, you have to make sure that you enter the same workgroup here as the one you entered on your Windows machines.

guest account is important only if you allow guest access to services. A guest is anyone on your network who has no account on your system; you may want to provide a special directory for them in the same way that some sites provide anonymous FTP access. In this case, the account specified here will provide the rights for the guest. keep alive specifies the interval in which the server checks whether a client connected to it is still alive and responding. This value can be between 0 (no checks) and 60 seconds. If your network is reliable enough, you can afford to set this to 0.

For now, we'll skip a few parameters that apply to printing services and cover them later. `preserve case`, `short preserve case`, and `case sensitive` specify how Samba should handle the fact that filenames on Unix systems are case sensitive while those on Windows are case insensitive. The settings shown in the previous example have proven very useful when you want to read and write files from both Unix and Windows, because they keep the case when saving (by default, everything would be saved with lowercase characters), but when looking for a file, matching is done without regard to case, as expected by Windows.

The following sections describe services that the Samba server provides to its clients. We'll start with `[usr]` and `[cdrom]` here, because those are straightforward entries applying to individual services. (`[homes]` and `[printers]` are special cases covering a number of services).

The group `[usr]` makes a directory available to Windows. In this case, the directory is named */usr*, but naming the service after the directory is just an administrative convenience. Because the service is named `usr`, it will show up in the users' browse lists (Network Neighborhood) that way. You could also have named the service `clinton` by describing it in the group `[clinton]`, but in that case the service would be announced as `clinton` to the clients in the Network Neighborhood window.

To make sure our share is visible in the browse list, we have set the value of the `browsable` parameter to `yes`. If we had not set this, you could still access the service, but you would have to know what it is called and could not access it via the browse list. `read only` specifies, of course, whether the clients may write to the directory tree provided by this service. Note that even if this value is `no`, users still need the usual Unix permissions to be able to read and write anything from that service. `create mode` specifies the permissions that files newly created by a client on this service will get. `directory` specifies the root of the directory tree to be exported by this service. Note that whether it is useful to export /usr to Windows machines depends on what you have stored there. If you keep only Linux programs and their utility files there, this is not useful, of course. Finally, `comment` specifies a string that is shown in the Properties dialog in Windows or in the detail view.

The service `cdrom` makes the Linux CD-ROM drive accessible to Windows clients. It has about the same format as `usr`, but of course specifies `read only = yes`, because you cannot write to a CD-ROM. `locking = no` means that Samba will not use locks to prevent one user from overwriting the files of another user; in this case the value makes sense because nobody can write to a CD-ROM and locking wastes time.

Now let's go to the more interesting sections. The section `[homes]` is special, because it does not describe a single service but a number of possible services. Use it to give each of your users a directory of his own that can be accessed from Windows systems on your LAN.

Each user to whom you want to offer a directory should have an account on your system; to make configuration easy, make the account name and the home directory the same as the login name the user has on the Windows network. All you need after that is a properly configured Samba with a [homes] section like the one shown in our example.

Whenever a user on a Windows client connects to the service, Samba checks the user name and asks for the password (which is then entered in a Windows dialog) and provides the home directory of the user. Thus, when a connection is set up, Samba creates a so-called *virtual service* for the home directory of the user in question. This is very useful, because you do not have to tell Samba explicitly about new users when you add them to your Unix system: once a user account is created and has a home directory, the user can access this home directory from Windows.

Chapter 8

This leaves us with the printing services. You can configure each printer that is configured on your Linux box separately, but in general, it is much easier to use the [printers] section. Just as [homes] specifies a number of file access services (each home directory), [printers] specifies a number of printing services: access is allowed to each printer configured in */etc/printcap*. As explained in "Managing Print Services" in Chapter 8, *Other Administrative Tasks*, the *printcap* file lists all the printers on your system and how they are accessed.

For the [printers] section to work, you need to set load printers = yes in the [global] section, which tells Samba to read */etc/printcap* to see which printers are available. Other important values in the global section with respect to printing are printing, which specifies the type of printer service your Linux box uses (normally bsd, the default) and printcap name, which tells Samba where your printer capabilities or *printcap* file is located. On Linux, the printer capabilities files is almost always */etc/printcap*, which is also the default used by Samba. If you use the alternative LPRng printing system, you must specify lprng here. There are other possibilities that are less likely to be used on Linux listed in the *smb.conf* manual page.

smb.conf (5)

You also need to specify in the [global] section which commands Samba can use to send files to the printer. These commands are simply those that would be issued on the command line by a user on your system, with placeholders (macros) beginning with % to refer to filenames and other changing parameters. The values shown in the example are crafted for a BSD printing system and are probably useful for you, too. They make use of a number of macros that Samba expands automatically when reading the configuration file: %p specifies the printer name, %s the name of the file to print and %j the job number of the print job. For more macros, please see the *smb.conf* manual page.

Most parameters in the [printers] section have already been explained, but there remains a very important one: printable = yes tells Samba that this section specifies printing services and not file services. Printer services should always be set to read-only, otherwise malicious users could interfere with other users' print jobs. The `directory` parameter specifies where Samba should store the temporary printing files.

Note that setting up the printing service on the Samba side is not enough to be able to print from Windows. You also need to configure a printer on all Windows clients and use a suitable printer driver for the printer in question. Samba supports the automatic installation of printer drivers onto Windows 95 and Windows 98 machines; read the manual page *smb.conf* for further details (look for the `printer driver file` option).

After you have made changes to your Samba configuration file, it is always a good idea to check the syntax with *testparm*, at least to ensure you haven't introduced a spelling or syntax error. You will probably also want to look at the values *testparm* outputs for all the parameters. There is also a tiny program called *testprns* that checks the validity of printer names, but it is not as helpful as *testparm*.

Normally, the Samba daemons *smbd* and *nmbd* should automatically reread the configuration file when it has been changed, but this does not always work correctly. You can always send the daemons the HUP signal to make them reread the *smb.conf* file, though:

```
tigger# killall -HUP smbd
tigger# killall -HUP nmbd
```

We have covered only a small number of the hundreds of options that Samba provides, but with the facts given here, you should already be able to set up file and printing services for Windows clients for a lot of situations, and you can always read up on further details in the Samba documentation.

Starting Samba

Depending on your distribution, there may already be a script to start the Samba service. In this case, it is best to use that script. For example, on Red Hat systems, you can start the Samba server (provided that you have installed the Samba package) with:

```
tigger# /etc/rc.d/smb start
```

and shut it down with:

```
tigger# /etc/rc.d/smb stop
```

On SuSE, the *smb* daemon is located by default in */sbin/init.d/smb* instead of */etc/rc.d/smb*, on Debian, it is */etc/init.d/samba*.

If you have installed Samba yourself, you have two options. You can either have the Samba daemons started by *inetd* or simply start them from the command line.

nmbd (8)

Since the latter is used more often and is better for testing, we describe that option here. The manual pages for *smbd* and *nmbd* describe how to use *inetd*.

To run Samba from the command line, simply start the daemon by entering the following commands (assuming that you have installed the Samba daemons in */usr/sbin*):

```
tigger# /usr/sbin/nmbd
tigger# /usr/sbin/smbd
```

Once you know that your Samba server works, you should start the daemons with the option *−D* which tells them to detach themselves from the shell they were started from, the normal mode of operation for a daemon:

```
tigger# /usr/sbin/nmbd -D
tigger# /usr/sbin/smbd -D
```

This also allows you to close the shell without killing the daemons.

The Samba daemons have a number of other options, but you can probably do without them; if necessary, you will find all the information in the manual pages. We have only touched the surface here of what Samba can do, but this should already give you an impression why Samba—despite being not specifically developed for Linux—is one of the software packages that have made Linux famous.

Utilities for Accessing DOS Filesystems: MTools

Most Linux users who want to run Linux programs on Windows files can do so simply by mounting their Windows partitions as we described earlier in the section "Mounting DOS, VFAT, and NTFS Partitions." Once you set up the mount correctly, you can use standard shell commands to move around in the directories and run *vi*, Perl scripts, or whatever other programs you know and love.

Before Linux contained support for nonnative file systems, a set of programs called MTools was quite important. It was a collection of simple commands that let you manipulate Windows directories and files while running Linux. Now, the main use we've found for MTools is to access Windows-formatted floppy disks, because MTools remove the need to mount the floppy disk just to read a file from it. Using Windows-formatted floppy disks can be a very useful and efficient way to transport smaller amounts of data from a Windows machine to a Linux machine and back if the two are not networked.

Here are summaries of the MTools utilities; they are further documented in manual pages that are part of the distribution:

mattrib
    Changes attributes of a Windows file

mcd
> Changes to a Windows directory

mcopy
> Copies files from Linux to Windows or from Windows to Linux

mdel
> Deletes a Windows file

mdir
> Displays a Windows directory

mformat
> Creates a Windows FAT filesystem on a floppy

mlabel
> Writes a Windows disk volume label to a Windows partition

mmd
> Creates a Windows directory

mrd
> Removes a Windows directory

mread
> Reads a Windows file to Linux

mren
> Renames a Windows file

mtype
> Displays the contents of a Windows file

mwrite
> Writes a Linux file to Windows

File Translation Utilities

As we already mentioned, one of the most prominent problems when it comes to sharing files between Linux and Windows is that the two systems have different conventions for the line endings in text files. Luckily, there are a few ways to solve this problem:

- If you access files on a mounted partition on the same machine, let the kernel convert the files automatically as described in the section "Mounting DOS, VFAT, and NTFS Partitions" earlier in this chapter. Use this with care!

- Sophisticated editors like Emacs can handle the conversion automatically at either load or save time for you.

- There are a number of small tools available that convert files from one line-end convention to the other. Some of these tools can also handle other conversion tasks as well.

We will look here at two of the small utilities mentioned here: *duconv* and *recode*.

duconv is a tiny program available with most distributions that converts the line-ends and can also convert some special characters used in European languages from their DOS encoding to their Unix encoding. Note that the latter is not necessary with text files written on newer versions of Windows (like Windows 95 and Windows 98), because Windows uses the same encoding for those special characters as Unix does, the international standard ISO Latin-1, also known as ISO 8859-1.

In order to convert a Windows text file to a Unix text file, call *duconv* as follows:

```
duconv -u dos_text_file unix_text_file
```

To convert the other way around (from Unix to Windows), use the option –d:

```
duconv -d unix_text_file dos_text_file
```

duconv is a nice little utility, but if you need something more full-blown, you should go for the GNU project's *recode*. This is a program that can convert just about any text-file standard to any other text-file standard. *recode* isn't as easy to use as *duconv*, however.

The normal way to use *recode* is to specify both the old and the new character sets (encodings of text file conventions) and the file to convert. *recode* will overwrite the old file with the converted one; it will have the same file name. For example, in order to convert a text file from Windows to Unix, you would enter:

```
recode ibmpc:latin1 textfile
```

textfile is then replaced by the converted version. You can probably guess that to convert the same file back to Windows conventions, you would use:

```
recode latin1:ibmpc textfile
```

In addition to `ibmpc` (as used on Windows) and `latin1` (as used on Unix), there are other possibilities available, among others `latex` for the LaTeX style of encoding diacritics (see TeX and LaTeX) and `texte` for encoding French email messages. You can get the full list by issuing:

```
recode -l
```

If you do not like *recode*'s habit of overwriting your old file with the new one, you can make use of the fact that *recode* can also read from standard input and write to standard output. To convert *dostextfile* to *unixtextfile* without deleting *dostextfile*, you could do:

```
recode ibmpc:latin1 < dostextfile > unixtextfile
```

With the two tools just described, you can handle text files quite comfortably, but this is only the beginning. Things are less easy when it comes to other files. For example, pixel graphics on Windows are usually saved as *bmp* files, which are very uncommon on Unix. Fortunately, there are a number of tools available that can convert *bmp* files to graphics file formats like *xpm* that are more common on Unix. Among these are the shareware image viewer and manipulation package *xv*, which is probably included with your distribution.

Things become even more hairy when it comes to proprietary file formats like those saved by office productivity programs. While the various incarnations of the *doc* file format of the Word for Windows word processor have become a de facto lingua franca for word processor files on Windows, until recently, it was hardly possible to read those files on Linux. Fortunately, a number of software packages have appeared lately that can read (and sometimes even write) those files. Among those are the word processor WordPerfect, the office productivity suite StarOffice, and the office productivity suite ApplixWare. Be aware though, that these conversions will never be perfect; it is very likely that you will have to edit the files by hand afterwards.

In general, the more common a file format is on Windows, the more likely it is that Linux developers will provide a means to read or even write those file formats as well. This might also be a good occasion to switch to open file formats like RTF (Rich Text Format) or XML (Extensible Markup Language) when you're on Windows, too. In the age of the Internet, where information is supposed to float freely, closed, nondocumented file formats are an anachronism.

Sharing Programs

The most popular non-Linux operating systems where compatibility is important—where people want to run its programs and files on Linux—are derivates of DOS: MS-DOS, PC-DOS, Novell DOS, and Windows 3.1 and later. You can use the Linux MTools package to search DOS filesystems, read and copy files, and write to a DOS filesystem. Still, compatibility with DOS obviously requires a lot more than handling a DOS filesystem.

There are two packages intended to provide Linux with the desired DOS compatibility. One is Dosemu and the other is Wine. We discuss them both in this chapter because of their importance to the Linux community.

It should be noted, though, that neither Dosemu nor Wine are finished products. While both development teams have made amazing progress, given the difficulty of their task, you should use them currently only if you are willing to fiddle around with them, trying to reconfigure things, and perhaps even trying to find and fix bugs. If you'd rather try a finished, commercial product, you can buy WABI (Windows Application Binary Interface) from Caldera, Inc., which is a port of the same product for Solaris and is quite stable, but it can run only Windows 3.1 programs.

Another remark: Two years ago, binary emulators like Dosemu and Wine were of utmost importance to the Linux community, because there was not much commercial software available. This situation has utterly changed, however. Many commercial software vendors are providing their products for Linux now, so you might be able to get what you want without running an emulator. Remember that emulation takes its toll; no emulated program can be faster or more stable than a native one.

Recently, new life was breathed into Wine because Corel announced that they would port their products (like CorelDRAW) to Linux by means of Wine, that is, they would support the further development of Wine. This is a notable acceptance of the outstanding work of the Wine team, but it remains to be seen whether these plans will be successful.

The development teams working on Dosemu and Wine are delighted to encourage more developers to pitch in and help, but if you are simply an end user, or a programmer with no access to the Internet and thus no ready access to the developer community, these packages may not be right for you.

There are also emulators for the Apple II and CP/M operating systems, as well as many other machines long forgotten by most users. They originally were run on other operating systems (such as MS-DOS) and have now been ported to Linux. You can get them from the usual Linux FTP sites that archive the emulator software, which are primarily *ftp://ftp.metalab.unc.edu* and its mirror sites in the path */pub/Linux/system/emulators*.

A demo of a commercial (but low-priced) Macintosh emulator is also available from *http://www.ardi.com* called Executor/Linux. This is a Linux version of a package that has been offered for several years on NeXT machines, and for more than a year on DOS machines. You might try it if only to gain the ability to read and write Mac floppy and SCSI disk formats, which the demo package provides. (The developers of this product have announced that they will release the source code for their Mac file browser to the public.)

If you want to keep up with developments on Executor/Linux, send mail to *majordomo@nacm.com* with nothing in the `Subject:` field, and with the message text `subscribe executor`.

DOS Emulators: Dosemu and xdos

First, we should make it clear that Linux's "DOS emulators," the Dosemu and *xdos* packages, aren't really emulators. They can be considered virtual machines that allow DOS and applications running on DOS to execute in real mode (virtual 8086 mode) in a "compatibility box" environment similar to the operation of DOS on a standard Intel 80286 or 80386. Because a necessary element of the compatibility box is the virtual 8086, only chipsets that implement the Intel real mode will ever have Dosemu or *xdos* ported to them. *xdos* is just a convenient wrapper for Dosemu that lets you run it in an X window, so for this discussion we'll focus primarily on Dosemu.

You should have 8 MB of RAM to use Dosemu, and it would be wise to also have a 12 MB swap partition set up on the hard disk.

Dosemu emulates the BIOS, CMOS memory, XMS and EMS memory, disk services, keyboard, serial devices and printer, and other necessary machine functions, letting DOS work in this controlled environment. Dosemu requires that you have a (licensed) copy of either OpenDOS (formerly known as DR-DOS) or MS-DOS 6.22, but other versions might work as well. Since OpenDOS is freely available, it is preferred by the Dosemu developers.

Dosemu tries to trap DOS and BIOS system calls and handle them in Linux, but it isn't always successful in doing this. DOS BIOS printer services are emulated with Unix file I/O, with the output intended for a printer spooled to a corresponding Linux file. Dosemu has problems with mouse support for some mice, particularly busmouse systems.

We don't encourage you to use Dosemu unless you are willing and able to contribute to the further development of the package and have Internet access to work with the development team. However, Dosemu appears to be useful enough and stable enough to justify discussing it as a package you should consider installing. You should be aware, though, that the development of documentation for Dosemu lags behind the development of software. If you aren't involved in Dosemu development, you may find it difficult to use new features; they may not be that safe anyhow.

More recent versions of Dosemu include some functions originally developed as part of Carnegie Mellon University's DOS emulator for Mach, so Dosemu distributions include the nonrestrictive CMU copyright notice. This notice asks that developers who build software using CMU's work provide a copy of their work to CMU and allow CMU the right to use and redistribute it. (The copyright notice *requires* that their notice be reproduced and included in any distribution that uses their software, whether or not their code is modified.) You should honor CMU's copyright, so if you will participate in developing Dosemu, be sure to read and observe its copyright notice.

The Dosemu package includes scripts and utilities to install and maintain the package. Dosemu is updated weekly, and each distribution includes a list of software known to run (or not to run) with the current release of the package.

Getting Dosemu and xdos

The FTP site guaranteed to maintain the latest public version of the Dosemu package is *ftp://tsx-11.mit.edu*. The files can be found in the */pub/linux/ALPHA/dosemu* directory. ("Alpha" refers to the state of development of the application, not to a distribution for Alpha architecture Linux.) This includes the most recent documentation files.

Dosemu does not itself support compressed filesystems, but you can use a special driver in the Linux kernel that can mount compressed filesystems and then access those mounted filesystems from within Dosemu.

Installing and Configuring Dosemu

Before you install the Dosemu package, you must first compile the Linux kernel with IPC (System V InterProcess Communication facilities). If you did not build Linux with IPC during the configuration process when installing Linux, you will have to rebuild the kernel to add the facilities before installing Dosemu, which uses System V–shared memory. We strongly recommend that you use a current release of Linux as a basis for running Dosemu and compile Dosemu with a current *gcc* compiler and libraries. Linux 2.0.28/2.1.15 and later include the needed kernel support for Dosemu.

You must have *gcc* Version 2.7.2 and *libc* Version 5.4.7 or later for this version of Dosemu. Later versions of Dosemu may require later versions of Linux, *gcc*, and C libraries.

Boot Linux and login as **root**. Place the Dosemu package in the / root directory and unpack it. (The Dosemu package name may vary from this example, whose name reflects our downloading the file via DOS before copying it into the Linux filesystem):

```
# gunzip dosemu-0.98.4.tgz
# tar -xvf dosemu-0.98.4.tar
```

The files unpack into the directory *dosemu-0.98.4* and its subdirectories.

Now read the documentation. A Dosemu HOWTO file comes with the distribution package in the */dosemu-0.98.4/doc* directory. Also read the file *QuickStart* that comes with the distribution. A script *ViewDocs* provided with Dosemu lets you view the documentation comfortably.

A file named *DANG* (Dosemu Novice's Altering Guide) contains notes for customizing source code. This file is extracted automatically from the source code itself, at each release. Additionally, the *dos(1)* manual page describes the state of the *dos* command for your version of Dosemu. There is a Texinfo document for Dosemu (*dosemu.texinfo*) that lags well behind the current state of development of the package. It contains information useful in preparing to install the Dosemu package.

If you need to rebuild your kernel to add IPC and DOS filesystem support and to install a kernel patch, do it now.

Still as **root**, go to the *dosemu-0.98.4* directory and verify that the distribution Makefile exists there. Enter the commands:

```
# make
# make install
```

You can now try your newly installed Dosemu with a tiny provided FreeDOS image by issuing:

```
# ./first-test
C:> exitemu
```

If this works for you, your Dosemu is probably built correctly.

Next, you will have to copy and edit some configuration files:

- Copy the file *etc/dosemu.conf* to */etc/dosemu.conf* and modify this file according to the documentation. Be sure to read the documentation, especially the file *doc/README.txt* to do this. You might also want to leave it as it is for now and come back here once you have gotten a little bit more feel for Dosemu.

- Depending on your security needs, copy either *etc/dosemu.users.easy* or *etc/dosemu.users.secure* to */etc/dosemu.users* and edit this file according to your needs.

Next, you need to create a DOS boot image. If you have a contemporary version of the MTools package (Version 3.8 or newer) and a bootable DOS partition or DOS boot floppy, you can run the program *setup-hdimage* provided with the Dosemu distribution as in the following example:

```
tigger: # ./setup-hdimage
checking your partitions, wait...
...done
I've seen the following DOS partitions (perhaps non-bootable):

    /dev/sdc1

If none of them are valid, you can continue any way using a bootable
floppy as input. Which one do you want to use as input?
Type in the full device name or ENTER to cancel
```

```
/dev/fd0

A normal MSDOS system has command.com as shell.
If you have a different one, please enter the name,
else just type ENTER



We now try to generate a bootable hdimage into /var/lib/dosemu/
hdimage.first and are calling ./dexe/mkdexe for this.

You will be prompted to edit the configuration files
(config.sys, autoexec.bat e.t.c).

Enter the name of your favorite editor, if you type just ENTER, the
editor given via the EDITOR environment variable will be used.



Starting ...
System type is IBMorOpenDos. sysfiles: ibmbio.com, ibmdos.com, command.com
1+0 records in
1+0 records out
Cannot create entry named . or ..

Skipping "config.sys", is not a directory

Skipping "autoexec.bat", is not a directory
 ... done
```

In this case, we use a bootable OpenDOS floppy disk. If everything goes well, the file */var/lib/dosemu/hdimage.first* should be generated and contain your DOS boot image. If there are problems, you might need to use the old method of creating a boot image; see the file *doc/README-tech.txt*, section 7, in the Dosemu distribution.

Next, check that there is a line like:

```
$_hdimage = "hdimage.first"
```

in your */etc/dosemu.conf*. There can be more than one image file present here, but *hdimage.first* should be the first one mentioned.

Now you are ready to start your Dosemu with:

```
dosemu -C
```

Dosemu should come up with something like:

```
Linux DOS emulator 0.98.4.0 $Date: 1999/08/05 02:46:39 $
Last configured at Mon Mar 22 13:05:19 CET 1999 on linux
This is work in progress.
Please test against a recent version before reporting bugs and problems.
Bugs, Patches & New Code to linux-msdos@vger.rutgers.edu
```

```
Starting DOS...

[Host File System] drive D: is directory /
[dosemu EMS 4.0 driver installed]

Caldera OpenDOS 7.01
Copyright (c) 1976, 1997 Caldera, Inc.
All rights reserved.

"Welcome to dosemu 0.98!"
C:\>
```

Now you are ready to try your DOS emulator. Be sure to read the documentation to see the many possibilities of configuring Dosemu. By editing */etc/dosemu.conf*, you can quickly solve problems that occur with specific DOS software, terminal modes, sound system support, and the like. You can add pointers to additional DOS directories on hard disks. When you are done working with Dosemu, you can exit it with:

```
C:\> exitemu
```

If you want to start Dosemu in an X window of its own, you can run the program *xdos* instead. You might need to execute:

```
xset fp rehash
```

first to make the newly installed DOS fonts available.

If you are adventurous, you can now even try to run Windows 3.x in real mode by installing it into your DOS hard-disk image and then typing:

```
win /r
```

Windows Emulation: Wine

Wine is the most ambitious DOS/Windows compatibility package, and it bears tremendous potential value to the Linux community. Wine is inspired by WABI, which originally was developed by Sun Microsystems to allow Microsoft Windows packages to run directly on Solaris. WABI has been licensed by Sun to other System V ports to the Intel PC, and a WABI development group comprised of several Unix vendors guides further the development of WABI. No Linux vendor that we are aware of is a member of the WABI development group. However, Caldera has licensed WABI from SunSoft. The WABI specifications are made available to the public, and the Linux Dosemu team has applied them to the Wine development effort. Wine is being developed for Linux, NetBSD, and FreeBSD at this time, and the first commercial support has been announced by Corel.

You need at least 16 MB of RAM to use Wine, and at least a 32 MB swap partition set up on the hard disk.

Wine consists primarily of a program loader that loads and executes 16-bit MS Windows application binaries and an emulation library that translates calls to MS Windows functions and translates them into Linux and X Window System function calls. As the Wine FAQ notes, Wine means either "WINdows Emulator, or Wine Is Not an Emulator. Both are right." When Wine is fully developed, most Windows applications will run under Wine in the Linux/X environment and will run about as fast under Wine as they do under windows. Maybe faster. A Linux-supported graphics coprocessor makes the X Window System perform a lot better and therefore makes a big difference to Wine performance.

At the time of this writing, Wine support for the Win32 ABI (used by 32-bit Windows 95 and NT applications) is progressing. Ultimately, Wine developers hope that it will be able to run both 16- and 32-bit Windows applications.

Wine is filesystem independent and can be used on any Linux (or Unix) filesystem. You must use the X Window System to run Wine; Wine is invoked from a window opened by your favorite Linux window manager:

```
wine /pathname/winapp.exe
```

where *pathname* is either a Linux- or a DOS-style pathname and *winapp.exe* is a Windows-based executable.

We can't encourage you to use Wine at this time unless you are a programmer who will contribute to the further development of this ambitious package. Wine is very much in alpha-stage development. As of this writing, Wine does not implement all of the MS-Windows application programming interface (API) functions. Because we think you won't be able to use Wine effectively at this stage unless you are a programmer with Internet access who can contribute to the project, we don't discuss how to install and configure Wine.

If you want to join the Wine developers team or are just looking for more information, your best bet is to check the Wine Headquarters web site at *http://www.winehq.com*; this is also where you can download the most current version of Wine.

CHAPTER THIRTEEN
PROGRAMMING LANGUAGES

There's much more to Linux than simply using the system. One of the benefits of free software is that it can be modified to suit the user's needs. This applies equally to the many free applications available for Linux and to the Linux kernel itself.

Linux supports an advanced programming interface, using GNU compilers and tools, such as the *gcc* compiler, the *gdb* debugger, and so on. A number of other programming languages, including Perl, Tcl/Tk, and LISP, are also supported. Whatever your programming needs, Linux is a great choice for developing Unix applications. Because the complete source code for the libraries and Linux kernel are provided, those programmers who need to delve into the system internals are able to do so.*

Chapter 10

Linux is an ideal platform for developing software to run under the X Window System. The Linux X distribution, as described in Chapter 10, *Installing the X Window System*, is a complete implementation with everything you need to develop and support X applications. Programming for X itself is portable across applications, so the X-specific portions of your application should compile cleanly on other Unix systems.

In this chapter, we'll explore the Linux programming environment and give you a five-cent tour of the many facilities it provides. Half of the trick to Unix programming is knowing what tools are available and how to use them effectively. Often the most useful features of these tools are not obvious to new users.

Since C programming has been the basis of most large projects (even though it is nowadays being replaced more and more by C++) and is the language common to most modern programmers—not only on Unix, but on many other systems as

---

* On a variety of Unix systems, the authors have repeatedly found available documentation to be insufficient. With Linux, you can explore the very source code for the kernel, libraries, and system utilities. Having access to source code is more important than most programmers would think.

well—we'll start out telling you what tools are available for that. The first few sections of the chapter assume you are already a C programmer.

But several other tools are emerging as important resources, especially for system administration. We'll examine two in this chapter: Perl and Tcl/Tk. They are both scripting languages like the Unix shells, taking care of grunt work like memory allocation, so you can concentrate on your task. But both Perl and Tcl/Tk offer a degree of sophistication that makes them more powerful than shell scripts and appropriate for many programming tasks.

Lots of programmers are excited about trying out Java, the new language from Sun Microsystems. While most people associate Java with interactive programs (applets) on web pages, it is actually a general-purpose language with many potential Internet uses. In a later section, we'll explore what Java offers above and beyond older programming languages and how to get started.

Programming with gcc

The C programming language is by far the most used in Unix software development. Perhaps this is because the Unix system itself was originally developed in C; it is the native tongue of Unix. Unix C compilers have traditionally defined the interface standards for other languages and tools, such as linkers, debuggers, and so on. Conventions set forth by the original C compilers have remained fairly consistent across the Unix programming board. To know the C compiler is to know the Unix system itself. Before we get too abstract, let's get to details.

The GNU C compiler, *gcc*, is one of the most versatile and advanced compilers around. Unlike other C compilers (such as those shipped with the original AT&T or BSD distributions or from various third-party vendors), *gcc* supports all the modern C standards currently in use—such as the ANSI C standard—as well as many extensions specific to *gcc* itself. Happily, however, *gcc* provides features to make it compatible with older C compilers and older styles of C programming. There is even a tool called *protoize* that can help you write function prototypes for old-style C programs.

gcc is also a C++ compiler. For those of you who prefer the obscure object-oriented environment, C++ is supported with all of the bells and whistles—including AT&T 3.0 C++ features, such as method templates. Complete C++ class libraries are provided as well, such as the *iostream* library familiar to many programmers.

For those with a taste for the particularly esoteric, *gcc* also supports Objective-C, an object-oriented C spinoff that never gained much popularity. But the fun doesn't stop there, as we'll see.

There's also a new kid on the block, *egcs*. *egcs* is not a completely new compiler, but is based on *gcc*. *egcs* has some advanced optimization features and is especially strong when it comes to newer C++ features like templates and namespaces. If you are going to do serious C++ programming, you will probably want to check it out. Alas, there is a problem with Version 2.0.*x* kernels that prevents them from being compiled with *egcs*. Newer kernels from the 2.1.*x* and those from the 2.2.*x* don't have this problem. But because of this, some distributors have opted to include the traditional *gcc* for C compilation and *egcs* for C++. You can read more about *egcs* at *http://egcs.cygnus.com*.

The Free Software Foundation has recently announced that *egcs* will become their default compiler, thus replacing *egcs*' own ancestor *gcc*.

In this section, we're going to cover the use of *gcc* to compile and link programs under Linux. We assume you are familiar with programming in C/C++, but we don't assume you're accustomed to the Unix programming environment. That's what we'll introduce here.

Quick Overview

Before imparting all of the gritty details of *gcc* itself, we're going to present a simple example and walk through the steps of compiling a C program on a Unix system.

Let's say you have the following bit of code, an encore of the much-overused "Hello, World!" program (not that it bears repeating):

```
#include <stdio.h>
int main() {
  (void)printf("Hello, World!\n");
  return 0; /* Just to be nice */
}
```

To compile this program into a living, breathing executable, there are several steps. Most of these steps can be accomplished through a single *gcc* command, but the specifics are left for later in the chapter.

First, the *gcc* compiler must generate an *object file* from this *source code*. The object file is essentially the machine-code equivalent of the C source. It contains code to set up the *main()* calling stack, a call to the mysterious *printf()* function, and code to return the value of 0.

The next step is to *link* the object file to produce an executable. As you might guess, this is done by the *linker*. The job of the linker is to take object files, merge them with code from libraries, and spit out an executable. The object code from the previous source does not make a complete executable. First and foremost, the code for *printf()* must be linked in. Also, various initialization routines, invisible to the mortal programmer, must be appended to the executable.

Where does the code for *printf()* come from? Answer: the libraries. It is impossible to talk for long about *gcc* without making mention of them. A library is essentially a collection of many object files, including an index. When searching for the code for *printf()*, the linker looks at the index for each library it's been told to link against. It finds the object file containing the *printf()* function and extracts that object file (the entire object file, which may contain much more than just the *printf()* function) and links it to the executable.

In reality, things are more complicated than this. As we have said, Linux supports two kinds of libraries: *static* and *shared*. What we have described in this example are static libraries: libraries where the actual code for called subroutines is appended to the executable. However, the code for subroutines such as *printf()* can be quite lengthy. Because many programs use common subroutines from the libraries, it doesn't make sense for each executable to contain its own copy of the library code. That's where shared libraries come in.

With shared libraries, all of the common subroutine code is contained in a single library "image file" on disk. When a program is linked with a shared library, *stub code* is appended to the executable, instead of actual subroutine code. This stub code tells the program loader where to find the library code on disk, in the image file, at runtime. Therefore, when our friendly "Hello, World!" program is executed, the program loader notices that the program has been linked against a shared library. It then finds the shared library image and loads code for library routines, such as *printf()*, along with the code for the program itself. The stub code tells the loader where to find the code for *printf()* in the image file.

Even this is an oversimplification of what's really going on. Linux shared libraries use *jump tables* that allow the libraries to be upgraded and their contents to be jumbled around, without requiring the executables using these libraries to be relinked. The stub code in the executable actually looks up another reference in the library itself—in the jump table. In this way, the library contents and the corresponding jump tables can be changed, but the executable stub code can remain the same.

But don't allow yourself to be befuddled by all this abstract information. In time, we'll approach a real-life example and show you how to compile, link, and debug your programs. It's actually very simple; most of the details are taken care of for you by the *gcc* compiler itself. However, it helps to have an understanding of what's going on behind the scenes.

gcc Features

gcc has more features than we could possibly enumerate here. Later, we present a short list and refer the curious to the *gcc* manual page and Info document, which will undoubtedly give you an eyeful of interesting information about this compiler.

Later in this section, we'll give you a comprehensive overview of the most useful *gcc* features to get you started. This in hand, you should be able to figure out for yourself how to get the many other facilities to work to your advantage.

For starters, *gcc* supports the "standard" C syntax currently in use, specified for the most part by the ANSI C standard. The most important feature of this standard is function prototyping. That is, when defining a function *foo()*, which returns an int and takes two arguments, a (of type char *) and b (of type double), the function may be defined like this:

```
int foo(char *a, double b) {
  /* your code here... */
}
```

This is in contrast to the older, nonprototype function definition syntax, which looks like:

```
int foo(a, b)
char *a;
double b;
{
  /* your code here... */
}
```

[34] C Progr.
Language

which is also supported by *gcc*. Of course, ANSI C defines many other conventions, but this is the one most obvious to the new programmer. Anyone familiar with C programming style in modern books, such as the second edition of Kernighan and Ritchie's *The C Programming Language*, can program using *gcc* with no problem. (C compilers shipped on some other Unix systems do not support ANSI features such as prototyping.)

The *gcc* compiler boasts quite an impressive optimizer. Whereas most C compilers allow you to use the single switch *−O* to specify optimization, *gcc* supports multiple levels of optimization. At the highest level of optimization, *gcc* pulls tricks out of its sleeve such as allowing code and static data to be shared. That is, if you have a static string in your program such as Hello, World!, and the ASCII encoding of that string happens to coincide with a sequence of instruction code in your program, *gcc* allows the string data and the corresponding code to share the same storage. How's that for clever?

Of course, *gcc* allows you to compile debugging information into object files, which aids a debugger (and hence, the programmer) in tracing through the program. The compiler inserts markers in the object file, allowing the debugger to locate specific lines, variables, and functions in the compiled program. Therefore, when using a debugger, such as *gdb* (which we'll talk about later in the chapter), you can step through the compiled program and view the original source text simultaneously.

Among the other tricks offered by *gcc* is the ability to generate assembly code with the flick of a switch (literally). Instead of telling *gcc* to compile your source to machine code, you can ask it to stop at the assembly-language level, which is much easier for humans to comprehend. This happens to be a nice way to learn the intricacies of protected-mode assembly programming under Linux: write some C code, have *gcc* translate it into assembly language for you, and study that.

gcc includes its own assembler (which can be used independently of *gcc*), just in case you're wondering how this assembly-language code might get assembled. In fact, you can include inline assembly code in your C source, in case you need to invoke some particularly nasty magic but don't want to write exclusively in assembly.

Basic gcc Usage

By now, you must be itching to know how to invoke all these wonderful features. It is important, especially to novice Unix and C programmers, to know how to use *gcc* effectively. Using a command-line compiler such as *gcc* is quite different from, say, using a development system such as Borland C under MS-DOS. Even though the language syntax itself is similar, the methods used to compile and link programs are not at all the same.

Let's return to our innocent-looking "Hello, World!" example. How would you go about compiling and linking this program?

The first step, of course, is to enter the source code. This is accomplished with a text editor, such as Emacs or *vi*. The would-be programmer should enter the source code and save it in a file named something like *hello.c*. (As with most C compilers, *gcc* is picky about the filename extension; that is, how it can distinguish C source from assembly source from object files, and so on. The *.c* extension should be used for standard C source.)

To compile and link the program to the executable *hello*, the programmer would use the command:

```
papaya$ gcc -o hello hello.c
```

and (barring any errors), in one fell swoop, *gcc* compiles the source into an object file, links against the appropriate libraries, and spits out the executable *hello*, ready to run. In fact, the wary programmer might want to test it:

```
papaya$ ./hello
Hello, World!
papaya$
```

As friendly as can be expected.

Obviously, quite a few things took place behind the scenes when executing this single *gcc* command. First of all, *gcc* had to compile your source file, *hello.c*, into an object file, *hello.o*. Next, it had to link *hello.o* against the standard libraries and produce an executable.

By default, *gcc* assumes that not only do you want to compile the source files you specify but also that you want them linked together (with each other and with the standard libraries) to produce an executable. First, *gcc* compiles any source files into object files. Next, it automatically invokes the linker to glue all the object files and libraries into an executable. (That's right, the linker is a separate program, called *ld*, not part of *gcc* itself—although it can be said that *gcc* and *ld* are close friends.) *gcc* also knows about the "standard" libraries used by most programs and tells *ld* to link against them. You can, of course, override these defaults in various ways.

You can pass multiple filenames in one *gcc* command, but on large projects you'll find it more natural to compile a few files at a time and keep the *.o* object files around. If you want only to compile a source file into an object file and forego the linking process, use the *−c* switch with *gcc*, as in:

```
papaya$ gcc -c hello.c
```

This produces the object file *hello.o* and nothing else.

By default, the linker produces an executable named, of all things, *a.out*. By using the *−o* switch with *gcc*, you can force the resulting executable to be named something different, in this case, *hello*. This is just a bit of left-over gunk from early implementations of Unix, and nothing to write home about.

Using Multiple Source Files

The next step on your path to *gcc* enlightenment is to understand how to compile programs using multiple source files. Let's say you have a program consisting of two source files, *foo.c* and *bar.c*. Naturally, you would use one or more header files (such as *foo.b*) containing function declarations shared between the two programs. In this way, code in *foo.c* knows about functions in *bar.c*, and vice versa.

To compile these two source files and link them together (along with the libraries, of course) to produce the executable *baz*, you'd use the command:

```
papaya$ gcc -o baz foo.c bar.c
```

This is roughly equivalent to the three commands:

```
papaya$ gcc -c foo.c
papaya$ gcc -c bar.c
papaya$ gcc -o baz foo.o bar.o
```

gcc acts as a nice frontend to the linker and other "hidden" utilities invoked during compilation.

Of course, compiling a program using multiple source files in one command can be time consuming. If you had, say, five or more source files in your program, the *gcc* command in the previous example would recompile each source file in turn before linking the executable. This can be a large waste of time, especially if you only made modifications to a single source file since last compilation. There would be no reason to recompile the other source files, as their up-to-date object files are still intact.

The answer to this problem is to use a project manager such as *make*. We'll talk about *make* later in the chapter, in the section "Makefiles."

Optimizing

Telling *gcc* to optimize your code as it compiles is a simple matter; just use the *−O* switch on the *gcc* command line:

```
papaya$ gcc -O -o fishsticks fishsticks.c
```

As we mentioned not long ago, *gcc* supports different levels of optimization. Using *−O2* instead of *−O* will turn on several "expensive" optimizations that may cause compilation to run more slowly but will (hopefully) greatly enhance performance of your code.

You may notice in your dealings with Linux that a number of programs are compiled using the switch *−O6* (the Linux kernel being a good example). The current version of *gcc* does not support optimization up to *−O6*, so this defaults to (presently) the equivalent of *−O2*. However, *−O6* is sometimes used for compatibility with future versions of *gcc* to ensure that the greatest level of optimization is used.

Enabling Debugging Code

The *−g* switch to *gcc* turns on debugging code in your compiled object files. That is, extra information is added to the object file, as well as the resulting executable, allowing the program to be traced with a debugger such as *gdb* (which we'll get to later in the chapter—no worries). The downside to using debugging code is that it greatly increases the size of the resulting object files. It's usually best to use *−g* only while developing and testing your programs and to leave it out for the "final" compilation.

Happily, debug-enabled code is not incompatible with code optimization. This means that you can safely use the command:

```
papaya$ gcc -O -g -o mumble mumble.c
```

However, certain optimizations enabled by *−O* or *−O2* may cause the program to appear to behave erratically while under the guise of a debugger. It is usually best to use either *−O* or *−g*, not both.

More Fun with Libraries

Before we leave the realm of *gcc*, a few words on linking and libraries are in order. For one thing, it's easy for you to create your own libraries. If you have a set of routines you use often, you may wish to group them into a set of source files, compile each source file into an object file, and then create a library from the object files. This saves you having to compile these routines individually for each program you use them in.

Let's say you have a set of source files containing oft-used routines, such as:

```
float square(float x) {
  /* Code for square()... */
}

int factorial(int x, int n) {
  /* Code for factorial()... */
}
```

and so on (of course, the *gcc* standard libraries provide analogs to these common routines, so don't be misled by our choice of example). Furthermore, let's say that the code for *square()* is in the file *square.c* and that the code for *factorial()* is in *factorial.c*. Simple enough, right?

To produce a library containing these routines, all that you do is compile each source file, as so:

papaya$ **gcc -c square.c factorial.c**

which leaves you with *square.o* and *factorial.o*. Next, create a library from the object files. As it turns out, a library is just an archive file created using *ar* (a close counterpart to *tar*). Let's call our library *libstuff.a* and create it this way:

papaya$ **ar r libstuff.a square.o factorial.o**

When updating a library such as this, you may need to delete the old *libstuff.a*, if it exists. The last step is to generate an index for the library, which enables the linker to find routines within the library. To do this, use the *ranlib* command, as so:

papaya$ **ranlib libstuff.a**

This command adds information to the library itself; no separate index file is created. You could also combine the two steps of running *ar* and *ranlib* by using the s command to *ar*:

papaya$ **ar rs libstuff.a square.o factorial.o**

Now you have *libstuff.a*, a static library containing your routines. Before you can link programs against it, you'll need to create a header file describing the contents of the library. For example, we could create *libstuff.h* with the contents:

```
/* libstuff.h: routines in libstuff.a */
extern float square(float);
extern int factorial(int, int);
```

Every source file that uses routines from *libstuff.a* should contain an #include "libstuff.h" line, as you would do with standard header files.

Now that we have our library and header file, how do we compile programs to use them? First of all, we need to put the library and header file somewhere the compiler can find them. Many users place personal libraries in the directory *lib* in their home directory, and personal include files under *include*. Assuming we have done so, we can compile the mythical program *wibble.c* using the command:

papaya$ **gcc -I../include -L../lib -o wibble wibble.c -lstuff**

The *–I* option tells *gcc* to add the directory *../include* to the *include path* it uses to search for include files. *–L* is similar, in that it tells *gcc* to add the directory *../lib* to the *library path*.

The last argument on the command line is *–lstuff*, which tells the linker to link against the library *libstuff.a* (wherever it may be along the library path). The *lib* at the beginning of the filename is assumed for libraries.

Any time you wish to link against libraries other than the standard ones, you should use the *–l* switch on the *gcc* command line. For example, if you wish to use math routines (specified in *math.h*), you should add *–lm* to the end of the *gcc* command, which links against *libm*. Note, however, that the *order* of *–l* options is significant. For example, if our *libstuff* library used routines found in *libm*, you must include *–lm* after *–lstuff* on the command line:

papaya$ **gcc -Iinclude -Llib -o wibble wibble.c -lstuff -lm**

This forces the linker to link *libm* after *libstuff*, allowing those unresolved references in *libstuff* to be taken care of.

Where does *gcc* look for libraries? By default, libraries are searched for in a number of locations, the most important of which is */usr/lib*. If you take a glance at the contents of */usr/lib*, you'll notice it contains many library files—some of which have filenames ending in *.a*, others ending in *.so.version*. The *.a* files are static libraries, as is the case with our *libstuff.a*. The *.so* files are shared libraries, which contain code to be linked at runtime, as well as the stub code required for the runtime linker (*ld.so*) to locate the shared library.

At runtime, the program loader looks for shared library images in several places, including */lib*. If you look at */lib*, you'll see files such as *libc.so.5.4.47*. This is the image file containing the code for the *libc* shared library (one of the standard libraries, which most programs are linked against).

By default, the linker attempts to link against shared libraries. However, there are several cases in which static libraries are used. If you enable debugging code with –*g*, the program will be linked against the static libraries. You can also specify that static libraries should be linked by using the –*static* switch with *gcc*.

Creating shared libraries

Now that you know how to create and use static libraries, it's very easy to make the step to shared libraries. Shared libraries have a number of advantages. They reduce memory consumption if used by more than one process, and they reduce the size of the executable. Furthermore, they make developing easier: when you use shared libraries and change some things in a library, you do not need to recompile and relink your application each time. You need to relink only if you make incompatible changes, such as adding arguments to a call or changing the size of a struct.

Before you start doing all your development work with shared libraries, though, be warned that debugging with them is slightly more difficult than with static libraries, because the debugger usually used on Linux, *gdb*, has some problems with shared libraries.

Code that goes into a shared library needs to be position independent. This is a just a convention for object code that makes it possible to use the code in shared libraries. You make *gcc* emit position-independent code by passing it one of the command-line switches –*fpic* or –*fPIC* (the former is preferred, unless the modules have grown so large that the relocatable code table is simply too small in which case the compiler will emit an error message, and you have to use –*fPIC*. To repeat our example from the last section:

```
papaya$ gcc -c -fPIC square.c factorial.c
```

This being done, it is just a simple step to generate a shared library:*

```
papaya$ gcc -shared -o libstuff.so square.o factorial.o
```

Note the compiler switch –*shared*. There is no indexing step as with static libraries.

Using our newly created shared library is even simpler. The shared library doesn't require any change to the compile command:

```
papaya$ gcc -I../include -L../lib -o wibble wibble.c -lstuff -lm
```

You might wonder what the linker does if there is a shared library *libstuff.so* and a static library *llibstuff.a* available. In this case, the linker always picks the shared

---

* In the ancient days of Linux, creating a shared library was a daunting task that even wizards were afraid of. The advent of the ELF object-file format a few years ago has reduced this task to picking the right compiler switch. Things sure have improved!

library. To make it use the static one, you will have to name it explicitly on the command line:

```
papaya$ gcc -I../include -L../lib -o wibble wibble.c libstuff.a -lm
```

Another very useful tool for working with shared libraries is *ldd*. It tells you which shared libraries an executable program uses. Here's an example:

```
papaya$ ldd wibble
        libstuff.so => libstuff.so (0x400af000)
        libm.so.5 => /lib/libm.so.5 (0x400ba000)
        libc.so.5 => /lib/libc.so.5 (0x400c3000)
```

The three fields in each line are the name of the library, the full path to the instance of the library that is used, and where in the virtual address space the library is mapped to.

If *ldd* outputs not found for a certain library, you are in trouble and won't be able to run the program in question. You will have to search for a copy of that library. Perhaps it is a library shipped with your distribution that you opted not to install, or it is already on your hard disk, but the loader (the part of the system that loads every executable program) cannot find it.

In the latter situation, try locating the libraries yourself and find out whether they're in a nonstandard directory. By default, the loader looks only in */lib* and */usr/lib*. If you have libraries in another directory, create an environment variable LD_LIBRARY_PATH and add the directories separated by colons.

Using C++

If you prefer object-oriented programming, *gcc* provides complete support for C++ as well as Objective-C. There are only a few considerations you need to be aware of when doing C++ programming with *gcc*.

First of all, C++ source filenames should end in the extension *.C* or *.cc*. This distinguishes them from regular C source filenames, which end in *.c.*

Second, the *g++* shell script should be used in lieu of *gcc* when compiling C++ code. *g++* is simply a shell script that invokes *gcc* with a number of additional arguments, specifying a link against the C++ standard libraries, for example. *g++* takes the same arguments and options as *gcc*.

If you do not use *g++*, you'll need to be sure to link against the C++ libraries in order to use any of the basic C++ classes, such as the cout and cin I/O objects. Also be sure you have actually installed the C++ libraries and include files. Some distributions contain only the standard C libraries. *gcc* will be able to compile your C++ programs fine, but without the C++ libraries, you'll end up with linker errors whenever you attempt to use standard objects.

Makefiles

Sometime during your life with Linux you will probably have to deal with *make*, even if you don't plan to do any programming. It's likely you'll want to patch and rebuild the kernel and that involves running *make*. If you're lucky, you won't have to muck with the makefiles—but we've tried to direct this book toward unlucky people as well. So in this section, we'll explain enough of the subtle syntax of *make* so that you're not intimidated by a makefile.

[46] make
[47] GNU make

For some of our examples, we'll draw on the current makefile for the Linux kernel. It exploits a lot of extensions in the powerful GNU version of *make*, so we'll describe some of those as well as the standard *make* features. A good introduction to *make* is provided in *Managing Projects with make* by Andrew Oram and Steve Talbott. GNU extensions are well documented by the GNU *make* manual.

Most users see *make* as a way to build object files and libraries from sources and to build executables from object files. More conceptually, *make* is a general-purpose program that builds *targets* from *prerequisites*. The target can be a program executable, a PostScript document, or whatever. The prerequisites can be C code, a TEX text file, and so on.

While you can write simple shell scripts to execute *gcc* commands that build an executable program, *make* is special in that it knows which targets need to be rebuilt and which don't. An object file needs to be recompiled only if its corresponding source has changed.

For example, say you have a program that consists of three C source files. If you were to build the executable using the command:

```
papaya$ gcc -o foo foo.c bar.c baz.c
```

each time you changed any of the source files, all three would be recompiled and relinked into the executable. If you only changed one source file, this is a real waste of time (especially if the program in question is much larger than a handful of sources). What you really want to do is recompile only the one source file that changed into an object file and relink all of the object files in the program to form the executable. *make* can automate this process for you.

What make Does

The basic goal of *make* is to let you build a file in small steps. If a lot of source files make up the final executable, you can change one and rebuild the executable without having to recompile everything. In order to give you this flexibility, *make* records what files you need to do your build.

Here's a trivial makefile. Call it *makefile* or *Makefile* and keep it in the same directory as the source files:

```
edimh: main.o edit.o
        gcc -o edimh main.o edit.o

main.o: main.c
        gcc -c main.c

edit.o: edit.c
        gcc -c edit.c
```

This file builds a program named *edimh* from two source files named *main.c* and *edit.c*. You aren't restricted to C programming in a makefile; the commands could be anything.

Three entries appear in the file. Each contains a *dependency line* that shows how a file is built. Thus the first line says that *edimh* (the name before the colon) is built from the two object files *main.o* and *edit.o* (the names after the colon). What this line tells *make* is that it should execute the following *gcc* line whenever one of those object files change. The lines containing commands have to begin with tabs (not spaces).

The command:

```
papaya$ make edimh
```

executes the *gcc* line if there isn't currently any file named *edimh*. But the *gcc* line also executes if *edimh* exists, but one of the object files is newer. Here, *edimh* is called a *target*. The files after the colon are called either *dependents* or *prerequisites*.

The next two entries perform the same service for the object files. *main.o* is built if it doesn't exist or if the associated source file *main.c* is newer. *edit.o* is built from *edit.c*.

How does *make* know if a file is new? It looks at the time stamp, which the filesystem associates with every file. You can see time stamps by issuing the *ls –l* command. Since the time stamp is accurate to one second, it reliably tells *make* whether you've edited a source file since the latest compilation or have compiled an object file since the executable was last built.

Let's try out the makefile and see what it does:

```
papaya$ make edimh
gcc -c main.c
gcc -c edit.c
gcc -o edimh main.o edit.o
```

If we edit *main.c* and reissue the command, it rebuilds only the necessary files, saving us some time:

```
papaya$ make edimh
gcc -c main.c
gcc -o edimh main.o edit.o
```

It doesn't matter what order the three entries are within the makefile. *make* figures out which files depend on which and executes all the commands in the right order. Putting the entry for *edimh* first is convenient, because that becomes the file built by default. In other words, typing make is the same as typing make edimh.

Here's a more extensive makefile. See if you can figure out what it does:

```
install: all
        mv edimh /usr/local
        mv readimh /usr/local

all: edimh readimh

readimh: read.o edit.o
        gcc -o readimh main.o read.o

edimh: main.o edit.o
        gcc -o edimh main.o edit.o

main.o: main.c
        gcc -c main.c

edit.o: edit.c
        gcc -c edit.c

read.o: read.c
        gcc -c read.c
```

First we see the target install. This is never going to generate a file; it's called a *phony target* because it exists just so you can execute the commands listed under it. But before install runs, all has to run, because install depends on all. (Remember, the order of the entries in the file doesn't matter.)

So *make* turns to the all target. There are no commands under it (this is perfectly legal), but it depends on edimh and readimh. These are real files; each is an executable program. So *make* keeps tracing back through the list of dependencies until it arrives at the *.c* files, which don't depend on anything else. Then it painstakingly rebuilds each of the targets.

Here is a sample run (you may need **root** privilege to install the files in the */usr/ local* directory):

```
papaya$ make install
gcc -c main.c
gcc -c edit.c
gcc -o edimh main.o edit.o
gcc -c read.c
gcc -o readimh main.o read.o
mv edimh /usr/local
mv readimh /usr/local
```

So the effect of this makefile is to do a complete build and install. First it builds the files needed to create *edimh*. Then it builds the additional object file it needs to create *readmh*. With those two executables created, the `all` target is satisfied. Now *make* can go on to build the `install` target, which means moving the two executables to their final home.

Many makefiles, including the ones that build Linux, contain a variety of phony targets to do routine activities. For instance, the makefile for the Linux kernel includes commands to remove temporary files:

```
clean:  archclean
        rm -f kernel/ksyms.lst
        rm -f core `find .  -name '*.[oas]' -print`
        .
        .
        .
```

and to create a list of object files and the header files they depend on (this is a complicated but important task; if a header file changes, you want to make sure the files that refer to it are recompiled):

```
depend dep:
        touch tools/version.h
        for i in init/*.c;do echo -n "init/";$(CPP) -M $$i;done > .tmpdep
        .
        .
        .
```

Some of these shell commands get pretty complicated; we'll look at makefile commands later in this chapter, in the section "Multiple Commands."

Some Syntax Rules

The hardest thing about maintaining makefiles, at least if you're new to them, is getting the syntax right. OK, let's be straight about it, the syntax of *make* is really stupid. If you use spaces where you're supposed to use tabs or vice versa, your makefile blows up. And the error messages are really confusing.

 Always put a tab at the beginning of a command—not spaces. And don't use a tab before any other line.

You can place a hash mark (#) anywhere on a line to start a comment. Everything after the hash mark is ignored.

If you put a backslash at the end of a line, it continues on the next line. That works for long commands and other types of makefile lines too.

Now let's look at some of the powerful features of *make*, which form a kind of programming language of their own.

Macros

When people use a filename or other string more than once in a makefile, they tend to assign it to a macro. That's simply a string that *make* expands to another string. For instance, you could change the beginning of our trivial makefile to read:

```
OBJECTS = main.o edit.o

edimh: $(OBJECTS)
        gcc -o edimh $(OBJECTS)
```

When *make* runs, it simply plugs in main.o edit.o wherever you specify $(OBJECTS). If you have to add another object file to the project, just specify it on the first line of the file. The dependency line and command will then be updated correspondingly.

Don't forget the parentheses when you refer to $(OBJECTS). Macros may resemble shell variables like $HOME and $PATH, but they're not the same.

One macro can be defined in terms of another macro, so you could say something like:

```
ROOT = /usr/local
HEADERS = $(ROOT)/include
SOURCES = $(ROOT)/src
```

In this case, HEADERS evaluates to the directory */usr/local/include* and SOURCES to */usr/local/src*. If you are installing this package on your system and don't want it to be in */usr/local*, just choose another name and change the line that defines ROOT.

By the way, you don't have to use uppercase names for macros, but that's a universal convention.

An extension in GNU *make* allows you to add to the definition of a macro. This uses a := string in place of an equal sign:

```
DRIVERS         =drivers/block/block.a

ifdef CONFIG_SCSI
DRIVERS := $(DRIVERS) drivers/scsi/scsi.a
endif
```

The first line is a normal macro definition, setting the DRIVERS macro to the filename drivers/block/block.a. The next definition adds the filename drivers/scsi/scsi.a. But it takes effect only if the macro CONFIG_SCSI is defined. The full definition in that case becomes:

```
drivers/block/block.a drivers/scsi/scsi.a
```

So how do you define CONFIG_SCSI? You could put it in the makefile, assigning any string you want:

```
CONFIG_SCSI = yes
```

But you'll probably find it easier to define it on the *make* command line. Here's how to do it:

```
papaya$ make CONFIG_SCSI=yes target_name
```

One subtlety of using macros is that you can leave them undefined. If no one defines them, a null string is substituted (that is, you end up with nothing where the macro is supposed to be). But this also give you the option of defining the macro as an environment variable. For instance, if you don't define CONFIG_SCSI in the makefile, you could put this in your *.bashrc* file, for use with the *bash* shell:

```
export CONFIG_SCSI=yes
```

Or put this in *.cshrc* if you use *csh* or *tcsh*:

```
setenv CONFIG_SCSI yes
```

All your builds will then have CONFIG_SCSI defined.

Suffix Rules and Pattern Rules

For something as routine as building an object file from a source file, you don't want to specify every single dependency in your makefile. And you don't have to. Unix compilers enforce a simple standard (compile a file ending in the suffix *.c* to create a file ending in the suffix *.o*) and *make* provides a feature called suffix rules to cover all such files.

Here's a simple suffix rule to compile a C source file, which you could put in your makefile:

```
.c.o:
        gcc -c $(CFLAGS) $<
```

The .c.o: line means "use a *.c* prerequisite to build a *.o* file." CFLAGS is a macro into which you can plug any compiler options you want: *-g* for debugging, for instance, or *-O* for optimization. The string $< is a cryptic way of saying "the prerequisite." So the name of your *.c* file is plugged in when *make* executes this command.

Here's a sample run using this suffix rule. The command line passes both the *-g* option and the *-O* option:

```
papaya$ make CFLAGS="-O -g" edit.o
gcc -c -O -g edit.c
```

You actually don't have to specify this suffix rule in your makefile, because something very similar is already built into *make*. It even uses CFLAGS, so you can determine the options used for compiling just by setting that variable. The make-file used to build the Linux kernel currently contains the following definition, a whole slew of *gcc* options:

```
CFLAGS = -Wall -Wstrict-prototypes -O2 -fomit-frame-pointer -pipe
```

While we're discussing compiler flags, one set is seen so often that it's worth a special mention. This is the *−D* option, which is used to define symbols in the source code. Since there are all kinds of commonly used symbols appearing in `#ifdefs`, you may need to pass lots of such options to your makefile, such as *−DDEBUG* or *−DBSD*. If you do this on the *make* command line, be sure to put quotation marks or apostrophes around the whole set. This is because you want the shell to pass the set to your makefile as one argument:

```
papaya$ make CFLAGS="-DDEBUG -DBSD" ...
```

GNU *make* offers something called *pattern rules*, which are even better than suffix rules. A pattern rule uses a percent sign to mean "any string." So C source files would be compiled using a rule like the following:

```
%.o: %.c
        gcc -c -o $@ $(CFLAGS) $<
```

Here the output file *%.o* comes first, and the prerequisite *%.c* comes after a colon. In short, a pattern rule is just like a regular dependency line, but it contains percent signs instead of exact filenames.

We see the `$<` string to refer to the prerequisite, but we also see `$@`, which refers to the output file. So the name of the *.o* file is plugged in there. Both of these are built-in macros; *make* defines them every time it executes an entry.

Another common built-in macro is `$*`, which refers to the name of the prerequisite stripped of the suffix. So if the prerequisite is *edit.c*, the string `$*.s` would evaluate to *edit.s* (an assembly language source file).

Here's something useful you can do with a pattern rule that you can't do with a suffix rule: you add the string _dbg to the name of the output file, so that later you can tell that you compiled it with debugging information:

```
%_dbg.o: %.c
        gcc -c -g -o $@ $(CFLAGS) $<

DEBUG_OBJECTS = main_dbg.o edit_dbg.o

edimh_dbg: $(DEBUG_OBJECTS)
        gcc -o $@ $(DEBUG_OBJECTS)
```

Now you can build all your objects in two different ways: one with debugging information and one without. They'll have different filenames, so you can keep them in one directory:

```
papaya$ make edimh_dbg
gcc -c -g -o main_dbg.o  main.c
gcc -c -g -o edit_dbg.o  edit.c
gcc -o edimh_dbg  main_dbg.o edit_dbg.o
```

Multiple Commands

Any shell commands can be executed in a makefile. But things can get kind of complicated because *make* executes each command in a separate shell. So this would not work:

```
target:
        cd obj
        HOST_DIR=/home/e
        mv *.o $HOST_DIR
```

Neither the *cd* command nor the definition of the variable HOST_DIR have any effect on subsequent commands. You have to string everything together into one command. The shell uses a semicolon as a separator between commands, so you can combine them all on one line like this:

```
target:
        cd obj ; HOST_DIR=/home/e ; mv *.o $$HOST_DIR
```

One more change: to define and use a shell variable within the command, you have to double the dollar sign. This lets *make* know that you mean it to be a shell variable, not a macro.

You may find the file easier to read if you break the semicolon-separated commands onto multiple lines, using backslashes so that *make* considers them one line:

```
target:
        cd obj ; \
        HOST_DIR=/home/e ; \
        mv *.o $$HOST_DIR
```

Sometimes makefiles contain their own *make* commands; this is called recursive *make*. It looks like this:

```
linuxsubdirs: dummy
        set -e; for i in $(SUBDIRS); do $(MAKE) -C $$i; done
```

The macro $(MAKE) invokes *make*. There are a few reasons for nesting makes. One reason, which applies to this example, is to perform builds in multiple directories (each of these other directories has to contain its own makefile). Another reason is to define macros on the command line, so you can do builds with a variety of macro definitions.

GNU *make* offers another powerful interface to the shell as an extension. You can issue a shell command and assign its output to a macro. A couple of examples can be found in the Linux kernel makefile, but we'll just show a simple example here:

```
HOST_NAME = $(shell uname -n)
```

This assigns the name of your network node—the output of the *uname −n* command—to the macro HOST_NAME.

make offers a couple of conventions you may occasionally want to use. One is to put an at-sign before a command, which keeps *make* from echoing the command when it's executed:

```
@if [ -x /bin/dnsdomainname ]; then \
    echo #define LINUX_COMPILE_DOMAIN \"`dnsdomainname`\"; \
else \
    echo #define LINUX_COMPILE_DOMAIN \"`domainname`\"; \
fi >> tools/version.h
```

Another convention is to put a hyphen before a command, which tells *make* to keep going even if the command fails. This may be useful if you want to continue after an *mv* or *cp* command fails:

```
- mv edimh /usr/local
- mv readimh /usr/local
```

Including Other Makefiles

Large projects tend to break parts of their makefiles into separate files. This makes it easy for different makefiles in different directories to share things, particularly macro definitions. The line:

```
include filename
```

reads in the contents of *filename*. You can see this in the Linux kernel makefile, for instance:

```
include .depend
```

If you look in the file *.depend*, you'll find a bunch of makefile entries: to be exact, lines declaring that object files depend on header files. (By the way, *.depend* might not exist yet; it has to be created by another entry in the makefile.)

Sometimes include lines refer to macros instead of filenames, as in:

```
include ${INC_FILE}
```

In this case, INC_FILE must be defined either as an environment variable or as a macro. Doing things this way gives you more control over which file is used.

Autoconf and Automake

Writing Makefiles for a larger project usually is a boring and time-consuming task, especially if the programs are expected to be compiled on multiple platforms. From the GNU project come two tools called *Autoconf* and *Automake* that have a steep learning curve but greatly simplify the task of creating portable makefiles once mastered. In addition, *libtool* helps a lot in creating shared libraries portably. Describing how to use those programs is well beyond the scope of this book, but you can get them from *ftp://ftp.gnu.org/gnu/*.

Shell Programming

Chapter 4

In the section "Shells" in Chapter 4, *Basic Unix Commands and Concepts*, we discussed the various shells available for Linux, but something should be said about them in terms of programming. The differences come through most clearly when it comes to writing shell scripts. The Bourne shell and C shell command languages are slightly different, but the distinction is not obvious with most normal interactive use. In fact, many of the distinctions arise only when you attempt to use bizarre, little-known features of either shell, such as word substitution or some of the more oblique parameter expansion functions.

The most notable difference between Bourne and C shells is the form of the various flow-control structures, including `if ...then` and `while` loops. In the Bourne shell, an `if ...then` takes the form:

```
if list
then
    commands
elif list
then
    commands
else
    commands
fi
```

where `list` is just a sequence of commands (more generally called "pipelines") to be used as the conditional expression for the `if` and `elif` (short for "else if") commands. The conditional is considered to be true if the exit status of the `list` is zero (unlike Boolean expressions in C, in shell terminology an exit status of zero indicates successful completion). The `commands` enclosed in the conditionals are simply commands to execute if the appropriate `list` is true. The `then` after each `list` must be on a new line to distinguish it from the `list` itself; alternately, you can terminate the `list` with a `;`. The same holds true for the `commands`.

An example is:

```
if [ "$PS1" ]; then
  PS1="\h:\w% "
fi
```

This sequence checks to see whether the shell is a login shell (that is, whether the prompt variable `PS1` is set) and if so, resets the prompt to `\h:\w%`, which is a prompt expansion standing for the hostname followed by the current working directory. For example:

```
loomer:/home/loomer/mdw%
```

The `[...]` conditional appearing after the `if` is a *bash* built-in command, shorthand for *test*. The *test* command and its abbreviated equivalent provide a convenient mechanism for testing values of shell variables, string equivalence, and so forth. Instead of using `[...]`, you could call any set of commands after the `if`, as long as the last command's exit value indicates the value of the conditional.

Under *tcsh*, an `if ...then` compound statement looks like the following:

```
if (expression) then
  commands
else if (expression) then
  commands
else
  commands
endif
```

The difference here is that the *expression* after the `if` is an arithmetic or logical expression evaluated internally by *tcsh*, while with *bash* the conditional expression is a command, and the expression returns true or false based on the command's exit status. Within *bash*, using *test* or `[...]` is similar to an arithmetic expression as used in *tcsh*.

With *tcsh*, however, if you wish to run external commands within the *expression*, you must enclose the command in braces: `{command}`.

The equivalent of the previous *bash* sequence in *tcsh* is:

```
if ($?prompt) then
  set prompt="%m:%/%% "
endif
```

where *tcsh*'s own prompt special characters have been used. As you can see, *tcsh* boasts a command syntax similar to the C language, and expressions are arithmetically and logically oriented. In *bash*, however, almost everything is an actual command, and expressions are evaluated in terms of exit status values. There are analogous features in either shell, but the approach is slightly different.

A similar change exists with the `while` loop. In *bash*, this takes the form:

```
while list
do
    commands
done
```

You can negate the effect by replacing the word `while` with `until`. Again, `list` is just a command pipeline to be executed, and the exit status determines the result (zero for success and nonzero for failure). Under *tcsh* the loop looks like:

```
while (expression)
    commands
end
```

where `expression` is a logical expression to be evaluated within *tcsh*.

bash(1)
tcsh(1)

[8] Learning
bash Shell
[9] Using
csh and tcsh

This example should be enough to get a head start on understanding the overall differences of shell scripts under *bash* and *tcsh*. We encourage you to read the *bash* and *tcsh* manual pages (although they barely serve as a tutorial—more as a reference) and Info pages, if you have them available. Various books and tutorials on using these two shells are available as well; in fact, any book on shell programming will do, and you can interpolate the advanced features of *bash* and *tcsh* over the standard Bourne and C shells using the manual pages. *Learning the bash Shell* by Cameron Newham and Bill Rosenblatt and *Using csh and tcsh* by Paul DuBois are also good investments.

Using Perl

Perl may well be the best thing to happen to the Unix programming environment in years; it is worth the price of admission to Linux alone. Perl is a text- and file-manipulation language, originally intended to scan large amounts of text, process it, and produce nicely formatted reports from that data. However, as Perl has matured, it has developed into an all-purpose scripting language, capable of doing everything from managing processes to communicating via TCP/IP over a network. Perl is free software developed by Larry Wall, the Unix guru who brought us the *rn* newsreader and various popular tools, such as *patch*.

Perl's main strength is that it incorporates the most widely used features of languages, such as C, *sed*, *awk*, and various shells, into a single interpreted script language. In the past, getting a complicated job done was a matter of juggling these various languages into complex arrangements, often entailing *sed* scripts piping into *awk* scripts piping into shell scripts and eventually piping into a C program. Perl gets rid of the common Unix philosophy of using many small tools to handle small parts of one large problem. Instead, Perl does it all, and it provides many different ways of doing the same thing. In fact, this chapter was written by an Artificial Intelligence program developed in Perl. (Just kidding, Larry.)

Perl provides a nice programming interface to many features that were sometimes difficult to use in other languages. For example, a common task of many Unix system administration scripts is to scan a large amount of text, cut fields out of each line of text based on a pattern (usually represented as a *regular expression*), and produce a report based on the data. Let's say that you want to process the output of the Unix *last* command, which displays a record of login times for all users on the system, as so:

```
mdw        ttypf      loomer.vpizza.co Sun Jan 16 15:30 - 15:54  (00:23)
larry      ttyp1      muadib.oit.unc.e Sun Jan 16 15:11 - 15:12  (00:00)
johnsonm   ttyp4      mallard.vpizza.c Sun Jan 16 14:34 - 14:37  (00:03)
jem        ttyq2      mallard.vpizza.c Sun Jan 16 13:55 - 13:59  (00:03)
linus      FTP        kruuna.helsinki. Sun Jan 16 13:51 - 13:51  (00:00)
linus      FTP        kruuna.helsinki. Sun Jan 16 13:47 - 13:47  (00:00)
```

If we wanted to count up the total login time for each user (given in parentheses in the last field), we could write a *sed* script to splice the time values from the input, an *awk* script to sort the data for each user and add up the times, and another *awk* script to produce a report based on the accumulated data. Or, we could write a somewhat complex C program to do the entire task—complex because, as any C programmer knows, text-processing functions within C are somewhat limited.

However, this task can be easily accomplished by a simple Perl script. The facilities of I/O, regular-expression pattern matching, sorting by associative arrays, and number crunching are all easily accessed from a Perl program with little overhead. Perl programs are generally short and to the point, without a lot of technical mumbo-jumbo getting in the way of what you want your program to actually *do*.

[39] Programming Perl
[38] Learning Perl

Using Perl under Linux is really no different than on other Unix systems. Several good books on Perl already exist, including *Programming Perl*, by Larry Wall, Randal L. Schwartz, and Tom Christiansen; *Learning Perl*, by Randal L. Schwartz and Tom Christiansen; *Advanced Perl Programming* by Sriram Srinivasan; and *Perl Cookbook* by Tom Christiansen and Nathan Torkington. Nevertheless, we think Perl is such a great tool that it deserves something in the way of an introduction. After all, Perl is free software, as is Linux; they go hand in hand.

[40] Advanced Perl Programming
[41] Perl Cookbook

A Sample Program

What we really like about Perl is that it lets you immediately jump to the task at hand; you don't have to write extensive code to set up data structures, open files or pipes, allocate space for data, and so on. All these features are taken care of for you in a very friendly way.

The example of login times, just discussed, serves to introduce many of the basic features of Perl. First, we'll give the entire script (complete with comments) and then a description of how it works. This script reads the output of the *last* command (see the previous example) and prints an entry for each user on the system, describing the total login time and number of logins for each. (Line numbers are printed to the left of each line for reference):

```
1       #!/usr/bin/perl
2
3       while (<STDIN>) {    # While we have input...
4          # Find lines and save username, login time
5          if (/^(\S*)\s*.*\((.*):(.*)\)$/) {
6             # Increment total hours, minutes, and logins
7             $hours{$1} += $2;
8             $minutes{$1} += $3;
9             $logins{$1}++;
10         }
11      }
12
13      # For each user in the array...
14      foreach $user (sort(keys %hours)) {
15         # Calculate hours from total minutes
16         $hours{$user} += int($minutes{$user} / 60);
17         $minutes{$user} %= 60;
18         # Print the information for this user
19         print "User $user, total login time ";
20         # Perl has printf, too
21         printf "%02d:%02d, ", $hours{$user}, $minutes{$user};
22         print "total logins $logins{$user}.\n";
23      }
```

Line 1 tells the loader that this script should be executed through Perl, not as a shell script. Line 3 is the beginning of the program. It is the head of a simple while loop, which C and shell programmers will be familiar with: the code within the braces from lines 4–10 should be executed while a certain expression is true. However, the conditional expression <STDIN> looks funny. Actually, this expression is true whenever there is input on the STDIN filehandle—which refers to standard input, as you might guess.

Perl reads input one line at a time (unless you tell it to do otherwise). It also reads by default from standard input, again, unless you tell it to do otherwise. Therefore, this while loop will continuously read lines from standard input, until there are no lines left to be read.

The evil-looking mess on line 5 is just an if statement. As with most programming languages, the code within the braces (on lines 6–9) will be executed if the expression that follows the if is true. But what is the expression between the parentheses? Those readers familiar with Unix tools such as *grep* and *sed* will peg this immediately as a *regular expression*: a cryptic but useful way to represent a pattern to be matched in the input text. Regular expressions are usually found between delimiting slashes (/.../).

This particular regular expression matches lines of the form:

```
mdw        ttypf     loomer.vpizza.co Sun Jan 16 15:30 - 15:54  (00:23)
```

This expression also "remembers" the username (**mdw**) and the total login time for this entry (00:23). You needn't worry about the expression itself; building regular expressions is a complex subject. For now, all that you need to know is that this if statement finds lines of the form given in the example, and splices out the username and login time for processing. The username is assigned to the variable $1, the hours to the variable $2, and the minutes to $3. (Variables in Perl begin with the $ character, but unlike the shell, the $ must be used when assigning to the variable as well.) This assignment is done by the regular expression match itself (anything enclosed in parentheses in a regular expression is saved for later use to one of the variables $1 through $9).

Lines 6–9 actually process these three pieces of information. And they do it in an interesting way: through the use of an *associative array*. Whereas a normal array is indexed with a number as a subscript, an associative array is indexed by an arbitrary string. This lends itself to many powerful applications; it allows you to associate one set of data with another set of data gathered on the fly. In our short program, the keys are the usernames, gathered from the output of *last*. We maintain three associative arrays, all indexed by username: hours, which records the total number of hours the user logged in; minutes, which records the number of minutes; and logins, which records the total number of logins.

As an example, referencing the variable $hours{'mdw'} returns the total number of hours that the user **mdw** was logged in. Similarly, if the username **mdw** is stored in the variable $1, referencing $hours{$1} produces the same effect.

In lines 6–9, we increment the values of these arrays according to the data on the present line of input. For example, given the input line:

```
jem        ttyq2     mallard.vpizza.c Sun Jan 16 13:55 - 13:59  (00:03)
```

Line 7 increments the value of the hours array, indexed with $1 (the username, **jem**), by the number of hours that **jem** was logged in (stored in the variable $2). The Perl increment operator += is equivalent to the corresponding C operator. Line 8 increments the value of minutes for the appropriate user similarly. Line 9 increments the value of the logins array by one, using the ++ operator.

Associative arrays are one of the most useful features of Perl. They allow you to build up complex databases while parsing text. It would be nearly impossible to use a standard array for this same task. We would first have to count the number of users in the input stream and then allocate an array of the appropriate size, assigning a position in the array to each user (through the use of a hash function or some other indexing scheme). An associative array, however, allows you to index data directly using strings and without regard for the size of the array in question. (Of course, performance issues always arise when attempting to use large arrays, but for most applications this isn't a problem.)

Let's move on. Line 14 uses the Perl foreach statement, which you may be used to if you write shell scripts. (The foreach loop actually breaks down into a for loop, much like that found in C.) Here, in each iteration of the loop, the variable $user is assigned the next value in the list given by the expression sort(keys %hours). %hours simply refers to the entire associative array hours that we have constructed. The function keys returns a list of all the keys used to index the array, which is in this case a list of usernames. Finally, the sort function sorts the list returned by keys. Therefore, we are looping over a sorted list of usernames, assigning each username in turn to the variable $user.

Lines 16 and 17 simply correct for situations where the number of minutes is greater than 60; it determines the total number of hours contained in the minutes entry for this user and increments hours accordingly. The int function returns the integral portion of its argument. (Yes, Perl handles floating-point numbers as well; that's why use of int is necessary.)

Finally, lines 19–22 print the total login time and number of logins for each user. The simple print function just prints its arguments, like the *awk* function of the same name. Note that variable evaluation can be done within a print statement, as on lines 19 and 22. However, if you want to do some fancy text formatting, you need to use the printf function (which is just like its C equivalent). In this case, we wish to set the minimum output length of the hours and minutes values for this user to 2 characters wide, and to left-pad the output with zeroes. To do this, we use the printf command on line 21.

If this script is saved in the file logintime, we can execute it as follows:

```
papaya$ last | logintime
User johnsonm, total login time 01:07, total logins 11.
User kibo, total login time 00:42, total logins 3.
User linus, total login time 98:50, total logins 208.
User mdw, total login time 153:03, total logins 290.
papaya$
```

Of course, this example doesn't serve well as a Perl tutorial, but it should give you some idea of what it can do. We encourage you to read one of the excellent Perl books out there to learn more.

More Features

The previous example introduced the most commonly used Perl features by demonstrating a living, breathing program. There is much more where that came from—in the way of both well-known and not-so-well-known features.

As we mentioned, Perl provides a report-generation mechanism beyond the standard print and printf functions. Using this feature, the programmer defines a report "format" that describes how each page of the report will look. For example, we could have included the following format definition in our example:

```
format STDOUT_TOP =
User            Total login time    Total logins
-------------   -------------------  -------------------
.
format STDOUT =
@<<<<<<<<<<<<  @<<<<<<<<            @####
$user,          $thetime,           $logins{$user}
.
```

The STDOUT_TOP definition describes the header of the report, which will be printed at the top of each page of output. The STDOUT format describes the look of each line of output. Each field is described beginning with the @ character; @<<<< specifies a left-justified text field, and @#### specifies a numeric field. The line below the field definitions gives the names of the variables to use in printing the fields. Here, we have used the variable $thetime to store the formatted time string.

To use this report for the output, we replace lines 19–22 in the original script with the following:

```
$thetime = sprintf("%02d:%02d", $hours{$user}, $minutes{$user});
write;
```

The first line uses the sprintf function to format the time string and save it in the variable $thetime; the second line is a write command that tells Perl to go off and use the given report format to print a line of output.

Using this report format, we'll get something looking like:

```
User            Total login time    Total logins
-------------   -------------------  -------------------
johnsonm        01:07                  11
kibo            00:42                   3
linus           98:50                 208
mdw             153:03                290
```

Using other report formats we can achieve different (and better-looking) results.

Perl comes with a huge number of modules that you can plug in to your programs for quick access to very powerful features. A popular online archive called CPAN (for Comprehensive Perl Archive Network) contains even more modules: net modules that let you send mail and carry on other networking tasks, modules for dumping data and debugging, modules for manipulating dates and times, modules for math functions—the list could go on for pages.

If you hear of an interesting module, check first to see whether it's already loaded on your system. You can look at the directories where modules are located (probably under */usr/lib/perl5*) or just try loading in the module and see if it works. Thus, the command:

```
$ perl -MCGI -e 1
Can't locate CGI in @INC...
```

Chapter 16

gives you the sad news that the CGI.pm module (which we'll use in "Writing the CGI script" in Chapter 16, *The World Wide Web and Electronic Mail,* to handle a web form) is not on your system. CGI.pm is popular enough to be included in the standard Perl distribution, and you can install it from there, but for many modules you will have to go to CPAN (and some don't make it into CPAN either). CPAN, which is maintained by Jarkko Hietaniemi and Andreas König, resides on dozens of mirror sites around the world because so many people want to download its modules. The easiest way to get onto CPAN is to visit *http://www.perl.com/CPAN-local/.*

The following program—which we wanted to keep short, and therefore we neglected to find a useful task to perform—shows two modules, one that manipulates dates and times in a sophisticated manner and another that sends mail. The disadvantage of using such powerful features is that a huge amount of code is loaded from them, making the runtime size of the program quite large:

```perl
#! /usr/local/bin/perl

# We will illustrate Date and Mail modules
use Date::Manip;
use Mail::Mailer;

# Illustration of Date::Manip module
if ( Date_IsWorkDay( "today", 1) )  {

    # Today is a work day
    $date = ParseDate( "today" );

}
else {

    # Today is not a work day, so choose next work day
    $date=DateCalc( "today" , "+ 1 business day" );

}

# Convert date from compact string to readable string like "April  8"
$printable_date = UnixDate( $date , "%B %e" );

# Illustration of Mail::Mailer module
my ($to) = "the_person\@you_want_to.mail_to";
my ($from) = "owner_of_script\@system.name";

$mail = Mail::Mailer->new;

$mail->open(
            {
                From => $from,
```

```
            To => $to,
            Subject => "Automated reminder",
        }
    );

print $mail <<"MAIL_BODY";
If you are at work on or after
$printable_date,
you will get this mail.
MAIL_BODY

$mail->close;

# The mail has been sent! (Assuming there were no errors.)
```

The reason packages are so easy to use is that Perl added object-oriented features in version 5. The Date module used in the previous example is not object oriented, but the Mail module is. The `$mail` variable in the example is a Mailer object, and it makes mailing a messages straightforward through methods like new, open, and `close`.

[38] Learning Perl

To do some major task like parsing HTML, just read in the proper CGI package and issue a new command to create the proper object—all the functions you need for parsing HTML will then be available.

perlobj(1)

If you want to give a graphical interface to your Perl script, you can use the Tk module, which originally was developed for use with the Tcl language, or the Gtk module, which uses the newer GIMP Toolkit (GTK). The book *Learning Perl/Tk* by Nancy Walsh shows you how to do graphics with that module. Both Tcl and Tk are discussed later in the chapter.

Another abstruse feature of Perl is its ability to (more or less) directly access several Unix system calls, including interprocess communications. For example, Perl provides the functions msgctl, msgget, msgsnd, and msgrcv from System V IPC. Perl also supports the BSD socket implementation, allowing communications via TCP/IP directly from a Perl program. No longer is C the exclusive language of networking daemons and clients. A Perl program loaded with IPC features can be very powerful indeed—especially considering that many client-server implementations call for advanced text-processing features such as those provided by Perl. It is generally easier to parse protocol commands transmitted between client and server from a Perl script, rather than write a complex C program to do the work.

As an example, take the well-known SMTP daemon, which handles the sending and receiving of electronic mail. The SMTP protocol uses internal commands such as recv from and mail to to enable the client to communicate with the server. Either the client or the server, or both, can be written in Perl, and can have full access to Perl's text- and file-manipulation features as well as the vital socket communication functions.

Perl is a fixture of CGI programming, that is, writing small programs that run on a web server and help web pages becoming more interactive.

As a far-out example of the kinds of things Perl and IPC can do, Larry Wall was reportedly considering rewriting the *rn* newsreader entirely in Perl.

Pros and Cons

One of the features of (some might say "problems with") Perl is the ability to abbreviate—and obfuscate—code considerably. In the previous script, we have used several common shortcuts. For example, input into the Perl script is read into the variable $_. However, most operations act on the variable $_ by default, so it's usually not necessary to reference $_ by name.

Perl also gives you several ways of doing the same thing, which can, of course, be either a blessing or a curse depending on how you look at it. In *Programming Perl*, Larry Wall gives the following example of a short program that simply prints its standard input. All of the following statements are equivalent:

```
while ($_ = <STDIN>) { print; }
while (<STDIN>) { print; }
for (;<STDIN>;) { print; }
print while $_ = <STDIN>;
print while <STDIN>;
```

The programmer can use the syntax most appropriate for the situation at hand.

Perl is popular, and not just because it is useful. Because Perl provides much in the way of eccentricity, it gives hackers something to play with, so to speak. Perl programmers are constantly outdoing each other with trickier bits of code. Perl lends itself to interesting kludges, neat hacks, and both very good and very bad programming. Unix programmers see it as a challenging medium to work with—because Perl is relatively new, not all of the possibilities have been exploited. Even if you find Perl too baroque for your taste, there is still something to be said for its artistry. The ability to call oneself a "Perl hacker" is a point of pride within the Unix community.

Programming in Tcl and Tk

Tool Command Language, or Tcl, (pronounced "tickle") is a simple, interpreted language that is similar, in some respects, to the Bourne shell or Perl. The real benefit of Tcl is that it can be extended as well as embedded in other applications. It is particularly popular when used with the Tk extension, which offers about the simplest interface you could get to program with windows. As an additional benefit, you can run your Tcl/Tk problems without much hassle on both Unix, Windows, and the Macintosh.

By *extended*, we mean that you can add new commands to the Tcl language, simply by writing a few routines in C. By *embedded*, we mean that you can link a C program to the Tcl libraries, giving that program full access to the Tcl language. Whereas most Tcl programs are written as scripts and executed by a precompiled Tcl interpreter, you can include the interpreter routines in your own application.

For example, let's say that you wanted to write a command-driven debugger similar in nature to *gdb*. The debugger would present a prompt and allow users to enter commands such as *step* and *breakpoint*.

If the command syntax for your debugger is simple, you could easily write your own routines in C to read a command and process it. However, this approach becomes more complex when you wish to allow the user to define variables, macros, new functions, and so forth.

Instead of writing these routines from scratch, it is easy to embed a Tcl interpreter into your debugger application. Every command entered by the user would be handled by the interpreter routines. These routines are available as a set of C library functions.

The Tcl language itself includes many, many commands of its own. It provides control structures such as `while` and `for` loops, the ability to define functions, string and list manipulation routines, arithmetic functions, and so forth.

On top of these core Tcl routines, your debugger must provide additional commands—such as the aforementioned *step* and *breakpoint*. You would implement these commands in C within your application and tell the Tcl interpreter how to use them.

Now your debugger application has all of the power of Tcl at its fingertips. For example, the user customization file for the debugger could be a simple Tcl script. Within this script, the user can define new functions and variables, using Tcl's built-in support for these features.

Chapter 10

Among the many extensions to Tcl is Tk, which provides many commands that allow your application to utilize the X Window System as a user interface. (X is introduced in Chapter 10.) Writing X-based applications as a Tk script is surprisingly easy. For example, the following Tcl/Tk application displays a text-entry widget in which a filename may be entered. It then runs an *xterm* containing a *vi* process to edit the file:

```
#!/usr/bin/wish -f

# Create a label widget, named .l
label .l -text "Filename:"
# Create an entry widget, named .e
entry .e -relief sunken -width 30 -textvariable fname

# Place the two widgets into the application window
pack .l -side left
```

```
pack .e -side left -padx 1m -pady 1m

# When the return key is pressed in the entry widget, run xterm
bind .e <Return> {
  exec xterm -e vi $fname
}
```

We will explain the syntax of this script shortly, but for now you can see that in less than 20 lines of code, we have developed a reasonably complex X application. When this script is executed, it will look like Figure 13-1.

An indication of Tk's usefulness is that the two scripting languages Perl and Python both have interfaces to it.

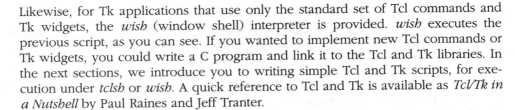

Figure 13-1: Simple Tk-generated window

For Tcl applications that use only the core Tcl routines, the precompiled interpreter *tclsh* is provided. This interpreter simply reads Tcl commands and executes them, one by one. In the case of our debugger application, we would write a new program that is linked to the Tcl interpreter library routines.

[43] Tcl/
Tk Nutshell

Likewise, for Tk applications that use only the standard set of Tcl commands and Tk widgets, the *wish* (window shell) interpreter is provided. *wish* executes the previous script, as you can see. If you wanted to implement new Tcl commands or Tk widgets, you could write a C program and link it to the Tcl and Tk libraries. In the next sections, we introduce you to writing simple Tcl and Tk scripts, for execution under *tclsh* or *wish*. A quick reference to Tcl and Tk is available as *Tcl/Tk in a Nutshell* by Paul Raines and Jeff Tranter.

Crash Course in Tcl

The Tcl language is easy to learn. If you are at all familiar with other scripting languages, such as the Bourne or C shell, Tcl/Tk will pose no threat to you.

[42] Tcl/Tk

For this reason, we will not spend a great deal of time on the Tcl language itself. It is straightforward and can be learned with the help of the various Tcl manual pages or John Ousterhout's excellent book, *Tcl and the Tk Toolkit*. This book describes not only how to write Tcl and Tk scripts but also how to use the Tcl/Tk libraries in your own applications.

Let's start with a simple example. The following Tcl script counts the lines in the given filename:

```
 1  #!/usr/bin/tclsh -f
 2
 3  if {$argc != 1} {
 4      error "lc <filename>"
 5  }
 6
 7  set thefile [open [lindex $argv 0] r]
 8  set count 0
 9
10  while {[gets $thefile line] >= 0} {
11      set count [expr $count + 1]
12  }
13
14  puts "Read $count lines."
```

Lines 3–5 use a simple `if` statement to ensure that there is one argument to the script—that being the filename containing lines to count. The `if` command takes two arguments: an expression and a block of code to execute if the expression evaluates as true. (Like C, zero indicates false, nonzero indicates true.)

Each of the arguments to the `if` command are contained in braces, which group a set of words (or lines) together as a single argument. Although this syntax may remind you of C or Perl, Tcl's command-parsing behavior is actually quite simple. For example, it allows a command argument (here, the body of code on lines 3–5 containing the `error` command) to span multiple lines only if the opening brace is at the end of a line. If we had written the `if` command as:

```
if {$argc != 1}
  { error "lc <filename>" }
```

Tcl would have given us the error:

```
Error: wrong # args: no script following "$argc != 1" argument
wrong # args: no script following "$argc != 1" argument
    while executing
"if {$argc != 1} "
    (file "./lc.tcl" line 3)
```

In other words, Tcl doesn't know that the second argument to `if` is on the following line.

The body of the `if` command, on line 4, uses the `error` command to display an error message and exit the Tcl script.

On line 7, we open the file given as the first command-line argument, and assign the resulting file pointer to the variable `thefile`. The `set` command must be used to assign values to variables. This is because all Tcl commands must begin with a command name; we can't set the variable `a` to 1 using something like:

```
a = 1
```

because a refers to a variable, not a command. Instead, we use:

```
set a 1
```

Later, to refer to the value of the variable a, we would use $a.

The first argument to set is the name of the variable to assign, and the second argument is the value. Here, we have:

```
set thefile [open [lindex $argv 0] r]
```

Square brackets [...] are used to specify a *subscript*, a sequence of commands to nest within the current command. The subscript is executed, and its return value substituted in the subscript's place.

For example, let's look at the subscript:

```
open [lindex $argv 0] r
```

This script executes the open command to open the file given as its first argument. The second argument, r, indicates that the file should be opened for reading.

The first argument to open is the subscript:

```
lindex $argv 0
```

The lindex command is used to index a list, or array, of items. In this case, we wish to obtain the 0th element of the $argv array, which contains the command-line arguments to the program, minus the command name itself. (This is unlike the use of argv in C programs.) Therefore, the 0th element of $argv is the first command-line argument.

Let's say that we named our script *lc.tcl*, and invoked it as:

```
eggplant$ lc.tcl /etc/passwd
```

Therefore, within the command:

```
set thefile [open [lindex $argv 0] r]
```

the nested subscript:

```
open [lindex $argv 0] r
```

will be replaced with:

```
open "/etc/passwd" r
```

which will, in turn, be replaced with the value of the file pointer corresponding to */etc/passwd*. The net result is that the file pointer value is assigned to the variable thefile.

On line 8, we set the variable count to 0, which acts as our line counter.

Lines 10–12 contain a simple while loop, which repeatedly reads lines from the file until end of file (EOF):

```
while {[gets $thefile line] >= 0} {
    set count [expr $count + 1]
}
```

As we can see, the while command takes two arguments: a condition and a block of code to execute while the condition is true. Here, the loop condition is:

```
[gets $thefile line] >= 0
```

We see the subscript:

```
gets $thefile line
```

which executes the gets command. This reads a single line from the file pointer $thefile and assigns it to the variable line. gets returns the count of the number of characters read, or -1 if EOF is reached. Therefore, the while loop will continuously read lines from the file until gets returns a value less than zero.

The body of the while loop is:

```
set count [expr $count + 1]
```

which increments the value of count. Remember that Tcl commands must begin with a command name. Therefore, arithmetic expressions are handled using the expr command. Here, the subscript:

```
expr $count + 1
```

returns the value of the variable count plus 1. This is the canonical way to increment variables within Tcl.

Finally, on line 14, we see:

```
puts "Read $count lines."
```

which uses the puts command to display a string to standard output.

Here is a sample run of this script:

```
eggplant$ lc.tcl /etc/passwd
Read 144 lines.
```

Writing Tk Applications

Even the basic Tcl knowledge given in the previous section is enough to allow you to write applications using Tk, the Tcl extensions for the X Window System. Tk is essentially a collection of Tcl commands that create and manipulate X widgets—such as buttons, scrollbars, menus, and so forth. As we will see, Tk is extremely versatile and greatly simplifies the task of building a graphical user interface under X.

A widget is an object you want to manipulate, such as a rectangle. Each widget requires memory and a bunch of properties, but Tk relieves you from thinking about all that. You just create a widget and tell Tk what you want it to look like.

In this section, we'll help the user create an oval and a rectangle: each of those is a widget. But we also need a place to draw them: something fixed where the oval and rectangle are free to move around. So before drawing, we'll create an empty space called a *canvas* widget. The canvas widget is a generic graphics widget with support for many types of objects, such as ovals, lines, text, and so forth. And to provide the kind of convenient user interface people expect, we'll create a menu widget and a frame widget to hold everything together. When executed, this application looks something like Figure 13-2.

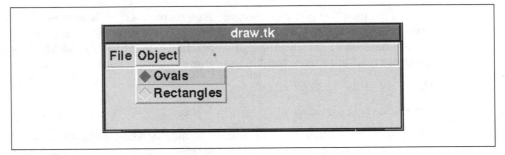

Figure 13–2: Window displayed by Tk program

Let's walk through the source for our application, *draw.tcl*:

```
#!/usr/bin/wish -f
# Global variables, used to keep track of objects and positions
set oval_count 0
set rect_count 0
set orig_x 0
set orig_y 0
```

No sweat here: we simply initialize a few variables to keep track of the oval and rectangle objects we create, as well as the location of the object as it is created.

The next portion of the source may be a bit daunting at first:

```
# This procedure enables ovals.
proc set_oval {} {
  # Allow us to access these global variables
  global oval_count orig_x orig_y

  # When button-1 is pressed, create an oval
  bind .c <ButtonPress-1> {
    set orig_x %x
    set orig_y %y
    set oval_count [expr $oval_count + 1]
```

```
   .c create oval %x %y %x %y -tags "oval$oval_count" -fill red
}

# When we drag button 1, delete the current oval and replace it
bind .c <B1-Motion> {
   .c delete "oval$oval_count"
   .c create oval $orig_x $orig_y %x %y -tags "oval$oval_count" -fill red
}
}
```

Here, we define a procedure named set_oval using the Tcl proc command. The first argument to proc is the list of arguments that the procedure will take; in this case, there are none. The second argument is the body of the procedure itself. This procedure is invoked when we select the Ovals item from the Objects menu, which is configured later in this section.

The first thing set_oval does is declare the variables oval_count, orig_x, and orig_y to be globals; otherwise, Tcl would assume we were using these variables locally within the procedure.

The next task is to bind an action to a ButtonPress event in the canvas widget we will be drawing into. This widget is named .c. Tk widgets are named hierarchically. The widget . (a period) refers to the main application window. Any widgets created within that window are given names beginning with a period, such as .c (for a canvas widget), .mbar (for a menu bar), and so on. Of course, the programmer can choose widget names, but those names must begin with a period. As we will see later, widgets may be contained within other widgets; for example, a menu is contained within a menu bar. A widget named:

.mbar.file.menu

might refer to the menu menu contained within the menu item file contained within the menu bar .mbar. This is demonstrated later in this section.

The bind command creates an event binding for a particular widget.* The first argument to bind is the widget in which to create the binding, the second argument is the event to track, and the third argument is the code to execute when that event occurs.

In this case, we wish to start drawing an oval whenever the user presses mouse button 1 in the canvas widget. The code of the binding sets the variables orig_x and orig_y to %x and %y, respectively. Within a binding, %x and %y refer to the x and y coordinates of the event in question. In this case, this would be the cursor position where the mouse button was pressed. We wish to save this location when the oval is resized. In addition, we increment the oval_count variable.

---

* An *event* is simply a message generated by the X server in response to a user action. For example, when the user presses mouse button 1 (usually the left mouse button) within a certain window, that window is sent a ButtonPress-1 event.

The `ButtonPress-1` binding also executes the command:

```
.c create oval %x %y %x %y -tags "oval$oval_count" -fill red
```

This creates an `oval` object within the canvas widget `.c`. The upper-left and lower-right coordinates of the oval are given as `%x` and `%y`, the location of the `ButtonPress` event. We fill the oval with the color `red`.

The `-tags` option to the canvas `create` command assigns a "name" to the newly created `oval` object. In this way, we can refer to this particular oval on the canvas widget by its name. To ensure that each oval has a unique name, we use the `oval_count` variable, which is incremented each time an oval is created.

When the mouse is dragged with button 1 pressed, we wish to resize the oval. This is accomplished by setting a binding for the `B1-Motion` event in the canvas widget. This binding executes the two commands:

```
.c delete "oval$oval_count"
.c create oval $orig_x $orig_y %x %y -tags "oval$oval_count" -fill red
```

The canvas `delete` command deletes the object named by the given tag. We then recreate the oval at its original upper-left corner position, but with the new lower-right corner given by the location of the `B1-Motion` event. In other words, we are replacing the original oval object with a new oval with different coordinates, corresponding to the position of the mouse. This effectively resizes the oval as the mouse moves across the canvas widget with button 1 pressed.

We define an analogous `set_rect` function, which is nearly identical to the one previously discussed, but creates canvas `rectangle` objects instead:

```
# Identical to set_oval, but uses rectangles
proc set_rect {} {
  global rect_count orig_x orig_y
  bind .c <ButtonPress-1> {
    set orig_x %x
    set orig_y %y
    set rect_count [expr $rect_count + 1]
    .c create rectangle %x %y %x %y -tags "rect$rect_count" -fill blue
  }
  bind .c <B1-Motion> {
    .c delete "rect$rect_count"
    .c create rectangle $orig_x $orig_y %x %y -tags "rect$rect_count" \
      -fill blue
  }
}
```

Another way to draw rectangles and ovals would be to have a generic "draw object" function that uses a variable, say `$objtype`, to keep track of the current object type. The menu settings (described later) select the object type by setting the value of this variable. In the drawing function, we could simply use a canvas command such as:

```
.c create $objtype %x %y %x %y -tags "obj$obj_count" -fill blue
```

However, this assumes that all objects will be drawn in the same way (by clicking on one position and dragging the mouse to size the object). Using separate functions for each object type allows us to specialize the interface for each if we wish to do so.

Now we are ready to define the various widgets that make up our application. First, we need to create a frame widget to be used as a menu bar. A frame widget merely acts as a container for other widgets:

```
# Create a frame widget to be used as a menubar.
frame .mbar -relief groove -bd 3
pack .mbar -side top -expand yes -fill x
```

Here, we create a frame widget named .mbar. The -relief option specifies the display style for this widget—in this case, we wish the menu bar to appear as though it has a "groove" running along its perimeter. The -bd option sets the width of the widget's border, which, in this case, defines the width of the groove.

The pack command places widgets within the application window, or within other widgets. It is one kind of "geometry manager" available for Tk. In order for a widget to be displayed within the application, a geometry manager must be called to place the widget. pack is provided with Tcl/Tk, and is versatile enough for almost any application. pack allows you to specify how widgets should be placed relative to one another, without having to specify absolute locations.

In this case, we pack the .mbar widget into the top edge of its parent widget, which is . (the main application window). The -fill x option tells pack that the widget should be allocated the entire width of the window in which it is contained; the -expand option specifies that the widget should grow to fill that space. If you are interested in the intricacies of pack, the Tk pack manual page provides a great deal of detail.

Next, we create two menubutton widgets within this menu bar—the File and Object menus:

```
# Create two menu items
menubutton .mbar.file -text "File" -menu .mbar.file.menu
menubutton .mbar.obj -text "Object" -menu .mbar.obj.menu
pack .mbar.file .mbar.obj -side left
```

The two widgets in question are named .mbar.file and .mbar.obj. Therefore, each widget is a direct child of the .mbar widget, not the main application window. When we pack the two widgets, they are packed into the left side of their parent, the menu bar.

The -menu option to the menubutton command specifies the menu widget that should be displayed when this pulldown menu is selected. We will create the .mbar.file.menu and .mbar.obj.menu widgets later:

```
# Create the file menu, and add a single "Quit" item to it
menu .mbar.file.menu
.mbar.file.menu add command -label "Quit" -command { exit }
```

First, we create the File menu itself, and add a single command item to it. A command item is like a button: when selected, the code given by the -command option is executed. In this case, selecting this option exits the Tk script:

```
# Create the object menu, and add two radiobutton objects to it
menu .mbar.obj.menu
.mbar.obj.menu add radiobutton -label "Ovals" -variable objtype \
   -command { set_oval }
.mbar.obj.menu add radiobutton -label "Rectangles" -variable objtype \
   -command { set_rect }
```

Here, we create the Objects menu, and add two objects of type radiobutton to it. Radiobuttons define a set of options where only one of the options may be selected at a given time. For example, when Ovals is selected, it is highlighted in the menu and Rectangles is dimmed.

In order to "link" the two radiobuttons (so that only one may be selected at a time), we use the -variable option to specify a "dummy" variable that keeps track of the current setting of the radio buttons. The -variable option may be used in conjunction with -value, which assigns a value to the named variable when the menu item is selected. Instead, we choose to execute a procedure (specified with the -command option) when the menu item is selected, which precludes the need for -value.

Next, we create our canvas widget and pack it into the application window:

```
# Create the canvas .c
canvas .c
pack .c -side top
```

Finally, we enable the Ovals option by artificially invoking the corresponding menu item. This is exactly what happens when the user selects the menu item using the mouse:

```
# Turn on ovals, by invoking the first item in the object menu
.mbar.obj.menu invoke 0
```

Here, in a few dozen lines of code, we have a complete, relatively complex X application. There are many easy ways to extend this program: for example, by adding new object types, allowing the user to save and load "pictures" created with it, and so on. In fact, the canvas widget even supports an option to dump a PostScript image of its contents, which then can be printed.

Using Tcl and Tk in Other Applications

As mentioned previously, you can use Tcl and Tk with other programs written in languages such as C or Perl. Writing a complex program as a Tcl/Tk script is possible, but it would probably be slower than coding it in a compiled language because Tcl is interpreted. Although Perl is interpreted as well, Perl is suited to many tasks that are more difficult to accomplish in Tcl or C.

The canonical way to use Tcl and Tk with a C program is to link the Tcl and Tk libraries with the C code. Tcl and Tk provide simple *.a* static libraries, as well as shared *.so* libraries on some systems. The Tcl interpreter is implemented as a series of functions that your program calls.

The idea is that you implement new Tcl commands as C functions, and the Tcl interpreter calls those functions when one of those commands is used. To do this you must structure your program to initialize the Tcl interpreter and use a Tcl "main loop," which reads Tcl commands from some location (such as a file) and executes them. This is roughly equivalent to building your own *tclsh* or *wish* interpreter with a few extra Tcl/Tk commands implemented in C.

This may not be the best solution for all applications. First of all, it requires some of your program to be restructured, and the Tcl interpreter ends up controlling the application—not the other way around. Also, unless you use shared Tcl and Tk libraries, having a complete Tcl/Tk interpreter embedded in your application can make the binary quite large—well over a megabyte. Also, your application may depend on some kind of Tcl script to drive it, which means that the executable is not enough to use the complete application: you need the driving script as well.

Another solution is to write an application in C or Perl that executes the *wish* interpreter as a separate process and communicates with it via pipes. In this case, you will need two pipes: one for the C program to write commands to *wish* and another for the C program to read responses from *wish*. This can be done with a single pipe, but synchronization becomes more difficult. For example, responses from *wish* may be asynchronous—generated from user events such as a button press—which makes the use of a single pipe a bit complex.*

The most straightforward way of setting this up is to write a C function that does the following (in pseudocode):

```
Create two pipes by calling pipe() twice;
Use fork() to start a child process;
   In the child process,
      close the read end of one pipe and the write end of another;
      Use dup2() to duplicate stdin and stdout to the appropriate pipes;
      Use execlp() to start wish;
```

---

* Remember that a pipe is a simple one-way data stream used to communicate from one process to another. The shell allows you to use single pipes between commands, as in *cat foo.txt.gz | gunzip -c | more.*

```
In the parent process;
    close the read end of the write pipe, and the write end of the
        read pipe;
    Use fdopen() on each pipe to get a FILE descriptor for use with
        fprintf() and fscanf();
```

Of course, you'll need some knowledge of Unix systems programming to use the previous example, but it's provided here for the adventurous.

The parent process (your C application) can now write Tcl/Tk commands to the write pipe and read responses from *wish* on the read pipe. The *select* function can be used to poll for data on the read pipe, in case you want your application to keep processing while waiting for data from the *wish* interpreter.

This way, we treat *wish* as a "server" for X Window System routines. Your program would send widget-creation commands down the write pipe. *wish* could be told to print a string to standard output when a response is required from the application. For example, a button widget could be created that prints the string okay button pressed when pressed by the user. Your program would read this string on the read pipe and respond to it. Other parts of the application could be controlled by *wish* without your application's knowledge. The computing-intensive, speed-critical parts of the application would be coded in C, and the interface handled by *wish*.

[35] Advanced Programming

Hopefully, the overview here should be enough to give you an idea of how to write a C or Perl program that uses *wish* in this way. It's a good idea to read a book on Unix systems programming that talks about interprocess communication using pipes, such as *Advanced Programming in the UNIX Environment* by Richard Stevens or *UNIX System Programming* by David Curry.

Java

Chapter 16

Java is a network-aware, object-oriented language developed by Sun Microsystems. Java has been causing a lot of excitement in the computing community as it strives to provide a secure language for running applets downloaded from World Wide Web sites. The idea is simple: allow web browsers to download Java applets, which run on the client's machine. The popular Netscape web browser (discussed in Chapter 16) includes support for Java, and the Java Developer's Kit and other tools have been ported to Linux. But Java is not only suitable for those applets, in recent time, it has been used more and more as a general purpose programming language that offers fewer obstacles for beginners and that—because of its built-in networking libraries—is often used for programming client/server applications.

The Promise of Java, or Why You Might Want to Use Java

All this may not sound too exciting to you. There are lots of object-oriented programming languages, after all, and with Netscape plug-ins you can download executable programs from web servers and execute them on your local machine.

But Java is more. One of its most exciting aspects is platform independence. That means that you can write and compile your Java program and then deploy it on almost every machine, whether it is a lowly 386 running Linux, a powerful Pentium II running the latest bloatware from Microsoft, or an IBM mainframe. Sun Microsystems calls this "Write Once, Run Anywhere." Unfortunately, real life is not as simple as design goals. There are tiny, but frustrating, differences that make a program work on one platform and fail on another. With the advent of the new GUI library Swing in Java 2.0, a large step has been made to remedy this.

This neat feature of compiling code once and then being able to run it on another machine is made possible by the Java Virtual Machine (JVM). The Java compiler does not generate object code for a particular CPU and operating system like *gcc* does, it generates code for the Java Virtual Machine. This machine does not exist anywhere in hardware (yet), but is instead a specification. This specification says which so-called opcodes the machine understands and what the machine does when it encounters them in the object file. The program is distributed in binary form containing so-called *byte codes* that follow the Java Virtual Machine specification.

Now all you need is a program that implements the Java Virtual Machine on your particular computer and operating system. These are available nowadays for just about any platform—no vendor can dare not provide a Java Virtual Machine for its hardware or operating system. This program is also called the Java interpreter, because it interprets the opcodes compiled for the Java Virtual Machine and translates them into code for the native machine.

This distinction, which makes Java both a compiled and an interpreted language, makes it possible for you to write and compile your Java program and distribute it to someone else, and no matter what hardware and operating system she has, she will be able to run your program as long as a Java interpreter is available for it.

Alas, Java's platform independence comes at a price. Because the object code is not object code of any currently existing hardware, it must pass through an extra layer of processing, meaning that programs written in Java typically run ten to twenty times slower than comparable programs written in, for example, C. While this does not matter for some cases, in other cases it is simply unacceptable. There are so-called Just-In-Time compilers available that first translate the object code for the Java Virtual Machine into native object code and then run this object code.

When the same object code is run a second time, the precompiled native code can be used without any interpretation and thus runs faster. But the speed that can be achieved with this is still inferior to that of C programs. Sun Microsystems is working on a technology that is said to provide an execution speed "comparable to C programs," but whether this promise can be fulfilled remains to be seen.

Java also distinguishes between applications and applets. Applications are standalone programs that are run from the command line or your local desktop and behave like ordinary programs. Applets, on the other hand, are programs (usually smaller) that run inside your web browser. (To run these programs, the browser needs a Java interpreter inside.) When you browse a web site that contains a Java applet, the web server sends you the object code of the applet, and your browser executes it for you. This can be used for anything from simple animations to complete online banking systems.*

When reading about the Java applets, you might have thought, "And what happens if the applet contains mischievous code that spies my hard disk or even maybe deletes or corrupts files?" Of course, this would be possible if the Java designers had not designed a multistep countermeasure against such attacks: All Java applets run in a so-called sandbox, which allows them access only to certain resources. For example, Java applets can output text on your monitor, but they can't read data from your local filesystem or even write to it unless you explicitly allow them to. While this sandbox paradigm reduces the usefulness of applets, it increases the security of your data. With recent Java releases, you can determine how much security you need and thus have additional flexibility.

[53] Thinking in Java
[54] Exploring Java
[55] Core Java 2

If you decide that Java is something for you, we would recommend that you get a copy of *Thinking in Java* by Bruce Eckel. It covers most of the things you need to know in the Java world and also teaches you general programming principles. Other Java titles that are well worth looking into include *Exploring Java* by Pat Niemeyer and Josh Peck and *Core Java* by Gary Cornell and Cay Horstmann.

Getting Java for Linux

Fortunately, there is a Linux port of the so-called JDK, the Java Developers Kit provided by Sun Microsystem for Solaris and Windows which serves as a reference implementation of Java. In the past, there was usually a gap between the appearance of a new JDK version for Solaris and Windows and the availability of the JDK for Linux. Sun Microsystems has now promised to work closely together with the developers doing the Linux port, so there is hope that future Linux versions will be available in a timely manner.

The "official" Java implementation JDK contains a compiler, an interpreter and several related tools. Other kits are also available for Linux, often in the form of Open Source software. We'll cover the JDK here, though, because that's the standard.

---

* One of us does all his financial business with his bank via a Java applet that his bank provides when browsing a special area of their web server.

One more note: Most distributions already contain the JDK for Linux, so it might be easier for you to simply install a prepackaged one. However, the JDK is moving fast, and you might want to install a newer version than the one your distribution contains.

Your one stop for shopping for Java software for Linux is *http://www.black-down.org*. Here, you will find documentation, news about the Linux ports, and links to the places where you can download a copy of the JDK for your machine.

After unpacking and installing the JDK according to the instructions, you have several new programs at your disposal. *javac* is the Java compiler, *java* is the interpreter, and *appletviewer* is a small GUI program that lets you run applets without using a full-blown web browser.

A Working Example of Java

The following program (which has been written for Java 1.1, but should also work with Java 1.2/2) is a complete Java program that can run as a stand-alone application as well as an applet. It is a small painting program that lets you scribble on a virtual canvas. It also utilizes some GUI elements like a push button and an option menu.

The part of Java that lets you use GUI elements like windows and menus is called the Abstract Window Toolkit (AWT). It, too, helps fulfill Java's promise of "Write once, run anywhere." Even though different operating systems like Linux, Windows, and the Macintosh have completely different windowing systems, you need to write your user interface code only once. The AWT then maps the platform-independent widgets to a native GUI library. Thus, your program will have the native look of the respective windowing systems, depending on the system you run it on.

The AWT has a number of drawbacks, such as the different look that the programs have on each platform (some people consider this an advantage, though, because the program looks like a native application), the speed, and the numerous bugs. With the recent advent of Java 2.0, AWT will be replaced by a new toolkit called Swing that is based on an internal layer of the AWT and implements all user interface elements in Java. Swing projects usually look very nice but are even slower.

Enough talk now. Here is the code for the little scribbling program:

```
import java.applet.*;
import java.awt.*;
import java.awt.event.*;
/** An applet that can also run as a standalone application */
public class StandaloneScribble extends Applet {
   /**
    * The main() method.  If this program is invoked as an application,
    * this method will create the necessary window, add the applet to it,
```

```
                 * and call init(), below.  Note that Frame uses a PanelLayout by
                 * default.
                 */
                public static void main(String[] args) {
                  Frame f = new Frame();                    // Create a window
                  Applet a = new StandaloneScribble();      // Create the applet panel
                  f.add(a, "Center");                       // Add applet to window
                  a.init();                                 // Initialize the applet
                  f.setSize(400, 400);                      // Set the size of the
                                                            // window
                  f.show();                                 // Make the window visible
                  f.addWindowListener(new WindowAdapter() { // Handle window close
                                                            // requests
                    public void windowClosing(WindowEvent e) { System.exit(0); }
                  });
                }
                /**
                 * The init() method.  If the program is invoked as an applet, the
                 * browser allocates screen space for it and calls this method to set
                 * things up.
                 */
                public void init() {
                  // Define, instantiate and register a MouseListener object
                  this.addMouseListener(new MouseAdapter() {
                    public void mousePressed(MouseEvent e) {
                      lastx = e.getX();
                      lasty = e.getY();
                    }
                  });
                  // Define, instantiate and register a MouseMotionListener object
                  this.addMouseMotionListener(new MouseMotionAdapter() {
                    public void mouseDragged(MouseEvent e) {
                      Graphics g = getGraphics();
                      int x = e.getX(), y = e.getY();
                      g.setColor(Color.black);
                      g.drawLine(lastx, lasty, x, y);
                      lastx = x; lasty = y;
                    }
                  });
                  // Create a clear button
                  Button b = new Button("Clear");
                  // Define, instantiate, and register a listener to handle button
                  // presses
                  b.addActionListener(new ActionListener() {
                    public void actionPerformed(ActionEvent e) {  // clear the scribble
                      Graphics g = getGraphics();
                      g.setColor(getBackground());
                      g.fillRect(0, 0, getSize().width, getSize().height);
                    }
                  });
```

```
      // And add the button to the applet
      this.add(b);
   }
   protected int lastx, lasty;  // Coordinates of last mouse click
}
```

Save this code in a file named *StandaloneScribble.java*. The name is important; it must be the same as the name of the class implemented in the file with *.java* attached. To compile this code, issue the following command:

`$tigger ` **`javac StandaloneScribble.java`**

This can take a while. The Java compiler is not particularly fast, mainly because it is written in Java itself. When it is done, it will have created a file *StandaloneScribble.class* together with some more *.class* files which we won't talk about here.

Now you can run this program from the command-line. Simply issue the command:

`$tigger ` **`java StandaloneScribble`**

If you have installed the JDK correctly, you should get a window to scribble in. Note that the argument passed to the Java command was *StandaloneScribble* without the *.class* extension. This is because, technically, the interpreter is not executing the file, but the class.

You can also run this program, in a web browser or in the *appletviewer* from the JDK. For this, you need a bit of HTML code. The following should be enough:

```
<APPLET code="StandaloneScribble.class" width=150 height=100>
</APPLET>
```

Save this code to a file and open it with either a web browser like Netscape Navigator or the *appletviewer*, and you'll see the program in the browser window.

To finish this section, let's go through some of the most interesting lines of the program: In the first three lines, other Java classes that come from the JDK are imported. This is roughly comparable to including header files in a C program although there is no linking step in Java. When the program is run, the Java interpreter needs to be able to find the imported classes. It does this by looking in the directories mentioned in the environment variable CLASSPATH that you should have set up according to the JDK documentation.

Lines 13 through 21 contain the `main()` method. When the program is run as a standalone application, this method is called by the interpreter to start the execution of the program. In this method, a window is set up which is then used for screen output.

Most of the remaining code is the method `init()`. It is called either from `main()` when run standalone or directly from the web browser when run as an applet. In the latter case, `main()` is not executed at all.

Executing Java Programs Like Ordinary Programs

Chapter 7

Since version 2.0, the Linux kernel has a nice feature that allows it to execute a Java program without explicitly invoking the interpreter. In order to enable this feature, you need to recompile your kernel (see Chapter 7, *Upgrading Software and the Kernel*) and turn on Java binary format support. When you have installed the new kernel and rebooted your machine, you can make your class file executable and just run it from the command line. The Linux kernel will call the Java interpreter for you in the background:

```
tigger$ chmod +x StandaloneScribble.class
tigger$ ./StandaloneScribble.class
```

Nice feature, isn't it? The big boys like IBM and Microsoft are still trying to get it working. In case it does not work for you, the most probable reason is that the Linux-Kernel cannot find the Java interpreter. Check the values of the two constants _PATH_JAVA and _PATH_APPLET in the file */usr/src/linux/fs/binfmt_java.c*. If these do not reflect the location of your Java interpreter and *appletviewer*, move the interpreter and the *appletviewer* to one of the directories shown. Alternatively, you can change the *binfmt_java.c* file to include the proper directory, after which you have to recompile and install your kernel.

Other Languages

There are many other popular (and not-so-popular) languages available for Linux. For the most part, however, these work identically on Linux as on other Unix systems, so there's not much in the way of news there. There are also so many of them that we can't cover them in much detail here. We do want to let you know what's out there, however, and explain some of the differences between the various languages and compilers.

Python has gained a lot of attention lately, because it is a powerful mixture of different programming paradigms and styles. For example, it is one of the very few interpreted object-oriented programming languages (Perl being another example, but only relatively late in its existence). Python fans say it is especially easily learned. Python was almost entirely written and designed by Guido van Rossum, who chose the name because he wrote the interpreter while watching reruns of the British TV show *Monty Python's Flying Circus*. You can read all about Python at *http://www.python.org* or in *Programming Python* by Mark Lutz.

[52] Program-
ming Python

LISP is an interpreted language used in many applications, ranging from artificial intelligence to statistics. It is used primarily in computer science, because it defines a clean, logical interface for working with algorithms. (It also uses a lot of parentheses, something computer scientists are always fond of.) It is a functional programming language and is very generalized. Many operations are defined in terms of recursion instead of linear loops. Expressions are hierarchical, and data is represented by lists of items.

There are several LISP interpreters available for Linux. Emacs LISP is a fairly complete implementation in itself. It has many features that allow it to interact directly with Emacs—input and output through Emacs buffers, for example—but it may be used for non-Emacs–related applications as well.

Also available is CLISP, a Common LISP implementation by Bruno Haible of Karlsruhe University and Michael Stoll of Munich University. It includes an interpreter, a compiler, and a subset of CLOS (Common LISP Object System, an object-oriented extension to LISP). CLX, a Common LISP interface to the X Window System, is also available, and it runs under CLISP. CLX allows you to write X-based applications in LISP. Austin Kyoto Common LISP, another LISP implementation, is available and compatible with CLX as well.

SWI-Prolog, a complete Prolog implementation by Jan Wielemaker of the University of Amsterdam, is also available. Prolog is a logic-based language, allowing you to make logical assertions, define heuristics for validating those assertions, and make decisions based on them. It is a useful language for AI applications.

Also available are several Scheme interpreters, including MIT Scheme, a complete Scheme interpreter conforming to the R^4 standard. Scheme is a dialect of LISP that offers a cleaner, more general programming model. It is a good LISP dialect for computer-science applications and for studying algorithms.

At least two implementations of Ada are available—AdaEd, an Ada interpreter, and GNAT, the GNU Ada Translator. GNAT is actually a full-fledged optimizing Ada compiler. It is to Ada what *gcc* is to C and C++.

Along the same vein, two other popular language translators exist for Linux—*p2c*, a Pascal-to-C translator, and *f2c*, a FORTRAN-to-C translator. If you're concerned that these translators won't function as well as bona fide compilers, don't be. Both *p2c* and *f2c* have proven to be robust and useful for heavy Pascal and FORTRAN use.

f2c is FORTRAN-77–compliant, and a number of tools are available for it as well. *ftnchek* is a FORTRAN checker, similar to *lint*. Both the LAPACK numerical methods library and the *mpfun* multiprecision FORTRAN library have been ported to Linux using *f2c*. *toolpack* is a collection of FORTRAN tools, such as a source-code pretty-printer, a precision converter, and a portability checker.

Among the miscellaneous other languages available for Linux are interpreters for APL, Rexx, Forth, ML, Eiffel, and a Simula-to-C translator. The GNU versions of the compiler tools *lex* and *yacc* (renamed to *flex* and *bison*, respectively), which are used for many software packages, have also been ported to Linux. *lex* and *yacc* are invaluable for creating any kind of parser or translator, most commonly used when writing compilers.

## CHAPTER FOURTEEN

TOOLS FOR PROGRAMMERS

Many judge a computer system by the tools it offers its programmers. Unix systems have won the contest by many people's standards, having developed a very rich set over the years. Leading the parade is the GNU debugger, *gdb*. In this chapter, we take a close look at this invaluable utility and a number of other auxiliary tools C programmers will find useful.

Even if you are not a programmer, you should consider using the Revision Control System (RCS). It provides one of the most reassuring protections a computer user could ask for—backups for everything you do to a file. If you delete a file by accident, or decide that everything you did for the past week was a mistake and should be ripped out, RCS can recover any version you want. If you are working on a larger project that involves either a large number of developers or a large number of directories, Concurrent Versioning System (CVS) might be more suitable for you. It is based on RCS, but provides some additional features.

Debugging with gdb

Are you one of those programmers who scoff at the very idea of using a debugger to trace through code? Is it your philosophy that if the code is too complex for even the programmer to understand, then the programmer deserves no mercy when it comes to bugs? Do you step through your code, mentally, using a magnifying glass and a toothpick? More often than not, are bugs usually caused by a single-character omission, such as using the = operator when you mean +=?

Then perhaps you should meet *gdb*—the GNU debugger. Whether or not you know it, *gdb* is your friend. It can locate obscure and difficult-to-find bugs that result in core dumps, memory leaks, and erratic behavior (both for the program and the programmer). Sometimes even the most harmless-looking glitches in your

[50] gdb

code can cause everything to go haywire, and without the aid of a debugger like *gdb*, finding these problems can be nearly impossible—especially for programs longer than a few hundred lines. In this section, we'll introduce you to the most useful features of *gdb* by way of examples. There's a book on *gdb*, too—the Free Software Foundation's *Debugging with GDB*.

gdb is capable of either debugging programs as they run, or examining the cause for a program crash with a core dump. Programs debugged at runtime with *gdb* can either be executed from within *gdb* itself or can be run separately; that is, *gdb* can attach itself to an already running process to examine it. First, we'll discuss how to debug programs running within *gdb* and then move on to attaching to running processes and examining core dumps.

Tracing a Program

Our first example is a program called *trymb* that detects edges in a grayscale image. *trymb* takes as input an image file, does some calculations on the data, and spits out another image file. Unfortunately, it crashes whenever it is invoked, as so:

```
papaya$ trymh < image00.pgm > image00.pbm
Segmentation fault (core dumped)
```

Now, using *gdb* we could analyze the resulting core file, but for this example, we'll show how to trace the program as it runs, instead.*

Before we use *gdb* to trace through the executable *trymb*, we need to ensure that the executable has been compiled with debugging code (see the section "Enabling Debugging Code" in Chapter 13, *Programming Languages*). To do so, we should compile *trymb* using the –g switch with *gcc*.

Chapter 13

Note that enabling optimization (–O) with debug code (–g) is not illegal but not recommended. The problem is that *gcc* is too smart for its own good. For example, if you have two identical lines of code in two different places in a function, *gdb* may unexpectedly jump to the second occurrence of the line, instead of the first, as expected. This is because *gcc* combined the two lines into a single line of machine code used in both instances.

Some of the automatic optimizations performed by *gcc* can be confusing when using a debugger. To turn off *all* optimization (even optimizations performed without specifying –O), use the –O0 (that's *dash-oh-zero*) option with *gcc*.

Now we can fire up *gdb* to see what the problem might be:

```
papaya$ gdb trymh
GDB is free software and you are welcome to distribute copies of it
  under certain conditions; type "show copying" to see the conditions.
```

---

* The sample programs in this section are not programs you're likely to run into anywhere; they were thrown together by the authors for the purpose of demonstration.

There is absolutely no warranty for GDB; type "show warranty" for details.
GDB 4.16 (i486-unknown-linux --target i486-linux),
Copyright 1996 Free Software Foundation, Inc.
(gdb)

Now *gdb* is waiting for a command. (The command *help* displays information on the available commands.) The first thing we want to do is start running the program so that we can observe its behavior. However, if we immediately use the *run* command, the program simply executes until it exits or crashes.

First, we need to set a *breakpoint* somewhere in the program. A breakpoint is just a location in the program where *gdb* should stop and allow us to control execution of the program. For the sake of simplicity, let's set a breakpoint on the first line of actual code, so that the program stops just as it begins to execute. The *list* command displays several lines of code (an amount that is variable) at a time:

```
(gdb) list
12        main() {
13
14          FloatImage inimage;
15          FloatImage outimage;
16          BinaryImage binimage;
17          int i,j;
18
19          inimage = (FloatImage)imLoadF(IMAGE_FLOAT,stdin);
20          outimage = laplacian_float(inimage);
21
(gdb) break 19
Breakpoint 1 at 0x289c: file trymh.c, line 19.
(gdb)
```

A breakpoint is now set at line 19 in the current source file. You can set many breakpoints in the program; breakpoints may be conditional (that is, triggered only when a certain expression is true), unconditional, delayed, temporarily disabled, and so on. You may set breakpoints on a particular line of code, a particular function, a set of functions, and in a slew of other ways. You may also set a *watchpoint*, using the *watch* command, which is similar to a breakpoint but is triggered whenever a certain event takes place—not necessarily at a specific line of code within the program. We'll talk more about breakpoints and watchpoints later in the chapter.

Next, we use the *run* command to start the program running. *run* takes as arguments the same arguments you'd give *trymh* on the command line; this can include shell wildcards and input/output redirection, as the command is passed to */bin/sh* for execution:

```
(gdb) run < image00.pgm > image00.pfm
Starting program: /amd/dusk/d/mdw/vis/src/trymh < image00.pgm >\
image00.pfm
```

```
Breakpoint 1, main () at trymh.c:19
19              inimage = (FloatImage)imLoadF(IMAGE_FLOAT,stdin);
(gdb)
```

As expected, the breakpoint is reached immediately at the first line of code. We can now take over.

The most useful program-stepping commands are *next* and *step*. Both commands execute the next line of code in the program, except that *step* descends into any function calls in the program, and *next* steps only to the next line of code in the same function. *next* quietly executes any function calls that it steps over but does not descend in their code for us to examine.

imLoadF is a function that loads an image from a disk file. We know this function is not at fault (you'll have to trust us on that one), so we wish to step over it using the *next* command:

```
(gdb) next
20              outimage = laplacian_float(inimage);
(gdb)
```

Here, we are interested in tracing into the suspicious-looking *laplacian_float* function, so we use the *step* command:

```
(gdb) step
laplacian_float (fim=0x0) at laplacian.c:21
21              i = 20.0;
(gdb)
```

Let's use the *list* command to get some idea of where we are:

```
(gdb) list
16          FloatImage laplacian_float(FloatImage fim) {
17
18              FloatImage mask;
19              float i;
20
21              i = 20.0;
22              mask=(FloatImage)imNew(IMAGE_FLOAT,3,3);
23              imRef(mask,0,0) = imRef(mask,2,0) = imRef(mask,0,2) = 1.0;
24              imRef(mask,2,2) = 1.0; imRef(mask,1,0) = imRef(mask,0,1) = i/5;
25              imRef(mask,2,1) = imRef(mask,1,2) = i/5; imRef(mask,1,1) = -i;
(gdb) list
26
27              return convolveFloatWithFloat(fim,mask);
28          }
(gdb)
```

As you can see, using *list* multiple times just displays more of the code. Because we don't want to *step* manually through this code, and we're not interested in the *imNew* function on line 22, let's continue execution until line 27. For this, we use the *until* command:

```
(gdb) until 27
laplacian_float (fim=0x0) at laplacian.c:27
27              return convolveFloatWithFloat(fim,mask);
(gdb)
```

Before we step into the *convolveFloatWithFloat* function, let's be sure the two parameters, fim and mask, are valid. The *print* command examines the value of a variable:

```
(gdb) print mask
$1 = (struct {...} *) 0xe838
(gdb) print fim

$2 = (struct {...} *) 0x0
(gdb)
```

mask looks fine, but fim, the input image, is null. Obviously, *laplacian_float* was passed a null pointer instead of a valid image. If you have been paying close attention, you noticed this as we entered *laplacian_float* earlier.

Instead of stepping deeper into the program (as it's apparent that something has already gone wrong), let's continue execution until the current function returns. The *finish* command accomplishes this:

```
(gdb) finish
Run till exit from #0  laplacian_float (fim=0x0) at laplacian.c:27
0x28c0 in main () at trymh.c:20
20          outimage = laplacian_float(inimage);
Value returned is $3 = (struct {...} *) 0x0
(gdb)
```

Now we're back in *main*. To determine the source of the problem, let's examine the values of some variables:

```
(gdb) list
15          FloatImage outimage;
16          BinaryImage binimage;
17          int i,j;
18
19          inimage = (FloatImage)imLoadF(IMAGE_FLOAT,stdin);
20          outimage = laplacian_float(inimage);
21
22          binimage = marr_hildreth(outimage);
23          if  (binimage == NULL) {
24            fprintf(stderr,"trymh: binimage returned NULL\n");
(gdb) print inimage
$6 = (struct {...} *) 0x0
(gdb)
```

The variable inimage, containing the input image returned from *imLoadF*, is null.

Passing a null pointer into the image-manipulation routines certainly would cause a core dump in this case. However, we know *imLoadF* to be tried and true because it's in a well-tested library, so what's the problem?

As it turns out, our library function *imLoadF* returns NULL on failure—if the input format is bad, for example. Because we never checked the return value of *imLoadF* before passing it along to *laplacian_float*, the program goes haywire when inimage is assigned NULL. To correct the problem, we simply insert code to cause the problem to exit with an error message if *imLoadF* returns a null pointer.

To quit *gdb*, just use the command *quit*. Unless the program has finished execution, *gdb* will complain that the program is still running:

```
(gdb) quit
The program is running.  Quit anyway (and kill it)? (y or n) y
papaya$
```

In the following sections we examine some specific features provided by the debugger, given the general picture just presented.

Examining a Core File

Do you hate it when a program crashes and spites you again by leaving a 10 MB core file in your working directory, wasting much-needed space? Don't be so quick to delete that core file; it can be very helpful. A core file is just a dump of the memory image of a process at the time of the crash. You can use the core file with *gdb* to examine the state of your program (such as the values of variables and data) and determine the cause for failure.

The core file is written to disk by the operating system whenever certain failures occur. The most frequent reason for a crash and the subsequent core dump is a memory violation—that is, trying to read or write memory that your program does not have access to. For example, attempting to write data into a null pointer can cause a *segmentation fault*, which is essentially a fancy way to say, "you screwed up." Other errors that result in core files are so-called "bus errors" and "floating-point exceptions." Segmentation faults are a common error and occur when you try to access (read from or write to) a memory address that does not belong to your process's address space. This includes the address 0, as often happens with uninitialized pointers. Bus errors result in using incorrectly aligned data and are therefore rare on the Intel architecture, which does not pose strong alignment conditions like other architectures, such as SPARC. Floating-point exceptions point to a severe problem in a floating-point calculation like an overflow, but the most usual case is a division by zero.

However, not all such memory errors will cause immediate crashes. For example, you may overwrite memory in some way, but the program continues to run, not knowing the difference between actual data and instructions or garbage. Subtle memory violations can cause programs to behave erratically. One of the authors once witnessed a bug that caused the program to jump randomly around but without tracing it with *gdb*, it still appeared to work normally. The only evidence of a bug was that the program returned output that meant, roughly, that two and two did not add up to four. Sure enough, the bug was an attempt to write one too many characters into a block of allocated memory. That single-byte error caused hours of grief.

You can prevent these kinds of memory problems (even the best programmers make these mistakes!) using the Checker package, a set of memory-management routines that replaces the commonly used *malloc()* and *free()* functions. We'll talk about Checker in the section "Using Checker."

However, if your program does cause a memory fault, it will crash and dump core. Under Linux, core files are named, appropriately, *core*. The core file appears in the current working directory of the running process, which is usually the working directory of the shell that started the program, but on occasion, programs may change their own working directory.

Some shells provide facilities for controlling whether core files are written. Under *bash*, for example, the default behavior is not to write core files at all. In order to enable core file output, you should use the command:

```
ulimit -c unlimited
```

probably in your *.bashrc* initialization file. You can specify a maximum size for core files other than `unlimited`, but truncated core files may not be of use when debugging applications.

Also, in order for a core file to be useful, the program must be compiled with debugging code enabled, as described in the previous section. Most binaries on your system will not contain debugging code, so the core file will be of limited value.

Our example for using *gdb* with a core file is yet another mythical program called *cross*. Like *trymh* in the previous section, *cross* takes as input an image file, does some calculations on it, and outputs another image file. However, when running *cross*, we get a segmentation fault:

```
papaya$ cross < image30.pfm > image30.pbm
Segmentation fault (core dumped)
papaya$
```

To invoke *gdb* for use with a core file, you must specify not only the core file-name but also the name of the executable that goes along with that core file. This is because the core file itself does not contain all the information necessary for debugging:

```
papaya$ gdb cross core
GDB is free software and you are welcome to distribute copies of it
 under certain conditions; type "show copying" to see the conditions.
There is absolutely no warranty for GDB; type "show warranty" for details.
GDB 4.8, Copyright 1993 Free Software Foundation, Inc...
Core was generated by `cross'.
Program terminated with signal 11, Segmentation fault.
#0  0x2494 in crossings (image=0xc7c8) at cross.c:31
31                  if ((image[i][j] >= 0) &&
(gdb)
```

gdb tells us that the core file terminated with signal 11. A *signal* is a kind of message that is sent to a running program from the kernel, the user, or the program itself. Signals are generally used to terminate a program (and possibly cause it to dump core). For example, when you type the interrupt character, a signal is sent to the running program, which will probably kill the program.

In this case, signal 11 was sent to the running *cross* process by the kernel when *cross* attempted to read or write to memory that it did not have access to. This signal caused *cross* to die and dump core. *gdb* says that the illegal memory reference occurred on line 31 of the source file *cross.c*:

```
(gdb) list
26              xmax = imGetWidth(image)-1;
27              ymax = imGetHeight(image)-1;
28
29              for (j=1; j<xmax; j++) {
30                for (i=1; i<ymax; i++) {
31                  if ((image[i][j] >= 0) &&
32                      (image[i-1][j-1] < 0) ||
33                      (image[i-1][j] < 0) ||
34                      (image[i-1][j+1] < 0) ||
35                      (image[i][j-1] < 0) ||
(gdb)
```

Here, we see several things. First of all, there is a loop across the two index variables i and j, presumably in order to do calculations on the input image. Line 31 is an attempt to reference data from image[i][j], a two-dimensional array. When a program dumps core while attempting to access data from an array, it's usually a sign that one of the indices is out of bounds. Let's check them:

```
(gdb) print i
$1 = 1
(gdb) print j
$2 = 1194
(gdb) print xmax
$3 = 1551
(gdb) print ymax
$4 = 1194
(gdb)
```

Here we see the problem. The program was attempting to reference element `image[1][1194]`, however, the array extends only to `image[1550][1193]` (remember that arrays in C are indexed from 0 to *max*-1). In other words, we attempted to read the 1195th row of an image that only has 1194 rows.

If we look at lines 29 and 30, we see the problem: the values `xmax` and `ymax` are reversed. The variable `j` should range from 1 to `ymax` (because it is the row index of the array), and `i` should range from 1 to `xmax`. Fixing the two `for` loops on lines 29 and 30 corrects the problem.

Let's say that your program is crashing within a function that is called from many different locations, and you want to determine where the function was invoked from and what situation led up to the crash. The *backtrace* command displays the *call stack* of the program at the time of failure. If you are like me and are too lazy to type `backtrace` all the time, you will be delighted to hear that you can also use the shortcut *bt*.

The call stack is the list of functions that led up to the current one. For example, if the program starts in function *main*, which calls function *foo*, which calls *bamf*, the call stack looks like:

```
(gdb) backtrace
#0   0x1384 in bamf () at goop.c:31
#1   0x4280 in foo () at goop.c:48
#2   0x218 in main () at goop.c:116
(gdb)
```

As each function is called, it pushes certain data onto the stack, such as saved registers, function arguments, local variables, and so forth. Each function has a certain amount of space allocated on the stack for its use. The chunk of memory on the stack for a particular function is called a *stack frame*, and the call stack is the ordered list of stack frames.

In the following example, we are looking at a core file for an X-based animation program. Using *backtrace* gives us:

```
(gdb) backtrace
#0   0x602b4982 in _end ()
#1   0xbffff934 in _end ()
#2   0x13c6 in stream_drawimage (wgt=0x38330000, sn=4)\
at stream_display.c:94
#3   0x1497 in stream_refresh_all () at stream_display.c:116
#4   0x49c in control_update_all () at control_init.c:73
#5   0x224 in play_timeout (Cannot access memory at address 0x602b7676.
(gdb)
```

This is a list of stack frames for the process. The most recently called function is frame 0, which is the "function" *_end* in this case. Here, we see that *play_timeout* called *control_update_all*, which called *stream_refresh_all*, and so on. Somehow, the program jumped to *_end* where it crashed.

However, _end is not a function; it is simply a label that specifies the end of the process data segment. When a program branches to an address such as _end, which is not a real function, it is a sign that something must have caused the process to go haywire, corrupting the call stack. (This is known in hacker jargon as "jumping to hyperspace.") In fact, the error "Cannot access memory at address 0x602b7676" is another indication that something bizarre has occurred.

We can see, however, that the last "real" function called was *stream_drawimage*, and we might guess that it is the source of the problem. To examine the state of *stream_drawimage*, we need to select its stack frame (frame number 2), using the *frame* command:

```
(gdb) frame 2
#2   0x13c6 in stream_drawimage (wgt=0x38330000, sn=4)\
at stream_display.c:94
94          XCopyArea(mydisplay,streams[sn].frames[currentframe],\
XtWindow(wgt),
(gdb) list
91
92          printf("CopyArea frame %d, sn %d, wid %d\n",currentframe,sn,wgt);
93
94          XCopyArea(mydisplay,streams[sn].frames[currentframe],\
XtWindow(wgt),
95              picGC,0,0,streams[sn].width,streams[sn].height,0,0);
(gdb)
```

Well, not knowing anything else about the program at hand, we can't see anything wrong here, unless the variable sn (being used as an index into the array streams) is out of range. From the output of *frame*, we see that *stream_drawimage* was called with an sn parameter of 4. (Function parameters are displayed in the output of *backtrace*, as well as whenever we change frames.)

Let's move up another frame, to *stream_refresh_all*, to see how *stream_display* was called. To do this, we use the *up* command, which selects the stack frame above the current one:

```
(gdb) up
#3   0x1497 in stream_refresh_all () at stream_display.c:116
116          stream_drawimage(streams[i].drawbox,i);
(gdb) list
113     void stream_refresh_all(void) {
114         int i;
115         for (i=0; i<=numstreams; i++) {
116            stream_drawimage(streams[i].drawbox,i);
117
(gdb) print i
$2 = 4
(gdb) print numstreams
$3 = 4
(gdb)
```

Here, we see that the index variable i is looping from 0 to numstreams, and indeed i here is 4, the second parameter to *stream_drawimage*. However, numstreams is also 4. What's going on?

The for loop on line 115 looks funny; it should read:

```
for (i=0; i<numstreams; i++) {
```

The error is in the use of the <= comparison operator. The streams array is indexed from 0 to numstreams-1, not from 0 to numstreams. This simple off-by-one error caused the program to go berserk.

As you can see, using *gdb* with a core dump allows you to browse through the image of a crashed program to find bugs. Never again will you delete those pesky core files, right?

Debugging a Running Program

gdb can also debug a program that is already running, allowing you to interrupt it, examine it, and then return the process to its regularly scheduled execution. This is very similar to running a program from within *gdb*, and there are only a few new commands to learn.

The *attach* command attaches *gdb* to a running process. In order to use *attach* you must also have access to the executable that corresponds to the process.

For example, if you have started the program *pgmseq* with process ID 254, you can start up *gdb* with:

papaya$ **gdb pgmseq**

and once inside *gdb*, use the command:

```
(gdb) attach 254
Attaching program '/home/loomer/mdw/pgmseq/pgmseq', pid 254
__select (nd=4, in=0xbffff96c, out=0xbffff94c, ex=0xbffff92c, tv=0x0)
    at __select.c:22
__select.c:22: No such file or directory.
(gdb)
```

The No such file or directory error is given because *gdb* can't locate the source file for __select. This is often the case with system calls and library functions, and it's nothing to worry about.

You can also start *gdb* with the command:

papaya$ **gdb pgmseq 254**

Once *gdb* attaches to the running process, it temporarily suspends the program and lets you take over, issuing *gdb* commands. Or you can set a breakpoint or watchpoint (with the *break* and *watch* commands) and use *continue* to cause the program to continue execution until the breakpoint is triggered.

The *detach* command detaches *gdb* from the running process. You can then use *attach* again, on another process, if necessary. If you find a bug, you can *detach* the current process, make changes to the source, recompile, and use the *file* command to load the new executable into *gdb*. You can then start the new version of the program and use the *attach* command to debug it. All without leaving *gdb*!

In fact, *gdb* allows you to debug three programs concurrently: one running directly under *gdb*, one tracing with a core file, and one running as an independent process. The *target* command allows you to select which one you wish to debug.

Changing and Examining Data

To examine the values of variables in your program, you can use the *print*, *x*, and *ptype* commands. The *print* command is the most commonly used data inspection command; it takes as an argument an expression in the source language (usually C or C++) and returns its value. For example:

```
(gdb) print mydisplay
$10 = (struct _XDisplay *) 0x9c800
(gdb)
```

This displays the value of the variable `mydisplay`, as well as an indication of its type. Because this variable is a pointer, you can examine its contents by dereferencing the pointer, as you would in C:

```
(gdb) print *mydisplay
$11 = {ext_data = 0x0, free_funcs = 0x99c20, fd = 5, lock = 0,
  proto_major_version = 11, proto_minor_version = 0,
  vendor = 0x9dff0 "XFree86", resource_base = 41943040,
  ...
  error_vec = 0x0, cms = {defaultCCCs = 0xa3d80 "",\
clientCmaps = 0x991a0 "'",
    perVisualIntensityMaps = 0x0}, conn_checker = 0, im_filters = 0x0}
(gdb)
```

`mydisplay` is an extensive structure used by X programs; we have abbreviated the output for your reading enjoyment.

print can print the value of just about any expression, including C function calls (which it executes on the fly, within the context of the running program):

```
(gdb) print getpid()
$11 = 138
(gdb)
```

Of course, not all functions may be called in this manner. Only those functions that have been linked to the running program may be called. If a function has not been linked to the program and you attempt to call it, *gdb* will complain that there is no such symbol in the current context.

More complicated expressions may be used as arguments to *print* as well, including assignments to variables. For example:

```
(gdb) print mydisplay->vendor = "Linux"
$19 = 0x9de70 "Linux"
(gdb)
```

assigns the value of the vendor member of the mydisplay structure the value "Linux" instead of "XFree86" (a useless modification, but interesting nonetheless). In this way, you can interactively change data in a running program to correct errant behavior or test uncommon situations.

Note that after each *print* command, the value displayed is assigned to one of the *gdb* convenience registers, which are *gdb* internal variables that may be handy for you to use. For example, to recall the value of mydisplay in the previous example, we need to merely print the value of $10:

```
(gdb) print $10
$21 = (struct _XDisplay *) 0x9c800
(gdb)
```

You may also use expressions, such as typecasts, with the *print* command. Almost anything goes.

The *ptype* command gives you detailed (and often long-winded) information about a variable's type or the definition of a struct or typedef. To get a full definition for the struct _XDisplay used by the mydisplay variable, we use:

```
(gdb) ptype mydisplay
type = struct _XDisplay {
    struct _XExtData *ext_data;
    struct _XFreeFuncs *free_funcs;
    int fd;
    int lock;
    int proto_major_version;
    ...
    struct _XIMFilter *im_filters;
} *
(gdb)
```

If you're interested in examining memory on a more fundamental level, beyond the petty confines of defined types, you can use the *x* command. *x* takes a memory address as an argument. If you give it a variable, it uses the *value* of that variable as the address.

x also takes a count and a type specification as an optional argument. The count is the number of objects of the given type to display. For example, x/100x 0x4200 displays 100 bytes of data, represented in hexadecimal format, at the address 0x4200. Use *help x* to get a description of the various output formats.

To examine the value of `mydisplay->vendor`, we can use:

```
(gdb) x mydisplay->vendor
0x9de70 <_end+35376>:    76 'L'
(gdb) x/6c mydisplay->vendor
0x9de70 <_end+35376>:    76 'L'   105 'i' 110 'n' 117 'u' 120 'x' 0 ''
(gdb) x/s mydisplay->vendor
0x9de70 <_end+35376>:       "Linux"
(gdb)
```

The first field of each line gives the absolute address of the data. The second represents the address as some symbol (in this case, _end) plus an offset in bytes. The remaining fields give the actual value of memory at that address, first in decimal, then as an ASCII character. As described earlier you can force *x* to print the data in other formats.

Getting Information

The *info* command provides information about the status of the program being debugged. There are many subcommands under *info*; use *help info* to see them all. For example, *info program* displays the execution status of the program:

```
(gdb) info program
Using the running image of child process 138.
Program stopped at 0x9e.
It stopped at breakpoint 1.
(gdb)
```

Another useful command is *info locals*, which displays the names and values of all local variables in the current function:

```
(gdb) info locals
inimage = (struct {...} *) 0x2000
outimage = (struct {...} *) 0x8000
(gdb)
```

This is a rather cursory description of the variables. The *print* or *x* commands describe them further.

Similarly, *info variables* displays a list of all known variables in the program, ordered by source file. Note that many of the variables displayed will be from sources outside of your actual program—for example, the names of variables used within the library code. The values for these variables are not displayed, because the list is culled more or less directly from the executable's symbol table. Only those local variables in the current stack frame and global (static) variables are actually accessible from *gdb*. *info address* gives you information about exactly where a certain variable is stored. For example:

```
(gdb) info address inimage
Symbol "inimage" is a local variable at frame offset -20.
(gdb)
```

By `frame offset`, *gdb* means that *inimage* is stored 20 bytes below the top of the stack frame.

You can get information on the current frame using the *info frame* command, as so:

```
(gdb) info frame
Stack level 0, frame at 0xbffffaa8:
 eip = 0x9e in main (main.c:44); saved eip 0x34
 source language c.
 Arglist at 0xbffffaa8, args: argc=1, argv=0xbffffabc
 Locals at 0xbffffaa8, Previous frame's sp is 0x0

 Saved registers:
  ebx at 0xbffffaa0, ebp at 0xbffffaa8, esi at 0xbffffaa4, eip at\
0xbffffaac
(gdb)
```

This kind of information is useful if you're debugging at the assembly-language level with the *disass*, *nexti*, and *stepi* commands (see the section "Instruction-level debugging").

Miscellaneous Features

gdb(1)

We have barely scratched the surface about what *gdb* can do. It is an amazing program with a lot of power; we have introduced you only to the most commonly used commands. In this section, we'll look at other features of *gdb* and then send you on your way.

[50] gdb
Chapter 9

If you're interested in learning more about *gdb*, we encourage you to read the *gdb* manual page and the Free Software Foundation manual. The manual is also available as an online Info file. (Info files may be read under Emacs, or using the *info* reader; see the section "Tutorial and Online Help" in Chapter 9, *Editors, Text Tools, Graphics, and Printing*, for details.)

Breakpoints and watchpoints

As promised, we're going to demonstrate further use of breakpoints and watchpoints. Breakpoints are set with the *break* command; similarly, watchpoints are set with the *watch* command. The only difference between the two is that breakpoints must break at a particular location in the program—on a certain line of code, for example—and watchpoints may be triggered whenever a certain expression is true, regardless of location within the program. Though powerful, watchpoints can be horribly inefficient; any time the state of the program changes, all watchpoints must be reevaluated.

When a breakpoint or watchpoint is triggered, *gdb* suspends the program and returns control to you. Breakpoints and watchpoints allow you to run the program (using the *run* and *continue* commands) and stop only in certain situations, thus saving you the trouble of using many *next* and *step* commands to walk through the program manually.

There are many ways to set a breakpoint in the program. You can specify a line number, as in *break 20*. Or, you can specify a particular function, as in *break stream_unload*. You can also specify a line number in another source file, as in *break foo.c:38*. Use *help break* to see the complete syntax.

Breakpoints may be conditional; that is, the breakpoint triggers only when a certain expression is true. For example, using the command:

```
break 184 if (status == 0)
```

sets a conditional breakpoint at line 184 in the current source file, which triggers only when the variable status is zero. The variable status must be either a global variable or a local variable in the current stack frame. The expression may be any valid expression in the source language that *gdb* understands, identical to the expressions used by the *print* command. You can change the breakpoint condition (if it is conditional) using the *condition* command.

Using the command *info break* gives you a list of all breakpoints and watchpoints and their status. This allows you to delete or disable breakpoints, using the commands *clear*, *delete*, or *disable*. A disabled breakpoint is merely inactive, until you reenable it (with the *enable* command); on the other hand, a breakpoint that has been deleted is gone from the list of breakpoints for good. You can also specify that a breakpoint be enabled once; meaning that once it is triggered, it will be disabled again—or enabled once and then deleted.

To set a watchpoint, use the *watch* command, as in:

```
watch (numticks < 1024 && incoming != clear)
```

Watchpoint conditions may be any valid source expression, as with conditional breakpoints.

Instruction-level debugging

gdb is capable of debugging on the processor-instruction level, allowing you to watch the innards of your program with great scrutiny. However, understanding what you see requires not only knowledge of the processor architecture and assembly language, but also some gist of how the operating system sets up process address space. For example, it helps to understand the conventions used for setting up stack frames, calling functions, passing parameters and return values, and so on. Any book on protected-mode 80386/80486 programming can fill you in on these details. But be warned: protected-mode programming on this processor is quite different from real-mode programming (as is used in the MS-DOS world). Be sure that you're reading about native *protected-mode* 386 programming, or else you might subject yourself to terminal confusion.

The primary *gdb* commands used for instruction-level debugging are *nexti, stepi,* and *disass. nexti* is equivalent to *next,* except that it steps to the next instruction, not the next source line. Similarly, *stepi* is the instruction-level analogue of *step.*

The *disass* command displays a disassembly of an address range that you supply. This address range may be specified by literal address or function name. For example, to display a disassembly of the function *play_timeout,* use the command:

```
(gdb) disass play_timeout
Dump of assembler code for function play_timeout:
to 0x2ac:
0x21c <play_timeout>:             pushl   %ebp
0x21d <play_timeout+1>:           movl    %esp,%ebp
0x21f <play_timeout+3>:           call    0x494 <control_update_all>
0x224 <play_timeout+8>:           movl    0x952f4,%eax
0x229 <play_timeout+13>:          decl    %eax
0x22a <play_timeout+14>:          cmpl    %eax,0x9530c
0x230 <play_timeout+20>:          jne     0x24c <play_timeout+48>
0x232 <play_timeout+22>:          jmp     0x29c <play_timeout+128>
0x234 <play_timeout+24>:          nop
0x235 <play_timeout+25>:          nop
...

0x2a8 <play_timeout+140>:         addb    %al,(%eax)
0x2aa <play_timeout+142>:         addb    %al,(%eax)
(gdb)
```

This is equivalent to using the command *disass 0x21c* (where `0x21c` is the literal address of the beginning of *play_timeout*).

You can specify an optional second argument to *disass,* which will be used as the address where disassembly should stop. Using *disass 0x21c 0x232* will only display the first seven lines of the assembly listing in the previous example (the instruction starting with `0x232` itself will not be displayed).

If you use *nexti* and *stepi* often, you may wish to use the command:

```
display/i $pc
```

This causes the current instruction to be displayed after every *nexti* or *stepi* command. *display* specifies variables to watch or commands to execute after every stepping command. `$pc` is a *gdb* internal register that corresponds to the processor's program counter, pointing to the current instruction.

Using Emacs with gdb

Chapter 9

Emacs (described in the section "The Emacs Editor" in Chapter 9) provides a debugging mode that lets you run *gdb*—or another debugger—within the integrated program-tracing environment provided by Emacs. This so-called "Grand Unified Debugger" library is very powerful and allows you to debug and edit your programs entirely within Emacs.

To start *gdb* under Emacs, use the Emacs command M-x gdb and give the name of the executable to debug as the argument. A buffer will be created for *gdb*, which is similar to using *gdb* alone. You can then use *core-file* to load a core file or *attach* to attach to a running process, if you wish.

Whenever you step to a new frame (e.g., when you first trigger a breakpoint), *gdb* opens a separate window that displays the source corresponding to the current stack frame. This buffer may be used to edit the source text just as you normally would with Emacs, but the current source line is highlighted with an arrow (the characters =>). This allows you to watch the source in one window, and execute *gdb* commands in the other.

Within the debugging window, there are several special key sequences that can be used. They are fairly long, though, so it's not clear that you'll find them more convenient than just entering *gdb* commands directly. Some of the more common commands include:

C-x C-a C-s
    The equivalent of a *gdb step* command, updating the source window appropriately

C-x C-a C-i
    The equivalent of a *stepi* command

C-x C-a C-n
    The equivalent of a *next* command

C-x C-a C-r
    The equivalent of a *continue* command

C-x C-a <
    The equivalent of an *up* command

C-x C-a >
    The equivalent of a *down* command

If you do type in commands in the traditional manner, you can use M-p to move backwards to previously issued commands and M-n to move forward. You can also move around in the buffer using Emacs commands for searching, cursor movement, and so on. All in all, using *gdb* within Emacs is more convenient than using it from the shell.

In addition, you may edit the source text in the *gdb* source buffer; the prefix arrow will not be present in the source when it is saved.

Emacs is very easy to customize, and there are many extensions to this *gdb* interface that you could write yourself. You could define Emacs keys for other commonly used *gdb* commands or change the behavior of the source window. (For example, you could highlight all breakpoints in some fashion or provide keys to disable or clear breakpoints.)

Programming Tools

Along with languages and compilers, there is a plethora of programming tools out there, including libraries, interface builders, debuggers, and other utilities to aid the programming process. In this section, we'll talk about some of the most interesting bells and whistles of these tools to let you know what's out there.

Debuggers

There are several interactive debuggers available for Linux. The de facto standard debugger is *gdb*, which we just covered in detail.

In addition to *gdb*, there are several other debuggers, each with features very similar to *gdb*. *xxgdb* is a version of *gdb* with an X Window System interface similar to that found on the *xdbx* debugger on other Unix systems. There are several panes in the *xxgdb* debugger's window. One pane looks like the regular *gdb* text interface, allowing you to input commands manually to interact with the system. Another pane automatically displays the current source file along with a marker displaying the current line. You can use the source pane to set and select breakpoints, browse the source, and so on, while typing commands directly to *gdb*. A number of buttons are provided on the *xxgdb* window as well, providing quick access to frequently used commands, such as *step*, *next*, and so on. Given the buttons, you can use the mouse in conjunction with the keyboard to debug your program within an easy-to-use X interface.

Another debugger similar to *xxgdb* is UPS, an X-based debugger that has been ported to a number of Unix platforms. UPS is much simpler than *xxgdb* and doesn't provide the same features, but it is a good debugger nonetheless and has a less demanding learning curve than *gdb*. It is adequate for most applications and straightforward debugging needs.

Two other graphical frontends for *gdb* deserve mention. DDD, the Data Display Debugger, has the same features as *xxgdb* with a nicer, Motif user interface. In addition, it can display structures and classes in a graphical manner, which is especially useful if you want to explore the data structures of an unknown program. *kdbg* comes from the KDE project and—in addition to the features that *xxgdb* provides—is fully integrated into the KDE desktop.

Profiling and Performance Tools

There are several utilities out there that allow you to monitor and rate the performance of your program. These tools help you locate bottlenecks in your code— places where performance is lacking. These tools also give you a rundown on the call structure of your program, indicating what functions are called, from where, and how often. (Everything you ever wanted to know about your program, but were afraid to ask.)

gprof is a profiling utility that gives you a detailed listing of the running statistics for your program, including how often each function was called, from where, the total amount of time that each function required, and so forth.

In order to use *gprof* with a program, you must compile the program using the *–pg* option with *gcc*. This adds profiling information to the object file and links the executable with standard libraries that have profiling information enabled.

Having compiled the program to profile with *–pg*, simply run it. If it exits normally, the file *gmon.out* will be written to the working directory of the program. This file contains profiling information for that run and can be used with *gprof* to display a table of statistics.

As an example, let's take a program called *getstat*, which gathers statistics about an image file. First, we compile *getstat* with *–pg*, and run it:

```
papaya$ getstat image11.pgm > stats.dat
papaya$ ls -l gmon.out
-rw-------    1 mdw      mdw          54448 Feb  5 17:00 gmon.out
papaya$
```

Indeed, the profiling information was written to *gmon.out*.

To examine the profiling data, we run *gprof* and give it the name of the executable and the profiling file *gmon.out*:

```
papaya$ gprof getstat gmon.out
```

If you do not specify the name of the profiling file, *gprof* assumes the name *gmon.out*. It also assumes the executable name *a.out* if you do not specify that, either.

gprof output is rather verbose, so you may want to redirect it to a file or pipe it through a pager. It comes in two parts. The first part is the "flat profile," which gives a one-line entry for each function, listing the percentage of time spent in that function, the time (in seconds) used to execute that function, the number of calls to the function, and other information. For example:

```
Each sample counts as 0.01 seconds.
  %   cumulative   self              self     total
 time   seconds   seconds    calls  ms/call  ms/call  name
45.11    27.49     27.49       41   670.51   903.13   GetComponent
16.25    37.40      9.91                              mcount
10.72    43.93      6.54  1811863     0.00     0.00   Push
10.33    50.23      6.30  1811863     0.00     0.00   Pop
 5.87    53.81      3.58       40    89.50   247.06   stackstats
 4.92    56.81      3.00  1811863     0.00     0.00   TrimNeighbors
```

If any of the fields are blank in the output, *gprof* was unable to determine any further information about that function. This is usually caused by parts of the code that were not compiled with the *–pg* option; for example, if you call routines in nonstandard libraries that haven't been compiled with *–pg*, *gprof* won't be able to gather much information about those routines. In the previous output, the function *mcount* probably hasn't been compiled with profiling enabled.

As we can see, 45.11% of the total running time was spent in the function *GetComponent*—which amounts to 27.49 seconds. But is this because *GetComponent* is horribly inefficient or because *GetComponent* itself called many other slow functions? The functions *Push* and *Pop* were called many times during execution: could they be the culprits?*

The second part of the *gprof* report can help us here. It gives a detailed "call graph" describing which functions called other functions and how many times they were called. For example:

```
index % time    self  children    called     name
                                              <spontaneous>
[1]     92.7    0.00    47.30                 start [1]
                0.01    47.29       1/1           main [2]
                0.00     0.00       1/2           on_exit [53]
                0.00     0.00       1/1           exit [172]
```

The first column of the call graph is the index: a unique number given to every function, allowing you to find other functions in the graph. Here, the first function, *start*, is called implicitly when the program begins. *start* required 92.7% of the total running time (47.30 seconds), including its children, but required very little time to run itself. This is because *start* is the parent of all other functions in the program, including *main*; it makes sense that *start* plus its children requires that percentage of time.

The call graph normally displays the children as well as the parents of each function in the graph. Here, we can see that *start* called the functions *main*, *on_exit*, and *exit* (listed below the line for *start*). However, there are no parents (normally listed above *start*); instead, we see the ominous word <spontaneous>. This means that *gprof* was unable to determine the parent function of *start*; more than likely because *start* was not called from within the program itself but kicked off by the operating system.

Skipping down to the entry for *GetComponent*, or function-under-suspect, we see the following:

```
index % time    self  children    called          name
                0.67    0.23       1/41               GetFirstComponent [12]
               26.82    9.30      40/41               GetNextComponent [5]
[4]     72.6   27.49    9.54      41              GetComponent [4]
                6.54    0.00 1811863/1811863          Push [7]
                3.00    0.00 1811863/1811863          TrimNeighbors [9]
                0.00    0.00       1/1                InitStack [54]
```

The parent functions of *GetComponent* were *GetFirstComponent* and *GetNextComponent*, and its children were *Push*, *TrimNeighbors*, and *InitStack*. As we can see,

---

* Always a possibility where this author's code is concerned!

GetComponent was called 41 times—one time from *GetFirstComponent* and 40 times from *GetNextComponent*. The *gprof* output contains notes that describe the report in more detail.

GetComponent itself requires over 27.49 seconds to run; only 9.54 seconds are spent executing the children of *GetComponent* (including the many calls to *Push* and *TrimNeighbors!*). So it looks as though *GetComponent* and possibly its parent *GetNextComponent* need some tuning; the oft-called *Push* function is not the sole cause of the problem.

gprof also keeps track of recursive calls and "cycles" of called functions and indicates the amount of time required for each call. Of course, using *gprof* effectively requires that all code to be profiled is compiled with the *–pg* option. It also requires a knowledge of the program you're attempting to profile; *gprof* can only tell you so much about what's going on. It's up to the programmer to optimize inefficient code.

One last note about *gprof*: running it on a program that calls only a few functions—and runs very quickly—may not give you meaningful results. The units used for timing execution are usually rather coarse—maybe one-hundredth of a second—and if many functions in your program run more quickly than that, *gprof* will be unable to distinguish between their respective running times (rounding them to the nearest hundredth of a second). In order to get good profiling information, you may need to run your program under unusual circumstances—for example, giving it an unusually large data set to churn on, as in the previous example.

If *gprof* is more than you need, *calls* is a program that displays a tree of all function calls in your C source code. This can be useful to generate either an index of all called functions or to produce a high-level hierarchical report of the structure of a program.

Use of *calls* is simple: you tell it the names of the source files to map out, and a function-call tree is displayed. For example:

```
papaya$ calls scan.c
     1    level1 [scan.c]
     2          getid [scan.c]
     3                getc
     4                eatwhite [scan.c]
     5                      getc
     6                      ungetc
     7                strcmp
     8          eatwhite [see line 4]
     9          balance [scan.c]
    10                eatwhite [see line 4]
```

By default, *calls* lists only one instance of each called function at each level of the tree (so that if *printf* is called five times in a given function, it is listed only once). The *−a* switch prints all instances. *calls* has several other options as well; using *calls −b* gives you a summary.

Using strace

strace is a tool that displays the system calls being executed by a running program.* This can be extremely useful for real-time monitoring of a program's activity, although it does take some knowledge of programming at the system-call level. For example, when the library routine *printf* is used within a program, *strace* displays information only about the underlying *write* system call when it is executed. Also, *strace* can be quite verbose: many system calls are executed within a program that the programmer may not be aware of. However, *strace* is a good way to quickly determine the cause for a program crash or other strange failure.

Take the "Hello, World!" program given earlier in the chapter. Running *strace* on the executable *hello* gives us:

```
papaya$ strace hello
execve("./hello", ["hello"], [/* 49 vars */]) = 0
mmap(0, 4096, PROT_READ|PROT_WRITE, MAP_PRIVATE|MAP_ANONYMOUS,\
 -1, 0) = 0x40007000
mprotect(0x40000000, 20881, PROT_READ|PROT_WRITE|PROT_EXEC) = 0
mprotect(0x8048000, 4922, PROT_READ|PROT_WRITE|PROT_EXEC) = 0
stat("/etc/ld.so.cache", {st_mode=S_IFREG|0644, st_size=18612,\
 ...}) = 0
open("/etc/ld.so.cache", O_RDONLY)       = 3
mmap(0, 18612, PROT_READ, MAP_SHARED, 3, 0) = 0x40008000
close(3)                                 = 0
stat("/etc/ld.so.preload", 0xbffff52c)   = -1 ENOENT (No such\
 file or directory)
open("/usr/local/KDE/lib/libc.so.5", O_RDONLY) = -1 ENOENT (No\
 such file or directory)
open("/usr/local/qt/lib/libc.so.5", O_RDONLY) = -1 ENOENT (No\
 such file or directory)
open("/lib/libc.so.5", O_RDONLY)         = 3
read(3, "ELF\1\1\1\0\0\0\0\0\0\0\0\0\3"..., 4096) = 4096
mmap(0, 770048, PROT_NONE, MAP_PRIVATE|MAP_ANONYMOUS, -1, 0) = \
0x4000d000
mmap(0x4000d000, 538959, PROT_READ|PROT_EXEC, MAP_PRIVATE|MAP_\
FIXED, 3, 0) = 0x4000d000
mmap(0x40091000, 21564, PROT_READ|PROT_WRITE, MAP_PRIVATE|MAP_\
FIXED, 3, 0x83000) = 0x40091000
mmap(0x40097000, 204584, PROT_READ|PROT_WRITE, MAP_PRIVATE|MAP_\
```

---

* Debian users may find the *ltrace* package useful as well. It's a library call tracer that tracks all library calls, not just calls to the kernel; users of other distributions can download the latest version of the source at *ftp://ftp.debian.org/debian/dists/unstable/main/source/utils/*.

```
FIXED|MAP_ANONYMOUS, -1, 0) = 0x40097000
close(3)                                      = 0
mprotect(0x4000d000, 538959, PROT_READ|PROT_WRITE|PROT_EXEC) = 0
munmap(0x40008000, 18612)                     = 0
mprotect(0x8048000, 4922, PROT_READ|PROT_EXEC) = 0
mprotect(0x4000d000, 538959, PROT_READ|PROT_EXEC) = 0
mprotect(0x40000000, 20881, PROT_READ|PROT_EXEC) = 0
personality(PER_LINUX)                        = 0
geteuid()                                     = 501
getuid()                                      = 501
getgid()                                      = 100
getegid()                                     = 100
fstat(1, {st_mode=S_IFCHR|0666, st_rdev=makedev(3, 10), ...}) = 0
mmap(0, 4096, PROT_READ|PROT_WRITE, MAP_PRIVATE|MAP_ANONYMOUS,\
 -1, 0) = 0x40008000
ioctl(1, TCGETS, {B9600 opost isig icanon echo ...}) = 0
write(1, "Hello World!\n", 13Hello World!
)             = 13
_exit(0)                                      = ?
papaya$
```

This may be much more than you expected to see from a simple program. Let's walk through it, briefly, to explain what's going on.

The first call *execve* starts the program itself. All the *mmap, mprotect,* and *munmap* calls come from the kernel's memory management and are not really interesting here. In the three consecutive *open* calls, the loader is looking for the C library and finds it on the third try. The library header is then read and the library mapped into memory. After a few more memory-management operations and the calls to *getuid, geteuid, getgid,* and *getegid,* which retrieve the rights of the process, there is a call to *ioctl.* The *ioctl* is the result of a *tcgetattr* library call, which the program uses to retrieve the terminal attributes before attempting to write to the terminal. Finally, the *write* call prints our friendly message to the terminal and *exit* ends the program.

The calls to *munmap* (which unmaps a memory-mapped portion of a file) and *brk* (which allocates memory on the heap) set up the memory image of the running process. The *ioctl* call is the result of a *tcgetattr* library call, which retrieves the terminal attributes before attempting to write to it. Finally, the *write* call prints our friendly message to the terminal, and *exit* ends the program.

strace sends its output to standard error, so you can redirect it to a file separately from the actual output of the program (usually on standard output). As you can see, *strace* tells you not only the names of the system calls, but also their parameters (expressed as well-known constant names, if possible, instead of just numerics) and return values.

make and imake

We have already introduced *make*, the project manager used to compile projects, among other things. One problem with *make* is that makefiles aren't always easy to write. When large projects are involved, writing a makefile with cases for each kind of source file can be tedious. Even with the built-in *make* defaults, this is often more work than should be necessary.

One solution is to use *imake*, an extension to *make* based on the use of the C pre-processor. *imake* is simply a makefile generator: you write an Imakefile that *imake* converts to a robust makefile. *imake* is used by programs in the X Window System distribution but is not limited to use by X applications.

We should note at this point that *imake* can simplify the process of writing make-files, especially for compiling C programs. However, *make* is more generally applicable than *imake* for this task. For example, you can use *make* to automatically format documents using *groff* or TEX. In this case, you need the flexibility of *make* alone, and *imake* may not be the best solution.

Here is a sample Imakefile that builds two programs, *laplacian* and *getstat*. At the top of the Imakefile, options for the entire compilation are specified (*imake* has its own defaults for these, but they aren't always useful). Following that, variables are defined for each program to be compiled, and the *imake* macros `AllTarget` and `NormalProgramTarget` create makefile rules for compiling these programs:

```
# Linker options:
LDOPTIONS = -L/usr/local/lib -L../lib
# The C compiler to use:
CC = gcc
# Flags to be used with gcc:
CFLAGS = -I. -I$(HOME)/include -g
# Local and system libraries to link against:
LOCAL_LIBRARIES = -lvistuff
SYS_LIBRARIES = -lm


# Specify the sources in the SRCS variable, and the corresponding object
# files in the variable LAP_OBJS.
SRCS = laplacian.c laplacian-main.c
LAP_OBJS = laplacian.o laplacian-main.o


# Create rules for building laplacian.
AllTarget(laplacian)
NormalProgramTarget(laplacian,$(LAP_OBJS),,$(LOCAL_LIBRARIES),\
$(SYS_LIBRARIES))


# Do the same thing for getstat. Note that SRCS can be redefined for each
# target, but LAP_OBJS can't, so we use a unique name for each target.
SRCS = getstat.c getstat-main.c component.c
GS_OBJS = getstat.o getstat-main.o component.o
```

```
AllTarget(getstat)
NormalProgramTarget(getstat,$(GS_OBJS),,$(LOCAL_LIBRARIES),\
$(SYS_LIBRARIES))
```

Note that we must use a different variable for the object files for each target, although SRCS can be redefined for each.

In order to translate the Imakefile into a makefile, use the command *xmkmf*. *xmkmf* will simply run *imake* with the options to do the translation correctly, using the default *imake* macros (such as AllTarget and NormalProgramTarget). You can then issue *make* to compile the program:

```
papaya$ xmkmf
mv Makefile Makefile.bak
imake -DUseInstalled -I/usr/X386/lib/X11/config
papaya$
```

imake(1)
xmkmf(1)
[53]imake

If you want to use your own *imake* macros, you can invoke *imake* by hand using the appropriate options. The *imake* and *xmkmf* manual pages should fill in the gaps. *Software Portability with imake* by Paul DuBois is another guide to the system.

If you find *imake* too complex for your taste, other "makefile makers" are available as well, such as *ICmake*, which generates makefiles using a macro language similar to C.

If you have compiled software packages yourself, you will often have found compilation instructions that told you to run a provided script called *configure*. This is produced by a Makefile generator called *autoconf*, which is often used together with another program called *automake*. *autoconf* and *automake* are not easy to use, but they give you way more flexibility than *imake*, *ICmake*, and all other Makefile generators. Unfortunately, the usage of *autoconf* is way beyond the scope of this book. If you're interested in this, get yourself a copy from the archives and start reading the documentation.

Using Checker

Checker is a replacement for the various memory-allocation routines, such as *malloc, realloc,* and *free,* used by C programs. It provides smarter memory-allocation procedures and code to detect illegal memory accesses and common faults, such as attempting to free a block of memory more than once. Checker displays detailed error messages if your program attempts any kind of hazardous memory access, helping you to catch segmentation faults in your program before they happen. It can also detect memory leaks—for example, places in the code where new memory is *malloc'*d without being *free'*d after use.

Checker is not just a replacement for *malloc* and friends. It also inserts code into your program to verify all memory reads and writes. It is very robust and therefore somewhat slower than the regular *malloc* routines. Checker is meant to be used during program development and testing; once all potential memory-corrupting bugs have been fixed, you can link your program with the standard libraries.

For example, take the following program, which allocates some memory and attempts to do various nasty things with it:

```
#include <malloc.h>
int main() {
  char *thememory, ch;

  thememory=(char *)malloc(10*sizeof(char));

  ch=thememory[1];      /* Attempt to read uninitialized memory */
  thememory[12]=' ';    /* Attempt to write after the block */
  ch=thememory[-2];     /* Attempt to read before the block */
}
```

We simply compile this program with the *–lchecker* option, which links it with the Checker libraries. Upon running it, we get the following error messages (among others):

```
From Checker:
        Memory access error
        When Reading at address 0x10033
        inside the heap
        1 bytes after the begin of the block

From Checker:
        Memory access error
        When Writing at address 0x1003e
        inside the heap
        2 bytes after the end of the block
From Checker:
        Memory access error
        When Reading at address 0x10030
        inside the heap
        2 bytes before the begin of the block
```

For each memory violation, Checker reports an error and gives us information on what happened. The actual Checker error messages include information on where the program is executing as well as where the memory block was allocated. You can coax even more information out of Checker if you wish, and, along with a debugger such as *gdb*, you can pinpoint problems easily.*

Checker also provides a garbage collector and detector you can call from within your program. In brief, the garbage detector informs you of any memory leaks: places where a function *malloc*'d a block of memory but forgot to *free* it before returning. The garbage collector routine walks through the heap and cleans up the results of these leaks. You can also call the garbage collector and detector

---

* We have edited the output somewhat in order to remove extraneous information and to increase readability for the purpose of the example.

manually when running the program from within *gdb* (as *gdb* allows you to directly call functions during execution).

Interface Building Tools

A number of applications and libraries let you easily generate a user interface for your applications under the X Window System. If you do not want to bother with the complexity of the X programming interface, using one of these simple interface-building tools may be the answer for you. There are also tools for producing a text-based interface for programs that don't require X.

The classic X programming model has attempted to be as general as possible, providing only the bare minimum of interface restrictions and assumptions. This generality allows programmers to build their own interface from scratch, as the core X libraries don't make any assumptions about the interface in advance. The X Toolkit Intrinsics (Xt) provides a rudimentary set of interface widgets (such as simple buttons, scrollbars, and the like), as well as a general interface for writing your own widgets if necessary. Unfortunately this can require a great deal of work for programmers who would rather use a set of pre-made interface routines. A number of Xt widget sets and programming libraries are available for Linux, all of which make the user interface easier to program.

In addition, the commercial Motif library and widget set is available from several vendors for an inexpensive single-user license fee. Also available is the XView library and widget interface, which is another alternative to using Xt for building interfaces under X. XView and Motif are two sets of X-based programming libraries that in some ways are easier to program than the X Toolkit Intrinsics. Many applications are available that utilize Motif and XView, such as XVhelp (a system for generating interactive hypertext help for your program). Binaries statically linked with Motif may be distributed freely and used by people who don't own Motif itself.

Before you start developing with XView or Motif, a word of caution is in order. XView, which was once a commercial product of Sun Microsystems, has been dropped by the developers and is no longer maintained. Also, while some people like the look, the programs written with XView look very nonstandard. Motif on the other hand is still being actively developed (albeit rather slowly), but has some problems itself. First, programming with Motif can be frustrating, because it is difficult, error prone, and cumbersome since the Motif API was not designed according to modern GUI API design principles. Also, Motif programs tend to run very slowly.

But there are other widget sets and interface libraries for X like:

Xaw3D
> A modified version of the standard Athena widget set which provides a 3D, Motif-like look and feel

Qt A C++ GUI toolkit written by the Norwegian company Troll Tech

GTK

A C GUI toolkit that was originally written for the image manipulation program GIMP

Many people complain that the Athena widgets are too plain in appearance. Xaw3D is completely compatible with the standard Athena set and can even replace the Athena libraries on your system, giving all programs that use Athena widgets a modern look. Xaw3D also provides a few widgets not found in the Athena set, such as a layout widget with a TEX-like interface for specifying the position of child widgets.

Chapter 11

Qt is an excellent package for GUI development in C++ that sports an ingenious mechanism for connecting user interaction with program code, a very fast drawing engine, and a comprehensive but easy-to-use API. Qt is considered by many as the successor to Motif as the de facto GUI programming standard, because it is the foundation of the desktop KDE (see "The K Desktop Environment" in Chapter 11, *Customizing Your X Environment*), which has gotten a lot of interest.

[45] Programming with Qt

Qt is a commercial product, but you can use it for free if you write free software for Unix (and hence Linux) systems with it. There is also a (commercial) Windows version of Qt, which makes it possible to develop for Linux and Windows at the same time and create an application for the other platform by simply recompiling. Imagine being able to develop on your favorite operating system Linux and still being able to target the larger Windows market! One of the authors, Kalle, uses Qt to write both free software (the KDE Desktop Environment just mentioned) and commercial software (often cross-platform products that are developed for Linux and Windows). Qt is being very actively developed; for more information, see *Programming with Qt* by Kalle Dalheimer.

For those who do not like to program in C++, *GTK* might be a good choice. *GTK* programs usually offer just as good response time as *Qt* programs, but the toolkit itself is not as complete. Documentation especially is lacking. For C-based projects, though, *GTK* is good alternative if you do not need to be able to recompile your code on Windows.

Many programmers are finding that building a user interface, even with a complete set of widgets and routines in C, requires much overhead and can be quite difficult. This is a question of flexibility versus ease of programming: the easier the interface is to build, the less control the programmer has over it. Many programmers are finding that prebuilt widgets are adequate enough for their needs, so the loss in flexibility is not a problem.

One of the problems with interface generation and X programming is that it is difficult to generalize the most widely used elements of a user interface into a simple programming model. For example, many programs use features such as buttons, dialog boxes, pull-down menus, and so forth, but almost every program uses these widgets in a different context. In simplifying the creation of a graphical interface, generators tend to make assumptions about what you'll want. For example, it is simple enough to specify that a button, when pressed, should execute a certain procedure within your program, but what if you want the button to execute some specialized behavior the programming interface does not allow for? For example, what if you wanted the button to have a different effect when pressed with mouse button 2 instead of mouse button 1? If the interface-building system does not allow for this degree of generality, it is not of much use to programmers who need a powerful, customized interface.

Writing
Tk Applications

The Tcl/Tk programming interface described in the previous chapter is growing in popularity, partly because it is so simple to use and provides a good amount of flexibility. Because Tcl and Tk routines can be called from interpreted "scripts" as well as internally from a C program, it is not difficult to tie the interface features provided by this language and toolkit to functionality in the program. Using Tcl and Tk is on the whole less demanding than learning to program Xlib and Xt (along with the myriad of widget sets) directly. It should be noted, though, that the larger a project gets, the more likely it is that you will want to use a language like C++ that is more suited towards large-scale development. For several reasons, larger projects tend to become very unwieldy with Tcl: the use of an interpreted language slows the execution of the program, Tcl/Tk design is hard to scale up to large projects, and important reliability features like compile- and link-time type checking are missing. The scaling problem is improved by the use of namespaces (a way to keep names in different parts of the program from clashing) and an object-oriented extension called [incr Tcl].

TclMotif, a version of Tcl bound with the popular Motif widget set, is also available for Linux. The Motif widgets are widely acclaimed to be easy to program and pleasant to use. The advantage of TclMotif is that the binary is freely distributable although Motif itself is a commercial product. Therefore, you do not have to own Motif to use TclMotif. TclMotif will in effect let you write programs that use Motif widgets and routines through the Tcl interface. A statically linked binary is available on a number of Linux FTP sites and from other sources. If you want to recompile TclMotif itself, for some reason, you need to own Motif in order to do so.

Wafe is another version of Tcl/Tk that includes the Athena widgets and miscellaneous other tools that make the programming model easier to use. If you are accustomed to programming Xt with the Athena widgets, but you want to move to Tcl and Tk, Wafe is a good place to start.

Chapter 13

Tcl and Tk allow you to generate an X-based interface complete with windows, buttons, menus, scrollbars, and the like, around your existing program. The interface may be accessed from a Tcl script (as described in the section "Writing Tk Applications" in Chapter 13) or from within a C program.

Another interface-building tool much like Tcl and Tk is *xtpanel*. *xtpanel* is meant primarily to generate an X interface "wrapper" around an existing text-based program. *xtpanel* allows you to set up a window with various panes, text editing regions, buttons, scrollbars, and so on, and bind the actions of these widgets to features in the program. For example, one could use *xtpanel* to produce an X-based interface for the *gdb* debugger, similar to *xxgdb*. You could define a "step" button which, when pressed, sends the *step* command to the regular *gdb* interface. A text-editing pane could be defined to interact with *gdb* in the regular way. Of course, doing something more complex, like setting up a source-view pane, would be difficult using something as general as *xtpanel*.

If you like the Tk toolkit, but do not like the programming language Tcl, you will be delighted to hear that you can use Tk with other languages as well; it has become the GUI toolkit of choice for the scripting languages Python and Perl, too.

If you require a nice text-based interface for a program, there are several options. The GNU *getline* library is a set of routines that provides advanced command-line editing, prompting, command history, and other features used by many programs. As an example, both *bash* and *gdb* use the *getline* library to read user input. *getline* provides the Emacs and *vi*-like command-line editing features found in *bash* and similar programs. (The use of command-line editing within *bash* is described in the section "Typing Shortcuts" in Chapter 4, *Basic Unix Commands and Concepts*.)

Chapter 4

Another option is to write a set of Emacs interface routines for your program. An example of this is the *gdb* Emacs interface, which sets up multiple windows, special key sequences, and so on, within Emacs. The interface is discussed in the earlier section "Using Emacs with gdb." (No changes were required to *gdb* code in order to implement this: look at the Emacs library file *gdb.el* for hints on how this was accomplished.) Emacs allows you to start up a subprogram within a text buffer and provides many routines for parsing and processing text within that buffer. For example, within the Emacs *gdb* interface, the *gdb* source listing output is captured by Emacs and turned into a command that displays the current line of code in another window. Routines written in Emacs LISP process the *gdb* output and take certain actions based on it.

The advantage to using Emacs to interact with text-based programs is that Emacs is a powerful and customizable user interface within itself. The user can easily redefine keys and commands to fit her own needs; you don't need to provide these customization features yourself. As long as the text interface of the program is straightforward enough to interact with Emacs, customization is not difficult to accomplish. In addition, many users prefer to do virtually everything within Emacs—from reading electronic mail and news, to compiling and debugging programs. Giving your program an Emacs frontend allows it to be used more easily by people with this mindset. It also allows your program to interact with other programs running under Emacs—for example, text can easily be cut and pasted between different Emacs text buffers. You can even write entire programs using Emacs LISP, if you wish.

Revision Control Tools — RCS

Revision Control System (RCS) has been ported to Linux. This is a set of programs that allow you to maintain a "library" of files that records a history of revisions, allows source-file locking (in case several people are working on the same project), and automatically keeps track of source-file version numbers. RCS is generally used with program source-code files, but is general enough to be applicable to any type of file where multiple revisions must be maintained.

Why bother with revision control? Many large projects require some kind of revision control in order to keep track of many tiny complex changes to the system. For example, attempting to maintain a program with a thousand source files and a team of several dozen programmers would be nearly impossible without using something like RCS. With RCS, you can ensure that only one person may modify a given source file at any one time, and all changes are checked in along with a log message detailing the change.

RCS is based on the concept of an *RCS file*, a file which acts as a "library" where source files are "checked in" and "checked out." Let's say that you have a source file *importrtf.c* that you want to maintain with RCS. The RCS filename would be *importrtf.c,v* by default. The RCS file contains a history of revisions to the file, allowing you to extract any previous checked-in version of the file. Each revision is tagged with a log message that you provide.

When you check in a file with RCS, revisions are added to the RCS file, and the original file is deleted by default. In order to access the original file, you must check it out from the RCS file. When you're editing a file, you generally don't want someone else to be able to edit it at the same time. Therefore, RCS places a lock on the file when you check it out for editing. A locked file may only be modified by the user who checks it out (this is accomplished through file permissions). Once you're done making changes to the source, you check it back in, which allows anyone working on the project to check it back out again for further work. Checking out a file as unlocked does not subject it to these restrictions; generally, files are checked out as locked only when they are to be edited but are checked out as unlocked just for reading (for example, to use the source file in a program build).

RCS automatically keeps track of all previous revisions in the RCS file and assigns incremental version numbers to each new revision that you check in. You can also specify a version number of your own when checking in a file with RCS; this allows you to start a new "revision branch" so that multiple projects can stem from different revisions of the same file. This is a good way to share code between projects but also to assure that changes made to one branch won't be reflected in others.

Here's an example. Take the source file *importrtf.c*, which contains our friendly program:

```
#include <stdio.h>

int main(void) {
  printf("Hello, world!");
}
```

The first step is to check it into RCS with the *ci* command:

```
papaya$ ci importrtf.c
importrtf.c,v  <--  importrtf.c
enter description, terminated with single '.' or end of file:
NOTE: This is NOT the log message!
>> Hello world source code
>> .
initial revision: 1.1
done
papaya$
```

The RCS file *importrtf.c,v* is created, and *importrtf.c* is removed.

In order to work on the source file again, use the *co* command to check it out. For example:

```
papaya$ co -l importrtf.c
importrtf.c,v  -->  importrtf.c
revision 1.1 (locked)
done
papaya$
```

will check out *importrtf.c* (from *importrtf.c,v*) and lock it. Locking the file allows you to edit it, and to check it back in. If you only need to check the file out in order to read it (for example, to issue a *make*), you can leave the *-l* switch off of the *co* command to check it out unlocked. You can't check in a file unless it is locked first (or it has never been checked in before, as in the example).

Now, you can make some changes to the source and check it back in when done. In many cases, you'll want to always have the file checked out and use *ci* to merely record your most recent revisions in the RCS file and bump the version number. For this, you can use the *-l* switch with *ci*, as so:

```
papaya$ ci -l importrtf.c
importrtf.c,v  <--  importrtf.c
new revision: 1.2; previous revision: 1.1
enter log message, terminated with single '.' or end of file:
>> Changed printf call
>> .
done
papaya$
```

This automatically checks out the file, locked, after checking it in. This is a useful way to keep track of revisions even if you're the only one working on a project.

If you use RCS often, you may not like all of those unsightly *importrtf.c,v* RCS files cluttering up your directory. If you create the subdirectory *RCS* within your project directory, *ci* and *co* will place the RCS files there, out of the way from the rest of the source.

In addition, RCS keeps track of all previous revisions of your file. For instance, if you make a change to your program that causes it to break in some way and want to revert to the previous version to "undo" your changes and retrace your steps, you can specify a particular version number to check out with *co*. For example:

```
papaya$ co -l1.1 importrtf.c
importrtf.c,v  -->  importrtf.c
revision 1.1 (locked)
writable importrtf.c exists; remove it? [ny](n): y
done
papaya$
```

checks out version 1.1 of the file *importrtf.c*. You can use the program *rlog* to print the revision history of a particular file; this displays your revision log entries (entered with *ci*) along with other information such as the date, the user who checked in the revision, and so forth.

RCS automatically updates embedded "keyword strings" in your source file at checkout time. For example, if you have the string:

```
/* $Header$ */
```

in the source file, *co* will replace it with an informative line about the revision date, version number, and so forth, as in:

```
/* $Header: /work/linux/hitch/programming/tools/RCS/rcs.tex
       1.2 1994/12/04 15:19:31 mdw Exp mdw $ */
```

(This line was broken to fit on the page, but in actuality it is supposed to be all on one line.)

Other keywords exist as well, such as $Author$, $Date$, and Log (the latter keeps a complete record of the log entries for each revision embedded in the source file).

Many programmers place a static string within each source file to identify the version of the program after it has been compiled. For example, within each source file in your program, you can place the line:

```
static char rcsid[] = "\@(#)$Header$";
```

co replaces the keyword $Header$ with a string of the form given here. This static string survives in the executable, and the *what* command displays these strings in a given binary. For example, after compiling *importrtf.c* into the executable *importrtf*, we can use the command:

```
papaya$ what importrtf
importrtf:
        $Header: /work/linux/hitch/programming/tools/RCS/rcs.tex
                1.2 1994/12/04 15:19:31 mdw Exp mdw $
papaya$
```

what picks out strings beginning with the characters @(#) in a file and displays them. If you have a program that has been compiled from many source files and libraries, and you don't know how up to date each of the components are, you can use *what* to display a version string for each source file used to compile the binary.

ci(1)
co(1)
rcs(1)

RCS has several other programs in its suite, including *rcs*, used for maintaining RCS files. Among other things, *rcs* can give other users permission to check out sources from an RCS file. See the manual pages for *ci*, *co*, and *rcs* for more information.

Revision Control Tools — CVS

CVS, the Concurrent Version System, is more complex than RCS and thus perhaps a little bit oversized for one-man projects. But whenever more than one or two programmers are working on a project or the source code is distributed over several directories, CVS is the better choice. CVS uses the RCS file format for saving changes, but employs a management structure of its own.

By default, CVS works with full directory trees. That is, each CVS command you issue affects the current directory and all the subdirectories it contains, including their subdirectories and so on. This recursive traversal can be switched off with a command-line option, or you can specify a single file for the command to operate on.

CVS has formalized the sandbox concept that is used in many software development shops. In this concept, there is a so-called *repository* containing the "official" sources that are known to compile and work (at least partly). No developer is ever allowed to directly edit files in this repository. Instead, each developer checks out a local directory tree, the so-called *sandbox*. Here, he can edit the sources to his heart's delight, make changes, add or remove files, and do all sorts of things that developers usually do (no, not playing Quake or eating marshmallows). When the developer has made sure that her changes compile and work, she transmits them to the repository again and thus makes them available for the other developers.

When you as a developer have checked out a local directory tree, all the files are writable. You can make any necessary changes to the files in your personal workspace. When you have finished local testing and feel sure enough of your work to share the changes with the rest of the programming team, you write any changed files back into the central repository by issuing a CVS commit command. CVS then checks whether another developer has checked in changes since you checked out your directory tree. If this is the case, CVS does not let you check your changes in, but asks you first to take the changes of the other developers over to your local tree. During this update operation, CVS uses a sophisticated algorithm to reconcile ("merge") your changes with those of the other developers. There are cases in which this is not automatically possible. In this case, CVS informs you that there have been conflicts and asks you to resolve those. The file in question is marked up with special characters so that you can see where the conflict has occurred and decide which version should be used. Note that CVS makes sure that conflicts can only occur in local developers' trees. There is always a consistent version in the repository.

Setting up a CVS repository

If you are working in a larger project, it is likely that someone else has already set up all the necessary machinery to use CVS. But if you are your project's administrator or you just want to tinker around with CVS on your local machine, you will have to set up a repository yourself.

First, set your environment variable CVSROOT to a directory where you want your CVS repository to be. CVS can keep as many projects as you like in a repository and makes sure they do not interfere with each other. Thus, you just have to pick a directory once to store all projects maintained by CVS, and you won't need to need to change it when you switch projects. Instead of using the variable CVS-ROOT, you can always use the command-line switch –d with all CVS commands, but since this is cumbersome to type all the time, we will assume that you have set CVSROOT.

Once the directory exists for a repository, you can create the repository itself with the following command (assuming that CVS is installed on your machine):

```
$tigger cvs init
```

There are several different ways to create a project tree in the CVS repository. If you already have a directory tree, but it is not yet managed by RCS, you can simply import it into the repository by calling:

```
$tigger cvs import directory manufacturer tag
```

where *directory* is the name of the top-level directory of the project, *manufacturer* is the name of the author of the code (you can use whatever you like here) and *tag* is a so-called release tag that can be chosen at will. For example:

```
$tigger cvs import dataimport acmeinc initial
... lots of output ...
```

If you want to start a completely new project, you can simply create the directory tree with *mkdir* calls and then import this empty tree like shown in the previous example.

If you want to import a project that is already managed by RCS, things get a little bit more difficult, because you cannot use *cvs import*. In this case, you have to create the needed directories directly in the repository and then copy all RCS files (all files that end in *,v*) into those directories. Do not use RCS subdirectories here!

Every repository contains a file named *CVSROOT/modules* that contains names of projects in the repository. It is a good idea to edit the *modules* file of the repository to add the new module. You can check out, edit, and check in this file like every other file. Thus, in order to add your module to the list, do the following (we will cover the various commands soon):

```
$tigger cvs checkout CVSROOT/modules
$tigger cd CVSROOT
$tigger emacs modules
... or any other editor of your choice, see below for what to enter ...
$tigger cvs commit modules
$tigger cd ..
$tigger cvs release -d CVSROOT
```

If you are not doing anything fancy, the format of the *modules* file is very easy: Each line starts with the name of module, followed by a space or tab and the path within the repository. There are many more things you can do with the *modules* file which you can find in the CVS documentation, especially in the Info pages or at *http://www.loria.fr/~molli/cvs-index.html*.

Working with CVS

In the following section, we will assume that either you or your system administrator has set up a module called `dataimport`. You can now check out a local tree of this module with the following command:

```
$tigger cvs checkout dataimport
```

If there is no module defined for the project you want to work on, you need to know the path within the repository. For example, something like the following could be needed:

```
$tigger cvs checkout clients/acmeinc/dataimport
```

Whichever version of the *checkout* command you use, CVS will create a directory called *dataimport* under your current working directory and check out all files and directories from the repository that belong to this module. All files are writable, and you can start editing them right away.

After you have made some changes, you can write back the changed files into the repository with one single command:

```
$tigger cvs commit
```

Of course, you can also check in single files:

```
$tigger cvs commit importrtf.c
```

But whatever you do, CVS will ask you—as RCS does—for a comment to include with your changes. But CVS goes a step beyond RCS in convenience. Instead of the rudimentary prompt from RCS, you get a full-screen editor to work in. You can choose this editor by setting the environment variable CVSEDITOR; if this is not set, CVS looks in EDITOR, and if this is not defined either, CVS invokes *vi*. If you check in a whole project, CVS will use the comment you entered for each directory in which there have been changes but will start a new editor every time to ask you whether you might want to change each file.

As already mentioned, it is not necessary to set *CVSROOT* correctly for checking files in, because when checking the tree out, CVS has created a directory *CVS* in each work directory. This directory contains all the information that CVS needs for its work, including where to find the repository.

While you have been working on your files, it may well be that a co-worker has checked in some of the files that you are currently working on. In this case, CVS will not let you check in your files but asks you to first update your local tree. Do this with the command:

```
$tigger cvs update
M importrtf.c
A exportrtf.c
? importrtf
U importword.c
```

(You can specify a single file here as well.) You should carefully examine the output of this command: CVS outputs the names of all the files it handles, each preceded by a single key letter. This letter tells you what has happened during the update operation. The most important letters are shown in Table 14-1.

Table 14-1: Key Letters for Files Under CVS

Letter	Explanation
P	The file has been updated. The P is shown if the file has been added to the repository in the meantime or if it has been changed, but you have not made any changes to this file yourself.
U	You have changed this file in the meantime, but nobody else has.
M	You have changed this file in the meantime, and somebody else has checked in a newer version. All the changes have been merged successfully.
C	You have changed this file in the meantime, and somebody else has checked in a newer version. During the merge attempt, conflicts have arisen.

Table 14-1: Key Letters for Files Under CVS (continued)

Letter	Explanation
?	CVS has no information about this file, that is, this file is not under CVS's control.

The c is the most important of those letters. CVS was not able to merge all changes and needs your help. Load those files into your editor and look for the string <<<<<<<. After this string, the name of the file is shown again, followed by your version, ending with a line containing =======. Then comes the version of the code from the repository, ending with a line containing >>>>>>>. You now have to find out—probably by communicating with your co-worker—which version is better or whether it is possible to merge the two versions by hand. Change the file accordingly and remove the CVS markings <<<<<<<, ======= and >>>>>>>. Save the file and once again commit it.

If you decide that you want to stop working on a project for a time, you should check whether you have really committed all changes. To do this, change to the directory above the root directory of your project and issue the command:

```
$tigger cvs release dataimport
```

CVS then checks whether you have written back all changes into the repository and warns you if necessary. A useful option is *–d*, which deletes the local tree if all changes have been committed.

CVS over the Internet

CVS is also very useful where distributed development teams* are concerned, because it provides several possibilities to access a repository on another machine.

If you can log into the machine holding the repository with *rsh*, you can use remote CVS to access the repository. To check out a module, do the following:

```
cvs -d :ext:user@domain.com:/path/to/repository checkout dataimport
```

If you cannot or do not want to use *rsh* for security reasons, you can also use the secure shell *ssh*. You can tell CVS that you want to use *ssh* by setting the environment variable CVS_RSH to *ssh*.

Authentication and access to the repository can also be done via a client/server protocol. Remote access requires a CVS server running on the machine with the repository; see the CVS documentation for how to do this. If the server is set up, you can login to it with:

---

* The use of CVS has burgeoned along with the number of free software projects which are developed over the Internet by people from different continents.

```
cvs -d :pserver:user@domain.com:path/to/repository
CVS password:
```

As shown, the CVS server will ask you for your CVS password, which has been assigned to you by the administrator of the CVS server. This login procedure is necessary only once for every repository. When you check out a module, you need to specify the machine with the server, your username on that machine, and the remote path to the repository; as with local repositories, this information is saved in your local tree. Since the password is saved with minimal encryption in the file *.cvspass* in your home directory, there is a potential security risk here. The CVS documentation tells you more about this.

When you use CVS over the Internet and check out or update largish modules, you might also want to use the −*z* option, which expects an additional integer parameter and transmits the data in compressed form.

Patching Files

Let's say that you're trying to maintain a program that is updated periodically, but the program contains many source files, and releasing a complete source distribution with every update is not feasible. The best way to incrementally update source files is with *patch*, a program by Larry Wall, author of Perl.

patch is a program that makes context-dependent changes in a file in order to update that file from one version to the next. This way, when your program changes, you simply release a patch file against the source, which the user applies with *patch* to get the newest version. For example, Linus Torvalds usually releases new Linux kernel versions in the form of patch files as well as complete source distributions.

A nice feature of *patch* is that it applies updates in context; that is, if you have made changes to the source yourself, but still wish to get the changes in the patch file update, *patch* usually can figure out the right location in the original file to apply the changes to. This way, your versions of the original source files don't need to correspond exactly to those that the patch file was made against.

In order to make a patch file, the program *diff* is used, which produces "context diffs" between two files. For example, take our overused "Hello World" source code, given here:

```
/* hello.c version 1.0 by Norbert Ebersol */
#include <stdio.h>

int main() {
  printf("Hello, World!");
  exit(0);
}
```

Let's say that you were to update this source, as in the following:

```
/* hello.c version 2.0 */
/* (c)1994 Norbert Ebersol */
#include <stdio.h>

int main() {
  printf("Hello, Mother Earth!\n");
  return 0;
}
```

If you want to produce a patch file to update the original *hello.c* to the newest version, use *diff* with the *−c* option:

papaya$ **diff −c hello.c.old hello.c > hello.patch**

This produces the patch file *hello.patch* that describes how to convert the original *hello.c* (here, saved in the file *hello.c.old*) to the new version. You can distribute this patch file to anyone who has the original version of "Hello, World," and they can use *patch* to update it.

Using *patch* is quite simple; in most cases, you simply run it with the patch file as input:*

```
papaya$ patch < hello.patch
Hmm...  Looks like a new-style context diff to me...
The text leading up to this was:
--------------------------
|*** hello.c.old      Sun Feb  6 15:30:52 1994
|--- hello.c    Sun Feb  6 15:32:21 1994
--------------------------
Patching file hello.c using Plan A...
Hunk #1 succeeded at 1.
done
papaya$
```

patch warns you if it appears as though the patch has already been applied. If we tried to apply the patch file again, *patch* would ask us if we wanted to assume that *−R* was enabled—which reverses the patch. This is a good way to back out patches you didn't intend to apply. *patch* also saves the original version of each file that it updates in a backup file, usually named `filename˜` (the filename with a tilde appended).

In many cases, you'll want to update not only a single source file but an entire directory tree of sources. *patch* allows many files to be updated from a single diff. Let's say you have two directory trees, *hello.old* and *hello*, which contain the

---

* The output shown here is from the last version that Larry Wall has released, Version 2.1. If you have a newer version of patch, you will need the *−−verbose* flag to get the same output.

sources for the old and new versions of a program, respectively. To make a patch file for the entire tree, use the *−r* switch with *diff*:

```
papaya$ diff -cr hello.old hello > hello.patch
```

Now, let's move to the system where the software needs to be updated. Assuming that the original source is contained in the directory *hello*, you can apply the patch with:

```
papaya$ patch -p0 < hello.patch
```

patch(1)

The *−p0* switch tells *patch* to preserve the pathnames of files to be updated (so it knows to look in the *hello* directory for the source). If you have the source to be patched saved in a directory named differently from that given in the patch file, you may need to use the *−p* option. See the *patch* manual page for details about this.

Indenting Code

If you're terrible at indenting code and find the idea of an editor that automatically indents code for you on-the-fly a bit annoying, you can use the *indent* program to pretty-print your code after you're done writing it. *indent* is a smart C-code formatter, and has many options allowing you to specify just what kind of indentation style you wish to use.

Take this terribly formatted source:

```
double fact (double n) { if (n==1) return 1;
else return (n*fact(n-1)); }
int main () {
printf("Factorial 5 is %f.\n",fact(5));
printf("Factorial 10 is %f.\n",fact(10)); exit (0); }
```

Running *indent* on this source produces the relatively beautiful code:

```
#include <math.h>

double
fact (double n)
{
  if (n == 1)
    return 1;
  else
    return (n * fact (n - 1));
}
void
main ()
{
```

```
    printf ("Factorial 5 is %f.\n", fact (5));
    printf ("Factorial 10 is %f.\n", fact (10));
    exit (0);
}
```

Not only are lines indented well, but whitespace is added around operators and function parameters to make them more readable. There are many ways to specify how the output of *indent* will look; if you're not fond of this particular indentation style, *indent* can accommodate you.

indent can also produce *troff* code from a source file, suitable for printing or for inclusion in a technical document. This code will have such nice features as italicized comments, boldfaced keywords, and so on. Using a command such as:

papaya$ **indent -troff importrtf.c | groff -mindent**

produces *troff* code and formats it with *groff*.

## CHAPTER FIFTEEN

TCP/IP AND PPP

So, you've staked out your homestead on the Linux frontier, and installed and configured your system. What next? Eventually you'll want to communicate with other systems—Linux and otherwise—and the Pony Express isn't going to suffice.

Fortunately, Linux supports a number of methods for data communication and networking. This includes serial communications, TCP/IP, and UUCP. In this chapter and the next, we will discuss how to configure your system to communicate with the world.

[4] Network Admin Guide

Linux Network Administrator's Guide, available from the Linux Documentation Project (see the Bibliography) and also published by O'Reilly & Associates, is a complete guide to configuring TCP/IP and UUCP networking under Linux. For a detailed account of the information presented here, we refer you to that book.

Networking with TCP/IP

Linux supports a full implementation of the Transmission Control Protocol/Internet Protocol (TCP/IP) networking protocols. TCP/IP has become the most successful mechanism for networking computers worldwide. With Linux and an Ethernet card, you can network your machine to a Local Area Network (LAN) or (with the proper network connections) to the Internet—the worldwide TCP/IP network.

Hooking up a small LAN of Unix machines is easy. It simply requires an Ethernet controller in each machine and the appropriate Ethernet cables and other hardware. Or if your business or university provides access to the Internet, you can easily add your Linux machine to this network.

Linux TCP/IP support has had its ups and downs. After all, implementing an entire protocol stack from scratch isn't something that one does for fun on a weekend. On the other hand, the Linux TCP/IP code has benefited greatly from the hoard of beta testers and developers to have crossed its path, and as time has progressed many bugs and configuration problems have fallen in their wake.

The current implementation of TCP/IP and related protocols for Linux is called NET-4. This has no relationship to the so-called NET-2 release of BSD Unix; instead, in this context, NET-4 means the fourth implementation of TCP/IP for Linux. Before NET-4 came (no surprise here) NET-3, NET-2, and NET-1, the last having been phased out around kernel Version 0.99.pl10. NET-4 supports nearly all the features you'd expect from a Unix TCP/IP implementation and a wide range of networking hardware.

Linux NET-2 also supports Serial Line Internet Protocol (SLIP) and Point-to-Point Protocol (PPP). SLIP and PPP allow you to have dial-up Internet access using a modem. If your business or university provides SLIP or PPP access, you can dial in to the SLIP or PPP server and put your machine on the Internet over the phone line. Alternatively, if your Linux machine also has Ethernet access to the Internet, you can configure it as a SLIP or PPP server.

In the following sections, we won't mention SLIP any more, because nowadays most people use PPP. If you want to run SLIP on your machine, you can find all the information in the *Linux Network Administrator's Guide*.

[74] Ethernet
HOWTO

Besides the *Linux Network Administrator's Guide*, the Linux NET-3 HOWTO contains more or less complete information on configuring TCP/IP and PPP for Linux. The Linux Ethernet HOWTO is a related document that describes configuration of various Ethernet card drivers for Linux.

[28] TCP/IP

Also of interest is *TCP/IP Network Administration* by Craig Hunt. It contains complete information on using and configuring TCP/IP on Unix systems. If you plan to set up a network of Linux machines or do any serious TCP/IP hacking, you should have the background in network administration presented by that book.

[30] DNS
and BIND

If you really want to get serious about setting up and operating networks, you will probably also want to read *DNS and BIND* by Cricket Liu and Paul Albitz. This book tells you all there is to know about name servers in a refreshingly funny manner.

TCP/IP Concepts

[26] Inter-
networking

In order to fully appreciate (and utilize) the power of TCP/IP, you should be familiar with its underlying principles. Transmission Control Protocol/Internet Protocol is a suite of *protocols* (the magic buzzword for this chapter) that define how machines should communicate with each other via a network, as well as internally to other layers of the protocol suite. For the theoretical background of the Internet protocols, the best sources of information are the first volume of Douglas Comer's *Internetworking with TCP/IP* and the first volume of W. Richard Stevens' *TCP/IP Illustrated*.

TCP/IP was originally developed for use on the Advanced Research Projects Agency network, ARPAnet, which was funded to support military and computer-science research. Therefore, you may hear TCP/IP being referred to as the "DARPA

Internet Protocols." Since then, many other TCP/IP networks have come into use, such as the National Science Foundation's NSFNET, as well as thousands of other local and regional networks around the world. All of these networks are interconnected into a single conglomerate known as the Internet.

On a TCP/IP network, each machine is assigned an *IP address*, which is a 32-bit number uniquely identifying the machine. You need to know a little about IP addresses to structure your network and assign addresses to hosts. The IP address is usually represented as a dotted quad: four numbers in decimal notation, separated by dots. As an example, the IP address 0x80114b14 (in hexadecimal format) can be written as 128.17.75.20.

The IP address is divided into two parts: the network address and the host address. The network address consists of the higher-order bits of the address and the host address of the remaining bits. (In general, each *host* is a separate machine on the network.) The size of these two fields depends upon the type of network in question. For example, on a Class B network (for which the first byte of the IP address is between 128 and 191), the first two bytes of the address identify the network, and the remaining two bytes identify the host (see Figure 15-1). For the example address just given, the network address is 128.17, and the host address is 75.20. To put this another way, the machine with IP address 128.17.75.20 is host number 75.20 on the network 128.17.

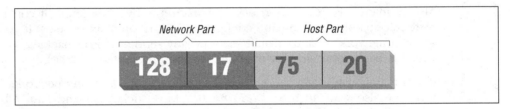

Figure 15–1: IP address

In addition, the host portion of the IP address may be subdivided to allow for a *subnetwork address*. Subnetworking allows large networks to be divided into smaller subnets, each of which may be maintained independently. For example, an organization may allocate a single Class B network, which provides two bytes of host information, up to 65,534 hosts on the network. The organization may then wish to dole out the responsibility of maintaining portions of the network, so that each subnetwork is handled by a different department. Using subnetworking, the organization can specify, for example, that the first byte of the host address (that is, the third byte of the overall IP address) is the subnet address, and the second byte is the host address for that subnetwork (see Figure 15-2). In this case, the IP address 128.17.75.20 identifies host number 20 on subnetwork 75 of network 128.17.*

---

* Why not 65,536 instead? For reasons to be discussed later, a host address of 0 or 255 is invalid.

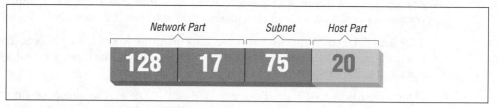

Figure 15-2: IP address with subnet

Processes (either on the same machine or on different machines) that wish to communicate via TCP/IP generally specify the destination machine's IP address as well as a *port address*. The destination IP address is used, of course, to route data from one machine to the destination machine. The port address is a 16-bit number that specifies a particular service or application on the destination machine that should receive the data. Port numbers can be thought of as office numbers at a large office building: the entire building has a single IP address, but each business has a separate office there.

Here's a real-life example of how IP addresses and port numbers are used. The *telnet* program allows a user on one machine to start a login session on another. On the remote machine, there is the *telnet* "daemon," *telnetd*, which is listening to a specific port for incoming connections (in this case, the port number is 23).*

The user executing *telnet* specifies the address of the machine to log in to, and the *telnet* program attempts to open a connection to port 23 on the remote machine. If it is successful, *telnet* and *telnetd* are able to communicate with each other to provide the remote login for the user in question.

Note that the *telnet* client on the local machine has a port address of its own. This port address is allocated to the client dynamically when it begins execution. This is because the remote *telnetd* doesn't need to know the port number of the incoming *telnet* client beforehand. When the client initiates the connection, part of the information it sends to *telnetd* is its port number. *telnetd* can be thought of as a business with a well-known mailing address. Any customers that wish to correspond with the *telnetd* running on a particular machine need to know not only the IP address of the machine to talk to (the address of the *telnetd* office building), but also the port number where *telnetd* can be found (the particular office within the building). The address and port number of the *telnet* client are included as part of the "return address" on the envelope containing the letter.

The TCP/IP family contains a number of protocols. Transmission Control Protocol (TCP) is responsible for providing reliable, connection-oriented communications between two processes, which may be running on different machines on the network. User Datagram Protocol (UDP) is similar to TCP except that it provides

---

* On many systems, *telnetd* is not always listening to port 23; the Internet services daemon *inetd* is listening on its behalf. For now, let's sweep that detail under the carpet.

connectionless, unreliable service. Processes that use UDP must implement their own acknowledgment and synchronization routines if necessary.

TCP and UDP transmit and receive data in units known as *packets.* Each packet contains a chunk of information to send to another machine, as well as a header specifying the destination and source port addresses.

Internet Protocol (IP) sits beneath TCP and UDP in the protocol hierarchy. It is responsible for transmitting and routing TCP or UDP packets via the network. In order to do so, IP wraps each TCP or UDP packet within another packet (known as an IP *datagram*), which includes a header with routing and destination information. The IP datagram header includes the IP address of the source and destination machines.

Note that IP doesn't know anything about port addresses; those are the responsibility of TCP and UDP. Similarly, TCP and UDP don't deal with IP addresses, which (as the name implies) are only IP's concern. As you can see, the mail metaphor with return addresses and envelopes is quite accurate: each packet can be thought of as a letter contained within an envelope. TCP and UDP wrap the letter in an envelope with the source and destination port numbers (office numbers) written on it.

IP acts as the mail room for the office building sending the letter. IP receives the envelope and wraps it in yet another envelope, with the IP address (office building address) of both the destination and the source affixed. The post office (which we haven't discussed quite yet) delivers the letter to the appropriate office building. There, the mail room unwraps the outer envelope and hands it to TCP/UDP, which delivers the letter to the appropriate office based on the port number (written on the inner envelope). Each envelope has a return address that IP and TCP/UDP use to reply to the letter.

In order to make the specification of machines on the Internet more humane, network hosts are often given a name as well as an IP address. The Domain Name Service (DNS) takes care of translating hostnames to IP addresses, and vice versa, as well as handles the distribution of the name-to-IP address database across the entire Internet. Using hostnames also allows the IP address associated with a machine to change (e.g., if the machine is moved to a different network), without having to worry that others won't be able to "find" the machine once the address changes. The DNS record for the machine is simply updated with the new IP address, and all references to the machine, by name, will continue to work.

[4] Network
Admin Guide
[28] TCP/IP
[30] DNS
and BIND

DNS is an enormous, worldwide distributed database. Each organization maintains a piece of the database, listing the machines in the organization. If you find yourself in the position of maintaining the list for your organization, you can get help from the *Linux Network Administrator's Guide* or *TCP/IP Network Administration.* If those aren't enough, you can really get the full scoop from the book *DNS and BIND.*

For the purposes of most administration, all you need to know is that a daemon called *named* (pronounced "name-dee") has to run on your system. This daemon is your window onto DNS.

Now, we might ask ourselves how a packet gets from one machine (office building) to another. This is the actual job of IP, as well as a number of other protocols that aid IP in its task. Besides managing IP datagrams on each host (as the mail room), IP is also responsible for routing packets between hosts.

Before we can discuss how routing works, we must explain the model upon which TCP/IP networks are built. A network is just a set of machines that are connected together through some physical network medium—such as Ethernet or serial lines. In TCP/IP terms, each network has its own methods for handling routing and packet transfer internally.

Networks are connected to each other via *gateways* (also known as *routers*). A gateway is a host that has direct connections to two or more networks; the gateway can then exchange information between the networks and route packets from one network to another. For instance, a gateway might be a workstation with more than one Ethernet interface. Each interface is connected to a different network, and the operating system uses this connectivity to allow the machine to act as a gateway.

In order to make our discussion more concrete, let's introduce an imaginary network, made up of the machines **eggplant**, **papaya**, **apricot**, and **zucchini**. Figure 15-3 depicts the configuration of these machines on the network. Note that **papaya** is connected to another network as well, which includes the machines **pineapple** and **pear**. These machines have the respective IP addresses:

Hostname	IP address
eggplant	128.17.75.20
apricot	128.17.75.12
zucchini	128.17.75.37
papaya	128.17.75.98, 128.17.112.3
pear	128.17.112.21
pineapple	128.17.112.40, 128.17.30.1

As you can see, **papaya** has two IP addresses—one on the 128.17.75 subnetwork and another on the 128.17.112 subnetwork. **pineapple** has two IP addresses as well—one on 128.17.112 and another on 128.17.30.

IP uses the network portion of the IP address to determine how to route packets between machines. In order to do this, each machine on the network has a *routing table*, which contains a list of networks and the gateway machine for that network. To route a packet to a particular machine, IP looks at the network portion of the destination address. If there is an entry for that network in the routing table,

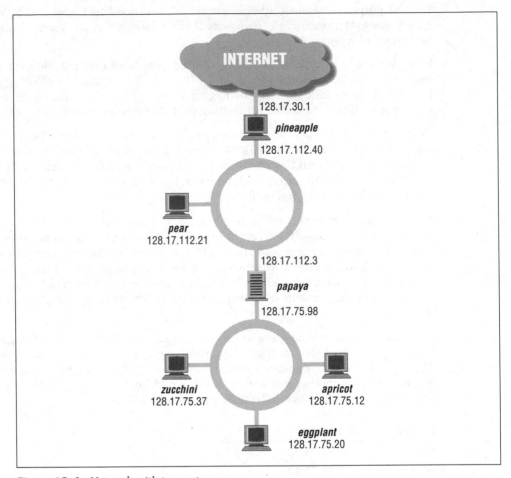

Figure 15–3: Network with two gateways

IP routes the packet through the appropriate gateway. Otherwise, IP routes the packet through the "default" gateway given in the routing table.

Routing tables can contain entries for specific machines as well as for networks. In addition, each machine has a routing table entry for itself.

Let's examine the routing table for **eggplant**. Using the command *netstat –rn*, we see the following:

```
eggplant:$ netstat -rn
Kernel IP routing table
Destination    Gateway       Genmask        Flags  MSS  Window irtt Iface
128.17.75.0    128.17.75.20  255.255.255.0  UN     1500 0         0 eth0
default        128.17.75.98  0.0.0.0        UGN    1500 0         0 eth0
```

```
127.0.0.1    127.0.0.1    255.0.0.0     UH    3584 0      0 lo
128.17.75.20 127.0.0.1    255.255.255.0 UH    3584 0      0 lo
```

The first column displays the destination networks (and hosts) that the routing table includes. The first entry is for the network 128.17.75 (note that the host address is 0 for network entries), which is the network that **eggplant** lives on. Any packets sent to this network should be routed through 128.17.75.20, which is the IP address of **eggplant**. In general, a machine's route to its own network is through itself.

The `Flags` column of the routing table gives information on the destination address for this entry; `U` specifies that the route is "up," `N` that the destination is a network, and so on. The `MSS` field shows how many bytes are transferred at a time over the respective connection, `Window` indicates how many frames may be sent ahead before a confirmation must be made, `irtt` gives statistics on the use of this route, and `Iface` lists the network device used for the route. On Linux systems, Ethernet interfaces are named *eth0*, *eth1*, and so on. *lo* is the loopback device, which we'll discuss shortly.

The second entry in the routing table is the default route, which applies to all packets destined for networks or hosts for which there is no entry in the table. In this case, the default route is through **papaya**, which can be considered the door to the outside world. Every machine on the 128.17.75 subnet must go through **papaya** to talk to machines on any other network.

The third entry in the table is for the address 127.0.0.1, which is the *loopback* address. This address is used when a machine wants to make a TCP/IP connection to itself. It uses the *lo* device as its interface, which prevents loopback connections from using the Ethernet (via the *eth0* interface). In this way, network bandwidth is not wasted when a machine wishes to talk to itself.

The last entry in the routing table is for the IP address 128.17.75.20, which is the **eggplant** host's own address. As we can see, it uses 127.0.0.1 as its gateway. This way, any time **eggplant** makes a TCP/IP connection to itself, the loopback address is used as the gateway, and the *lo* network device is used.

Let's say that **eggplant** wants to send a packet to **zucchini**. The IP datagram contains a source address of 128.17.75.20 and a destination address of 128.17.75.37. IP determines that the network portion of the destination address is 128.17.75 and uses the routing table entry for 128.17.75.0 accordingly. The packet is sent directly to the network, which **zucchini** receives and is able to process.

What happens if **eggplant** wants to send packets to a machine not on the local network, such as **pear**? In this case, the destination address is 128.17.112.21. IP attempts to find a route for the 128.17.112 network in the routing tables, but none exists, so it selects the default route through **papaya**. **papaya** receives the packet and looks up the destination address in its own routing tables. The routing table for **papaya** might look like this:

Destination	Gateway	Genmask	Flags	MSS	Window	irtt	Iface
128.17.75.0	128.17.75.98	255.255.255.0	UN	1500	0	0	eth0
128.17.112.0	128.17.112.3	255.255.255.0	UN	1500	0	0	eth1
default	128.17.112.40	0.0.0.0	UGN	1500	0	0	eth1
127.0.0.1	127.0.0.1	255.0.0.0	UH	3584	0	0	lo
128.17.75.98	127.0.0.1	255.255.255.0	UH	3584	0	0	lo

As you can see, **papaya** is connected to the 128.17.75 network through its *eth0* device and to 128.17.112 through *eth1*. The default route is through **pineapple**, which is a gateway to the Wild Blue Yonder (as far as **papaya** is concerned).

Once **papaya** receives a packet destined for **pear**, it sees that the destination address is on the network 128.17.112 and routes that packet to the network using the second entry in the routing table.

Similarly, if **eggplant** wants to send packets to machines outside the local organization, it would route packets through **papaya** (its gateway). **papaya** would, in turn, route outgoing packets through **pineapple**, and so forth. Packets are handed from one gateway to the next until they reach the intended destination network. This is the basic structure upon which the Internet is based: a seemingly infinite chain of networks, interconnected via gateways.

Hardware Requirements

You can use Linux TCP/IP without any networking hardware at all; configuring "loopback" mode allows you to talk to yourself. This is necessary for some applications and games that use the loopback network device.

Chapter 1
[74] Ethernet
HOWTO

However, if you want to use Linux with an Ethernet TCP/IP network, obviously you'll need an Ethernet adapter card. Many Ethernet adapters are supported by Linux for the ISA, EISA, and PCI buses, as well as pocket and PCMCIA adapters. In Chapter 1, *Introduction to Linux*, we provided a partial list of supported Ethernet cards; see the Linux Ethernet HOWTO for a complete discussion of Linux Ethernet hardware compatibility.

[4] Network
Admin Guide

Linux also supports SLIP and PPP, which allow you to use a modem to access the Internet over the phone line. In this case, you'll need a modem compatible with your SLIP or PPP server; for example, many servers require a 56kbps V.90 modem (most also support K56flex). In this book, we describe the configuration of PPP, because it is what most Internet service providers offer. If you want to use the older SLIP, please see the *Linux Network Administrator's Guide*.

Configuring TCP/IP with Ethernet

In this section, we discuss how to configure an Ethernet TCP/IP connection on a Linux system. Presumably this system will be part of a local network of machines that are already running TCP/IP; in which case your gateway, name server, and so forth are already configured and available.

The following information applies primarily to Ethernet connections. If you're planning to use PPP, read this section to understand the concepts, and follow the PPP-specific instructions in the section "Dial-up PPP" later in this chapter.

On the other hand, you may wish to set up an entire LAN of Linux machines (or a mix of Linux machines and other systems). In this case, you'll have to take care of a number of other issues not discussed here. This includes setting up a name server for yourself, as well as a gateway machine if your network is to be connected to other networks. If your network is to be connected to the Internet, you'll also have to obtain IP addresses and related information from your access provider.

In short, the method described here should work for many Linux systems configured for an existing LAN—but certainly not all. For further details, we direct you to a book on TCP/IP network administration, such as those mentioned at the beginning of this chapter.

First of all, we assume that your Linux system has the necessary TCP/IP software installed. This includes basic clients such as Telnet and FTP, system-administration commands, such as *ifconfig* and *route* (usually found in */etc* or */sbin*), and networking configuration files (such as */etc/hosts*). The other Linux-related networking documents described earlier explain how to go about installing the Linux networking software if you do not have it already.

Chapter 7

We also assume that your kernel has been configured and compiled with TCP/IP support enabled. See the section "Building a New Kernel" in Chapter 7, *Upgrading Software and the Kernel*, for information on compiling your kernel. To enable networking, you must answer yes to the appropriate questions during the *make config* or *make menuconfig* step, rebuild the kernel, and boot from it.

Once this has been done, you must modify a number of configuration files used by NET-4. For the most part this is a simple procedure. Unfortunately, however, there is wide disagreement between Linux distributions as to where the various TCP/IP configuration files and support programs should go. Much of the time, they can be found in */etc*, but in other cases may be found in */usr/etc*, */usr/etc/inet*, or other bizarre locations. In the worst case, you'll have to use the *find* command to locate the files on your system. Also note that not all distributions keep the NET-2 configuration files and software in the same location; they may be spread across several directories.

This section also assumes use of one Ethernet device on the system. These instructions should be fairly easy to extrapolate if your system has more than one network connection (and hence acts as a gateway).

Here, we also discuss configuration for loopback-only systems (systems with no Ethernet or PPP connection). If you have no network access, you may wish to configure your system for loopback-only TCP/IP, so that you can use applications that require it.

Your network configuration

Before you can configure TCP/IP, you need to determine the following informa-tion about your network setup. In most cases, your local network administrator or network-access provider can provide you with this information:

Your IP address

This is the unique machine address in dotted-decimal format. An example is 128.17.75.98. Your network administrators will provide you with this number.

If you're configuring loopback mode (i.e., no PPP, no Ethernet card, just TCP/IP connections to your own machine), your IP address is 127.0.0.1.

Your subnetwork mask

This is a dotted quad, similar to the IP address, which determines which por-tion of the IP address specifies the subnetwork number and which portion specifies the host on that subnet.

The subnetwork mask is a pattern of bits, which, when bitwise-ANDed with an IP address on your network, will tell you which subnet that address belongs to. For example, your subnet mask might be 255.255.255.0. If your IP address is 128.17.75.20, the subnetwork portion of your address is 128.17.75.

We distinguish here between "network address" and "subnetwork address." Remember that for Class B addresses, the first two bytes (here, 128.17) specify the network, while the second two bytes specify the host. With a subnet mask of 255.255.255.0, however, 128.17.75 is considered the entire subnet address (e.g., subnetwork 75 of network 128.17), and 20 the host address.

Your network administrators choose the subnet mask and therefore can pro-vide you with this information.

This applies as well to the loopback device. Since the loopback address is always 127.0.0.1, the netmask for this device is always 255.0.0.0.

Your subnetwork address

This is the subnet portion of your IP address as determined by the subnet mask. For example, if your subnet mask is 255.255.255.0 and your IP address 128.17.75.20, your subnet address is 128.17.75.0.

Loopback-only systems don't have a subnet address.

Your broadcast address

This address is used to broadcast packets to every machine on your subnet. In general, this is equal to your subnet address (see previous item) with 255 replaced as the host address. For subnet address 128.17.75.0, the broadcast address is 128.17.75.255. Similarly, for subnet address 128.17.0.0, the broadcast address is 128.17.255.255.

Note that some systems use the subnet address itself as the broadcast address. If you have any doubt, check with your network administrators.

Loopback-only systems do not have a broadcast address.

The IP address of your gateway

This is the address of the machine that acts as the default route to the outside world. In fact, you may have more than one gateway address—for example, if your network is connected directly to several other networks. However, only one of these will act as the *default* route. (Recall the example in the previous section, where the 128.17.112.0 network is connected both to 128.17.75.0 through **papaya**, and to the outside world through **pineapple**.)

Your network administrators will provide you with the IP addresses of any gateways on your network, as well as the networks they connect to. Later, you will use this information with the *route* command to include entries in the routing table for each gateway.

Loopback-only systems do not have a gateway address. The same is true for isolated networks.

The IP address of your name server

This is the address of the machine that handles hostname-to-address translations for your machine. Your network administrators will provide you with this information.

You may wish to run your own name server (by configuring and running *named*). However, unless you absolutely must run your own name server (for example, if there is no other name server available on your local network), we suggest using the name-server address provided by your network administrators. At any rate, most books on TCP/IP configuration include information on running *named*.

Naturally, loopback-only systems have no name-server address.

The networking rc files

rc files are systemwide resource configuration scripts executed at boottime by *init*. They run basic system daemons (such as *sendmail*, *crond*, and so on) and are used to configure network parameters. *rc* files are usually found in the directory */etc/rc.d*.

Note that there are *many* ways to carry out the network configuration described here. Every Linux distribution uses a slightly different mechanism to help automate the process. What we describe here is a generic method that allows you to create two *rc* files that will run the appropriate commands to get your machine talking to the network. Most distributions have their own scripts that accomplish more or less the same thing. If in doubt, first attempt to configure networking as suggested by the documentation for your distribution and, as a last resort, use the methods described here. (As an example, the Red Hat distribution uses the script */etc/rc.d/ init.d/network*, which obtains network information from files in */etc/sysconfig*. The *control-panel* system administration program provided with Red Hat configures networking automatically without editing any of these files. The SuSE distribution, on the other hand, distributes the configuration over several files, such as */sbin/init.d/network* and */sbin/init.d/route*, among others, and lets you configure most networking aspects via the tool *yast*.)

Here, we're going to describe the *rc* files used to configure TCP/IP:

Red Hat

> Networking is scattered among files for each *init* level that includes networking. For instance, the */etc/rc.d/rc1.d* directory controls a level 1 (single-user) boot, so it doesn't have any networking commands, but the */etc/rc.d/rc3.d* controlling a level 3 boot has files specifically to start networking.

SuSE

> All the startup files for all system services, including networking, are grouped together in the */sbin/init.d* directory. They are actually quite generic and get their actual values from the system-wide configuration file */etc/rc.config*. The most important files here are */sbin/init.d/network*, which starts and halts network interfaces, */sbin/init.d/route*, which configures routing, and */sbin/init.d/ serial*, which configures serial ports. If you have ISDN hardware, the files */sbin/init.d/i4l* and */sbin/init.d/i4l_hardware* are applicable, too. Note that in general, you do not need to (and should not) edit those files; edit */etc/rc.config* instead.

Debian

> The network configuration (Ethernet cards, IP addresses, and routing) is set up in the file */etc/init.d/network*. The base networking daemons (*portmap* and *inetd* themselves are initialized by the start-stop script */etc/init.d/netbase*).

Slackware

> Networking is started by files named *rc.inet1* and *rc.inet2*. *rc.inet1* is used to configure the basic network parameters (such as IP addresses and routing information), and *rc.inet2* fires up the TCP/IP daemons (*telnetd*, *ftpd*, and so forth).

init uses the file */etc/inittab* to determine what processes to run at boot time. In order to run the files */etc/rc.d/rc.inet1* and */etc/rc.d/rc.inet2* from *init*, */etc/inittab* might include entries such as:

```
n1:34:wait:/etc/rc.d/rc.inet1
n2:34:wait:/etc/rc.d/rc.inet2
```

Chapter 5

The *inittab* file is described in the section "init, inittab, and rc files" in Chapter 5, *Essential System Management*. The first field gives a unique two-character identifier for each entry. The second field lists the runlevels in which the scripts are run; on this system, we initialize networking in runlevels 3 and 4. The word `wait` in the third field tells *init* to wait until the script has finished execution before continuing. The last field gives the name of the script to run.

While you are first setting up your network configuration, you may wish to run *rc.inet1* and *rc.inet2* by hand (as **root**) in order to debug any problems. Later you can include entries for them in another *rc* file or in */etc/inittab*.

As mentioned earlier, *rc.inet1* configures the basic network interface. This includes your IP and network address and the routing table information for your system. Two programs are used to configure these parameters: *ifconfig* and *route*. Both of these are usually found in */sbin*.

ifconfig is used for configuring the network device interface with certain parameters, such as the IP address, subnetwork mask, broadcast address, and the like. *route* is used to create and modify entries in the routing table.

For most configurations, an *rc.inet1* file similar to the following should work. You will, of course, have to edit this for your own system. Do not use the sample IP and network addresses listed here; they may correspond to an actual machine on the Internet:

```
#!/bin/sh
# This is /etc/rc.d/rc.inet1 - Configure the TCP/IP interfaces

# First, configure the loopback device

HOSTNAME=`hostname`

/sbin/ifconfig lo 127.0.0.1    # uses default netmask 255.0.0.0
/sbin/route add 127.0.0.1      # a route to point to the loopback device

# Next, configure the ethernet device. If you're only using loopback or
# SLIP, comment out the rest of these lines.

# Edit for your setup.
IPADDR="128.17.75.20"      # REPLACE with your IP address
NETMASK="255.255.255.0"    # REPLACE with your subnet mask
NETWORK="128.17.75.0"      # REPLACE with your network address
BROADCAST="128.17.75.255"  # REPLACE with your broadcast address
GATEWAY="128.17.75.98"     # REPLACE with your default gateway address

# Configure the eth0 device to use information above
/sbin/ifconfig eth0 ${IPADDR} netmask ${NETMASK} broadcast ${BROADCAST}

# Add a route for our own network
/sbin/route add ${NETWORK}
```

```
# Add a route to the default gateway
/sbin/route add default gw ${GATEWAY} metric 1

# End of Ethernet Configuration
```

As you can see, the format of the *ifconfig* command is:

```
ifconfig interface device options...
```

For example:

```
ifconfig lo 127.0.0.1
```

assigns the *lo* (loopback) device the IP address 127.0.0.1, and:

```
ifconfig eth0 127.17.75.20
```

assigns the *eth0* (first Ethernet) device the address 127.17.75.20.

In addition to specifying the address, Ethernet devices usually require that the sub-network mask be set with the *netmask* option and the broadcast address be set with *broadcast*.

The format of the *route* command, as used here, is:

```
route add [ -net | -host ] destination [ gw gateway ]
[ metric metric ] options
```

where *destination* is the destination address for this route (or the keyword default), *gateway* the IP address of the gateway for this route, and *metric* the metric number for the route (discussed later).

We use *route* to add entries to the routing table. You should add a route for the loopback device (as seen earlier), for your local network, and for your default gateway. For example, if our default gateway is 128.17.75.98, we would use the command:

```
route add default gw 128.17.75.98
```

route takes several options. Using *–net* or *–host* before *destination* will tell *route* that the destination is a network or specific host, respectively. (In most cases, routes point to networks, but in some situations you may have an independent machine that requires its own route. You would use *–host* for such a routing table entry.)

The *metric* option specifies a *metric value* for this route. Metric values are used when there is more than one route to a specific location, and the system must make a decision about which to use. Routes with lower metric values are preferred. In this case, we set the metric value for our default route to 1, which forces that route to be preferred over all others.

How could there possibly be more than one route to a particular location? First of all, you may use multiple *route* commands in *rc.inet1* for a particular destination—if you have more than one gateway to a particular network, for example. However, your routing tables may dynamically acquire additional entries in them if you run *routed* (discussed further below). If you run *routed*, other systems may broadcast routing information to machines on the network, causing extra routing table entries to be created on your machine. By setting the `metric` value for your default route to 1, you ensure that any new routing table entries will not supersede the preference of your default gateway.

You should read the manual pages for *ifconfig* and *route*, which describe the syntax of these commands in detail. There may be other options to *ifconfig* and *route* that are pertinent to your configuration.

Let's move on. *rc.inet2* is used to run various daemons used by the TCP/IP suite. These are not necessary in order for your system to talk to the network, and are therefore relegated to a separate *rc* file. In most cases you should attempt to configure *rc.inet1*, and ensure that your system is able to send and receive packets from the network, before bothering to configure *rc.inet2*.

Among the daemons executed by *rc.inet2* are *inetd*, *syslogd*, and *routed*. The version of *rc.inet2* on your system may currently start a number of other servers, but we suggest commenting these out while you are debugging your network configuration.

The most important of these servers is *inetd*, which acts as the "operator" for other system daemons. It sits in the background and listens to certain network ports for incoming connections. When a connection is made, *inetd* spawns off a copy of the appropriate daemon for that port. For example, when an incoming Telnet connection is made, *inetd* forks *in.telnetd*, which handles the Telnet connection from there. This is simpler and more efficient than running individual copies of each daemon. This way, network daemons are executed on demand.

syslogd is the system logging daemon; it accumulates log messages from various applications and stores them into log files based on the configuration information in */etc/syslogd.conf*.

routed is a server used to maintain dynamic routing information. When your system attempts to send packets to another network, it may require additional routing table entries in order to do so. *routed* takes care of manipulating the routing table without the need for user intervention.

Here is a sample *rc.inet2* that starts up *syslogd*, *inetd*, and *routed*:

```
#! /bin/sh
# Sample /etc/rc.d/rc.inet2

# Start syslogd
if [ -f /usr/sbin/syslogd ]
```

```
then
        /usr/sbin/syslogd
fi

# Start inetd
if [ -f /usr/sbin/inetd ]
then
        /usr/sbin/inetd
fi

# Start routed
if [ -f /usr/sbin/routed ]
then
        /usr/sbin/routed -q
fi
```

Among the various additional servers you may want to start in *rc.inet2* is *named*. *named* is a name server; it is responsible for translating (local) IP addresses to names, and vice versa. If you don't have a name server elsewhere on the network, or if you want to provide local machine names to other machines in your domain, it may be necessary to run *named*. *named* configuration is somewhat complex and requires planning; we refer interested readers to *DNS and BIND*.

[30] DNS and BIND

/etc/hosts

/etc/hosts contains a list of IP addresses and the hostnames they correspond to. In general, */etc/hosts* contains entries only for your local machine and perhaps other "important" machines (such as your name server or gateway). Your local name server provides address-to-name mappings for other machines on the network transparently.

For example, if your machine is **eggplant.veggie.com** with the IP address 128.17.75.20, your */etc/hosts* would look like this:

```
127.0.0.1               localhost
128.17.75.20            eggplant.veggie.com eggplant
```

If you're using only loopback, the only line in */etc/hosts* file should be for the address 127.0.0.1.

/etc/networks

The */etc/networks* file lists the names and addresses of your own and other networks. It is used by the *route* command and allows you to specify a network by name instead of by address.

Every network you wish to add a route to using the *route* command (generally called from *rc.inet1*) should have an entry in */etc/networks* for convenience; otherwise, you will have to specify the network's IP address instead of the name.

As an example:

```
default       0.0.0.0          # default route      - mandatory
loopnet       127.0.0.0        # loopback network - mandatory
veggie-net    128.17.75.0      # Modify for your own network address
```

Now, instead of using the command:

```
route add 128.17.75.20
```

we can use:

```
route add veggie-net
```

/etc/host.conf

The */etc/host.conf* file specifies how your system resolves hostnames. It should contain the two lines:

```
order hosts,bind
multi on
```

These lines tell the resolver libraries to first check the */etc/hosts* file and then ask the name server (if one is present) for any names it must look up. The `multi` entry allows you to have multiple IP addresses for a given machine name in */etc/hosts*.

On systems that use the new *glibc2* (like Red Hat from Version 5.0, SuSE from Version 6.0 and Debian from Version 2.0), */etc/nsswitch.conf* is used instead of */etc/host.conf*. In this case, this file should contain the lines `hosts: files dns` and `networks: files dns`.

/etc/resolv.conf

This file configures the name resolver, specifying the address of your name server (if any) and domains that you want to search by default if a specified hostname is not a fully specified hostname. For example, if this file contains the line:

```
search vpizza.com vpasta.com
```

then using the hostname **blurb** will try to resolve the names **blurb.vpizza.com** and **blurb.vpasta.com** (in this order). This is convenient, because it saves you typing in the full names of often-used domains. On the other hand, the more domains you specify here, the longer the DNS lookup will take.

For example, the machine **eggplant.veggie.com** with a name server at address 128.17.75.55 would have the following lines in */etc/resolv.conf*:

```
domain       veggie.com
nameserver  128.17.75.55
```

You can specify more than one name server; each must have a `nameserver` line of its own in *resolv.conf*.

Setting your hostname

You should set your system hostname with the *hostname* command. This is usually executed from */etc/rc.d/rc.sysinit* (*/sbin/init.d/boot* on SuSE systems); simply search your system *rc* files to determine where it is invoked. For example, if your (full) hostname is **eggplant.veggie.com**, edit the appropriate *rc* file to execute the command */bin/hostname eggplant.veggie.com*. Note that the *hostname* executable may be found in a directory other than */bin* on your system.

Trying out your network

Once you have the various networking configuration files modified for your system, you should be able to reboot (using a TCP/IP-enabled kernel) and attempt to use the network.

When first booting the system, you may wish to disable execution of *rc.inet1* and *rc.inet2* and run them by hand once the system is up. This allows you to catch any error messages, modify the scripts, and retry. Once you have things working, you can enable the scripts from */etc/inittab*.

One good way of testing network connectivity is to simply *telnet* to another host. You should first try to connect to another host on your local network, and if this works, attempt to connect to hosts on other networks. The former will test your connection to the local subnet; the latter, your connection to the rest of the world through your gateway.

You may be able to connect to remote machines, via the gateway, whereas connecting to machines on the subnet fails. This is a sign that there is a problem with your subnetwork mask or the routing table entry for the local network.

When attempting to connect to other machines, you should first try to connect using only the IP address of the remote host. If this seems to work, but connecting via hostname does not, there may be a problem with your name server configuration (e.g., */etc/resolv.conf* and */etc/host.conf*) or with your route to the name server.

The most common source of network trouble is an ill-configured routing table. You can use the command:

```
netstat -rn
```

netstat(8)

to display the routing table; in the previous section, we described the format of the routing tables as displayed by this command. The *netstat* manual page provides additional insight as well. Using *netstat* without the *−n* option forces it to display host and network entries by name instead of address.

route(8)

To debug your routing tables, you can either edit *rc.inet1* and reboot, or use the *route* command by hand to add or delete entries. The manual page for *route* describes the full syntax of this command. Note that simply editing *rc.inet1* and re-executing it will not clear out old entries in the routing table; you must either reboot or use *route del* to delete the entries.

If absolutely nothing seems to work, there may be a problem with your Ethernet device configuration. First, be sure that your Ethernet card was detected at the appropriate address and/or IRQ at boot time. The kernel boot messages will give you this information; if you are using *syslogd*, kernel boot-time messages are also saved in a file, such as */var/log/messages*.

[74] Ethernet HOWTO

If detection of your Ethernet card is faulty, you may have to modify kernel parameters to fix it. The Linux Ethernet HOWTO includes much information on debugging Ethernet card configurations. In many cases, the fix is as simple as specifying the appropriate IRQ and port address at the LILO boot prompt. For example, booting via LILO with the command:

```
lilo: linux ether=9,0x300,0,1,eth0
```

will select IRQ 9, base address 0x300, and the external transceiver (the fourth value of 1) for the *eth0* device. To use the internal transceiver (if your card supports both types), change the fourth value of the `ether` option to 0.

Also, don't overlook the possibility that your Ethernet card is damaged or incorrectly connected to your machine or the network. A bad Ethernet card or cable can cause no end of trouble, including intermittent network failures, system crashes, and so forth. When you're at the end of your rope, consider replacing the Ethernet card and/or cable to determine if this is the source of the problem.*

If your Ethernet card is detected, but the system is still having problems talking to the network, the device configuration with *ifconfig* may be to blame. Be sure you have specified the appropriate IP address, broadcast address, and subnet mask for your machine. Invoking *ifconfig* with no arguments displays information on your Ethernet device configuration.

Dial-up PPP

In order to communicate over TCP/IP using a modem (such as through a dial-up account to an Internet service provider) or through some other serial device (such as a "null modem" serial cable between two machines), Linux provides the Point-to-Point Protocol software suite, commonly known as PPP. PPP is a protocol that takes packets sent over a network (such as TCP/IP) and converts them to a format that can be easily sent over a modem or serial wire. Chances are, if you have an

---

* One of the authors once spent three hours trying to determine why the kernel wouldn't recognize an Ethernet card at boot time. As it turned out, the 16-bit card was plugged into an 8-bit slot—mea culpa.

Internet account with an ISP, the ISP's server uses PPP to communicate with dialup accounts. By configuring PPP under Linux, you can directly connect to your ISP account in this way.

SLIP (Serial Line Internet Protocol) is an earlier protocol that has the same basic features as PPP. However, it lacks certain important qualities, such as the ability to negotiate IP addresses and packet sizes. These days SLIP has more or less been supplanted entirely by PPP; however, some older ISPs may still use SLIP rather than PPP. If this is the case, we refer you to other sources of information, such as the *Linux Network Administrator's Guide*.

[4] Network Admin Guide

In this section, we will cover configuration of a PPP *client*—that is, a system that will connect to an ISP (or other PPP server) in order to communicate with the Internet. Setting up a Linux machine as a PPP server itself is also possible but is somewhat more involved; this is covered in the *Linux Network Administrator's Guide*.

Basic PPP Configuration for Modems

In the United States and many parts of the world, people use traditional dial-up modems to send digital data over telephone lines. So we'll cover configuration for modems first. Then we'll show how to configure PPP for the faster and more convenient type of line called Integrated Services Digital Network (ISDN), which is especially popular in Europe and available but not very well marketed in most of the United States.

Requirements

Most Linux systems come preinstalled with all of the software needed to run PPP. Essentially, you need a kernel compiled with PPP support and the *pppd* daemon and related tools, including the *chat* program.

Most Linux distributions include PPP support in the preconfigured kernel or as a kernel module that is loaded on demand. However, it may necessary to compile kernel PPP support yourself; this is a simple matter of enabling the PPP options during the kernel configuration process and rebuilding the kernel. PPP is usually compiled as a separate module, so it is sufficient to recompile only the kernel modules if this is the case. See "Building the Kernel" in Chapter 7 for information on compiling the kernel and modules.

Chapter 7

The *pppd* and *chat* utilities are user-level applications that control the use of PPP on your system; they are included with nearly every Linux distribution. On Red Hat systems, these utilities are installed in */usr/sbin* and are found in the *ppp* RPM package.

Also required for PPP usage is a modem that is compatible with both Linux and the type of modems used by your ISP's server. Most 14.4, 28.8, 56K and other standard modem types fit into this category; there are very few modem types not supported by Linux, and it would be unusual for an ISP to use anything so eso-teric as to require you to buy something else.

One type of modem to watch out for is the so-called "Winmodem." This was origi-nally a product sold by US Robotics but has now been produced in several vari-eties by other vendors. Winmodems use the host CPU to convert digital signals into analog signals so they can be sent over the phone line, unlike regular modems which have a special chip to perform this function. The problem with Winmodems is that, as of this writing, the programming details for these devices are proprietary, meaning that there are no Linux drivers for this class of devices. (Besides, some people scoff at the idea of wasting precious CPU cycles to gener-ate modem signals, a job best left to specialized hardware. One perceived advan-tage of these so-called "software modems," on the other hand, is that upgrading their functionality is simply a matter of upgrading the operating system driver which controls them, rather than buying new hardware.)

Serial device names

Under Windows 95/98 and MS-DOS, modems and other serial devices are named COM1 (for the first serial device), COM2 (for the second), and so forth, up to COM4. (Most systems support up to four serial devices, although multiport cards are available that can increase this number.) Under Linux, these same devices are referred to as */dev/ttyS0*, */dev/ttyS1*, on up to */dev/ttyS3*.* On most systems, at installation time a symbolic link called */dev/modem* will be created. This link points to the serial device on which the modem can be found, as shown in the fol-lowing listing:

```
% ls -l /dev/modem
lrwxrwxrwx   1 root       root        10 May  4 12:41 /dev/modem -> /dev/ttyS0
```

If this link is incorrect for your system (say, because you know that your modem is not on */dev/ttyS0* but on */dev/ttyS2*), you can easily fix it as **root** by entering:

```
# ln -sf /dev/ttyS2 /dev/modem
```

Setting up PPP

There are several steps involved in PPP configuration. The first is to write a so-called "chat script," which performs the "handshaking" necessary to set up a PPP connection between your machine and the ISP. During this handshaking phase, various pieces of information might be exchanged, such as your ISP username and password. The second step is to write a script that fires up the *pppd* daemon; run-ning this script causes the modem to dial the ISP and start up PPP. The final step is to configure your system's */etc/resolv.conf* file so it knows where to find a domain name server. We'll go through each of these steps in turn.

---

* Older versions of Linux also used special "callout" devices, called */dev/cua0* through */dev/ cua3*. These are obsolete as of Linux kernel Version 2.2.

Before you start, you need to know the following pieces of information:

- The ISP dialin account phone number

- Your ISP username and password

- The IP address of the ISP's domain name server

Your ISP should have told you this information when you established the account.

In addition, you might need to know the following:

- The IP address of the ISP's server

- The IP address of your system (if not dynamically assigned by the ISP)

- The subnet mask you should use

These last three items can usually be determined automatically during the PPP connection setup; however, occasionally this negotiation does not work properly. It can't hurt to have this information in case you need it.

chat is a program that can perform simple handshaking between a PPP client and server during connection setup, such as exchange usernames and passwords. *chat* is also responsible for causing your modem to dial the ISP's phone number and other simple tasks.

chat itself is automatically invoked by *pppd* when started (this is discussed later). All you need to do is write a simple shell script that invokes *chat* to handle the negotiation. A simple chat script is shown in the following example. Edit the file */etc/ppp/my-chat-script* (as **root**) and place in it the following lines:

```
#!/bin/sh
# my-chat-script: a program for dialing up your ISP
exec chat -v            \
     '' ATZ             \
     OK ATDT555-1212    \
     CONNECT ''                 \
     ogin: mdw          \
     assword: my-password
```

Be sure that the file *my-chat-script* is executable; the command chmod 755 /etc/ ppp/my-chat-script will accomplish this.

Note that each line ending in a backslash should not have any characters *after* the backslash; the backslash forces line-wrapping in the shell script.

The third line of this script runs *chat* itself with the options on the following lines. Each line contains two whitespace-delimited fields: an "expect" string and a "send" string. The idea is that the chat script will respond with the send string when it receives the expect string from the modem connection. For example, the last line of the script informs chat to respond with my-password when the prompt assword* is given by the ISP's server.

The first line of the handshaking script instructs *chat* to send ATZ to the modem, which should cause the modem to reset itself. (Specifying an expect string as ' ' means that nothing is expected before ATZ is sent.) The second line waits for the modem to respond with OK, after which the number is dialed using the string ATDT555-1212. (If you use pulse dialing, rather than tone dialing, change this to ATDP555-1212. The phone number, of course, should be that of the remote system's modem line.)

When the modem responds with CONNECT, a newline is sent (indicated by ' ' as the send string). After this, *chat* waits for the prompt ogin: before sending the username and assword: before sending the password.

The various send strings starting with AT in the previous example are simply Hayes–modem-standard modem control strings. The manual that came with your modem should explain their usage; this is not specific to Linux or any other operating system. As one example, using a comma in a phone number indicates that the modem should pause before sending the following digits; one might use ATDT9,,,555-1212 if a special digit (9 in this case) must be dialed to reach an outside line.

Note that this is a very simple *chat* script that doesn't deal with timeouts, errors, or any other extraordinary cases that might arise while you're attempting to dial into the ISP. See the *chat* manual pages for information on how to spruce up your script to deal with these cases. Also, note that you need to know in advance what prompts the ISP's server will use (we assumed login and password). There are several ways of finding out this information; possibly, the ISP has told you this information in advance, or supplied a handshaking script for another system such as Windows 95 (which uses a mechanism very similar to *chat*). Otherwise, you can dial into the ISP server "by hand," using a simple terminal emulator, such as *minicom* or *seyon*. The man pages for those commands can help you to do this.

Now, we're ready to configure the *pppd* daemon to initiate the PPP connection using the *chat* script we just wrote. Generally, this is done by writing another shell script that invokes *pppd* with a set of options.

The format of the *pppd* command is:

```
pppd device-name baudrate options
```

Table 15-1 shows the options supported by *pppd*. You almost certainly won't need all of them.

---

* This is not meant as an expletive. Rather, leaving off the first letter of the prompt admits the possibility of either Password: or password: to be used as the prompt!

Table 15-1: Common *pppd* Options

Option	Effect
lock	Locks the serial device to restrict access to *pppd*.
crtscts	Uses hardware flow control.
noipdefault	Doesn't try to determine the local IP address from the hostname. The IP is assigned by the remote system.
user *username*	Specifies the hostname or username for PAP or CHAP identification.
netmask *mask*	Specifies the netmask for the connection.
defaultroute	Adds a default route to the local system's routing table, using the remote IP address as the gateway.
connect *command*	Uses the given *command* to initiate the connection. *pppd* assumes this script is in */etc/ppp*. If not, specify the full path of the script.
local_IP_address: *remote_IP_address*	Specifies the local and/or remote IP addresses. Either or both of these could be 0.0.0.0 to indicate that the address should be assigned by the remote system.
debug	Logs connection information through the syslog daemon.

It is common to invoke the *pppd* command from a shell script. Edit the file */etc/ppp/ppp-on* and add the following lines:

```
#!/bin/sh
# the ppp-on script

exec /usr/sbin/pppd /dev/modem 38400 lock crtscts noipdefault \
    defaultroute 0.0.0.0:0.0.0.0 connect my-chat-script
```

As with the *my-chat-script* file in the earlier example, be sure this is executable and watch out for extra characters after a backslash at the end of a line.

With this script in place, it should be possible to connect to the ISP using the command:

```
% /etc/ppp/ppp-on
```

You need not be **root** to execute this command. Upon running this script, you should hear your modem dialing, and if all goes well, after a minute PPP should be happily connected. The *ifconfig* command should report an entry for ppp0 if PPP is up and running:

```
# ifconfig
lo        Link encap:Local Loopback
          inet addr:127.0.0.1  Bcast:127.255.255.255  Mask:255.0.0.0
          UP BROADCAST LOOPBACK RUNNING  MTU:3584  Metric:1
```

```
                   RX packets:0 errors:0 dropped:0 overruns:0 frame:0
                   TX packets:0 errors:0 dropped:0 overruns:0 carrier:0
                   collisions:0

ppp0               Link encap:Point-to-Point Protocol
                   inet addr:207.25.97.248  P-t-P:207.25.97.154  Mask:255.255.255.0
                   UP POINTOPOINT RUNNING  MTU:1500  Metric:1
                   RX packets:1862 errors:0 dropped:0 overruns:0 frame:0
                   TX packets:1288 errors:0 dropped:0 overruns:0 carrier:0
                   collisions:0
                   Memory:73038-73c04
```

Here, we can see that PPP is up, the local IP address is 207.25.97.248, and the remote server IP address is 207.25.97.154.

If you wish to be notified when the PPP connection is established (the *ppp-on* script returns immediately), add the following line to */etc/ppp/ip-up*:

```
/usr/bin/wall "PPP is up!"
```

/etc/ppp/ip-up is executed when PPP establishes an IP connection, so you can use this script to trigger the *wall* command when the connection is complete.

Another simple shell script can be used to kill the PPP session. Edit the file */etc/ppp/ppp-off* as follows:

```
#!/bin/sh
# A simple ppp-off script

kill `cat /var/run/ppp0.pid`
```

Running */etc/ppp/ppp-off* now kills the PPP daemon and shuts down the modem connection.

By itself, use of *pppd* along with *chat* only establishes a PPP connection and assigns you an IP address; in order to use domain names, you need to configure the system to be aware of the domain name server provided by your ISP. This is done by editing */etc/resolv.conf*. The man page for *resolver* describes this file in detail, however, for most purposes it suffices to simply include lines of two forms: one that specifies the list of domains to search whenever a domain name is used and another that specifies the address of a DNS server.

A sample */etc/resolv.conf* file might look like:

```
# Sample /etc/resolv.conf
search cs.nowhere.edu nowhere.edu
nameserver 207.25.97.8
nameserver 204.148.41.1
```

The first line indicates that every time a domain name is used (such as **orange** or **papaya**), it should be searched for in the list of specified domains. In this case, resolver software would first expand a name like **papaya** to **papaya.cs.nowhere.edu** and try to find a system by that name, then expand it to **papaya.nowhere.edu** if necessary and try again.

The lines beginning with `nameserver` specify the IP address of domain name servers (which should be provided by your ISP) that your system contacts to resolve domain names. If you specify more than one `nameserver` line, the given DNS servers will be contacted in order, until one returns a match; in this way, one DNS server is treated as a primary and the others as backups.

The PPP configuration described here is meant to be very simple and will certainly not cover all cases; the best sources for additional information are the man pages for *pppd* and *chat* as well as the Linux PPP HOWTO and related documents.

Happily, both *chat* and *pppd* log messages on their progress, as well as any errors, using the standard syslog daemon facility. By editing */etc/syslog.conf*, you can cause these messages to be captured to a file. To do this, add the following lines:

```
# Save messages from chat
local2.*                                        /var/log/chat-log

# Save messages from pppd
daemon.*                                        /var/log/pppd-log
```

This will cause messages from *chat* to be logged to */var/log/chat-log* and messages from *pppd* to be logged to */var/log/pppd-log*.

Note that these log messages will contain private information, such as ISP usernames and passwords! It is important that you leave this logging enabled only while you are debugging your PPP configuration; after things are working, remove these two log files and remove the lines from */etc/syslog.conf*.

chat will also log certain errors to */etc/ppp/connect-errors*, which is not controlled through the syslog daemon. (It should be safe to leave this log in place, however.)

Some ISPs may require you to use a special authentication protocol, such as PAP (Password Authentication Protocol) or CHAP (Challenge Handshake Authentication Protocol). The protocols rely on some form of "shared secret" known to both the client and the server; in most cases, this is just your ISP account password.

If PAP or CHAP is required by your ISP, they are configured by adding information to the files */etc/ppp/pap-secrets* and */etc/ppp/chap-secrets*, respectively. Each file has four fields separated by spaces or tabs. Here is an example of a *pap-secrets* file:

```
# Secrets for authentication using PAP
# client       server          secret          IP or Domain
mdw            *               my-password
```

The first field is your system's name as expected by the remote system, usually your ISP username. The second field specifies the ISP's server name; an asterisk allows this entry to match all ISP servers to which you might connect. The third field specifies the shared secret provided by your ISP; as stated earlier, this is usually your ISP password. The fourth field is primarily used by PPP servers to limit the IP addresses to which users dialing in have access. These addresses can be specified as either IP addresses or domain names. For most PPP client configurations, however, this field is not required.

The *chap-secrets* file has the same four fields, but you need to include an entry other than * for the service provider's system; this is a secret the ISP shares with you when you establish the account.

If PAP or CHAP is being used, it's not necessary for the *chat* script to include handshaking information after CONNECT is received; *pppd* will take care of the rest. Therefore, you can edit */etc/ppp/my-chat-script* to contain only the lines:

```
#!/bin/sh
# my-chat-script: a program for dialing up your ISP
exec chat -v              \
    '' ATZ                \
    OK ATDT555-1212   \
    CONNECT ''
```

You will also need to add the user option to the *pppd* command line in */etc/ppp/ppp-on*, as so:

```
#!/bin/sh
# the ppp-on script

exec /usr/sbin/pppd /dev/modem 38400 lock crtscts noipdefault \
    user mdw defaultroute 0.0.0.0:0.0.0.0 connect my-chat-script
```

PPP over ISDN

ISDN has offered convenient, high-speed data communications—at a price—for many years; it is particularly popular in Europe where rates and marketing have been more favorable to its use than in the United States. ISDN, which integrates data and regular voice transmission over a single line, offers both a faster connection setup and much better throughput than traditional modems.

ISDN lines can transfer 64 kbits/second. And unlike analog lines, they can achieve this speed all the time, because their transmission does not depend on the vagaries of analog transmission with interference by various kinds of noise. A newer protocol called ADSL (Asymmetric Digital Subscriber Line) is upping the ante for fast data access over phone lines, but ISDN still has a bigger market right now.

In this section, we describe how to configure dial-up access to your Internet provider over an ISDN line. We'll cover only the most common style of connection, synchronous PPP, not the special mode called *Raw IP* over ISDN. Furthermore, this section discusses just internal ISDN boards, which require a very different kind of setup from the dial-up access covered in the previous section. To set up external ISDN devices, or the so-called ISDN modems (a term that is an oxymoron, because there is no modulation and demodulation), you can use commands similar to those in the previous section, because these devices present themselves to the computer and the operating system like a normal modem that offers some additional commands, faster connection setup, and higher throughput.

In a way, setting up ISDN connections is much easier than setting up analog connections, because many of the problems (bad lines, long connection setup times, and so on) simply cannot occur with digital lines. Once you dial the number, the connection is set up within milliseconds. But this can lead to problems. Since the connections are set up and shut down so fast, a misconfigured system that dials out again and again can cost you a fortune. This is even more so because with internal ISDN cards, you hear no clicking and whistling like with modems, and there are no lights that inform you that a connection has been made. You can check the status of your ISDN line with some simple programs, though.

Setting up dial-up PPP over ISDN is done in two steps:

1. Configure your ISDN hardware.

2. Configure and start the PPP daemon and change the routing table to use your ISDN line.

We will cover those steps in the next sections.

Configuring Your ISDN Hardware

The first step involves making your ISDN board accessible to the kernel. Like with any other hardware board, you need a device driver that must be configured with the correct parameters for your board.

Linux supports a large number of ISDN hardware boards. We cannot cover every single board here, but the procedure is more or less the same for each one. Reading the documentation for your specific card in the directory *Documentation/isdn* in the Linux kernel sources will help you a lot if your board is not covered here.

We will concentrate here on boards that use the so-called *HiSax* driver. This device driver works with most cards that use the Siemens HSCX chipset. That includes, for instance, the USR Sportster internal TA and the well-known Teles, ELSA, and Fritz boards. Other boards are similarly configured.

The first thing you need to do is configure the kernel so that it includes ISDN support. It is very advisable to compile everything ISDN-related as modules, especially while you are experimenting with setting it up. You will need the following modules:

- ISDN support.

- Support for synchronous PPP.

- One device driver module for your hardware. If you pick the HiSax driver, you will also have to specify which specific brand of ISDN card you have and which ISDN protocol you want to use. The latter is almost certainly EURO/DSS1, unless you live in Germany and have had your ISDN for a long time in which case it might be 1TR6. When in doubt, ask your phone company.

Chapter 7

Compile and install the modules as described in Chapter 7. Now you are ready to configure your ISDN hardware. Some distributions like SuSE make setting up ISDN lines very easy and comfortable. We cover the hard way here in case your distribution is not so user friendly, the automatic configuration does not work, or you simply want to know what is going on behind the scenes.

Now you need to load the device driver module using *modprobe*. This will automatically load the other modules as well. All the device driver modules accept a number of module parameters; the `hisax` modules accepts, among others, the following:

`id=boardid`

Sets an identifier for the ISDN board. You can pick any name you like here, but you cannot have the same identifier for more than one board in your system.

`type=boardtype`

Specifies the exact board brand and type. For example, a value of 16 for *boardtype* selects the support for the USR Sportster internal TA. See *Documentation/isdn/README.hisax* in the kernel sources for the full list of board types.

`protocol=protocoltype`

Selects an ISDN subprotocol. Valid values for *protocoltype* are 1 for the old German 1TR6 protocol, 2 for the common EDSS1 (so-called Euro ISDN) and 3 for leased lines.

`irq=irqno`

Specifies the interrupt line to use. Not all boards need this.

`io=addr`

Specifies the I/O address to use. Not all boards need this. Some boards need two I/O addresses. In this case, the parameters to use are `io0` and `io1`.

For example, the following command loads the HiSax driver for use with a Teles 16.3 board, Euro ISDN, IO address 0x280, and IRQ line 10 (a very common case):

```
tigger # modprobe hisax type=3 protocol=2 io=0x280 irq=10
```

Please see *Documentation/isdn/README.HiSax* or the equivalent file for your hardware for more information.

This module is not much of a talker; if there is no output from the *modprobe* command, it is likely that everything went well. You might also want to check your system log at */var/log/messages*. You should see a few lines starting with HiSax: (or the name of the driver you are using), ending with:

```
HiSax: module installed
```

If the module did not load, you will most likely find the answer also in */var/log/ messages*. The most common problem is that the IRQ or I/O address was wrong or that you selected the wrong card type. If all else fails, and you have Windows installed on the same machine, boot up Windows and check what it reports for the IRQ and I/O address lines.

You should do one more check before you jump to the next section, and this check involves calling yourself. This can work because, with ISDN, you always have two phone lines at your disposition. Thus one line will be used for the outgoing "phone call" and the other line will be used for the incoming one.

In order to have the ISDN subsystem report what is going on with your phone lines, you will need to configure it to be more verbose than it is by default. You do this by means of three utility programs that are all part of the isdn4k-utils package that you can find at your friendly Linux FTP server around the corner.

The isdn4k-utils contain, among other things, the three utilities *hisaxctrl* for configuring the device driver, *isdnctrl* for configuring the higher levels of the ISDN subsystem, and *isdnlog*, a very useful tool that logs everything happening on your ISDN lines. While you can use *hisactrl* and *isdnctrl* without any configuration, you will need to provide a small configuration file for *isdnlog*. For now, we will content ourselves with a quick solution, but once your ISDN connection is up and running, you will want to configure *isdnlog* to see where your money is going. So for now, copy one of the sample configuration files contained in the *isdnlog* package to */etc/isdn/isdn.conf.* You will at least need to edit the following lines:

COUNTRYCODE=
> Add your phone country code here, for example, 1 for the United States and Canada, 44 for the United Kingdom, 46 for Sweden, and so on.

AREAPREFIX=
> If the area codes in your country are prefixed by a fixed digit, put this in here. The prefix is 0 for most European countries, 9 for Finland, and nothing for the United States, Denmark, and Norway.

AREACODE=

Put your area code in here. If you have specified an AREAPREFIX in the last step, don't repeat that here. For example, Stockholm, Sweden, has the area code 08. You put 0 into AREAPREFIX and 8 into AREACODE.

Once you have set this up, execute the following commands to make your ISDN system more verbose:

```
tigger # /sbin/hisaxctrl boardid 1 4
tigger # /sbin/isdnctrl verbose 3
tigger # /sbin/lsdnlog /dev/isdnctrl0 &
```

If you need to use a different driver from HiSax, you might need to use a different command. For example, for the PCBit driver, the command *pcbitctl* is available in the isdn4k-utils package.

Now you can go ahead and phone yourself. You should try all your MSNs (multiple subscriber numbers, which are your ISDN phone numbers) to see that the board can detect all of them. During or after each call, check */var/log/messages*. You should see lines like the following:

```
Mar 16 18:34:22 tigger kernel: isdn_net: call from 4107123455,1,0 -> 123456
Mar 16 18:34:33 tigger kernel: isdn_net: Service-Indicator not 7, ignored
```

This shows that the kernel has detected voice call (the service indicator is 0) from the phone number 123455 in the area with the area code (0)4107 to the MSN 123456.

Note how the number called is specified, because you will need this information later. The number is sent with the area code in some phone networks, but without the area code in others. Anyway, congratulations if you have come this far. Your ISDN hardware is now correctly configured.

Setting Up Synchronous PPP

Setting up the PPP daemon again involves several substeps. On Linux, the ISDN board is treated like a network interface that you have to configure with special commands. In addition, you need to specify the username and password that your ISP has assigned you. When everything is configured, you start up the *ipppd* daemon, which lurks in the background until a connection request is made.

First, let's configure the "network interface." This involves a number of commands that most system administrators simply put into a script that they store in a file like */sbin/pppon*. Here is a sample file that you can modify to your needs:

```
/sbin/isdnctrl addif ippp0
/sbin/isdnctrl addphone ippp0 out 0123456789
/sbin/isdnctrl dialmax ippp0 2
/sbin/isdnctrl eaz ippp0 123456
/sbin/isdnctrl huptimeout ippp0 100
```

```
/sbin/isdnctrl 12_prot ippp0 hdlc
/sbin/isdnctrl 13_prot ippp0 trans
/sbin/isdnctrl encap ippp0 syncppp
/sbin/ifconfig ippp0 1.1.1.1 pointopoint 123.45.67.89 metric 1
```

Let's go through these commands one by one:

isdnctrl addif ippp0
> Tells the kernel that a new ISDN interface with the name `ippp0` will be used.
> Always use names starting with `ippp`.

isdnctrl addphone ippp0 out 0123456789
> Tells the ISDN interface which phone number to use. This is the phone number that you use to dial up your provider. If you have used analog dial-up so far, check with your provider, because the phone number for ISDN access could be different.

isdnctrl dialmax ippp0 2
> Specifies how many times the kernel should dial if the connection could not be established before giving up.

isdnctrl eaz ippp0 123456
> Specifies one of your own MSNs here. This is very important—without this, not much will work. In case your provider verifies your access via your phone number, make sure that you specify the MSN here that you have registered with your provider.

isdnctrl huptimeout ippp0 100
> Specifies the number of seconds that the line can be idle before the kernel closes the connection (specified by last number in this command.) This is optional, but can save you a lot of money if you do not have a flat phone rate. Thus, if you forget to shut down the connection yourself, the kernel will do that for you.

isdnctrl 12_prot ippp0 hdlc
> Specifies the layer 2 protocol to use. Possible values here are `hdlc`, `x75i`, `x75ui`, and `x75bui`. Most providers use `hdlc`. When in doubt, ask your provider.

isdnctrl 13_prot ippp0 trans
> Specifies the layer 3 protocol to use (the 1 in the option is the letter L). Currently, only `trans` is available.

isdnctrl encap ippp0 syncppp
> Specifies the encapsulation to use. A number of values are possible here, but if you want to use synchronous PPP (or your provider demands that), you have to specify `syncppp` here. Another not-so-uncommon value is `rawip`. But since this provides only very weak authentication facilities, few providers still use it, even though it gives slightly better throughput because it has less overhead.

```
ifconfig ippp0 1.1.1.1 pointopoint 123.45.67.89 metric 1
```
> Creates the new network interface. If your IP address is not assigned dynamically (as is the case with most dial-up connections), you need to specify your IP address instead of the 1.1.1.1 here. Also, you need to change the 123.45.67.89 to the IP address of your provider's dial-up server.

Phew! But we are not finished yet. Next, you need to configure the *ipppd* daemon itself. This is done in the file */etc/ppp/ioptions*. You can also have a configuration file specific to each *ipppd* daemon, but that is necessary only if you want to be able to use different ISDN connections, that is, if you have multiple dial-up accounts.

ipppd (8)

The following is an *ioptions* file that is generic enough to work with most providers. It does not give maximum throughput but is quite stable. If you want to optimize it, ask your provider about the possible settings and read the manual page for *ipppd*:

```
debug
/dev/ippp0
user yourusername
name yourusername
mru 1500
mtu 1500
ipcp-accept-local
ipcp-accept-remote
noipdefault
-vj -vjccomp -ac -pc -bsdcomp
defaultroute
```

You have to change only two things here: change yourusername in the third and fourth lines to the username that your provider has assigned you for connecting to his system. We won't go through all the options here; see the manual page when in doubt.

ISDN access requires the same security as an analog modem. See the section "PAP and CHAP" earlier in this chapter for directions on setting up your *pap-secrets* or *chap-secrets* file as required by your service provider.

Now we have got our things together and can start having fun! First run the *ipppd* daemon:

```
tigger # /sbin/ipppd pidfile /var/run/ipppd.ippp0.pid file /etc/ppp/ioptions &
```

The *ipppd* daemon will now wait for connection requests. Since we have not configured it yet to automatically make a connection, we have to manually trigger the connection. This is done with the following command:

```
tigger # isdnctrl dial ippp0
```

You should now check */var/log/messages*. There should be lots of messages that start with ipppd. The last of those messages should be contain the words local

IP address and remote IP address together with the IP addresses. Once you find those messages, you are done. Because we have used the defaultroute option previously, the kernel has set up the default route to use the ISDN connection, and you should now be able to access the wide, wide world of the Internet. Start by pinging your provider's IP address. Once you are done and want to shut down the connection, enter:

```
tigger # isdnctrl hangup ippp0
```

And If It Does Not Work?

If you have no connection even though your hardware was successfully recognized and you have set up everything as described here, */var/log/messages* is again your friend. It is very likely that you will find the cause of the error there, even though it might be buried a bit.

The most common error is specifying the password or the username incorrectly. You know that you have a problem with the authentification if you see a line like:

```
PAP authentification failed
```

or:

```
CHAP authentification failed
```

in the log file. Check your *chap-secrects* or *pap-secrets* very carefully. Your provider might also be able to see from her log files where exactly the authentification went wrong.

Of course, it could also be the case that your provider does not support synchronous PPP as described here, even though most providers do nowadays. If this is the case, ask your provider for exact settings.

If it still does not work, ask your provider. A good ISP has a phone support line and can help you connect your Linux box. If your provider tells you that they "only support Windows," then it's time to switch. There are many Linux-friendly providers out there. Often the support staff is using Linux and can help you even though the provider's official policy is not to support Linux.

If for some reason you are stuck with an uncooperative provider, try finding other customers of this provider that also use Linux. Setting up your connection in nonstandard cases means fiddling with the options and parameters of the ISDN subsystem in the kernel and the *ipppd* daemon, and if somebody else has already found out what to do, you don't have to.

Where to Go from Here?

Once your ISDN connection works and you can access the Internet, you might want to set up some conveniences or other customizations. Here are some suggestions:

- Make *ipppd* dial your remote site automatically. This can be done by setting the default route to the *ippp0* device like this:

```
/sbin/route add default netmask 0.0.0.0 ippp0
```

  Now, whenever the kernel needs to send an IP packet to an IP address for which it has no specific route configured, it will trigger the *ipppd* daemon to build a connection. Use this only if you have also specified the `huptimeout` option of the ISDN subsystem, otherwise you could pay a fortune to your telephone company (unless you have a flat rate).

  Since there are programs that try to build up Internet connections from time to time (Netscape is one of those candidates), setting this up can be dangerous for your wallet. If you use this, make sure to check the state of the connection often (see later in this section).

- Try tools that monitor your ISDN connection. The *isdn4k-utils* package contains a number of those tools, including the command-line tools *imon* and *imontty* and X-based tools.

- Configure *isdnlog* to log exactly what you need, and use *isdnrep* to get detailed reports about the usage of your ISDN line. This works not only for calls to and from computer systems but for calls to other ISDN-enabled devices like phones and fax machines. There is only one caveat: Your ISDN board cannot capture outgoing phone numbers for connections being set up by other devices. Most telephone companies provide a service, though, that echos this phone number back to you and thus lets the ISDN subsystem pick it up. This service is often available for free or for a nominal fee. Ask your telephone company.

- For the truly adventurous: Experiment with Multilink-PPP. As you know, with ISDN you have at least two lines. If you need extra high capacity, why not use both? That's what Multilink-PPP does. In order to use this, you need to turn on the `Support generic MP` option during kernel configuration and see the files *Documentation/isdn/README.syncppp* and *Documentation/isdn/syncppp.FAQ* in the kernel sources for hints on how to do this. Of course, your provider has to support this, too.

NFS and NIS Configuration

Once you have TCP/IP enabled on your system, you may wish to configure your system to use the Network File System (NFS) or Network Information Service (NIS). NFS allows your system to share files directly with a network of machines. File access across NFS is transparent; you simply access the files as if they were stored on your local disk. In system administration terms, one system mounts another's filesystem on a local directory, just as a local filesystem can be mounted. NFS also allows you to export filesystems, allowing other systems on the network to mount your disks directly.

NIS (formerly known as the Yellow Pages, or YP, service) is a system that allows your host to obtain information automatically on user accounts, groups, filesystem mount points, and other system databases from servers on the network. For example, let's say you have a large collection of machines that should have the same user accounts and groups (information usually found in */etc/passwd* and */etc/group*). Users should be able to log into any of these machines and access their files directly (say, by mounting their home filesystem from a central location using NFS). Obviously, maintaining user accounts across many machines would be problematic; in order to add a new user, you would need to log into each machine and create the user account on each. When you use NIS, however, the system automatically consults centrally maintained databases across the network for such information, in addition to local files such as */etc/passwd*. NIS+ is an enhanced NIS service that is coming into use at some sites.

If your Linux system is to interact with other systems on a LAN, it's quite possible that NFS and NIS are in wide use on your LAN. In this section, we'll show you how to configure your system as an NFS and NIS client; that is, to mount remote filesystems and to participate in an existing NIS domain. It is possible to configure your system as an NFS and NIS server, but there are many subtle issues involved in configuring any Unix or Linux system as an NFS/NIS server. Instead of providing a dangerously incomplete account of server configuration here, we refer you to O'Reilly's *Managing NFS and NIS* by Hal Stern. If you are already familiar with NFS/NIS configuration on other Unix systems, Linux is really no different; the manual pages and Linux HOWTO documents provide all of the specifics.

[31] NFS
and NIS

Configuring NFS

Configuring your system to mount remote filesystems over NFS is a breeze. Assuming that you have TCP/IP configured and hostname lookup works correctly, you can simply add a line to your */etc/fstab* file such as the following:

```
# device            directory           type      options
allison:/usr        /fsys/allison/usr   NFS       defaults
```

As with regular filesystem mounts, be sure to create the mount-point directory (in this case */fsys/allison/usr*) first. The line in */etc/fstab* example allows your system to mount the directory */usr* from the machine **allison** on the network.

Before the example NFS mount will work, however, the system administrator for the NFS server (here **allison**) must configure the system to *export* the given directory (here, */usr*) to your system. On most Unix systems, this is simply a matter of editing a file, such as */etc/exports*, or running a simple command. Exporting a directory makes it available for other systems to mount it using NFS. It is not necessary for the exported directory to be the root of a filesystem itself; that is, you can export */usr* even if */usr* does not have its own separate filesystem.

In exporting a directory, the administrator may choose to make the directory available for *read-only* access. In this case you will not be able to write to the filesystem when mounted on your system. You should set the `options` field of the */etc/fstab* line in the previous example to `ro` instead of `defaults`.

A few words of warning about NFS. First of all, NFS is not very happy when the servers for remote filesystems go down or the network connection fails. When the NFS server is unreachable for any reason, your system prints warning messages to the console (or system logs) periodically. If this is a problem, you can attempt to unmount any remote filesystems from the affected servers.

Another detail to watch out for when mounting NFS filesystems is the owner (UIDs) and group IDs (GIDs) of the files on the remote filesystem. In order to access your own files via NFS, the user and group ID for your own account must match those on the NFS server. One easy way to check this is with an *ls -l* listing: If the UID or GID does not match any local user, *ls* displays the UID/GID of files as numbers; otherwise, the user or group name is printed.

If IDs do not match, you have a few ways to remedy this problem. One is to simply change the UID of your user account (and the GID of your primary group) to match those on the NFS server (say, by editing your local */etc/passwd*). This approach requires you to *chown* and *chgrp* all of your local files after making the change. Another solution is to create a separate account with matching UID/GID. However, the best approach may be to use NIS to manage your user and group databases. With this solution, you do not create your user and group accounts locally; instead, they are provided to you by an NIS server. More on this later.

Another NFS caveat is the restriction of **root** permissions on NFS-mounted filesystems. Unless the NFS server explicitly grants your system **root** access on NFS-mounted filesystems, you will not have total access to files when logged in as **root** on your local system. The reason for this is security: allowing unlimited **root** access to files on a remote-mounted NFS filesystem opens itself up to abuse, especially when the NFS server and the NFS client are maintained or owned by different people. For this reason, you will not have omnipotent power to access or modify remote-mounted files when logged in as **root** on your local system.

Configuring NIS

NIS is a complex system, simply because it is so flexible. NIS is a general-purpose network database system, allowing your machine to transparently access information on user accounts, groups, filesystems, and so forth, from databases stored across the network. One goal of NIS is to ease network management. Allowing user account information (such as that stored in *etc/passwd*), for example, to be maintained on a single server makes it easy for many machines to share the same user accounts. In the previous section on NFS, we showed how user and group IDs on the NFS server and client should match in order to effectively access your files remotely. Using NIS allows your UID and GID to be defined from a remote site, not locally.

If your machine is connected at a site where NIS is used, chances are you can add your machine as an NIS client, thus allowing it to obtain user, group, and other databases directly from the network. To some extent this makes it unnecessary to create local user accounts or groups at all; apart from the locally defined users such as **root**, **bin**, and so forth, all other users will be created from the NIS server. If you couple the use of NIS with mounting user home directories from an NFS server, it's also unnecessary to set aside local storage for users. NIS can greatly lessen the amount of work you need to do as a system administrator.

In an NIS configuration, there may be NIS *servers*, *slaves*, and *clients*. As you can guess, servers are the systems where NIS databases originate and are maintained. NIS slaves are systems to which the server copies its databases. The slaves can provide the information to other systems, but changes to the databases must be made from the server. NIS clients are those systems that request database information from servers or slaves. Slaves are simply used as a way to ease the load on the NIS server; otherwise, all NIS requests would have to be serviced by a single machine.

To completely understand how NIS works and to maintain an NIS server is enough material for a whole book (again, *Managing NFS and NIS*). However, when reading about NIS you are likely to come across various terms. NIS was originally named YP. This usage has been discontinued as Yellow Pages is trademarked in the United Kingdom (it's the phone book, after all).

There are at least two implementations of NIS for Linux: the "traditional" NIS implementation and a separate implementation known as "NYS" (standing for NIS+, YP, and Switch). The NIS client code for the "traditional" implementation is contained within the standard C library and is already installed on most Linux systems. (This is necessary to allow programs such as *login* to transparently access NIS databases as well as local system files.) The NYS client code is contained within the Network Services Library, *libnsl*. Linux systems using NYS should have compiled programs such as *login* against this library. On the other hand, the new *glibc2* standard C library comes with support for NIS+. Different Linux distributions use different versions of the NIS or NYS client code, and some use a mixture of the two. To be safe, we'll describe how to configure a system for both traditional the NIS and NYS implementations, meaning that no matter which is installed on your system, it should be able to act as a client.

We do assume here that you have installed and started all the necessary NIS daemon processes (such as *ypbind*) used by traditional NIS to talk to the NIS server. If your Linux system does not appear to have any NIS support, consult documents such as the Linux NIS HOWTO to configure it from scratch. Nearly all current Linux distributions come prepackaged with NIS client (and server) support, and all that's required of you is to edit a few configuration files.

The first step is to set the NIS domain in which your system will be operating. Your network administrators can provide this information to you. Note that the NIS domain name is not necessarily identical to the DNS domain name, which can be set with the *hostname* command. For example, if the full hostname of your system is **loomer.vpizza.com**, your DNS domain name is **vpizza.com**. However, your NIS domain name could be entirely different, for example, **vpizzas**. The NIS domain name is selected by the NIS server administrators and is not related to the DNS domain name described earlier.

Setting the domain name is usually a matter of running the *domainname* command at boot time, perhaps in one of your system *rc* files (such as */etc/rc.d/ rc.inet1* described earlier). You should first check that *domainname* is not being executed in one of the existing *rc* files. The command takes the format:

```
domainname domain-name
```

for example, `domainname vpizzas`. The command itself is usually found in */sbin/ domainname* and may have a slightly different name, such as *domainname-yp*.

A slightly different method sets the domain name under NYS. You should create (or edit) the file */etc/yp.conf.* This file should contain two lines: one specifying the name of your NIS domain and another specifying the hostname of the NIS server. As an example:

```
domain vpizzas
ypserver allison.vpizza.com
```

sets the NIS domain name to **vpizzas** and specifies that **allison.vpizza.com** should be used as the NIS server. If no `ypserver` line is included in this file, the system broadcasts a message on the network at boot time to determine the name of the NIS server. Your network administrators can provide you with the hostname of your preferred NIS server.

Once these two steps are complete, your system should be able to transparently access NIS databases. One way to test this is to query the system for a password database entry from the NIS server. The *ypwhich* queries specific NIS databases, for example:

```
ypwhich username passwd
```

If this returns the line from the NIS *passwd* database for the given user, you have successfully queried the NIS database. (One way to verify that the information returned is correct is to run this same command on another system in your NIS domain whose NIS configuration is known to be working.) The NIS *passwd* database is not identical to the */etc/passwd* file on your system, although it is in the same format. The Linux HOWTO documents contain additional information on troubleshooting your NIS configuration.

CHAPTER SIXTEEN

THE WORLD WIDE WEB AND ELECTRONIC MAIL

T he previous chapter put you on a network. It may have been hard work, but the result was quite an accomplishment: your system is now part of a community. If you are connected to the Internet, the next step is to get access to all the riches this medium offers. People generally agree that the most useful applications on the Internet are the World Wide Web and electronic mail; they are the subjects of this chapter.

The World Wide Web

The World Wide Web (WWW or Web, for short) is a relative newcomer to the Internet information hierarchy. The WWW project's goal is to unite the many disparate services available on the Internet into a single, worldwide, multimedia, hypertext space. In this section we'll show you how to access the WWW with your Linux machine. We'll also describe how to configure your own WWW server to provide documents to the Web.

The World Wide Web project was started in 1989 by Tim Berners-Lee at the European Center for Particle Physics (CERN). The original goal of the project was to allow groups of researchers in the particle-physics community to share many kinds of information through a single, homogeneous interface.

Before the Web, each type of information available via the Internet was provided by its own unique client/server pair. For example, to retrieve files via FTP, one used the FTP client, which connected to the *ftpd* daemon on the server machine. Gopher (an old hierarchical document system that was considered quite flashy before the Web), Usenet news, *finger* information, and so forth all required their own individual clients. The differences between operating systems and machine architectures compounded the problem; in theory, these details should be hidden from the user who is trying to access the information.

The Web provides a single abstraction for the many kinds of information available from the Internet. One uses a single Web "client," a so-called *browser*—such as Netscape Navigator or Lynx—to access the Web. On the Web, information is provided as documents (also known as "pages"), where each document may have links to others. Documents may be located on any machine on the Internet that is configured to provide web access. Representing information in this way is commonly referred to as "hypertext," which is an important concept underlying the entire Web.

For example, the Linux Documentation Project provides various Linux-related documents via the Web. The LDP home page, which can be found at *http://www.linuxdoc.org*, contains links to a number of other Linux-related pages around the world. The LDP home page is shown in Figure 16-1.

The highlighted regions of text in the document are links. When the user selects a link (e.g., by clicking on the text with the mouse), the document pointed to by the link is retrieved. The documents can reside on virtually any machine on the Internet; the actual "locations" of web documents are hidden from the user.

Many of the documents available via the Web are in the form of multimedia hypertext pages, as seen in Figure 16-1. These pages may contain links to pictures, sounds, MPEG video files, PostScript documents, and much more. This multimedia information is provided by a protocol known as HyperText Transfer Protocol (HTTP). The Web is also capable of accessing documents provided via FTP, Gopher, Usenet news, and so on.

For example, when accessing a document via HTTP, you are likely to see a page such as that displayed in Figure 16-1—with embedded pictures, links to other pages, and so on. When accessing a document via FTP, you might see a directory listing of the FTP server, as seen in Figure 16-2. Clicking on a link in the FTP document either retrieves the selected file or displays the contents of another directory.

Given this kind of abstraction, we need a way to refer to documents available on the Web. *Uniform Resource Locators*, or URLs, are the answer. A URL is simply a pathname uniquely identifying a web document, including the machine it resides on, the filename of the document, and the protocol used to access it (FTP, HTTP, etc.). For example, when you visit LDP's home page:

> *http://www.linuxdoc.org*

it redirects you to the URL:

> *http://metalab.unc.edu/LDP/index.html*

Let's break this down. The first part of the URL, *http:*, identifies the protocol used for the document, which in this case is HTTP. The second part of the URL, *//metalab.unc.edu*, identifies the machine where the document is provided. The final portion of the URL, *LDP/index.html*, is the logical pathname to the document on

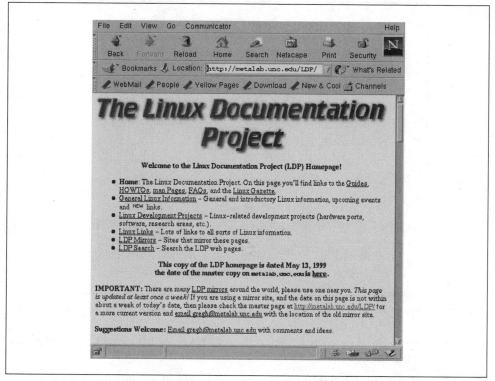

Figure 16–1: Linux Documentation Project (LDP) Home Page on the World Wide Web

metalab.unc.edu. This is similar to a Unix pathname, in that it identifies the file *index.html* in the directory *LDP*. Therefore, to access the LDP home page, you'd fire up a browser, telling it to access *http://metalab.unc.edu/LDP/index.html*. What could be easier?

Actually, the conventions of web servers do make it easier. If you specify a directory as the last element of the path, the server understands that you want the file *index.html* in that directory. So you can reach the LDP home page with a URL as short as:

http://metalab.unc.edu/LDP/

To access a file via anonymous FTP, we can use a URL such as:

ftp://tsx-11.mit.edu/pub/linux/docs/INFO-SHEET/

This URL retrieves the introductory Linux information on *tsx-11.mit.edu*. Using this URL with your browser is identical to using *ftp* to fetch the file by hand.

The best way to understand the Web is to explore it. In the following section we'll explain how to get started with a browser. Later in the chapter, we'll cover how to

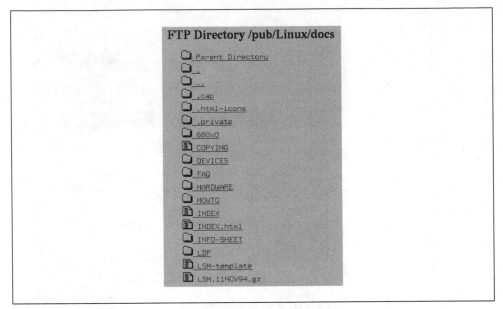

Figure 16–2: FTP directory as displayed in the Netscape Navigator Web browser

configure your own machine as a web server for providing documents to the rest of the Web.

Of course, in order to access the Web, you'll need a machine with direct Internet access (via either Ethernet or PPP). In the following sections, we assume that you have already configured TCP/IP on your system and that you can successfully use clients such as *telnet* and *ftp*.

Using Netscape Navigator

Netscape Navigator is one of the most popular browsers. Versions are available for the Macintosh, Microsoft Windows, and, of course, the X Window System on Unix machines. As you would expect, there is a Linux binary version available, which you can obtain from the Netscape FTP sites, such as *ftp://ftp.netscape.com.*

Netscape Navigator exists in two incarnations. First, there is the product developed and distributed by Netscape Communications Inc., which is available only in binary, but may now (unlike in earlier times) be freely redistributed. Second, there is Mozilla, which in a way is the "Open Source" version of Netscape Navigator. Netscape has made the source code available for everybody to hack on under a license similar to the GPL, but of course they do not assume responsibility for those versions. In this book, we will cover only the "official" version from Netscape, but you can find full information about the Open Source version at *http://www.mozilla.org.*

In addition, there are two versions of the software shipped by Netscape. First, there is Navigator, the standalone web browser. Second, there is Netscape Communicator, which really is a suite of programs, including Navigator, a mail and news client, and several other, less often used programs. When you want to use only the web browser, it suffices to get just Navigator. If you want to use the other tools as well, get the full Communicator suite. In the following description, we will assume that you use Communicator, because that's what is on most Linux distributions. If you have Navigator, things should be the same except that you won't have the mail and news client.

Here, we assume that you're using a networked Linux machine running X and that you have obtained a copy of the Netscape Navigator binary. As stated before, your machine must be configured to use TCP/IP, and you should be able to use clients such as *telnet* and *ftp*.

Starting Netscape Navigator is simple. Run the command:

```
eggplant$ netscape url
```

where `url` is the complete web address, or URL, for the document you wish to view. If you don't specify a URL, Netscape should display the Netscape home page as shown in Figure 16-3 by default, but you can specify another page to be displayed on startup, even a blank page.

The Netscape home page is a good place to start if you're interested in Web exploration. It contains links to information about the software itself, as well as demonstration documents showing off the power of the Web. (See the next section "Navigating the Web," for more information on finding your way around the Web.)

While using Netscape Navigator, you can scroll the document using the scrollbars on the edge of the window. Alternatively, you can use the space bar and Delete key to move back and forth by pages or the arrow keys to scroll the document in smaller steps.

Links appear as highlighted text (usually in blue, on color systems, or underlined on monochrome). To follow a link, simply click on it with the mouse. Netscape remembers the links that you have followed; after you have selected a link, it appears in a darker color (or with dotted underlines) in the future.

Keep in mind that retrieving documents on the Web can be slow at times. This depends on the speed of the network connection from your site to the server, as well as the traffic on the network at the time. In some cases, web sites may be so loaded that they simply refuse connections; if this is the case, Netscape displays an appropriate error message. At the bottom edge of the Netscape window, a status report is displayed, and while a transfer is taking place, the Netscape Navigator logo in the upper-right corner of the window animates. Clicking on the logo takes you back to the Netscape home page.

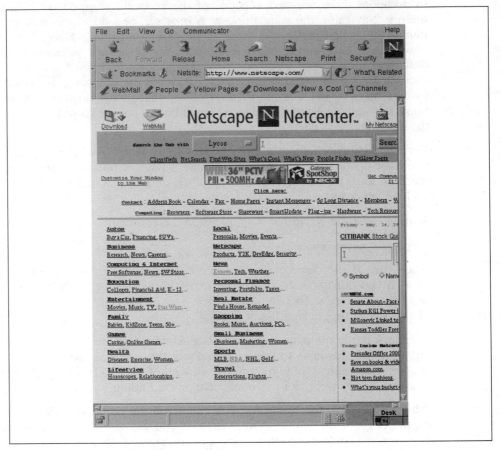

Figure 16–3: Netscape home page

As you traverse links within Netscape Navigator, each document is saved in the *window history*, which can be recalled using the Go menu. Pressing the Back button at the top edge of the Netscape window moves you back through the window history to previously visited documents. Similarly, the Forward button moves you forward through the history.

You can also bookmark frequently visited web sites (or URLs) to Netscape's "bookmarks file." Whenever you are viewing a document that you might want to return to later, choose Add Bookmark from the Communicator/Bookmarks menu. You can display your bookmarks by choosing the Bookmarks menu. Selecting any item in this menu retrieves the corresponding document from the Web.

As mentioned previously, you can access new URLs by running *netscape* with the URL as the argument. However, you can also select Open Page... from the File menu. Just type the name of the URL into the text-entry field, press the Enter key, and the corresponding document is retrieved.

Netscape Navigator is a powerful application with many options. There are many ways to customize Netscape's behavior; however, many of the customization details tend to change from release to release. Fortunately, Netscape has provided complete documentation for Navigator online, via the Web (where else?). This information is available on Netscape's home page at *http://www.netscape.com*. Recent versions of Navigator also include the documentation as a local copy.

Netscape is not the only browser that reads Web documents. The National Center for Supercomputing Applications (NCSA), which developed the first modern Web browser, Mosaic, has recently released a powerful new version called Vosaic.

Chapter 11

Another browser for the X Window System that currently does not have all the bells and whistles but is fast and easy to use is *kfm* from the KDE project (see "The K Development Environment" in Chapter 11, *Customizing Your X Environment*). Yet another versatile browser is Lynx. It is a text-based browser, so you miss the pictures when you use it. But this makes it fast, and you may find it convenient. You can also use it without the X Window System. And finally, for those who never want to leave Emacs, there is Emacs/W3, a fully featured web browser you can use within Emacs or XEmacs.

Navigating the Web

The Web is growing at a tremendous rate. In fact, by the time you read this book, the Web may have completely changed in appearance from the descriptions given here. Hundreds of thousands of web servers have emerged since the Web's inception.

As the Web expands to encompass countless servers from all over the world, it becomes more difficult to find the information that's out there. Unless you happen to run across a URL or hyperlink to an interesting site, how can you locate information by subject?

Fortunately, a number of services have appeared on the Web to simplify this task. While none of these services provide a complete listing of web sites, the high degree of connectivity on the Web ensures that if whatever you're looking for is out there, you'll find it.

First, keep in mind that the Web is a dynamic place. We've made every attempt to certify that the information here is current, but by the time you read this book, several of these links may have moved, or may no longer exist.

A popular index of web sites is *Yahoo!*, available at:

> *http://www.yahoo.com*

but there are now many such "portals" offering a slice of interesting sites.

One of the largest search engines is:

> *http://www.altavista.com*

which indexes millions of web sites. Also interesting is:

> *http://www.dejanews.com*

where news articles are indexed and searchable.

Configuring Your Own WWW Server

Now that you've seen what the Web provides, you're ready to set up your own gas station on the information superhighway. Running your own web server is easy. It consists of two tasks: configuring the *httpd* daemon and writing documents to provide on the server.

httpd is the daemon that services HTTP requests on your machine. Any document accessed with an `http` URL is retrieved using *httpd*. Likewise, `ftp` URLs are accessed using *ftpd*, `gopher` URLs using *gopherd*, and so on. There is no single web daemon; each URL type uses a separate daemon to request information from the server.

There are several HTTP servers available. The one discussed here is the *Apache httpd*, which is easy to configure and very flexible. In this section, we'll discuss how to install and configure the basic aspects of this version of *httpd*. Later in the chapter, we talk about how to write your own documents in HTML (the markup language used by web pages) as well as more advanced aspects of server configuration, such as providing interactive forms.

The first step, of course, is to obtain a Linux *httpd* binary. Your Linux distribution may come with *httpd* installed, but make sure that this in fact is the Apache *httpd* and not one of the older ones. If you do not find Apache in your distribution, you can obtain the *httpd* sources from *http://www.apache.org* and build it yourself. The *apache.org* web site contains complete documentation for the software.

[33] Apache

Apache—The Definitive Guide by Ben Laurie and Peter Laurie covers everything about Apache, including sophisticated configuration issues.

Where the various files of an Apache installation go depends on your distribution or the package you installed, but the following is a common setup. You should locate the various pieces in your system before continuing:

/usr/sbin/httpd

    Is the binary executable, which is the server itself. On Debian, this is */usr/sbin/ apache* instead.

/etc/httpd

    Contains the configuration files for *httpd*, most notably *httpd.conf.* We discuss how to modify these files later. On Debian systems, this is */etc/apache* instead of */etc/httpd*.

/usr/local/httpd

    Contains the HTML scripts to be served up to the site's clients. This directory and those below it, the *web space*, are accessible to anyone on the Web and therefore pose a severe security risk if used for anything other than public data.

/var/log/httpd

    Holds log files stored by the server.

Our task now is to modify the configuration files in the configuration subdirectory. You should notice at least the following four files in this directory: *access.conf-dist*, *httpd.conf-dist*, *mime.types*, and *srm.conf-dist*. Copy the files with names ending in *-dist* and modify them for your own system. For example, *access.conf-dist* is copied to *access.conf* and edited.

The latest version of Apache pretty much configures itself, but in case things go wrong, we'll tell you here how to do it manually so that you can fix things yourself.

At *http://www.apache.org*, you will find complete documentation on how to configure *httpd*. Here, we'll present sample configuration files that correspond to an actual running *httpd*.

httpd.conf

The file *httpd.conf* is the main server-configuration file. First, copy *httpd.conf-dist* to *httpd.conf* and edit it. In the following example, a sample *httpd.conf* is presented with comments explaining each field:

```
# This is the main server configuration file.
# See URL http://www.apache.org for instructions.

# Do NOT simply read the instructions in here without understanding
# what they do, if you are unsure consult the online docs. You have been
# warned.

# Originally by Rob McCool. Copyright (c) 1995-1999 The Apache Group.
# All rights reserved. See http://www.apache.org/LICENSE.txt for license.

# ServerType is either inetd, or standalone.
```

```
ServerType standalone

# If you are running from inetd, go to "ServerAdmin".

# Port: The port the standalone listens to. For ports < 1023, you will
# need httpd to be run as root initially.

Port 80

# HostnameLookups: Log the names of clients or just their IP numbers
#    e.g.   www.apache.org (on) or 204.62.129.132 (off)
# You should probably turn this off unless you are going to actually
# use the information in your logs, or with a CGI.  Leaving this on
# can slow down access to your site.
HostnameLookups on

# If you wish httpd to run as a different user or group, you must run
# httpd as root initially and it will switch.

# User/Group: The name (or #number) of the user/group to run httpd as.
#   On SCO (ODT 3) use User nouser and Group nogroup
#   On HPUX you may not be able to use shared memory as nobody, and the
#   suggested workaround is to create a user www and use that user.
User wwwrun
Group #-2

# The following directive disables keepalives and HTTP header flushes for
# Netscape 2.x and browsers which spoof it. There are known problems with
# these

BrowserMatch Mozilla/2 nokeepalive

# ServerAdmin: Your address, where problems with the server should be
# e-mailed.

ServerAdmin mdw@zucchini.veggie.org

# ServerRoot: The directory the server's config, error, and log files
# are kept in

ServerRoot /usr/local/httpd

# BindAddress: You can support virtual hosts with this option. This
# option is used to tell the server which IP address to listen to.
# It can either contain "*", an IP address, or a fully qualified
# Internet domain name. See also the VirtualHost directive.

#BindAddress *

# ErrorLog: The location of the error log file. If this does not start
# with /, ServerRoot is prepended to it.
```

```
ErrorLog /var/log/httpd.error_log

# TransferLog: The location of the transfer log file. If this does not
# start with /, ServerRoot is prepended to it.

TransferLog /var/log/httpd.access_log

# PidFile: The file the server should log its pid to
PidFile /var/run/httpd.pid

# ScoreBoardFile: File used to store internal server process information.
# Not all architectures require this.  But if yours does (you'll know
# because this file is created when you run Apache) then you *must*
# ensure that no two invocations of Apache share the same scoreboard file.
ScoreBoardFile /var/log/apache_status

# ServerName allows you to set a host name which is sent back to clients
# for your server if it's different than the one the program would get
# (i.e. use "www" instead of the host's real name).
#
# Note: You cannot just invent host names and hope they work. The name you
# define here must be a valid DNS name for your host. If you don't
# understand this, ask your network administrator.

#ServerName www.veggie.org

# CacheNegotiatedDocs: By default, Apache sends Pragma: no-cache with each
# document that was negotiated on the basis of content. This asks proxy
# servers not to cache the document. Uncommenting the following line
# disables this behavior, and proxies will be allowed to cache the
# documents.

#CacheNegotiatedDocs

# Timeout: The number of seconds before receives and sends time out

Timeout 300

# KeepAlive: Whether or not to allow persistent connections (more than
# one request per connection). Set to "Off" to deactivate.

KeepAlive On

# MaxKeepAliveRequests: The maximum number of requests to allow
# during a persistent connection. Set to 0 to allow an unlimited amount.
# We reccomend you leave this number high, for maximum performance.

MaxKeepAliveRequests 100

# KeepAliveTimeout: Number of seconds to wait for the next request

KeepAliveTimeout 15
```

```
# Server-pool size regulation.  Rather than making you guess how many
# server processes you need, Apache dynamically adapts to the load it
# sees --- that is, it tries to maintain enough server processes to
# handle the current load, plus a few spare servers to handle transient
# load spikes (e.g., multiple simultaneous requests from a single
# Netscape browser).

# It does this by periodically checking how many servers are waiting
# for a request.  If there are fewer than MinSpareServers, it creates
# a new spare.  If there are more than MaxSpareServers, some of the
# spares die off.  These values are probably OK for most sites ---

MinSpareServers 5
MaxSpareServers 10

# Number of servers to start --- should be a reasonable ballpark figure.

StartServers 5

# Limit on total number of servers running, i.e., limit on the number
# of clients who can simultaneously connect --- if this limit is ever
# reached, clients will be LOCKED OUT, so it should NOT BE SET TOO LOW.
# It is intended mainly as a brake to keep a runaway server from taking
# Unix with it as it spirals down...

MaxClients 150

# MaxRequestsPerChild: the number of requests each child process is
#  allowed to process before the child dies.
#  The child will exit so as to avoid problems after prolonged use when
#  Apache (and maybe the libraries it uses) leak.  On most systems, this
#  isn't really needed, but a few (such as Solaris) do have notable leaks
#  in the libraries.

MaxRequestsPerChild 30

# Proxy Server directives. Uncomment the following line to
# enable the proxy server:

#ProxyRequests On

# To enable the cache as well, edit and uncomment the following lines:

#CacheRoot /usr/local/etc/httpd/proxy
#CacheSize 5
#CacheGcInterval 4
#CacheMaxExpire 24
#CacheLastModifiedFactor 0.1
#CacheDefaultExpire 1
#NoCache a_domain.com another_domain.edu joes.garage_sale.com
```

```
# Listen: Allows you to bind Apache to specific IP addresses and/or
# ports, in addition to the default. See also the VirtualHost command

#Listen 3000
#Listen 12.34.56.78:80


#
# Read config files from /etc/httpsd
#
ResourceConfig   /etc/httpd/srm.conf
AccessConfig     /etc/httpd/access.conf
TypesConfig      /etc/httpd/mime.types
```

The `ServerType` directive is used to specify how the server will run—either as a standalone daemon (as seen here) or from *inetd*. For various reasons, it's usually best to run *httpd* in standalone mode. Otherwise, *inetd* must spawn a new instance of *httpd* for each incoming connection.

One tricky item here is the port number specification. You may wish to run *httpd* as a user other than **root** (that is, you may not have **root** access on the machine in question and wish to run *httpd* as yourself). In this case, you must use a port numbered 1024 or above. For example, if we specify:

```
Port 2112
```

then we may run *httpd* as a regular user. In this case, HTTP URLs to this machine must be specified as:

http://www.veggie.org:2112/...

If no port number is given in the URL (as is the usual case), port 80 is assumed.

srm.conf

srm.conf is the Server Resource Map file. It configures a number of facilities provided by the server; for example, the directory where HTML documents are stored on your system, or what directory the various CGI binaries are located in. Let's walk through a sample *srm.conf*:

```
# The directory where HTML documents will be held.
DocumentRoot /usr/local/httpd/htdocs

# Personal directory for each user where HTML documents will be held.

UserDir public_html
```

Here, we specify the `DocumentRoot` directory, where documents to be provided via HTTP are stored. These documents are written in the HyperText Markup Language (HTML), which is discussed in the section "Writing HTML Documents."

For example, if someone were to access the URL:

http://www.veggie.org/fruits.html

the actual file accessed would be */usr/local/httpd/htdocs/fruits.html*.

The `UserDir` directive specifies a directory each user may create in his home directory for storing public HTML files. For example, if we were to use the URL:

http://www.veggie.org/~mdw/linux-info.html

the actual file accessed would be *~mdw/public_html/linux-info.html*.

```
# If a URL is received with a directory but no filename, retrieve this
# file as the index (if it exists).
DirectoryIndex index.html

# Turn on 'fancy' directory indexes
FancyIndexing on
```

Here, we enable the indexing features of *httpd*. In this case, if a browser attempts to access a directory URL, the file *index.html* in that directory is returned, if it exists. Otherwise, *httpd* generates a "fancy" index with icons representing various file types. Figure 16-2 shows an example of such an index.

Icons are assigned using the `AddIcon` directive, as seen here:

```
# Set up various icons for use with fancy indexes, by filename
# E.g., we use DocumentRoot/icons/movie.xbm for files ending
#      in .mpg and .qt
AddIcon /icons/movie.xbm .mpg
AddIcon /icons/back.xbm ..
AddIcon /icons/menu.xbm ^^DIRECTORY^^
AddIcon /icons/blank.xbm ^^BLANKICON^^
DefaultIcon /icons/unknown.xbm
```

The icon filenames (such as */icons/movie.xbm*) are relative to `DocumentRoot` by default. (There are other ways to specify pathnames to documents and icons—for example, by using aliases. This is discussed later.) There is also an `AddIconBy-Type` directive, which lets you specify an icon for a document based on the document's MIME type and an `AddIconByEncoding` directive, which lets you specify an icon for a document based on the document's encoding (i.e., whether and how it is compressed). These encodings are described further later in the section "An aside: MIME types."

You can also specify an icon to be used when none of the above match. This is done with the `DefaultIcon` directive.

The optional `ReadmeName` and `HeaderName` directives specify the names of files to be included in the index generated by *httpd*:

```
ReadmeName README
HeaderName HEADER
```

Here, if the file *README.html* exists in the current directory, it will be appended to the index. The file *README* will be appended if *README.html* does not exist. Likewise, *HEADER.html* or *HEADER* will be included at the top of the index generated by *httpd*. You can use these files to describe the contents of a particular directory when an index is requested by the browser:

```
# Local access filename
AccessFileName .htaccess

# Default MIME type for documents
DefaultType text/plain
```

The `AccessFileName` directive specifies the name of the *local access file* for each directory. (This is described later, along with the discussion about the *access.conf* file.) The `DefaultType` directive specifies the MIME type for documents not listed in *mime.types*. This is described further in the section "An aside: MIME types":

```
# Set location of icons
Alias /icons/ /usr/local/html/icons/

# Set location of CGI binaries
ScriptAlias /cgi-bin/ /usr/local/httpd/cgi-bin/
```

The `Alias` directive specifies a pathname alias for any of the documents listed in *srm.conf* or accessed by a URL. Earlier, we used the `AddIcon` directive to set icon names using pathnames such as */icons/movie.xbm*. Here, we specify that the pathname */icons/* should be translated to */usr/local/html/icons/*. Therefore, the various icon files should be stored in the latter directory. You can use `Alias` to set aliases for other pathnames as well.

The `ScriptAlias` directive is similar in nature, but it sets the actual location of CGI scripts on the system. Here, we wish to store scripts in the directory */usr/local/httpd/cgi-bin/*. Any time a URL is used with a leading directory component of */cgi-bin/*, it is translated into the actual directory name. More information on CGI and scripts is included in the section "Writing the CGI script."

access.conf

The last configuration file that requires your immediate attention is *access.conf*, which is the global access configuration file for *httpd*. It specifies which files may be accessed and in what ways. You may also have a per-directory access configuration file if you require greater specificity. (Recall that we used the `AccessFile-Name` directive in *srm.conf* to set the local access file for each directory to *.htaccess*.)

Here is a sample *access.conf* file. It consists of a number of <Directory> items, each of which specifies the options and attributes for a particular directory:

```
# Set options for the cgi-bin script directory.
<Directory /usr/local/html/cgi-bin>
Options Indexes FollowSymLinks
</Directory>
```

Here, we specify that the CGI script directory should have the access options Indexes and FollowSymLinks. There are a number of access options available. These include:

FollowSymLinks
> Symbolic links in this directory should be followed to retrieve the documents they point to.

ExecCGI
> Allow the execution of CGI scripts from this directory.

Indexes
> Allow indexes to be generated from this directory.

None
> Disable all options for this directory.

All
> Enable all options for this directory.

There are other options as well; see the *httpd* documentation for details.

Next, we enable several options and other attributes for */usr/local/httpd/htdocs*, the directory containing our HTML documents:

```
<Directory /usr/local/httpd/htdocs>

Options Indexes FollowSymLinks

# Allow the local access file, .htaccess, to override any attributes
# listed here
AllowOverride All

# Access restrictions for documents in this directory
<Limit GET>
order allow,deny
allow from all
</Limit>

</Directory>
```

Here, we turn on the Indexes and FollowSymLinks options for this directory. The AllowOverride option allows the local access file in each directory (*.htaccess*, set in *srm.conf*) to override any of the attributes given here. The *.htaccess* file has the same format as the global *access.conf* but applies only to the directory in which it is located. This way, we can specify attributes for particular directories by including a *.htaccess* file in those directories instead of listing the attributes in the global file.

The primary use for local access files is to allow individual users to set the access permissions for personal HTML directories (such as `~/public_html`) without having to ask the system administrator to modify the global access file. There are security issues associated with this, however. For example, a user might enable access permissions in her own directory such that any browser can run expensive server-side CGI scripts. If you disable the `AllowOverride` feature, users cannot get around the access attributes specified in the global *access.conf*. This can be done by using:

```
AllowOverride None
```

which effectively disables local *.htaccess* files.

The `<Limit GET>` field is used to specify access rules for browsers attempting to retrieve documents from this server. In this case, we specify `order allow,deny`, which means that `allow` rules should be evaluated before `deny` rules. We then instate the rule `allow from all`, which simply means any host may retrieve documents from the server. If you wish to deny access from a particular machine or domain, you could add the line:

```
deny from .nuts.com biffnet.biffs-house.us
```

The first entry denies access from all sites in the *nuts.com* domain. The second denies access from the site *ftp://biffnet.biffs-house.us*.

Starting httpd

Now you're ready to run *httpd*, allowing your machine to service HTTP URLs. As mentioned previously, you can run *httpd* from *inetd* or as a standalone server. Here, we describe how to run *httpd* in standalone mode.

All that's required to start *httpd* is to run the command:

```
httpd -f configuration-file
```

where `configuration-file` is the pathname of *httpd.conf*. For example:

```
/usr/sbin/httpd -f /etc/httpd/httpd.conf
```

starts up *httpd*, with configuration files found in */etc/httpd*.

Watch the *httpd* error logs (the location of which is given in *httpd.conf*) for any errors that might occur when trying to start up the server or when accessing documents. Remember you must run *httpd* as **root** if it is to use a port numbered 1023 or less. Once you have *httpd* working to your satisfaction, you can start it automatically at boot time by including the appropriate *httpd* command line in one of your system *rc* files, such as */etc/rc.d/rc.local*.

Modern releases of Apache also provide a utility called *apachectl* that controls the starting, stopping, reloading, and so on of the *httpd* process.

Before you can request documents via HTTP from your browser, you'll need to write them. This is the subject of the next section.

Writing HTML Documents

Documents requested by HTTP may be in several forms. These forms include images, PostScript files, sounds, MPEG movies, and so forth. The *mime.types* configuration file describes the document types that *httpd* understands.

The most common type of document serviced by HTTP is an HTML file. HTML documents support text, links to other documents, inline images, and so forth. Most documents that you'll see on the Web are written in HTML. A more powerful alternative named XML has been getting a lot of press, but its strength lies in supporting specialized web applications, such as documents maintained in multiple languages and everybody's favorite buzzword—electronic commerce. HTML is sufficient for traditional, standalone pages.

HTML is surprisingly easy to learn. With the tutorial included here, you should be on your way to writing HTML documents and providing information to the Web in less than an hour.

Many tools allow you to convert other markup languages (such as LaTeX, Microsoft RTF, and so forth) to HTML, and vice versa. If you have particularly long documents in another formatting language that you wish to provide on the Web, it might be easier to convert them automatically to HTML or provide a PostScript or DVI image of the documents instead.

The canonical source for HTML information is the URL:

http://www.ncsa.uiuc.edu/General/Internet/www/HTMLPrimer.html

[25] HTML

which is a beginner's guide to writing HTML documents. Here, we'll present the essentials of HTML to get you up to speed.

HTML basics

If you're used to other formatting languages, such as TeX, HTML appears quite simple in comparison. Here is a minimal HTML document (which to be precise is not exactly correct HTML but something that all browsers understand):

```
<html>
<head>
<title>Ye Olde Generic HTML Document</title>
</head>
<body>
<h1>Writing HTML for Fun and Profit</h1>
```

```
Although writing HTML documents may not be a commmon source
of income, <em>authors</em> tend to bend the rules in this
respect.

<p> The advantage? It's really too easy for words.
</body>
</html>
```

Within HTML documents, *elements* are denoted by a <tag>...</tag> pair.*

As you can see, we begin the document with a header that contains the line:

```
<title>Ye Olde Generic HTML Document</title>
```

which defines the title for this document. In the body that follows is an <h1> element, which is a top-level heading. Under Netscape Navigator for X, the title generally appears in the *Document Title* window and the heading within the document itself.

All HTML documents should have a title, but headings are, of course, optional. To HTML, a heading is just a portion of text that is set in a larger and/or bolder font. It has no bearing on the actual document structure.

HTML supports six levels of headings:

```
<h1>First-level heading</h1>
<h2>Second-level heading</h2>
...
<h6>Sixth-level heading</h6>
```

Following the heading is the body of the document. As you can see, we use the <em> tag to emphasize text:

```
...of income, <em>authors</em> tend to bend the rules in this...
```

Paragraphs are separated by a <p> tag. HTML ignores blank lines and indentation in the document. Therefore, to skip a line and begin a new paragraph, using <p> is necessary (unlike TEX, for example, which causes paragraph breaks at blank lines).

Viewing the document

Before we go much further with HTML, let's describe how to look at your first work of hypertext art. Most web browsers allow you to open a local HTML document and view it. For example, under Navigator, selecting Open Page from the File menu and then clicking Choose File... allows you to view an HTML file. Other browsers, such as Lynx, provide similar mechanisms. You should first save your HTML document in a file (such as *sample.html*) and view it with your web browser.

---

* HTML is really a Document Type Definition in Standard Generalized Markup Language (SGML). SGML defines the <tag>...</tag> conventions.

When viewed in Netscape Navigator, our sample document looks like Figure 16-4. As you can see, Navigator does the actual "text formatting" for you; all that is required on your end is to write the document and point your web browser at it.

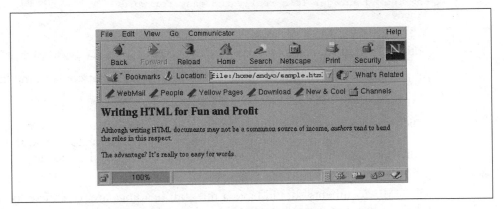

Figure 16–4: Sample HTML document displayed by Netscape

It's also quite easy to make your new HTML documents available via the Web. Assuming you have configured *httpd* as described in the previous section, you can place the HTML file in the *httpd* DocumentRoot directory (in our case, this is */usr/local/httpd/htdocs*).

Therefore, assuming the previous document is saved as */usr/local/httpd/htdocs/ sample.html*, and *httpd* is running on your system, anyone can access the document by opening the URL:

   http://www.veggie.org/sample.html

with a web browser. (Of course, substituting your own hostname for *www.veggie.org*.)

Note that you can create directories, symbolic links, and so forth within the DocumentRoot directory. Any HTTP URLs to your system will access filenames that are relative to DocumentRoot. So if we create the directory */usr/local/httpd/htdocs/my-docs* and place *sample.html* there, the corresponding URL is:

   http://www.veggie.org/my-docs/sample.html

Using links

In order to refer to other documents, or sections within the same document, *links* are used within the HTML source. For example:

```
<p> You can find more information about HTML
<a href="http://www.w3.org/MarkUp/"> here </a>.
```

Within Navigator, this sentence will look like Figure 16-5.

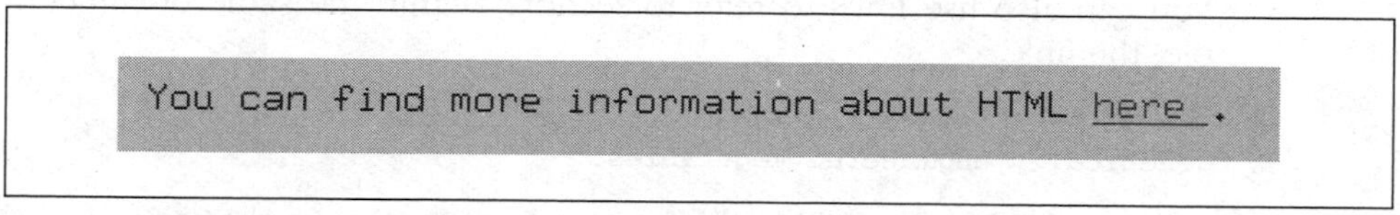

```
You can find more information about HTML here .
```

Figure 16–5: Link displayed by Netscape

The word "here" is highlighted, indicating that it is a link. Clicking on the link within Netscape retrieves the document pointed to by the URL:

http://www.w3.org/MarkUp/

The <a> element is known as an *anchor*; it specifies a link that is associated with a particular region of text (in this case, the word "here").

The <a> element we used is known as an *absolute link*. That is, the URL includes the complete machine and pathname specification. For documents on the same machine, you should use *relative links*, such as:

```
<p> You can also access the <a href="gardening.html">Vegetable Gardening
    Home Page</a>.
```

URL names in relative links are relative to the directory in which the current HTML document is located. The *type* of URL (e.g., *http*, *ftp*, and so on) is assumed to be identical to that of the URL of the current document. That is, if the previous text is found within the document:

http://www.veggie.org/my-docs/sample.html

the link points to the URL:

http://www.veggie.org/my-docs/gardening.html

If the filename used in a relative link begins with a slash (/), as in:

```
Click <a href="/info/veggie.html">here</a> for more information.
```

the URL is assumed to be relative to the DocumentRoot directory. In this case, the URL is equivalent to:

http://www.veggie.org/info/veggie.html

Relative links can also point to the parent directory, as in:

```
<a href="../plants/plants.html">Here</a> is more about plants.
```

The use of relative links is important for documents that are related. They allow you to rearrange the directory hierarchy of HTML files without rendering all your links obsolete. However, when accessing unrelated documents on the same system, it might be best to use an absolute link. In this way, the location of your document does not depend on the location of others on the same system.

You can also use links to refer to sections within the same document. For example, the link:

```
See <a href="#Genetics">below</a> for information on
genetically engineered vegetables.
```

refers to the location within the current document, tagged as so:

```
<a name="Genetics">
<h1>Genetically Engineered Vegetables: Our Specialty</h1> </a>
```

Here, the anchor uses the `name` attribute, instead of `href`. In addition, the text within the anchor is the entire heading name. It's not required that you use headings as `name` anchors, but it usually makes sense to do so when you want to have cross references to other "sections" of the document. For instance, when a user selects the link pointing to this anchor, they will see the section heading:

Genetically Engineered Vegetables: Our Specialty

at the top of the Netscape Navigator document window.

Links can also refer to particular locations within other documents. For example:

```
<a href="tomatoes.html#Genetics">Here</a> is more information on
our mutated tomatoes.
```

refers to the section labeled with `<a name="Genetics">` in the document *tomatoes.html*.

As you might guess, you are not limited to making links to other HTML documents. Links can point to image files, sounds, PostScript files, as well as other URL types such as FTP, Gopher, or WAIS services. In short, any valid URL can serve as a link. For example:

```
Click <a href="ftp://ftp.veggie.org/pub/">here</a> to access our
anonymous FTP archive.
```

provides a link to the named FTP URL.

An aside: MIME types

MIME stands for *Multipurpose Internet Mail Extensions*. As the named suggests, it was originally developed for electronic mail and is a standard for transporting documents that contain data other than plain printable ASCII text. You can find more information about MIME types at:

> *http://www.w3.org/TR/REC-html40/ types.html#b-6.7*

When you link to images or sounds, the range of valid image and sound types you may use depends on the abilities of the browser. For example, when accessing the URL:

> *http://www.veggie.org/pics/artichoke.gif*

the browser will be responsible for running a separate program to display the image. However, the server providing the image must tell the browser what type of data the incoming image is. This is handled by the *mime.types* file, in the *httpd* configuration directory. This file contains lines such as:

```
image/gif                    gif
image/jpeg                   jpeg jpg jpe
audio/basic                  au snd
application/postscript       ai eps ps
text/html                    html
text/plain                   txt
```

The first field in each line defines the MIME type name for the document in question. The remaining fields indicate filename extensions that the MIME type corresponds to. In this case, any filenames ending in *.gif* are treated as `image/gif` type documents.

When the browser (say, Netscape Navigator) retrieves a document, it also gets information on the MIME type associated with it from the server. In this way, the browser knows how to deal with the document. For `text/html` documents, Navigator simply formats the HTML source text and displays it in the document window, for `image/gif` documents, it uses internal image viewing code to display the graphic. For `image/png` documents, Navigator runs a separate image viewer, such as *xv*. Similarly, `application/postscript` documents are viewed using Ghostview on most Unix systems.

How individual MIME types are dealt with is up to the browser. Navigator provides an option that allows you to specify a program to be run to process documents of a particular type.

The *srm.conf* file can also contain a `DefaultType` directive, which specifies which MIME type to use when all the other types do not apply. We use:

```
DefaultType    text/plain
```

If the server is unable to determine the type of document, it assumes `text/plain`, which is used for unformatted text files. Netscape displays these text files in a constant-width font in the document window.

Embedded images

One of the nicer features provided by HTML is the ability to include images directly in the document. This is accomplished with the `<img>` element:

```
<img src="pics/cat.gif">
Tristessa, the Best Cat in the Universe.
```

This embeds the image pointed to by the relative URL `pics/cat.gif` in the document, as seen in Figure 16-6. Absolute URLs can be used with `<img>` as well.

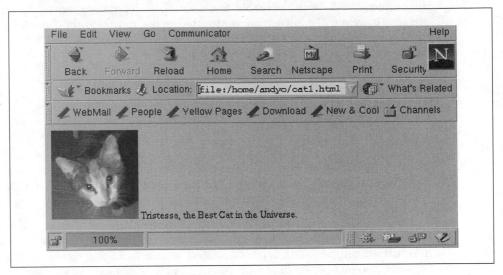

Figure 16–6: Image displayed by Netscape

In theory, the `<img>` element can be used to embed "any" document into the current one. However, it is most commonly used for small images. The kind of images that can be inline depends on the particular browser. GIF and JPEG images seem to be universally accepted. However, note that not all browsers can display inline images—most notably text-based browsers such as Lynx.

You can also use `<img>` within an anchor, as in:

```
<a href="cat.html">
<img src="pics/cat.gif"></a>
Tristessa, the Best Cat in the Universe.
```

The display won't look any different, but a user who clicks on the picture will be taken to the page *cat.html* in the same subdirectory as the current page. To make it clear that another page is available, you should probably include both image and text in the anchor. This can be accomplished just by moving the closing `</a>` tag:

```
<a href="cat.html">
<img align="center" src="pics/cat.gif" alt="Photo of cat">
Tristessa, the Best Cat in the Universe.
</a>
```

As a slight aesthetic improvement (and to show that you have control over the placement of items) we centered the text next to the image by specifying `align="center"`. We also conformed to modern accessibility guidelines by providing an `alt` tag that displays explanatory text for people who can't see the image, such as blind readers or anyone using a text-only browser. The final version of our little page is shown in Figure 16-7.

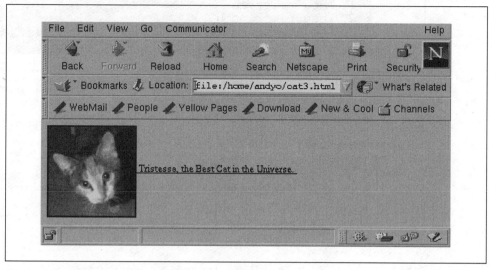

Figure 16–7: Image and link displayed by Netscape

More HTML features

Obviously, you need more than section headings, links, and inline images to write nicely formatted HTML documents. HTML provides many other text-layout features.

A numbered list can be obtained with the `<ol>` element, using `<li>` for each item in the list.

```
Zucchinis have the following nice features:
<ol>
<li> They're green.
<li> They're crunchy.
<li> They taste great in salads.
</ol>
```

This list appears as shown in Figure 16-8 when formatted by Netscape Navigator.

An unnumbered list can be obtained by using `<ul>` in place of `<ol>`. Unnumbered list items are marked with bullets instead of incremental numbers.

Lists can be nested as well. When unnumbered lists are nested, the bullet style usually changes at each level, as in Figure 16-9. The HTML source used to produce this list is:

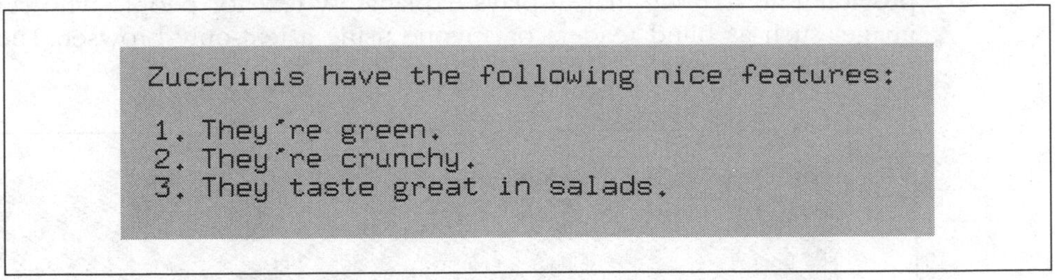

```
Zucchinis have the following nice features:

1. They're green.
2. They're crunchy.
3. They taste great in salads.
```

Figure 16–8: List displayed by Netscape

```
Here is an example of a nested list.
<ul>
<li> The first item.
<li> The second item.
    <ul>
    <li> The first nested item.
    <li> Another item.
        <ul>
        <li> Yet another level of nesting.
        </ul>
    </ul>
</ul>
```

The indentation is used strictly to make the source easier to read; feel free to use whatever indentation style you deem appropriate.

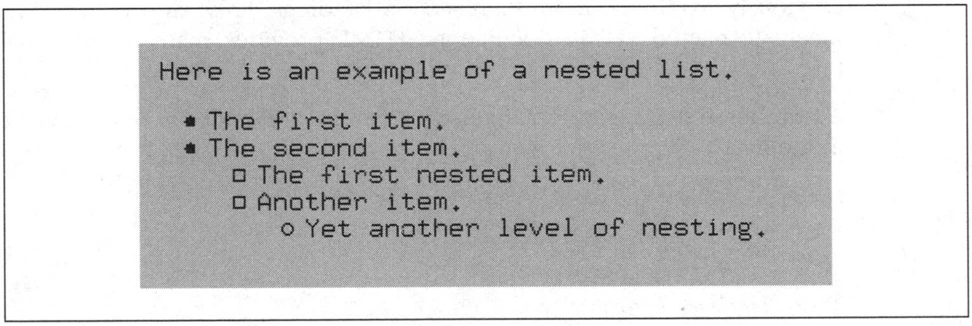

```
Here is an example of a nested list.

* The first item.
* The second item.
    □ The first nested item.
    □ Another item.
        o Yet another level of nesting.
```

Figure 16–9: Nested lists displayed by Netscape

Various types of text emphasis are available. We've already seen <em>, which usually causes words to be placed in italics. Note that how these items are displayed depends entirely on the browser. The most commonly used emphasis tags are:

<em>
    Emphasized text, usually rendered as italics

```
<code>
```
Program source code, usually rendered in a constant-width font

```
<samp>
```
Sample output from a program, also in constant width

```
<kbd>
```
User keyboard input

```
<strong>
```
For strong emphasis, usually in boldface

Here is an example that uses several of these elements.

```
<p> <em>Amazing</em>, she thought. The <kbd>find</kbd> command can be
used for almost <strong>anything!</strong>
```

This is displayed within Navigator as seen in Figure 16-10.

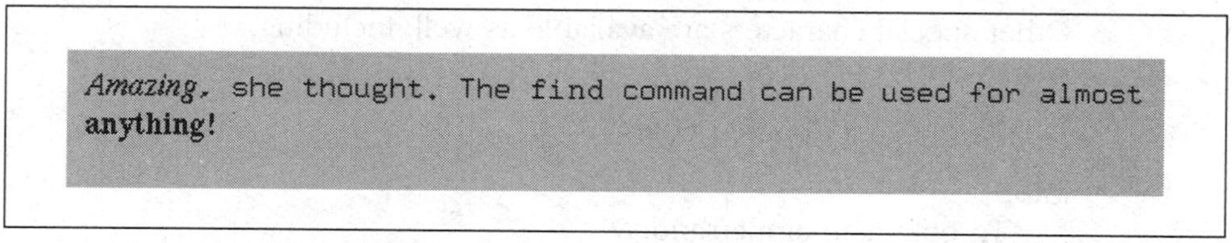

Figure 16–10: Fonts displayed by Netscape

Note that <code>, <samp>, and <kbd> are all usually displayed as a constant-width typewriter font. However, it is important to distinguish between different types of logical emphasis in documents. In this way, we can change the typeface used to display <kbd> items (for example, to a slanted font), but allow <code> and <samp> to remain the same.

HTML also provides the <b>, <i>, and <tt> tags to produce boldface, italic, and constant-width text, respectively, should you wish to specify fonts directly.

The <pre> element allows you to include "preformatted" or "verbatim" text within an HTML document:

```
The source code for <code>hello.c</code> is as follows.
<pre>
#include &lt;stdio.h&gt;

void main() {
  printf("Hello, world!");
}
</pre>
```

This text will be displayed as seen in Figure 16-11.

```
The source code for hello.c is as follows.

#include <stdio.h>

void main() {
  printf("Hello, world!");
}
```

Figure 16–11: Preformatted text displayed by Netscape

Note the use of < to obtain < and > to obtain >. This is necessary because the < and > characters have a special meaning within HTML documents. Even within a <pre> element, substitution is necessary.

Other special characters are available as well, including:

"
> To obtain a double-quote: "

&
> To obtain an ampersand: &

é
> To obtain an acute-accented *e*: é

ö
> To obtain an *o*-umlaut: ö

The complete HTML specification, located at:

> *http://www.w3.org/TR/REC-html40/*

lists all the available codes.

You'll often seen a horizontal rule used in HTML documents to visually divide the page. This is obtained with the <hr> element, as so:

```
All right, I dare you to cross this line: <p><hr>
<p> All right, I dare you to cross this one: <p><hr>
```

Finally, the <address> element is often used at the end of HTML documents to specify the name and address of the author, or maintainer, of the page. For example:

```
<p><hr><p>
<address>Mr. P. Head, potatoe@veggie.org</address>
```

Many people link the name within the `<address>` item to a personal home page.

Finding out more

Within Netscape Navigator, you can view the HTML source for any document on the Web. While viewing the document in question, select the Document Source option from the View menu. This gives you an inside look at how the page was written. The Lynx web browser provides a similar option in the form of the backslash (\) command.

Building Interactive Forms

As mentioned in previous sections, Netscape Navigator and Apache *httpd* include support for *forms*, which allow the user to provide input (in the form of text-entry fields, buttons, menus, and so forth) to a script, executed on the server. For example, one form might include a text field for entering a username. Submitting the form causes the server to run a *finger* script, displaying the output as an HTML document.

The ability to use forms depends on the capabilities of both the browser and *httpd* server. Not all browsers can view forms, but nowadays most do. Also, not all implementations of *httpd* understand forms. We suggest using Apache *httpd*, discussed earlier in this chapter, which provides extensive forms support.

The canonical example of an interactive form is one where users can send electronic mail to the maintainer of the form page. In this section, through the use of this example, we'll demonstrate how to write forms and the server scripts that are executed by the forms. Of course, with a browser that includes a mail client of its own or that can be connected to a mail program, just putting `mailto:` `mail_address` into the HTML page would suffice. But a form could also be part of a larger application; for example, you might not only want to send feedback via mail, but also order goods in an online shopping application.

The HTML form document

The first step in building a form is to write an HTML document that corresponds to the form itself. These HTML pages contain a `<form>` element, which in turn contains several other elements denoting buttons, text-entry fields, and so forth.

Here, we present a small cross section of what forms can do. For an extensive example of forms use, see the URL:

> *http://us.imdb.com*

which is a comprehensive database of information on over 30,000 movies, allowing you to search by title, genre, actors, directors, and so forth.

Here is the HTML document for our simple mail form:

```
1   <title>Ye Olde Generic Mail Form</title>
2   <h1>Send mail to me</h1>
3   <p>You can use this form to send me mail.
4
5   <p><hr><p>
6   <form method="POST" action="/cgi-bin/mailer.pl">
7   <input name="from"> Your email address<p>
8   <input name="subject"> Subject<p>
9   <input type=hidden name="to" value="mdw@veggie.org">
10  <hr>
11  Enter message body below:<br>
12  <hr>
13  <textarea name="body" cols=60 rows=12></textarea><p>
14  <hr>
15  <input type=submit value="Send mail"><p>
16  </form>
```

When viewed within Netscape Navigator, this form looks like Figure 16-12.

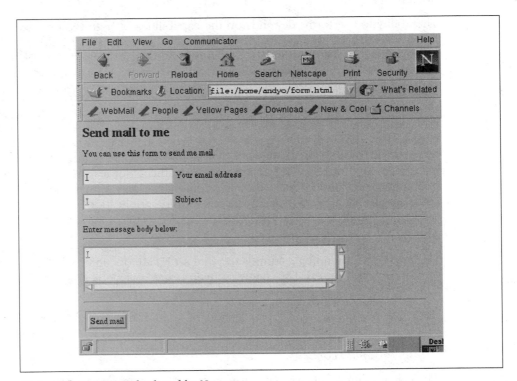

Figure 16–12: Form displayed by Netscape

As you can see, the form uses several additional features of HTML. Let's walk through the file and describe them all.

Line 6 uses the `<form>` element, which encloses the entire form itself. There are several options, or attributes, associated with the `<form>` element.

The `method` attribute specifies the means by which form information is sent to the server script. Valid methods are `GET` and `POST`. The `GET` method passes information as command-line arguments to the server script; the `POST` method passes information to the script's standard input. This option has bearing only on how you implement your server script; for various reasons, it's strongly suggested that you use the `POST` method.

The `action` attribute specifies the URL of the script that this form executes on the server. CGI scripts are usually stored in a directory named *cgi-bin* that must be specified in the `ScriptAlias` directive in the *srm.conf* file.

Here, we specify that the script:

```
/cgi-bin/mailer.pl
```

should be executed when the form is submitted. The next section describes how to write this script.

Lines 7–9 use the `<input>` element. This is the most common element found within a form; it specifies some kind of input item, such as a text field, button, or checkbox. The `<input>` element has several attributes.

The `name` attribute specifies a unique string that identifies this element to the server script. The `type` attribute specifies the type of input element. Its value can be `text`, `radio`, `checkbox`, `password`, `submit`, `reset`, or `hidden`. If no `type` is specified (as on lines 7 and 8), `text` is the default. The `value` attribute specifies the default value associated with this input item.

Several other attributes for `input` are also available; these set the maximum length of input for text entry fields, and so forth.

Lines 7 and 8 define input elements named `from` and `subject`, both of type `text`. These text-entry fields are used to enter the sender's email address and the subject of the message.

Line 9 defines a `hidden` element named `to`, which sets the email address that mail should be sent to. This is a "trick" that allows us to specify the recipient's email address within the HTML form itself. Otherwise, we'd have to specify the recipient address within the server script (*mailer.pl*), which would require each user that wished to use the mail form to have a private copy of the script. This way, any user on the system can use the script, as long as he specifies his own address as the value of the `to` item. The reasons for this will become clear in the next section, where we discuss the *mailer.pl* script itself.

On line 13, we use the `<textarea>` element. This element denotes a multiline text-entry field, with scrollbars on the right and bottom edges. As with `<input>`, the `name` attribute names the element. The `cols` and `rows` attributes set the size of the `textarea`.

Note that unlike `<input>`, the `<textarea>` element has a corresponding `</textarea>` end tag on the same line. Any text that appears between `<textarea>` and `</textarea>` is the default contents of the entry field.

On line 15, we use another `<input>` element, of type `submit`. This defines a button which, when pressed, submits the form and runs the server script associated with it. The `value` attribute specifies the text of the button as displayed; in this case, it is `"Send mail"`.

Finally, on line 16, we end the form with a `</form>` end tag.

[25] HTML

Multiple forms can be used within a single HTML document; however, you cannot nest one `<form>` within another. A good book where you can learn about HTML and forms is *HTML: The Definitive Guide* by Chuck Musciano and Bill Kennedy.

Writing the CGI script

Scripts executed by forms use the CGI convention, which specifies how data is passed from the form to the script. At this point, it is not important to understand the details of the CGI specification; however, you should be aware that data is passed to scripts as a set of name/value pairs. For example, given our sample form, let's say the user entered the address:

```
bsmarks@norelco.com
```

in the `from` `<input>` field. The value `bsmarks@norelco.com` would then be associated with the name `from` when passed to the script.

As mentioned previously, the mechanism by which these name/value pairs are passed to the server script depends upon the form method (`GET` or `POST`) used. In general, name/value pairs are encoded in the form:

```
action?name=val&name=val&...
```

and passed to the server script either on the command line (in the case of `GET`-method forms) or as standard input (in the case of `POST`-method forms). In addition, certain characters (such as `=`, `&`, and so on) must be escaped. Several environment variables pass certain parameters to the script.

Server scripts can be written in practically any language, such as C, Perl, or even shell scripts. Because decoding the name/value pairs within a C program can be a bit harrowing, we instead show how to implement a script in Perl, in which text-processing facilities are more suited for this task.

The following example is the Perl script *mailer.pl*. Put this script in the directory you have set aside to hold CGI scripts when you configured the system:

```
#!/usr/bin/perl

use CGI qw(:standard);

print header(), start_html( "Mail form results" ),\
h1( "Mail form results" );

my $to = parse( "to" );
my $from = parse( "from" );
my $subject = parse( "subject" );
my $body = parse( "body" );

open (MAIL,"|/usr/lib/sendmail $to") ||
  die "<p>Error: Couldn't execute sendmail.\n";

print MAIL "To: $to\n";
print MAIL "From: $from\n";
print MAIL "subject: $subject\n\n";
print MAIL "$body\n";
close MAIL;

print p( "All right, mailed the following to <tt>$to</tt>:" );
print p( "<pre>\nTo: $to\nFrom: $from\nsubject:\
$subject\n\n$body\n</pre>" );
print end_html();
```

Chapter 13

If you're new to Perl, refer to the introduction given in Chapter 13, *Programming Languages*. However, you need not be a Perl wizard to follow this code.

This script first loads the module *CGI.pm*, which has been included in the Perl distribution since Perl 5.004; it will help you a great deal when it comes to writing CGI scripts. We first use its methods header(), ()start_html(), and h1() to write the header, including the crucial line:

```
Content-type: text/html
```

which informs the server to watch for the MIME type of data coming from the script, and to start the HTML code. With *CGI.pm* you do not even need to worry about the HTML syntax!

After printing out those initial lines, we use the routine parse() from *CGI.pm*, which parses the parameters passed to the CGI script. While this doesn't sound like much, parsing those parameters is actually no small feat, because lots of things have to be taken into consideration. With parse, you simply pass the name of the parameter and get its value back.

The script then opens a pipe to */usr/lib/sendmail* in the program that sends the mail message. (If you use a mail handler other than *sendmail* on your system, this filename should be modified.) We then pass the message to *sendmail*, prefixing it with an appropriate header containing the To:, From:, and Subject: fields derived from the data given on the form.

Note that there is a security risk here when you are using *sendmail* like this, because you do not know what is in the $to variable. In addition, the pipe technique is not very portable. In a production system, you would probably use the Perl module `Mail::Mailer` to send the mail, but since this has nothing to do with CGI scripting in particular, we leave this to your own explorations.

After closing the pipe to *sendmail*, we print the message as sent to standard output to allow the user to verify that the message was processed correctly. Again, we use the method p() from *CGI.pm* to output the HTML code. Finally, we use end_html() to correctly close the HTML tags.

Keep in mind that there are always security issues at work when dealing with HTML-based forms. Be certain that your scripts cannot be used to execute unauthorized processes on your system. If your server scripts are CPU-intensive, you might want to limit access to them to prevent heavy system load. In general, be sure that you know what you're doing when providing forms on your web server.

Electronic Mail

Electronic mail (email) is one of the most desirable features of a computer system. You can send and receive email on your Linux system locally between users on the host and between hosts on a network. You have to set up three classes of software to provide email service. These are the *mail user agent* or mailer, the *mail transport agent* (MTA), and the *transport protocol.*

The mailer provides the user interface for displaying mail, writing new messages, and filing messages. Linux offers you many choices for mailers. They are always being improved, and a particular mailer may provide certain features, such as the ability to serve as a newsreader or to serve as a web browser.

The mailer relies on the MTA to route mail from one user to another, whether locally or across systems. The MTA in turn uses a transport protocol, usually either UUCP (Unix-to-Unix Copy) or Simple Mail Transport Protocol (SMTP), to provide the medium for mail transfer.

There are a number of possible scenarios when using email on a Linux system, and depending on those scenarios, you will have to install a different set of software packages. However, no matter which option you choose, you will always need a mailer.

The first scenario applies to dial-up access to the Internet via an Internet Service Provider (ISP). In this scenario, there is often only one user on the Linux machine, even though this is not a requirement. The ISP accepts your mail from then Internet and stores it for you on its hard disks. You can then retrieve the mail whenever you want by using the common POP3 (Post Office Protocol) protocol or the newer protocol IMAP. Outgoing mail in this scenario is almost exclusively sent via the protocol SMTP (Simple Mail Transfer Protocol) that is generally used to transport mail over the Internet.

In the easiest case, you use your mailer both to retrieve the mail via POP3 or IMAP and to send it back via SMTP. When you do this, you do not even need to set up an MTA, because the mailer handles everything. This is not terribly flexible, but if all you want is to access your mail easily, this might be an option for you. Mailers that support this include Netscape Messenger (see later) and KMail from KDE.

If you want more flexibility (which comes at the price of more configuration and maintenance work), you can install an MTA (like *smail*, described in the next section). You will need a program that transports the mail from your provider's POP3 or IMAP server. This program fetches your mail when you ask it to and passes the messages on to the MTA running on your system, which then distributed the mail to the recipients' mail folders. One program that does exactly that is *fetchmail*, which we will cover later in this chapter. Outgoing mail is again sent via SMTP, but with an MTA running on your machine, you can choose not to send the outgoing messages directly to your provider's SMTP server, but rather to your own server, which is provided by the MTA. The MTA then forwards the mail to your provider, which in turn sends it to the recipients. With this setup, you can instruct your MTA to send outgoing mails at certain intervals only, so that you do not always have to make a dial-up connection.

The third scenario is meant for machines that have a permanent connection to the Internet, either because they are in a network that has a gateway with a permanent connection, or because your machine is using a leased line to your Internet provider. In this case, you might want to receive mail messages as soon as they arrive at your provider and not have them stored there. This also requires setting up an MTA. Incoming mails will be directed to your SMTP server (i.e., your MTA). Your provider will have to set things up accordingly for this to work.

[4] Network
Admin Guide
[32] sendmail

Of course, there are many more scenarios how to get your mail, and mixtures between the three mentioned are possible as well. If you are going to set up a mail service for a whole network, you will most certainly want to read the *Linux Network Administrator's Guide* as well as *sendmail*.

You have a number of software choices for setting up email on a Linux host. We can't describe all the available email solutions, but we do describe some packages that are often used and quite suitable for their respective tasks. We document what we think is the most popular Linux solution at this time: the Elm mailer (Version 2.4 at the time of this writing), the Netscape Messenger (Version 4.5), the *smail* (*smail3.1.29*) mail transport agent, and the *fetchmail* implementation of the POP3 and IMAP protocols. These are relatively simple to configure but provide all the features most users need. In addition, with these tools, you can cover all the scenarios described earlier.

The smail Mail Transport Agent

There are two major MTAs available on Linux: *smail* and *sendmail*. They both support the SMTP and UUCP protocols for handling mail. The *sendmail* package has been around for a long time. It is generally considered somewhat more difficult to use than *smail*, but it is thoroughly documented in the book *sendmail*, by Costales, Allman, and Rickert. The *smail* package is reportedly easier to configure and manage than *sendmail* and is perhaps more robust on systems with limited memory. It is very popular on Linux. We've decided to go with the most popular Linux MTA, *smail*, and describe its essential configuration and use here. However, if you need to configure a mail host that has many connections and handles lots of mail, you really need *sendmail*. Recently, other mail transport agents like *qmail*, *exim*, and *zmailer* have become popular as well, but *smail* (for its easy installation) and *sendmail* (for demanding requirements) should cover about everything you need.

[32] sendmail

smail can be invoked in many modes by a specific invocation name that establishes its special uses. For example, *smail* can be invoked as *rmail*, and it replaces the original *rmail* in that function. It also can be invoked as a daemon process (*smtpd* or *in.smtpd*) and replaces other mail utilities, such as *mailq*. *smail* is compatible with the *sendmail* MTA and interfaces satisfactorily with it.

[4] Network
Admin Guide

Olaf Kirch's *Linux Network Administrator's Guide* provides information specific to installing *smail* on Linux hosts. Also, the *smail3* package has an excellent guide to installing and maintaining *smail*, entitled *Smail—Installation and Administration Guide* by Karr and Noll. Finally, you should also print out the manual pages for *smail*, which describe in detail all the configuration files and directories that *smail* uses.

The *smail* package is bundled with some Linux distributions. On the distributions that bundle *smail*, most use the Linux installation script to perform basic configuration of *smail* as well. One problem with this approach is that you need to periodically update your *smail* installation, and there is no convenient script to do this unless you reinstall Linux at the same time. Another problem is that some major Linux distributions seem to miss some detail or another in configuring the *smail* utilities, so that you need to go in and add a file link, edit a resource file, or something of the kind.

But take heart: even though patches are applied and features are added, your same old *smail* configuration files almost always continue to work just fine. You usually only need to update your binaries to stay up to date.

That's the good news. The bad news is that different distributions of *smail* install the files in different places. If you grab a set of binaries from an FTP site and install it over your obsolete installation, you might find that you have one version of *smail* installed in */usr/bin* and another in */sbin*. Because *smail* functions, as a number of mail utilities do, through the use of file links, this kind of inconsistency can cause real problems with your installation.

If you build a distribution from scratch, though, you may find that it is a generic installation not tailored for Linux. (However, a generic Unix FTP site is likely to have the full set of documentation that seems to be missing from some of the Linux sites we've checked.)

What can you do? Well, if you take a distribution from a particular FTP site, it might help to stick with that site, even if it means you don't get the latest and greatest update at the earliest possible moment. This works particularly well if the site is a binary distribution site—your configuration files will be left untouched. Or you can just jump in and install updated files and then use *find* or *whereis* to sort out tangled up links and duplicated files. In any case, you will likely find that even if your Linux installation script installed and configured *smail* correctly on your system, you don't like all the selected behaviors. If this is the case, often your best bet is to simply edit the *smail* configuration file for your system.

Getting and installing smail

An excellent FTP site that contains an up-to-date Linux binary distribution (at the time of this writing) is *ftp://metalab.unc.edu*. The *smail* package can be found in */pub/Linux/system/mail/mta/smail-linuxbin-3.1.29.1.tar.gz*. The specific filename will presumably change with each update to the source files, but the path will probably remain the same.

We should perhaps add that nobody seems to be currently working on *smail*. It works as it is, but you shouldn't hold your breath waiting for enhancements or bug fixes.

You can also get *smail* as a source package to compile yourself from the same location. In this case, get the file *smail-3.1.29.1.tar.gz*.

To install the binary Linux distribution:

1. FTP the file in binary mode.

2. Move the file to the Linux root directory as */smail.tar.gz*.

3. Run *gunzip* on the file, which results in a file named *smail.tar*.

4. Execute *tar –xvf smail.tar* on the file in the root directory. The *smail.tar* unpacks into a directory tree.

Chapter 7

The section "Archive and Compression Utilities" in Chapter 7, *Upgrading Software and the Kernel*, tells you all you need to know about *gunzip* and *tar*.

If you should run across a package called *smailcfg* when browsing an FTP site, you might think it is a configuration utility for *smail*. It isn't; it's a configuration utility for *sendmail*.

Configuring a Linux-installed smail package

Some Linux distributions come with *smail* already packaged, and *smail* is installed when you run the Linux installation program. Linux systems typically install the various parts of the *smail* package to the following directories: */bin, /usr/bin, /usr/lib/smail,* and */usr/man/man?.* The *smail* configuration may be stored in */var/lib/smail/config.*

Many of the variables *smail* uses are assigned based on information collected from the Linux configuration. If you installed Linux with TCP/IP, for example, *smail* will be configured to use SMTP with it. There are some *smail* variables you still need to set, however. These include:

postmaster

This variable supplies a user ID to serve as postmaster on the local system. The mail administrator on the system is normally the designated postmaster. It is almost a moral obligation of a system on an open network (with links beyond a LAN) to have a designated postmaster. If there is a problem with email on a system, any user (anywhere) should be able to send a message to *postmaster@hostname* to have it investigated. In the most rudimentary system, the postmaster can be the **root** user, but it is preferable for the postmaster to be assigned to an ordinary user ID. (Some systems set up a "phony" account for the postmaster, so the duties can be rotated.)

smart_path

This is an important variable to set, especially when you are a fledgling mail host. smart_path should be the name of the "smart host" to which your system routes all mail that it doesn't already know how to deliver. In the simplest setup, anything that isn't local mail is routed to the smart_path host you specify. If you have a connection to an Internet host, it should be your smart host.

visible_name

This variable specifies a name *smail* uses as the return address for all mail sent by your host. For example, if your full hostname is **deus.x-machina.org**, you might prefer the visible name to be **x-machina.org**. A **user** on the host *deus* would have her From address set to *user@x-machina.org* instead of *user@deus.x-machina.org.* This is especially useful if there are several hosts that users on the local network have accounts on, or if names of specific host systems in the domain change.

smart_user

The smart_user isn't necessarily a user. You can leave smart_user with no value assigned, in which case any mail that cannot be delivered will be bounced (returned to sender). If you assign a user ID to smart_user, improperly addressed mail sent to your system will be forwarded to the smart_user.

Often, `smart_user` is the same user as **postmaster**, but for a small system, it is probably best to bounce the mail. `smart_user` is intended to allow manual rerouting of mail when a user moves, loses an account, and so on. It has little use on a system with few users.

smail(5)

There are additional variables that you can set. The online manual page describes them all in its discussion of the *config* file. Your distribution might not contain the documents in printable form, but you should print your own if you need to, by entering one of the following commands. (The first generates plain text for every printer; the second assumes you have configured *ghostscript* to drive your specific printer by default):

```
$ man 5 smail | col -b | lpr
$ gtroff -man /usr/man/man5/smail.5 | ghostscript | lpr
```

There has been a configuration script floating around some distributions (look for */usr/lib/smail/tools.linux/config*), but on the other hand, all you really need is *smail(5)* and your trusty ASCII editor to fix up your *smail* configuration files. (Though we would also use the *Linux Network Administrator's Guide* and the *Smail—Installation and Administration Guide*.)

[4] Network
Admin Guide

Configuring smail

Fortunately, *smail* default values for the Linux *smail* distribution are decent, and the *mkconfig* script largely automates the remaining *smail* installation issues. With any luck you can accept all default values and just run *smail* "out of the box."

Look for a *README* text file in the current distribution. You should begin by reading this file if it exists. On a typical Linux distribution of *smail*, the *README* file is found in */usr/lib/smail/linux.tools/README*. The *README* file describes the release and provides any special notes and general instructions for installing and configuring the current version of the software. If your distribution does not have a *README* file for *smail*, you will have to make do with the manual pages, which should give you all the information you need.

smail EDITME file

The first step in configuring *smail* from a Linux distribution is to go to the */usr/lib/smail/linux.tools* directory (or wherever your distribution stores the *smail* configuration files) and copy the *EDITME-dist* file to *EDITME*. There are some distributions out there in netland where even the *EDITME* file is missing. These distributions typically contain only the binary files needed, but no configuration files whatsoever. If this is case, look again at the place where you downloaded your *smail* package; sometimes you can find another package that contains configuration files. If all else fails, download the source package and take the *EDITME-dist* file you find there.

Once you are the lucky owner of an *EDITME* file, edit it to alter any variables you need to. Some of the values you can assign in *EDITME* are better handled in a later step, when you run */usr/lib/smail/linux.tools/mkconfig* to complete the *smail* installation. Variable assignments in the *EDITME* file are in the form of `variable=value`. The following are variables to which you might wish to give special attention to in the *EDITME* file:

`OS_TYPE=linux`

> The `OS_TYPE` should already have a value of `linux` if you are using a standard Linux distribution of *smail*. Check this just in case.

`HAVE=HDB_UUCP`

> If you've installed some other UUCP package than the usual Taylor UUCP, you should study the comments about the `HAVE` variable. For Taylor UUCP, you don't want to set a value for `HAVE`.

`UUCP_ZONE`

> If you are on a UUCP network, and you are not going to be on the Internet, look at the comments on the `UUCP_ZONE` variable. You may need to set `UUCP_ZONE=true` to achieve the address-handling behavior you want for certain UUCP networks.

`DOMAINS`

> You may need to set `DOMAINS` to a domain name if you did not perform a standard Linux installation and configuration. If you did, however, you will probably want to omit setting `DOMAINS` in the *EDITME* file, and make any changes you need when you run *mkconfig*.

`SMAIL_BIN_DIR`

> Linux normally sets */usr/bin* as the `SMAIL_BIN_DIR` value. This variable establishes the path to the primary mailer on the system. If you've put your primary mailer somewhere else, you'll have to change this variable's value.

`LIB_DIR`

> Linux normally sets */usr/lib/smail* as the `LIB_DIR` path. If you put *smail* files somewhere other than */usr/lib/smail*, you need either to change `LIB_DIR` to reflect this or to link the directory you use to */usr/lib/smail*.

`NEWALIASES`

> The *mkaliases* command functions as the *newaliases* utility if you set this variable; otherwise you must invoke the utility as *mkaliases*. The default behavior is the latter. If you want to enable invocation as *newaliases*, the argument to `NEWALIASES` should be set to the path of the *newaliases* command.

UUCP_SYSTEM_FILE

If you are using a UUCP package other than Taylor UUCP, you may need to set this variable to something different from its current value. Currently, it is set as UUCP_SYSTEM_FILE=/usr/lib/UUCP/Systems, which is typical for a BNU or HoneyDanBer UUCP distribution.

SPOOL_DIRS

By default, SPOOL_DIRS is set to */var/spool/smail*, but you may want more than one spool directory available if you think you will need more inodes to handle the volume of pending mail or if you change the directory specified. To specify more than one spooling directory, enter each spooling directory's path, separated by a colon. If you have set aside a fast disk drive for spooling operations, you may need to change the path in order to place the primary spooling directory in that mounted path. For example, if your fast disk drive is mounted as */var/spool*, you might have something like:

```
SPOOL_DIRS=/var/spool/smail:/usr/spool/smail
```

NEWS_SPOOL_DIR

This is normally set to */var/spool/news*; considerations are similar to SPOOL_DIRS variable, except, of course, that Netnews volume is getting huge, so you really might need more spooling directories.

The mkconfig file

After you are satisfied with the state of your *EDITME* file (and in fact, you may have determined that you need not set any special values in an *EDITME* file), you are ready to run */usr/lib/smail/tools.linux/mkconfig*. This utility creates a supplementary file that overrides or supplements other *smail* variables; the file is */usr/lib/smail/tools.linux/config.state*. We'll provide responses to a few of these questions and show you the resulting output file. These are the considerations you should be ready to resolve when *mkconfig* is run:

Extra hostnames

mkconfig already knows a hostname if you installed Linux using one of the standard distributions or if you gave a value in the *EDITME* file. Now you are asked if you want your host to be known by multiple hostnames. This is useful if the host is on more than one network, for example. For our configuration run, the host value was already set to *pond.walden.com* (composed from the hostname value of *pond* and from the domain name value of *walden.com*). We answered the query by entering an additional hostname of *pond.conserve.org*, because we'd like to be known to some correspondents on the outside by that domain name.

System's visible name

You can set the visible name to something other than the actual hostname. The purpose of this is to provide a single visible mailing address for mail coming from a cluster of machines. You should specify the machine that all mail coming from outside the local network will be sent to. If the visible name value isn't set, the primary host and domain names form the name used.

Smart host

This is a very important consideration; you should have a *smart host*, which is a host to which you route all mail you can't deliver. If you don't answer this question when you run *mkconfig*, you should edit the */usr/lib/smail/config* file to provide this data when you are ready to designate a smart host. We responded to this query with *ruby.ora.com*, because we are using it as our connection to the outside world.

Smart transport

This specifies the preferred mail-transport medium; the default is TCP.

Smart user

This is for email wizards who can figure out forwarding addresses for mis-routed mail. You should probably leave it unset, so mail that is routed to an unknown user on the local host is bounced back to the sender.

Postmaster

Someone should take responsibility for email. If you are performing *mkconfig*, you are probably "it" and should provide your own user ID in response. If the postmaster isn't designated, all mail sent to **postmaster** goes to the **root** user. We supplied **lark** as the user ID for postmaster.

Primary mailer

Basically, *mkconfig* checks to see if */bin/mail* exists, and if it does (as it does on most Linux systems), it regretfully accepts this as the primary mailer. You can edit your customization file to use another mailer, like Elm.

The file that results from the interactive *mkconfig* procedure looks like this:

```
more_hostnames=pond.walden.com:pond.conserve.org
visible_name=
smart_path=ruby.ora.com
smart_user=
postmaster=lark
```

Final smail installation notes

When your *smail* installation is complete, make sure you remove or rename any existing *rmail*, *sendmail*, or other commands that *smail* is intended to replace. (The *smail* installation script probably already has created these links, but you need to verify the situation; if you had existing utilities before installing *smail*, they may not have been replaced with links to *smail*.) Create the *smail* links that are needed to carry out all of its many roles, so programs that depend on these utilities can find them:

```
# ln /usr/bin/smail /usr/bin/mailq
# ln /usr/bin/smail /usr/bin/rmail
# ln /usr/bin/smail /usr/bin/rsmtp

# ln /usr/bin/smail /usr/bin/runq
# ln /usr/bin/smail /usr/sbin/sendmail
# ln /usr/bin/smail /usr/bin/smtpd
# ln /usr/bin/smail /usr/bin/mkaliases
```

[4] Network
Admin Guide

When you have established these links, the utilities that rely on them can be configured for full network operation. For good instructions on that process, refer to (of course) the *Linux Network Administrator's Guide*.

If *smail* is configured correctly on your system, there is a line in the */etc/services* file that says:

```
smtp        25/tcp          mail
```

There is also a line in the */etc/services* file that says:

```
SMTP    stream  tcp    nowait  root  /usr/sbin/tcpd  /usr/bin/rSMTP -bs
```

smail runtime configuration files

The *smail* binary is preconfigured and needs only minor tuning. Usually the changes can be made through the *EDITME* script, the *linux.tools/config* script, or directly to the */var/lib/smail/config* (*/etc/smail/config* on Debian 1.3) file. Normally, you need no other configuration, but there are some other files *smail* uses to alter configuration at runtime. If you should ever need any of these, build them according to "Setting Up Runtime Configuration Files" in *Smail—Installation and Administration Guide*. Also use *smail(5)* to provide information about the meanings of the variables you set.

A second host configuration file, */private/usr/lib/smail/config*, redefines mailer behavior on a local workstation. This is intended for use on a LAN, in cases where your local system might need to behave differently from the central *smail* configuration file that controls the site as a whole.

The *directors*, *routers*, and *transports* files redefine attributes of the *smail* director, router, or transport MTA functions. Again, these normally apply to LAN and multipathed network connections.

A *methods* file is used in conjunction with runtime configuration files to assign different transport protocols to use with different hosts. This isn't necessary for mixed

UUCP and TCP/IP use, but it can be employed when you want to do something unusual, such as using an SMTP protocol over UUCP or a UUCP batch protocol over TCP/IP. The technique is useful, but is not for the novice mail administrator.

A *qualify* file tells a host the domain to route mail to if a bare hostname is given as a mail address. This is an easily abused feature and should normally be avoided. However, it can define UUCP mail routing to a UUCP system that keeps full and accurate UUCP maps (with the cooperation of that host's mail administrator).

A *retry* file modifies retry and timeout behavior of *smail*. This file sets minimum delivery intervals, maximum durations, and the number of attempts separately for each target domain that the mail host connects to. Its use is beyond the scope of this book, but you may need to use this file at some point.

Getting the Mail to Your Computer with Fetchmail

If your provider stores your mail for you until you fetch it, and you do not want to use your mailer to download the mail, you need a program that retrieves the mail from your provider's computer. There are a lot of programs for doing this; we will discuss *fetchmail* here briefly, because it is both robust and flexible and can handle both POP3 and IMAP.

You can get *fetchmail* from your friendly Linux archive; chances are that your distribution carries it, too. In case you download a source distribution of *fetchmail*, unpack, build, and install it according to the installation instructions.

You can control *fetchmail*'s behavior both via command-line options or by a configuration file. It is a good idea to first try to fetch your mail by passing the necessary information on the command line, and when this works, to write the configuration file.

As an example, let's assume that my provider is running the POP3 protocol, that my username there is **joeuser** and that my password is secret. The hostname of the machine where the POP3 server is running is **mail.isp.com**. I can then retrieve my mail with the following command:

```
fetchmail --protocol POP3 --username joeuser mail.isp.com
```

fetchmail then asks me for my password, and after I specify it correctly, retrieves the mail waiting for me and passes it on to my MTA for further delivery. This assumes that a SMTP server is running on port 25 of my machine, but this should be the case if I have set up my MTA correctly.

While you are experimenting with *fetchmail*, it might be a good idea to also specify the option *--keep*. This prevents *fetchmail* from deleting the messages from your POP3 account. Normally, all messages are deleted from your provider's hard disk once they are safely stored on your own machine. This is a good thing, because most providers limit the amount of mail you can store on their machines before retrieving them, and if you don't delete the messages after fetching them, you might reach this limit quite soon. On the other hand, while testing, it is a good idea to be on the safe side and use *--keep* so as not to lose any mail.

fetchmail (1)

With the options just shown to *fetchmail*, you should already be able to get your mail in most cases. For example, if your provider uses the newer IMAP protocol, simply specify `IMAP` in the command line instead of `POP3`. If your provider has some unusual setup, you might need one of the other options that the *fetchmail* manual page tells you about.

Once you are satisfied with the download process, you can write a *fetchmail* configuration file in order not to have to enter all the options each time you use the command. This configuration file is called *.fetchmailrc* and should reside in your home directory. Once you are done editing it, make sure it has the permission value 0600 so that nobody except yourself can read it, because this file might contain your password:

```
chmod 0600 ~/.fetchmailrc
```

The full syntax of the configuration file is detailed in the *fetchmail* man page, but in general you need only very simple lines that start with `poll`. To specify the same data as on the command line in the previous example, but this time include the password, put the following line into your configuration file:

```
poll mail.isp.com protocol pop3 username joeuser password secret
```

Now you can run *fetchmail* without any parameters. Since *fetchmail* already knows about your password from the configuration file, it will not prompt you for it this time. If you want to play safe while testing, add the word `keep` to the `poll` line.

Using *fetchmail* with a configuration file has one additional advantage: You can fetch mail from as many mailboxes as you want. Just add more `poll` lines to your *.fetchmailrc*, and *fetchmail* happily retrieves your mail from one server after the other.

When and how you run *fetchmail* depends on what kind of connection to the Internet you have. If you have a permanent connection or a cheap, flat rate, you might want to have *fetchmail* invoked by *cron* at a suitable interval (like once an hour). However, if your Internet connection is nonpermanent (dial-up) and costly, you might want to choose to run *fetchmail* by hand whenever you actually want to fetch and read your mail so as to minimize your Internet connection time. Finally, if you are using PPP for dialing in to your Internet service provider, you might want to invoke *fetchmail* from the *ip-up* script, which is invoked as soon as an Internet connection is made. With this setup, when you browse a web page and your computer dials up your provider, your mail is fetched automatically.

Other Email Administrative Issues

In this section we describe tasks, services, and some additional utilities involved in managing your electronic mail system.

You should normally use only one Internet host to get all your mail. It is possible to use a more complex arrangement, but this is frowned upon because of the possibility of setting up loops—virtual Sargasso Seas of lost network information. Loops can route mail in circles, passing over and over through the same machines until they "time out" by exceeding the limit on the number of machines they can pass through.

Registering an address

If you want to get your mail directly from the Internet, you need to register an Internet domain name for your system. You may have the domain name of your Internet connecting host, but you could have some other domain name entirely. It doesn't matter; the Domain Name System (DNS) database routes mail for your domain to your Internet host connection. We call this host your *gateway* connection. (If your system routes all mail back only to this gateway connection, your system is called a *leaf* system.)

In turn, the gateway host that connects you to the Internet normally holds your MX (mail exchanger) record. A host that holds an MX record for a system acts as the mail forwarder to that system. It must know the exact paths to deliver mail to all the machines in your domain, if you use more than one host as a mail host. The gateway host connects directly to your system, generally either by Ethernet or by UUCP connection over a switched telephone line.

Your own mail host should be configured so that all email not sent to the local host, or not otherwise sent directly to a host you connect to, is routed to your Internet mail gateway—your smart host.

[28] TCP/IP
[30] DNS
and BIND

The *Linux Network Administrator's Guide* tells how to register domain names, fill out MX records, and configure both sides of the gateway-leaf mail connection. Two other books that can help you manage your Internet connection are *TCP/IP Network Administration* and *DNS and BIND*.

It should be noted that registering a domain does not automatically imply that you'll be doing all the mail handling yourself. Many Internet service providers offer the service of registering a domain of your choice and then do all the mail handling for you, that is, you still get the mail in your mailbox.

Mail system maintenance

You should set up a *cron* task to occasionally check the mail queue (usually */var/spool/smail*) and force an attempt to deliver mail that wasn't previously delivered for some reason. Mail can be queued because a host is temporarily

Chapter 8

unreachable, or a filesystem is full, or for myriad other little reasons. *cron* is discussed in the section "Scheduling Jobs Using cron" in Chapter 8, *Other Administrative Tasks.*

The mail administrator also should occasionally check the mail queue and make sure there are no messages "stuck" there:

```
$ mailq -v
```

This command generates a report on any mail in the queue, along with log information that informs you if there is a persistent mail-delivery problem.

Installing Elm

Now you can get mail to your system, and it is sitting in a spool directory waiting to be read. Your last job is to install a mailer that provides a convenient interface for reading, composing, and filing mail messages.

The Elm mailer was created by Dave Taylor, of the Elm Development Group, and continues to be developed through the Usenet Community Trust. Copyrights on Elm are held by Dave Taylor and the Usenet Community Trust.

Elm isn't the most powerful mailer available, but it is robust and suits the needs of most users. It has a simple user interface with menus and built-in help. Most other screen-oriented mailers available on Linux support much the same basic mailer features, using a similar display interface. Once you know Elm, you can easily switch to another mailer if you find one more to your taste. Other popular text-mode mailers are *pine* and *mutt*; the supporters of the different mailers can start arguments that are no less violent than those between Emacs supporters and *vi* lovers. In addition, there are now also a great number of X-based GUI mailers that are often easier to set up and use than the traditional text-mode mailers like Elm. We will cover one of them, Netscape Messenger, later in this chapter.

In this discussion, we mention different directories and files that Elm uses. These are defaults; the mail administrator can set up some different locations, and each Elm user can change the setup of files and directories.

Preparing for installation

Before you install Elm, you should already have set up communications links to any UUCP and TCP/IP hosts with which you exchange mail directly. If these connections change, you may have to reinstall Elm or edit some files. During installation, you need to supply the Elm configuration program with essential data about the host domain name and system name, about the routing of mail, and so on. Specific information you need includes:

Domain name

If you are on the Internet, you need to register a domain name, or (more commonly) become part of an established domain—probably the domain of the host that will provide you with mail service and hold your MX record.

Hostname

This is the name of the mail host you are configuring.

Absolute name

This is the complete hostname, including the domain.

Locking methods

Elm uses mail spool files, and sometimes it needs to lock files. Elm supports UUCP "dotlock," locking, BSD *flock* locking, and System V *fcntl* locking. Linux possesses both *fcntl* and *flock* functions. If you are also using UUCP on your system, you need dotlock and you should also enable *fcntl* locking. Elm will ask you interactively when you run *Configure* what forms of locking to support.

Content-length control

MTAs can now transmit binary messages embedded in email. However, to do so, they cannot tolerate changes in message content by mailers. A Content-Length: header is used to specify the message length, and you should allow this header to be used. However, honoring Content-Length: headers requires that the mailer not insert escapes or buffering characters in front of instances of the text string From occurring at the start of a line.

Dot-message termination

By default, Elm turns off dot-termination of mail (where a line containing only a . causes the mailer to end the message). You don't want to enable dot termination if you enable content-length control, which you probably want to allow in the brave new multimedia world.

Before using *Configure* to install Elm, read the *Elm Configuration Guide* to make sure you have the answers you need to complete the process successfully. There are a number of lesser issues to decide in addition to the issues just mentioned. Some of them require knowledge of your Linux file tree, so you should investigate these first to avoid having to abort or reinstall later. You may also find it useful to refer to the chapter in the *Linux Network Administrator's Guide* that gives an introduction to electronic mail, for a broader view of electronic mail issues, including mail addressing and routing and use of UUCP as a mail-routing agent.

[4] Network Admin Guide

If you reinstall Elm, you may need to replace system alias files and have all the users replace their alias files. A *newalias* command is provided for the purpose and should be run by each Elm user.

Installation Procedure

First, get the latest released sources for Elm and put the source files in a build directory, such as */usr/local/bin/elm2.4*. Elm may have been included with your Linux distribution and could have been built when installing or reinstalling the Linux package. If this is the case, you should test the installation to make sure it is complete and up to date.

At least one major distribution of Linux that includes the Elm package includes only the executable and omits example configuration files and installation instructions. You can get the rest of the package (including documentation) through FTP sites that have the full package. These are not necessarily Linux source sites.

The Elm package contains a *Configure* shell script you should run to install Elm. A file named *Instruct* contains fundamental directions for installing the current version of Elm on your system, but it probably doesn't tell you the information you should have on hand when you run *Configure*. We'll try to tell you the needed key information, but if we miss something, reinstalling Elm is as easy as running *Configure* again. From your Elm build directory, as the **root** user, execute *Configure*:

```
# sh Configure
```

Configure installs localized configuration files after asking you some questions.

Next, you need to build the Elm document set:

```
# make documentation
```

Then run a full *make* process, building a log file and showing messages in case of *make* errors:

```
# make all > MAKELOG 2>&1 &
# tail -f MAKELOG
```

This assumes you are using the *bash* shell. If you use *csh* or *tcsh*, enter the *make* command this way:

```
% make all >& MAKELOG &
```

This process takes a while. On successful completion, you should find most of these commands in */usr/bin*: *answer, checkalias, elm, fastmail, filter, frm, listalias, messages, newalias, newmail, printmail,* and *readmsg*. There should also be equivalent online reference pages in */usr/man/man1* and */usr/man/man8*.

Next, install your software on the system:

```
# make install
```

As of the time of this writing (Elm Version 2.4), there is a known security risk with *arepdaemon* and *autoreply*. These should be removed from your system. The manual pages for these utilities should also be removed before you update your *whatis* database by running *makewhatis*. If you are using Elm 2.4 PL 24 or later, these programs have already been removed from the ELM distribution.

Before running Elm, read and dispose of any queued mail for the **root** user. You will be testing the Elm configuration as **root**, and you don't want to lose any pending messages.

Now test your installation by running Elm. First, check that Elm correctly detects that you have no existing mail (still as the **root** user):

```
# elm -z
```

Elm should display the message `no mail` and exit. (If there is mail for **root**, Elm will come up in interactive mode and list the messages at the Index screen.)

Next, check for correct mailbox handling. (Elm creates a test mail folder when it installs):

```
# elm -f test/test.mail
```

Exit without marking any messages for deletion. Elm should prompt you for correct handling of the messages.

Assume a nonprivileged user identity and run *elm −z*. Elm should not load unless there is pending mail. If there is pending mail and you have not previously had Elm installed (don't have a *$HOME/.elm* directory), Elm should prompt you to create the directory. You need to edit the *SYSTEM_ALIASES* file to set up at least one alias, defining the identity of the system postmaster so that mail sent to the postmaster at your site is handled correctly. Then, the *newaliases* command must be run to set up the aliases table. The procedure is described in the *Elm Configuration Guide* for your version of Elm.

Once you are satisfied that Elm is configured and installed properly, you can propagate the installation of Elm on your whole LAN, if you maintain mail services on more than one host. The directions for the *make* process are included in the *Instruct* file of the Elm distribution.

Elm documentation

There is a set of documents for Elm that may be useful for tuning Elm or building scripts for advanced mail management. The Elm document set on your system most likely matches the version of Elm you are running, which is a critical advantage. These are the guides available in the Elm document set:

Elm User's Guide
> Provides some history of Elm, fundamental usage, and credits for contributors to the continued development of Elm. This guide provides basic usage

information but is thin on concepts, some of which are described in the *Elm Reference Guide* or in other guides. Unless your version of Elm is later than Version 2.4, you probably won't need this except to satisfy your curiosity.

Elm Reference Guide

Discusses Elm and the options within the Elm environment, Elm advanced features and debugging, *elmrc* options file customization, and more. This guide provides some of the conceptual information that the *Elm User's Guide* omits as well as useful practical and conceptual information on various Elm features and utilities. This volume can be handy when configuring Elm, and it contains some information of interest only to mail administrators.

Elm Alias User's Guide

Tells how to set up and maintain mail aliases in Elm and the related files.

Elm Filter System User's Guide

Tells how to use Elm mail-filter utilities to automate some mail handling.

Elm Configuration Guide

Discusses all the available options of the current version of Elm to help you fine-tune your configuration. You can get into trouble if you rely only on this volume, so if you decide to tinker with some of the more arcane options, we recommend you change them one by one and test the results rather than make wholesale changes. This volume is of practical interest to mail administrators, though, who should use it in conjunction with a printout of a complete *elmrc* file and the *sysdefs.h* file on the system.

Elm Forms Mode Guide

Describes the use of AT&T Mail Forms, which Elm supports. This feature isn't useful to most Elm mail users, but if you need the feature, you need this guide as well.

Elm reference pages

Elm has online reference pages you can access using the *man* command for each utility that you can invoke from the command line and a reference page that describes files that Elm creates and uses in mail management. These are always useful, and you should use them generously at any time. They describe the command-line options for each command and provide technical detail that may not be available anywhere else. Some sites may keep these files in a printable format as well—in PostScript, text, or another format—so you can have them at hand for personal reference.

Elm also contains internal help, which is stored in a set of files you can print for convenient hardcopy reference. These files are:

elm-help.0

Help for Elm Actions (internal commands) available from the Index screen

elm-help.1
> Help for Elm Options (user customization) menu

elm-help.2
> Help for the Elm Alias menu

elm-help.3
> Help for Elm Actions available from the message display screen

Using Netscape Messenger

Netscape Navigator, the web browser that you learned about at the beginning of this chapter, is accompanied by a suite of other programs. These include the mailer, Netscape Messenger. If you have downloaded (or installed from your distribution media) the full Netscape Communicator package, you already have Netscape Messenger. If not, get Netscape Communicator, because Messenger is currently not available standalone.

Many people criticize Netscape Messenger for being slow and for missing some features. But on the other hand, Messenger is easy to set up and has some nice features like hierarchical folders and tight integration with the web browser.

Once you have installed Netscape Communicator, you can run the web browser Netscape Navigator as usual and then open up the Messenger window by selecting Messenger from the Communicator menu or by pressing the key combination Alt-2.

The Messenger window (see Figure 16-13) is divided by default into three parts. On the left, you see the tree of folders (at first startup, you will have only the default folders, of course), the upper part of the right side shows a listing of mails in the currently selected folder, and the lower part of the right side shows the currently selected mail. You can change how the space is distributed between these parts by dragging on the knob on the separator line between them.

Before you can first use Messenger, you have to set up some things first. Select Edit from the Preferences menu and then open the configuration group Mail & Newsgroups by clicking on the little arrow next to it. You have to fill out at least the Identity and Mail Servers forms. First click on Identity and enter your name and email address as indicated in the dialog box.

Next, click on Mail Servers. The upper half of the dialog box shows a list of mail servers that Messenger should retrieve mail from. Unfortunately, even though there is a whole list provided here, you can have only one mail server unless you use the IMAP protocol.

To configure an Incoming Mail Server, click on the Add . . . button and fill out the form that appears. Your system administrator or your Internet provider will be able to give you all the data you need. Note that you can choose between three server types. For POP3 and IMAP, you will have to specify your username and password

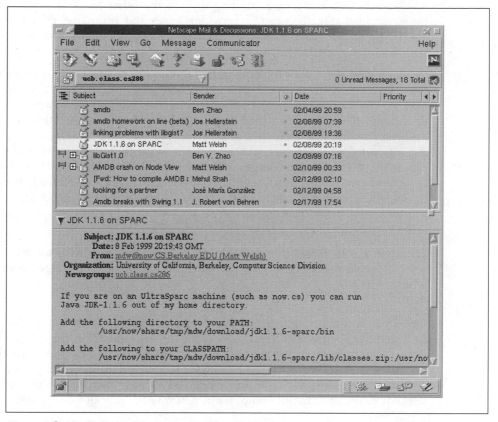

Figure 16–13: Netscape Messenger window

as they appear on your provider's server in addition to protocol-specific parameters. If you use one of those two server types, you do not need an MTA on your machine; Messenger automatically retrieves the mail and sorts the messages into your mail folders without any other programs intervening.

The option `movemail`, on the other hand, is used when you have set up other software like the MTA *smail* and the mail-fetching program *fetchmail*, both described earlier in this chapter. In this case, those programs will retrieve your mail and put them into your mail folder somewhere on your system, often */var/spool/mail/username*. In this case, tell Messenger where *movemail* should pick up your mail from.

The next thing to set up is the outgoing mail server. If you have set up your own SMTP server because you have installed an MTA, enter either `localhost` (if the SMTP is running on the same machine as Messenger) or the hostname of the machine the SMTP server is running on. On the other hand, if you want to send outgoing mail directly to your provider, enter the hostname of your provider's SMTP server here. Depending on your provider, you might also need to specify your account name here again.

Once you are done with the configuration, you can tell Messenger to get your mail from wherever you specified and sort it into your folders. This is done by either clicking the Get Msg toolbar button or selecting File/Get New Messages from the File menu. If you get your mail from a POP3 or IMAP server, Messenger will first ask you for your password and then fetch your mail. All messages will be put into the Inbox folder where you can read them, store them into other folders, or simply delete them. How messages are dealt with is quite intuitive. You will be able to guess most of the functionality from the user interface. But when you are in doubt, you can always use the Help menu which, when you select an entry, opens a browser window (or reuses an already existing one) and shows the documentation on Netscape's web server.

To write a mail message, press Alt-M, click on the New Msg toolbar button, or select Message/New Message from the Message menu. Messenger opens a form where you can enter the recipients, the subject and, of course, the text of your mail.

Once you are done editing your mail you can press Alt-Enter, click on the Send toolbar button, or select Send Now from the File menu of the composition window. Messenger then directly contacts the SMTP server that you have configured and tries to send your mail. Of course, if you are using your provider's SMTP server, this requires that you are connected to your provider at that time or that you have configured your computer or gateway to dial out on demand.

If you have configured Messenger to use your provider's SMTP server and you have only a dial-up connection to the Internet, you might want to use another nifty feature of Messenger: if you send your mail by pressing Alt-Shift-Enter or selecting Send Later from the composition window's File menu, the message is not directly sent out, but instead stored in the Unsent Messages folder. You can collect your messages there until you have opened an Internet collection and then send them all at once by choosing Send Unsent Messages from the File menu. This is especially useful if dialing up to the Internet is costly where you live, because you can save yourself a lot of connection time.

We have only scratched the surface of what Messenger can do, and you might want to experiment further with it. A fairly basic thing to try out is to create new folders by selecting New Subfolder... from the File menu and then have Messenger sort your incoming messages automatically into the folders by subject, sender, or a number of other criteria. Sorting is accomplished by a feature called filters, which you can configure by selecting Message Filters... from the Edit menu.

SOURCES OF LINUX INFORMATION

Bibliography

This appendix contains information on various online sources of Linux information. While all of these documents are available electronically from the Internet or BBS systems, many are also available in printed form. Many Linux distributions also include much of this documentation in the distribution itself, so after you have installed Linux, these files may be present on your system. The Bibliography lists a number of books and other materials that relate to topics we have discussed in this book.

The best place for free documentation on Linux is the Linux Documentation Project site, which Matt Welsh set up. The URL for the main site is:

> *http://www.linuxdoc.org*

but there are many mirror sites around the world, one of which may be more convenient for you because it's closer or has less traffic. The site contains all of the online Linux documents, manuals, HOWTOs, and pointers to many other locations.

Online Documents

These documents should be available on any of the Linux FTP archive sites. If you do not have direct access to FTP, you will probably also find them on any decent Linux distribution CD-ROM.

In particular, the following documents may be found on *ftp://metalab.unc.edu* in the directory */pub/Linux/docs*. Many sites mirror this directory; however, if you're unable to locate a mirror site near you, this is a good one to fall back on. HOW-TOs and Linux Documentation Project manuals are listed in the Bibliography, which also lists other useful documents:

The Linux Frequently Asked Questions List
> The Linux Frequently Asked Questions (FAQ) list is a list of common questions (and answers!) about Linux. This document is meant to provide a general source of information about Linux, common problems and solutions, and a list of other sources of information. Every new Linux user should read this document. It is available in a number of formats, including plain ASCII, PostScript,

and Lout typesetter format. The Linux FAQ is maintained by Robert Kiesling at *kiesling@ix.netcom.com*.

The Linux META-FAQ

The META-FAQ is a collection of "metaquestions" about Linux—that is, sources of information about the Linux system and other general topics. It is a good starting place for the Internet user wishing to find more information about the system. It is maintained by Michael K. Johnson at *johnsonm@red-hat.com*.

The Linux INFO-SHEET

The Linux INFO-SHEET is a technical introduction to the Linux system. It gives an overview of the system's features and available software and also provides a list of other sources of Linux information. The format and content is similar in nature to the META-FAQ; incidentally, it is also maintained by Michael K. Johnson.

The Linux Software Map

The Linux Software Map (LSM) is a list of many applications available for Linux—where to get them, who maintains them, and so forth. The list is far from complete; to compile a complete list of Linux software would be nearly impossible. However, it does include many of the most popular Linux software packages. If you can't find a particular application to suit your needs, the LSM is a good place to start. The LSM is maintained by Aaron Schrab at *Aaron.Schrab@execpc.com*.

The Linux HOWTO Index

The Linux HOWTOs are a collection of "how to" documents, each describing in detail a certain aspect of the Linux system. They are maintained by the Linux Documentation Project and the current maintainer can be reached through the email alias *linux-howto@metalab.unc.edu*. The HOWTO Index lists the available HOWTO documents; see the Bibliography for a partial list of HOWTOs.

Other online documents

If you browse the *docs* subdirectory of any Linux FTP site, you'll see many other documents that are not listed here: a slew of FAQs, interesting tidbits, and other important information. This miscellany is difficult to categorize here; if you don't see what you're looking for on this list, just take a look at one of the Linux archive sites.

Linux Documentation Project Manuals

The Linux Documentation Project is working on developing a set of manuals and other documentation for Linux, including manual pages. These manuals are in various stages of development, and any help revising and updating them is greatly appreciated.

These books are available via anonymous FTP from a number of Linux archive sites, including *ftp://metalab.unc.edu* in the directory */pub/Linux/docs/LDP*. A number of commercial distributors are selling printed copies of these books; you may already be able to find the LDP manuals on the shelves of your local bookstore. A complete list of manuals can be found in the Bibliography.

Linux News and Information Sites

Recently, a number of sites that feature news about Linux have been created. If you need to get your daily dose of Linuxish reading, try one (or more) of the following:

http://lwn.net

> Has articles and feature stories about different Linux-related topics.

http://www.linuxgazette.com

> Now a subsidiary of the print magazine *Linux Journal*, *Linux Gazette* does not contain news so much as articles about setting things up and finding your way through your Linux system. Mainly targetted at beginners to intermediary users.

http://www.linuxfocus.org

> Calls itself "the first and (for the moment) only multilingual magazine about Linux." Contains longer reviews and articles about Linux-related things in several languages.

http://linux.miningco.com

> Contains longer reviews and articles about Linux-related things; often very well written.

http://www.freshmeat.net

> A very useful list of new software available for Linux. If you are wondering whether the rest of the Linux community is sleeping or working, check this site and watch the new applications coming in.

http://slashdot.org

> Brings often updated headlines from computing in general (but with a focus on Linux and free software) and is probably best known for its bulletin-board system where people can comment on the news and on other comments. The low quality of some comments (both orthographic and content-wise) sometimes makes a sort of fun of its own. (This does not apply to the news themselves, though.)

http://www.chariott.com/linapps.html
> The *Linux Applications and Utilities Page* is a very useful list of Linux software, grouped by category. You won't find everything available here, but it is a very good start if you are looking for a piece of software for a certain task but do not know any product names. Contains both free and commercial software.

http://www.linux-center.org
> One more web site that collects Linux-related resources and is well organized.

http://www.linuxberg.com
> Lists thousands of Linux programs by category with short descriptions and a rating. It's more difficult to find something than at the *Linux Application and Utilities Page*, but is way more complete, too.

http://linas.org/linux/
> This page, *Linux Enterprise Computing*, lists many other resources about using Linux in commercial settings. Very worth looking through even if you don't plan to use Linux commercially.

http://sal.kachinatech.com
> On this page, *Scientific Applications on Linux*, you can find lists and descriptions of applications for using Linux in science and research, an area Linux is traditionally strong in.

http://www.debian.org, *http://www.redhat.com*, *http://www.calderasystems.com* and *http://www.suse.com*
> Web sites of various Linux distributors; you should find a lot of information about your distribution here.

General Software FTP Sites

Since most software that runs on Linux comes from existing, well-established sources like the Free Software Foundation and the Berkeley Software Distribution, you can obtain most of it by visiting just a few places on the Internet. If your distribution doesn't have a certain package you need, don't despair; try going to the original source.

Here are popular sites for the main sources of software that run on Linux; all are heavily loaded. The first thing you should do when getting to the site is look for a listing of mirror sites (other computer systems that download the software from the primary site on a regular basis) that is closer to you; a mirror site is usually easier to connect to and runs faster:

The Linux kernel itself
> *http://www.kernel.org*

General Linux Software Repository
> Site *ftp://metalab.unc.edu* in directory */pub/Linux*

GNU software (Free Software Foundation)
> Site *ftp://ftp.gnu.org* in directory */gnu*

X Window System
> Site *ftp://ftp.x.org* in directory */pub/R6.3**

XFree86
> Site *ftp://ftp.xfree86.org* in directory */pub/XFree86*

FreeBSD
> Site *ftp://ftp.freebsd.org* in directory */pub/FreeBSD/LOCAL_PORTS*

Requests For Comments

Proposals, standards, and other information have historically been passed around the Internet community through documents called Requests for Comments (RFCs). All RFCs are available via anonymous FTP or the Web. Any RFCs of interest to you are likely to be listed at *http://info.internet.isi.edu/in-notes/rfc/files/*. Since the listing is enormous, it's more efficient just to enter a URL in the form:

> *http://info.internet.isi.edu/in-notes/rfc/files/rfcn.txt*

where *n* is the number of the RFC.

The Bibliography lists a number of RFCs that interest Linux network administrators and users.

---

* Get information about the state of the release by retrieving */pub/R6/RELNOTES.TXT* or */pub/R6/RELNOTES.PS*.

THE GNOME PROJECT

*by Miguel de Icaza, Instituto de Ciencias
Nucleares, UNAM; Nat Friedman, International
GNOME Support; Federico Mena, Red Hat Soft-
ware; and Elliot Lee, Red Hat Software*

What Is GNOME?

Unix has never been considered an extremely user-friendly operating system. Because it was originally designed by programmers for programmers,
the primary interface has long been the command line. Although this is a
very powerful interface, it has a very steep learning curve, especially for people
who are not acquainted with computers.*

Then, the appearance of the X Window System brought forth a proliferation of
GUI toolkits. The result was twofold: Unix programmers suddenly had the ability
to create easy-to-use human-friendly software interfaces. But the market was fragmented; programmers were divided into many camps, each using a different GUI
toolkit. This fragmentation delayed the development and deployment of a standard
graphical interface and powerful graphical applications.

And fragmentation in the Unix world has had other consequences as well; while
Unix developers tried to unify their splintered marketplace, the Unix technology
and core design—originated in the 1970s—began to stagnate. Meanwhile, other
operating systems were keeping up with technological progress in areas which
Unix had long ignored.

The user interface is an important component of today's desktop systems, but a
full desktop system and its applications need a lot more to provide all the needed
consistency and all the features users expect from modern systems. A software
development infrastructure must be in place as well.

GNOME, which stands for GNU Network Object Model Environment, is the GNU
effort to address these problems. It consists of a set of libraries, component interfaces, and applications. The GNOME project provides Unix-like systems with the

---

* This article originally appeared in *Linux Magazine* and can be found on their web site at
  http://www.linux-mag.com. It has been minimally edited from the authors' version.

technologies that it has lacked for decades. But although GNOME is bringing new technologies to Unix, it is not a research project: the GNOME team develops and implements ideas that have been tried on other systems in the past and have been proven succesful. Of course, the team doesn't mind trying new ideas, but there is a lot of catching up to be done for the time being.

The Windowing System Foundation

Integrated operating systems like the MacOS or Microsoft Windows hide the fact that many programs work together to create the desktop. With Linux, it's necessary to know a little bit about how this illusion is created. Under Linux and other Unix-like operating systems, there are essentially three different software packages that work together in order to create a GUI environment.

The lowest level piece of software is the X Window System itself also called X11. X11 is the foundation software that interacts directly with the computer's hardware. It handles the interaction between input devices (keyboard and mouse) and output devices (monitor).

Higher-level applications can draw graphics to the screen and receive input from the keyboard and mouse by just talking to the X Window System. Individual applications don't have to know anything about how the hardware actually works. X is a standard component of most Unix-derivatives nowadays.

X does does this in a network-transparent fashion, which means that applications running under the X system can be running anywhere on the network.

The X Window System does not specify a policy for either the user interface used by each of the applications being displayed or by the decoration frame and window managing features. X actually relays the responsibility for managing windows to a special application called the Window Manager

The Window Manager controls the placement and appearance of windows on the screen. It works in coordination with X and instructs X where and how to draw windows. There are many window managers available that offer different customization options, but they all perform the same basic functions.

This is the way most people use X these days: the basic windowing system, a window manager, and some X applications.

The Role of GNOME

The user interface part of GNOME is built on top of the X foundation, and it consists roughly of:

The GNOME desktop system
> This is a set of tools that provides a desktop abstraction to users plus various utility applications for day-to-day work.

The GNOME application framework libraries
These libraries ensure that GNOME applications look and behave consistently.

Productivity GNOME applications
A number of productivity applications have been written as part of the GNOME project and they are distributed as part of the GNOME system.

The GNOME system can work with any window manager, but the desktop experience is enhanced if the window manager is GNOME-compliant. As of this writing, IceWM, *fvwm2*, Enlightenment, and WindowMaker are GNOME compliant.

GNOME is part of the GNU project. GNU stands for "GNU's not Unix" (it's a recursive acronym) and was a project begun in 1984 with the goal of creating a freely-redistributable Unix-like operating environment.

Aside from providing users with a friendly desktop and various productivity applications, GNOME addresses several important deficiencies encountered by Unix programmers:

- Lack of a framework for writing consistent and easy-to-use GUI applications

- Lack of inter-application communication standards

- Lack of a standard for writing interoperable, re-useable software components

- Lack of a standard printing architecture and high-quality imaging model

Before we explore how GNOME works its magic to solve these problems, a brief history of the project is in order.

A Brief History of the GNOME Project

Before the GNOME project as we know it was created, there were two earlier projects, the "libapp" project and the "old-GNOME" project. libapp was intended to supply programmers with a standardized method of storing, using, and retrieving various bits of information about the system and the user preferences; it was a library that anyone could use. On the other hand, Old-GNOME was aimed at providing Unix with a standard software component model, allowing programs to be used as components within other programs.

Chapter 11

When the KDE project (see "The K Desktop Environment" in Chapter 11, *Customizing Your X Environment*) emerged as a serious attempt to create a usable desktop environment for Unix, a number of people became worried about its licensing. The KDE team had chosen to build their project on top of the Qt GUI tool kit, which at that time was not truly free software. Although Qt has since changed its licensing terms and now qualifies as free software, at that time many people felt its use represented a step backwards for software freedom. This led to the emergence of the GNOME project as an attempt to develop a completely free desktop environment based on the original old-GNOME and libapp ideas.

Another important goal of the GNOME project was to make sure that the work done on any foundation libraries could be used from every programming language in Unix. To successfully create this standard, it was essential that every programmer had access to these technologies, no matter the choice of programming language.

The people on the original GNOME team had a good mix of backgrounds revolving around free software issues, graphics, and programming language design. The original team included the programmers who worked on the GNU Image Manipulation Program (the GIMP), Peter Mattis and Spencer Kimball. Richard Stallman, the founder of the GNU project, was involved, as were Erik Troan and Mark Ewing of Red Hat Software. Additionally, there were significant contributions from the members of the Free Software and GUILE mailing lists. (GUILE is GNU's Unique Intelligent Language for Extensions, a programming language that can be embedded in other programs to make them extensible through scripting. GUILE was one of the first scripting languages that could be used with GNOME.)

Since the project's inception, there have been regular releases of the GNOME source code base. After 18 months of development, GNOME 1.0 was officially released in March 1999. Updates and bug fixes are already being released on a continual basis, and as of this writing, the GNOME 1.0 series is at version 1.0.10.

GNOME 1.0 is a significant milestone in the history of the project because it represents a contract between the GNOME development team, independent software developers, and users everywhere. Release 1.0 provides a stable Application Programming Interface (API), on top of which new applications can be developed. Independent developers can take advantage of all the functions available in the libraries while feeling assured that their applications will continue to work in the future.

The GNOME Desktop: A User's Point of View

GNOME gives users an intuitive desktop metaphor, a file manager, an easy way to launch applications installed on the system, and built-in support for themes, which allow users to change the aesthetic characteristics of their desktop and applications. For example, the "steel" theme makes the desktop and applications appear to be made of steel, and a "wooden" theme makes them appear to be made of wood. Various desktop productivity tools such as a calendar, calculator, address book and spreadsheet are also included. The user can easily change the look of their applications by using the GNOME control center. Most GNOME distributions include numerous pre-designed desktop themes. Many other contributed themes can be found at *http://gtk.themes.org*, a web site dedicated to themes.

The GNOME desktop provides a number of powerful shortcuts that make it easy to interact with the computer. One of these is support for drag and drop: a file can be dropped onto the desktop to create a shortcut to it; a picture can be dropped onto the desktop setup program to change the desktop background; a color can be dragged from the color selector to the panel to change its background; and documents can be dragged onto the printer icon to print them.

Another key feature is GNOME's support for session management, which allows GNOME to remember the state of the desktop between logins. So, when users log in, they see the same desktop and running applications that were in use when they last logged off. In addition, GNOME applications can work together, by sharing a common clipboard, for example.

Some GNOME Applications

An increasing number of GNOME-compliant applications have become available. Some of the most popular include:

DIA
> An application for creating all sorts of sophisticated diagrams.

The GIMP

Chapter 9

> The GNU Image Manipulation Program (the project that started it all), described in Chapter 9, *Editors, Text Tools, Graphics, and Printing*. The GIMP is a powerful image editing and painting application. It performs common image manipulation functions such as painting, color correction, and cropping. It also supports advanced features such as layers and selections and is extensible via a sophisticated plug-in system. The plug-ins are separate programs that provide specialized image manipulation functions or special effects.

Gnumeric
> A powerful spreadsheet application. Gnumeric has all the features you would expect from any commercial offering but is free software. An exceptionally useful feature of Gnumeric is its ability to import and export Microsoft Excel files. For more information, check out *http://www.gnome.org/gnumeric*.

Guppi
> A basic graphics application. This is also the tool that Gnumeric uses to plot graphics.

AbiWord
> A full-featured word processor that uses the GNOME libraries as its engine and in the future will take full advantage of all of GNOME's component technology. This means users will be able to link and embed spreadsheets from Gnumeric or graphics from the GIMP into AbiWord documents or link AbiWord documents back into those programs.

GNOME as a Development Platform

While GNOME can certainly make Unix-based operating systems more palatable to ordinary users, the GNOME team devotes a lot of energy to making GNOME fun to hack on, too.

From the developer's perspective, GNOME is made up of a set of core libraries, an infrastructure for component programming, and a set of reusable language-neutral components.

The GNOME Foundation Libraries

Many powerful features work across all GNOME applications in a standardized way, thanks to these libraries.

GTK+ (GIMP toolkit)

GTK+ is GNOME's object oriented graphics toolkit. It was originally designed by the GIMP programmers to simplify their work in building the GIMP. GTK+ was chosen for GNOME primarily because it implemented an object system rich in functionality and it already had interface bindings for a wide range of programming languages. This meant that GTK+ already went a long way towards achieving GNOME's goal of programming language neutrality. For more information, see *http://www.gtk.org*.

Guidelines have been developed that specify the method for adding new language bindings (wrappers) for the GTK+/GNOME libraries. Developers following these guidelines have contributed support for a number of languages, including C++, Objective-C, TOM, PERL, Python, GUILE, ADA, and others. Other bindings are in various stages of development, which is understandable, considering the large number of libraries that make up GNOME.

GTK+'s object system is very elegant in its design and allows for classical single-inheritance, dynamic creation of new methods and classes, and a signal mechanism that dynamically attaches signal handlers to events that occur in the user interface (e.g., a mouse click).

Another reason for choosing GTK+ is that it advances the second goal of the project—to create an intuitive desktop metaphor. It does this by providing support for two drag-and-drop protocols—Xdnd (X Drag and Drop) and Motif DnD. This makes it possible to drag and drop objects between programs written in GNOME (like the desktop), and programs that were written using other tools (like Netscape). Because all this is handled by GTK+, application writers get this functionality for free.

Imlib

This is an imaging library and engine that provides for fast loading, saving, and displaying of images. Imlib provides sophisticated image caching and color-management functions which operate efficiently even on low-end displays or 8-bit video cards. Due to limitations in X's color management scheme, developers writing directly to the X Window System libraries and artists creating icons or images for X need to be concerned about how many colors a given image might use. Imlib frees them from these worries by providing automatic color reduction and dithering facilities.

XML/DOM libraries

The WWW Consortium (the organization that ratifies standards for the World Wide Web) recently introduced two new standards: XML and DOM. XML is the eXtensible Mark-up Language, which can be used to describe and create other mark-up languages such as HTML. With a well-written XML library in-place, GNOME developers can very easily add support to their applications for portably loading and saving structured data. DOM (Document Object Model) is a model that describes how applications can modify chunks of data in an XML document. Implementing these standards as a GNOME library makes it easier for programmers to write XML/DOM aware applications.

The Canvas/Libart engines

The Canvas is an engine for creating structured graphics that allows programmers to easily create interactive graphics displays. Its features include unlimited scrolling and completely flicker-free operation. The programmer simply creates a canvas item (stock items include text, images, polygons, and Gtk widgets) and specifies its location. The Canvas handles the rest.

The Canvas is designed to be an extensible, but generic, display engine. The Gnumeric spreadsheet application, for example, uses the Canvas to display the spreadsheet but provides its own custom extensions. Applications like the GNOME calendar and the Midnight Commander file manager use the basic functionality of the canvas in their displays.

Libart is a vector manipulation and rendering engine that uses anti-aliasing and alpha-compositing. The canvas is built upon Libart, which it uses to render its objects into an RGB buffer. Libart makes it easy for the canvas to create anti-aliased, alpha-composited output. Libart provides a superset of the PostScript imaging model for extremely high-quality output.

The Bonobo component and document model

Bonobo is the name of the GNOME project to create a component model and a standard for the interactions between the components of a compound document.

It's a framework similar in concept to Microsoft's Object Linking and Embedding (OLE). Bonobo allows programmers to create reusable software component objects (similar to Active X Controls). It is also a document model that defines a system where these objects can seamlessly interact within shared container documents (Similar to Linking and Embedding).

To use an example that many people are familiar with, in Microsoft Office, an Excel document can be embedded within a Word document. The Word document in this case is a container document. It contains both the Word data and the Excel data. However, clicking on the Excel data allows you to work on it as though you were working in Excel, even though it is embedded in the Word document. The Excel application functions as a piece of component software, creating the illusion that the user is only interacting with one application.

Bonobo is a set of CORBA interfaces that are necessary for component design and interaction. The Bonobo interfaces are both language- and toolkit-independent, and Bonobo components can be both written and used in any language. The reference implementation of Bonobo is based on the Gtk object system and maps CORBA interfaces to Gtk objects which can be easily manipulated by the application author.

Note that while many programmers associate OLE with great complexity, much of that is due to the way Microsoft was forced to design OLE so that it would work well with Windows. While sharing much of the same functionality as OLE, Bonobo is inherently a much simpler system to understand and design software with.

The Common Object Request Broker Architecture (CORBA)

Unix has long been praised for making it easy for users to take a bunch of small filter programs (like *grep* and *sed*) and tie them together using pipes to compose a more complex, makeshift application. Sadly, pipes and filters do not scale to more complex applications (especially graphical applications). GNOME is an environment in which software objects can talk to each other (even over networks) in a standard fashion without knowing anything about each other. This is made possible by GNOME's CORBA foundation.

CORBA is a software system based on completely open standards, specifying methods for software objects to interact with each other. These objects speak to each other through an Object Request Broker (ORB), which directs traffic between all of the different pieces of software. The CORBA standard specifies the functionality that an ORB must provide to client programs that make requests of it. The objects don't need to know anything about each other; they can be programs that can be written in different languages and perform different functions, and they can even be located on different machines. As long as they communicate through the ORB, they can all speak to each other.

CORBA is woven throughout GNOME and provides application developers with a rich set of services. Among them are:

A general IPC mechanism (Inter-Process Communication)

In the past, it was quite common in a Unix environment for programmers to invent a customized protocol in order for two applications to communicate. Needless to say, the situation did not do much to encourage software reuse or interoperability. Now, whenever GNOME applications need to communicate, they can just use CORBA.

A means of exporting an application's internal engine

Many applications in GNOME export their internal functionality to the outside world. This allows other programs—both GNOME and non-GNOME—to use the services exported by an application, making these applications especially accessible to scripting languages. In particular, exporting makes these applications accessible to scripting languages so that advanced users can write scripts that automate common tasks. In the not-too-distant future, the user will be able to write a Python script to manipulate a Gnumeric spreadsheet, perform customized spell checking, or automate repetitive presentation creation tasks. This is similar to the functionality that Microsoft's Visual Basic provides Microsoft Office under Windows. The Guppi graphics application, the file manager, and the Gnumeric spreadsheet are currently scriptable in this fashion.

A method for creating re-usable, interoperable software components

As previously mentioned, the Bonobo component and document model expands upon the services CORBA offers, creating a framework that offers both programmers and users a very high level of flexibility.

CORBA is a series of specifications for designing Object Request Brokers (ORBs), but it is not an actual piece of software. Many ORBs have been written to the CORBA specification, but they are all implemented differently, and not all of those ORBs suit every software project's needs. The GNOME team spent a long time searching for a suitable CORBA implementation. It required an ORB that supported C language bindings and that was both thin and fast. Eventually, a decision was made to write a CORBA ORB from scratch. Dick Porter, Elliot Lee (while working for Red Hat Labs), and Andrew Veliath wrote an all new high-performance CORBA ORB named ORBit. ORBit finally provides the plumbing that allows you to deploy CORBA throghout GNOME. It is described at *http://www.labs.red-hat.com/orbit.*

Programming Tools

As the GNOME system matures, new development tools are emerging to aid developers in designing GUI applications. Of particular interest is Damon Chaplin's Glade. Glade greatly simplifies the creation of complex UIs in much the same way that NeXT's Interface Builder simplifies this task under NeXTStep.

Databases can now be accessed in a uniform fashion through GNOME DB, which is a modified CORBA interface to various databases. GNOME DB also includes a designer front-end. This project is being managed by Michael Lausch, who handles the back-end and CORBA elements, and Rodrigo Moya, who is writing the GUI-builder code.

The GNOME Printing Architecture

The free software community, and Unix in general, have long lacked a standard printing architecture and high-quality imaging model. GNOME provides a sophisticated printing engine intended to standardize the way applications print.

GNOME-print (*http://www.levien.com/gnome/print-arch.html*) is the implementation of GNOME's printing architecture. It consists of a pluggable rendering engine and a set of standard widgets and dialog boxes for selecting and configuring printers. In addition, GNOME-print is responsible for managing outline fonts and contains scripts that automatically find fonts already installed on the system.

The GNOME-print imaging model is based upon the PostScript imaging model. Basic operations include vector and bezier path construction, stroking, filling, clipping, text printing (using Type1 fonts, with TrueType to follow shortly), and image printing.

At the time of this writing, GNOME-print generates only PostScript output. However, the design of the imaging model is closely linked to the rendering engine for the Canvas, and it is expected that these two modules will soon be interoperable. In particular, it will be possible to print into a Canvas, which is useful for providing a high quality print preview, and it will also be possible to print the contents of a Canvas. This feature should simplify the design of applications that use the Canvas, as very little extra code will be needed to support printing.

The GNOME-print engine will also be used to render printed pages directly without going through an intermediate PostScript step. This is especially exciting because it will allow high quality, high performance printing of complex pages to color inkjet printers. Complex pages could include transparency, gradients, and other elements considered tricky in the traditional PostScript imaging model.

Getting and Installing GNOME

Tested source code releases of GNOME are available at *ftp://ftp.gnome.org/pub/ GNOME.*

It is also possible to get the very latest GNOME developments from the anonymous CVS servers. Check the GNOME web page at *http://www.gnome.org* for details on how to pull the latest version straight from the CVS servers.

Fast-breaking news about GNOME is also posted to the GNOME web site, along with documents to get you started on installing GNOME and developing GNOME applications. If you are in need of assistance, check out the GNOME FAQ.

The Future of GNOME

The GNOME system is constantly being updated, fixed, and improved. Following the lead of other free software projects such as Linux, the GNOME team maintains two branches of the GNOME software. New technologies are distributed in a development branch which developers can use and experiment with. As the technologies mature and the software becomes more stable, the code is released with the stable branch, which is targeted at deployed systems.

The evolution of GNOME is not decided by one person or a comittee: GNOME evolves in the direction that the GNOME programmers consider important or interesting. And you can be one of those programmers; the GNOME team welcomes your code, patches, opinions, and help.

How Can You Help with GNOME?

The GNOME project welcomes people who want to assist in creating the best possible Open Source desktop environment. There are opportunities for all kinds of talent to be utilized. Programmers can help writing programs and reviewing existing code or updating or maintain the programs. Language teams can make sure that the GNOME system contains up-to-date translations for their languages. Other people can contribute to the project in many ways: helping other GNOME users; getting proprietary-based business to realize the importance of free software; documenting the system; and communicating to other people what is GNOME all about.

If you would like more information on how you can help out, please email *webmaster@gnome.org.*

INSTALLING LINUX ON DIGITAL/ COMPAQ ALPHA SYSTEMS

by Barrett G. Lyon, Lar Kaufman, and Richard Payne

In 1992, Digital introduced a 64-bit, superscaler, RISC-based architecture called the Alpha, winning impressive reviews in the industry for speed. Linux is an attractive alternative to the official operating systems shipped with the Alpha. But installation varies from system to system because the Alpha has evolved rapidly and has been shipped over the years with a wide variety of hardware and firmware (startup programs stored in ROM). This appendix is an introduction to the main issues and tasks in installing Linux, but you will also need to carefully read the documents for Linux installation and your hardware, and show a somewhat adventurous willingness to experiment.

A discussion of Alpha systems must cover years of hardware evolution from the older style UDB system to the current DS and AS series systems, as well as standard OEM configurations. Because there are so many different BIOS configurations and boot options, it's impossible to give detailed installation instructions for every type of Alpha system. We hope this discussion will be a guide to help users who are new to the Alpha architecture understand what to do when installing a new system.

NOTE   This discussion does not cover VAX, MIPS, AMD, or Intel CPU-based systems or hardware that share peripheral and packaging technologies with Alpha-based systems. We will focus only on the installation of Linux on Alpha systems and components manufactured by Compaq or licensees of Alpha technology, such as Samsung Semiconductor USA or Mitsubishi Semiconductor.

Alpha History and Status

In 1992, Digital Equipment Corporation, also known as DEC or Digital, introduced the Alpha with support for seven hardware platforms, three operating systems, multiple networking protocols, and multiple language compilers.

The Alpha constitutes the largest engineering project ever undertaken by Digital, involving more than 30 engineering groups spread across 10 countries. It was not the first RISC-based semiconductor that Digital produced, but it was the first that Digital decided to sell in the open market. Digital Semiconductor (DS) was created as an internal business group to manufacture, sell, and distribute Digital's semiconductors on the merchant market.

To keep up with demand and evolving semiconductor manufacturing technology, Digital outsourced manufacturing of the Alpha semiconductor, which included agreements with Samsung Electronics and Mitsubishi Electric to manufacturer current and future implementations of the Alpha semiconductors. In addition, the agreements granted Samsung and Mitsubishi licenses to market, sell, and distribute Alpha semiconductors worldwide and included joint development projects related to the Alpha semiconductor family.

The relatively small installed base of Alpha systems and the fact that most existing systems are "development platforms" that allow tinkering and tuning supported by massive archives of hardware documentation have encouraged continued development of Alpha chipsets. However, it also makes it hard for Linux developers to gather the wide range of systems under one simple installation procedure.

Compaq had its eyes set on having its own enterprise server architecture and operating system—an alternative to Microsoft and Intel. On January 26, 1998, Digital and the Compaq Computer Corporation announced a $9.6 billion-dollar merger where Digital became a wholly owned subsidiary of Compaq. DS came with the multibillion dollar package, and the name Digital was absorbed into Compaq as a brand name.

To summarize, Alpha architecture is a superscaler, open-industry standard, 64-bit, RISC-based architecture that is engineered by Compaq and manufactured in volume by Samsung, Mitsubishi, and their subsidiaries.

The Linux Port

The Alpha port of Linux did not happen overnight. It began as a rather humble patch to the Linux kernel. The first kernel patch was developed with funding and support from Digital. Even with all the patches to the kernel, most of the drivers and "userland" of distributions were not "64-bit clean." The mainstream kernel itself was not 64-bit clean until the 2.1.x development kernels. When development work on the 2.1.x kernels began, the Alpha port was adopted directly into the Linux kernel source tree. At this stage, the Alpha port of the Linux kernel was supported directly by the mainstream kernel distributions.

During the development efforts of the 2.1.x kernel, the Linux kernel and its drivers were made 64-bit clean. Most of the unaligned traps in the kernel were corrected, and the userland became much more 64-bit aware. At this time, Red Hat Software, Inc., quickly saw that 64-bit architecture was the direction of the semiconductor market and released a full Alpha port of their Linux distribution, Red Hat Linux 2.1. Other distributions followed, including Debian and SuSE. The distributions are described in the following list:

Debian

The Debian Linux distribution is the "official" Free Software Foundation GNU/Linux distribution, providing extensive GNU software solutions by preference when choices are available. A vendor-packaged GNU/Linux distribution is under development by Stampede Software and has a full Alpha port. See *http://www.debian.org* or *http://www.stampede.com.*

Red Hat

Red Hat Software, Inc. puts together one of the larger distributions of Linux. It supports many useful features such as RPM for package management and has a full Alpha port of all of its current releases. See *http://www.redhat.com.*

SuSE

SuSE's Linux distributions are developed with attention to internationalization needs and graphics interface support. (SuSE is sensitive to European market needs.) SuSE also uses RPM to provide updates and has a full Alpha port. See *http://www.suse.com.*

Identifying Your Alpha System

There are many different Alpha systems, each requiring different installation methods. Because different Linux kernels are compiled to meet these variations in CPU and system designs, you must identify your Alpha hardware to correctly choose boot disks and kernel disks for various distributions.

Before you install an operating system, you must know the machine's graphics options and audio components, system memory, CPU class, disk-drive interfaces and sizes, existing operating systems/filesystems (if any), and attached peripherals, especially any CD-ROM drive and floppy drives. Some Alpha systems require firmware configuration changes and even actual hardware changes to complete a Linux installation.

Which Linux distribution you choose to install may depend on the hardware you have and any other operating systems that you run on it. After you gather your hardware information, you can determine which distribution best suits your needs. You can always build any source packages from other installations once you have a bootable system. Here are a few examples of hardware factors that dictate your choice of distribution or method of installation:

- Some Alpha systems require setting jumpers to load Linux and install it as a native, firmware-bootable operating system.

- If your system has no floppy disk drive, you may not be able to install the Linux distribution you want on your system, because of firmware constraints in supporting filesystems and devices on systems that do not have floppy disk devices. We recommend that you install or attach a floppy drive to your system. If your system's floppy drive simply "died," it's very inexpensive to replace.*

- If your Linux installation shares the computer with another operating system (installed on different hard-disk partitions or different hard disks), different versions of Linux offer different levels of filesystem and utility compatibility with co-resident operating systems. For example, if you want to run Tru64 Unix (Digital Unix, or DU) on your system as well as the Debian Linux Alpha distribution, their default disk filesystem, partitioning, and labeling would conflict. Likewise, if you apply BSD-style disk labeling from Linux, that partition will not be accepted as valid by DU. If you want to set up Linux co-resident with another operating system on an Alpha system, the safest way is to partition the disk from within that operating system and define the partition for Linux to be installed to.

- The Linux *fdisk* utility fails to label DOSFS filesystems so that SRM and other firmware utilities will access them. Therefore, as a general rule, format your MS-DOS diskettes for configuring your system using MS-DOS or Windows NT (or buy preformatted MS-DOS diskettes).

- The first time you install Linux on older machines (especially UDB/Multias), your installation may fail if your system's internal battery is not charged. Reports of motherboards shipped from a vendor with a dead battery are common. Some systems have a rechargeable battery that nevertheless will not recharge on a powered-up system if the battery is discharged when the system is turned on. For instance, the monitor will not work, and firmware changes that you need to complete a self-booting installation will not be saved.

Once you have gathered your hardware data and selected your Linux distribution, choose your installation method. Alpha systems vary more than typical PC systems (having been engineered to be used as everything from basic display terminals to supercomputers), so you should evaluate your hardware and choose the booting method you will use with your Linux distribution. Otherwise, you may find that

---

* Even the extra-thin 3.5 inch floppy used in the older Multia and Alphabook 1 "systems" can be replaced with a standard laptop drive. On newer Alpha systems hardware, most hardware is interchangeable with standard OEM PC hardware.

you cannot complete the installation as you expected, or that Linux will be difficult to boot without rebuilding the installation.

Most Alpha installations use Milo, which is the easiest and most reliable method for installing Linux. The Milo utility is a mini-kernel that shares some of the same low-level PALcode (the language in which the firmware of an Alpha system is written) with the Linux kernel. Milo passes its hardware configuration definitions to Linux when it bootstraps the kernel, and Linux uses those definitions to interface with the PALcode segment that is co-resident in system memory with the Linux kernel. While there are alternatives to the Milo miniloader, you cannot use the usual Intel Linux boot management utilities to prepare an Alpha system for Linux installation, because they cannot provide the necessary firmware interface support.

If you add a CD-ROM drive to your system to install Linux, check your hardware documentation and Linux package documentation to determine that the CD-ROM will be recognized natively in the BIOS or that your Milo loader will support that drive. Standard SCSI CD-ROM drives are supported by Milo using integral SCSI controllers and several popular add-on controllers,* and an ATAPI(EIDE) CD-ROM is supported for some systems, especially those with a built-in ATAPI controller. But if the CD-ROM drive is not accessible as a native drive expected on a particular system, your system firmware or the Milo miniloader that bootstraps the Linux kernel may not recognize it.

Although network installation of Linux (storing the files on one machine and downloading them over the network to the machine where you want Linux to run) should be possible, major distributions have had persistent problems supporting this capability. We are not going to describe the technique. We assume you are installing Linux on a stand-alone Alpha system. You can configure it for network use later.

NOTE Configuring and setting booting behavior on some older Alpha systems requires changing jumper settings on the motherboard or changing system data stored in nonvolatile RAM, or both. You may need to change jumper settings initially for installation and again afterward to configure the system.

In typical Linux CD-ROM installation, you generally proceed as follows:

1. Collect system hardware information to select the correct installation files and procedures. Look at your system hardware manuals or system administration manuals. Get bug reports and review patches to the current software distribution that you will use to install your package. Collect current software

---

* The current Red Hat distribution of Milo recognizes the NCR 810 family of SCSI controllers; Adaptec1740, 2940, and 3940 series SCSI controllers; and QLOGIC ISP controllers. The Milo SHOW command causes Milo to display a list of its supported devices.

installation documentation if you believe the information provided by the vendor is obsolete or incomplete.

2. Consider the size of your hard-disk drives and decide how they are (or will be) partitioned for Linux. "Drives and Partitions Under Linux" in Chapter 3, *Installation and Initial Configuration* , offers basic considerations for allocating disk space and partitioning, although you must adjust the numbers for Alpha. The installation utilities that you choose will support one or another disk-partitioning method, but cannot be used for all partitioning requirements.

Chapter 3

3. Determine how you want Linux to boot when the installation is complete. This may affect your choice of installation method.

4. Choose your Linux installation method based on your hardware and its firmware, your disk-partitioning requirements, and Linux's booting behavior. For almost all installations, we think that Milo is the best firmware utility for loading Linux.

5. Create the correct data diskettes (Milo, kernel image, and ramdisk image) diskettes for your system.

6. Configure your system hardware as needed to support the installation of Linux.

7. If you use the usual Milo installation procedure, create the correct Milo image diskette for your system.

8. Power up the system, access its console (older systems use ARC, while newer ones use AlphaBIOS or SRM as described later), and load your Linux loader (usually the LINLOAD.EXE program, which is then used to load Milo). If you have Windows NT installed on your system, you can use the NT OSloader to load Milo; otherwise you will use system firmware to load a bootstrap loader that will then be used to prepare the system to install Linux.

9. Load Milo, use Milo to boot the kernel, and run the CD-ROM installation program.

10. Perform any additional disk partitioning and formatting for your system booting requirements.

11. Load additional Linux utilities, applications, compilers, and programming languages or libraries. Recompiling a current, stable release of the Linux kernel tailored to your system requirements is highly recommended.

12. When you are happy with your Linux installation, set it up to autoboot or boot from a boot manager selection menu. For some older systems, this may also require setting jumpers. Most systems require changes in the firmware console or installation of a bootstrap program (probably a Milo version) in system nonvolatile RAM.

An alternate procedure is required for those systems that Milo cannot configure; these alternatives are dependent on your system configuration and maintenance firmware. Like other systems, each Alpha contains at least one firmware program stored in system ROM or flash ROM that provides a configuration-program execution environment. Systems set up for Tru64 Unix or Open VMS have a System Reference Maintenance console or SRM. Systems set up for Windows NT usually have the Alpha Reference Console (ARC) firmware. Newer systems may have an AlphaBIOS instead of ARC; SRM is usually provided if the system was sold with DU.

NOTE   Firmware programs are small and efficient. Alpha system ROMs typically include space to hold several of them, along with other essential programs, such as debugging and diagnostic tools (which should not be overwritten).

Once Linux is installed, many systems provide a flash-RAM management utility (FMU) to allow you to "blow" a Milo image into system nonvolatile RAM. Other such utilities may come with your purchase of a commercial OS release or a developer package. Some are distributed on an EPROM chip that you install. Because ARC and AlphaBIOS firmware provide a graphical interface environment, they take more space, and you will not find both of them on a standard system. AlphaBIOS is a replacement for ARC that attempts to make OS installation on Alpha systems more uniform and automatic—more like OS installation on an Intel-architectured PC.

Booting Linux can be made as automatic as booting MS-DOS or Windows. We do not recommend that you use an FMU until you are satisfied with your tuned-up Linux installation.

Because all systems that are configured to run Windows NT are provided with a floppy drive that Milo can use to install Linux, the two main installation paths involve Milo (and ARC or AlphaBIOS), SRM and Milo, or other loader utilities. We focus on Milo-based installation methods for consistent and predictable results and offer an installation solution for any significant Alpha platform. If you do not like the specific solution that we describe, you will learn about other installation options as you review your resource materials.

Limitations of ARC Firmware

Most older systems have ARC firmware to set up hardware configurations, specify boot options, and perform other system maintenance tasks. This firmware is the usual starting point for installing Linux. It has several limitations. It knows how to access files only in MS-DOS, HPFS, and ISO9660 filesystems. When accessing files in MS-DOS or ISO9660, the system only recognizes 8.3 filenames. ARC offers a simple menu-driven console interface for managing your system hardware.

Limitations of AlphaBIOS Firmware

Newer systems use AlphaBIOS firmware instead of ARC. AlphaBIOS firmware is still in active development. If your system has AlphaBIOS, install the latest AlphaBIOS firmware update before installing Linux. AlphaBIOS knows how to access files only in MS-DOS and ISO9660 filesystems. When accessing files, the system only recognizes 8.3 filenames. AlphaBIOS implements a graphical interface for system configuration.

Limitations of the SRM Console Firmware

The SRM console can load data from IDE/ATAPI, SCSI, or floppy drives. It uses a system's native SCSI drive controller to access a recognized SCSI device for booting. SRM can read a SCSI floppy drive. SRM can access authentic MS-DOS–format filesystems (but not those created by Linux *fdisk*), BSD-labeled UFS filesystems (but not BSD-style filesystems labeled by Linux), and ISO9660 filesystems. An SRM console is available firmware for any system that does not provide or have ARC or AlphaBIOS.

The SRM console allows you to boot the system by transferring control to the secondary bootstrap loader that it loads blindly. SRM knows little about disk partitions or filesystems and treats disk devices as block devices. It reads from the first 512-byte sector of the storage device. This sector should contain a sector address and offset from which SRM can begin reading the size of data block. SRM goes to that location and loads contiguous data into memory. The data should be an image file of the secondary loader that boots the system.

Alpha systems usually have two secondary waders: the "raw" loader from the Linux kernel and the separate *aboot* utility. The *aboot* utility is more flexible than the raw loader if you must install Linux using the SRM console. However, you can use the SRM console to load the Milo loader for a more consistent installation procedure. Some machines do not currently have a MILO available (DS20), so, in those cases, using SRM and a secondary boot loader is mandatory.

When you use SRM and *aboot* to boot Linux, the first partition of the disk should start at cylinder number 2. This leaves room at the beginning of the disk to install *aboot*. The third partition on the disk (partition C) should be the entire size of the disk, from cylinder 1 to the end. The SRM Howto provides more information for those who will install using SRM and *aboot* at *http://www.alphalinux.org/faq/ srm.html.*

Limitations of Milo Miniloader

The Milo miniloader does not know how to boot itself from disk before booting Linux; it must be initially loaded either from system flash memory or from disk using an operating system loader (OSloader) developed for Alpha systems, such as Windows NT Alpha's boot manager. Linux distributions provide *linload.exe.*

When Milo is loaded from disk, it is bootstrap-loaded by ARC, AlphaBIOS, or SRM console after you use *linload.exe*. *linload.exe* knows MS-DOS (FAT) filesystems, but does not recognize HPFS or VMS filesystems. Milo is apparently limited to MS-DOS, ISO9660, and *ext2* filesystems when it has been loaded by *linload.exe*.

Milo will read *ext2* filesystems by default and can load operating system images in ISO9660 or MS-DOS (FAT) formats using a command-line option. Milo should load compressed kernel image files made using *gzip*, if given the full filename (e.g., *vmlinux.gz*), but we have found that at least some Milo distributions cannot process such files, at least not when loaded from ISO9660 or MS-DOS filesystems. For more information go to *http://www.alphalinux.org/faq/milo.html*.

Collecting System Hardware Information

Before you choose a Linux distribution, use the considerable resources about Linux and Alpha on the Internet. Indeed, a wealth of detailed hardware information about Alpha chips and platforms designed to support it are available for downloading and printing, including generously supplied technical manuals that would be expensive to purchase (or unavailable) through marketing channels. Be aware that much useful documentation may be supplied by a different vendor than the manufacturer of your CPU or system and from other distribution resources as well.

Sources of Information

Following is a partial list of important Internet sources for Alpha hardware information and information about installing Linux on Alpha systems.

AlphaLinux sites

The AlphaLinux Organization
 The Official AlphaLinux web site is at *http://www.alphalinux.org*.

The Digital Alpha OEM site
 This site is home for a lot of information about Alpha OEM products (including technical information). It's located at *http://www.digital.com/alphaoem/*.

The Compaq AlphaLinux web site
 This site contains interesting information on the use of Linux on Alpha hardware. It's at *http://www.unix.digital.com/linux/*.

AlphaLinux mailing lists

AXP-List from RedHat
> Send email to the following address and type `subscribe` into the subject line: *axp-list-request@redhat.com.*

Debian Alpha mailing list
> Send email to the following address and type `subscribe` into the body: *debian-alpha-request@lists.debian.org.*

AlphaLinux FTP sites

The official AlphaLinux FTP site
> This site is located at *ftp://ftp.alphalinux.org.*

The digital FTP site
> This site is located at *ftp://gatekeeper.dec.com.*

CPU, Support Chipset, Board, and System Identification

There are four classes of Alpha CPU: the 21064, 21066, 21164, and 21264. The 21064 and 21066 classes are both first-generation Alpha architectures, but the 21066 incorporates functions normally supplied on support chips into the CPU itself, creating distinctive platform characteristics and requirements. The 21164 and 21264 classes represent second- and third-generation chip architectures, respectively. Various chip architectures have been coupled with different system busses and interfaces, which subdivide the CPU types into different families of Alpha computers from desktop systems to supercomputing clusters.*

For purposes of installing Linux from a CD-ROM distribution, the subdivisions differ in the support that the Linux kernel provides for the features of the chips and in system assemblies and interfaces that use those features. If you cannot boot a kernel that appears to match your system, try a similar kernel from a related system or try a generic kernel. And, if that does not work, go to the AlphaLinux FTP site and try an earlier kernel or a later, developmental kernel. For the most part, however, your installation should be straightforward if you have selected the right image files to load and install Linux.

The subclass your system falls into determines whether you follow a routine Linux diskette-load installation procedure or use an alternative procedure. Even the routine AlphaLinux installation procedure is more complex than a Linux installation on the usual Intel PC. While the Intel PC provides the system hardware interface in the onboard BIOS, Alpha systems require that the system bootstrap itself by defining and loading a firmware interface before loading the operating system. For our installation purposes, we must usually use a firmware console that is resident on

---

* We will not discuss embedded systems and display terminal uses of Alpha CPUs here.

the system to load Milo (or another miniloader), which then loads Linux on the system.

Different Alpha systems offer the following console software:

- If the firmware was configured for Tru64 Unix or Open VMS, the system will have the SRM command-line console. The only exceptions are systems based around the UX motherboard, which have their own ARCS BIOSfirmware.

- If the firmware was configured for Windows NT, the system will have the ARC menu-interface console or AlphaBIOS graphical user interface console.

Some systems have more than one firmware console interface,* and most systems also have additional methods of bootstrapping an OS in firmware.

The standard firmware is initially loaded by accessing a system console when the system is booted and instructing it to load a Milo from diskette. Then the current Milo miniloader image is loaded from diskette, and it in turn is told to load the Linux kernel from the CD-ROM or boot diskette.

While you can get by using a slightly old Red Hat Milo for your hardware with the latest Red Hat Linux, you could not use a NetBSD Milo image (based on DU PAL-code) or a Milo image prepared for a very different Alpha system. Milo must be compatible with the system firmware used to load it as well as the Linux kernel that it loads. For instance, a Milo designed for ARC may not work if loaded with SRM even if it is for the correct system. Sometimes system firmware must be updated before using it to load the Milo image into memory. AlphaBIOS firmware, in particular, is updated frequently, and if your system uses AlphaBIOS you should assume that you need to update it before installing Linux. Your CD-ROM distribution may contain images for updated AlphaBIOS, ARC, or SRM firmware, if there is a known need for the updated version.

Preparing for Installation of Linux Alpha

We can now return to the steps we listed earlier to get Linux running. You must also decide how you want your Alpha to boot after Linux is installed and configured; Alpha systems support a number of alternatives.

---

* SRM console firmware for Multia, AlphaStation, AlphaServer, AlphaPC164, and AXPpcisystems from *ftp://gatekeeper.dec.com* or *http//ftp.digital.com/pub/DEC/Alpha/firmware*. The SRM is described in an online manual at *ftp://ftp.digital.com/pub/Digital/info/semiconductor/literature/srmcons.pdf*.

Minimum Hardware

You can run Linux on Alpha systems using as little as 8 MB of RAM, but most installation programs, like the Red Hat installer, require a minimum of 32 MB. The mininum disk space for the installation is 170 MB. To run the full X Window System and a desktop comfortably and have adequate storage for applications, you need a minimum of 16 MB RAM and 500 MB of hard-disk storage.

Many users of more recent Linux distributions have found that 24 MB or 32 MB of RAM is required to complete the installation. While it should still require no more than 16 MB to run Linux on a properly configured Alpha system (with a kernel compiled to support just that system's features), you may need more memory to install some distributions. An alternative is to install an earlier, smaller kernel.

Installation takes a huge amount of RAM because of the combined memory requirements of the bootstrap loader and Milo and the loading Linux kernel image, not because of the memory requirements of the Linux kernel itself. If you cannot complete your initial installation, you can also try to use an earlier and smaller Milo to boot your Linux distribution or a Milo that has been stored in nonvolatile RAM. You can select compact applications to conserve memory and storage. For more information, see *http://www.alphalinux.org*.

IDE/ATAPI Drive Support

Some Alpha systems, especially those intended for use as network servers, do not support IDE or ATAPI drives.* We recommend a fast SCSI drive as a basic system element, whether installed internally or attached externally. However, if your system has a free PCI slot, add a current PCIbus ATAPI/EIDE controller card supported by Linux so that you can also use a cheaper EIDE hard disk or fast CD-ROM drive. See the next section for more details on firmware limitations.

Firmware/BIOS Peripheral Device Support

Alpha systems recognize a number of peripheral devices through a configurable native Alpha system BIOS. The devices recognized vary, depending on whether the system was initially set up to run Windows NT, DU, or VMS.

Milo incorporates code from the original Windows NT firmware console for Windows NT systems, and ARC. An SRM console is provided for DU and VMS systems. If you install Linux using default system devices, you shouldn't have problems, but if you need to tailor the system to support your input device, you will find installation more complex. One list of supported peripherals in current Alpha systems is

---

* Early Alpha systems provided 10 mbps SCSI-2, and some of the latest Alpha system boards provide "fast and wide" 40 mbps SCSI-3. The very earliest (Jensen) provided an Adaptec 1740 ISA bus controller, but most SCSI controllers are integral NCR 810 family controllers that were considered high-performance controllers when adopted.

the "Hardware Compatibility List" in Samsung Semiconductor's *Alpha Resource Book*, found at *http://www.samsungsemi.com/Products/alpha/alpha-page1.html*.

If your system was set up for VMS, install system firmware for Windows NT or DU before installing Linux. Any SRM firmware from VMS should be replaced by SRM firmware for DU.

Updated Firmware

Your system firmware (ARC, AlphaBIOS, or SRM) should be up to date. In many cases, it won't matter whether it is an older version. But generally, we recommend updating your firmware before installing Linux. In the case of AlphaBIOS software, updating is expected and necessary.

Follow your hardware manual's directions for upgrading firmware. You can get firmware upgrades from *http://ftp.digital.com/pub/DEC/Alpha/firmware/*.

Some users advise you not to update firmware unless you know you need to do so. In other words, you can upgrade firmware if Linux fails to install properly on your system. Indeed, some Linux installations require some systems to be "downgraded" to an earlier firmware version to succeed.

Mice and Serial Ports

A commonly reported problem in Linux installations is connecting a serial mouse to the system. Some Linux installation programs map device definitions to the serial ports incorrectly during kernel configuration. Most of these complaints involve autodetection of a mouse installed on the first serial port. We recommend that you install a three-button PS/2-type mouse, if your system has a PS/2 hardware port rather than a serial mouse. Moreover, do not put a modem on serial port 1 as Milo will echo its output to serial port 1 and this can cause some strange results.

Installing Linux

Okay, you have collected your hardware manuals and selected the Linux distribution to install (one that meets your requirements based on the hardware you have). You should probably have at least a hardware manual for your system, which will describe hardware configuration and the use of the firmware consoles for your system, as well as provide useful error codes and diagnostics if there are difficulties. There will be an appendix near the end of each of Digital's system or evaluation board manuals that lists related documents, some of which are also useful. The document numbers will identify the files that you want from the Alpha library archive.

There are web sites providing FAQ files and other useful information for some specific Alpha systems as well.

You should also have the installation documents and addenda for your CD-ROM installation and information regarding any bugs and fixes for the distribution you are installing. Where your documentation is incomplete or describes a generic Linux installation, rather than the specific Linux Alpha installation, you may want to use the following sequence as a guide for installation.

Preparing Software for Installation

Check the web site of the company that provided your CD-ROM distribution for bug reports, patches, and later versions of the software version you are installing. Also check the AlphaLinux web site for independent verification of bug fixes and patches. Check Compaq's "System and Software and Driver Updates" web page for updated (Windows NT) software and drivers for your system at *http://ftp.digital.com/pub/DEC/Alpha/firmware/*. In particular, if your system uses AlphaBIOS, make sure you have the latest version, which you can get from the previously listed web page.

Check the AlphaLinux FTP site for updates in firmware that you need.

Create the failsafe recovery diskette, which is a linear-format block-data disk from an image file using an MS-DOS system and RAWRITE.EXE. This is a reserve parachute on your installation journey. If your ARC or SRM firmware needs updating, you can retrieve the files from the same location.

Next, make the three boot diskettes that you need for the Linux installation. To determine what diskette you may need for booting, visit the chart located on the Compaq FTP site at:

> *ftp://gatekeeper.dec.com/pub/DEC/Linux-Alpha/Kernels/systypes.txt*

You can make the diskettes on an IBM PC/MS-DOS system by invoking RAWRITE.EXE to create image file disks or using *dd* under Unix.

Preparing Hardware for Installation

The key issues here are disk-drive partitions and filesystems and supported video adapters. During disk configuration, we recommend that you use basic *fdisk* tools for reliability rather than use a GUI-based utility.

Your hardware manual will assist you in any required troubleshooting, such as providing beep code definitions. The UDB, for example, has a diagnostic LED character array that flashes a number or letter if a necessary firmware program in nonvolatile RAM (NV-RAM) or system ROM (SROM) error is detected on system boot.

If your system has been idle for some time, make sure that the cooling fans are working, too. Overheating your system in the middle of firmware reconfiguration would be particularly annoying.

Booting the Alpha System and Preparing to Load Milo

Because we cannot possibly cover all BIOS configurations in this book, we will give pointers on where to find detailed installation and configuration information for each type of firmware used with Milo.

Firmware	Location of Information
ARC Console	*http://www.alphalinux.org/faq/alphabios-howto.html*
AlphaBIOS	*http://www.alphalinux.org/faq/alphabios-howto.html*
SRM	*http://www.alphalinux.org/faq/srm.html*

Loading Milo and the Linux Boot Kernel

After you have successfully configured your BIOS to load Milo, you will see the Milo prompt. Because Milo is a microkernel, it has many options you may want to explore before bootstrapping the Linux kernel.

You should see the following Milo prompt:

```
MILO>
```

To see Milo options, enter Milo's help command:

```
MILO> help
```

To see how Milo has set up, what devices it knows, and the filesystems that it recognizes, enter the show command:

```
MILO> show
```

If everything looks fine, you can continue with the installation and load Linux from the prepared Linux kernel image.

Bootstrapping the kernel is very straightforward—you can do it in one command:

1. To load the Linux kernel from the first disk drive, type the following:

   ```
   MILO> boot fd0:vmlinux.gz root=/dev/fd0 load_ramdisk=1
   ```

   Note that this assumes you use the floppy image file that you prepared from a disk image file; Milo assumes an *ext2* partition by default and that *fd0* is the correct floppy drive. If you wanted to boot from an MS-DOS–formatted disk, such as the alternate disk previously prepared, you could enter:

```
MILO> boot fd0 -t msdos -fi vmlinux.gz load_ramdisk=1
```

2. Insert the ramdisk floppy when prompted.

3. Run your CD-ROM distribution's installation and configuration program.

4. After you finish installation, install Milo on a small disk partition on your machine to use for reconfiguring. If you want Milo to be able to load on booting, this partition must be a primary MS-DOS partition. You can create it using MS-DOS's or Window NT's *fdisk*.

Tuning and Post-Installation Considerations

Linux should now boot and work adequately. However, we recommend several enhancements.

Kernel Tuning

Once you have completed the installation, compile your own kernel, because the kernel shipped with your distribution probably contains more device drivers than you need. You can find information on compiling a kernel at the AlphaLinux web site (*http://www.alphalinux.org*), as well as in the kernel *Howto* (available from any Linux archive site).

Performance and Library Tuning

To increase the performance of AlphaLinux, you can replace the standard math libraries with the Compaq Portable Math Library (CPML). The CPML is identical in content to the Compaq Tru64 Unix *libm* and replaces the AlphaLinux *libm* directly. For more information on the CPML, visit:

http://www.unix.digital.com/linux/cpml.htm.

A good resource for AlphaLinux performance tuning is available at:

http://cyclone.ncsa.uiuc.edu/ PCA/PerformanceTuning.html

Binary Emulation

AlphaLinux is mostly binary compatible with Tru64 Unix (Digital Unix or DU); however, not all the system calls have been implemented. To run Tru64 Unix binaries on AlphaLinux, you need some of the shared libraries from Tru64 Unix, which requires a legal license of Tru64 Unix. More detailed explanation on how to set this up can be found in the AlphaLinux FAQ at *http://www.alphalinux.org/faq/ FAQ.html*.

AlphaLinux can also execute i386 Linux binaries through a program called em86. Information on this is also available in the AlphaLinux FAQ. Please note that patching the kernel is no longer necessary, although you must compile in support for i386 binaries when building the kernel.

Graphical Browser Considerations

Netscape has not ported the Netscape Communicator to AlphaLinux. But do not despair, because with binary emulation for x86 andTru64 Unix, the x86 and Tru64 native binaries will run on AlphaLinux.

The Mozilla browser is also an alternative. Information on Mozilla and other browser options can be found at *http://www.alphalinux.org/software*.

Some other options available are the KDE file manager from the K desktop environment (*http://www.kde.org*). If your Linux installation's port is not useable, a fairly stable earlier binary is available at *ftp://www.netstat.ne.jp/pub/Linux/Linux-Alpha-JP/Mozilla/mozilla-19981008-2/*

APPENDIX D

LINUXPPC: INSTALLING LINUX ON POWERPC COMPUTERS

by Jason Haas, LinuxPPC Inc.

Linux/PPC is the native port of the Linux operating system to the PowerPC processor. The effort to port Linux to PowerPC began in 1995 by Gary Thomas, and Australian developer Paul Mackerras initiated work on porting Linux to the Power Macintosh hardware. Linux now runs on almost every implementation of the PowerPC processor, including the 60x and 750, and the less-known 840 and 860 processors.

While the Linux port itself is called Linux/PPC (note the slash in the name), the most popular distribution, and the company maintaining the distribution, are called LinuxPPC (no slash). In this appendix, I provide information about the general port as much as possible, but some details will change in the next release (5.0) of LinuxPPC in any case.

Linux on PowerPC has become popular in the past two years as Mac OS users have started to search for alternatives to the Mac OS. For one thing, it's fast. When people install Linux, they're amazed at how fast their Macs really are. Linux can turn an old PowerMac 7500 into a responsive and capable machine, and it really unleashes 604 and 750 (G3) machines. It's also quite stable. When a Linux application crashes, it doesn't crash the OS as well.

And then there's multitasking. Linux can run a lot of programs at the same time and not slow down. When you click on a menu in the Mac OS, everything stops until you release the mouse button. The Mac OS can't do anything but draw that menu. A Mac OS-based web server that I used to administer was disabled overnight because of this. When the mouse button was unstuck the next morning, the server promptly crashed when the listserver tried to process all of the backlogged email messages that had accumulated overnight. All this because of the mouse button being stuck! (Linux has no such problems with the mouse buttons.)

Another excellent example of the benefits of Linux multitasking: Photoshop can run only one filter at a time. And the whole Mac is tied up in running the filter.

LinuxPPC ships with a Photoshop-like graphics application called The GIMP. Unlike Photoshop, GIMP can execute several filters simultaneously, and you can switch to other applications and keep working while GIMP runs the filters. (You can even hold down the mouse button.)

The most popular distribution for the PowerPC is called LinuxPPC (without the slash), which is developed and sold by LinuxPPC, Inc. You can order LinuxPPC on CD-ROM from *http://www.linuxppc.org*.

Another Linux distribution that is popular among very advanced Linux users is called Debian. The Debian for the PowerPC distribution is not as polished as the LinuxPPC Inc. distribution and is not available on CD-ROM. However, users who are familiar with Debian for other platforms may wish to use it. The Debian GNU/ Linux web site, *http://www.debian.org/ports/powerpc/*, should provide up-to-date information about the status of the Debian project. The instructions for installing Debian GNU/Linux on top of a base LinuxPPC are available from:

http://www.dartmouth.edu/cgibin/cgiwrap/jonh/lppc/faq.pl?file=572

LinuxPPC Inc. is an active supporter of the Debian project and has contributed hardware to the Debian organization.

LinuxPPC Inc. has developed a demonstration version of LinuxPPC that can be booted straight from the Mac OS. This version, called LinuxPPC Live, is a 105 MB version of LinuxPPC and doesn't require any installation or configuration on the part of the user. To download LinuxPPC Live, see the list of mirror sites at *http://www.linuxppc.org/mirrors.shtml*.

Compatible Hardware

LinuxPPC runs on any PCI-based Power Macintosh, which includes the iMac, the PowerMac G3, and the PowerBook 3400 and G3 models. As of this writing, the iMac is a little difficult to get Linux running on. Special iMac installation instructions are at *http://www.linuxppc.org/iMac/*. We hope the upcoming LinuxPPC 5.0 will have better iMac support.

Other PowerPC Platforms

When the AIM (Apple-IBM-Motorola) coalition designed the PowerPC processor, they created two reference designs for future hardware. The first design was called PReP, the PowerPC Reference Platform. PReP machines were intended to be servers and high-end workstations. Apple, Motorola, and IBM all made PReP boxes: the Apple Network Server 500 and 700, the Motorola FirePower and Power-STACK, and various IBM RS/6000 computers. These machines could run IBM's Unix variant, AIX, and a version of Windows NT for PowerPC. (Very few people knew that NT for PPC existed. Even fewer used it.)

Apple and Motorola abandoned their PReP boxes, and IBM stopped using the PReP design in favor of the newer Common Hardware Reference Platform (CHRP) design. Many Apple Network Servers have been successfully resurrected with LinuxPPC, much to the delight of their owners.

The CHRP platform was going to be the basis of cheap Macintosh cloning. The CHRP boards had both PC and Macintosh serial and keyboard ports and booted the Mac OS from a ROM DIMM chip. When Apple canceled its Mac OS licensing program in 1996, the hope of inexpensive Mac clones evaporated. But CHRP has resurfaced in 1998: the Apple iMac and Blue & White G3s are CHRP-based. IBM's RS/6000 workstations are also CHRP-based. IBM has become very interested in Linux on PowerPC and has been assisting with the port Linux/PPC to their newest RS/6000 models.

Unsupported PowerMacs

The PowerMac 6100, 7100, and 8100; and Workgroup Server 6150, 8150, and 9150 cannot run LinuxPPC. These machines used the NuBus architecture and don't have the PCI or Open Firmware circuitry that LinuxPPC depends on to boot.

There is a variant of Linux that runs on these early machines called MkLinux. MkLinux is really the Mach microkernel (also used in Apple's Mac OS X Server) running the Linux kernel in server mode. For most practical purposes, MkLinux is just another version of Linux, albeit one that runs on the old NuBus PowerMacs. Also, MkLinux is binary compatible with Linux/PPC, which means that applications compiled for Linux/PPC will run on MkLinux, and vice vera. MkLinux is a little bit slower than LinuxPPC, but it's the only option available for the oldest PowerMacs right now. You can find information on MkLinux at *http://www.mklinux.org*.

The PowerMac/Performa 5200, 5300, 6200 and 6300 series can't run any version of Linux at all. The only exceptions to this are the Performa 6360, a PCI-based machine that is capable of running LinuxPPC and the Performa 61xx-series (relabelled as PowerMac 6100 computers) which can run MkLinux.

Other Hardware Issues

There are a few types of hardware that LinuxPPC can't use. Some of them, such as specialized SCSI cards, video cards, and USB expansion cards, can't run on Linux because they lack a driver. LinuxPPC can't use the Apple GeoPort modems* that shipped with the Apple Performa series.

---

* The GeoPort modems are "software modems." Software modems are 90 percent software, which the Mac uses to emulate a hardware modem. The tradeoffs are speed, stability, and compatibility. Under the Mac OS, GeoPort modems are very slow and unstable, and they can't function at all under Linux since there aren't any drivers available for them. The only solution for these machines is to remove the modem, which may be an expansion card inside the computer, and replace it with an external modem. Relatively fast 33.6 and 57.6 kbps modems can be picked up for $50 to $100.

Kernel and Library Issues

LinuxPPC Release 5.0 was the first version of LinuxPPC to use Version 2.0 of the GNU C libraries (*glibc*). Previous versions used glibc 1.99, which has caused some porting headaches for developers. Kernel support has been quite good on PowerPC. When the 2.2 kernel was released, PowerPC was the first processor after x86 to get the new kernel ported and running. Version 2.2.1 of the kernel introduced drivers for Ultra/Wide SCSI cards and greatly improved support for the PowerBook G3 series, adding trackpad tapping, and screen brightness control support.

Preparing to Boot LinuxPPC

To get LinuxPPC installed on your Mac, you will have to partition your hard disk, install the OS, and configure your system for dual-booting LinuxPPC. Each step will be explained in detail later.

Booting LinuxPPC was revolutionized in 1998 when Benjamin Herrenschmidt released a utility called BootX, which gave PowerMac owners easy dual-boot capability. The BootX utility runs in the Mac OS as an application and comes with an extension that runs at system startup. Prior to BootX, the only way to boot Power-Macs was to edit their Open Firmware settings, which was a tricky proposition, at best. BootX also provides basic video support for machines that don't have video drivers.

With the BootX system, the Linux kernel is stored on the Macintosh hard disk. When the user gives the command to boot into Linux, BootX issues shutdown commands to the Mac OS. Just when the Mac is about to restart, the Mac OS is kicked out of the computer's RAM, and Linux begins to boot.

Getting the Mac Ready for Linux

Before you can see how fast your Mac really is, you have to do some work. You'll need a hard disk or removable disk, preferably a gigabyte or larger, that you can repartition. If you have only one hard disk, you'll need to get either an external hard drive or additional internal drive (if your machine has room for one) or erase the internal hard disk and repartition it! Unfortunately, there isn't any non-destructive partition software for the Macintosh.

If you have a LinuxPPC CD-ROM, you can boot from the CD-ROM straight into the Red Hat installer. The installer can run the *fdisk* utility (just a more familiar name for the LinuxPPC partitioning utility called *pdisk*), which you can use to partition your hard disk.

> *NOTE*   If you don't have a CD-ROM, but do have a fast Internet connection, you can perform an FTP-based installation of LinuxPPC. Instructions for FTP installation are at *http://www.linuxppc.org/userguide/ftpinstall.shtml*. You need to have a direct connection with a static IP number.

Partitioning the Hard Disk

Chapter 3

Chapter 2, *Preparing to Install Linux*, discusses the reasons for partitioning and general concepts behind it, while Drives and Partitions Under Linux" in Chapter 3, *Installation and Initial Configuration*, explains the names and sizes typically used for Linux partitions. Read those sections for background; here I discuss information specific to LinuxPPC.

A full installation of LinuxPPC takes up about 650 MB. You'll want to have more available for adding files and software. For a robust installation, we recommend devoting at least one gigabyte partition. Give it more if you can spare the disk space. It is possible to pare down the installation to fit on a 100 MB ZIP disk, but there's not much you can fit on there.

Before partitioning a disk, make a complete backup of the disk. Once you partition the hard disk, all of the data on the disk will be destroyed, and it will not be possible to recover it after it has been partitioned.

If you only have one hard disk, back up the whole disk! After you've backed up your data, boot the computer from the Mac OS CD-ROM that came with the machine, and use Apple's Drive Setup utility to format and partition the hard disk into two HFS partitions. Then install the Mac OS on the first partition, reboot into the Mac OS, restore your data, and resume the partitioning and installation process.

In this sample installation, we will use a 4 GB hard drive that has been split into two partitions of 2 GB each. The first will become an Apple HFS partition and will need to be installed on that partition. The second will be further partitioned into a pair of Linux partitions.

To partition the hard disk, you'll need the Mac OS version of *pdisk*, the disk partition utility. This is provided by the Red Hat installer under the name *fdisk* and can also be grabbed from *ftp://ftp.linuxppc.org/pub/linuxppc/linuxppc-R4/RedHat/tools/pdisk.hqx*. (Please use an FTP mirror site to lighten the load on the LinuxPPC system, especially if you're not in the United States. The mirror list is at *http://www.linuxppc.org/mirrors.shtml*.)

Unlike most Mac OS programs, *pdisk* is entirely text-based. It's also a very literal program, in that it will do exactly what you tell it to do. It won't delete your hard disk—unless you tell it to. To make it harder to accidentally wipe everything out, *pdisk* has a few safeguards built in:

• It won't save any changes unless you specifically tell it to do so.

• If you quit the program (In the File menu, choose Quit), it will not save the changes you've made to your hard disk. You have to tell it to save the changes with the *w* (write) command.

The *pdisk* commands are shown in Table D-1.

Table D-1: pdisk Partitioning Commands

Command	Purpose
e	Edits a device's map. A "device" is a hard disk.
b	Prints the available commands.
l	Lists a device's partition map.
L	Lists all devices' maps.
q	Quits the program.
v	Prints the version number and release date.

When you use *pdisk*, you're actually editing your hard disk's partition map. The partition map is a scary sounding name for a file that contains a list of all the partitions on your hard disk. The partition map is stored on a partition all its own.

When you're in the Mac OS, you see only one partition, which you think of as your hard disk. The other four partitions are invisible, and you don't have any reason to directly interact with them. (Unless you've decided to go and install Linux.) The first partition holds the partition map. The next three are device drivers, pieces of software that tells the Mac how to use the hard disk and where to look for the Mac OS partition. Your Mac OS software and the OS are stored on the fifth partition, which is an Apple HFS or HFS Plus partition.

NOTE   As of this writing, LinuxPPC cannot read HFS Extended (also known as HFS Plus) disks, including hard disks. Research is under way to get HFS Plus support working, but there isn't a date set for when we'll have HFS Plus compatibility. Check on *http://www.linuxppc.org* for an announcement.

When you start up *pdisk*, it presents you with a text prompt:

```
Top level command (? for help):
```

Now what? Type L and press Return. The system will print out a list of every SCSI and IDE device attached to your computer, including hard disks, CD-ROM drive, ZIP drive, and so on:

```
Top level command (? for help): L
pdisk: can't open file '/dev/sda'   (No such device)
pdisk: can't open file '/dev/sdb'   (No such device)
pdisk: can't open file '/dev/sdc'   (No such device)
pdisk: can't open file '/dev/sde'   (No such device)
pdisk: can't open file '/dev/sdf'   (No such device)
pdisk: can't open file '/dev/sdg'   (No such device)

Partition map (with 512 byte blocks) on '/dev/hda'
 #:                    type name          length    base      ( size )
 1: Apple_partition_map Apple                 63 @ 1
 2:         Apple_Driver43*Macintosh          54 @ 64
 3:         Apple_Driver43*Macintosh          74 @ 118
 4:     Apple_Driver_ATA*Macintosh           54 @ 192
 5:     Apple_Driver_ATA*Macintosh           74 @ 246
 6:         Apple_Patches Patch Partition    512 @ 320
 7:             Apple_HFS untitled       4194304 @ 832      (  2.0G)
 8:             Apple_HFS untitled       4256944 @ 4195136  (  2.0G)
```

If you don't have any SCSI devices on your machine, you'll see a bunch of error messages go whizzing by that say things similar to:

```
pdisk: can't open file '/dev/sda'   (No such device)
pdisk: can't open file '/dev/sdb'   (No such device)
```

The can't open file messages are *pdisk*'s cryptic way of reporting that it didn't find any device attached to your computer at that address. Instead of referring to a device as CD-ROM Drive at SCSI ID 4 or ATAPI HD 1, *pdisk* uses Linux's device name format. To Linux, everything is a device. Your modem, your hard disk, the floppy drive, even the RAM are considered devices.

The name of a hard disk depends on whether it's an IDE or SCSI hard disk. IDE disks are referred to as */dev/hdx*, and SCSI disks are */dev/sdx*. The variable *x* is one of the letters a, b, c, d, e, f, or g. The letter on the end of the name is how Linux distinguishes between drives.

Did you notice that IDE drives are hd and SCSI drives are sd? Those letters just denote which bus the devices are on. The letter after hd or sd is what you really need to pay attention to. If your computer has one IDE hard disk in it, it will be listed as */dev/hda*. You also will get an error on */dev/hdb*, which is your CD-ROM drive. Don't worry about it, though. (Trust me!)

If you have SCSI drives in your computer, *pdisk* will first display their names with "fake" SCSI names in the format */dev/scsibus.scsi_id*, such as */dev/sdc1.5*. Fortunately, it also lists their device name in proper */dev/sdletter* format. Linux refers to SCSI devices with the */dev/sdletter* scheme, so use that format when working with the device.

If you have an Ultra/Wide SCSI card by Adaptec or Apple, and you're planning on installing Linux on the hard disk attached to the card, prepare to be a little confused. Linux might say that your hard disk is in a different place than *pdisk* says it's in. This is because when Linux boots, it looks at the names of the devices attached to it. The Adaptec and Apple Ultra-Wide SCSI cards show up on the letter A. The Mac's SCSI controller is called the MESH chip, which is alphabetically after "Adaptec."

A hard disk on an Adaptec card will be at */dev/sda*. Devices on the regular internal SCSI bus will follow at */dev/sdb* and */dev/sdc*. If your machine has only one device on the SCSI card, you're in the clear. If you have other devices attached to it, the naming game can get a little hairy.

And now, we partition:

1. Choose the partition you're going to edit. In *pdisk*, type the letter e:

```
Top level command (? for help): e
Name of device: /dev/hda
Edit /dev/hda -
Command (? for help):
```

2. Delete the second HFS partition. You have to delete the partition in order to create free space, which you will use to make Linux partitions. Looking at the partition map, the seventh partition is the HFS partition, which will be erased. To delete a partition, type the letter d followed by the number of the partition you wish to delete:

```
Command (? for help): d8
Command (? for help): p
```

Typing p again will display the partition map. The Apple HFS partition has turned into free space, which you can use to make new partitions:

```
7:            Apple_HFS untitled      4194304 @ 832      (  2.0G)
8:            Apple_Free Extra        4256944 @ 4195136  (  2.0G)
```

3. Create the swap partition:

```
Command (? for help): c   "c" is the command to make a new partition.
First block: 8p  "8p": Use the first block of the free space partition,
                      which is the eighth partition.
Length in blocks: 30m  Make it 30MB. k = kb, m = mb, g = gb
Name of partition: swap  The partition will be called swap.
Command (? for help):
```

There! You've created your swap partition. Print out the partition map again. Examine the eighth and ninth partitions:

```
8:     Apple_UNIX_SVR2 swap           61440 @ 4195136 ( 30.0M)
9:        Apple_Free Extra          4195504 @ 4256576 (  2.0G)
```

The free space is now the ninth partition, and the new swap partition is at */dev/ hda7*. Next, make the root partition. Once you make root, you will be done partitioning.

When creating the root partition, instead of typing the length in megabytes, use the free-space partition's length in blocks. In this example, the Apple_Free partition is 4,195,504 blocks long, which is roughly 2 GB. By typing the partition's exact length in blocks, you will use up all the available disk space and not have wasted space left over after partitioning:

```
Command (? for help): c
First block: 9p
Length in blocks: 4195504
Name of partition: root
Command (? for help): p
```

```
Partition map (with 512 byte blocks) on '/dev/hda'
   #:                type name           length     base    ( size )
   1: Apple_partition_map Apple               63 @ 1
   2:        Apple_Driver43*Macintosh        54 @ 64
   3:        Apple_Driver43*Macintosh        74 @ 118
   4:    Apple_Driver_ATA*Macintosh          54 @ 192
   5:    Apple_Driver_ATA*Macintosh          74 @ 246
   6:       Apple_Patches Patch Partition    512 @ 320
   7:           Apple_HFS untitled        4194304 @ 832     (  2.0G)
   8:     Apple_UNIX_SVR2 swap               61440 @ 4195136 ( 30.0M)
   9:     Apple_UNIX_SVR2 root             4195504 @ 4256576 (  2.0G)
```

In this example, partition */dev/hda9* will become your root device. Write down which partition is your root device. You will need to know that later. If you have a SCSI hard disk, it would be */dev/sda7*. Also note that if you are planning on installing Linux on a drive other than your startup disk, you don't have to have the Apple_HFS partition on the disk. You can devote the entire drive to Linux.

When you're done partitioning, type w:

```
Command (? for help): w
Writing the partition map will permanently save changes.
Save changes? (y/N): y
```

pdisk will come back to the Top level command prompt. At this point, the changes to your hard disk will have been saved. Type q to quit *pdisk*.

Tips for partitioning include the following:

- If you make a mistake, it's not fatal. You can quit *pdisk* at any time without saving changes.

- Changes are not final until you tell *pdisk* to write the new partition map with the *w* command.

Installing BootX

The BootX software makes it very easy to boot LinuxPPC. It consists of three files, which need to go in specific places on your hard disk. The software includes the following:

The BootX application
> This is called Boot LinuxPPC on LinuxPPC CD-ROMs. The application can go anywhere on your hard disk. You can make multiple copies of it and place them in convenient locations.

The BootX Extension
> Place this in your Mac's Extensions folder. (The Extensions folder is inside the System folder.)

The vmlinux file (which is the Linux kernel)
> This needs to go directly inside the System folder—not the Extensions folder.

After you have placed the *vmlinux* file and BootX Extension in their respective places, double-click the BootX application. Make sure that the No Video Driver and Use RAM Disk boxes are checked. You don't need to enter anything in the `Root Device` or `More Kernel Arguments` field.

Make sure that the LinuxPPC CD-ROM is in the CD-ROM drive, and click the Linux button, and LinuxPPC will boot into the Red Hat installer.

Using the Red Hat Installer

The Red Hat installer is used in LinuxPPC 4.0 and 5.0, although new installers will be available in 5.0. The installer used in LinuxPPC 5.0 will work differently from the version described here.

To boot into the installer, double-click the BootX application. The BootX application may be called Boot LinuxPPC if you're using a LinuxPPC 4.1 or 5.0 CD-ROM.

First, the installer asks if you are using a color monitor. Press the space bar to make the installer operate in color mode, which has a blue background with red and grey buttons. Press the space bar or Return key when you are done reading the `Welcome to Powermac/Linux` message. The next screen lets you tell the computer what kind of keyboard you're using. The default is the U.S. keyboard. After selecting your keyboard type, the installer asks for the source of the installation files, which will probably be a CD-ROM.

Next, the installer automatically picks the partitions that will become root and swap. Formatting all of the partitions can take quite a while, but it is recommended when installing on a previously used hard disk.

You then choose which packages you want to install. The default installation is acceptable for most users. If you want to add more software, such as other servers, or want to pare down the installation, you can add or remove items to be installed at this screen. If you want the installer to install other packages, such as the bundled C compilers, use the arrow keys to move up and down through the installer screen, and use the Space bar to select and deselect items.

When you have selected the packages you want to install, tab over to the OK button and press Space. The installer begins putting the system in place. Depending on the speed of your CD-ROM drive, installation will take 10 to 45 minutes. After the computer has finished putting packages in place, the Network Configuration screen appears. However, instead of using this screen to set up your network interface, you should use the *netcfg* utility, which is available once you're in LinuxPPC. So skip this step.

Next, select the time zone that you are in. The default is U.S./Eastern time zone. After that, you'll need to assign the **root** password for the system. Please be sure to protect yourself by choosing a good password with a mixture of letters and numbers.

Type in your **root** password and press Return. The password will not appear on the screen, but the system will remember it. Type the password one more time to confirm it, and then press Return. Press Return one more time to press the OK button. You can skip the next two screens, "Quik Installation" and "Change Boot Variables." Leave the fields on these screens blank. They're not used for this installation process.

That's all! The computer will congratulate you on installing the system and should reboot into the Mac OS.

Post-Installation: Setting Up the BootX Software

BootX is very easy to configure after you've partitioned your hard disk. Type in the device name of your root partition. If you followed the example, the root device will be *sda7* or *hda9*, depending on what kind of disk is in your hard disk.

Make sure that the Use RAM Disk option is not checked. If this option remains on, the computer will boot into the installer instead of booting into Linux from the hard disk.

The No Video Driver option should be turned on. This option provides a video display on most systems, including those with cards that have no Linux video driver.

LinuxPPC R4 boots directly into the X Window System and boots the KDE window manager. If you would prefer Linux not to boot into KDE, it's very easy to modify the system. Like all things in Linux, there's a file that controls this aspect of the system. KDE is started in */etc/inittab*.

Use your favorite Unix text editor (such as *pico* or *vi*) to edit the file. The line you need to modify is at the very end of the file. It's the third line in this text:

```
# Run xdm in runlevel 5
#x:5:respawn:/usr/bin/X11/xdm -nodaemon
x:3:once:/opartition/kde/bin/kdm -nodaemon
```

Change the 3 to 5. That's it! The next time you boot LinuxPPC, it will stay at the console instead of booting X. If you want to start X from the console, type `startx`.

Getting Hardware to Do What You Want It to Do

Although the PowerMac does not present the variety of hardware—and therefore the variety of configuration problems—that come with Intel systems, there are some issues you may run into when running Linux on it.

Single-Button Mice

The fact that every Mac ships with a one-button mouse is a bit of a problem in a three-button mouse universe. To get around that, LinuxPPC's developers have used keyboard emulation of the other two buttons. On an ADB keyboard, Option-2 and Option-3 act as the middle and right mouse buttons, respectively. On the iMac and Blue G3 keyboards, the numeric keypad's Clear and Equal sign (=) act as the middle and right mouse buttons.

You can also buy inexpensive three-button mice and trackballs for both ADB and USB Macintoshes. LinuxPPC ships with a tiny program called *mousemode*, which lets you configure LinuxPPC for multibutton mice.

PowerBook Trackpads

Owners of Apple PowerBooks can use the trackpad to its fullest extent with versions 2.1.130 and higher of the Linux/PPC kernel. A tiny utility built into the system, called *trackpad*, lets you configure how the trackpad functions under LinuxPPC. The *trackpad* program can be run only by root.

To enable tapping, dragging, and drag lock, type `trackpad drag lock`. To turn off everything but tapping, type `trackpad tap`. And if you want the trackpad completely disabled, except for being able to move the pointer, type `trackpad notap`.

LinuxPPC 4.0 and 4.1 Video Issues

You have to use LinuxPPC for only a few minutes to notice that the video is rather slow, especially on the newer Apple G3 computers. The reasons for this are twofold. First, the portion of X Window System software that draws the GUI has no video acceleration. The second is that the version of KDE that shipped with R4 and 4.1 is also very slow, especially compared to KDE 1.1 and later versions. To improve the situation, you can do a few things:

- Upgrade to Version 2.2.4 or higher of the Linux/PPC kernel. Graphics are noticeably faster in the 2.2.4 kernel and will continue to improve in subsequent versions. The newest version of the kernel is available from *ftp://ftp.linuxppc.org/linuxppc/kernel/*.

- Install KDE 1.1 or use a different window manager.

    LinuxPPC 4.x shipped with the KDE, AfterStep, *twm*, and *fvwm2* window managers. Release 5.0 has GNOME and WindowMaker, as well as a new version of KDE. (GNOME and WindowMaker are also available for Release 4.0.)

- Upgrade to Release 5.0 if you're using LinuxPPC Feb98, 4.0 or 4.1. The new release has accelerated X servers built in. If you don't want to upgrade to R5, you can install the Xpmac_mga X server. The Xpmac_mga server runs on Power Macintoshes with IxMicro TwinTurbo cards, most ATI video cards, and Matrox MGAxx64 cards. Instructions for installing the Xpmac_mga server are at *http://www.linuxppc.org/userguide/xpmac_mga.shtml*.

INSTALLING LINUX/M68K ON MOTOROLA 68000-SERIES SYSTEMS

by Chris Lawrence, Linux/m68k Documentation Supremo

Linux/m68k is the port of the Linux operating system to the Motorola 680x0 (or m68k) processors. Linux/m68k, the first project to port Linux to a non-Intel processor, was begun in 1993 by Hamish Macdonald and Greg Harp, who ported the kernel to the Amiga. Several Atari users, including Björn Brauel, Roman Hodek, and Andreas Schwab, adapted Hamish's kernel beginning later that year to run on Atari's 32-bit ST series of computers.

Since 1996, Linux/m68k has been adapted to run on a number of other systems, including the pre-PowerPC Apple Macintosh line, several models of VMEbus single-board computers from Motorola and BVM Ltd., Apollo Domain workstations, the HP 9000 series and Sun 3 workstations, and NeXT. Most recently, there has been a port to the Q40 and Q60, two new 680x0-based computers that are being manufactured in Europe. A related project, Linux/APUS, has ported Linux/PPC (discussed in Appendix D, *LinuxPPC: Installing Linux on PowerPC Computers*) to Amigas with PowerPC processor cards; it is very much a hybrid of Linux/m68k and Linux/PPC.

Appendix D

As you can see from the diverse list of systems that Linux/m68k runs on, the challenge facing the m68k port was introducing enough flexibility into the kernel to cope with the variety of possible environments. Many of these abstractions—most notably, Martin Schaller and Geert Uytterhoeven's framebuffer and console abstractions—have since been incorporated into the mainstream kernel. These abstractions have meant that virtually every binary ever written for Linux/m68k—including the kernel image itself—can be run on every m68k platform without recompilation.

Linux/m68k has proven its robustness in the real world: several publicly accessible web servers, such as *http://shadow.cabi.net* and *http://amiga.nvg.org*, are running on Linux/m68k and one of the developers uses an Amiga running Linux as a web and mail server for his dormitory. Thousands of other users use Linux for myriad tasks from software development to text processing to academic research.

Linux, along with other free Unix clones, continues to provide m68k users with a dynamic, rapidly improving operating system not seen on these platforms since the heyday of the late 1980s and early 1990s.

NOTE	Apple's choice of the name MkLinux for its microkernel-based Linux for PowerPCs and other platforms has caused no end of confusion; this confusion has been further compounded because an early port of Linux to the m68k Macs (now believed to be vapor as no code has ever been released) was called MacLinux.
	The correct name for Linux on 680x0 processors is Linux/m68k; in particular, Linux for the pre-PowerPC Macintoshes should be called Linux/m68k for the Macintosh to avoid confusion with other projects. Neither of these is based on the microkernel or MkLinux.

Software Versions

As of this writing, active development of the 2.0 kernel series has stopped; the focus is now on producing a rock-solid 2.2 kernel in the near future. The latest Linux/m68k kernels can always be downloaded at *http://sunsite.auc.dk/ftp/projects/680x0/*; precompiled images are provided for stable kernels, and complete source trees and patches (relative to both previous versions and Linus's releases) are available for all versions.

Like other platforms, Linux/m68k has followed the *libc* roller coaster closely; thanks to the hard work of Andreas Schwab, our resident *gcc* and *libc* guru, we've never been left too far behind. At present, both major distributions ship with *glibc* 2.0 (*libc* 6); work is underway to prepare for the transition to *glibc* 2.1 (*libc* 6.1) in upcoming releases of Linux/m68k distributions. However, the kernel still supports both *libc* 4 and *libc* 5 applications, for those users who need them.

Supported Hardware

As a general rule, the 68020, 68030, 68040, and 68060 processors are supported.

For the 68020, a separate MMU (memory management unit) is necessary. The EC models of the 68030, 68040, and 68060 are missing MMUs and cannot run Linux.

For the 68020 and 68030, an FPU (floating point unit) is also recommended. A kernel-level FPU emulator is on the verge of release (as of this writing), but 68882 FPUs can be found for around U.S. $25 and will improve performance with many applications. Users of the 68LC040 can also take advantage of the FPU emulator; however, many of the 68LC040 chips produced have bugs that make FPU emulation unstable.

Generally, the minimum RAM requirement is between 4 and 8 MB of RAM; more RAM is generally better, though, and every little bit helps. Amiga users should note that Linux cannot use chip RAM except for the video, sound, and floppy drivers. The X Window System is usually comfortable only with at least 12–16 MB of RAM and an accelerated video card; however, it can run on the standard Amiga and Atari video modes with less memory.

While you can probably install a minimal Linux system on a 20–30 MB partition, for any serious work you'll need over 100 MB, including a separate swap partition. A useful approach is to purchase the largest hard drive you can afford and install Linux on it, and then watch it fill itself up. Many SCSI and IDE controllers are supported on various platforms, although the support is not as extensive as we would like because of the small developer base and relatively expensive hardware (the least expensive Ethernet card for a "big box" Amiga costs around U.S. $120!). All Amiga models are supported by Linux if they have the right CPU. Clones that do not include the Amiga's custom chips, such as the DraCo, are not supported at the moment; other clones, such as the BoXeR, may or may not work (we have not had any machines for testing).

Most 32-bit Ataris (ST/Mega ST/TT/Falcon) are supported although many people have had trouble with the Afterburner040 CPU card. The Medusa and Hades clones are also supported.

Macintosh models appear to be a hit-or-miss affair. Apple went through many permutations of hardware in the m68k line and not all of those permutations are currently supported; the porting work is further complicated by Apple's reluctance to release documentation to free software developers. In particular, Powerbook support is limited because of the different ADB (Apple Desktop Bus) design on those laptops. Even so, at least 27 Mac models are reported to have keyboard, mouse, and display support.

VMEbus single-board computers from several manufacturers are supported; these machines are widely used in industrial and research applications. Motorola's MVME 147, 162, 166, 167, 172, and 177 are currently supported, thanks to Richard Hirst. Richard has also ported Linux/m68k to BVM Ltd's BVME 4000 and 6000 computers and the Tadpole TP34V.

Other platforms have more limited support, due to a lack of people working on porting Linux/m68k to those systems. For example, only 25 MHz NeXTs are currently working.

For more information about support for your specific configuration (including expansion cards), consult the Linux/m68k FAQ at *http://www.linux-m68k.org/faq/ faq.html*; Mac users may also want to look at the Macintosh-specific hardware support pages at *http://www.mac.linux-m68k.org*.

Distributions

There are two major multiplatform distributions of Linux available for m68k. They include kernels that can handle most, if not all, of the supported hardware:

Debian (http://www.debian.org)

Debian is the only multiplatform distribution that officially supports Linux/m68k. Debian 2.1 was the second Debian release to include Linux/m68k packages and installation tools; this release, with more than 860 MB of compressed package files, is almost certainly the largest distribution of free software for 680x0-based systems ever produced.

Debian is developed by a worldwide team of volunteers, and the Debian/m68k team is in many respects a microcosm of this structure, including members from Europe and North America working on Amigas, Ataris, Macs, and VMEbus systems.

Two commercial distributions, Whiteline Linux/68k and Eagle Linux M68K, have been based on the 2.0 Debian release, and may be updated for 2.1. In addition, the official Debian CD-ROMs are reproduced and sold by more than two dozen vendors worldwide, for between U.S. $5 and $20 for a two CD-ROM binary-only set, and the complete distribution can be downloaded for free from Debian's worldwide mirror network.

Additional information specific to Debian/m68k can be found at *http://www.debian.org/ports/m68k/*.

In addition, there are two commercial distributions from Germany that are based on older versions of Debian:

Whiteline (Atari)
http://www.atari-world.com/dlm/linux.htm

Eagle (Amiga)
http://www.eagle-cp.com/www/m68k.html

Red Hat (http://www.redhat.com)

While Red Hat Software does not officially support Jes Sørensen's m68k port of its distribution, it is available on CD-ROM from the company as part of its Rough Cuts package. Red Hat for m68k releases generally follow the official releases by Red Hat Software. The current m68k release, as of this writing, is Version 5.1; a beta release of 5.2 is also available for testing, which features Red Hat's *Xconfigurator* program to simplify configuration of the X Window System. Like Debian, the distribution is available on CD-ROM from several vendors and can be downloaded via FTP from sites in the United States, Italy, and Denmark. The unofficial Red Hat port comes with an installer for Amigas; Atari and Mac users have reported some success with manual installations. More information can be found in Ron Flory's unofficial Red Hat installation FAQ at *http://www.feist.com/~rjflory/linux/rh/index.html*.

The choice of distribution is largely a matter of taste; generally, people who run Debian on one system will want to run it on others, and the same goes for Red Hat. If you've never used Linux before, however, the choice can be somewhat daunting (and one us early hackers never had to face). Debian certainly has the edge in package availability, although its increasing size does make it more cumbersome to install. The commercial distributions from Germany may be of interest if you can take advantage of their technical support (which means you probably would find a strong knowledge of German helpful).

However, Debian and Red Hat for m68k can be purchased for much less than you'd spend to buy Red Hat's official package for Intel, so you may want to try them both. In any event, there is a wide user base for both noncommercial distributions, which is more than willing to help users with their questions.

Installation

Each distribution uses a different installation method; in addition, the procedure for each major platform is somewhat different. Hence, it is impossible to go into any great depth in this appendix. A few particular issues are worth examining, however.

Booting Linux

While it is technically possible to boot directly into Linux on virtually any system, there are numerous challenges involved in writing a bootloader that can operate outside any operating system. At the moment, Amigas, Ataris, and VME systems can be booted without launching native operating systems (using m68k-specific versions of LILO).

For other platforms, and for specialized applications on Amigas, booters that run under the native OS (similar to Loadlin on Intel) are available. The Amiga and Atari booters are fairly rudimentary, although the latter does include some support for obtaining kernels over the network. The Macintosh booter, called Penguin, is a native MacOS application that provides a more user-friendly interface and allows configuration of some settings (such as screen settings) that the Mac porters haven't been able to determine how to change under Linux. Other systems are currently using hacked bootloaders from other operating systems or are launched from hardware boot managers.

Allowed boot options for Linux/m68k are covered in the file *kernel-options.txt* in the *Documentation/m68k* directory of the kernel source tree.

Partitioning and Filesystems

Each platform uses its own partitioning scheme or one adapted from another operating system. As a general rule, however, the partitioning schemes are more straightforward than those based on MS-DOS systems. Amigas, Ataris, and Macs don't distinguish between primary and logical partitions and can generally be configured without the disk-size issues that plague Intel systems (the 1024-cylinder limit, for example). Because of the extensive support in the Linux kernel for myriad disk-partitioning schemes, native HP/UX and SunOS partition tables can be used on those platforms.

Although each partitioning scheme is different, under Linux they generally use *fdisk* utilities based on the original *fdisk* for DOS-based platforms, so the menus are similar with a few exceptions; for example, the Amiga *fdisk* program provides the ability to set the AmigaOS mountable flag in the partition table.

Appendix D

Before booting Linux for the first time, some people may want to use a more familiar GUI-based partitioning tool under their existing OS. Amiga users should use either *HDToolbox* or the tool that came with their SCSI controller; Atari users should use a TOS-partition editor like SCSITool; and Mac users can use Apple's *HD SC Setup* or the m68k version of the *pdisk* utility from LinuxPPC Inc. (see Appendix D for detailed instructions on how to use it). VME systems, along with the Q40 and Q60, use the MS-DOS partition format (like Linux on Intel and Alpha). Users of other platforms should consult their native operating system's documentation.

Native filesystems are highly supported in recent kernels. All of the Amiga's filesystem formats (OFS and FFS) are supported, as are the Atari's GEMDOS (actually a variant of the MS-DOS filesystem) and the Mac's HFS. The native filesystems on other platforms are generally available as well, through the kernel's support for System V and Berkeley FFS filesystems.

The X Window System

Most people have a love-hate relationship with configuring X. On Linux/m68k, the situation is no different; however, due to the capabilities of the framebuffer device interface, configuration is somewhat easier than on other platforms.

Linux/m68k uses the FBDev X server from XFree86, which is a standard XFree86 server designed for the framebuffer device. This allows video settings to be inherited from the Linux console instead of requiring you to extensively edit your *XF86Config* file. You may want to adjust the depth settings, but you can leave other settings alone.

Users of machines with high-resolution graphics cards may be interested in using one resolution for the console and higher resolutions for X. This option requires that the framebuffer driver in question supports programming the video mode (i.e., it does not inherit the mode from the machine's native boot loader or it has only one fixed mode). Programmable video modes may be added to the *XF86Config* file. The format of the mode information is identical to the format used in *XF86Config* on all other architectures; you can also output appropriate mode lines from the *fbset* utility.

The X server and console also work together in that you can adjust framebuffer settings on the command line using the *fbset* program and then output the settings in a format that can be copied into your *XF86Config* file for switching modes within X.

Unfortunately, the *XF86Config* files shipped with distributions usually include extraneous information that is not relevant to m68k users (and only serves to confuse them). This is an area of concern that the Linux/m68k team plans to address in the near future.

Rebooting the System

Chapter 5

Linux/m68k uses the PC-style Ctrl-Alt-Del key combination to reboot the system. Because of hardware limitations, Linux/m68k is not able to safely trap the machine-specific reboot keys (like the Amiga's Ctrl-Amiga-Amiga sequence) and reset buttons. You can also reboot the system using the *shutdown* command as described in Shutting Down the System in Chapter 5, *Essential System Management*.

Registration

We keep a registry of Linux/m68k users to help track the use of our port and identify people who can help test drivers for new hardware. The Linux/m68k registration site is at *http://www.cs.kul- euven.ac.be/~geert/Linux/m68k/*. It is maintained by Geert Uytterhoeven.

For More Information

Linux/m68k users should consult the *comp.os.linux.m68k* newsgroup with any questions that they may have. There are a number of users who are happy to answer questions—at least the ones that aren't already answered elsewhere. The FAQ is another valuable resource at *http://www.linux-m68k.org/faq/faq.html*.

There are also mailing lists for Debian and Red Hat users; see *http://www.linux-m68k.org/mail.html* for details on how to subscribe to these lists.

More information on Linux/m68k, including pointers to all of the information discussed here and the complete FAQ, can be found at the Linux/m68k Home Pages, at *http://www.linux-m68k.org*, or their main U.S. mirror, *http://www.lordsutch.com/linux/*.

Installing Linux on Sun SPARC Systems

by David S. Miller, Red Hat Software

The SPARC port of Linux supports a wide range of systems, from the very low end to the extremely high end. Most people who have a Sun workstation or server around and would like to try Linux on it are likely to find that it is fully supported and works rather well. There are some small gaps here and there, but development is closing them as time goes on.

Supported Hardware

Support for Linux varies not only by series but by subseries. All series except the Enterprise 10000 and ancient sun4 systems are now fully supported. Work is under way to bring the others into line. Symmetric multiprocessing (SMP) kernels run on all series except sun4c.

In addition to the systems listed in this section, several clone vendors exist. If their clones are truly compatible with the equivalent Sun systems, Linux will work on them.

Sun4c Systems

These systems are supported by both the 2.0.x and 2.2.x series Linux kernels:

SPARCStation SLC
SPARCStation ELC
> These two sun4c systems have the motherboard right behind the monitor tube in the same encasement. I like to jokingly refer to them as "SPARCintosh" systems due to this layout. The SLC systems were the first Sun hardware ever to successfully run Linux.

SPARCStation IPX
SPARCStation IPC
> These machines are enclosed in a small shoebox-like case and use an external monitor.

SPARCStation 1
SPARCStation 1+
SPARCStation 2
> These were the first "pizza box"–style Sun workstations. They also introduced SBUS slots to allow for the addition of expansion cards.

Sun4m Systems

These systems are supported by both the 2.0.x and 2.2.x series Linux kernels. Multi-processor configurations are also supported:

SPARCServer 6xxMP
> These systems have a mainboard with two sun4m CPU module slots and SBUS slots as well. A VME bus is present but Linux does not provide any support for VME devices at this time.

SPARCStation LX
SPARCClassic
SPARCClassic X
> These enclosures are much like the IPC/IPX sun4c systems, but inside, they have the sun4m architecture. The CPUs are on the motherboard and graphics cards are also integrated in this way.

SPARCStation 4
SPARCStation 5
SPARCStation 10
SPARCStation 20
> The sun4m pizza-box workstations. The first two have the CPU on the motherboard, while the latter two systems have two sun4m CPU module slots. SBUS expansion slots are present in all four. The SS5 possesses a special expansion slot for graphics cards, such as the 24-bit TCX.

Sun4d Systems

These systems are supported only by the 2.2.x Linux kernels. As with the sun4m, multiprocessor configurations are supported:

SPARCServer 1000
SPARCCenter 2000
> The only difference between these two is that the latter has more expansion slots than the former.

UltraSPARC 64-bit Systems

All the UltraSPARC-based systems mentioned here (with one disclaimer about the Enterprise 10000) are supported by the 2.2.x Linux kernel only. Multiprocessor configurations are fully supported.

The systems include two classes of I/O architectures, SBUS and PCI. The older systems use SBUS while the newer ones are all PCI based:

Ultra 1
Ultra 2
Enterprise 2

> These are the desktop SBUS systems. The first two are uniprocessor only, whereas the Enterprise 2 can host two processors. All of them have SBUS expansion slots. The Ultra 2 and Enterprise 2 have a UPA slot for high-end Creator/Creator3d graphics cards.

Enterprise 3000, 3500, 4000, 4500, 6000, 6500, and 10000

> These are SBUS servers. The Enterprise x000 family have a high-speed packet switched bus, into which I/O or CPU/MEMORY expansion boards can be plugged. The I/O boards each have three SBUS slots and some standard onboard devices (Ethernet, SCSI, and fibrechannel). CPU boards have two cpus and SIMM slots for memory.

> The Enterprise 10000 is slightly different, in that each system board holds up to four processors, SBUS I/O systems, and memory SIMMS. Although support for this system has been written for the Linux kernel, it is untested, so I cannot claim that it is supported at this time. Systems with a base price of U.S. $1 million are hard to come by for testing.

Ultra 30
Ultra 60

> These are PCI-based UltraSPARC workstations made by Sun. Both come in a tower case, have four or so PCI expansion slots, and have standard devices onboard, such as Ethernet and SCSI. Both also have a UPA slot for Creator graphics cards. The Ultra 30 is a uniprocessor, whereas the Ultra 60 can have up to two processors.

> When Sun produced these workstations, it also produced a reference PCI UltraSPARC motherboard that OEMs could buy and resell with their own cases, disks, power supplies, and so on. This motherboard had an onboard IDE controller for disk storage instead of a SCSI.

Enterprise 250
Enterprise 450

> These are Sun's PCI servers. They have more PCI slots than the UltraSPARC workstations and boast the addition of various environmental control (fans

and temperature monitors) and the ability to diagnose remotely. The Enterprise 450 can also support up to four processors. Both systems use onboard NCR SCSI controllers for storage.

Ultra 5
Ultra 10

These are the PCI desktop UltraSPARCs. The Ultra 5 is in a more pizza-box–like enclosure, whereas the Ultra 10 uses a tower case. The Ultra 5 has one PCI expansion slot, the Ultra 10 has four. The Ultra 10 also provides a UPA slot for Creator graphics. The onboard storage I/O provided by both is IDE.

Ultra AXi
Ultra AXmp

Sun has also made two more PCI reference motherboards suitable for OEMs. The first is for workstations, the latter for rack-mount SMP systems. IDE is the onboard storage I/O for the AXi, while SCSI is on the AXmp. The AXmp has various environment control, fans, the ability to diagnose remotely, and support for up to four processors.

System Libraries

Early in the dark ages of the SPARC port of Linux, we first used an *a.out libc4* as the system C library. Several factors were behind this. First, we used *a.out* SunOS binaries to bootstrap the first-ever Linux/SPARC systems, so we knew that *a.out* worked. Second, this was the most stable *libc* source base at the time. I hope that not very many (if any) SPARC systems running this C library exist any longer. All native Linux binaries using *libc4* were statically linked.

ELF-based *libc5* was the next library for Linux/SPARC. The earliest complete distributions used this for the system libraries. Shared ELF libraries were fully supported on SPARC.

Today, most Linux/SPARC systems are *glibc*/ELF based and will probably remain this way for the foreseeable future.

Installation Differences from Intel

Most of the installation procedures for Linux/SPARC systems are identical to those of Intel-based Linux systems. The differences that do exist are just a side effect of different hardware, different booting procedures, and other similar divergences.

Graphics and X

Graphics cards are different on each system, and Linux/SPARC systems use different X servers. All SBUS-based and several onboard SPARC graphics cards use the Xsun series of servers. They are named:

Server	Purpose
XsunMono	For monochrome graphics cards only
Xsun	For 8-bit color and monochrome displays
Xsun24	For 24-bit color graphics cards only, including Creator/Creator3d

Unlike Xfree86 on Intel, these X servers do not use a server configuration file for several reasons. First, the mouse and keyboard types are known on SPARC systems. Second, the graphics card and resolution can be completely autodetected and configured, so no specification of these parameters is needed in a configuration file.

The PCI systems start to bring in some exception cases for graphics cards. Several of the desktop systems (such as Ultra 5 and Ultra 10) have an ATI Mach–64 derived graphics card on the motherboard. Also ATI Mach64 PCI expansion boards are available as well. These graphics cards do use the Xfree86 servers and thus have a configuration file to set up.

For these ATI cards, you set up the XF86Config file just as you would for ATI cards on an Intel system. There are a few sticking points to be aware of:

- Several PCI UltraSPARC systems provide the option of using either a traditional Sun-type [45] keyboard and mouse or a PC-style keyboard with a PS/2 mouse. If you're using the Sun keyboard, the keyboard configuration should look something like this:

```
XkbKeycodes      "sun(type5)"
XkbTypes         "default"
XkbCompat        "default"
XkbSymbols       "sun/us(sun5)"
XkbGeometry      "sun"
XkbRules         "xfree86"
XkbModel         "sun"
XkbLayout        "sun/us"
```

whereas for the PC-style keyboard you want something like this:

```
XkbRules     "xfree86"
XkbModel     "pc101"
XkbLayout    "us"
```

The X configuration tools, such as *xf86config* and *XConfigurator*, should be able to get the options right all by themselves. But if they don't, this description helps you.

- Monitor timing configuration can be a pain with Sun monitors. They are really Sony monitors with Sun's brand name on the case. There is no definitive tabulation of what Sony model is "underneath the hood" of the various Sun monitors. All is not lost—use the following rules of thumb and you will get a working X configuration when using tools like *XConfigurator* or *xf86config*.

  Simply take your monitor size (17-inch, 19-inch, and so on) and choose the most common Sony monitor of the same size.

  If you attach a standard off-the-shelf SVGA monitor to your PCI graphics card, you can simply select it from the X configuration tool monitor listing.

  Multihead X configurations are supported currently, but with some limitations. Mach64 ATI cards cannot be multiheaded. The rest of the ATI cards can be multiheaded within the same card type. (That is to say, two cards that both work with the Xsun server can be multiheaded, whereas an Xsun24 and an XsunMono cannot.) The restrictions in this paragraph will disappear in a future release of the X server.

The SILO Boot Loader

SPARC stations also differ from Intel-based systems in the boot loader. SPARC systems use a bootloader named SILO (for SPARC Improved LOader).

From the user's perspective, SILO behaves just like Intel's LILO. The main noticeable difference is that you don't need to run a special */sbin/silo* program each time a new kernel image is added to the *config* file (which is */etc/silo.conf*) as you need to do with Intel. Also, SILO is capable of loading any kernel image found on your *ext2*, UFS, or ISO9660 filesystems by name.

The reason SILO is able to do this is OBP (Open Boot Prom, the firmware used on SPARC systems). It provides a way for the bootloader code to read blocks off of boot devices, such as disks. With the kernel filename and device name you tell it to use, SILO simply reads your *ext2* partition and loads it. (Note: in another light this creates a slight limitation. See the section that follows on bootable devices and consoles.)

It is possible to use SILO to dual boot both Linux and some other SPARC OS. Some helpful hints on how to do this can be found at *http://www.sun.com/software/linux/dual_boot.html*.

Partitioning Disks

We now tackle the peculiarities of disk partitioning on Linux/SPARC systems. You can treat this process just like you would on an Intel system with the following exceptions:

- Disk slice c is special: it must exist, and it must encompass the entire disk. Most disk partitioning programs, such as *fdisk* and Disk Druid, automatically take care of this for you on SPARC systems.

  The reason for disk slice c being this way is that OBP uses this slice to determine the span of blocks on your disk and the location of the boot block for loading SILO from disk.

- If you are creating a partition for something other than an *ext2* or UFS filesystem, the partition must not start on the first block. The reason is that other uses, such as swap partitions and RAID slices, will end up overwriting the disk label and making your disk unusable.

  This is an issue only for Linux/SPARC on 2.0.x-based kernels. Sun has added facilities such that new RAID and swap partitions created under 2.2.x kernel–based distributions will take care of this issue transparently for you.

  The easiest way to deal with skipping the first block on 2.0.x–based distributions is to just start the partition at cylinder 1 instead of 0.

Installation from a Serial Console

Most SPARC users have grown accustomed to being able to install an OS using a serial line as the console. Linux/SPARC provides this facility as well.

The installation mechanisms I know about at this time all support the use of vt100 terminals only. When you boot the installer for your favorite distribution, it will automatically figure out if you have booted it on a serial console, and it will use whatever is appropriate for the installation procedure.

The installer will assume that if you installed the machine using a serial console, you will use the serial console for the running system. That is to say, if you install using a serial console, and then hook up a monitor and graphics card for the first boot, it won't work.

This does not mean you cannot change back to a framebuffer console from a serial one, and vice versa, after installation. A special shell script exists specifically for this purpose, called setconsole. Here are some sample uses:

setconsole ttya
> This will use the first serial line as the console.

setconsole ttyb
> This will use the second serial line as the console.

setconsole video
> Use the graphics card as the console.

SPARC-specific Issues After Installation

On UltraSPARC systems, the current provided userland is still 32-bit (even though the processor and the kernel itself are 64-bit). One advantage of this is that nearly all Linux/SPARC applications run unchanged between different Linux/SPARC machines. A 64-bit userland is (at the time of this writing) scheduled to be deployed in the summer of 1999. The 32-bit libraries will remain in the distribution so that users can still run their legacy 32-bit Linux/SPARC binaries.

One side effect of the current UltraSPARC 32-bit userland is that you need to take some care when compiling applications from source. Since the machine (and kernel) is 64-bit, the *uname* facility will report sparc64 as the system type, instead of just plain sparc (which is what all the non-UltraSPARC systems report).

Several build scripts used to drive the compilation of source packages (such as GNU *autoconf*) use this identification string to determine various aspects about the compilation environment (the sizes of various types in the C languages, and so on). The GNU utilities are going to do the wrong thing, because they see a 64-bit SPARC system type being reported, yet the userland runtime is 32-bit.

To overcome this issue, a tool called *sparc32* is provided on Linux/SPARC systems. Before you configure and build to compile some source-code package, invoke a subshell with a *sparc32 sh* command. This will cause all *uname* queries done in that subshell (and thus by the programs run from it) to report plain sparc as the system type. This solves the problem.

Bootable Devices and Consoles

Some devices, while fully supported, have limitations for booting. Sometimes a device's firmware doesn't adhere to the conventions expected by the OBP firmware found on SPARC systems. In such cases, neither Linux nor any other operating system can boot from the device. The core OBP firmware does not know how to operate any particular SCSI controller or graphics card. It knows only the details of your particular CPU type and the arrangement of your memory SIMMs.

So each device that OBP can be expected to talk to must have its very own firmware, which describes how the device is operated. This firmware is used to teach OBP how to read a block off a disk on a particular SCSI controller type, for example.

The net result is that if a device lacks the appropriate OpenBoot firmware, it cannot be used for booting the OS or be used as the console.

But this is not so much a limitation as it may seem. All SPARC systems have some sort of onboard boot device (which does have the appropriate firmware) and console.

On PCI UltraSPARC systems, Linux happens to support several PCI devices even if they lack the special firmware. So you can place a cheap Ethernet card into one of the PCI slots and Linux will happily use it. You just can't boot from it.

LILO BOOT OPTIONS

The most popular way to boot Linux on Intel platforms is the LInux LOader, LILO, whose configuration and use are described in the sectionx "Using LILO" in Chapter 5, *Essential System Management*. This appendix summarizes the options you can specify in the */etc/lilo.conf* file and on the */sbin/lilo* command line.

The configuration file starts with a section of global options, described in the next section. Global options are those that apply to every system boot, regardless of what operating system you are booting.

Following the global section, there is one section of options for each Linux kernel. While the variety of kernel options—many of them hardware specific—make it unfeasible to list them all here, the section "Kernel Options" later in this chapter describes the most common ones.

Finally, the configuration file contains a section for each non-Linux operating system that you want LILO to be able to boot. Each of those sections is referred to as an image section, because each boots a different kernel image (shorthand for a binary file containing a kernel) or another operating system. Each Linux image section begins with an `image=` line. Options found in these sections are described in the section "Image Options" later in this chapter.

Global Options

In addition to the options listed here, the kernel options `append`, `read-only`, `read-write`, `root`, and `vga` (described in the section "Kernel options" later) can also be set as global options:

`backup=backup-file`
    Copies the original boot sector to `backup-file` instead of to the file */boot/ boot.nnnn*, where *nnnn* is a number that depends on the disk device type.

`boot=`*`boot-device`*

> Sets the name of the device that contains the boot sector. `boot` defaults to the device currently mounted as the root, such as */dev/hda2*. Specifying a device, such as */dev/hda* (without a number), indicates that LILO should be installed in the master boot record; the alternative is to set it up on a particular partition, such as */dev/hda2*.

`compact`

> Merges read requests for adjacent disk sectors to speed up booting. Use of `compact` is particularly recommended when booting from a floppy disk. Use of `compact` may conflict with `linear`.

`default=`*`name`*

> Uses the image *name* as the default boot image. If `default` is omitted, the first image specified in the configuration file is used.

`delay=`*`tsecs`*

> Specifies, in tenths of a second, how long the boot loader should wait before booting the default image. If `serial` is set, `delay` is set to 20 at a minimum. The default is not to wait.

`disk=`*`device-name`*

> Defines parameters for the disk specified by *device-name* if LILO can't figure them out. Normally, LILO can determine the disk parameters itself and this option isn't needed. When `disk` is specified, it is followed by one or more parameter lines:

```
disk=/dev/sda
  bios = 0x80   # First disk is usually 0x80, second is usually 0x81
  sectors= ...
  heads= ...
```

> Note that this option is not the same as the disk geometry parameters you can specify with the `hd` boot command-line option. With `disk`, the information is given to LILO; with `hd`, it is passed to the kernel. The parameters that can be specified with `disk` are briefly listed here. They are described in detail in the *LILO User's Guide* which comes with the LILO distribution.

`bios=`*`bios-device-code`*

> Specifies the number the BIOS uses to refer to the device. See the previous example.

`cylinders=`*`cylinders`*

> Specifies the number of cylinders on the disk.

`heads=`*`heads`*
> Specifies the number of heads on the disk.

`inaccessible`
> Tells LILO that the BIOS can't read the disk; this option is used to prevent the system from becoming unbootable if LILO thinks the BIOS can read it.

`partition=`*`partition-device`*
> Starts a new section for a partition. The section contains one variable, `start=`*`partition-offset`* that specifies the zero-based number of the first sector of the partition:

```
partition=/dev/sda1
  start=2048
```

`sectors=`*`sectors`*
> Specifies the number of sectors per track.

`disktab=`*`disktab-file`*
> Superceded by the `disk=` option.

`fix-table`
> If set, allows LILO to adjust 3D addresses (addresses specified as sector/head/cylinder) in partition tables. This is sometimes necessary if a partition isn't track aligned and another operating system, such as MS-DOS, is on the same disk. See the *lilo.conf* manpage for details.

`force-backup=`*`backup-file`*
> Is like `backup`, but overwrites an old backup copy if one exists.

`ignore-table`
> Tells LILO to ignore corrupt partition tables.

`install=`*`boot-sector`*
> Installs the specified file as the new boot sector. If `install` is omitted, the boot sector defaults to */boot/boot.b*.

`linear`
> Generates linear sector addresses, which do not depend on disk geometry, instead of 3D (sector/head/cylinder) addresses. If LILO can't determine your disk's geometry itself, you can try using `linear`; if that doesn't work, then you need to specify the geometry with `disk=`. Note, however, that `linear` sometimes doesn't work with floppy disks, and it may conflict with `compact`.

`map=`*`map-file`*
> Specifies the location of the map file. Defaults to */boot/map*.

`message=message-file`
> Specifies a file containing a message to be displayed before the boot prompt. The message can include a formfeed character (Ctrl-L) to clear the screen. The map file must be rebuilt by rerunning the *lilo* command if the message file is changed or moved. The maximum length of the file is 65,535 bytes.

`nowarn`
> Disables warning messages.

`optional`
> Specifies that any image that is not available when the map is created should be omitted and not offered as an option at the boot prompt. Like the per-image option `optional`, but it applies to all images.

`password=password`
> Specifies a password that the user is prompted to enter when trying to load an image. The password is not encrypted in the configuration file, so if passwords are used, permissions should be set so that only the superuser is able to read the file. This option is like the per-image `password` option, except that all images are password protected and they all have the same password.

`prompt`
> Automatically displays the boot prompt without waiting for the user to press the Shift, Alt, or Scroll Lock key. Note that setting `prompt` without also setting `timeout` prevents unattended reboots.

`restricted`
> Can be used with `password` to indicate that a password needs to be entered only if the user specifies parameters on the command line. It is like the per-image `restricted` option, but applies to all images.

`serial=parameters`
> Allows the boot loader to accept input from a serial line as well as from the keyboard. Sending a break on the serial line corresponds to pressing a Shift key on the console to get the boot loader's attention. All boot images should be password protected if serial access is insecure (e.g., if the line is connected to a modem). Setting `serial` automatically raises the value of `delay` to 20 (i.e., two seconds) if it is less than that. The parameter string *parameters* has the following syntax:

`port[,bps[parity[bits]]]`

> For example, to initialize COM1 with the default parameters:

`serial=0,2400n8`

The parameters are:

`port`

Specifies the port number of the serial port. The default is 0, which corresponds to COM1 (*/dev/ttys0*). The value can be from 0 through 3, for the four possible COM ports.

`bps`

Specifies the baud rate of the serial port. Possible values of `bps` are 110, 300, 1200, 2400, 4800, 9600, 19200, and 38400. The default is 2400 bps.

`parity`

Specifies the parity used on the serial line. Parity is specified as n or N for no parity, e or E for even parity, and o or O for odd parity. However, the boot loader ignores input parity and strips the eighth bit.

`bits`

Specifies whether a character contains 7 or 8 bits. The default is 8 with no parity and 7 otherwise.

`timeout=`*tsecs*

Sets a timeout (specified in tenths of a second) for keyboard input. If no key has been pressed after the specified time, the default image is automatically booted. `timeout` is also used to determine when to stop waiting for password input. The default timeout is infinite.

`verbose=`*level*

Turns on verbose output, where higher values of *level* produce more output. If −v is also specified on the LILO command line, the level is incremented by one for each occurrence of −v. The maximum verbosity level is 5.

Image Options

The following options are specified for a particular image:

`alias=`*name*

Provides an alternate name for the image that can be used instead of the name specified with the `label` option.

`image=`*pathname*

Specifies the file or device containing the boot image of a bootable Linux kernel. Each per-image section that specifies a bootable Linux kernel starts with an `image` option. See also the `range` option.

`label=`*`name`*

Specifies the name that is used for the image at the boot prompt. Defaults to the filename of the image file (without the path).

`loader=`*`chain-loader`*

For a non-Linux operating system, specifies the chain loader to which LILO should pass control for booting that operating system. The default is */boot/ chain.b*. If the system will be booted from a drive that is neither the first hard disk nor a floppy, the chain loader must be specified.

`lock`

Tells LILO to record the boot command line and use it as the default for future boots until it is overridden by a new boot command line. `lock` is useful if there is a set of options that you need to enter on the boot command line every time you boot the system.

`optional`

Specifies that the image should be omitted if it is not available when the map is created by the *lilo* command. Useful for specifying test kernels that are not always present.

`password=`*`password`*

Specifies that the image is password protected and provides the password that the user is prompted for when booting. The password is not encrypted in the configuration file, so if passwords are used, only the superuser should be able to read the file.

`range=`*`sectors`*

Used with the `image` option, when the image is specified as a device (e.g., image=*/dev/fd0*), to indicate the range of sectors to be mapped into the map file. *sectors* can be given as the range *start–end* or as *start+number*, where *start* and *end* are zero-based sector numbers and *number* is the increment beyond *start* to include.

If only *start* is specified, only that one sector is mapped. For example:

```
image = /dev/fd0
   range = 1+512   # take 512 sectors, starting with sector 1
```

`restricted`

Specifies that a password is required for booting the image only if boot parameters are specified on the command line.

`table=`*`device`*

Specifies, for a non-Linux operating system, the device that contains the partition table. If `table` is omitted, the boot loader does not pass partition information to the operating system being booted. Note that */sbin/lilo* must be rerun if the partition table is modified. This option cannot be used with `unsafe`.

unsafe

>Can be used in the per-image section for a non-Linux operating system to indicate that the boot sector should not be accessed when the map is created. If unsafe is specified, some checking isn't done, but the option can be useful for running the *lilo* command without having to insert a floppy disk when the boot sector is on a fixed-format floppy-disk device. This option cannot be used with table.

Kernel Options

The following kernel options can be specified in */etc/lilo.conf* as well as on the boot command line:

append=*string*

>Appends the options specified in *string* to the parameter line passed to the kernel. This is typically used to specify certain hardware parameters. For example, if your system has more than 64 MB of memory (i.e., more than your BIOS can recognize), you can use append:

```
append = "mem=128M"
```

initrd=*filename*

>Specifies the file to load into */dev/initrd* when booting with a RAM disk. See also the options load_ramdisk, prompt_ramdisk, ramdisk_size, and ramdisk_start.

literal=*string*

>Is like append, but replaces all other kernel boot options.

noinitrd

>Preserves the contents of */dev/initrd* so they can be read once after the kernel is booted.

prompt_ramdisk=*n*

>Specifies whether the kernel should prompt you to insert the floppy disk that contains the RAM disk image, for use during Linux installation.

>Values of *n* are:

>*0* Don't prompt. Usually used for an installation where the kernel and the RAM disk image both fit on one floppy.

>*1* Prompt. This is the default.

ramdisk=*size*

>Is obsolete. This option should be used only with kernels older than Version 1.3.48. For newer kernels, see the options load_ramdisk, prompt_ramdisk, ramdisk_size, and ramdisk_start.

`ramdisk_size=n`
> Specifies the amount of memory, in kilobytes, to be allocated for the RAM disk. The default is 4096, which allocates 4 MB.

`ramdisk_start=offset`
> Used for a Linux installation where both the kernel and the RAM disk image are on the same floppy. `offset` indicates the offset on the floppy where the RAM disk image begins; it is specified in kilobytes.

`root=root-device`
> Specifies the device that should be mounted as the root. If the special name `current` is used, the root device is set to the device on which the root filesystem is currently mounted. This option defaults to the root-device setting contained in the kernel image.

`vga=mode`
> Specifies the VGA text mode that should be selected when booting. `mode` defaults to the VGA mode setting in the kernel image. The values are not case-sensitive. They are:

`ask`
> Prompts the user for the text mode. Pressing Enter in response to the prompt displays a list of the available modes.

`extended` *(or* ext*)*
> Selects 80x50 text mode.

`normal`
> Selects normal 80x25 text mode.

`number`
> Uses the text mode that corresponds to *number*. A list of available modes for your video card can be obtained by booting with `vga=ask` and pressing Enter.

lilo Command Options

The following list describes the *lilo* command options. Multiple options are given separately:

```
% lilo -q -v
```

`-C config-file`
> Specifies an alternative to the default configuration file (*/etc/lilo.conf*). *lilo* uses the configuration file to determine what files to map when it installs LILO.

-I *label*

>   Prints the path to the kernel specified by *label* to standard output or outputs an error message if no matching label is found. For example:

```
% lilo -I linux
/boot/vmlinuz-2.0.34-0.6
```

-q
>   Lists the currently mapped files. LILO maintains a file, by default */boot/map*, containing the name and location of the kernels to boot. Running *lilo* with this option prints the names of the files in the map file to standard output, as in this example (in which the asterisk indicates that linux is the default):

```
% lilo -q
linux           *
test
```

-r *root-directory*

>   Specifies that before doing anything else, LILO should chroot to the indicated directory. This option is used for repairing a setup from a boot floppy–you can boot from a floppy but have LILO use the boot files from the hard drive. For example, if you issue the following commands, LILO will get the files it needs from the hard drive:

```
% mount /dev/hda2 /mnt
% lilo -r /mnt
```

-R *command-line*

>   Sets the default command for the boot loader the next time it executes. The command executes once and then is removed by the boot loader. This option is typically used in reboot scripts, just before calling shutdown -r.

-t
>   Indicates that this is a test and does not really write a new boot sector or map file. It can be used with -v to find out what LILO would do during a normal run.

-u *device-name*

>   Uninstalls LILO by restoring the saved boot sector from */boot/boot.nnnn* after validating it against a timestamp. *device-name* is the name of the device on which LILO is installed, such as */dev/hda2*.

-U *device-name*

>   Is like -u, but does not check the timestamp.

-v
>   Specifies verbose output.

-V
>   Prints the LILO version number.

ZMODEM FILE TRANSFER

The Zmodem protocol is a robust and fast data-transfer protocol. It includes 32-bit cyclic redundancy checking (CRC) to ensure error-free data transfer. On Unix platforms, the RZSZ package provides the dominant tools for implementing Zmodem protocols. Related protocols, such as Xmodem and Ymodem, are also supported by commands that are part of the RZSZ package.

These commands are available in the current RZSZ package:

rz Receives files using the Zmodem batch protocol. If the sending program doesn't send Zmodem protocol files within 50 seconds, *rz* switches to *rb* mode.

rb Receives files using the Ymodem or Ymodem-g protocol. *rb* is an alternative invocation for the *rz* command.

rx Receives a file using the Xmodem protocol.

sz Sends files using the Zmodem batch protocol.

sb Sends files using either the Ymodem or Ymodem-g protocol. *sb* is an alternative invocation for the *sz* command.

sx Sends a file using the Xmodem protocol.

sz provides automatic downloading in response to an incoming *rz* request, and *rz* automatically processes incoming Ymodem or Zmodem files. *sz* can also be used as a filter to send standard input to the receiving host.

The RZSZ tools display information about the file transfers, including projections of transmission time, incremental crash recovery, recognition of wildcard file-selection arguments, and user notification on completion of transfer. Because most popular PC terminal-emulation packages (Professional-YAM, ZCOMM, ProComm, Telix, and a host of others) support Zmodem transfer, the RZSZ package makes it simple to transfer files between Linux systems, MS-DOS, Macintosh, VMS, and other operating systems.

Interestingly, although some Linux distributions include the *sz* and *rz* commands, they may omit portions of the RZSZ package (including the manual pages). So we'll give you some FTP sites to get the whole package in the next section.

Most of the time, you won't need to use Xmodem or Ymodem, so we will restrict our discussion to the *sz* and *rz* features.

Getting RZSZ

The RZSZ package isn't acknowledged as such in the Linux tools, which may mean that you won't find the whole package collected and compiled for Linux. However, we have found a number of FTP sites that carry the source, such as a subdirectory of NetBSD packages called *lrzsz* at *ftp://ftp.cs.umn.edu*.

The primary source for state-of-the-art RZSZ is *ftp://ftp.cs.pdx.edu*, maintained in directory */pub/zmodem* by Chuck Forsberg of Omen Technology, Inc.

Omen Technology (*http://www.omen.com*) offers a hardcopy manual for its RZ/SZ package (as well as detailed documentation for the PC terminal-emulation package Professional-YAM) that you can buy if the manual pages seem insufficient. You can download these packages on a shareware basis (meaning you are expected to pay a small fee) from the web site. Technical support is offered for registered RZ/SZ users. Omen Technology reports that almost all technical support problems with RZ/SZ are caused by the network, OS kernel bugs, or problems with third-party programs, not the RZ/SZ code itself.

Sending and Receiving Files

Most communications programs invoke *rz* and *sz* automatically. You can also connect to a remote system, log in, and manually invoke *sz* with the flags you want to use. Zmodem automatically downloads the files to your home system using the same filenames. (Zmodem tools aren't clever about filenames, so when you download to MS-DOS, be careful about getting files with names that can't be squeezed into the *filename.ext* DOS filename limit. If you transfer *filename.extension*, it arrives on your DOS host converted to *filename.ext*, which is probably OK. But, if you try to transfer *filename.more.extension*, most Zmodem utilities will give up, probably with a misleading message that the transfer completed.)

One of the most confusing things about Zmodem transfer is determining the command to use to perform the transfer. You have to remember which system you are invoking the command from and which system contains the files to transfer. A consistent way to perform Zmodem transfer is to always invoke the transfer on the remote host, whether uploading (sending to the remote host) or downloading (receiving from the remote host). For example, if you are logged in to a remote host (using C-Kermit, or Telix, or whatever) and want to send some text files from that system to your home system, you might enter something like this:

```
$ sz -a *.txt
```

sz would queue the files and successively send them back to the local system. The −*a* option stands for ASCII and ensures that carriage returns and newlines appear as they should on the system where the file ends up.

On the other hand, if you want to upload some files (receive them on the remote host), you would simply enter the following command:

```
$ rz
```

The remote system would then prompt something like this:

```
rz ready to begin transfer, type "sz file ..." to your modem program
**B0100000023be50
```

rz waits patiently for you to switch back to the local host and give it a Zmodem send command, using *sz* directly, or through the software you are using. For example, if you call the remote host using ProComm, you would press Page Up and select Zmodem transfer from the pop-up menu and then enter the files to send on the input line ProComm provides.

When sending files from a Macintosh system to a Unix or Linux host via Zmodem protocol, remember that the filenames cannot have spaces in them.

The following command checks some text files and sends only the *.txt* and *.doc* files that exist on both systems and that are newer on the sending system. Conversion of Unix newlines to DOS-style carriage return/linefeed is performed automatically by most receiving Zmodem packages:

```
$ sz -Yan *.txt *.doc
```

In many versions (not all, unfortunately) you can pipe the output of a process from a remote host to *sz* using a dash argument (*sz* −), and *sz* automatically sends the file on to you. A filename for the output is generated by putting an *s* in front of the process ID of the process that pipes the standard input to *sz* and appending a *.sz* suffix. For example, to get a printout of the *sz.1* manual page on the remote system (versions of *sz* software vary, of course), you might enter:

```
man sz | col -b | sz -
```

where col −b strips out the backspacing that was put into the formatted output by the *man* command to implement highlighting and underscoring on the display. The dash argument to *sz* tells it to send the file back to your local system. When you get offline and check, you might find the file saved locally as something like */tmp/s7750.sz.* (the */tmp* directory is the most common receiving directory that a given communications program uses unless the current directory is used.)

Summary of rz and sz Options

Because of the prevailing poor state of RZSZ documentation in the standard Linux distributions and because RZSZ tools don't have interactive help, we're providing you with summaries of the important flags for using the Zmodem protocol for file transfer. However, you should get the manual pages and possibly other documentation you need from an FTP site or a BBS; see the earlier section "Getting RZSZ." When you use RZSZ on another system, you should be aware that the utilities may have been modified to support additional features or to disable standard features. Check the local documentation.

The *rz* utility recognizes the following flags:

−+ Appends to any existing file of the same name, rather than overwrite it. (This can cause a malformed file if you are retransmitting an interrupted Zmodem transfer.)

−*a* Receives ASCII text and converts files to Unix newline conventions, stripping carriage returns and all characters beginning with a Ctrl-Z (the end-of-file character for the CP/M OS).

−*b* Receives binary and saves the file in exactly the form it was received.

−*D* Discards output. It sends data to */dev/null*; this is useful for tests.

−*e* Escapes the control characters. By default, *sz* escapes XON, XOFF, and (in older versions) DLE. This option forces the sending Zmodem program to escape others as well.

−*p* Protects destination files. This option skips Zmodem transfer if a destination file of the same name already exists. (Be aware that this prevents completion of an interrupted Zmodem transfer.)

−*q* Quiet exchange. Suppresses informational messages to standard output.

−*t n*

   Changes timeout to *n* tenths of seconds.

−*v* Turns on verbose. Not like a typical Unix utility "verbose." This flag causes a list of transferred filenames to be appended to a log file, normally */tmp/rzlog*. If multiple −*v* flags are used, additional information is also stored to the log.

Now for *sz*. Most *sz* options are simply passed to the receiving program that performs the operation. Not all Zmodem receiving programs can execute the requested options. If *sz* is invoked with the $SHELL environment variable set to a restricted shell (e.g., *rsh*), *sz* restricts pathnames to the current directory and to the value of the $PUBDIR variable if set (often used with UUCP), as well as subdirectories of these directories.

The meanings of the most common *sz* options are:

−+ Has the Zmodem receiver utility append the transmitted data to an existing file.

−*a* Sends ASCII text and converts each newline character (Unix style) in the transmitted file to a carriage return/linefeed (DOS style).

−*b* Transfers the file without any translation and tells the receiving Zmodem program not to make any translation. This option is used for binary sites.

−*d* Diverts path and compensates for filename and pathname incompatibilities between systems. (It's more reliable to rename files before you send them, though.) All periods (.) in a filename are changed to path-subpath separators in the transmitted pathname. (In Unix, change to / characters, and in DOS, change to backslashes. A file named *foobar.bazbuzzy*, for example, is transmitted as *foobar/bazbuzzy*.) If a stem filename has more than eight characters, a period is inserted to allow up to 11 characters. For example, a Unix file named *foo.barbazbuzzy* would be transmitted as *foo/barbazbuzzy*, but when received by the DOS Zmodem program would be stored as *foo\barbazbu.zzy*. (If the file is longer than that, and the receiving program cannot handle the length, the file is truncated at the limit—depending on the "wisdom" of the DOS Zmodem program.)

−*e* Escapes control characters.

−*f* Preserves full path. Directory prefixes are usually omitted; this forces the entire path to be sent in the transmitted filename.

−*L bytes*
   Sets the Zmodem subpacket length in bytes. (These are not the same as Xmodem, Ymodem, or Kermit packets.) The default packet length is 128 below 300 baud, 256 above 300 baud, or 1024 above 2400 baud. A larger packet gives slightly higher throughput, while a smaller packet speeds error recovery. This isn't worth messing with for modern modems that implement an error-correcting protocol in hardware.

−*l num*
   Sets the packet length in bytes. The receiver acknowledges correct data every *num* characters, where *num* is a value between 32 and 1024. You can use this to avoid overrun when XOFF flow control is lacking between the systems.

−*n* Newer file preservation. Send the file if the destination file of the same name does not exist, and overwrite the destination file only if the source file is newer than the destination file.

−N Newer/longer file preservation. Send the file if the destination file of the same name does not exist, and overwrite the destination file only if the source file is newer or longer than the destination file.

−p Protects destination files. Doesn't transfer the file if the destination file exists.

−q Suppresses reporting to the standard error.

−r Resumes an interrupted file transfer. If the source file is longer than the desti-nation file, the transfer begins at the offset in the source file that equals the length of the destination file. (This mode is automatically assumed in some Zmodem receiving programs.)

−t num

Timeout. Set the timeout to *num* tenths of seconds.

−u Breaks file links after successful transmission. Conveniently implements a way to "collect" files to a directory they can all be sent from.

−w bytes

Limits the transmit window size to the specified number of bytes to impose flow control and limit buffering.

−v Turns on verbose. Appends the list of transmitted filenames to the */tmp/szlog* record. Extra *−v* options cause additional information about the transfer to be added to the record.

−y Tells the receiving Zmodem program to overwrite any existing files having the same name.

−Y Tells the receiving Zmodem program to overwrite any existing file with the same name, but skip sending source files that have a file with the same path-name on the destination system.

Some Zmodem Usage Notes

You can invoke *sz* with a special terminal test mode:

```
$ sz -TT
```

This form of invocation causes *sz* to output all 256 8-bit character code combina-tions to your terminal. If you are having problems transferring files intact, this command lets you isolate the character codes that are being trapped by the oper-ating systems.

Calling an RZSZ utility from most versions of the UUCP *cu* usually fails, because most *cu* implementations contend for characters from the modem with RZSZ tools. (C-Kermit apparently now can call RZSZ, but this is a new feature we haven't tried.)

Other Interesting Packages

There are several other packages commonly available on Linux systems that you may be interested in using. You can find out about them by reading the appropriate HOWTO files and other accompanying documentation.

The *term* utility is a client/server system that allows you to multiplex your serial line—that is, you can log in multiple times over a single dial-up connection. *term* includes additional features allowing you to run network clients (such as Telnet, FTP, and Netscape Navigator) over the serial line. You can even use *term* to display remote X Window System clients on your local machine. So you can simultaneously run a remote X session, download files, and send mail, for example. This capability is most useful if your modem can handle high-speed data transfer; you can get comfortable performance with a 28.8 Kbps (preferably v.34-compliant) modem.

Chapter 15

term is somewhat like PPP (discussed in the section "Dial-up PPP" in Chapter 15, *TCP/IP and PPP*) but *term* can be executed as a normal user: no need for **root** access on either the client or server side, and no need for a special PPP dial-in server.

To use *term*, you need a dial-in shell account on a Unix system. You build the *term* software both on that Unix system and on your Linux machine. You dial in to the remote system and execute *term* there; it now handles all data to and from your dial-in connection. On your local machine, you place the communications program in the background and execute *term* to control the dial-in connection from your Linux system. The two instances of *term* are now communicating over the modem line.

To log in to the remote session over the *term*-controlled line, you can use *trsh*. This starts a remote shell over the modem line. You can run *trsh* many times (in different windows or virtual consoles), starting multiple logins to the remote machine, for example.

You can also use various network clients with *term*. These include Telnet, FTP, mail readers, and the like. These clients must be specially compiled to use *term*. Many of them are available for Linux. In order for them to work, the remote system must be connected to the Internet (or another local network); network requests are redirected to the remote system over the modem line. This way, it appears as though your system is connected to the network; you can *telnet* or *ftp* to any other system on the Internet directly from your Linux machine. The WWW browser Netscape Navigator, discussed in the section "Using Netscape Navigator" in Chapter 16, *The World Wide Web and Electronic Mail*, works with *term* as well.

Chapter 16

Two other packages are worth mentioning. *pcomm* is a data-communications package that intentionally resembles the ProComm for DOS package, the most popular DOS communications package. *Seyon* offers a powerful suite of terminal-emulation and data-communications tools.

If we've missed your favorite file-transfer or data-communications tool, we apologize. This is certainly an area where available Linux tools offer an embarrassment of riches. On the other hand, if you are clinging to more primitive utilities, we hope this appendix has given you the opportunity to learn and use more powerful tools.

BIBLIOGRAPHY

Linux Documentation Project Manuals

[1] Welsh, Matt et. al. *Linux Installation and Getting Started*. 1992–1994.

A user's guide for Linux, a prototype for this book. The manual is targeted primarily for the Unix novice and as such does not contain the broad scope of information that is in this book. If you are new to Unix and need more information, *Linux Installation and Getting Started* is a great place to look.

[2] Greenfield, Larry. *Linux Users' Guide*. 1993–1994.

An introduction to the most important commands and programs people use on Linux. It is not limited to common Unix utilities and the use of the shell (although it has a lot of essential information in these areas). It also covers a wide range of activities that you will find yourself doing on Linux, such as manipulating windows on the X Window System and using the *vi* and Emacs editors. The book is particularly helpful for people who have not used Unix or X before.

[3] Wirzenius, Lars. *The Linux System Administrator's Guide*. 1995.

This is a guide to running and configuring a Linux system. There are many issues relating to systems administration that are specific to Linux, such as the needs for supporting a user community, filesystem maintenance, backups, and more. This guide covers many of the associated tasks.

[4] Kirch, Olaf. *Linux Network Administrator's Guide*. O'Reilly & Associates. 1995.

An extensive and complete guide to networking under Linux, including TCP/IP, UUCP, SLIP, and more. This book is a very good read; it contains a wealth of information on many subjects, clarifying the many confusing aspects of network configuration. It has been published by O'Reilly & Associates as a companion volume to this book.

[5] Goldt, Sven, Harper, John D., van der Meer, Sven, and Welsh, Matt. *Linux Programmer's Guide*. 1995.

A listing of functions and programming techniques, some familiar to those who have programmed on other common versions of Unix and some quite specific to Linux. While there are some hints and examples, it currently is a brief description of what is available. Contains particularly full sections on interprocess communication, curses, and porting from other Unix systems to Linux.

[6] Rusling, David A. *The Linux Kernel*. 1999.

Principals and concepts behind the design of Linux.

Unix and Unix Shells

[7] Todino, Grace, Strang, John, and Peek, Jerry. *Learning the Unix Operating System, Fourth Edition*. O'Reilly & Associates. 1997.

A good introductory book on learning the Unix operating system. Most of the information should be applicable to Linux as well. We suggest reading this book if you're new to Unix and just want a quick start. It introduces basic networking commands, email, and the X Window System to novice users.

[8] Newham, Cameron, and Rosenblatt, Bill. *Learning the bash Shell, Second Edition*. O'Reilly & Associates. 1998.

Introduces the *bash* shell as a user interface and as a programming language.

[9] DuBois, Paul. *Using csh and tcsh*. O'Reilly & Associates. 1995.

A guide to the interactive features (not programming constructs) of *csh* and the version more commonly used on Linux systems, *tcsh*.

[10] Siever, Ellen, and the Staff of O'Reilly & Associates. *Linux in a Nutshell, Second Edition*. O'Reilly & Associates. 1999.

Summarizes all commands and options, along with generous descriptions and examples that put the commands in context.

[11] Quercia, Valerie, and O'Reilly, Tim. *Volume 3M: X Window System User's Guide Motif Edition*. O'Reilly & Associates. 1993.

A complete tutorial and reference guide to using the X Window System for users who have installed X on their Linux systems and who want to know how to get the most out of it. Unlike some windowing systems, a lot of the power provided by X is not obvious at first sight. Includes the *twm* window manager and has been revised for X11 Release 5.

Applications and Technologies

[12] Tranter, Jeff. *Linux Multimedia Guide*. O'Reilly & Associates. 1996.

Describes how to install, configure, and write C programs to manipulate multimedia devices, including sound cards, CD-ROM drives, and joysticks. Also lists useful utilities and libraries for multimedia development.

[13] Stallman, Richard M. *Emacs manual: Eleventh Edition, Version 19.29*. Free Software Foundation. 1995.

Describes the widely used and powerful GNU Emacs editor. Written by the software's creators, this manual is the same as the comprehensive online Info documentation.

[14] Cameron, Debra, and Rosenblatt, Bill. *Learning GNU Emacs, Second Edition*. O'Reilly & Associates. 1996.

Provides a congenial introduction to GNU Emacs and includes a brief introduction to Emacs customization and to GNU Emacs LISP programming.

[15] Lamb, Linda, and Robbins, Arnold. *Learning the vi Editor, Sixth Edition*. O'Reilly & Associates. 1998.

Provides a complete guide to text editing with the standard features of *vi*, an editor available on nearly every Unix system and now on some non-Unix operating systems (in the form of Elvis, Vile, and other clones). Covers the use of the *ex* command (mode) and advanced features of *vi*.

[16] Dougherty, Dale, and Robbins, Arnold. *sed & awk, Second Edition*. O'Reilly & Associates. 1997.

Describes the use of *sed* and *awk* as powerful editors to create and modify text files. *sed* and *awk* are stream editors that process multiple files and save many hours of repetitive work in achieving the same results as a standard text editor.

[17] Peek, Jerry, O'Reilly, Tim, and Loukides, Mike. *Unix Power Tools, Second Edition*. O'Reilly & Associates. 1997.

Offers Unix utility tips, tricks, concepts, and freeware. Covers add-on utilities and how to take advantage of clever features in the most popular Unix utilities. It includes a CD-ROM with source and popular binaries.

[18] Knuth, Donald E. *The TEXbook*. Addison-Wesley Publishing Co. 1986.

Provides the first, and still definitive, reference to the TEX text-formatting language. Written by the creator of TEX.

[19] Lamport, Leslie. *LATEX—A Document Preparation System*. Addison-Wesley Publishing Co. 1994.

A very readable guide to the LATEX extension to TEX, by the creator of LATEX.

[20] van Herwijnen, Eric. *Practical SGML, Second Edition*. Kluwer Academic Publishers. 1994.

Provides an excellent introduction to the Standard Generalized Markup Language (ISO 8879-1986) for creating structured documents. There are several flawed books on this subject out there, but this one is just about right.

[21] Goldfarb, Charles F. *The SGML Handbook*. Clarendon Press. 1991.

Provides the authoritative "bible" on Standard Generalized Markup Language. Contains the complete text of the standard for SGML, ISO 8879-1986, with the author's annotations. Charles Goldfarb is the father of SGML and was the technical leader of the committee that developed the standard. This book is expensive, but costs less than ISO 8879 alone. It is an essential resource for the serious SGML tools or documentation-systems developer.

The Internet

[22] Conner, Kiersten, and Krol, Ed. *The Whole Internet: The Next Generation*. O'Reilly & Associates. Forthcoming.

Provides a comprehensive, bestselling introduction to the Internet, but it's helpful to both novices and veterans. The book pays special attention to tools to help you find World Wide Web information. It has chapters on email, news, browsing, security, online banking and personal finance, games, creating web pages, esoteric and emerging technologies, and commerical and financial resources. There's also a catalog of useful web resources.

[23] Kehoe, Brendan P. *Zen and the Art of the Internet: A Beginner's Guide, Fourth Edition*. PTR Prentice Hall. 1995.

Introduction to the Internet, aimed at the novice user. It covers topics ranging from email to Usenet news to Internet folklore. An electronic text version of the first edition (1992) of this book is available via anonymous FTP and may be freely distributed and printed. See "Internet Resources" later in this bibliography.

[24] Quarterman, John S. *The Matrix: Computer Networks and Conferencing Systems Worldwide*. Digital Press. 1989.

A massive listing of different networks around the world.

[25] Musciano, Chuck, and Kennedy, Bill. *HTML: The Definitive Guide, Third Edition*. O'Reilly & Associates. 1998.

A comprehensive guide to the use of current HTML features for writing World Wide Web pages, including browser-specific extensions.

Networks and Communications

[26] Comer, Douglas R. *Internetworking with TCP/IP, Volume 001: Principles, Protocols, Architecture*. Prentice-Hall International. 1995.

Provides a comprehensive background for understanding the Internet suite of protocols and how they are used in modern networking.

[27] Stevens, W. Richard. *TCP/IP Illustrated, Volume 1: The Protocols*. Addison-Wesley. 1995.

The first volume in a comprehensive series of three books about the protocols used in the Internet. Makes extensive use of the *tcpdump* program to show what network packets look like.

[28] Hunt, Craig. *TCP/IP Network Administration, Second Edition*. O'Reilly & Associates. 1997.

A complete guide to setting up and running a TCP/IP network. While this book is not Linux specific, roughly 90 percent of it is applicable to Linux. Coupled with the Linux NET-3-HOWTO and *Linux Network Administrator's Guide*, this is a great book discussing the concepts and technical details of managing TCP/IP. Covers setting up a network, configuring network applications, routing mail and resolving addresses, troubleshooting, and setting up security.

[29] Blair, John D. *Samba—Integrating Unix and Windows*. 1998.

A comprehensive guide to setting up Samba that contains lots of examples and a good introduction into Windows networking protocols.

[30] Liu, Cricket, and Albitz, Paul. *DNS and BIND, Third Edition*. O'Reilly & Associates. 1998.

Provides thorough treatment of the Internet Domain Name System and of the Unix implementation: Berkeley Internet Name Domain (BIND). An important resource for system administrators, because this book shows how to set up and maintain the DNS software on a network.

[31] Stern, Hal. *Managing NFS and NIS*. O'Reilly & Associates. 1991.

Describes management of the Network File System and the Network Information System for system administrators who need to set up and manage a network filesystem installation and network-information services. Includes PC/NFS and automounter configuration.

[32] Costales, Bryan, and Allman, Eric. *sendmail, Second Edition*. O'Reilly & Associates. 1997.

A hefty and possibly intimidating book, but really a fine and complete description of how to configure *sendmail*. Includes extensive reference material.

[33] Laurie, Ben, and Laurie, Peter. *Apache—The Definitive Guide*. O'Reilly & Associates. 1997.

Explains how to install and configure the Apache web server, including Server-Side. Covers how to write external modules using the Apache API.

Programming Languages and Utilities

[34] Kernighan, Brian, and Ritchie, Dennis. *The C Programming Language, Second Edition*. Prentice Hall. 1988.

The classic reference on the C language, by its creators. Updated to cover ANSI C in the second edition.

[35] Stevens, Richard. *Advanced Programming in the Unix Environment*. Addison-Wesley Publishing Co. 1992.

Introduces and describes the use of Unix system calls in detail.

[36] Stallman, Richard M. *Using and Porting GNU CC for Version 2.8*. Free Software Foundation.

Discusses many *gcc* command options, language extensions, and other considerations in using the GNU C compiler.

[37] Kochan, Stephen, and Wood, Patrick. *Unix Shell Programming*. Hayden Press. 1990.

A well-known guide to writing shell scripts.

[38] Schwartz, Randal L., and Christiansen, Tom. *Learning Perl, Second Edition*. O'Reilly & Associates. 1997.

Provides a hands-on tutorial designed to get you writing useful Perl scripts as quickly as possible. Perl provides a portable replacement (Unix, DOS, and other operating systems) for shell programming that incorporates a superset of *sed* and *awk* functionality.

[39] Wall, Larry, and Schwartz, Randal L. *Programming Perl, Second Edition*. O'Reilly & Associates. 1996.

Provides an authoritative guide to the powerful and portable Perl programming language, co-authored by its creator, Larry Wall.

[40] Srinivasan, Sriram. *Advanced Perl Programming*. O'Reilly & Associates. 1997.

Covers many difficult and rarely described topics in Perl programming like embedding and extending the Perl interpreter, networking, and building complex data structures.

[41] Christiansen, Tom, and Torkington, Nathan. *Perl Cookbook*. O'Reilly & Associates. 1998.

Contains literally hundreds of ready-to-use Perl code snippets for Perl programs.

[42] Ousterhout, John K. *Tcl and the Tk Toolkit*. Addison-Wesley Publishing Co. 1994.

Describes the Tcl and Tk languages. Written by the inventor, most of the book is devoted to a discussion of Tk commands and widgets. Also tells how to embed Tcl and Tk in C programs.

[43] Raines, Paul, and Tranter, Jeff. *Tcl/Tk in a Nutshell*. O'Reilly & Associates. 1999.

A quick-ref to all Tcl and Tk commands as well as popular extensions.

[44] Flanagan, David. *Java in a Nutshell, Second Edition*. O'Reilly & Associates. 1997.

A reference work on the Java language with some tutorial sections and examples.

[45] Dalheimer, Matthias Kalle. *Programming with Qt*. O'Reilly & Associates. 1999.

A thorough introduction to the Qt toolkit. This readable guide is a good source of information on advanced Qt programming topics.

[46] Oram, Andrew, and Talbott, Steve. *Managing Projects with make, Second Edition*. O'Reilly & Associates. 1991.

Describes all the basic features of the *make* utility and provides guidelines to programmers on using *make* for managing large compilation projects.

[47] Stallman, Richard M., and McGrath, Roland. *GNU Make, Version 3.77*. Free Software Foundation. 1998.

Describes the powerful GNU version of the *make* utility—both basic use and advanced features.

[48] DuBois, Paul. *Software Portability with imake, Second Edition*. O'Reilly & Associates. 1996.

Describes the *imake* utility, which works with *make* to let code be compiled and installed on different Unix machines.

[49] Lewine, Donald. *POSIX Programmer's Guide*. O'Reilly & Associates. 1991.

Explains the X/Open POSIX standards and is a reference for the POSIX.1 programming library, helping you write more portable programs. Linux is intended to be POSIX-compliant, although its compliance is uncertified.

[50] Stallman, Richard M., and Cygnus Solutions. *Debugging with GDB: The GNU Source-Level Debugger for GDC Version 4.18*. Free Software Foundation. 1999.

Describes how to use the *gdb* debugger, the standard debugger on Linux and probably the most popular debugger in the Unix world.

[51] Lutz, Mark, and Asher, David. *Learning Python*. O'Reilly & Associates. 1999.

A gentle introduction to Python.

[52] Lutz, Mark. *Programming Python*. O'Reilly & Associates. 1996.

Teaches you everything you ever wanted to know about Python, including text processing, writing graphical user interfaces, and embedding Python.

[53] Eckel, Bruce. *Thinking in Java*. Prentice-Hall PTR. 1998.

Covers most Java topics and also includes valuable general programming hints.

[54] Niemeyer, Patrick, and Peck, Joshua. *Exploring Java, Second Edition*. O'Reilly & Associates. 1997.

A general introduction to the Java programming language from the very extensive O'Reilly Java series.

[55] Cornell, Gary, and Horstmann, Cay S. *Core Java 2, Volume 1: Fundamentals, Fourth Edition*. Prentice Hall. 1999.

A thorough—if lengthy—introduction to all basic Java topics. Part of the SunSoft Press Java series.

System Administration

[56] Nemeth, Evi, Snyder, Garth, and Seebass, Scott. *Unix System Administration Handbook, Second Edition*. Prentice Hall. 1995.

The most frequently recommended book on the subject.

[57] Frisch, Æleen. *Essential System Administration, Second Edition*. O'Reilly & Associates. 1995.

Guides you through the system administration tasks on a Unix system.

[58] Garfinkel, Simson, and Spafford, Gene. *Practical Unix and Internet Security, Second Edition*. O'Reilly & Associates. 1996.

An excellent book on Unix system security. It taught us quite a few things that we didn't know, even with several years of Unix system-administration experience. As with most Unix books, this book is geared for large systems, but almost all of the content is relevant to Linux. Explains network security (including UUCP, NFS, Kerberos, and firewall machines) in detail.

[59] Mui, Linda, and Pearce, Eric. *Volume 8: X Window System Administrator's Guide*. O'Reilly & Associates). 1992.

Covers detailed system-administration guidance for the X Window System and X-based networks for X administrators. Can be purchased with or without a CD-ROM.

Personal Computer Hardware

[60] Rosch, Winn L. *The Winn L. Rosch Hardware Bible*. Brady Publishing Div. Macmillan Computer Publishing. 1994.

A comprehensive guide to PC components and peripherals. You will find this book useful when purchasing, maintaining, repairing, and upgrading PCs. Though oriented primarily toward the Intel and clone systems, it is broadly useful because it covers technology, theory, and practice in computer architecture. It is applicable to all significant personal computer systems, as well as containing information specific to the ISA, EISA, and Microchannel systems (and the various secondary buses). This book can probably tell you what you need to know about microprocessors, memory, modems, MIDI, and more.

HOWTOs (Partial List)

[61] *Installation HOWTO*, by Eric Raymond.

Describes how to obtain and install a distribution of Linux, similar to the information presented in Chapter 3, *Installation and Initial Configuration*.

[62] *The Linux Distribution HOWTO*, by Eric Raymond.

Lists Linux distributions available via mail order and anonymous FTP. It also includes information on other Linux-related goodies and services.

[63] *XFree86 HOWTO*, by Eric Raymond.

Describes how to install and configure the X Window System software for Linux. See Chapter 10, *Installing the X Window System*, for more about the X Window System.

[64] *Bootdisk HOWTO*, by Tom Fawcett.

Discusses the creation and uses of Linux boot disks, covering various methods and systems. A good resource for new Linux users because it covers basic information on disk types and disk components. Gives example file setups as well as references to an FAQ, related software, and other HOWTOs.

[65] *Linux BootPrompt HOWTO*, by Paul Gortmaker, ed.

Offers an overview of boot-prompt arguments and explains the commonly used LILO booting program. Includes a comprehensive list of kernel parameters and device parameters, as well as popular software and hardware options for booting a Linux system.

[66] *The CD Writing HOWTO*, by Winfried Trümper.

Covers the installation of devices that write CD-ROMs and how to use them to burn a CD-ROM.

[67] *UUCP HOWTO*, by Guylhem Aznar.

A brief introduction to installing UUCP, with special attention to the Taylor version that is standard for Linux.

[68] *Hardware Compatibility HOWTO*, by Patrick Reignen.

Contains an extensive list of hardware supported by Linux. While this list is far from complete, it should give users a general picture of which hardware devices are supported by the system.

[69] *SCSI Programming HOWTO*, by Heiko Eissfeldt.

Information on programming the generic Linux SCSI interface.

[70] *PCI HOWTO*, by Michael Will.

Offers a comprehensive look at PCI-Linux compatibility. Contains a thorough description of why to use PCI and explains how PCI can be used with Linux, including sections on Ethernet cards, video cards, and motherboards. Summarizes the author's research on PCI-Linux compatibility, with specific reports on both successes and problems, and recommends hardware to use with PCI.

[71] *The Linux CD-ROM HOWTO*, by Jeff Tranter.

Lists supported CD-ROM drives and explains how to install, configure, and read from a drive. Also describes some useful utilities that can be used with a CD-ROM drive.

[72] *Kernel HOWTO*, by Brian Ward.

Deals with configuring, compiling, and patching the kernel. Provides additional information on related material, including programs and modules, warns of several common problems, and discusses tips for using the kernel. Includes a list of applicable HOWTOs.

[73] *NET-3 HOWTO*, by Terry Dawson.

Describes installation, setup, and configuration of the NET-3 TCP/IP software under Linux, including SLIP. If you want to use TCP/IP on your Linux system, this document is a must read.

[74] *The Linux Ethernet HOWTO*, by Paul Gortmaker, ed.

Describes the various Ethernet devices supported by Linux and explains how to configure each of them for use by the Linux TCP/IP software. This document is closely related to the NET-3-HOWTO.

[75] *PPP HOWTO*, by Robert Hart.

Focuses on connecting PCs running Linux to a PPP server. Covers configuring kernels and modems, setting up the PPP files and connection, and automating and shutting down connections. Includes troubleshooting and debugging tips and sources of further PPP information.

[76] *DNS HOWTO*, by Nicolai Langfeldt.

Focuses on setting up a simple DNS name server. Includes sample files for DNS configuration, tips on maintaining a bug-free server, and scripts for automatic setup. Also provides a brief reference list of online and printed DNS documentation.

[77] *NIS HOWTO*, by Thorsten Kukuk.

Compares NIS versus NIS+ and NIS versus NYS. Describes setup for both NIS and NYS, including tips on installation, common problems, and server programs. Presents both a helpful glossary of NIS-related terms and an FAQ address.

[78] *Firewall HOWTO*, by Mark Grennan.

Defines firewalls and their pros and cons. Details the basic setup for firewalls on a PC running Linux, focusing on proxy servers. Includes a small section on advanced firewall configuration.

[79] *ISP Hookup HOWTO*, by Egil Kvaleberg.

Deals with basic Internet Service Provider configuration. Covers surfing the Net, sending and receiving email, reading news, and establishing automated connections. Summarizes related information with a helpful list of online documentation, including other HOWTOs.

[80] *GCC HOWTO*, by Daniel Barlow.

Describes the installation and setup of the *gcc* compiler. Covers compiling, debugging, linking, and dynamic loading of programs with *gcc*.

[81] *Shadow Password HOWTO*, by Michael H. Jackson.

Deals with installing, compiling, and configuring Shadow Suite, a Linux password program. Explains why you should shadow the *passwd* file and lists other programs that need to work in conjunction with Shadow Suite. Includes an FAQ and changes from the previous release.

[82] *The Linux Printing HOWTO*, by Grant Taylor.

Describes how to configure printing software under Linux, such as *lpr*. Configuration of printers and printing software under Unix can be confusing at times; this document sheds some light on the subject.

[83] *DOSEMU HOWTO*, by Uwe Bonnes and David Hodges.

Introduces Dosemu with a run down on the particulars of development and versions. Explains compiling and installing it, then discusses compatibility with hardware and software for X, Windows, and Netware, as well as video and sound. Includes sections on identifying and fixing problems.

[84] *UMSDOS HOWTO*, by Jacques Gelinas.

Explains the availability, documentation, installation, and operation of UMSDOS, a Linux filesystem. Includes explanations of pseudo-root, booting with UMSDOS, and DOS partitions. Discusses reasons to use UMSDOS and compares it to *Ext2*.

[85] *Commercial HOWTO*, by Mr. Poet.

Less of a "HOWTO" than a list of commercial software and applications, the Linux Commercial HOWTO is more for those interested in commercial Linux opportunities. Discusses methods of marketing applications and lists currently available Linux products.

[86] *Linux Access HOWTO*, by Michael De La Rue.

Focuses on information for users with physical disabilities or who may have difficulty using Linux with standard computer hardware. Includes suggestions for obtaining aids (such as voice-recognition software) and lists other sources where related information can be obtained.

[87] *Ftape HOWTO*, by Kevin Johnson.

Describes the installation and use of the floppy tape driver that works on QIC-80 and QIC-40 compatible drives. This driver lets you attach tape drives to a floppy-disk controller.

Internet Requests For Comments

[88] RFC 1597. *Address Allocation for Private Internets*. Rekhter, Y., Watson, T. J., and Watson, T. J.

Lists the IP network numbers private organizations can use internally without having to register these network numbers with the Internet Assigned Numbers Authority (IANA). The document also discusses the advantages and disadvantages of using these numbers.

[89] RFC 1340. *Assigned Numbers*. Postel, J., and Reynolds, J.

Defines the meaning of numbers used in various protocols, such as the port numbers standard TCP and UDP servers are known to listen on, and the protocol numbers used in the IP datagram header.

[90] RFC 1144. *Compressing TCP/IP Headers for Low-Speed Serial Links*. Jacobson, V.

Describes the algorithm used to compress TCP/IP headers in CSLIP and PPP.

[91] RFC 1033. *Domain Administrators Operations Guide*. Lottor, M.

Together with its companion RFCs, RFC 1034, and RFC 1035, this is the definitive source on DNS, the Domain Name System.

[92] RFC 1034. *Domain Names–Concepts and Facilities*. Mockapetris, P.V.

A companion to RFC 1033.

[93] RFC 1035. *Domain Names—Implementation and Specification*. Mockapetris, P.V.

A companion to RFC 1033.

[94] RFC 974. *Mail Routing and the Domain System*. Partridge, C.

Describes mail routing on the Internet. It tells the full story about MX records.

[95] RFC 977. *Network News Transfer Protocol*. Kantor, B., and Lapsley, P.

Defines NNTP, the common news transport used on the Internet.

[96] RFC 1094. *NFS: Network File System Protocol specification*. Nowicki, B.

The formal specification of the NFS and mount protocols (Version 2).

[97] RFC 1055. *Nonstandard for Transmission of IP Datagrams over Serial Lines: SLIP*. Romkey, J.L.

Describes SLIP, the Serial Line Internet Protocol.

[98] RFC 1057. *RPC: Remote Procedure Call Protocol Specification: Version 2*. Sun Microsystems, Inc.

The formal specification of the encoding used for remote procedure calls, which underlie both NFS and NIS.

[99] RFC 1058. *Routing Information Protocol*. Hedrick, C.L.

Describes RIP, which is used to exchange dynamic routing information within LANs and WANs.

[100] RFC 1535. *A Security Problem and Proposed Correction with Widely Deployed DNS Software*. Gavron, E.

Discusses a security problem with the default search list used by older versions of the BIND resolver library.

[101] RFC 1036. *Standard for the Interchange of Usenet messages*. Adams, R., and Horton, M.R.

Describes the format of Usenet news messages and how they are exchanged on the Internet as well as on UUCP networks. A revision of this RFC is expected to be released in the near future.

[102] RFC 822. *Standard for the Format of ARPA Internet Text Messages*. Crocker, D.

The definitive source of wisdom regarding, well, RFC-conformant mail. Everyone knows it; few have really read it.

[103] RFC 821. *Simple Mail Transfer Protocol.* Postel, J.B.
Defines SMTP, the mail transport protocol over TCP/IP.

INDEX

B

About the Authors

Matt Welsh is a Ph.D. student at the University of California, Berkeley, settling in sunny California after spending time wandering around Europe and braving the harsh winters of upstate New York. He has been a long-time Linux advocate and developer, a role which saw him field questions from thousands of Linux users over the years. Matt was the original coordinator of the Linux Documentation Project and author of the seminal *Linux Installation and Getting Started* guide. More recently, he has been promoting the use of Linux for supercomputing applications through the Extreme Linux working group. At Berkeley, his research involves the intersection of next-generation Internet systems and high-performance computing. His varied and sundry interests include world travel, Zen Buddhism, experimental music, and backpacking.

Matthias Kalle Dalheimer was born and grew up in Hamburg, Germany, where he also acquired his MS in computer science at the University of Hamburg. After working two and a half years for Star Division GmbH, where he was head of the Unix group and responsible for porting the company's office productivity suite StarOffice to Unix and Linux systems, he founded his own consulting company, which specializes in designing and implementing cross-platform software solutions. Kalle also works as a technical editor for the German branch of O'Reilly & Associates, and has translated several American O'Reilly books to German (among these are *Advanced Perl Programming* and *Java Examples in a Nutshell: A Desktop Quick Reference*). Kalle now lives in a tiny village in the North German country-side with his wife and his two-year-old son. In his spare time, he enjoys playing with his son, hiking in the forest and along the seaside, and traveling to Sweden as often as possible. Since he has recently acquired an old farm in Sweden, he is now planning to relocate there.

Lar Kaufman is a law student at Boston University, living in Concord, Massachusetts. He has worked as a documentation consultant for many years, and began writing about Unix in 1983. Since then, he has written about System V, BSD, Mach, OSF/1, and Linux. His hobbies include interactive media as art/literature, home-built and antique aircraft (he's a licensed aircraft mechanic), and natural history. Formerly a BBS operator, in 1987 Lar founded the Fidonet echoes (newsgroups) Biosphere and BioNews. He is currently working on a project to develop a media lab incorporating adaptive technology for print-disabled use through the law library where he studies. The lab will use a Linux server and provide user services on Windows NT, Macintosh, and Linux systems.

Colophon

Our look is the result of reader comments, our own experimentation, and feedback from distribution channels. Distinctive covers complement our distinctive approach to technical topics, breathing personality and life into potentially dry subjects.

The image on the cover of *Running Linux, Third Edition* is a rearing horse. A horse will rear often to avoid going forward—as a way to avoid either further work or a frightening object. Other factors may include poorly fitted tack or an overly aggressive rider. For some horses, rearing is a learned behavior. Often a very difficult vice to correct, rearing is not a very common problem with most reasonably trained horses, and it is not breed-specific or discipline-specific. Rearing is an unsettling, difficult move to ride, not to mention dangerous. When a horse rears, its rider must lean forward on the horse's neck, to avoid shifting the weight and flipping the horse over backwards.

Edie Freedman designed the cover of *Running Linux, Third Edition* using Quark-Xpress 3.32. The cover image of a rider on a rearing horse is adapted from a 19th-century engraving from *Marvels of the New West: A Vivid Portrayal of the Stupendous Marvels in the Vast Wonderland West of the Missouri River*, by William Thayer (The Henry Bill Publishing Co., Norwich, CT, 1888).

Jeffrey Liggett was the production editor for *Running Linux, Third Edition*; Alva Ware-Bevacqui was the copyeditor; John Files was the proofreader; Sebastian Banker provided production assistance; Nancy Kotary, Claire Cloutier LeBlanc, and Abigail Myers provided quality control. Chris Reilley, Robert Romano, and Rhon Porter created the illustrations using Adobe Photoshop 5 and Macromedia Free-Hand 8. Seth Maislin wrote the index.

Kathleen Wilson produced the cover layout with QuarkXPress 3.32 and Adobe Photoshop 5 software, using the ITC Garamond Condensed font. Edie Freedman, Jennifer Niederst, and Alicia Cech designed the interior layout. Chapter opening graphics are from the Dover Pictorial Archive and *Marvels of the New West*. Whenever possible, our books use RepKover™, a durable and flexible lay-flat binding. If the page count exceeds RepKover's limit, perfect binding is used.

Interior fonts are Adobe ITC Garamond. Text was prepared in SGML using the DocBook 2.1 DTD. The print version of this book was created by translating the SGML source into a set of gtroff macros using a filter developed at O'Reilly by Norman Walsh. Steve Talbott designed and wrote the underlying macro set on the basis of the GNU gtroff -gs macros; Lenny Muellner adapted them to SGML and implemented the book design. The GNU gtroff text formatter version 1.10 was used to generate PostScript output.

 # More Titles from O'Reilly

Linux

Linux in a Nutshell, 2nd Edition

By Ellen Siever &
the Staff of O'Reilly & Associates
2nd Edition February 1999
628 pages, ISBN 1-56592-585-8

This complete reference covers the core commands available on common Linux distributions. It contains all user, programming, administration, and networking commands with options, and also documents a wide range of GNU tools. New material in the second edition includes popular LILO and Loadlin programs used for dual-booting, a Perl quick-reference, and RCS/CVS source control commands.

Linux Multimedia Guide

By Jeff Tranter
1st Edition September 1996
386 pages, ISBN 1-56592-219-0

Linux is increasingly popular among computer enthusiasts of all types, and one of the applications where it is flourishing is multimedia. This book tells you how to program such popular devices as sound cards, CD-ROMs, and joysticks. It also describes the best free software packages that support manipulation of graphics, audio, and video and offers guidance on fitting the pieces together.

Linux Network Administrator's Guide

By Olaf Kirch
1st Edition January 1995
370 pages, ISBN 1-56592-087-2

One of the most successful books to come from the Linux Documentation Project, *Linux Network Administrator's Guide* touches on all the essential networking software included with Linux, plus some hardware considerations. Topics include serial connections, UUCP, routing and DNS, mail and News, SLIP and PPP, NFS, and NIS.

Linux Device Drivers

By Alessandro Rubini
1st Edition February 1998
442 pages, ISBN 1-56592-292-1

This practical guide is for anyone who wants to support computer peripherals under the Linux operating system or who wants to develop new hardware and run it under Linux. It shows step-by-step how to write a driver for character devices, block devices, and network interfaces, illustrated with examples you can compile and run. Focuses on portability.

Learning the bash Shell, 2nd Edition

By Cameron Newham & Bill Rosenblatt
2nd Edition January 1998
336 pages, ISBN 1-56592-347-2

This second edition covers all of the features of bash Version 2.0, while still applying to bash Version 1.x. It includes one-dimensional arrays, parameter expansion, more pattern-matching operations, new commands, security improvements, additions to ReadLine, improved configuration and installation, and an additional programming aid, the bash shell debugger.

The Cathedral & the Bazaar

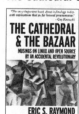

By Eric S. Raymond
1st Edition October 1999
288 pages, ISBN 1-56592-724-9

After Red Hat's stunning IPO, even people outside the computer industry have now heard of Linux and open-source software. This book contains the essays, originally published online, that led to Netscape's decision to release their browser as open source, put Linus Torvalds on the cover of Forbes Magazine and Microsoft on the defensive, and helped Linux to rock the world of commercial software. These essays have been expanded and revised for this edition, and are in print for the first time.

Linux

Using Samba

By Peter Kelly, Perry Donham & David Collier-Brown
1st Edition November 1999
416 pages, Includes CD-ROM
ISBN 1-56592-449-5

Samba turns a UNIX or Linux system into a file and print server for Microsoft Windows network clients. This complete guide to Samba administration covers basic 2.0 configuration, security, logging, and troubleshooting. Whether you're playing on one note or a full three-octave range, this book will help you maintain an efficient and secure server. Includes a CD-ROM of sources and ready-to-install binaries.

Learning Red Hat Linux

By Bill McCarty
1st Edition September 1999
394 pages, Includes CD-ROM
ISBN 1-56592-627-7

Learning Red Hat Linux will guide any new Linux user through the installation and use of the free operating system that is shaking up the world of commercial software. It demystifies Linux in terms familiar to Windows users and gives readers only what they need to start being successful users of this operating system.

MySQL & mSQL

By Randy Jay Yarger, George Reese & Tim King
1st Edition July 1999
506 pages, ISBN 1-56592-434-7

This book teaches you how to use MySQL and mSQL, two popular and robust database products that support key subsets of SQL on both Linux and UNIX systems. Anyone who knows basic C, Java, Perl, or Python can write a program to interact with a database, either as a stand-alone application or through a Web page. This book takes you through the whole process, from installation and configuration to programming interfaces and basic administration. Includes ample tutorial material.

Programming with Qt

By Matthias Kalle Dalheimer
1st Edition April 1999
384 pages, ISBN 1-56592-588-2

This indispensable guide teaches you how to take full advantage of Qt, a powerful, easy-to-use, cross-platform GUI toolkit, and guides you through the steps of writing your first Qt application. It describes all of the GUI elements in Qt, along with advice about when and how to use them. It also contains material on advanced topics like 2D transformations, drag-and-drop, and custom image file filters.

Open Sources: Voices from the Open Source Revolution

Edited by Chris DiBona, Sam Ockman & Mark Stone
1st Edition January 1999
280 pages, ISBN 1-56592-582-3

In *Open Sources*, leaders of Open Source come together in print for the first time to discuss the new vision of the software industry they have created, through essays that explain how the movement works, why it succeeds, and where it is going. A powerful vision from the movement's spiritual leaders, this book reveals the mysteries of how open development builds better software and how businesses can leverage freely available software for a competitive business advantage.

Programming with GNU Software

By Mike Loukides & Andy Oram
1st Edition December 1996
260 pages, Includes CD-ROM
ISBN 1-56592-112-7

This book and CD combination is a complete package for programmers who are new to UNIX or who would like to make better use of the system. The tools come from Cygnus Support, Inc., and Cyclic Software, companies that provide support for free software. Contents include GNU Emacs, gcc, C and C++ libraries, gdb, RCS, and make. The book provides an introduction to all these tools for a C programmer.

UNIX Tools

The UNIX CD Bookshelf

By O'Reilly & Associates, Inc.
1st Edition November 1998
444 pages, Includes CD-ROM
ISBN 1-56592-406-1

The UNIX CD Bookshelf contains six books
from O'Reilly plus the software from *UNIX
Power Tools* – all on a convenient CD-ROM.
A bonus hard-copy book, *UNIX in a Nutshell:
System V Edition*, is also included. The
CD-ROM contains *UNIX in a Nutshell: System V Edition; UNIX
Power Tools, 2nd Edition* (with software); *Learning the UNIX
Operating System, 4th Edition; Learning the vi Editor, 5th Edition;
sed & awk, 2nd Edition;* and *Learning the Korn Shell*.

sed & awk, 2nd Edition

By Dale Dougherty & Arnold Robbins
2nd Edition March 1997
432 pages, ISBN 1-56592-225-5

sed & awk describes two text manipulation
programs that are mainstays of the UNIX
programmer's toolbox. This edition covers
the sed and awk programs as they are
mandated by the POSIX standard and
includes discussion of the GNU versions of these programs.

lex & yacc, 2nd Edition

By John Levine, Tony Mason & Doug Brown
2nd Edition October 1992
366 pages, ISBN 1-56592-000-7

Shows programmers how to use two
UNIX utilities, lex and yacc, in program
development. You'll find tutorial sections
for novice users, reference sections for
advanced users, and a detailed index.
Major MS-DOS and UNIX versions of lex
and yacc are explored in depth. Also covers Bison and Flex.

Managing Projects with make, 2nd Edition

By Andrew Oram & Steve Talbott
2nd Edition October 1991
152 pages, ISBN 0-937175-90-0

make is one of UNIX's greatest contributions
to software development, and this book is the
clearest description of make ever written. It
describes all the basic features and provides
guidelines on meeting the needs of large,
modern projects. Also contains a description
of free products that contain major enhancements to make.

Writing GNU Emacs Extensions

By Bob Glickstein
1st Edition April 1997
236 pages, ISBN 1-56592-261-1

This book introduces Emacs Lisp and tells
you how to make the editor do whatever
you want, whether it's altering the way text
scrolls or inventing a whole new "major
mode." Topics progress from simple to
complex, from lists, symbols, and keyboard commands to
syntax tables, macro templates, and error recovery.

UNIX Power Tools, 2nd Edition

By Jerry Peek, Tim O'Reilly & Mike Loukides
2nd Edition August 1997
1120 pages, Includes CD-ROM
ISBN 1-56592-260-3

Loaded with practical advice about almost
every aspect of UNIX, this second edition of
UNIX Power Tools addresses the technology
that UNIX users face today. You'll find
thorough coverage of POSIX utilities, including GNU versions,
detailed bash and tcsh shell coverage, a strong emphasis on
Perl, and a CD-ROM that contains the best freeware available.

O'REILLY®

TO ORDER: **800-998-9938** • **order@oreilly.com** • **http://www.oreilly.com/**
OUR PRODUCTS ARE AVAILABLE AT A BOOKSTORE OR SOFTWARE STORE NEAR YOU.
FOR INFORMATION: **800-998-9938** • **707-829-0515** • **info@oreilly.com**

UNIX Tools

Applying RCS and SCCS

By Don Bolinger & Tan Bronson
1st Edition September 1995
528 pages, ISBN 1-56592-117-8

Applying RCS and SCCS is a thorough introduction to these two systems, viewed as tools for project management. This book takes the reader from basic source control of a single file, through working with multiple releases of a software project, to coordinating multiple developers. It also presents TCCS, a representative "front-end" that addresses problems RCS and SCCS can't handle alone, such as managing groups of files, developing for multiple platforms, and linking public and private development areas.

Software Portability with imake, 2nd Edition

By Paul DuBois
2nd Edition September 1996
410 pages, ISBN 1-56592-226-3

This handbook is ideal for X and UNIX programmers who want their software to be portable. The second edition covers version X11R6.1 of the X Window System, using imake for non-UNIX systems such as Windows NT, and some of the quirks about using imake under OpenWindows/Solaris.

Practical Internet Groupware

By Jon Udell
1st Edition October 1999
524 pages, ISBN 1-56592-537-8

This revolutionary book tells users, programmers, IS managers, and system administrators how to build Internet groupware applications that organize the casual and chaotic transmission of online information into useful, disciplined, and documented data.

In a Nutshell Quick References

UNIX in a Nutshell: System V Edition, 3rd Edition

By Arnold Robbins
3rd Edition September 1999
616 pages, ISBN 1-56592-427-4

The bestselling, most informative UNIX reference book is now more complete and up-to-date. Not a scaled-down quick reference of common commands, *UNIX in a Nutshell* is a complete reference containing all commands and options, with descriptions and examples that put the commands in context. For all but the thorniest UNIX problems, this one reference should be all you need. Covers System V Release 4 and Solaris 7.

Year 2000 in a Nutshell

By Norman Shakespeare
1st Edition September 1998
330 pages, ISBN 1-56592-421-5

This reference guide addresses the awareness, the managerial aspect, and the technical issues of the Year 2000 computer dilemma, providing a compact compendium of solutions and reference information useful for addressing the problem. Includes a comprehensive Cobol quick reference, plus reference for date-related functions in many other languages. Also includes templates, worksheets, and action plans.

Tcl/Tk in a Nutshell

By Paul Raines & Jeff Tranter
1st Edition March 1999
456 pages, ISBN 1-56592-433-9

The Tcl language and Tk graphical toolkit are powerful building blocks for custom applications. This quick reference briefly describes every command and option in the core Tcl/Tk distribution, as well as the most popular extensions. Keep it on your desk as you write scripts, and you'll be able to quickly find the particular option you need.

O'REILLY®

TO ORDER: **800-998-9938** • *order@oreilly.com* • *http://www.oreilly.com/*
OUR PRODUCTS ARE AVAILABLE AT A BOOKSTORE OR SOFTWARE STORE NEAR YOU.
FOR INFORMATION: **800-998-9938** • **707-829-0515** • *info@oreilly.com*

In a Nutshell Quick References

Perl in a Nutshell

By Ellen Siever, Stephen Spainhour &
Nathan Patwardhan
1st Edition December 1998
674 pages, ISBN 1-56592-286-7

The perfect companion for working
programmers, *Perl in a Nutshell* is a
comprehensive reference guide to the
world of Perl. It contains everything you
need to know for all but the most obscure
Perl questions. This wealth of information is packed into an
efficient, extraordinarily usable format.

SCO UNIX in a Nutshell

By Ellie Cutler & the Staff of O'Reilly & Associates
1st Edition February 1994
590 pages, ISBN 1-56592-037-6

The desktop reference to SCO UNIX and
Open Desktop(R), this version of *UNIX
in a Nutshell* shows you what's under the
hood of your SCO system. In addition to
all commands and options, this reference
covers shell syntax for the Bourne, Korn, C,
and SCO shells; compiler and debugging commands; networking
with email, TCP/IP, NFS, and UUCP; and system administration
commands.

UML in a Nutshell

By Sinan Si Alhir
1st Edition September 1998
290 pages, ISBN 1-56592-448-7

The Unified Modeling Language (UML),
for the first time in the history of systems
engineering, gives practitioners a common
language. This concise quick reference
explains how to use each component of the
language, including its extension mechanisms
and the Object Constraint Language (OCL). A tutorial with realistic
examples brings those new to the UML quickly up to speed.

How to stay in touch with O'Reilly

1. Visit Our Award-Winning Web Site

http://www.oreilly.com/

★ "Top 100 Sites on the Web" —*PC Magazine*
★ "Top 5% Web sites" —*Point Communications*
★ "3-Star site" —*The McKinley Group*

Our web site contains a library of comprehensive product information (including book excerpts and tables of contents), downloadable software, background articles, interviews with technology leaders, links to relevant sites, book cover art, and more. File us in your Bookmarks or Hotlist!

2. Join Our Email Mailing Lists

New Product Releases

To receive automatic email with brief descriptions of all new O'Reilly products as they are released, send email to:
listproc@online.oreilly.com
Put the following information in the first line of your message (*not* in the Subject field):
subscribe oreilly-news

O'Reilly Events

If you'd also like us to send information about trade show events, special promotions, and other O'Reilly events, send email to:
listproc@online.oreilly.com
Put the following information in the first line of your message (*not* in the Subject field):
subscribe oreilly-events

3. Get Examples from Our Books via FTP

There are two ways to access an archive of example files from our books:

Regular FTP

- ftp to:
  ftp.oreilly.com
  (login: anonymous
  password: your email address)
- Point your web browser to:
  ftp://ftp.oreilly.com/

FTPMAIL

- Send an email message to:
  ftpmail@online.oreilly.com
  (Write "help" in the message body)

4. Contact Us via Email

order@oreilly.com
To place a book or software order online. Good for North American and international customers.

subscriptions@oreilly.com
To place an order for any of our newsletters or periodicals.

books@oreilly.com
General questions about any of our books.

software@oreilly.com
For general questions and product information about our software. Check out O'Reilly Software Online at **http://software.oreilly.com/** for software and technical support information. Registered O'Reilly software users send your questions to: **website-support@oreilly.com**

cs@oreilly.com
For answers to problems regarding your order or our products.

booktech@oreilly.com
For book content technical questions or corrections.

proposals@oreilly.com
To submit new book or software proposals to our editors and product managers.

international@oreilly.com
For information about our international distributors or translation queries. For a list of our distributors outside of North America check out:
http://www.oreilly.com/www/order/country.html

5. Work with Us

Check out our website for current employment opportunites:
www.jobs@oreilly.com
Click on "Work with Us"

O'Reilly & Associates, Inc.
101 Morris Street, Sebastopol, CA 95472 USA
TEL   707-829-0515 or 800-998-9938
          (6am to 5pm PST)
FAX   707-829-0104

Titles from O'Reilly

International Distributors

UK, Europe, Middle East and Africa (except France, Germany, Austria, Switzerland, Luxembourg, Liechtenstein, and Eastern Europe)

INQUIRIES
O'Reilly UK Limited
4 Castle Street
Farnham
Surrey, GU9 7HS
United Kingdom
Telephone: 44-1252-711776
Fax: 44-1252-734211
Email: information@oreilly.co.uk

ORDERS
Wiley Distribution Services Ltd.
1 Oldlands Way
Bognor Regis
West Sussex PO22 9SA
United Kingdom
Telephone: 44-1243-779777
Fax: 44-1243-820250
Email: cs-books@wiley.co.uk

France

INQUIRIES
Éditions O'Reilly
18 rue Séguier
75006 Paris, France
Tel: 33-1-40-51-52-30
Fax: 33-1-40-51-52-31
Email: france@editions-oreilly.fr

ORDERS
GEODIF
61, Bd Saint-Germain
75240 Paris Cedex 05, France
Tel: 33-1-44-41-46-16 (French books)
Tel: 33-1-44-41-11-87 (English books)
Fax: 33-1-44-41-11-44
Email: distribution@eyrolles.com

Germany, Switzerland, Austria, Eastern Europe, Luxembourg, and Liechtenstein

INQUIRIES & ORDERS
O'Reilly Verlag
Balthasarstr. 81
D-50670 Köln
Germany
Telephone: 49-221-973160-91
Fax: 49-221-973160-8
Email: anfragen@oreilly.de (inquiries)
Email: order@oreilly.de (orders)

Canada (French language books)

Les Éditions Flammarion ltée
375, Avenue Laurier Ouest
Montréal (Québec) H2V 2K3
Tel: 00-1-514-277-8807
Fax: 00-1-514-278-2085
Email: info@flammarion.qc.ca

Hong Kong

City Discount Subscription Service, Ltd.
Unit D, 3rd Floor, Yan's Tower
27 Wong Chuk Hang Road
Aberdeen, Hong Kong
Tel: 852-2580-3539
Fax: 852-2580-6463
Email: citydis@ppn.com.hk

Korea

Hanbit Media, Inc.
Chungmu Bldg. 201
Yonnam-dong 568-33
Mapo-gu
Seoul, Korea
Tel: 822-325-0397
Fax: 822-325-9697
Email: hant93@chollian.dacom.co.kr

Philippines

Global Publishing
G/F Benavides Garden
1186 Benavides Street
Manila, Philippines
Tel: 632-254-8949/637-252-2582
Fax: 632-734-5060/632-252-2733
Email: globalp@pacific.net.ph

Taiwan

O'Reilly Taiwan
No. 3, Lane 131
Hang-Chow South Road
Section 1, Taipei, Taiwan
Tel: 886-2-23968990
Fax: 886-2-23968916
Email: taiwan@oreilly.com

China

O'Reilly Beijing
Room 2410
160, FuXingMenNeiDaJie
XiCheng District
Beijing, China PR 100031
Tel: 86-10-66412305
Fax: 86-10-86631007
Email: beijing@oreilly.com

India

Computer Bookshop (India) Pvt. Ltd.
190 Dr. D.N. Road, Fort
Bombay 400 001 India
Tel: 91-22-207-0989
Fax: 91-22-262-3551
Email: cbsbom@giasbm01.vsnl.net.in

Japan

O'Reilly Japan, Inc.
Yotsuya Y's Building
7 Banch 6, Honshio-cho
Shinjuku-ku
Tokyo 160-0003 Japan
Tel: 81-3-3356-5227
Fax: 81-3-3356-5261
Email: japan@oreilly.com

All Other Asian Countries

O'Reilly & Associates, Inc.
101 Morris Street
Sebastopol, CA 95472 USA
Tel: 707-829-0515
Fax: 707-829-0104
Email: order@oreilly.com

Australia

Woodslane Pty., Ltd.
7/5 Vuko Place
Warriewood NSW 2102
Australia
Tel: 61-2-9970-5111
Fax: 61-2-9970-5002
Email: info@woodslane.com.au

New Zealand

Woodslane New Zealand, Ltd.
21 Cooks Street (P.O. Box 575)
Waganui, New Zealand
Tel: 64-6-347-6543
Fax: 64-6-345-4840
Email: info@woodslane.com.au

Latin America

McGraw-Hill Interamericana
Editores, S.A. de C.V.
Cedro No. 512
Col. Atlampa
06450, Mexico, D.F.
Tel: 52-5-547-6777
Fax: 52-5-547-3336
Email: mcgraw-hill@infosel.net.mx

O'REILLY™

O'Reilly & Associates, Inc.
101 Morris Street
Sebastopol, CA 95472-9902
1-800-998-9938

Visit us online at:
http://www.ora.com/
orders@ora.com

O'REILLY WOULD LIKE TO HEAR FROM YOU

Which book did this card come from?

_____

Where did you buy this book?
- ❏ Bookstore
- ❏ Direct from O'Reilly
- ❏ Bundled with hardware/software
- ❏ Computer Store
- ❏ Class/seminar
- ❏ Other _____

What operating system do you use?
- ❏ UNIX
- ❏ Windows NT
- ❏ Other _____
- ❏ Macintosh
- ❏ PC(Windows/DOS)

What is your job description?
- ❏ System Administrator
- ❏ Network Administrator
- ❏ Web Developer
- ❏ Programmer
- ❏ Educator/Teacher
- ❏ Other _____

❏ Please send me O'Reilly's catalog, containing a complete listing of O'Reilly books and software.

Name _____ Company/Organization _____

Address _____

City _____ State _____ Zip/Postal Code _____ Country _____

Telephone _____ Internet or other email address (specify network) _____

Nineteenth century wood engraving
of a bear from the O'Reilly &
Associates Nutshell Handbook®
Using & Managing UUCP.

POST CARD

PLACE
STAMP
HERE

NO POSTAGE
NECESSARY IF
MAILED IN THE
UNITED STATES

BUSINESS REPLY MAIL

FIRST CLASS MAIL   PERMIT NO. 80   SEBASTOPOL, CA

Postage will be paid by addressee

O'Reilly & Associates, Inc.
101 Morris Street
Sebastopol, CA 95472-9902